Architectural Guide
China

Architectural Guide China

Evan Chakroff, Addison Godel and Jacqueline Gargus

Contents

成都 Chengdu

Traditions in Chinese Architecture, Art, Aesthetics and Space

Jacqueline Gargus

China is a vast and ancient land, stretching from the northern steppes of Inner Mongolia down to the tropical rainforests of Yunnan. Its history spans ten millennia and its population is comprised of fifty-six different ethnic groups. Religious and philosophical traditions include Neolithic Animism, Geomancy, Legalism, Confucianism, Taoism, Buddhism, Islam, Christianity, and more. How can such a varied assembly of peoples, practices, landforms, cultures, climates, and historical moments be collected together and discussed as a unity? In the introduction to *Art in China,* Craig CLUNAS warns against an Orientalising tendency to lump Chinese artefacts together under the catch phrase, "Chinese Art." Hence his title stresses the common geographical locus, "in China," rather than the Chinese-ness of the objects, or the common cultural, ritual, or aesthetic role they share. With architecture in China, the problem is a bit different. The word "architecture" only came into being in China in the twentieth century, after a group of young Chinese students returned from the West and brought it with them.[1] Yet even in the absence of a professional practice or body of ancient architectural theory, historical works of Chinese architecture from all over the country share a remarkable similarity of style as well as common constructional, material, site planning, and organisational strategies. Indeed conferences have been held in an attempt to parse out nuanced stylistic changes over the millennia, because even connoisseurs quibble about when, and if, stylistic distinctions emerged.

Neolithic archaeology reveals the presence of round structures in the most ancient of Chinese sites, such as the annular Neolithic houses at Banpo, 2000 BCE, and regional variations occur, often motivated by extremes in climate, local availability of materials, or the need for additional security. Syncretic adoption of new building types and practices arose with the arrival of religions from abroad and trade along the silk route. The hemispherical Indian *stupa* melded with native, stacked roof timber traditions to yield the Buddhist pagoda.[2] Hindu cave structures inspired carved sanctuaries, like the **Yungang Grottoes** (p. 391).[3] However, the dominant building practice throughout China was post and beam timber frame construction, mounted on rammed earth platforms.[4] It is tempting to emphasise the universality of architectural tropes, like Gottfried SEMPER's Caribbean hut, by observing parallels with ancient Chinese examples, as illustrated in drawings from the fifteenth-century *Carpenter's*

Opposite: Hall of Supreme Harmony, **Forbidden City** (p. 074).

Han dynasty ceramic model of a tower, Henan Provincial Museum

Songyue Pagoda, 523 CE; China's oldest extant pagoda

Gary Lee Todd, Ph.D., Sias International University | GaryLeeTodd.com

Han tomb tile

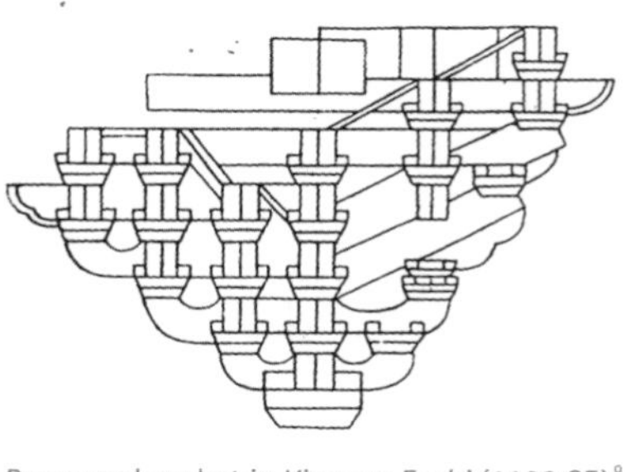

Dougong bracket in *Yingzao Fashi* (1103 CE)[9]

All photos this page: Gary Lee Todd, Ph.D.

Manual of LU Ban (*Lu Ban Jing*)[5] or the even older Han dynasty ceramic models.

The "elements" in Chinese timber construction differ slightly from those identified by Semper. Both share the tectonic element of wooden supports and roof structure, as well as an earthwork, which serves as an elevated platform. Even Semper's textile, or woven wall, is a feature in Chinese structures in southern climes, although in northern areas earthen walls are used to provide additional warmth. Instead of Semper's knot as the fundamental joint, Chinese architecture uses the elaborate wooden bracket, the *dougong,* comprised of an impost block, called the *dou* and stacked cantilevered brackets, the *gong.*[6] The orthogonal arms of the bracket often extend to create a reticulated truss system, rather than triangulated trusses. Since wood is an ephemeral material, there are no remaining structures dating back to extreme antiquity.[7] The earliest extant timber structure in China is the Nanchan Temple of 782 CE. Yet the record shows that timber frame construction came into use by the Spring and Autumn Period, when legendary master carpenter LU Ban (c. 507–444 BCE) is claimed to have invented many carpentry tools, including the saw, the plane, and the ladder, as well as a flying wooden bird.[8] Furthermore, ceramic models from the Han dynasty show that the framing system had already achieved a refined form by the third century BCE. Masonry architecture also exists in China, but detailing is mimetic of timber architecture. When masonry architecture was used, it was usually for funerary architecture and bridges.

Numerous reasons support the Chinese preference for timber architecture. Timber was a cheap and readily available material. Large structures could be erected quickly, without the use of highly skilled craftsmen or slave labour, required for the

Han era house, ceramic model

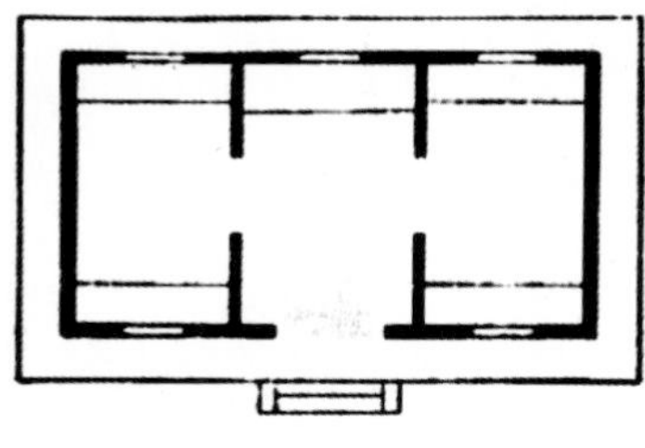
Three-bay traditional plan

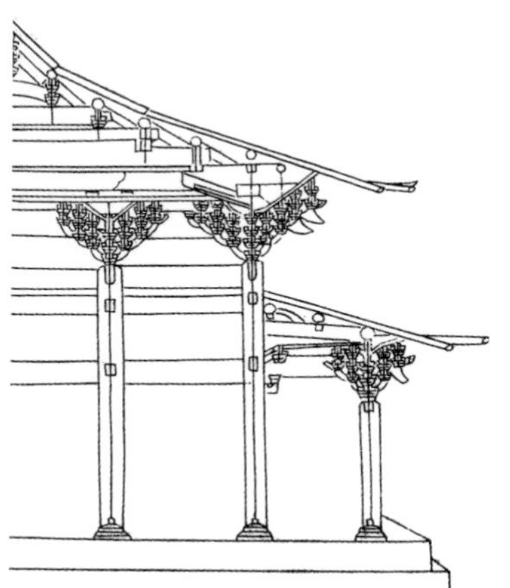
Framing system, showing the extension of the *dougong* into stacked trusses, from *Yingzao Fashi* (1103 CE)

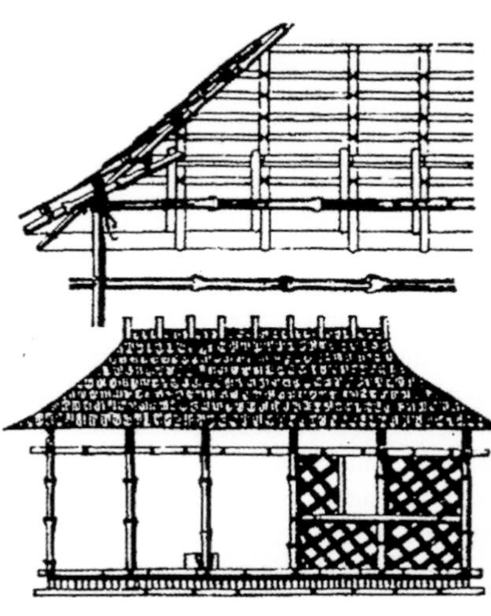
Gottfried Semper, Caribbean Hut, from *Four Elements of Architecture* (1851)

construction of monumental masonry architecture. If timber elements rotted, they could be easily replaced. Like the free plan, timber post and beam structures provided great flexibility and could be easily reprogrammed, expanded and adjusted to accommodate different uses over time. The elaborate *dougong* bracket also had practical applications. Held together with mortise and tenon connections, wooden brackets were effective in controlling expansion and contraction due to changing temperature and humidity. They were also flexible joints, capable of withstanding strong lateral wind loads and the shaking of earthquakes. The use of timber frame construction also served as an extension of philosophical interests. Confucianism placed little value on the immortality of material things and thereby favoured the use of ephemeral material, like timber.[10] Taoism stressed the desire to live in harmony with nature, not to harness and transform it. Wooden posts resting gently on stone foundation blocks do not disturb the flow of energy of the site, the *qi,* and therefore offer the most propitious way of building.

One explanation for the longevity and stylistic unity in historical Chinese architecture is that architecture was not considered to be a fine art, but rather an instrument of statecraft. Since before the Han dynasty, China had a strong centralised government run by a literate class of state functionaries, or scholar-officials, who rose to high rank by excelling in the national civil service examination. The English word "Mandarin," (from the Sanskrit for "counsellor," via Portuguese) was the name for someone in one of the nine top grades of the Chinese Imperial Civil Service, and even the language of Mandarin Chinese was a kind of bureaucratic Esperanto, based on the northern dialects and created by officials to facilitate communication

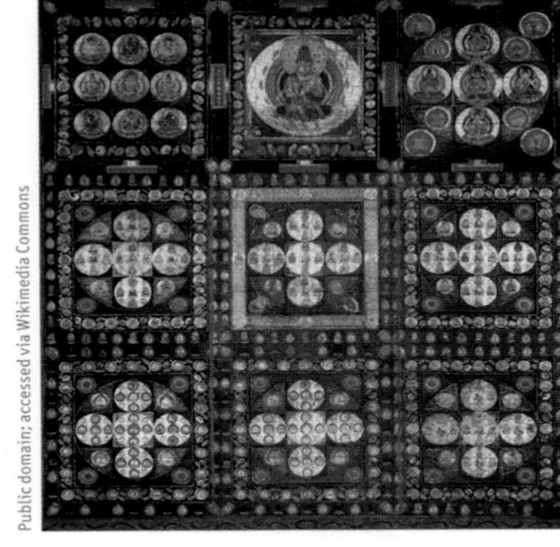

Chinese-inspired Buddhist Kongokai mandala, from Japan's Heian period

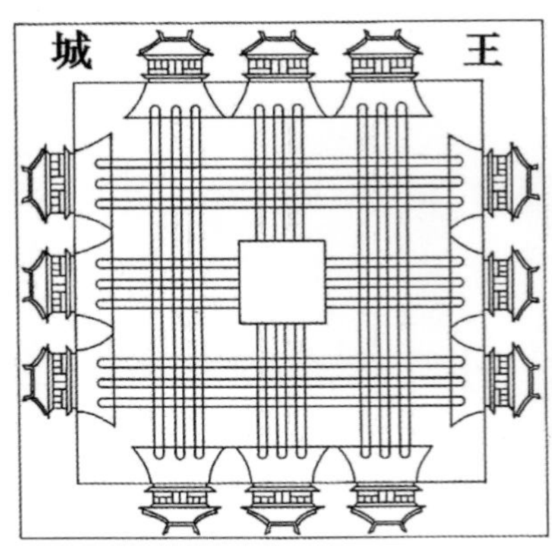

Wangcheng, ideal city, 2nd c. BCE, from *Rites of Zhou*

among people from far-flung regions. All aspects of life were tightly organised by government rules, codes and standards. Architecture, and with it city planning, was no different. With the rise of Confucianism in the Zhou dynasty (fifth century BCE) a link was forged between a well-ordered government and a moral, ethical, society. Confucian thought instantiated the legacy of the pre-imperial Sage-Kings, mythical ideal rulers, who were believed to have marshalled virtue, wisdom, and kingly power to create rules and institutions for the good of later generations. The desire to preserve that ancient legacy led to the inherent conservatism of Confucian thought. In the *Analects,* Confucius says, "I detest purple for displacing vermilion," a phrase sometimes interpreted as a defence of severe, ritualised tradition against the encroachment of frivolous pleasure.[11] The uniform planning strategies for imperial capitals over time also served to manifest the legitimacy of the government. At this period, Chinese architecture was not considered to be an art and had no aesthetic dimension. Rather, carefully constructed buildings and towns were valued as palpable evidence of imperial power and its moral rectitude. Because the Confucian belief system held that Heavenly action mirrored earthly action, merit, decorum, and propriety were rewarded in all aspects of life, including the construction of the built environment.[12]

While neither architectural theory nor even architectural design existed in ancient China *per se,* books of standards, rules, and codes proliferated and offered highly detailed building instructions with Confucian exactitude.[13] There were no master builders, in the European medieval sense. Instead, buildings were constructed by craftsmen, and work was overseen by vast state bureaucracies, such as the Imperial Ministry of Works in the Zhou dynasty (1046 BCE–256 CE) or the Imperial Offices of Royal Building in the Qing dynasty (1644–1911 CE).[14] Structures were organised with entry on the long side, and had hip or gable roofs, eventually transforming to curved roofs in the Tang dynasty (perhaps simply to throw snow farther from the foundations). Numerology played a part, and structures typically had an odd number of bays, ranging from one to eleven (in the Hall of Supreme Harmony in Beijing's **Forbidden City**, p. 074). Buildings were commissioned by specifying the required number of bays and roof purlins, and dimensions were organised according to a proportional ratio of around 3:2.[16] The size, function, siting, exposure, colour, proportions, modular relationships, and decorative programme of buildings or town plans were strictly prescribed, with the aim of making visible the elaborate, hierarchical structure of society. For example, eleven different ranks of household were stipulated, and a different set of building standards applied to each.

During the Song dynasty, scholar LI Jie composed an illustrated building manual, the *Yingzao Fashi* (c. 1103 CE) by editing, revising, and compiling bits of older building treatises, just as Vitruvius assembled his *Ten Books of Architecture* from fragments of Greek and Roman building texts.[17]

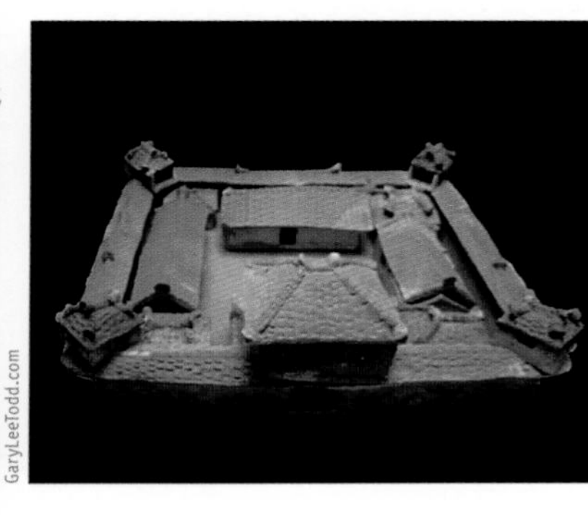

GaryLeeTodd.com

Pottery residential courtyard complex, or *siheyuan* (*circa*. 475 CE, Wu Kingdom)

Nine Domains of Zhou, from *Rites of Zhou*[15]

LIANG Sicheng, the father of Chinese architectural history, called it the "grammar book of Chinese architecture."[18] Used all over China for several centuries, the *Yingzao Fashi* was not so much a book of theory as an administrative tool, which proposed a unified set of architectural standards which helped to fix and proliferate a national style. Topics ranged from large-scale issues, like site planning, to specific technical questions, such as timber joinery, or even mathematical formulae and poetic, metaphorical ways of understanding architectural elements.[19] An eight-graded modular system was prescribed for buildings of each social rank, and all dimensions were developed from the basic module of the *dou,* the impost block of a bracket.[20] Such construction manuals assured that best practices were applied nationwide, leading to efficiency, clarity, and economy, especially in court projects, where the rules were followed most strictly. Timber could be pre-sized and precut, since all building projects for the same rank of household followed the same regulations. More importantly, because the architectural marking of social rank was standardised, it was thereby decipherable to everyone across the empire. Almost everything about a building was determined by social rank. Certain colours and materials were reserved for people of the highest rank. For example, yellow ceramic roof tile could only be used on imperial projects.

An even older building manual, *Rites of the Zhou Dynasty, Artificers' Record* (second century BCE), gives instructions for the building of Wangcheng, an ideal city for a ruler. The town is configured as a nine-square grid, with a palace in the centre and each position assigned a particular function: "The capital is a rectangle of nine square *li.* On each side of the wall are three gates... the altar of the ancestors is to the left (east) and that of the earth, right (west). The court is held in front, and marketing is done in the rear."[21] Architecture and town planning corresponded to and embodied the hierarchical structure of society but also manifested the transcendental aspirations of that society. The nine-square town diagram recalls the organisation of Buddhist mandalas, meditation tools, thought to be microcosms of the universe. Because ancient Chinese cosmology considered the earth to be a nine-part square, the design of the town produced a habitable mandala, to promote virtue and good works.[22] LI Hua, a Tang era scholar, wrote: "between the carpenter's weight strings and marking lines [is something] close to government order and enlightenment."[23] The directive to build cities as microcosms of divine order did not only reside in literature. Most historic imperial towns were built according to this model, including **Beijing** (p. 064) and **Pingyao** (p. 387), among many others.

On a smaller scale, vernacular courtyard residential complexes (called *siheyuan* in the area around Beijing; see p. 066) follow the same structured arrangement of parts as town plans. On an even smaller scale, each house follows the same hierarchical disposition of spaces as

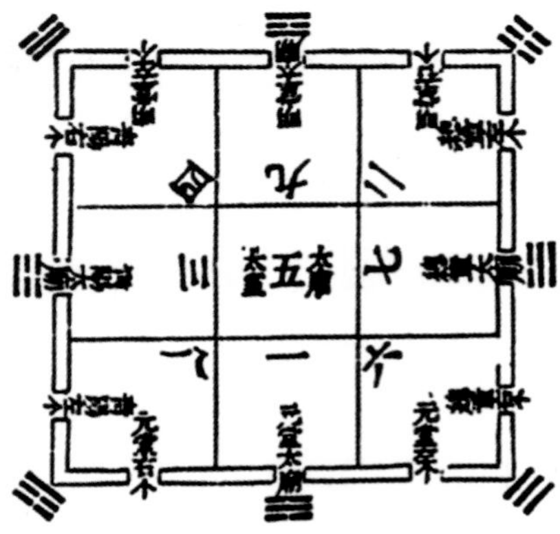

Mingtang, Hall of 9 Chambers of the Luminous Hall, organising magic square numbers and eight trigrams in the *I Ching*

Animal symbolism in *feng shui:* black tortoise (north), white tiger (east), red phoenix (south), azure dragon (west)

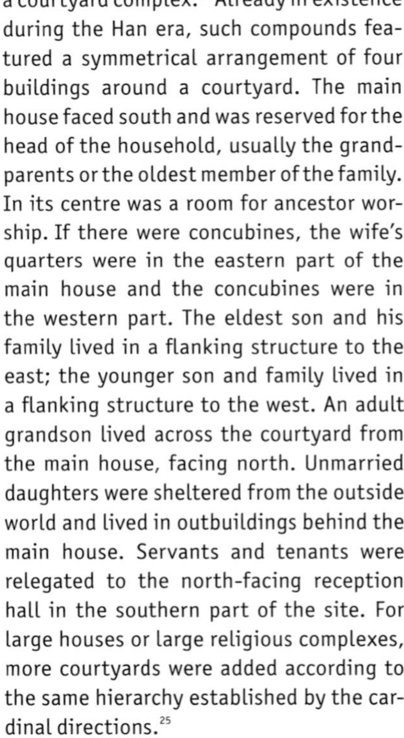

a courtyard complex.[24] Already in existence during the Han era, such compounds featured a symmetrical arrangement of four buildings around a courtyard. The main house faced south and was reserved for the head of the household, usually the grandparents or the oldest member of the family. In its centre was a room for ancestor worship. If there were concubines, the wife's quarters were in the eastern part of the main house and the concubines were in the western part. The eldest son and his family lived in a flanking structure to the east; the younger son and family lived in a flanking structure to the west. An adult grandson lived across the courtyard from the main house, facing north. Unmarried daughters were sheltered from the outside world and lived in outbuildings behind the main house. Servants and tenants were relegated to the north-facing reception hall in the southern part of the site. For large houses or large religious complexes, more courtyards were added according to the same hierarchy established by the cardinal directions.[25]

Design in harmony with nature, as practised in the Chinese art of geomancy, *feng shui,* is characteristic of the Taoist roots of Chinese culture, just as the expression of administrative hierarchies and social rank is characteristic of Confucian practice. In site planning, Taoist concerns usually held sway. In ancient China, building was not considered to be mere shelter, but rather an intervention in the universe, a disruption in cosmic flow of energy. *Feng shui* provided a ritual practice to re-establish balance, order, and harmony on a site by suggesting proper alignments with the cardinal axes, and adjacent geological features, such as mountains, rocks, rivers, lakes, valleys, etc. The words *feng* and *shui* themselves mean wind and water, dynamic and phenomenal qualities of the site. Many *feng shui* directives also make sense on a practical level. Opening up to southern exposure affords warmth and light; protecting buildings from the north shields against inhospitable winds and the advance of northern invaders.

Further insights into Chinese space can be found in the work of Taoist philosopher LAOZI (fifth or sixth century BCE, often referred to as Lao-Tzu). For Laozi, space is not a terrain to be surveyed and apportioned. Instead, space is the void. Laozi observed that one must carve out a void to create a room, for "only where there is emptiness does the room acquire utility."[26] American architect Frank Lloyd WRIGHT was strongly influenced by the Taoist emphasis on the primacy of space as well as its attention to designing with nature. He stated: "It was Lao Tzu, who lived five hundred years before Christ, who first claimed that housing is not just four walls and a roof, but is rather about the internal space... it turned the concept of the house completely upside down. As long as one can accept such an idea, they are bound to reject classical architecture."[27] Yet in Taoism, the concept of the void, *wu,* did not merely describe a preference for space over mass, as Wright construed it. Instead emptiness was thought to provoke inward reflection and provide a "mirror of the universe" and the "pure mind."[28]

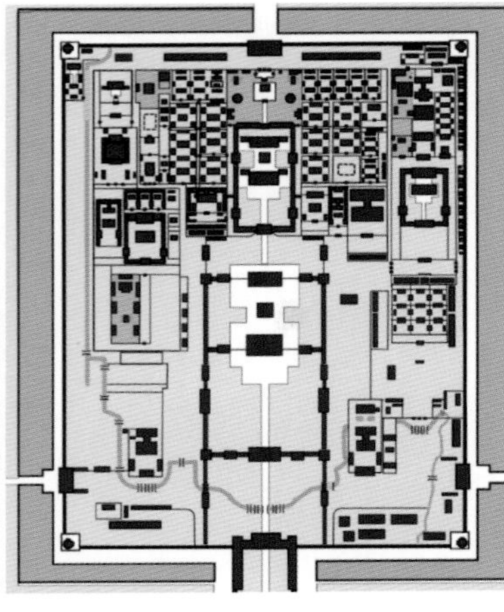

The Imperial City, Beijing, overall plan

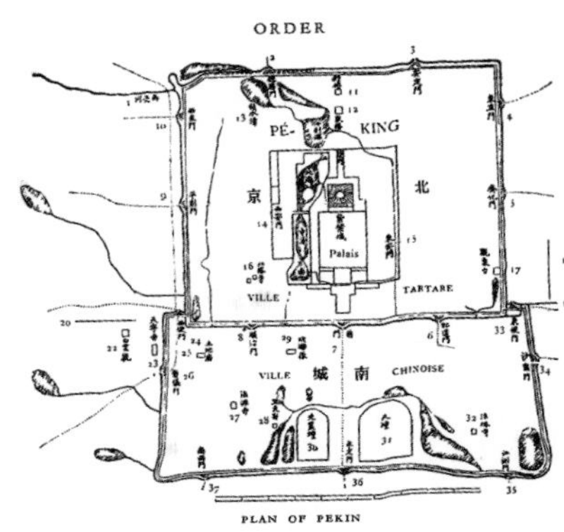

Beijing plan, used to illustrate "Order" in Le Corbusier 's *City of Tomorrow* (1929)

Traditional Chinese geomancy provides other terms that prove useful for understanding architectural and spatial composition in China: the complementary opposites of *"xing"* or form and *"shi"* or dynamic configuration.[29] *Xing* is familiar to Westerners, and describes the visible physical properties of isolated elements, understood from close up. *Shi* is more specific to an active way of seeing space, and describes distant views, aggregations, and dynamic, ever shifting relationships that constellate to form "global outlines."[30] According to WANG Qiheng, *xing* and *shi* are "mutually opposing and mutually generating at the same time."[31] *Shi* is translated by François JULLIEN as "propensity," i.e. "power," "position" or "circumstances," that arise from the disposition of things.[32] Robin WANG parses Jullien's discussion of these terms and states: "... *Shi* is entailed in *xing* and *xing* relies on *shi*. Their relationship is like the ocean to waves or galloping to a horse. *Xing* is the shape of the waves or the horse itself. *Shi* is hidden energy, the potential force in the wave or in the horse. It is powerful and is ready to mobilise a given entity..."[33]

In discussing the Zhou-era ideal city, and Chinese imperial city planning in general, historian CAI Yanxin refers to the *feng shui* underpinnings of Chinese space: "the philosophical foundation of the development of square-shaped cities in ancient China was determined by ancient philosophies, such as the philosophy of *yin yang*, along with the principles of the "Five Elements" of water, fire, earth, wood, and metal. The theme of duality, which features in these philosophies, led to an emphasis on forming a central axis in the basic layout of cities and also promoted symmetry."[34] Cai's idea that a strong central axis and a nine-square grid communicate duality and the oppositional tension of *yin* and *yang* does not ring true to Western ears. In rough terms, *yin* is associated with the feminine, darkness, inaction, and the negative, while *yang* is associated with the masculine, light, action, and the positive. Yet in Western thought, an axis enforces an equalising symmetry and a nine-square grid confers organisation around a singular centre, while providing sameness of cells, commensurability, recursive order, and scalable uniformity, not the reciprocal embrace of opposites associated with the *yin* and *yang*.

The paradox may have to do with different ways of understanding space. Western space, at least in modern times, is abstract, denatured, Cartesian space, mathematical, commodifiable, and reducible to points on a chart. In historical China and even today, space unfolds on a ground plane surging with flows of subterranean energy, *qi*, the "material force" or "breath of life."[35] The cardinal directions are not just points on a compass. Rather, they are governed by animal spirits, whose alignment and interrelationships play an important role in creating auspicious environments, as studied in *feng shui*. The Red Phoenix (or bird) and the element fire are associated with the south, the Black Tortoise and the element water with the north, the Azure Dragon and the element wood with the West,

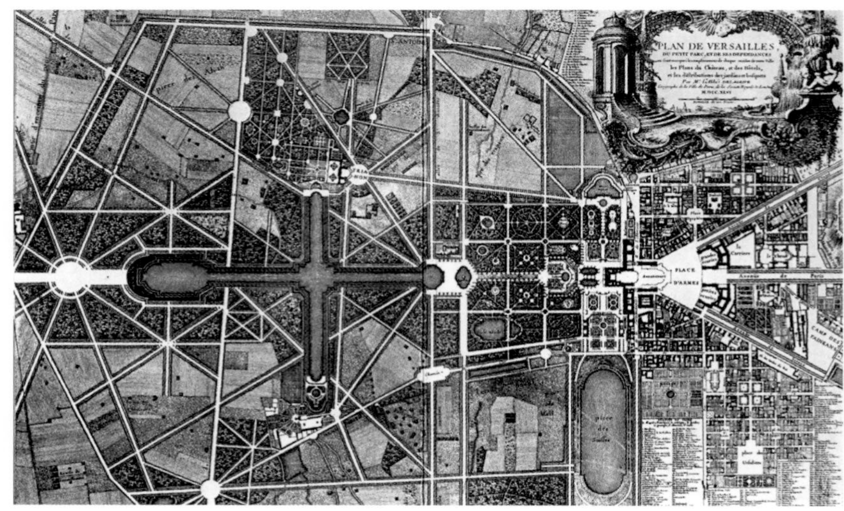

Delagrive, Plan of Versailles, 1746

and the White Tiger and the element metal with the East. The fifth Chinese cardinal direction, Centre, is associated with the Yellow Dragon and the element earth.[36] Each creature and each substance has distinct and very different attributes. In the *Rites of Zhou* a procession is described in terms of the relative position of these guardian creatures: "In front there is a Red Bird, followed by a slow moving Turtle at the rear, to the left is the Azure Dragon and to the right a White Tiger."[37] In other words, an axial arrangement is called for, but it is described in terms that stress the balance and reconciliation of difference across a line, rather than the uniform unfolding of matched entities framing an axis. If conventional notions of axial symmetry can be put aside, then anyone would have to admit that east is profoundly different from west, north from south. The leveling and neutralising role played by Cartesian coordinates has no place in the lived world. An axis calls out difference across the line as much as it authorises the mirroring of equal qualities. A classical Chinese history book, *Discussion of the States* (*Guoyu*) includes a speech from 779 BCE, which discusses beauty as the reconciliation of difference: "When unlike is joined to like, the result is called harmony *(he)*... But if sameness is added to sameness, exhaustion is reached and matters are at an end... Where there is but one sound, hearing ceases; where there is but one kind of material, pattern is absent; where there is but one kind of taste, there is no sweetness; where there is but one kind of example, there is no persuasion."[38]

More can be said about the role of the axis in Chinese city plans and how it seems to exercise strategies familiar from Western examples, while in fact doing something quite different. Compare, for example, the use of the axis in two vast, axially organised royal projects for rulers who both claimed a celestial pedigree: the Son of Heaven's Imperial City in Beijing (begun 1406) and the Sun King's chateau and gardens of Versailles (rebuilt from the 1660s onwards). Both use sheer scale and relentless order to demonstrate the power of the state. Both integrate landscape and architecture to orchestrate a complex narrative about the relationship of culture and nature. Both use geometry and pattern to construct a habitable diagram of society. However, beyond that, the deployment of the axis is quite different and serves different ends. For one thing, Versailles is linear, while the Imperial City is simultaneously linear and concentric. At Versailles, the axis is generative of a continuous, telescoping path, and stretches out along an infinite east-west axis, vanishing below the horizon line, like the sun. In the Imperial City, the axis is an organisational device, but it cannot be experienced in its entirety. Instead of a continuous swath of space, the path proceeds through a network of courtyards, opening up towards the south, and growing dense towards the north. Each courtyard delimits space

Adam Perelle, View of Versailles, 1690

and view behind walls and gates. Instead of a grand axial vista revealing all, as at Versailles, the Imperial City is revealed episodically, the vista is discontinuous, and new views open up at each threshold.

The centres in the two schemes are therefore very different. At Versailles the centre is implied and unstable, originating in the palace, but projected outwards, constantly displaced and repositioned along the axis, moving towards infinity. In Beijing, the centre is at the core of the embedded concentric layers. Hierarchy is established by stipulating and reaffirming centrality. Indeed, the Chinese name for China (*Zhongguo*) means "Middle Kingdom," thus claiming for the nation the same hierarchical status on the world map as the Forbidden City has in Beijing. Yet at the Imperial City the centre is at once unitary and dispersed, with the architectural object dissolving into a tightly knit, expanding field. The emphasis on centre in Beijing also has cosmological meaning. Ancient Chinese astronomers organised the constellations around the North Star, called the "Purple Palace," and believed it to be the home of the celestial emperor.[39] The dwelling of the earthly emperor, the Son of Heaven, marked its kinship with the celestial Purple Palace both by its central position and by its Chinese name, *Zijin Cheng,* literally the "Purple Forbidden City." Furthermore, the Forbidden City is purported to have 9,999 and one-half rooms, just shy of the 10,000 rooms in the celestial palace.[40]

Different ways of seeing and understanding the world come to the fore in the two palace designs. The axis in Versailles skewers space, uniting foreground, middle ground and background along an unbroken visual vector. The best view of the complex is from the King's bedroom window, which frames converging paths, like a diagram of Renaissance mathematical perspective as described by Leon Battista ALBERTI in 1435. In 1927, Erwin PANOFSKY argued that perspective was not merely a neutral descriptive tool, but rather a symbolic form, carrying with it larger attitudes about the world.[41] Each culture and each epoch has its own way of seeing, and the methods of representation do not merely delineate that vision, but also create it. Panofsky notes that Albertian perspective requires a point of view and an immobile, monocular viewer, gazing fixedly in one direction. Moreover, because mathematical perspective requires a vantage point outside the picture plane, the viewer is pulled away from the depicted scene and territory is opened up for dispassionate scientific scrutiny of the image as something apart from self. A complete separation of subject and object is called for, illustrated in Albrecht DÜRER's drawing of an artist with a perspective machine, in which a gridded screen separates the artist from his object of scrutiny. Panofsky recognised the shortcomings of mathematical perspective: "The structure of an infinite, unchanging, and homogeneous space – in short, a purely mathematical space – is unlike the structure of

Albrecht Dürer, "Draftsman's Net," c. 1532

psychophysiological space: 'Perception does not know the concept of infinity.'"[42] The removal of subject from object is also marked formally in the layout of Versailles, where the mass of the palace complex coagulates at one end, while vectors of sight and space project forward and away. The visual unfolding of events at Versailles corresponds to Plato's emission theories of vision, which posited that rays of sight emanated outwards from the eyes. If the use of axes in western architecture favours views that conform to Platonic theories of vision and Alberti's perspective window on the world, then what is it like to look at and experience the axis of the Imperial City? Andrew BOYD, Jianfei ZHU and others suggest that it is a bit like looking at a Chinese scroll painting, where episode follows episode as one unrolls the scroll.[43] Moreover, the ritual of revealing and concealing, necessary to view a scroll painting or to walk through the Forbidden City, connects to Taoist ideas that concealment enhances the sacrality of a place.[44]

There are fundamental differences in the purpose and experience of Eastern and Western pictorial space. In traditional Western painting, the whole can be taken in at a glance to create a plausible representation of the world. The mathematisation of space and the conceit of the passive, stationary viewer permit everyone, using reason, to decipher perspective space in exactly the same way. By contrast, viewing a Chinese painting requires action over time: both the physical action of rolling and unrolling a scroll or leafing through an album, and the visual tracing of path with the eye. Rather than the separation of subject and object, enforced by Western perspective, Chinese painting requires the viewer to imaginatively immerse himself and wholly enter into the painting. To see a Chinese painting is to journey through its space, using memory and imagination to anticipate or recall hidden images or to connect paths through large expanses of void or mist. The viewer is invited to experience the texture of the path, the smell of the air, the blowing wind, the dewy mist, and the light through the leaves. The task of the Chinese painting is not verisimilitude or the mapping of the world, but rather the evocation and re-creation of the feeling experienced by the painter. As Dawn DELBLANCO observes: "The experience of seeing a scroll for the first time is like a revelation. As one unrolls the scroll, one has no idea what is coming next: each section presents a new surprise."[45] An extreme example of the unfolding of narrative over the length of a scroll is the twenty-six metre Ming dynasty scroll, "Departure Herald," which depicts a procession of the Emperor and his entourage. The pace of viewing a scroll depends on the level of engagement of the viewer. The eye moves through the space to link it with other depicted scenes, and each viewing permits a different path and a different feeling. Multiple viewpoints are often included, thus fragmenting the singularity of the subject-object relationship to a dispersed field of possibilities. There is no compositional centre, nor any focal point which organises the painting as a whole. The marginalisation of human presence in such landscape paintings corresponds to Taoist beliefs that people are minute and insignificant in the context of the vast cosmos, and thereby unworthy of holding the over-arching vantage point mandated by perspective.

Because traditional Chinese painting was not a mirror or window to the world, but a tool to evoke strong experience, Jullien characterised it as "nonobject" in his

Shitao, "10,000 Ugly Inkblots," 1685, detail

provocatively named book, *The Great Image Has No Form, or On the Nonobject through Painting* (2009). Viewing a Chinese painting is not about understanding the formal properties of the work, but participating in the dynamic fusion of subject into object. The viewer must take part in the atmosphere and energy of the work. The immersive spatial experience called for in Chinese painting reflects Taoist belief in a continuum of existence, creating a unity of art, reality and imagination. Zhu states that engaging with a Chinese painting requires "a dissolution of the viewing subject into the world."[46] Hence landscape painting was the most highly valued genre in the East, since it served to enhance awareness and spiritual advancement.[47]

The focus on the re-creation of experience assigned great value to quickness of execution, energy, and looseness of images. Tracing the calligraphic gesture of the brush and motion of the painter's hand was a way to better embrace his state of mind and also to intuit the intensive training and discipline that made possible such apparently casual brushstrokes. Ming dynasty painter TANG Zhiqi stated: "When you paint there is no need to paint all the way; if with each brushstroke you paint all the way, it becomes common." A Chan (Chinese for Zen) saying dwells on a related theme: "The one who is good at shooting does not hit the centre of the target," suggesting that the act of archery, like the act of painting, is not aimed at an outcome, but at a fully inhabited, immediate experience. "10,000 Ugly Inkblots," by the painter Shitao (born ZHU Rueji), from 1685, is a good illustration of how the experience of the painter supersedes the apparent aesthetic qualities of the work. Shitao deliberately violates accepted standards of beauty as he becomes more and more energised and immersed in the work. The horizontal scroll painting is covered in a dense web of splashes, splatters, lines, and blots, seeming to anticipate Jackson POLLOCK's all-over action painting by more than 250 years. At the same time it contains a critique of the role of the image in painting. The left side of the work contains an orderly drawing of pavilions in a landscape, but as one journeys on, moving to the right, the wildness of the paint and the energy of the painter escalate, ultimately forgoing representation entirely in favour of pure embodiment of passion, mood, spiritual energy, and the physicality of paint and painter. The contrast between the two sides forces the viewer to understand that the painting is something quite different than a mere record of a view. In Shitao's poem about the painting he declares: "I have broken out of the mold and liberated my 'mind's eyes!' Like a Transcendent riding the wind, whose flesh and bones have etherealised."[48] The sketchiness of the image increases its immediacy and enhances its value. Tang dynasty scholar CHANG Yen-yuan wrote: "If the spirit-resonance is sought for, the outward likeness will be obtained at the same time."[49]

Since Gotthold LESSING's *Laocoön* (1766), it has been accepted in Western art that poetry and painting have fundamentally different characteristics. Poetry, like music, is dynamic and temporal, gaining meaning and richness by signs (words, notes, beats) sequenced in time and coming one after another (*nacheinander*). The visual arts, by contrast, are static for Lessing, spatial rather than temporal, in which signs (shapes, lines, colours) gain meaning based on their relative position in a defined spatial field (*nebeneinander*).[50] The viewing of a Chinese scroll

Shitao, "Flower," circa 1690

Ni Zan, "Six Gentlemen," fourteenth century

confounds Lessing's dualistic categories and requires a new kind of seeing, conflating Lessing's modes of spatiality and temporality. Indeed, the Chinese word for looking at a painting is *du hua*, meaning *to read*.[51]

Moreover, in China the art of painting is integrally wrapped up with the art of writing. Chinese calligraphy established techniques of disciplined, expressive brush handling used by master painters. In fact, the very nature of Chinese writing arises from image making, with each ideogram drawn from an abstracted and condensed image of things, and not the sound of words, as in the West. Painter ZHAO Mengfu (1254–1322) described his art as "writing" rather than "painting."[52] Calligraphy, painting and poetry were seen as part of a continuum, called "the three perfections," and all were practised together by accomplished scholars.[53] The meaning of a painted image is completed by accompanying calligraphs and poems, and vice versa. The surface of a painting was not only used to collect images and poetic notations from the artist, but also seals, calligraphy and poetic responses from successive generations of viewers. Looking at an annotated scroll enabled viewers to experience the history of the painting, the history of seeing, and to enter into a dialogue with highly cultivated viewers from the past. Such notations were artfully and deliberately composed, and contribute to the dense, layered meaning of the work, as in NI Zan's "Six Gentlemen," an image of six stately trees, inscribed with subsequent notations and responses over generations. The poet, Ezra POUND, believed so strongly in the legibility and transparency of the image in Chinese written characters that he translated Chinese poetry, even though he had no understanding of the language.[54] He further used his loose sense of how Chinese characters collect and overlay related but different meanings in his own Imagist poetry. Pound observed that Westerners lost the original metaphors that "our ancestors built ... into structures of language," while Chinese writing, by contrast, "bears its metaphors on its face."[55]

Landscape painting was not the only way that scholars, officials, *literati,* and aristocrats engaged with and contemplated nature: they also created gardens. After the collapse of the Han dynasty there was a renewed interest in indigenous Tao practices, and especially landscape and

Zhao Mengfu, "Autumn Colours on the Qiao and Hua Mountains," Song dynasty

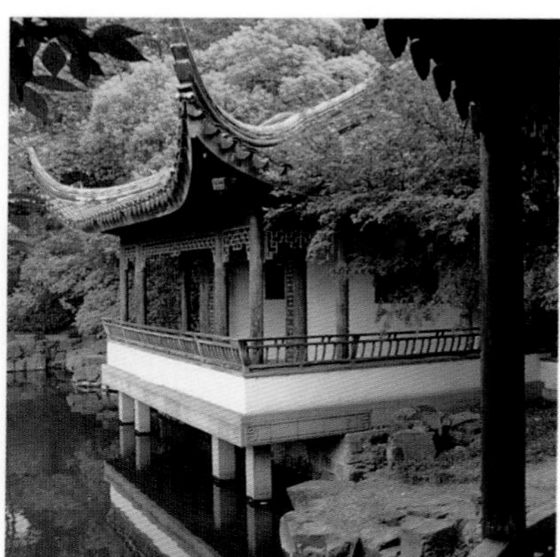

North Temple Garden, Suzhou (p. 228)

garden design. The Chinese word for landscape is *shan shui* (literally "mountain," "water"). Not surprisingly, standard features in all Chinese gardens were water and mountains, or rather miniaturised mountains in the form of lavish rock compositions, called rockeries, and also paths, plants, flowers, pavilions, and an enclosing garden wall, usually painted white. Water and rock were opposing elements in Taoist thought, *yin* and *yang,* and their opposition, reconciliation and balance were key to creating a harmonious design. Contrasting the ever-changing, smooth fluidity of water against the unchanging, rough solidity of rock heightened awareness and provoked pensive reflection. At the same time, deeply eroded, eccentrically twisted rockeries in Chinese gardens were reminders that rock and water were complexly interrelated, for water eroded rock and gave it form.

The first gardens in China were vast holdings of the Emperor, but as scholar-officials retired from court, they began to construct gardens at a more modest scale. The purpose of the gardens was to create a spot where they could commune with nature and study, philosophise, write poetry, practise calligraphy, and paint, although gardens were also the sites of banquets, drinking and administrative activity. Another purpose of the garden was to display the refinement and taste of the owner. The names of garden pavilions offer clues to their expected use: the **Humble Administrator's Garden** (p. 218) has forty-eight pavilions with evocative names, like "Watching the Pines and Appreciating Paintings Hall" or "Listening to the Rain Pavilion"; the Lingering Garden holds the "Spot of Return for Reading" and the "Peak-Worshipping Pavilion." Extreme aesthetic sensitivity was sought and the gardens provided an ideal setting for the cultivation of such refined taste. A seventeenth-century epigram provides insight into the sophisticated aesthetic and literary culture of the scholars who cultivated and curated these gardens: "The sounds of pine trees, of brooks, of mountain beasts, of nocturnal insects, of cranes, of lutes, of chess pieces falling, of rain dripping on steps, of snow splashing on windows and of tea boiling are all sounds of the utmost purity. But the sound of someone reading is supreme."[56]

The gardens of scholar-officials were much smaller than imperial gardens, not only because scholars did not have the means to finance vast projects, but also because sumptuary laws forbade the display of excessive wealth on the part of commoners. Perhaps the "Humble Administrator" gave his rich and extensive garden such a self-effacing name to avoid inviting close scrutiny and running afoul of the law. Even though scholar gardens were relatively small, they were nonetheless expected to contain a miniaturised universe and sometimes the mythical settings of Chinese legends. To conjure up the illusion of a much larger and varied space, such gardens took advantage of complex spatial strategies. Frequently designed by skilled painters, it is not surprising that many of the garden

Matteo Ripa, plate from "36 views of the Imperial Summer Palace at Jehol," 1714

J. B. Fischer von Erlach, "artificial mountain," from *Outline of a History of Architecture*, 1721

designs made use of pictorial devices to extend space. Plays of scale and proximity created illusions of depth and simulacra of vast, remote landscapes. Rocks stood for mountains, moss for forests, ponds for oceans. "Borrowed" scenery *(jiejing)* permitted the experience of the garden to be further extended by framing views of surrounding mountains or capturing sound from the chants and bells of nearby monasteries.[57] The illusion of deep space in a shallow plenum was evoked by means of layering, fragmentation, disorientation, dislocation, displacement, folding, zig-zagging, and framing. Irregular shapes were preferred for landforms, rockeries, ponds, and even trees, because their lineaments could not be anticipated. Edges were concealed so that surprise and discovery were around every corner. Zig-zag paths and passageways provided a varied sequence of composed views from multiple vantage points, sometimes framing views with round moon doors or decorative lattices. (Accustomed to such ingenious illusionism and spatial artifice, a Chinese friend once remarked at the grand French garden of Vaux-le-Vicomte, "it could be smaller.") Circuitous movement through Chinese gardens followed the Chinese proverb, "By detours, access to secrets."[58] Similar to the fragmentation of the axial experience at the Forbidden City, the experience of the garden is a series of discoveries and discrete environments. In both cases, the episodic revelation of elements parallels the sequential presentation of scenes in scroll painting. Indeed, during the Qing dynasty, the design of gardens was overseen by the Imperial Institution of Paintings.

Chinese architecture did not have much of an influence in the West, except as an inspiration for the decorative programme and colour palette of Rococo architecture and as a source for exotic imagery in garden follies. Perhaps Chinese traditional architecture was too strongly linked to bureaucratic prescriptions to survive export, or perhaps simple, timber post-and-beam structures, dominant throughout China, were already plentiful and widely adopted throughout Europe and America. However, Chinese garden design had a powerful legacy in the West. The first Chinese garden seen by a Westerner was KUBLAI Khan's garden at Xanadu, visited by Marco POLO in 1275,[59] and celebrated in Samuel Taylor COLERIDGE's poem as "a stately pleasure dome ... with twice five miles of fertile ground with walls and towers ... girdled round."[60] Western contact with the East intensified once Jesuit priests began to set up missions in China. Saint Francis XAVIER was first to arrive in 1552, and Father Matteo RICCI followed in 1582, creating a dictionary and a map of China. Louis XIV's court mathematician travelled to China in 1685,[61] reporting on the Chinese preference for informal, naturalistic rock piles, grottos, and hills, rather than the strict geometric order favoured in Louis XIV's court in France. Austrian court architect Johann Bernhard FISCHER VON ERLACH included several plates on China in his *Outline of a History of Architecture* (1721), based solely on early publications, and perhaps portrayals of Chinese scenes on teacups and brocades. Throughout the eighteenth century, the trade in Chinese decorative arts flourished, fueling a taste for Chinese decorative motifs, called

Sir William Chambers, "House of Confucius" at Kew Gardens, London, 1762

Johann Gottfried BÜRING, "Chinese House," Schloß Sanssouci, Potsdam, c. 1760

chinoiserie. Schloß Pillnitz in Dresden and the Chinese House at Schloß Sanssouci in Potsdam are particularly strong examples of the *chinoiserie* style.

Between 1711 and 1723, Father Matteo RIPA spent time in China, where he introduced the art of copper engraving to the Chinese and produced a series of landscape engravings, including *Thirty-six Views of the Imperial Summer Palace at Jehol,* 1714. Upon returning to Europe in 1724, Ripa stopped in London and probably met Lord BURLINGTON, who had a copy of *Thirty-six Views* in his library.[62] Influenced by Ripa's evocations of the wild spontaneity of Chinese gardens, as well as landscape paintings by Claude LORRAIN and Nicolas POUSSIN, Burlington and William KENT went on to design one of the first English picturesque gardens, at Chiswick. They adopted Chinese compositional strategies of a seemingly natural, uncontrived layout, and carefully sited follies on irregular terrain. The style of natural, deliberately variegated, picturesque gardens subsequently became known throughout Europe as the *jardin anglo-chinois.* Rudolf WITTKOWER has argued that the enthusiastic reception of Chinese garden design in eighteenth-century England was not simply an aesthetic choice, but also reflective of political values.[63] Anti-royalist Whigs (like Burlington) felt an affinity for Chinese Confucian ideals which celebrated advancement through merit, study, filial duty, and service, as opposed to conservative Tory beliefs in the divine right of kingship and immovable social classes, thought to be expressed in grand, axial Baroque compositions.[64]

Of the eighteenth-century British architects who adopted Chinese motifs and spatial strategies, Sir William CHAMBERS had the most direct experience of Chinese architecture, ornament, and landscape. Chambers visited Guangzhou in the 1740s (on a Swedish trading vessel) and did much to promote the Western taste for naturalistic gardens and China-inspired garden pavilions. Chambers believed that English gardens were monotonous and lacked life – especially gardens designed by his contemporary, Lancelot "Capability" BROWN. In his writings on Chinese gardens, *On the Art of Laying Out Gardens Among the Chinese* (1757), and *Dissertation on Oriental Gardening* (1773), Chambers adduced the Chinese garden as an alternative model and antidote to the dull uniformity of the English landscape. Chambers identified three kinds of Chinese landscapes: the "pleasing," the "terrible," and the "surprising." These categories, like Chambers's outlandish descriptions, had little to do with Chinese garden tradition, but rather reflected theories of the beautiful and sublime, recently promulgated by Edmund BURKE, and even more closely Joseph ADDISON's categories of the beautiful, the great and the uncommon. Chambers said: "Gardeners, like poets, should give a loose to their imagination, and even fly beyond the bounds of truth, whenever it is necessary to elevate, to embellish, to enliven, or to add novelty to their subject."[65] In addition to writing theoretical tracts, Chambers also designed garden structures derived from Chinese and other exotic sources, most notably the Pagoda and "House of Confucius" in London's Kew Gardens (1762).

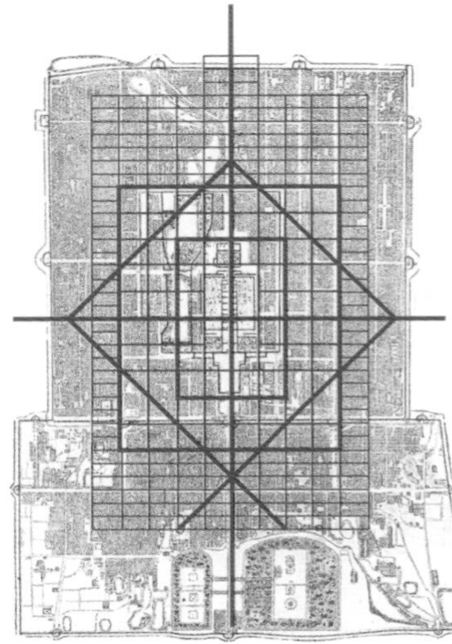

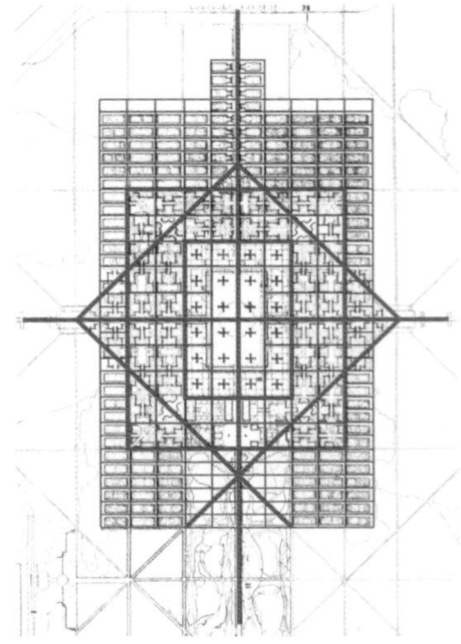

Comparison of planning and geometric structure in the Imperial City (per the 1875 Bretschneider Plan), and Le Corbusier's 1922 *Ville Contemporaine*

In the twentieth century, while architects like Wright discovered Taoist aspects of Chinese architecture, which valorised space and the sensitive melding of architecture and landscape, Le Corbusier (born Charles-Édouard JEANNERET-GRIS) instead drew inspiration from the taut Confucian order and enormity of the Imperial City in Beijing. He also admired the well-organised power structure that made possible such large-scale building. Decrying the tangled network of medieval alleys that characterised European cities of his day and the timidity of contemporary architects and urban planners, Le Corbusier urged strong action, free from nostalgia. In *The City of Tomorrow* (1929), Le Corbusier saw the architect as a surgeon who could cut away tumorous antiquated urban fabric and open the city up to light, space, greenery, free-flowing traffic, and order. Looking back at a time when bolder action was possible, Le Corbusier dedicated *Ville Radieuse* to "Authority," and illustrated it with an image of Louis XIV, the "great urbanist." In *The City of Tomorrow* Le Corbusier twice illustrates the plan on Beijing with the remark: "compare this plan with that of Paris... And we Westerners felt called on to invade China in the cause of civilisation."[66] Le Corbusier's admiration for the plan of Beijing was not merely passive. His *Ville Contemporaine* (1922) is a refashioning of the plan of imperial Beijing, extracting from it the strategy of a strong axial disposition of concentrically nested grids of different densities and scales, with tight fabric at one end and looser fabric and park land at the other. Furthermore, Le Corbusier borrows the footprint for his *Ville Contemporaine* from the Plan of the Imperial City, or at least from the 1875 Bretschneider Plan of the Imperial City, illustrated in his writings.

Our brief examination of traditions in Chinese architecture, painting, and conceptions of space has shown that two different traditions underlie most aspects of Chinese culture: Taoism and Confucianism, *yin* and *yang*. While the former favours asymmetry and a surrender to the natural features of the site, the latter fosters order, uniformity, modularity, and standardisation. It's hard to guess how this double history prepared territory for contemporary architecture in China, but it's easy to see that Chinese architecture today has not yet found an adequate response. Geomancers are still called in to help site buildings, and property values for favourably sited dwellings by far outstrip the price of units with inauspicious *feng shui*. However, when faced with demands for efficient land use, maximum floor area ratio, ever-expanding infrastructure, and the need to accommodate a vast population, there is not much the *feng shui* can do to allow the natural landscape to hold its own against buildings and site "improvements." The present Chinese leadership shares the ancient emperors' belief that

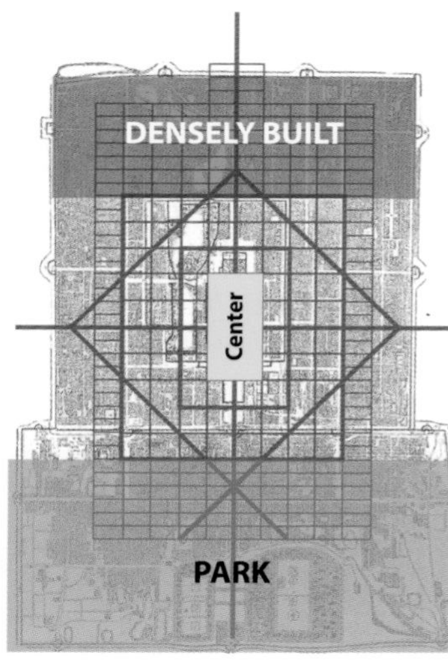

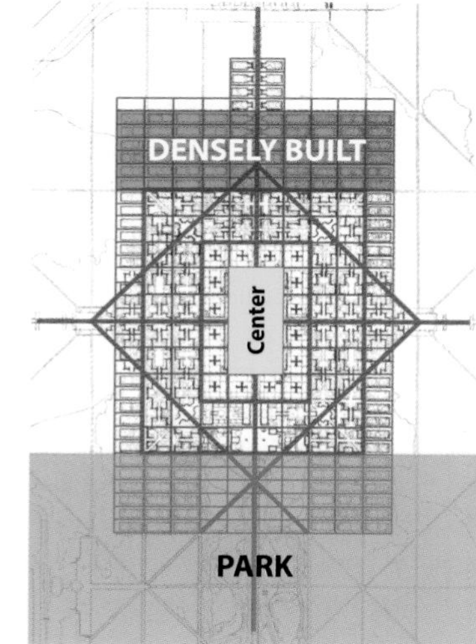

Comparison between the distribution of programme in the Imperial City and Le Corbusier's *Ville Contemporaine* (1922)

architecture is an effective tool to represent the power and ambitions of the state, hence no project is too vast to be undertaken. Yet if the overwhelming scale of Mao's parade grounds at **Tian'anmen Square** (p. 072) created one kind of architectural symbol for China, then the **2008 Olympic grounds** (p. 095 forward) and the explosion of avant-gardist shopping malls, corporate headquarters, luxury housing complexes, and themed new towns offer another. In both kinds of undertaking, vast areas of traditional urban fabric and even traditional villages, are laid waste to make room for rapacious development. The traditional architectural heritage of China thereby shrinks, and that is cause for concern.

Chinese architects and planners have long been aware of the difficulty of holding onto traditions while adapting technologies to regain the superiority and political strength the nation held throughout its history. Nuanced responses to the question of a Chinese architecture in the twenty-first century are being explored by a young generation of architects tapping materiality, typology, circulation, landscape, and the fostering of community in their designs. Perhaps the spatial concepts of *xing* (form) and *shi* (global composition) also need more careful consideration, so that instead of creating a new China full of eccentric object-buildings, the unity and harmony of the whole shall be taken into account.

Notes

1. Nancy STEINHARDT, *Chinese Architecture,* New York: Cambridge University Press, 2011, p.2
2. Andrew BOYD, *Chinese Architecture 1500 BC – AD 1911,* Chicago: University of Chicago Press, 1962, p.127.
3. CAI Yanxin, *Chinese Architecture,* New York: Cambridge University Press, 2011, p. 83.
4. Steinhardt, *op. cit.* p. 7.
5. Klaas RUITENBEEK, *Carpentry and Building in Late Imperial China: a Study of the Fifteenth Century Carpenter's Manual Lu Ban Jing* (Leiden & New York: E.J. Brill, 1993), p. 287, Figures 57– 59, Vol. 3.
6. Steinhardt, *op. cit.* p. 7.
7. LI Jie, (1035–1110), *Yingzao fashi zhushi.* ed. Liang Sicheng (Beijing: *Zhongguo jianzhu gongye chubanshe*, 1983), p. 114.
8. DU Shiran et al., *Biographies of Ancient Chinese Scientists Series One: Lu Ban* (Beijing: Kexue Chubanshe, 1992), pp. 22–25.
9. Li Jie, *Yingzao fashi zhush*i. See images in Joseph NEEDHAM, *Science and Civilisation in China: Volume 4, Part 3, Civil Engineering and Nautics,* p. 96; and Liang Sicheng, ed., *Yingzao fashi zhushi, op cit.*
10. Puay-Peng HO, "China II, 1, I: Architecture: Structure and Materials: Timber," in *Oxford Art Online*, www.oxfordartonline.com
11. Confucius, *The Analects*, Book 17, No. 18, translation Lau, p. 146, cited in "Chinese Aesthetics," *Oxford Art Online*, www.oxfordart-online.com.
12. William Theodore de BARY, *Sources of Chinese Tradition,* Vol. 1. New York: Columbia University Press, 1999, p. 295.

13. The *Yingzao fashi,* and other traditional building manuals, were less bodies of theory than sets of technical instructions and regulations. Feng, *op. cit.* p.7. Architecture was outside the scope of thoughtful consideration among the *literati.*

14. Cai Yanzin, *op. cit.*, p. 5.

15. This image is included in John B. HENDERSON's essay, *op. cit,* with the caption: "This diagram depicts the type of geometrised political geography devised by Han cosmographers. All the domains in this schema are centered on the royal capital, which occupies the central square. According to this schema, the degree of barbarism increases with the square of the distance from the center..." p. 207.

16. "China II, 1, I : Architecture: Structure and Materials: Timber," in *Oxford Art Online,* www.oxfordartonline.com.

17. The purpose of the *Yingzao Fashi* and other building manuals was to disseminate correct, useful building knowledge to people in the construction practice, and to establish standards which marked rank, not to theorise and speculate about architecture in an abstract sense.

18. LIANG Ssu-Ch'eng, *Chinese Architecture: A Pictorial History,* Cambridge, Mass. MIT Press, 1984, p.14.

19. Jiren FENG, *Chinese Architecture and Metaphor,* p. 138.

20. Puay-Peng Ho, *Oxford Art Online,* "China II, 1, I : Architecture: Structure and Materials: Timber," www.oxfordartonline.com, after Liang Sicheng.

21. Nelson WU, *Chinese and Indian Architecture,* New York, Braziller, 1963, p. 37.

22. John B. Henderson, "Chinese Cosmological Thought: The High Intellectual Tradition," *The History of Cartography, vol.20: Cartography in Traditional East and Southeast Asian Societies,* ed. J. B. Harley and David Woodward. Chicago: University of Chicago Press, 1994, p. 204.

23. LI Hua, "Hanyuandian fu," cited by Jiren Feng, *op. cit.*, p. 1.

24. Cai Yanzin, *op. cit.*, p. 133.

25. *Ibid.*, pp. 129 – 132.

26. Laozi, cited by Li Xiaodong, "The Aesthetic of the Absent," *The Journal of Architecture,* Vol 7, Spring 2002, p. 87.

27. Cai Yanzin, op. cit. p. 65.

28. Chang Tzu, *Teachings and Sayings of Chuang Tzu,* New York: Dover, 2001, p. 86.

29. Robin WANG, *Yinyang: The Way of Heaven and Earth in Chinese Thought and Culture,* United States of America: Cambridge University Press, 2012, p. 151.

30. Jianfei ZHU, *Chinese Spatial Strategies,* London and New York: Routledge, 2004, p. 225.

31. WANG Qiheng, *Fengshui xingshi shuo,* cited by Zhu, op. cit.

32. François JULLIEN, *The Propensity of Things,* p. 91, cited by Zhu, op. cit., p. 277.

33. Robin Wang, *Yinyang: The Way of Heaven and Earth in Chinese Thought and Culture,* 2012, *op. cit.,* p. 151.

34. Cai Yanzin, *op. cit.*, p. 9.

35. LU & BOZOVIC,"The Spatial Concept of Chinese Architecture," 2.3 & 2.4. *Built Spaces: The Cultural Shaping of Architectural and Urban Spaces,* Vol. 9, No. 1, Nov. 2004.

36. Derek WALTERS, *Chinese Mythology: An Encyclopedia of Myth and Legend,* New York: Harper Collins, 1992.

37. *Zhou Book of Rites, The LÎ KÎ, A Collection of Treatises on the Rules of Propriety or Ceremonial Usages,* translated by James LEGGE, 1885, *Sacred Books of the East Vol. 27, The Sacred Books of China* Vol. 4. Part Y, 1.1, Section I, Part V, 1.1

38. Haun Sassy, "Chinese Aesthetics: The Archaic Period: Music as the Measure," *Oxford Art Online.*

39. Emmanuelle MORGEN, Deborah KAUFMAN eds., *Beijing and Shanghai,* p. 12, Fodor's, 2005.

40. Zhuoyun YU, *Palaces of the Forbidden City.* New York: Viking, 1984, p. 18.

41. Erwin PANOFSKY, *Perspective as Symbolic Form,* trans. Christopher S. Wood. New York: Zone Books, 1997, p. 30.

42. Ernst CASSIRER, *The Philosophy of Symbolic Forms,* quoted by Panofsky in *Perspective as Symbolic Form,* p. 28–29.

43. Boyd, *op cit.,* p.73, Zhu, Jianfei, *Chinese Spatial Strategies: Imperial Beijing 1420–1911,* London: Routledge, 2004, p. 227.

44. Jeffrey MEYER, *The Dragons of Tiananmen,* pp 61–2, cited by Zhu, *Ibid.,* p. 224.

45. Dawn DELBANCO, catalog note, *Metropolitan Museum of Art.*

46. Zhu, *op. cit.*, p. 230.

47. Jessica RAWSON, ed., *The British Museum Book of Chinese Art,* (2nd edition), London: British Museum Press, 2007, p. 112.

48. "Ten Thousand Ugly Ink Blots" belongs to a series of four paintings made in 1685. The poem is included on the fourth painting. http://www.hyo-shinna.com/html/ten_thousand_ugly_ink_blots_.html

49. CHANG Yen-yuan, *Origin and Development of Painting,* c.845 CE, cited by François Jullien, *The Propensity of Things, op. cit.,* p. 92.

50. Gotthold Lessing, *Laocoön: An Essay on the Limits of Painting and Poetry*, 1766, translation E.C. Beasley, London: Longman, Brown, Green, and Longmans, 1853, p. 101.
51. Maxwell HEARN, *How to Read Chinese Paintings*, Metropolitan Museum of Art, 2008, p.1.
52. *Ibid.*, p. 4.
53. Michael SULLIVAN, *The Three Perfections: Chinese Painting, Poetry, and Calligraphy,* New York: George Braziller, 1999.
54. Pound also made use of notebooks by Italian Sinologist Ernesto Fenollosa, and Chinese assistants, but he believed the main import of the poems could be found in the ideograph itself.
55. Ezra Pound, *The ABCs of Reading,* (1934) New York: New Directions, 1960, p. 96.
56. Stanislaus Fung, *Oxford Art Online,* "Garden," §VI: "East Asia," v: "Qing period (1644–1911)."
57. Maggie KESWICK, *Chinese Garden: History, Art & Architecture,* New York: Rizzoli, 1978, p. 181.
58. CAO Xueqin, *Dream of the Red Chamber,* 1868, cited by Michel Baridon in *Les Jardins*, p. 443.
59. Marco POLO, *The Travels of Marco Polo, Book 1,* translated by Henry Yule, New York: Dover, 1903/1993, Chapter 61, "Of the City of Chandu, and the Kaan's Palace There," p. 289.
60. Samuel Taylor Coleridge, "Xanadu," 1797.
61. Catherine PAGANI, *Eastern Magnificence and European Ingenuity: Clocks of Late Imperial China*, 2001, p.182.
62. John Dixon HUNT, *The Genius of the Place: The English Landscape Garden, 1620-1820,* Cambridge, Mass. MIT Press, 1988, p.283.
63. Rudolf WITTKOWER, "English Neo-Palladianism, the Landscape Garden, China and the Enlightenment," in *Palladio and English Palladianism*, London: Thames & Hudson, 1974, p. 51.
64. Vittoria de PALMA, *Wasteland: A History,* New Haven and New York: Yale University Press, 2014, p 231.
65. Sir William CHAMBERS, *A Dissertation on Oriental Gardening,* Dublin: W. Wilson, 1773, p. 16.
66. Le Corbusier, City of To-Morrow, trans. Frederick Etchells. New York: Dover, reissue 1987, p. 88.

Sources and Recommended Reading

CAI Yanxin, *Chinese Architecture,* London: Cambridge University Press, 2010.

FENG Jiren, *Chinese Architecture and Metaphor: Song Culture in the Yingzao Fashi Building Manual,* Honolulu: University of Hawaii Press, 2012.

HEARN, Maxwell, *How to Read Chinese Paintings,* New York: Metropolitan Museum of Art, 2008.

JULLIEN, François, *The Great Object has No Form,* Chicago: Chicago University Press, 2012.

JULLIEN, François, *The Propensity of Things,* Cambridge, Mass. MIT Press 1995.

LU & BOZOVIC, "The Spatial Concept of Chinese Architecture," *Built Spaces. The Cultural Shaping of Architectural and Urban Spaces*, Vol. 9, No.1, Singapore, 2004.

STEINHARDT, Nancy, *Chinese Architecture,* New Haven, Yale University Press, 2002.

STEINHARDT, Nancy, *Chinese Imperial City Planning,* Honolulu: University of Hawaii Press, 1990.

WANG, Robin, *Yinyang: The Way of Heaven and Earth in Chinese Thought and Culture,* London: Cambridge University Press, 2012.

ZHU Jianfei, *Chinese Spatial Strategies: Imperial Beijing 1420–1911,* London: Routledge, 2004.

中国铁建十
中国铁建
Pine's
铁八号

A History of Modernities: Some Cautionary Notes

Addison Godel

The prospect of a "modern" architecture for China has remained an open question for over a century, bound up as it is in larger issues of China's relationship to the West and to its own past. The complex stew of mutually reinforcing trends that constituted Western modernity – industry, capital, bureaucracy, science, urbanisation, state centralisation, rapid technological change, alienation, avant-garde art, and so on – also made its way to China, but in different forms and under different circumstances, sometimes anticipated by established features of Chinese culture. One would hardly expect the results to play out the same way, even if there were not already a fundamental contrast between the modernist belief in "progress" and the historical Chinese picture of the world.

Architecture, unsurprisingly, has repeatedly borne witness to the complicated translation and reinvention of what it means to be modern. My goal in this text is not to attempt a comprehensive history of these reckonings and adaptations, but merely to sketch a few episodes that may give the visitor some reference points when exploring China's architectural and urban landscape. Consideration of these past moments may also suggest a few pitfalls to be avoided in evaluating recent Chinese work, which exhibits a great variety of thematic concerns and formal devices often lost in the shorthand of project summaries and online chatter. Too often, casual commentators reduce all designs to stand-ins for larger trends (real or imaginary), doing a disservice to those who expend months or years of intellectual energy on a design project.

Historically, despite many earlier European encounters, it was the nineteenth century that crystallised Chinese points of view on foreign "modernity." In that time, China suffered a long series of paralysing and humiliating defeats at the hands of people previously understood as barbarians. These experiences prompted protracted attempts by some Chinese thinkers to adopt or adapt "modern" (European) technologies, institutional forms and cultural practices to their own needs. This fundamental sea change in China's concept of itself and of the world is often seen as the precondition for the toppling of the Qing dynasty and the establishment of the doomed Republic of China in 1912. But even under the last emperors, industrialisation (to name one customary benchmark of modernity) was well under way: factories had sprung up in many of the port cities, railroads and telegraph lines crisscrossed the east coast, and catalytic enterprises like coal mining had begun in earnest.

Opposite: Construction near **Nanluogu Xiang** (p. 114)

As they did in Europe, industrialisation, capitalisation and urbanisation exposed architecture to new materials and new programmatic requirements. In China, however, the process was imposed from without, by foreign capital and military force. Nonetheless, Chinese architects, a newly recognised profession in a country where building had historically been an art or trade passed down from master to apprentice, began to explore the expressive potential latent in these challenging circumstances. But except in purely industrial buildings, Chinese designers for the most part eschewed the raw, unornamented massing of German functionalism or the "International Style." Instead, they favoured a streamlined, Moderne take on European classicism, in line with international Art Deco. Many examples still survive, especially in the period's cosmopolitan metropolis, Shanghai.

The architects of these buildings were often Westerners or Western-trained; for example, a programme for funding Chinese students at the University of Pennsylvania (then a Beaux-Arts school) was in place from the beginning of the century. Public buildings like the **Sun Yat-Sen Mausoleum** (p. 133) and **Jiangwan Stadium** (p. 190), designed by American-trained Chinese architects, incorporated traditional references (some more obvious than others), but took their typological cues from recent Beaux-Arts monuments. To the policymakers of the Republic of China, to be "modern" meant fitting in with the mainstream of European and American practice, not the fringe *avant-gardes* which architectural history recognises as the heart of "Modernism." While these buildings may look American or European, it is helpful to remember that they were built to do things which were specific to the China of the 1930s. At the same time, for many Chinese observers, Westernised cities like Shanghai represented the decadent barbarism that came from foreign influence.

It's hard to say what directions these developments might have taken, had the Republic endured; following the triumph of the People's Liberation Army in 1949, modernisation would proceed primarily along Soviet models. Particularly in the early years, this did allow for variants on the earlier Beaux-Arts approach. High-profile buildings, such as the museums around **Tian'anmen Square** (p. 072) and the **Shanghai Exhibition Centre** (p. 166), resemble Stalinist Socialist-Realism, with varying degrees of pompous scale, "Chinese" ornamentation, and propagandistic imagery applied to Beaux-Arts volumes. The costs of such projects at times made them a target of suspicion in a People's Republic, even as industrially oriented Soviet and East German advisors were displacing Beaux-Arts convention. Until the Sino-Soviet split of 1960, these figures helped outline central economic plans along Soviet Five-Year models, emphasising heavy industry over consumer goods. As in the Soviet Union during Khrushchev's tenure (1953–1964), they also favoured industrial building and purportedly rationalised, radically modern urban planning. To this day, much of the Chinese building code is Soviet in origin, accounting for the peculiar densities and "towers-in-a-park" planning of many otherwise contemporary schemes. Tough, economically oriented goals, and the persistence of the Beaux-Arts, mean that China boasts few postwar modern monuments, but industrial spaces like those of the **798 Arts District** (p. 100) suggest that even the rational engineers were not without aesthetic preferences. Meanwhile, architectural production itself was reorganised on the Soviet model, with private firms abolished and replaced by huge state "design institutes." Rigid standards proliferated, and boxy concrete Modernism of the Eastern European variety prevailed in the construction of housing, factories and offices.

Ultimately, architectural development after the Revolution was considerably disrupted by the wider convulsions of Chinese society in the Mao era. While standards of living improved through the 1950s, the famine brought on by the Great Leap Forward (1958–1961), and the total chaos of the Cultural Revolution (beginning 1966), made intellectual pursuits almost impossible. The Cultural Revolution's radical proposition was that Communist China had not yet made enough of a break from its capitalist and

The Great Hall of the People at **Tian'anmen Square,** 1959 (p. 072). Monumentally-scaled Beaux Arts classicism, dressed with "lotus" motifs and yellow tiles.

dynastic past. With schools closed and many intellectuals suppressed, exiled or killed, the decade from 1966 to 1976 effectively left a generational hole in China's architectural lineage. At the same time, the nation's heritage was put in the cross-hairs, with innumerable historic sites destroyed as relics of "old ways of thinking" (see the **Ming Tombs**, p. 110).

After order was restored in the second half of the 1970s, DENG Xiaoping began experimenting with the capitalisation of the economy in the 1980s. Even so, the state design institutes long maintained their monopoly. The Western model of an individual practising architect was tentatively explored in the Special Economic Zones, beginning in 1995, then rolled out nationwide in 2000. The institutes, often associated with major universities, are still around, and building constantly. Architects often start their careers within the institutes before striking out on their own; some high-profile designers remain within these agencies, exerting power over administrative sub-units as *de facto* design offices. These key figures do not always display distinctive design signatures or concerns, and it is easy for visitors to pass over institute work in housing, shopping and office developments as generic, derivative and repetitious. Doing so may render invisible the important issues as Chinese architects themselves see them, but it may be inevitable when one is trained to look for unique, innovative and discursively engaged projects.

The other key development since Deng has been the return of foreign architects to the Chinese field. Though they would not be permitted to set up offices in China until the latter half of the 1990s, collaborations began at the turn of the 1980s (for example, the **Fragrant Hill Hotel,** p. 092). At that time, Chinese production of concrete and steel simply could not meet project requirements, and construction methods on-site were not up to Western standards. A self-conscious desire to "catch up" was spurred by the example of the surrounding "Asian Tiger" economies, whose big cities glittered with new, high-tech towers. The example of Hong Kong, close at hand but still British territory, might have been a particular stimulus to the dreams of Chinese architects. Once again, it was thought that up-to-date architectural ideas from abroad would be necessary to meet Chinese goals.

The 1980s, in fact, bore witness to a broad debate within architectural culture, in short between "national form" and "Modernism." "National form" meant the use of Chinese historical styles, to a point that the "modernists" found absurd. Stan FUNG and ZHAO Yang discuss Beijing's giant new **Western Railway Station** (p. 103), a fundamentally modern

Billboard promoting a new-town development

structure embellished with an enormous (and functionless) pavilion-style building on top. But what did "Modernism" mean, besides rejecting Chinese historical types? And how did the rejection of history sit with designers, reflecting on the destructive excesses of the Cultural Revolution that had marked their formative years? China's "closed" condition meant that international modernist discourse was not available until the 1980s, and then only sparingly until the 1990s. For example, WANG Shu recalls that Japanese Metabolist projects of the 1960s were very popular in Chinese schools in the 1980s – but via texts published with only partial translations alongside the evocative images. Things have changed; today, China's leading architectural magazines are arguably more robust and varied in content than their Western equivalents, and juxtapose glossy and eye-catching content from around the world with thematic roundtable debates and multi-part translations of obscure twentieth century treatises (see p. 397). Some nuances of foreign discourse may of course be as obscure to Chinese audiences as the details of Chinese practice are to American architects, but today, it's Western observers like myself who struggle with partial translations of project summaries, sensing the scope of debates that we can only incompletely grasp.

All this would seem to place Chinese production on an essentially parallel track with the West, although the eagerness of the local design pool and client base to assimilate Western modernity has led to a proliferation of buildings which appear generically contemporary, or at least generically Postmodern. As LU Xin argues, the gulf in design culture is compounded by another tendency in Chinese professional practice: emphasising the project's image over the diagrammatic processes (formalist or programmatic) treasured in certain Western circles. Foreign architects often deride Chinese design as superficial, but to the Chinese, the functionalist-derived Western approach misses the forest for the trees. These differences also reflect boom-time planning and construction schedules. Chinese construction schedules are short, Chinese competitions are *very* short, and the expected quantity of presentation imagery is great. Lu tells the story of a competition for which her team produced a bidding document of thirteen pages; the worldly wise printer advised them to add more. Working around the clock, the designers expanded the document to forty-three pages and won the job – though the client found the brochure "rather thin."[1] This may be an extreme example, but it hints at the expectations of clients: the architect should be prepared, hard-working, serious about the client's needs – in short, ready to build.

If influential sectors of the Chinese market are disinclined towards the minute critical distinctions that separate various

Modern Chinese urbanism: freestanding, linear mid-rises, with newer high-rises looming

strains of contemporary Western architecture, and favour an image-oriented approach to projects generally, then the eager embrace of foreign "starchitects" is not surprising. At least, that's the line taken by some critics (at home and abroad) who find the whole affair faddish and simple-minded. In the boom, they say, China missed the potential for really substantive mediations between things international and things Chinese. We'll return to this theme in a moment, but it's certainly true that many of the "star" projects of the decade leading up to the 2008 Olympics seem as if they could have been built anywhere, assuming massive budgets, underpaid labour, and minimal regulation. But, as in the early modern period, the significance of these buildings (to many Chinese), is *that they are in China,* and thus fulfil a narrative of national progress and achievement.

Similar points might be made about the dominant urban forms, whose Modern and Soviet models are widely seen as discredited in the West. As Carlo RATTI writes of mega-scaled, zoned-based planning, "this is an unpopular city type with many Westerners, but one that is still interpreted as a symbol of modernity by Chinese deputies that must account for their actions not to the citizens, but to superiors obsessed by the idea of economic progress."[2] But we could look for simpler explanations: there are many Chinese, they would like to live somewhere, and the efficiencies of large-scale planning serve a purpose. It's understandable if Westerners are tempted to call upon the Chinese to build their cities more smartly, more sustainably, more artfully, than we have built our own lately. But do such demands implicitly carry the requirement that China not become as "modern" as the countries whose economies it now eclipses? Building an OMA skyscraper, a sprawling American-style suburb of "European" style villas, or a colossally vast "People's Square," could be a bit like putting a man in space – or simply providing "what the market wants." It is wholly appropriate to critique such claims, and lay bare their underlying assumptions, but it may not be appropriate for Western designers, who now think they have the city all figured out, to insist that China do things their way.

With a little hindsight, it's also now clear that the early years of the twenty-first century were an overheated period of icon-oriented architecture globally. China became, for many, a scapegoat for the "Bilbao effect," as grandiose super-buildings promised to give meaning to life in what turned out to be bubble years of unrestrained global capital. Setting aside what such projects mean to the Chinese population at large, their symbolic value to China's government – which remains autocratic and repressive despite its market "reforms" – seems clear. The 2008 Beijing Olympics, for example, were seen internationally as a sort of coming-out party for the New China, with the state

FAKE Design (AI Weiwei), Three Shadows Photographic Gallery at **Caochangdi** (p. 102). The surface depth of grey brickwork is dictated by computer-aided study of natural light falling through existing trees – commingling natural and artificial, familiar and strange.

presenting itself as both a global force to be reckoned with, and a team player, hosting a venerable ceremony of friendly athletic rivalry. Architecture provided the setting, with the two most celebrated buildings produced in collaboration with foreign lead designers (p. 097, p. 098). Are such team-ups a natural reflection of China's position on the world stage, and the exciting prospect of doing business in a country experiencing rapid growth and urbanisation? Or do they give tacit support to a regime as notable for its crackdowns on free speech as for its embrace of private ownership? These questions seemed extraordinarily potent in the mid-2000s, as a number of (often very thoughtful) books and exhibitions gathered up recent Chinese architectural production for non-Chinese audiences.

The pace of such publications has slowed considerably since the Olympics, which may reflect many things: the death of the book, the collapse of the global economy, or the fair-weather trend-following of readers. But in our estimation, there has been a real decline in the trend of mega-projects touting foreign star names. It's not that there's been a slowdown in Chinese architectural production, or even in the generation of monumental buildings; the infamous epidemic of regional and municipal art museums with nothing to exhibit appears to continue apace, reflecting the constant emergence and growth of newly urbanised centres. Under construction right now in **Datong** (p. 390) is a cultural super-square with a foursome of signature buildings, very much along the lines of Shenzhen's creation a decade earlier (p. 320). However, in general, these days the buildings are perhaps a little *less* big, while foreign designers (as distinct from foreign engineering and construction consultancies) seem no longer to be shoo-ins for the biggest projects. With the opening up of private practice, China is beginning to produce its own crop of big-name architects.

As in the early modern period, many of these practitioners are foreign-educated, or have worked in the Chinese offices of Western firms. But, without necessarily privileging a Western idea about what marks success in architecture (an individual voice, etc.), it's clear that the generation which came of age in the 1980s and 1990s has its own priorities and is willing to explore the ambiguities and conflicts of being Chinese in the age of globalisation. When Amateur Architecture's WANG Shu was awarded the Pritzker Prize in 2012, the possibility appeared that European and American design students would someday be obliged to know and reckon with Chinese work, rather than encountering it occasionally as a novelty.[3]

Atelier Deshaus, **Qingpu Private Enterprise Office** (p. 187). Corbusian plan geometry and Nouvel-esque plays of surface and interior combine to repeatedly complicate the building's relationship to its under-planned new-town context.

In any case, the new work in China is varied, not just in style but in ambitions. Atelier Deshaus develop a precise, neo-Modern aesthetic (p. 174, p. 187), while Archi-Union explore advanced digital design and fabrication (maps p. 201, p. 205, p. 389). Amateur Architecture hybridise traditional Chinese architectural forms and severe, elemental geometry (p. 242, p. 264); Urbanus and MADA s.p.a.m. assert the importance of urban space in cities gone mad for private development (p. 322, p. 240). XU Tiantian's arts buildings, alternately boxy and free-form, play on the difference between art's exhibition and its production, probing the meaning of postindustrial "art spaces" in an art world driven by dollars and government management (p. 105). Of course, individual firms address themselves to multiple themes. Pei ZHU (formerly of Urbanus) riffs on the vanishing Beijing *siheyuan* in one project, and starkly architecturalises the microchip in the next (p. 078, p. 096). In Chengdu, LIU Jiakun uses traditional brick masonry as formwork for concrete structures that suggest the ghosts of an earlier way of working; in Jinhua, he builds wiry, high-tech platforms for drinking tea (p. 281, p. 389). AI Weiwei's "architecture park" in Jinhua (p. 276) tests the medium's capacity to prompt new ways of thought through form, while in other projects he seems to call for some simple peace, quiet, and time to think (p. 102, p. 287).

Many of these firms are still young, evolving, watching each other while finding their own voices. The greatest pitfall in evaluating this work would be to read it solely as an archetypal *synthesis between modernity and tradition*. While the lens of critical regionalism can give us a new appreciation of all sorts of architectural work, it can also become a kind of self-fulfilling straitjacket: once you're looking for syntheses of the modern and the traditional, or the global and the local, you tend to find (and praise) them, without questioning the assumptions that lay behind the individual terms. Without intending to, one arrives at a position where architects from countries that are expected to be "modern" are permitted to pursue whatever concerns they please, while the Non-West is sentenced to eternally meditate on its own "local"-ness, poetically redrawing the line between China and the rest of the world. This manoeuvre is neo-colonial in its effect; moreover, by praising the "sensitive" tradition-addressing work exclusively, it denies legitimacy to firms that dedicate themselves to formal or technological experimentation, to wittily reinventing the assumed building programme, or to problems involving plan, section, light, material and space – concerns elsewhere regarded as being essential to the development of architecture.

Anyway, the supposed power of "local" and "traditional" signifiers, to reach something "deep" in the "soul of a people," is suspect for a number of reasons. Such thinking risks a dangerous blood-and-soil reading of a culture and its art forms. It may be particularly problematic here, given the past European tendency to conceive of China's "traditional" ways as evidence of an unchanging society, effectively bereft of history. This in turn provided background intellectual justification for colonial domination: with Europe placed in a progressive narrative, but the rest of the world languishing in cyclical non-history, non-Europeans existed only to provide plot points in the West's grand narrative of self-discovery.[4] When Western observers posit a frictionless present-day access to a single, timeless, pan-Chinese "tradition," they unwittingly redraw a nineteenth-century intellectual map.

China is not "timeless," but fundamentally timed. Attempts to stir "memory" through form, even in less problematic appeals to individual memories, are unlikely to succeed on their own terms. If the goal is to evoke a sense of "belonging" or "home," designers and commentators would do well to remember that these feelings are shaped by experience, not by blood. Of course, as an American raised in the South in the 1980s, I can't guess what forms speak most profoundly to my Chinese peers. I do know that for my own sake, evocations of white-columned plantation houses make me profoundly uncomfortable, and a designer hoping to poetically reach my deepest feelings of rootedness and harmony would do better to exploit crinkled plastic photo albums, VHS cassettes, and wood panelling.Indeed, some of the most interesting work in China is concerned with the immediate past, and the spatial legacies of the twentieth century. Even the urban landscapes of the Deng era are already decades old; they are the worlds within which today's architects have lived, loved and found themselves. They are thus as natural a source of design inspiration as anything else. Projects that re-imagine premodern urban forms might be seen not so much as rediscoveries of a forgotten past – since these forms have hardly disappeared from everyday Chinese life – but as interventions in the current event that is their transformation or destruction.

To illustrate just how complicated these issues may be, let us conclude by turning from architecture to fast food, and the evident Chinese popularity of American fast food. Does the ubiquity of Colonel Sanders's smiling portrait represent a "modern" desire for American industrial junk food? Is the Colonel simply the mirror image of the profusion of "Chinese" cuisines available in the United States? Or, as the science-fiction author Neal Stephenson suggests in *The Diamond Age,* does it reflect both a "traditional" taste for fried chicken itself, and the quasi-Confucian values suggested by the discreet and elderly Sanders? If the latter reading seems a stretch, one need only consider a Chinese rival: Uncle Fast Food, a similarly silver-haired gentleman serving up efficient, industrialised Chinese cooking in hard plastic renditions of earthenware dishes. If Uncle Fast Food is not exactly "Chinese" and "traditional," can the Colonel really be simply "foreign" and "modern"? If both figures split the difference, then clearly there are complexities in play that would be lost if one simply marked both as vaguely thought-provoking curios of globalisation.

The "modern," complicated from the start by the circumstances of its imposition onto China, means something different in 2015 than it did in 1911, 1949, or even 1989. The revolutionary campaigns against the past did succeed, to a great extent, in dissolving the traditional family and social structure; the resurgence of capitalism has done its work as well. To some, China's building boom reflects this trajectory, revealing a country of itinerant, cash-hungry migrants, upwardly mobile young professionals and nuclear families in rented apartments, replacing extended families gathered in a courtyard house. The vast sweep and ambitious forms of grand construction projects may represent progress and prestige in some eyes, and a society gone mad in others. Lost in the shuffle are the tens of millions of profoundly underpaid and marginalised migrant workers who construct these wonders. They are routinely forgotten by the foreign architects, who are simply dazzled by the speed

Colonel Sanders and Uncle Fast Food, side by side in Shanghai (near **Yu Bazaar**, p. 154)

and cheapness of Chinese construction as it seems to fulfil their creative dreams. To the developers and government entities that sponsor building projects, what is at stake may be mere competitive branding, regional status, or, a quick return on investment.

As I write this, Chinese architecture may stand at another turning point. In October 2014, Chinese president XI Jinping made a much-discussed call for an end to "weird architecture." It is still uncertain whether this constitutes a personal opinion or a policy shift; whether it applies equally to foreign and homegrown firms; whether it is principally aimed at style, or at budgetary excesses; and, of course, how the "weird" might be identified and eliminated. Architects and local policy-makers are scrambling to interpret these remarks, once again seeking appropriate ways of building in the complex field of economic, political, and cultural forces. More than a century after China first began to explore what it meant to make a "modern" building, the question is no less charged than ever.

Notes

1. LU Xin, *China, China,* p. 45. Full cite below.
2. Carlo RATTI, "Rebuilding Beijing," in *Domus* #864, November 2003, page 53.
3. Why the Pritzker was awarded solely to Wang, excluding his wife and partner LU Wenyu, remains obscure. Lu has since expressed polite disinterest in the award.
4. Here I am indebted to Denise FERREIRA DA SILVA, whose work on the racial underpinnings of post-Enlightenment Western thought is fascinating, though not for the theoretically faint of heart.

Sources and Recommended Reading

Jeffrey CODY, Nancy S. STEINHARDT & Tony ATKIN, eds., *Chinese Architecture and the Beaux-Arts*, Honolulu: University of Hawaii Press, 2011. In-depth coverage of the various Beaux-Arts lineages.

Edward DENISON, *Modernism in China: Architectural Visions and Revolutions*, Chichester: Wiley, 2008. An exhaustive history going back to the seventeenth century, and up until the Civil War.

DING Guanghui, "'Experimental Architecture' in China," in *Journal of the Society of Architectural Historians,* March 2014. What "experimental" meant on the Chinese scene circa 2000.

Claudio GRECO and Carlo SANTORO, "2(0), 1, 0...CHINA!" in *Lotus International* #141, March 2010. A short but spirited essay on the Olympic era and its fallout.

LU Xin, *op cit., China, China... Western Architects and City Planners in China,* Ostfildern: Hatje Cantz, 2008. Working reference for architects practising in China.

Charlie Q. L. XUE, *Building a Revolution: Chinese Architecture Since 1980*, Hong Kong: Hong Kong University Press, 2006. Chinese architectural and urban debates of the 1980s and 1990s.

北京
Beijing

© iStockphoto / TommL

北京 Beijing

Beijing (formerly Peking) is the capital of the People's Republic of China. With a few interruptions, it was also the capital of Imperial China from 1279 to 1912, and of the Republic of China from 1912 to 1928. In short, it has been at the centre of one of the great world civilisations for millennia. It has accumulated tremendous historical and cultural significance, even as its physical fabric has undergone several major changes – most recently, a wave of demolitions and new construction which has transformed the majority of the city from one-storey courtyard dwellings on narrow alleys into something entirely different. Almost simultaneously, Beijing became one of the first cities in China to conspicuously embrace the construction of major projects by foreign architects. The largest of these commissions were awarded in the period leading up to the 2008 Olympics, as China used architecture to assert its self-image as a bold, prosperous, forward-looking country. To understand how this came about, it's necessary to see the city both as a top-down planning project, and a bottom-up manifestation of social forces.

Beijing wasn't always a bustling powerhouse, but it was almost always important. As far back as the eleventh century BCE, this area was home to a series of trading towns, owing to the intersection of the north-going road through the mountains and the north-eastern road to Manchuria. Much later, connection to the **Grand Canal** (see p. 226) plugged the region more directly into the heartland's economy. While these towns sometimes became regional capitals, they were really border outposts at the northern fringe of the empire, not far from the ongoing **Great Wall** project (p. 108).

While later Beijing might appear to be a "copy" of these earlier cities, at slight geographic remove, in actuality all of the cities on this site were designed according to principles which can be observed in countless ancient Chinese walled cities. (For a well-preserved example, those planning on longer stays in China should consider trekking to **Pingyao,** p. 387) Generally speaking, traditional Chinese urban planning reflects a fusion of Confucian social hierarchy, imperial political symbolism, and considerably older traditions concerning the fortune-setting roles played by geometry, geomancy and numerology. According to these traditions, the ideal capital is a nine-square grid, with its main entry from the south and the seat of government in the centre. A grid of major streets links up the sub-modules of the squares,

Previous spread: The **Forbidden City** (p. 074) and **National Grand Theatre** (p. 077)

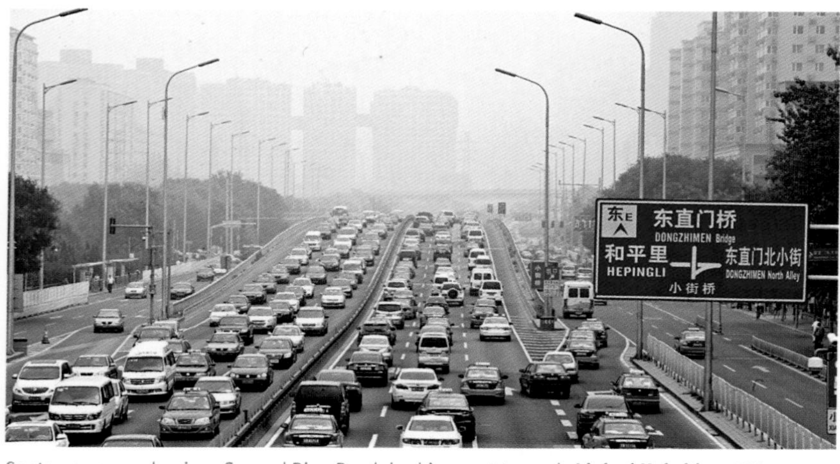

Contemporary urbanism: Second Ring Road, looking east towards **Linked Hybrid**, p. 090

Alfred Schinz, *The Magic Square* (1996), p. 327. Courtesy Edition Axel Menges.

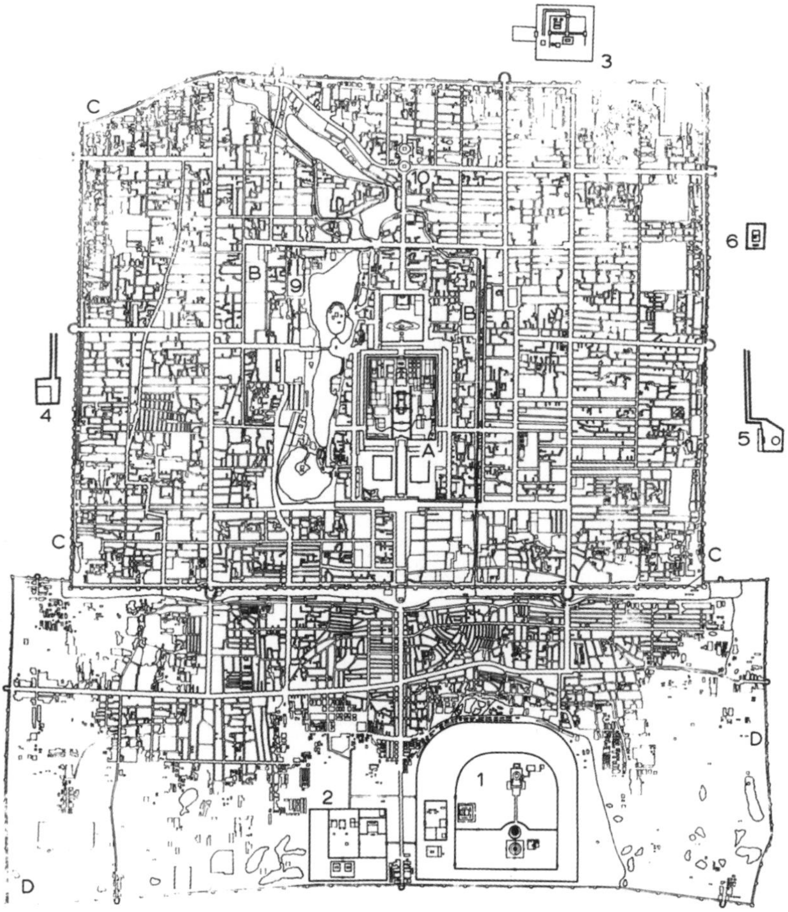

Ming-era Beijing

and a square perimeter (however difficult to secure) reflects the clear order of the universe: the king is at the centre of his palace, the palace is at the centre of the city, and the city is at the centre of the world. Old maps show this concentric-square diagram extending to encompass the empire, reflecting the Chinese name for China itself: *Zhōngguó,* or "Middle Kingdom" (see also p. 039).

A new ruler hoping to govern this vast territory would naturally want to tap into such powerful symbolism. Indeed, this seems

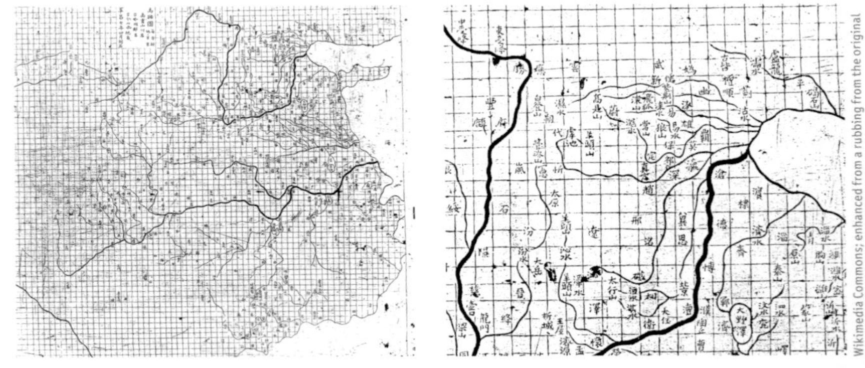

Wikimedia Commons; enhanced from a rubbing from the original

Yu Ji Tu (the "Map of the Tracks of Yu") and detail. Stone Carving, 1137 CE. Grid lines every 100 *li* (today, 1 *li* equals 500 metres, though historically the measurement varied).

to have influenced Kublai Khan's choice, in 1271, to build a new capital based on the same principles. Since his conquering grandfather Genghis had invaded China from the north, this Mongolian empire's approximate north-south centre fell close to the former trade and defence outpost. Many of Beijing's essential features (the street grid's major axes, the rough position of the central palace city, and the series of artificial lakes) date back to the Khan's city of Dadu, founded in 1267. The lakes, unfortunately, threw off the number of north-south streets, and put Dadu's palace considerably south of the geographic centre. It could be argued this inauspicious siting doomed the Khan's dynasty, which was overthrown by the founding Ming in 1386. Shortly run out of Nanjing ("southern capital") by scandal and slaughter, the Ming re-established their court at Dadu, renaming it Beijing, or "northern capital."

Under the Ming Emperor Yongle (1360–1424), several changes were made to the city's layout. The palace city was completely rebuilt (on the same spot), the northern third of Kublai Khan's grid was abandoned, and major new temple complexes (eventually including the **Temple of Heaven**, p. 080, and **Temple of Earth**, map p. 114) were established to the south. These changes shifted the city south to surround the palace, returning to the ideal nine-square diagram, with the Emperor's seat at the true centre. This may have paid off, as the following centuries of Ming rule are considered a high point of Chinese civilisation. The succeeding Qing retained this basic order, simply adding some temples, refreshing the imperial gardens, and building a southern wall to enclose the Outer City, which had grown up around the temple complexes. When the last Emperor abdicated in 1912, the city would not have been unrecognisable to Marco Polo.

That's the story of old Beijing from the perspective of top-down rulers and master planners. But the gridded, concentric Chinese city can also be read from the bottom up, as the macro-scale multiplication of the city's fundamental tissue: the narrow residential lane, or *hutong*. Until the late twentieth century, most of Beijing was a network of thousands of these lanes, fronted by single-storey courtyard houses or *siheyuan*. This typology, which solidified by the Ming period, formed a low-rise, moderately dense "carpet" of a city that was easy to navigate (if sometimes repetitious), due to the differentiated grain of the *hutong*: the residential alleys run east to west, while the larger streets (parallel to the city's fundamental north-south axis), contained shopping and artisan workshops.

The hierarchy of city and dwelling directly reflected cultural norms. The extended family, living together, was sorted out in a Confucian hierarchy: the elders got the best-appointed northern rooms, younger members got the east and west, and servants and support programme went to the south. A wall screened views from the street, making the courtyard into a private, discrete world. The arrangement suited northern China's climate, with the south-facing halls catching the southern sun, while the blank northern walls provided shelter from winter winds. The *siheyuan* thus corresponded with *feng shui* principles, which

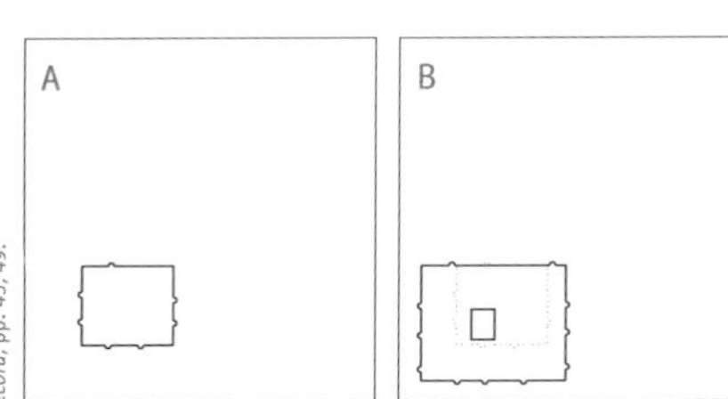

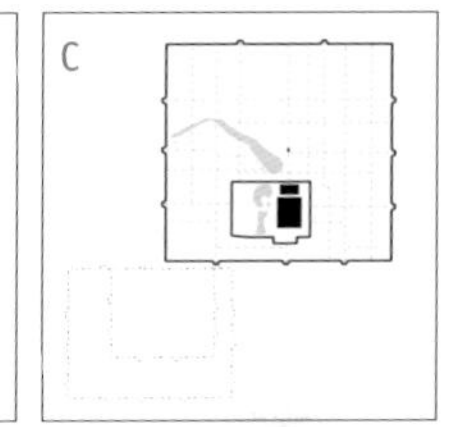

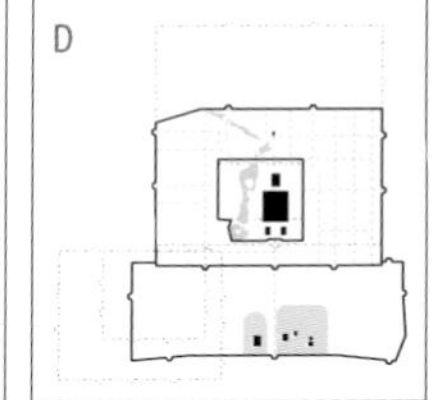

Urban succession, with previous iterations in dashed lines. **A.** Southern capital of the Mongolian/Khitan Liao dynasty, established 938 CE. **B.** Zhongdu, capital of the Jin dynasty, established 1153. **C.** Dadu, capital of the Yuan dynasty, established by Kublai Khan in 1271. **D.** Ming/Qing dynasty Beijing, established 1403; shown after the completion of the Outer City Wall in 1553 enclosed the Temples of Heaven and Agriculture.

to be in the public domain, edited. Diagrams redrawn based on images in Wang, *Beijing Record*, pp. 45, 49.

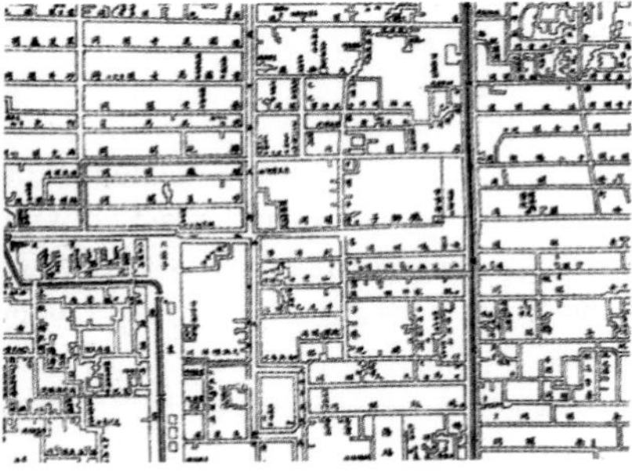

Detail from a 1930s' map, showing Beijing's east-west "grain"

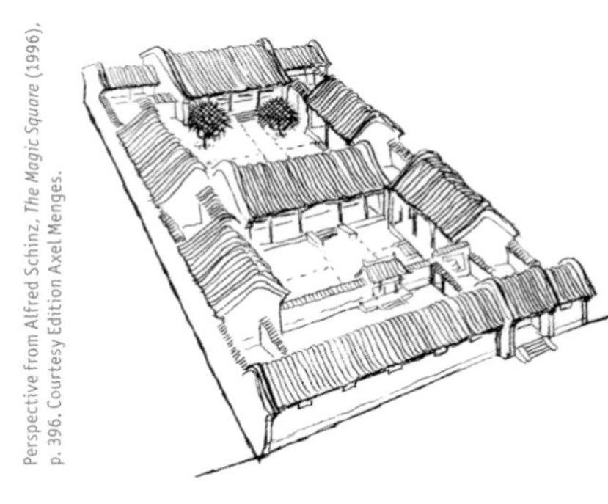

Perspective from Alfred Schinz, *The Magic Square* (1996), p. 396. Courtesy Edition Axel Menges.

Perspective view, two-courtyard *siheyuan*

A *hutong* in 2013

Looking into the first courtyard of a *siheyuan*

labelled certain orientations, functions and numbers as auspicious (see p. 036). Indeed, the courtyard dwelling was seen as a microcosm of the square planet, with the open earth in the centre, reflecting the open heavens above.

The courtyard house not only symbolised the rigid social structure; it also helped realise it. The closed world of the *siheyuan* is a machine for domination by the family patriarch (a sort of miniature emperor) and both the family's business and its women can be kept hidden from the larger world. None of this was limited to the dwellings of ordinary people; there were upscale *siheyuan* with more courts, more rooms and finer ornament. Social class was reinscribed by material and details – commoners could use only grey tile and black doors, while in the imperial palace one finds glazed tile and red doors. Indeed, the **Forbidden City** palace complex (p. 074) can be seen as a kind of massively scaled-up *siheyuan*, thus corroborating the essentially pyramidal organisation of pre-modern Chinese society.

The finely grained yet tightly structured order of *hutongs* and *siheyuan* has been under pressure for decades. In 1949, following the Republic of China's brief use of Nanjing as the capital, the new Communist government once again restored Beijing's administrative centrality, and almost immediately a debate broke out about where the new government should be housed. Certainly the people's party could not be based in the old imperial palace, but it would need offices, meeting halls, even national monuments. One faction argued for preservation of the old city on the grounds of its historical significance, but this was a time of revolution, and exuberant hope of great social transformation. Chairman MAO was happy to capitalise on the historical symbolism of taking over the old capital, but he was fundamentally suspicious of history as a thing of value in itself. Mao chose to build within the city, by demolition if necessary, and the preservationists never really had much hope. Still, the Mao-era demolitions were confined to certain specific sites. The largest was **Tian'anmen Square** (p. 072), where space was demanded for an enormous public assembly grounds along with new museums and the "Great Hall of the People," cranked out in 1959 as one of the "Ten Great Buildings" celebrating the Republic's decennial (see also map p. 114). Communist urban planners, working with Soviet advisors, also knocked down the old city walls, filled in moats, and planned for the concentric expansion of the city with successive ring roads, ultimately saddling the city with today's desperate traffic jams and awkward subway routes. A few remnants of the walls survive, for example at the City Wall Relics Park (明城墙遗址公园), just south of **Beijing Railway Station** (map p. 114).

Despite these substantial changes to the historic centre, most government-directed development in this period was focused on new industrial towns, another Soviet-inspired idea. These were easier to construct on new peripheral sites than through demolition, so Beijing remained largely intact. In the same era, large tracts of low-rise, unornamented Modernist housing (often associated with *danwei* work units) began to appear beyond the Second Ring Road, which traced the path of the old city wall. Interestingly, some of contemporary Beijing's most animated street life can be found in these places. They're not much to look at (though their trees have grown in well), but they were built quite densely, with space for retail and services.

Beijing's pedestrian-scale, low-rise urban fabric first came under serious pressure during the Cultural Revolution period of the 1960s and '70s. In a policy aimed at creating a new urban proletariat, the government increased the population of Beijing beyond what the available *siheyuan* could practically support (even as a parallel movement forced city dwellers back to the farm to be "re-educated"). Residents filled in their courtyards to create more rooms; while the street network remained the same, the lifestyle it supported was pushed to the breaking point. Given the ambitions of the Cultural Revolution, such erosion and destabilisation of traditional culture were probably by design. Meanwhile, the overpopulated *siheyuan* became a kind of urbanistic time bomb – a bit like American tenements during the Depression and war decades, they were storing up a huge, unresolved demand for housing. When DENG Xiaoping's capitalist-oriented economic reforms (see **Shenzhen,** p. 316) finally came to Beijing in the 1990s, it became possible to meet this demand through new construction. The value of *hutong* land would rise far above what could possibly be made off one-storey courtyard dwellings. Those who held control of property began a wave of demolition and construction virtually unmatched in human history. As an array of tall object-buildings, standing free on their lots and seemingly indifferent to the surrounding streets, Beijing has finally become the "modern" city its zoning anticipated sixty years ago. Comparisons could of course be made to other Chinese cities in this period, most famously Shenzhen. But Shenzhen was not a capital with centuries worth of historic fabric and millions of pre-established inhabitants; Beijing thus raises distinct questions about preservation, urban fabric, and the appropriate role of the state in shepherding a city's transformation. A single major project can involve relocating thousands or tens of thousands of people, and by the turn of the millennium, two thirds of the *hutongs* had been demolished – even before Olympic preparations prompted another round of demolition and construction.

A 1999 master plan finally established twenty-five historic neighbourhoods to be preserved, and in fact the most recent trend has been to build enormous high-rise tracts on greenfield sites, especially to the city's east. This in turn intensifies traffic and pollution, among other problems, and

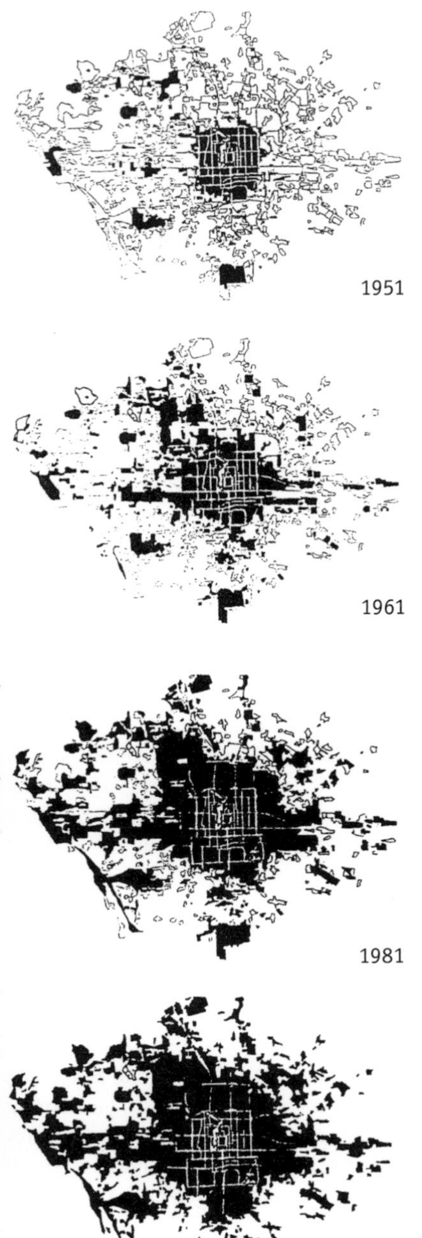

Source: Unpublished statistics from the Beijing Municipal Institute of Urban Planning and Design, 1991. Courtesy UBC Press.

Growth of Beijing's built-up area in the Communist era

Courtesy Paul Reuber Architect; see note p. 396

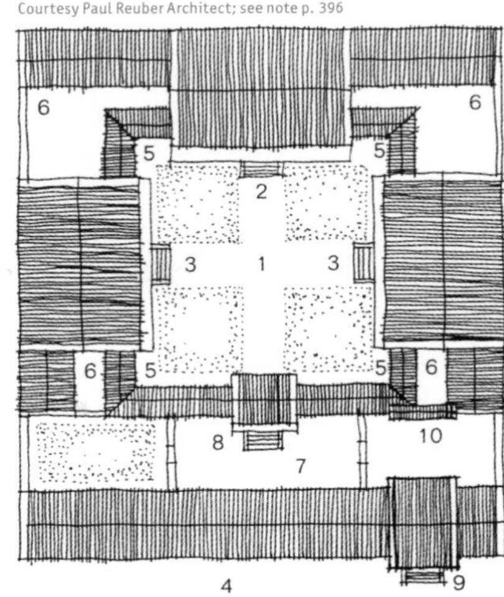

Roof plan of a typical *siheyuan*

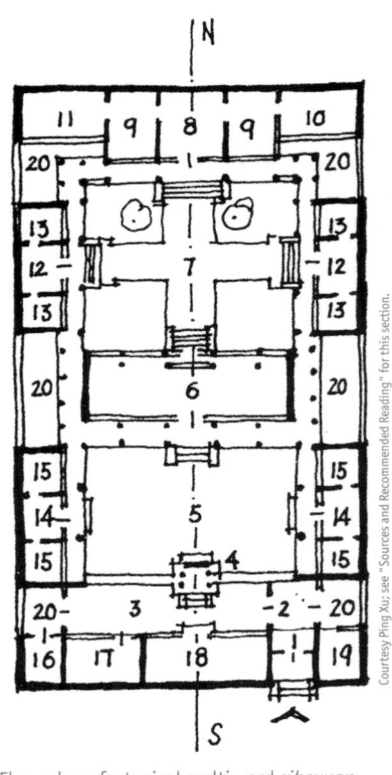

Courtesy Ping Xu; see "Sources and Recommended Reading" for this section.

Floor plan of a typical multi-yard *siheyuan*

subway planners struggle to keep pace with the geographic spread of the city. For the *siheyuan*, however, the damage has been done, and it's not clear how strict the new limitations are in practice. Some large *hutong* blocks still remain (mainly around the Forbidden City and Tian'anmen Square, where code limits building height), and the surviving clusters do give some sense of the animated, multi-programmed street life that must have once been universal in Beijing. Yet the mere fact that they are clusters robs them of their strength. A city's economy works through aggregations and multiplications. One is reminded of the strips of weedy landscape preserved as highway medians; technically, they may add up to a large open green space, but being discontinuous, they hardly constitute a park, let alone an ecosystem.

Hutong fabric, including a temple, competes with mid-rise slabs and towers

Beijing is more populous than ever, but if the *hutong* blocks are surrounded by wide automobile roads, how can the shops hope to have customers? How can residents hope to walk to their places of business? The demolition may indeed be a self-accelerating cycle: once the city is damaged enough for life within the *hutong* to become affected, the incentives to cash in and move out become more convincing. As more people do so, more of the city is wiped out, and more of what remains is unable to function. Of course, there are efforts to preserve and restore small sections, either as tourist attractions or specialised shopping districts. Some of the extant *hutong* zones have found a kind of salvation in expatriate bohemians and hipster entrepreneurs, who predictably find these places quite charming; we, too, recommend them as great places to come into contact with regional Chinese culture (especially street food) alongside import liquor and the globally ubiquitous "night life." In this way, the terms for a city's survival seem similar to those found in many places: some quantity of old fabric will persist, put to different uses, by different people, in smaller numbers.

To be fair, Beijing's demand for new construction was also driven by the perceived obsolescence of *siheyuan* housing. High rise developments may not make possible the close-knit communities of the old neighbourhoods, but they do offer modern conveniences that many Westerners would consider essentials. Life along a *hutong* involves dealing with unreliable utilities, failing infrastructure, and shared latrines. It's understandable that many Chinese might see the change as an unmitigated improvement, even while it's tempting for outsiders to read the fate of Beijing as a retread of the errors of Western urban renewal. Similarly, it's worth noting that Beijing's historical layout (the squares, the grid) is still largely legible in plan. This is not always true of Western cities which carried out reconstruction schemes in the twentieth century.

Today we can observe ways of redeveloping former *hutong* sites that go beyond the free-standing object model. In the 1980s, concerned Chinese designers and educators attempted to intervene with schemes (most famously the **Ju'er Hutong**, p. 114) that retained the basic grid-and-courtyard layout, while upping the density with multi-storey arrangements. Not architecturally flashy (indeed, deliberately "backgrounded"), these schemes prefigure more commercially-driven "new old" developments which now pop up here and there in the city. More broadly, architects building in Beijing at various scales have in many cases attempted to recreate the lively urbanism which their clients' projects would replace, sometimes picking up the "courtyard" as social organiser or formal motif. The meteoric rise of the developer SOHO China (**S**mall **O**ffice/**H**ome **O**ffice) is noteworthy here; their desire to associate mixed-use developments and live-work units with stylish design has led them to hire a number of "name" architects for their projects in Beijing (See pp. 081, 083, 085-087, 089, 103). Most of these eschew traditional details and materials, but are concerned in some way with producing a pedestrian, "urban" experience, even when stuck with twenty-first century mega-sites. Of course, a city composed only of high-end retail and cocktail options presents its own considerable problems.

Hutongs aren't the only form of Beijing fabric undergoing transformation. Many of the suburban, Mao-era factory districts mentioned above have since been engulfed by the sprawling city, even as they've been rendered obsolete or redundant by the shift of industrial production to more remote and larger-scale complexes elsewhere in China. Beijing's cosmopolitan class, and its steady flow of international travellers, have encouraged the transformation of many former factories and warehouses into galleries, theatres, and whole "art villages" as in **798** (p. 100), **Caochangdi** (p. 102), the **Red Brick Art Museum** (map 118), and the more remote **Songzhuang** (p. 105) – as well as smaller interventions at industrial sites in the old city centre, like **Studio-X** (p. 079) and **Meridian Space** (p. 078). While these places vary in their success (and their levels of government management), they tend to function surprisingly well as little pedestrian worlds, since they were originally planned as self-contained complexes of closely-spaced buildings. The popularity of these places, like the SOHO developments, suggests a way out of the era of super-block "icon" buildings, though of course plenty of those are in progress as of this writing. Without overstating architects' fantasies of a re-pedestrianised twenty-first century defined by "street life" and face-to-face interaction, it would appear that Beijing may still be a vibrant laboratory for urban alternatives.

Practical Considerations

Thanks to the overlay of Communist-modernist mega-blocks onto the denser grid of the old city, Beijing's mapped scale is often deceptive. Walking between districts can consume your entire visit, and cabs can get bogged down in traffic. A subway trip, though rarely the shortest distance between two points, is cheap and comparatively painless; we recommend grouping sites by subway line rather than overall proximity (see p. 112 for more suggestions). In general, you would need the better part of a week to begin to do the city justice, but depending on how thoroughly you treat the very large, must-see historic complexes (Forbidden City, Ming Tombs, Temple of Heaven), it is possible to group some of the major contemporary sites into a single (long) day – enough to at least get a sense of the trends. We do recommend exploring the older monuments and *hutong* blocks first; they are justifiably world-famous, and many contemporary projects draw from the principles of traditional urbanism.

Sources and Recommended Reading

Daniel ABRAMSON, "The aesthetics of city-scale preservation policy in Beijing" in *Planning Perspectives* #22, 2007. Historic preservation, and the lack thereof.

Domus #864, November 2003. Fascinating critical essays on contemporary Beijing, by Carlo RATTI, Yung Ho CHANG, Deyan SUDJIC, others.

Claudio GRECO & Carlo SANTORO, *Beijing: The New City*, Milan: Skira, 2008. Thorough treatment of spaces and buildings, ancient and new, with excellent historic maps.

Wu HUNG, *Remaking Beijing: Tiananmen Square and the Creation of a Political Space*, Chicago: University of Chicago Press, 2005. Penetrating case study of Tian'anmen Square as a microcosm of political changes in Beijing and China as a whole.

Michael MEYER, *The Last Days of Old Beijing*, New York: Walker & Co., 2008. Readable and personality-filled account of *hutong* life, interspersed with historical background.

Paul REUBER, "Beijing's 'Hutongs' and 'Siheyuan'" in *Canadian Architect* #43:10, 1998. *Hutongs*, and their destruction; see also p. 396.

Alfred SCHINZ, *The Magic Square*, Stuttgart: Axel Menges, 1996. See p. 396. A good general reference, but particularly useful concerning dynastic-era planning.

WANG Jun, *Beijing Record*, Singapore, London: World Scientific, 2011 (2008). A blow-by-blow account of Beijing's Mao-era transformations, as told by policy-makers, architects, and ordinary citizens.

Ping XU, "Feng-Shui Models Structured Traditional Beijing Courtyard Houses" in *Journal of Architectural and Planning Research* #15:4, 1998. Informative background on the social-symbolic role of *hutongs*.

Tian'anmen Square
Various; 1651, 1958+

BJ 01

天安门广场
❖ 39.9031, 116.3914

Originally, the space in front of the Forbidden City's South Gate (the Tian'anmen) was just the intersection of two axial streets. Starting in 1651, the emperors developed it into a T-shaped "Corridor of 1,000 Steps," ringed by a colonnade that emphasised its length and the sense of ceremonial procession towards the palace. With the end of the empire, it became a centre of protest activity, such as the nationalist May 4th Movement (1919). It was here that MAO Zedong proclaimed the People's Republic of China in 1949; almost immediately, he called for the square to be remade (through massive demolitions) to fit the new, notionally egalitarian, state. Though Mao had hoped to draw crowds one million strong, the completed plaza held only 500,000, still the largest public space in the world at the time. Tian'anmen Square was flanked by new monuments to the people (mostly in a Chinese-Socialist-Realist style) and bounded on the north by the vastly widened Chang'an Avenue. As Wu HUNG has argued, this shifted the city's centre south from an imperial solid to a citizen's void, while monuments in the centre cut off the old imperial axis. Mao's mausoleum would later complete the process, putting a solid block on the very spot of the former gate. Meanwhile, smaller versions of Tian'anmen appeared in other cities, becoming sites of Maoist indoctrination and the public humiliation of suspected Rightists. In 1976, and again in 1989, Tian'anmen was the site of major, unscripted mass protests; since 1989 the government has moved to depoliticise the space. In this effort, slogans have been removed, a few trees have been planted, and large LED screens have been installed, displaying videos of appealing Chinese landscapes on loop. Nothing commemorates the 1989 protest and its violent suppression. Tian'anmen is well-staffed by uniformed and plain-clothes police officers, and with enormous roads on all sides, entry to the square can be easily controlled via underground access passages. Here, autocracy wears the bland, implacable face of the genial washed-out bureaucrat, almost apologetic about having to inconvenience you with the tedious metal-detector process. It's hard to shake off the ghosts of Mao's cheering crowds, amassed by choice or by force to give the impression of popular approval of uncountable atrocities. His portrait, increasingly rare in China, still hangs on the Tian'anmen, although it seems to have been downgraded from an object of idolistic adoration to a backdrop for family photos. If one could block out the square's political associations, its spatial properties would still be stultifying and exhausting in their own right. Fully deserving of the ubiquitous epithet "wind-swept," this is regularised, emptied-out, Modernist space at its worst. One bright spot, in design terms: the National Museum on the eastern edge was designed by China's great architectural historian and preservationist LIANG Sicheng, in a quasi-Modern style with a flattened façade and airy forecourt. An appealingly bright overhaul by GMP (2007–2011) wisely preserves and extends these features. ZHANG Bo's stolid

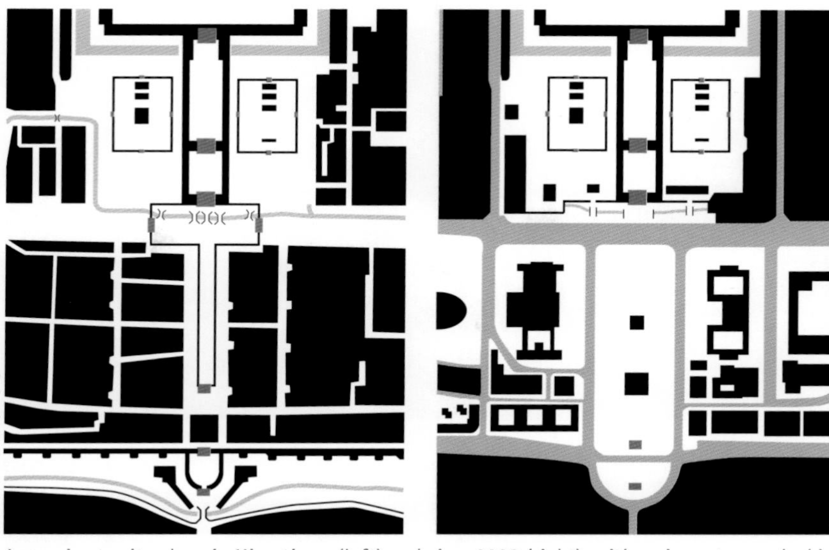

maps reprinted in Wang, *Beijing Record*.

Approximate site plans in Ming times (left) and circa 2008 (right), with major gates marked in orange and the moat of the **Forbidden City** proper (p. 074) at the north edge. The **National Grand Theatre** (p. 077) is partially visible at the left edge of the later plan.

Security fences on the boulevard

Mausoleum of Mao Zedong

© Christian Gahl, courtesy GMP

New National Museum, interior

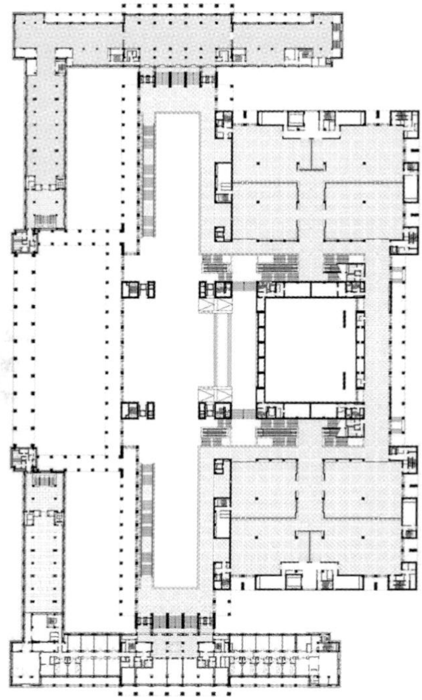

Courtesy: GMP

New National Museum, plan

Great Hall of the People (1959) faces the museum at a distance. HUA Guofeng's Mausoleum of Mao Zedong (1977) anchors the composition, occupying the site of the Gate of China, former entrance to the imperial city.

Forbidden City

Various; 1406–1420, with additions

BJ 03

紫禁城

❖ 39.9157, 116.3908

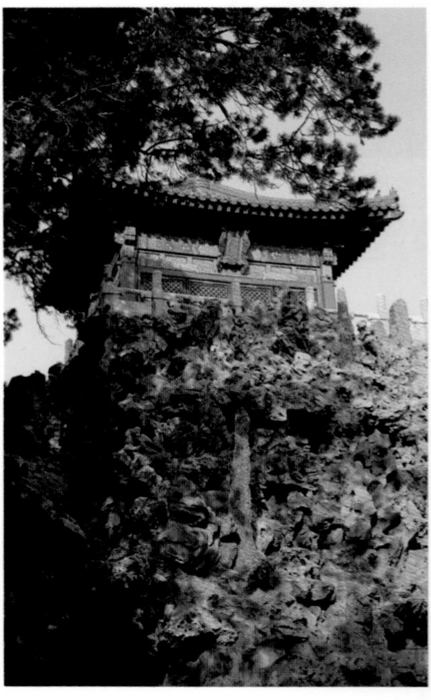

Shortly after relocating the capital to Beijing, the Yongle Emperor (reign: 1402–1424) began building a new palace city, roughly on the site of the recently-abandoned Mongol capital. It took two to three hundred thousand workers fourteen years to complete the mammoth complex, which still survives today (after minor additions and periodic renovations). The palace city follows the classic concentric-rectangle diagram (see Beijing introduction, p. 064). The hierarchy is reinforced within the complex: at dead centre are the great halls of the Outer Court, where the Emperor would oversee essential ceremonies. Beyond this to the north are the imperial residences, flanked by the homes of guards and eunuchs. Each function has its own separate pavilion, and the entire ensemble was off-limits to the general public – "forbidden" – until it became the Palace Museum in 1925. Its organisation is also, essentially, a scaled-up *siheyuan* courtyard house, just as the traditional social hierarchy is a macrocosm of the Confucian order of the individual family. The palace is thus modelled on, and a model for, the city and the rest of the country. While the most impressive and famous spaces are the central courts and their halls, don't miss out on exploring the northern reaches of the complex, which scales down to a more intimate grain and becomes a matrix of differently-sized and differently-composed courtyards. At the north end is the imperial garden. Compared with private, "southern" Chinese gardens (see **Suzhou,** p. 210), imperial gardens seem rigidly orthogonal and axial, like extensions of the palace's logic, or miniatures of imperial funeral complexes (see **Ming Tombs,** p. 110). This regularity only highlights the organic twists of the carefully-crafted trees and rockeries.

View down one of the side lanes within the complex

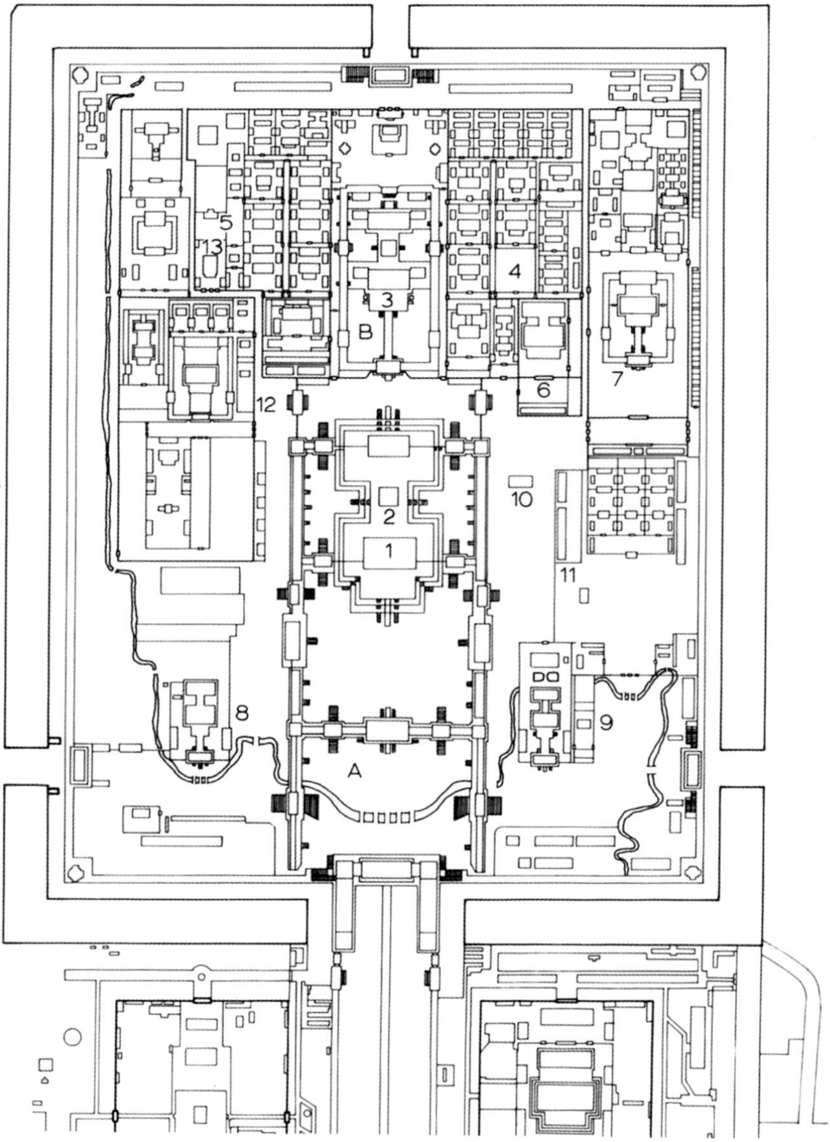

Alfred Schinz, *The Magic Square*, p. 322. After YU Zhouyun. Courtesy Edition Axel Menges.

Plan

Jingshan Park

BJ 04

1400+

景山公园

❖39.9233, 116.3903

Originally an imperial garden attached directly to the **Forbidden City** (p. 074), Jingshan Park (literally "Prospect Hill") was constructed using fill dirt from the excavation of the palace moat, and served as one of the Yongle Emperor's projects to reorganise Beijing. The separation of palace and garden by a roadway, completed in 1928, was one of Beijing's first major twentieth-century projects. The park offers respite from the clamour of the city, but the real reason to visit is to enjoy the views from atop the hill, which give a great sense of the scope and texture of the palace complex below. Other landmarks may be visible, depending on the haze.

Beihai Park

BJ 05

1179+

北海公园

❖39.9243, 116.3829

Organised around one of the string of lakes that slink through the historic city centre, this large imperial garden features a number of historic structures. The famous White Dagoba (1271+, with several reconstructions), is the most prominent; from it, one may journey back down the hill through a novel set of caves. In imperial times, the park acted as a collection of pieces, re-creating in miniature the country's best gardens. If you have time to wander and explore, there are a number of fine spaces strung around the perimeter of the big island, and along the park's east edge (a bit back from the lake). If you're not travelling to Suzhou or Hangzhou, this and the **Summer Palace** (p. 093) offer a taste of classical Chinese garden design.

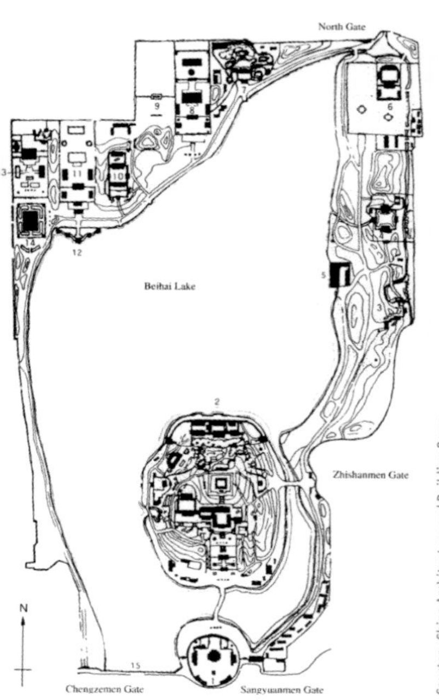

Plan

Courtesy China Architecture and Building Press

National Grand Theatre
Paul ANDREU, 1999–2007

BJ 06

国家大剧院 西城区西长安街2号
2 W Chang'an Ave, Xicheng
❖39.9031, 116.3834

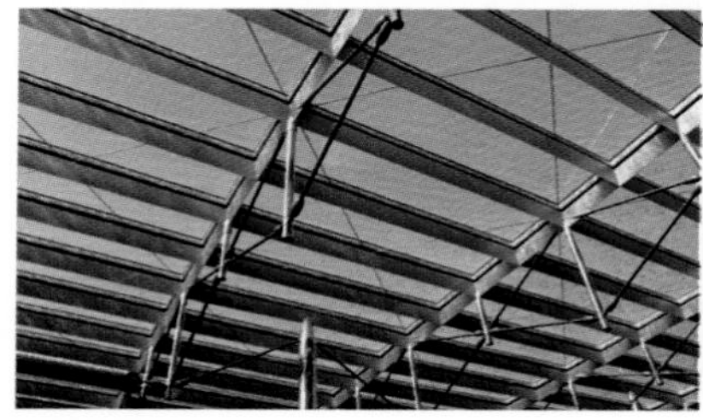

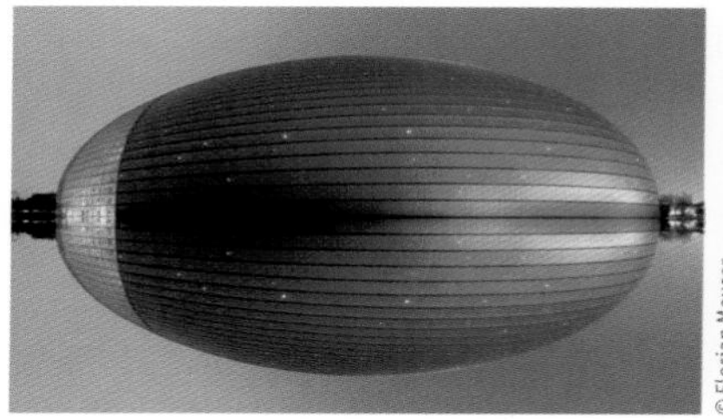

© Florian Meuser

This performing arts centre – containing a 2,500-seat opera house, a 2,000-seat concert hall, and a 500-seat theatre – disguises its bulk by burying all the circulation and support spaces under a vast reflecting pool. This frees the building to present itself as a shining, apparently seamless island. The state had sought a symbol for its commitment to the arts, while the selection of a foreign architects working in a high-tech mode implied the vibrant creative spirit of the *New China*. Andreu described the building as "an open and popular forum rather than an elitist cultural institution," and asserted that on the inside, the scale is broken down, making something "like a neighbourhood." Nonetheless, some Beijingers called it "the alien egg," or less printable nicknames; other critics felt the project contributed to an urbanistic void spreading out from Tian'anmen Square, and noted the thousands of *siheyuan* bulldozed to make room. All of the positive symbolic weight attached to the project means that Andreu has also had to bear the brunt of any backlashes – not just against the building but against the forces and trends that produced it. But it could be argued that the building is actually contextual: next to the Forbidden City and Tian'anmen Square, a lesser building might have seemed like a consolation prize. As other Chinese cities have rushed to build their own, fussier eggs, spheres, and crescent-moons, do the simplicity and studied retreat of this project invoke the monolithic state, or the reflective autonomy of the arts?

Hotel Kapok/Blur Hotel

BJ 10

Studio Pei-Zhu, 2004–2006

木棉花酒店
东城区东华门大街16号
16 Donghuamen Ave, Dongcheng
❖ 39.9137, 116.3993

Using a strategy of "urban acupuncture," the architects modify an ageing government office building with internal light wells meant to operate like *siheyuan* courtyards. Refusing to demolish even this less "historic" part of the street fabric, a gridded fibreglass skin (meant to evoke a Chinese lantern) conveys the hotel's contemporary boutique sensibility and camouflages the old building.

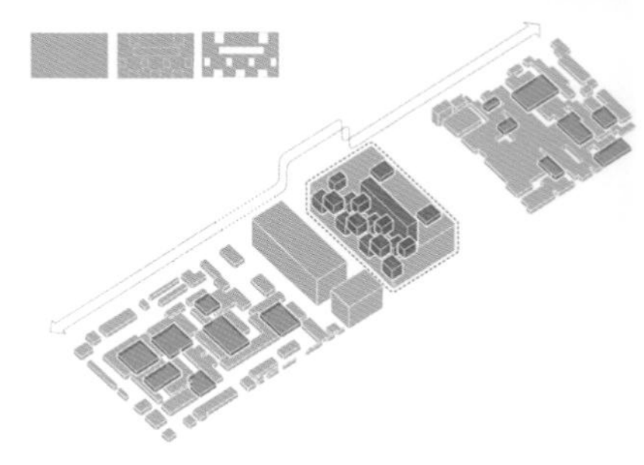

Courtyard diagram

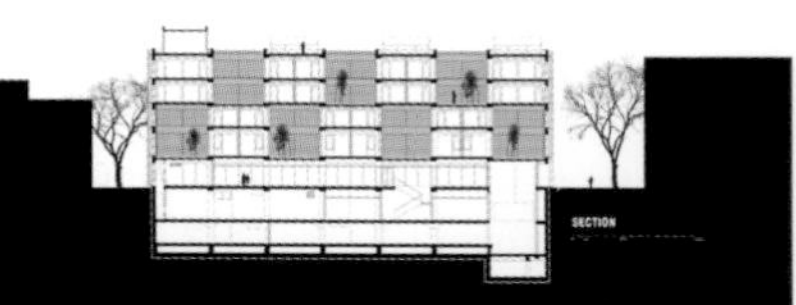

Longitudinal Section

Drawings courtesy Studio Pei-Zhu

Meridian Space

BJ 12

ORIGIN Architect (LI Ji), 2014

77剧场
东城区美术馆后街77号77文创园内
77 Meishuguan Hou Jie, Dongcheng
❖39.9263, 116.4027

This small printing factory complex, nestled in Beijing's historic grid, dates back to the 1960s, with various additions over time. The recent renovation, converting it into an arts and night-life zone, is more than skin-deep. Portions of the existing complex were strategically removed to create a set of courtyards and lanes appropriate to the *hutong* context. The sense of spatial texture is enhanced by

Photographs © Dorian Cave | Meridian Space

the array of catwalks and stairs unfolding from the rooftop terrace towards the rear of the site. The show-stopping, "folding" front wall of the central theatre is meant to enable the indoor performance space to spill out into the large front courtyard. The existing industrial materials, with the variety built up over time, are embraced.

Studio-X Beijing

BJ 18

OPEN Architecture, 2009

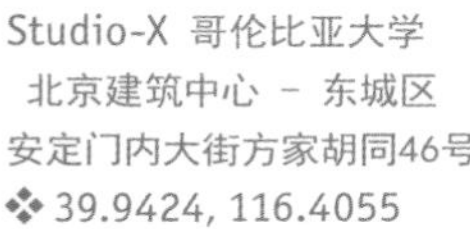

Studio-X 哥伦比亚大学
北京建筑中心 – 东城区
安定门内大街方家胡同46号
❖ 39.9424, 116.4055

This research, teaching, and exhibition space for Columbia University's Graduate School of Architecture, Planning and Preservation is one of several stylish interventions on this courtyard, formerly a munitions factory and now a creative-industry compound. Industrial objects are juxtaposed with craft details, and ventilating skylights open up the space. The lobby's metal floor covers a six-metre pit (connecting to a bomb shelter). Movable furniture (book cases, storage lockers, and partitions) is used to subdivide the space. With Columbia expected to leave the space in Spring 2015, its future is uncertain.

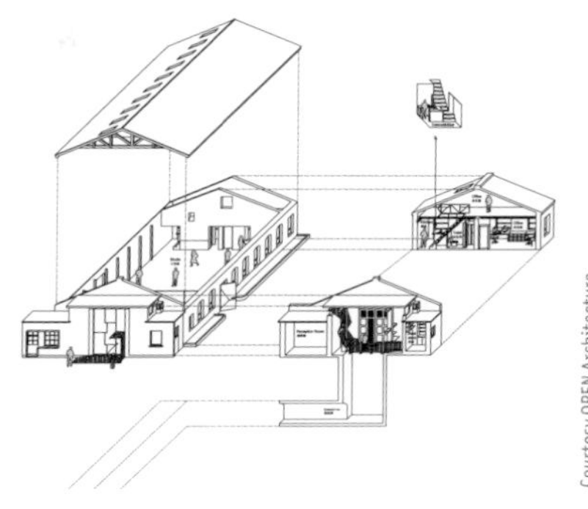

Courtesy OPEN Architecture

Exploded isometric

Confucius Temple & Imperial Academy

BJ 19

1302+

北京孔庙/北京孔廟 ， 国子监
东城区国子监街15号
15 Guozijian Street, Dongcheng
❖ 39.9447, 116.4085

The nearby **Lama** and **Earth Temples** (map p. 114) may be bigger attractions, but this joint complex, including a key site in imperial civil service training, has an interesting sense of shear as two lines of pavilions (of different layout) slide past one another other. The *steles,* engraved with important works, possess architectural presence; contemporary designers might take note. The Hall of Classics (in the pond) is a model negotiation between square and circle. Current structures mostly date to the Ming or Qing dynasties.

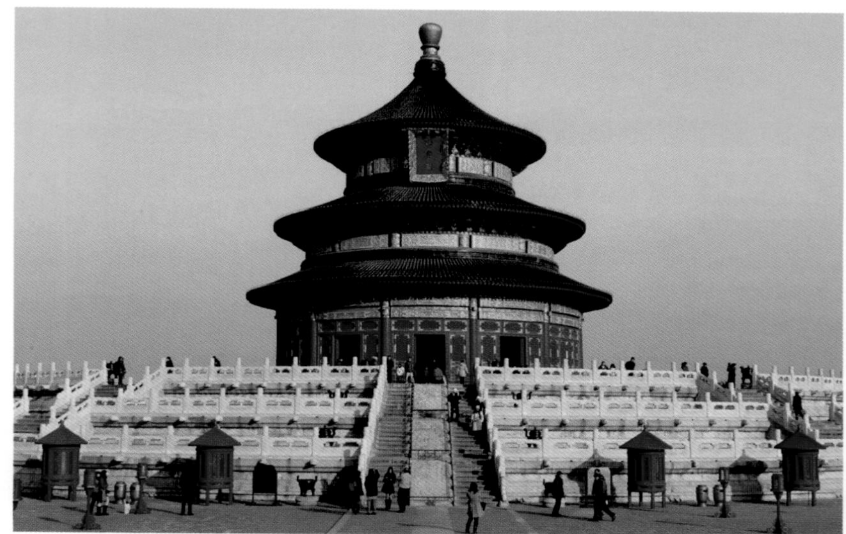

Temple of Heaven (Tiantan)

1406–1420+

BJ 23

天坛
东城区天坛内东里7号
7 Tiantan Neidongli, Dongcheng District
❖ 39.8789, 116.4073

Justifiably one of Beijing's most famous (and sacred) sites, the Temple of Heaven is a master-work of traditional Chinese architecture, though it's an exception in terms of temple typology; it eschews the hall-courtyard-hall diagram for a more concentric, centralised plan and form. While the Temple dates back to the 1400s, the structure we see today was built sometime in the 1700s under the Qianlong Emperor, and restored several times in the twentieth century. The temple complex sits to the east of the city's central axis, balanced (asymmetrically) by the Temple of Agriculture to the west; together they mark the southern extent of Beijing's old city wall. The design of the famous tiered *Qinian Dian* ("Hall of Prayer for Good Harvests," towards the north end) is cosmologically significant, reflecting the traditional belief that the the heavens are round and the Earth square. Here the two meet in the architecture of the circular temple atop its rectangular base. Today, the extensive temple grounds make one of Beijing's largest and most pleasant parks, indeed one of its best-used public spaces, enthusiastically occupied by local exercise groups, plus players of cards and Mahjong. Compare to **Tuanjiehu Park** (p. 084).

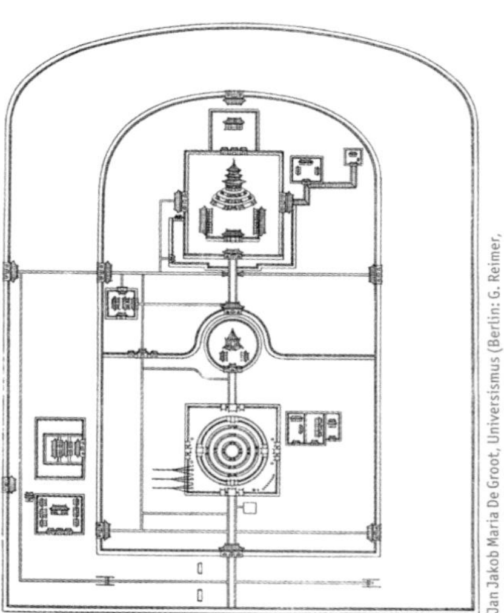

Diagrammatic plan

Jan Jakob Maria De Groot, Universismus (Berlin: G. Reimer, 1918). Believed to be in the public domain.

Galaxy SOHO

Zaha HADID Architects, 2008–2013

BJ 25

银河SOHO
东城区南竹杆胡同2号
2 South Zhugan Hutong (at East 2nd Ring Road), Dongcheng District
❖ 39.9203, 116.4276

In the 2000s and 2010s, the "towers-on-a-podium" mixed-use typology was arguably the dominant architectural form in mainland China. While such developments were typically disengaged from the surrounding context and offered little in the way of civic engagement, the buildings of SOHO China tended to buck the trend by including public pedestrian routes and a surprising level of porosity at the edges, which theoretically help stitch the new development into the existing urban fabric. Galaxy SOHO hews closely to the well-defined typological model: towers flank an open-air pedestrian boulevard, connected at their base by several retail floors. Here, the towers take on a sculpted, plastic form that seems to recall the karst formations of southern China, or (as at the **Guangzhou Opera,** p. 300) "rocks in a stream" – a reading emphasised by the central water feature. HADID's designers seem to have come to terms with the expertise of local contractors: where the Opera showed some detailing issues with doubly-curved surfaces, here the complex curvature appears smooth and confident, and is smartly achieved through a series of stacked plates.

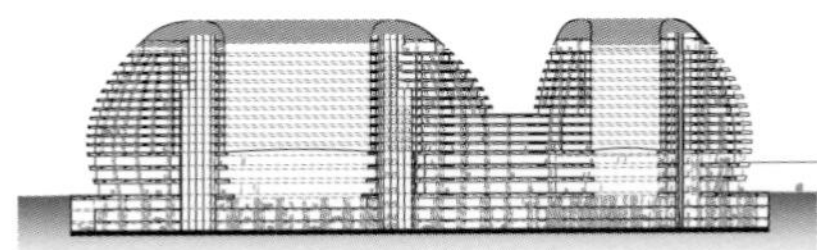

Longitudinal section

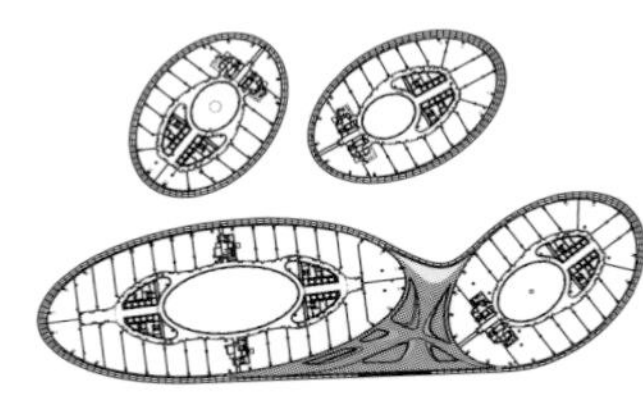

Eighth-floor plan

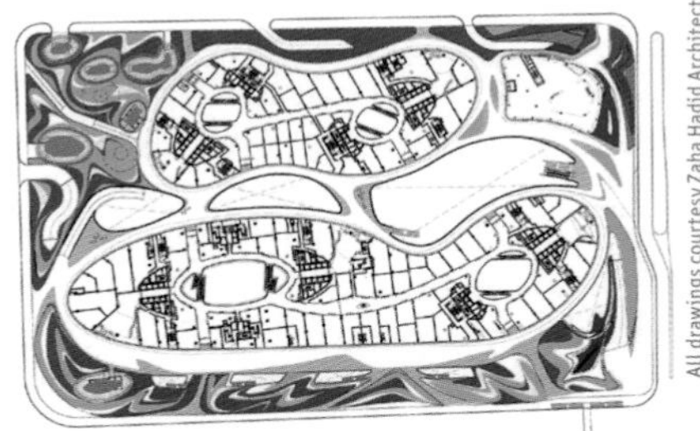

Ground-floor plan

All drawings courtesy Zaha Hadid Architects

Courtesy LOT-EK

LOT-EK, Sanlitun South

SHoP, Sanlitun South

Courtesy LOT-EK

LOT-EK, Sanlitun North

Courtesy LOT-EK

Kuma, Sanlitun South

Sanlitun Village

BJ 28

KUMA Kengo and Associates, various architects, 2005–2008

三里屯太古里
北京市朝阳区三里屯路19号
19 Sanlitun Road, Chaoyang
❖ 39.9335, 116.4486

This mixed-use, low-rise development is not a SOHO project (see p. 070), but it feels like one, both in the signature architecture and the attempt at recreating the context's varied, lively urbanism. Sanlitun is a famous night-life district, especially for expatriates working in the nearby diplomatic compounds; the area is changing fast, but appealingly seedy, and quasi-bohemian establishments can still be found on the upper floors of run-down Communist-era blocks. Kuma's master plan for the "Village" reaches for an older, denser urbanism and breaks the buildings into small volumes, separated by narrow lanes and a few larger plazas, shielded from the roadway. There are actually two sites, a few blocks apart; this helps the project feel slightly more integrated into its surroundings. More important is the selection of several different firms to design the buildings, with most contributing both to the "north" and "south" schemes. Several buildings have been altered, and may not match the photos above.

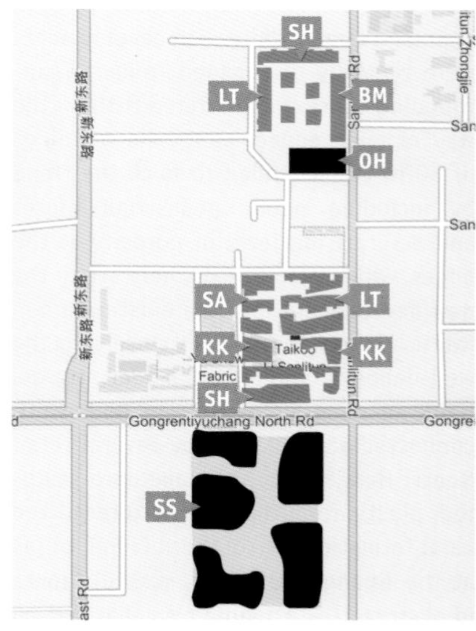

Area map
BM Beijing Matsubara & Architects
KK KUMA Kengo and Associates
LT LOT-EK
OH Opposite House (KUMA Kengo, opposite)
SA Sako
SH SHoP
SS Sanlitun SOHO (KUMA Kengo, opposite)

The Opposite House

BJ 29

KUMA Kengo and Associates (KUMA Kengo), 2005–2008

瑜舍,
朝阳区三里屯路11号
11 Sanlitun Road, Chaoyang
❖ 39.9360, 116.4491

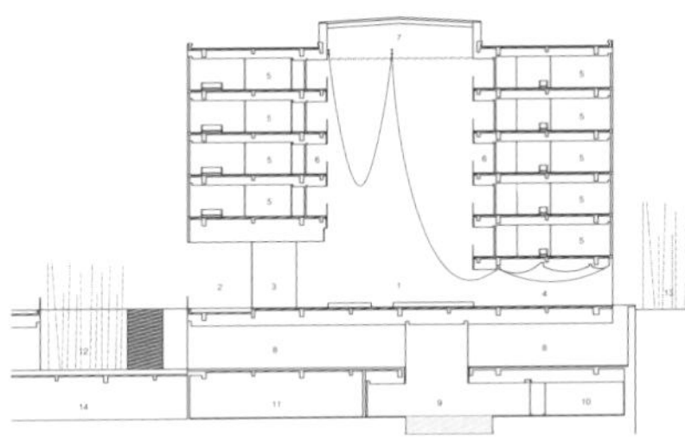

Cross section

This luxury hotel is effectively a part of **Sanlitun Village** (opposite), anchoring one end of that development, and providing a distinctive icon for this rapidly-gentrifying district. The hotel is defined by its jade-green curtain wall, (silk-screened with a pattern inspired by traditional latticework), and by its central atrium. The latter represents the architects' attempt to recreate the vitality of a traditional courtyard home. The design picks up on other classical design strategies, creating spatial ambiguity and subtle public-private divisions through the use of layered, translucent screens.

Sanlitun SOHO

BJ 30

KUMA Kengo and Associates (KUMA Kengo), 2007–2010

三里屯SOHO, 工人体育场北路8号
8 Worker's Stadium N. Rd. (at Sanlitun Rd.)
❖ 39.9309, 116.4477

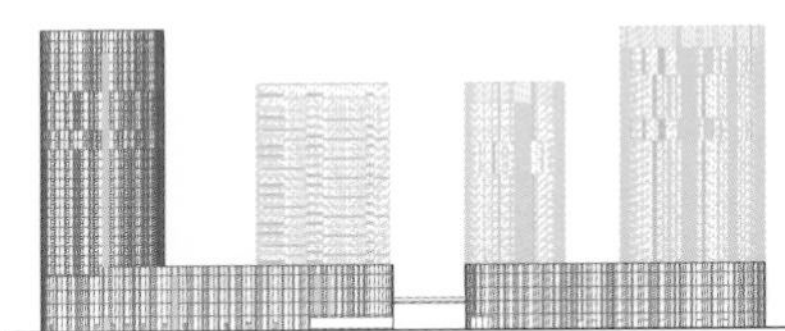

West Elevation

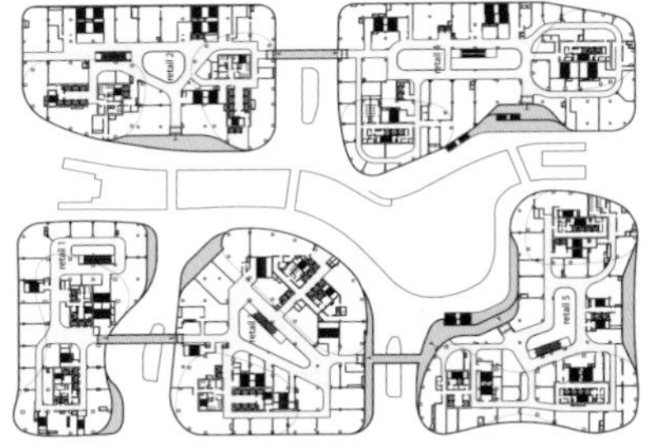

Ground-floor Plan

This mixed-use commercial development, similar to the smaller "Village" across the street (opposite), strives to create pedestrian-friendly outdoor space. The curvaceous plan forms are meant to soften the scheme's monumentality and produce an "urban Grand Canyon," or a "compact city" within a single complex. Compare to SOHO's **Galaxy** (p. 081) and **Jian Wai** (p. 089).

Photo by Xia Zhi, courtesy MAD

Photo by Xia Zhi, courtesy MAD

Hotel Conrad

BJ 31

MAD, Metamax, BIAD, 2008–2013

康莱德酒店
朝阳区东三环北路29号
29 N Dong San Huan Rd, Chaoyang
❖ 39.9264, 116.4550

Developed in parallel to the firm's dramatically twisting Absolute Towers in Toronto (2006–2012), this smaller project tested similar geometry in simplified form – as a wrapped sheet of variegated openings keyed to the grid of a more straightforward volume. The stated agenda mixes several organic metaphors – a "neural network," a "mutation," and a "plant rising through a crack" in the sidewalk. Keep an eye on the firm's **Chaoyang Park towers** (map p. 115), under construction nearby, anticipated for 2016.

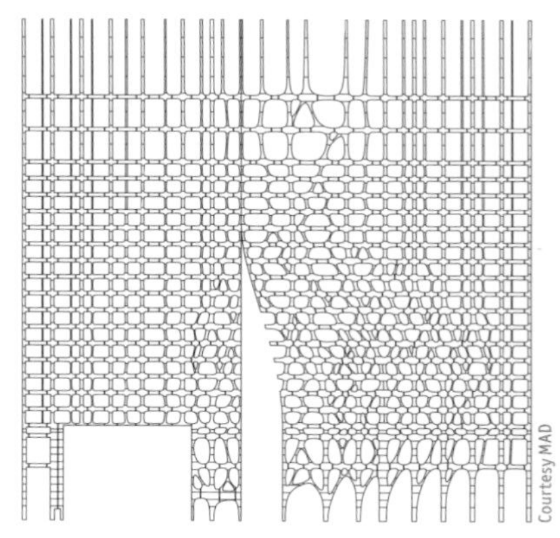

Courtesy MAD

Unwrapped drawing of façade

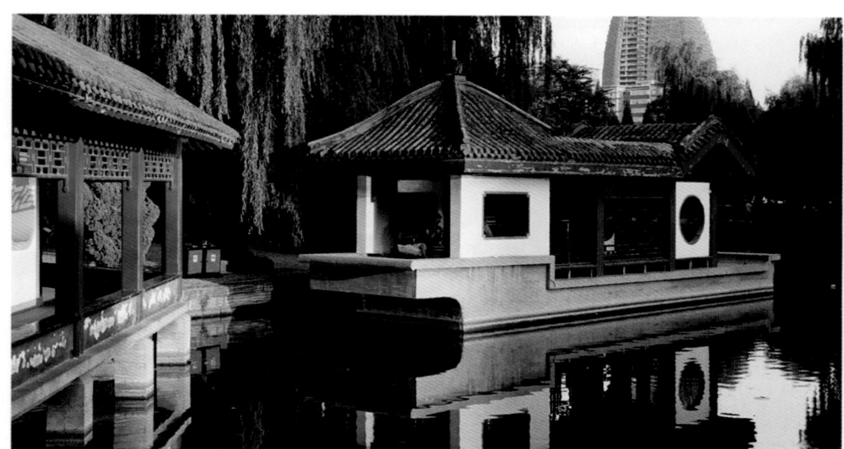

Tuanjiehu Park

BJ 32

1958+

团结湖公园
朝阳区 团结湖南里16号
16 Tuanjiehu Nanli, Chaoyang District
❖ 39.9244, 116.4585

An easily-missed treat: locals exercising, playing cards, and watching the kids ride novelty paddle-boats, all in a twentieth-century facsimile of a classical Chinese garden. The park is free to enter, and thus very well-used, like the **Temple of Heaven** (p. 080), *sans* temple.

Phoenix International Media Centre

BJ 33

BIAD/UFo (Un-Forbidden Office), 2008–2012

凤凰国际传媒中心
朝阳公园路（朝阳公园西南角）
Chaoyang Park Rd. (SE corner of the park)
❖ 39.9332, 116.4676

Inspired by Moebius strips, this twisting, well-detailed doughnut is meant to smoothly resolve the different spatial demands of repetitive small offices and large media studios. The fit between form and programme isn't a complete match, so the leftover spaces are free to be shaped into dramatic, tubular circulation zones. The building lifts up from the ground to permit a public route through to Chaoyang Park, though it remains to be seen how consistently that will be open. UFo is an arm of BIAD (a state design agency), dedicated to researching digital techniques. The work seems to be paying off; this building displays a much more confident handling of complex curvature than typical institute work of even a few years ago.

Chaowai SOHO

BJ 35

SEUNG H-Sang/IROJE architects & planners, 2006+

朝外 SOHO
北京市朝阳区朝外大街乙6号
6B Chaowai Da Jie, Chaoyang
❖ 39.9187, 116.4485

This relatively introverted SOHO scheme renders shopping and offices as a geode: a rocky and semi-opaque volume is split open and shifted, to reveal glass-walled courtyards and passageways within. The courtyards are appealingly cool in summer, and welcome for the light and sense of orientation they give to the shopping-mall levels.

Ground-floor plan

Parkview Green Fangcaodi

BJ 36

Integrated Design Associates (Winston SHU), Arup, 2010

芳草地 2芳草地北巷 朝阳区
2 Fangcaodi North Alley, Chaoyang
❖ 39.9183, 116.4434

This glassy pyramid contains a luxury mall and terraced mid-rise blocks of office and hotel space. The monumental form, spectacular section, and enormous moat-like trench give the impression that this could be the *final* mall, whose coming other malls have long awaited. But while this is far more self-contained and object-like than the nearby SOHO schemes, the expression of individual volumes within the big tent still seems to suggest an interest in urban space. It earned a LEED Platinum rating through natural ventilation, daylighting of spaces, recycling of rainwater, etc. Shu previously worked for Norman Foster; compare to **HSBC** (p. 352) and **Chek Lap Kok** (p. 365). To obtain the best views, check out the gallery near the top, on the northeast side.

Shangdu SOHO

BJ 37

LAB Architecture Studio, 2004–2007

尚都SOHO
北京市朝阳区东大桥路8号
8 Dongdaqiao Road, Chaoyang
❖ 39.9175, 116.4453

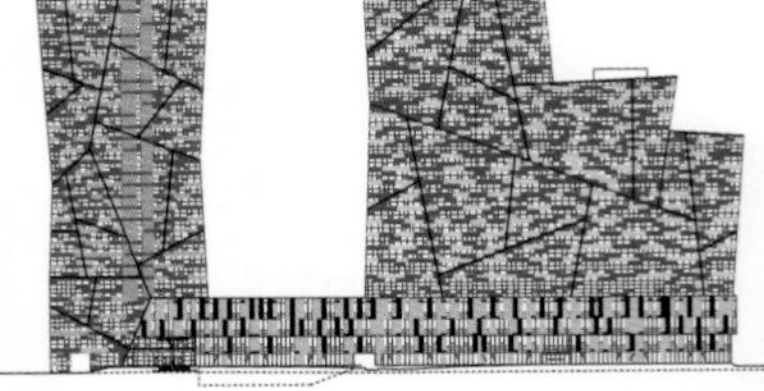

Elevation

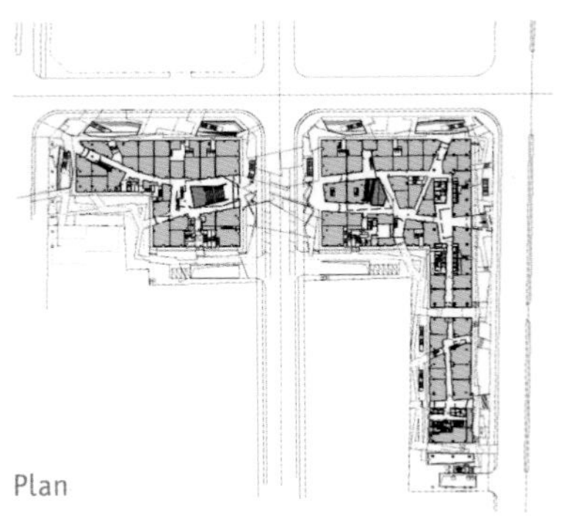

Plan

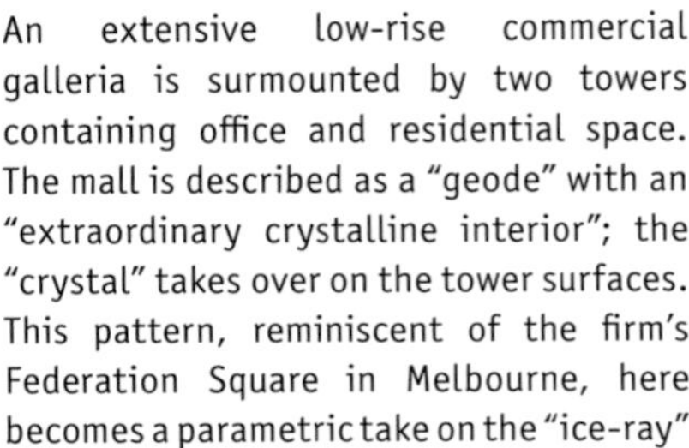

An extensive low-rise commercial galleria is surmounted by two towers containing office and residential space. The mall is described as a "geode" with an "extraordinary crystalline interior"; the "crystal" takes over on the tower surfaces. This pattern, reminiscent of the firm's Federation Square in Melbourne, here becomes a parametric take on the "ice-ray" screen designs seen in traditional gardens. Inside, varied paths and road-spanning sky-bridges recreate urban continuities lost in Beijing's contemporary super-scale. Shifts between floor plates, dramatised by lighting at night, correspond to the desired variety of leasable floor areas.

The Place

Kritzinger & Rao, 2000s

BJ 38

世贸天阶 – 朝阳区光华路9号
9 Guanghua Rd, Chaoyang
❖ 39.9151, 116.4460

© Florian Meuser

Reflecting a national taste for all things European, this piece of Western-style Postmodernism features two shopping malls that face each other across a supersized Italian *piazza*. The space is sheltered and framed by an enormous LED screen, co-designed by Jeremy RAILTON (whose résumé includes TV's *Pee-Wee's Playhouse*). On the mall's lowest level, you may still find Zhong SONG's Music Bar, a curvaceous contemporary interior.

© Florian Meuser

Guanghualu SOHO

MADA s.p.a.m. (Qingyun MA), 2008

BJ 39

光华路SOHO
北京市朝阳区光华路22号
22 Guanghua Road, Chaoyang
❖ 39.9116, 116.4461

Referring to flattering puns on the client's name ("SoHILL" and "SoROCK"), the architects created a "hill-like" building with "caves" and a penthouse "rock" at the top. The glassy voids light the interior; separating the volume into eight shifting bars reduces the mall's monolithic scale. The polka-dot motif is described as an "eternal" fashion statement. Details aside, the interior is a familiar mall.

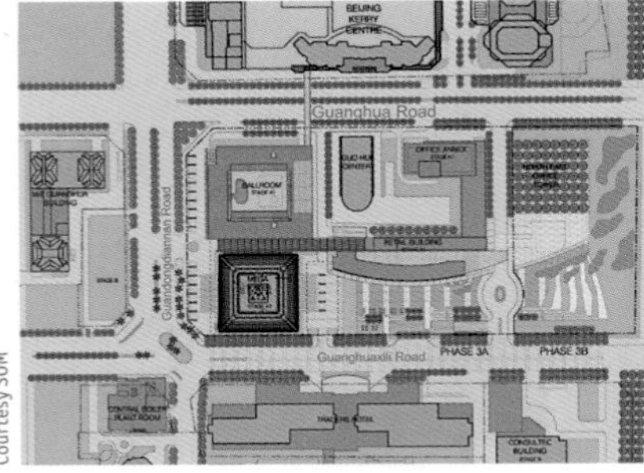

Courtesy SOM

Site plan

China World Trade Centre, Tower III

SOM, 2010

BJ 40

中国国际贸易中心 – 大厦三期
朝阳区建国门外大街1号
1 Jianguomen Outer St, Chaoyang
❖ 39.9109, 116.4521

The tallest building in Beijing as of 2014, the CWTC Tower marks the centre of Beijing's new Central Business District (CBD). The mixed-use tower features the typical combination of hotel and office suites, accessed via separate lobbies on the east and west sides of the block, respectively.

Photo courtesy SOM | © Tim Griffith

The rippling, textured façade was designed to maximise daylighting while minimising heat gain, an environmentally-conscious design that helped earn the building a LEED Gold certification. The tapered form is a major presence on Beijing's modern skyline, and its sheer verticality is a symbol of the city's ongoing process of modernisation, for better or worse.

CCTV Station & Headquarters

OMA (Rem KOOLHAAS), ECADI, 2002–2013

BJ 41

中央电视台
北京市朝阳区东三环中路32号
32 East Third Ring Road, Chaoyang
❖ 39.9140, 116.4581

The headquarters of China's state TV agency is the apogee of China's "starchitect" boom of the early 2000s. Mocked on internet forums as "the big pants" (and raunchier things), the building is nonetheless a major component of Beijing's international image, a startling feat of structural engineering, and the culmination of decades of architectural theory. Koolhaas attempts to undercut the authoritarian monumentality of the project with a number of humane gestures: the three-dimensional loop, defying the phallic convention of skyscrapers, was intended to provide a visitors' route, increasing the organisation's transparency. A pleasant podium landscape was intended to encourage public engagement. Clearly, Koolhaas's belief in the liberatory potential of the tall

building survives (see 1978's *Delirious New York*), but these elements of the design didn't, or did so in limited ways. The complex is heavily-guarded and inaccessible, disconnected from the surrounding blocks by concrete walls and barbed wire. This looming object, with its predatory posture, could now suggest paranoid surveillance. On the other hand, the gravity-defying, scaleless form (which marks the density of its diagonal structure in order to render it insubstantial pattern) has a certain totemic presence, which may inspire free-thinking in a vaguer way. The smaller building in the back is "TVCC," the production facility (which famously caught fire partway through construction).

Jian Wai SOHO

BJ 43

YAMAMOTO Riken, 2004

建外SOHO
朝阳区东三环中路39号
39 East Third Ring Road, Chaoyang
❖ 39.9040, 116.4521

The most emphatically Modernist SOHO project makes a statement by refusing ornament and styling, beyond the anti-style style of the white grid. The success of the project depends on its ground-level public space, which is animated by cuts down to lower-level retail, parking, and the commercial ground floors of the condo towers. A few retail and gallery buildings complete the complex. Yamamoto, like a number of postwar Modernists (especially those of Team X), claims as his inspiration the dense weave of traditional cities in the Arab world, yet this could just as easily be seen as a critique of Beijing's over-scaled, post-1949 grid, which Yamamoto refuses by a slight rotation in plan. High rises and cars do not rule out a pleasant pedestrian atmosphere, including pathways to coffee shops as well as places to sit with friends under a tree, buying nothing. If there is something slightly anemic about the end product, this probably has more to do with the uniform sheen on the mid- and up-scale retail establishments (and their customers) than with the minimalist aesthetic, which really is a breath of fresh air in Beijing.

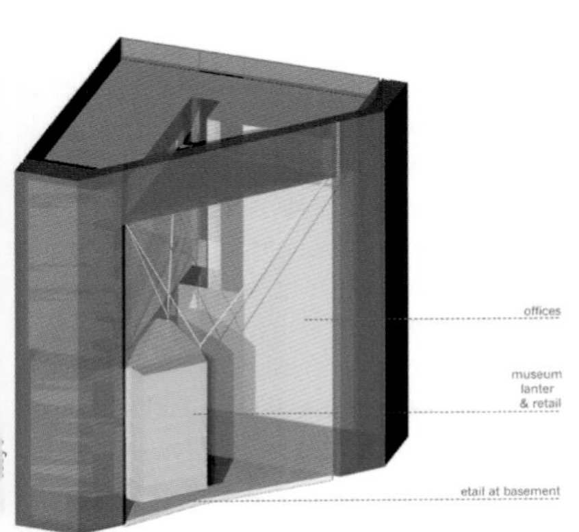

Massing diagram

Photo courtesy SOM | © Tim Griffith

Photo courtesy SOM | © Tim Griffith

New Poly Plaza

BJ 45

SOM, 2007

新保利大厦，朝阳门北大街1号
1 North Chaoyangmen Avenue
❖ 39.9312, 116.4260

This triangular office atrium features most of one face given over to a vast cable-net curtain wall (one of the world's largest of this type). Given the over-scaled, polluted and generally unpleasant public realm in this part of Beijing, the light-filled atrium offers a nice compromise between openness and introversion. If Beijing someday caps or at least landscapes its highways, office-workers here will be glad of the view. Compare to the firm's Poly International Plaza, for the same client, in Guangzhou (p. 307).

© Shu He, courtesy Steven Holl Architects

© Shu He, courtesy Steven Holl Architects

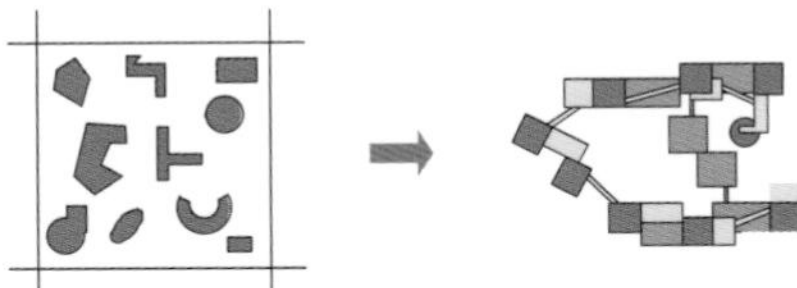
"City of objects" vs. "city of spaces"

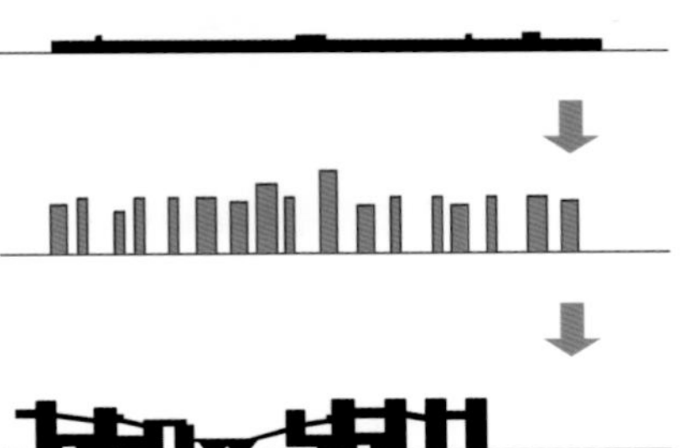
Beijing before the 1980s ("Horizontality"), after the 1980s ("Verticality"), and Linked Hybrid ("Vertical Horizontality")

Linked Hybrid

BJ 47

Steven HOLL Architects, 2003–2009

当代MOMA
东城区东直门外香河园路1号
1 Xiangheyuan Road, Dongzhimen
❖ 39.9491, 116.4318

This set of upscale housing towers – confusingly dubbed "Beijing MOMA" – is linked together by a "bridge" of shared programme, including a gym, restaurant, gallery space, and so on. These spaces are lifted into the air in an effort to make the project more urbanistically porous, while hybridising the high-rise "object building" with the low-rise courtyard fabric. Another "local" touch: the colours around the windows were supposedly chosen at random using the *I Ching*. Holl describes the promenade in filmic terms – "jump cuts" on elevators, "panning" views from raised passages – and stresses that he would like to see it evolve on its own, acquiring new programmes. Critics have charged that because the building is cut off by a ring road, its upmarket status and its security forces, it will not be able to sustain these ambitions. Indeed, it can be tough to reach the courtyard without a ticket to the complex's conveniently located movie theatre. A sequel of sorts can be seen in **Chengdu** (map p. 388), where Holl abandons the bridges but broadens and dramatises the openings to the sidewalk, making it clearer that at least the *architecture* intends to create a public space. However these problems are resolved, Linked Hybrid merits close attention. The idea of a building as a bridge (apparent also in the **Vanke headquarters,** p. 331) runs back through Holl's work to early, unbuilt projects for the Bronx (1977) and the now-famous High Line (1979). Realised here, these ideas seem like a refreshed treatment of the old Modernist dream of "streets in the air," looking somehow airier despite Beijing's smog. It's as if the dramatic late-Modern forms of 1960s concrete Brutalism have been married to that period's minimalist sculpture – or to the simplified "white" material palette of the 1920s. The elementary gridded surface, which clearly broadcasts the lines of diagonal structure, also seems like a Modernist refusal of imagery and references, *I Ching* or no.

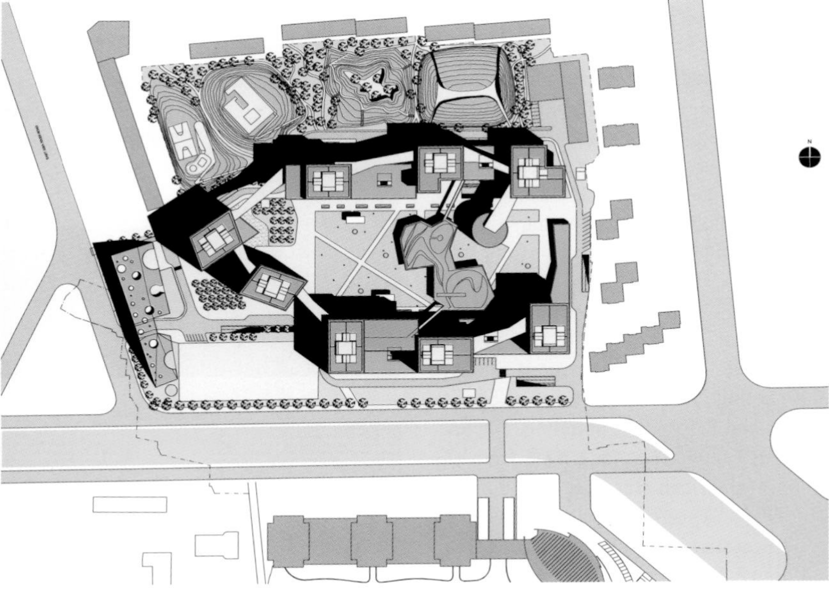

Site plan

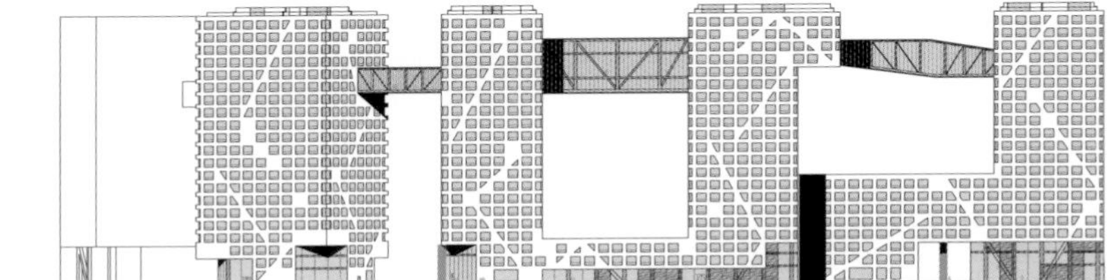

South elevation

It's not unlike **Jian Wai SOHO** (p. 089), and contrasts with the juggling of structure and image-making at **CCTV** (p. 088) and the **National Stadium** (p. 098). Significant to the success of all of Holl's Chinese projects of this period was then-partner and Beijing office head LI Hu. Li is now a principal of OPEN Architecture (based in this building) and a rising star; see **Studio-X** (p. 079), and much bigger things coming soon.

Perspective, collaged into landscape image

Fragrant Hill Hotel

BJ 50

Pei Cobb Freed (Ieoh Ming PEI), 1979–1982

香山饭店
北京市海淀区买卖街40号
40 Maimai Street, Haidian
❖ 39.9886, 116.1885

After Pei joined a successful effort to talk the government out of building high-rises in central Beijing, the state commissioned a hotel complex in this former imperial hunting park. Pei saw historicism as "a man in a tailored suit wearing a coolie hat" – think here of the later **Beijing West Station** (p. 103). He also resented the dominance of Soviet-style Modernism and its "slavish" imitators. His design thus abstracted Chinese courtyard houses and gardens, with smatterings of Suzhou details and polycentric planning. The government, expecting Modernism from the Chinese-American star, was disappointed, while Pei's Western fans feared they saw a good Brutalist going Postmodern. China's building industry was still recovering from the years of instability, and the difficult construction process culminated in Pei's immediate family having to personally install the potted plants for the grand opening. For all that, it's well-detailed, and thus in better shape than many much more recent buildings. Pei would not do another building in mainland China until the **Suzhou Museum** (p. 216). Both projects find a mature architect returning to his country of birth and trying to make sense of several design traditions. Here, the programme of guest rooms lends itself to a pavilionisation and attenuation of plan typical of gardens. Compare to the **Bank of China in Beijing** (map p. 117), completed nearly twenty years later, in which a similar synthesis gives the Modern elements (in the mode of Pei's National Gallery wing in Washington, D.C.) greater emphasis.

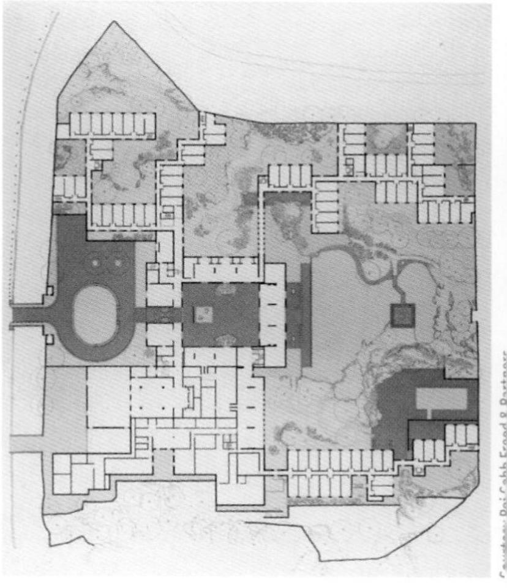

Plan

Summary Palace

BJ 52

Various, twelfth century onwards

颐和园

❖ 39.9969, 116.2755 (East Gate)

Although this hill was long home to a palace complex, most of the current construction dates from the reign of the Qianlong Emperor (1711–1799), who also developed the back garden of the Forbidden City. The palace was reconstructed by the Dowager Empress in the 1880s, after being damaged in the same British and French assault that completely wiped out the nearby **Old Summer Palace** (p. 094). Garden historian CHENG Liyao divides the Summer Palace into four conceptual areas: a highly formal court/residential section to the east (with the "small but exquisite" Xiequyuan Garden to the north); the northern side of the hill (a "naturalised" landscape with a group of Tibetan Buddhist temples); the southern face of the hill (with towers dramatically sited on a short but steep axis); and, further away, the South and West Lakes, sprinkled with islands and pavilions. These last are inspired by southern gardens (particularly **West Lake,** p. 256). As with the Forbidden City garden, this complex is a bit of a hybrid, with the axial, imperial arrangement (very much apparent in plan) played against a looser sensibility. Due to the topography and the presence of the lake (a former reservoir), one experiences the axial sequences mostly in the oblique or in severe perspective, and the whole north side of the hill unfolds as winding paths leading to surprising reveals. If all this reads as "Picturesque" in the British sense, that's because European gardens of the eighteenth and nineteenth centuries were indebted to Chinese ones, or at least to vague descriptions of them. The Summer Palace is considerably larger than a **Suzhou** garden, and does not aspire to the same kind of spatial intricacy – but then, emperors are not mere poet-officials. Those with extra time in the region should consider a comparative visit to the larger imperial resort at **Chengde** (map p. 119).

Overall plan

Courtesy China Architecture and Building Press

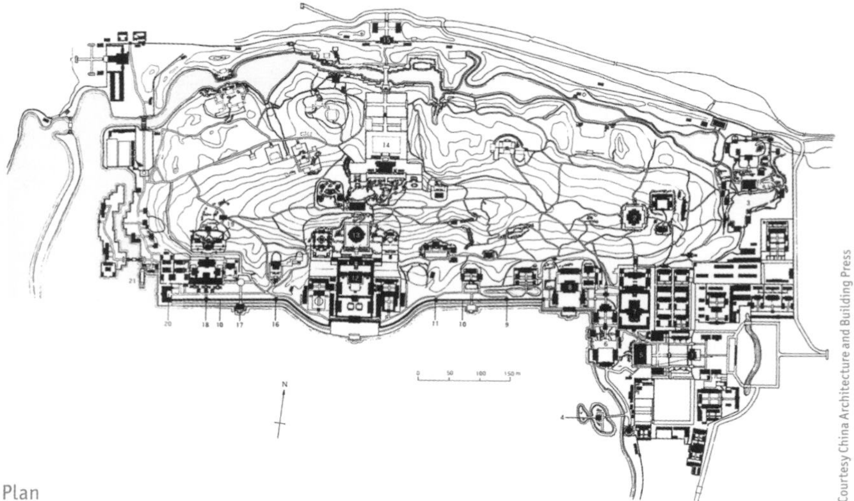

Plan

Courtesy China Architecture and Building Press

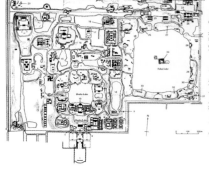

Ruins of the Old Summer Palace

BJ 53

Various designers, 1709+

Reconstructed plan of the Yuanmingyuan

圆明园遗址公园
北京市海淀区清华西路28号
28 Tsinghua University West Road, Haidian
❖ 40.0056, 116.3085 (south gate)

This linked complex of three gardens, the primary residence of the Qing emperors, now forms the backdrop to Beijing's university district. It was destroyed by the British and French in an act of cultural vandalism at the end of the Second Opium War (1860); some was reconstructed, then destroyed again by Europeans during the Boxer Rebellion (1900). Visitors thus find only a pleasant park and some scenic ruins. Note a set of Baroque pieces, including a small maze, added to the *Changchun Yuan* (just off the above plan; see map p. 116) by the Jesuit Giuseppe CASTIGLIONE in the 1750s. Known as the "Western Mansions" (西洋楼), they are among the first pieces of European architecture built in China as self-conscious acts of representation, rather than colonial expedients. Whether seen as amusing novelties, tributes from foreign barbarians, or symbols of encroaching Western values, they mark an architectural turning point.

Christian Church

BJ 58

GMP (von GERKAN, MARG, and Partners), 2004–2007

基督教堂
海淀区彩和坊路9号
9 Cai He Fang Rd, Haidian
❖ 39.9821, 116.3015

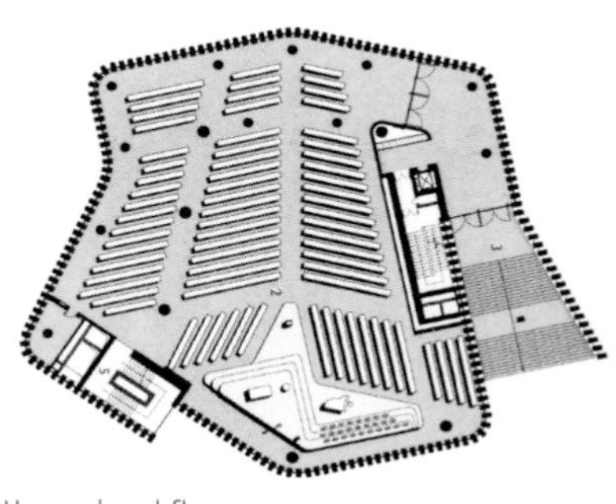

Upper-level floor

While some estimate that China is home to as many as fifty-four million Christians, a long tradition of state atheism has left few local precedents to draw from in building large churches. The architects seem to have taken cues from the mid-century work of Alvar AALTO: undulating wall and altar, abstract bell-tower, and lots of white paint. The concrete rib structure itself carries meaning – becoming a cross at the entryway – and modulates sunlight for environmental comfort. These are fair responses to the drab glitziness of Zhongguancun's high-tech commercialism. (The drapes are later additions.)

Olympic Green & Forest Park

BJ 62

Sasaki Associates, with Tsinghua University (implementation of Forest Park) and Steven HANDEL (ecological strategies)
2002–2008

北京奥林匹克公园
❖ 39.9931, 116.3871

Rendering, with distant **Bird's Nest** (p. 098)

Organised around a long central spine (lining up with the historic north-south line of Beijing, through the Forbidden City), the Olympic Park's monumental expanses are offered in counterbalance to the more picturesque, sculptural landscape created just to the north, around the new "Dragon Lake." The "Dragon's Tail" water feature links these spaces, together with the existing 1990 Asian Games complex (the southern "loop" in the plan at right). To the designers, contemporary planning for a sustainable environmental was "rooted in the myths and legends of ancient China," and so the journey from forest to park is also meant to symbolise a historical evolution, with different spots along the way representing particular dynasties and cultural achievements. Sasaki's plan also called for mixed-use, pedestrian-oriented developments, with an eye on post-Games integration into the larger fabric of the city. Unfortunately, this has not happened, and the site is now rather barren. The parking-lot tracts just east of the "Dragon's Tail," for years a missed opportunity, are to be the site of Jean NOUVEL's National Museum (date TBD).

Master plan

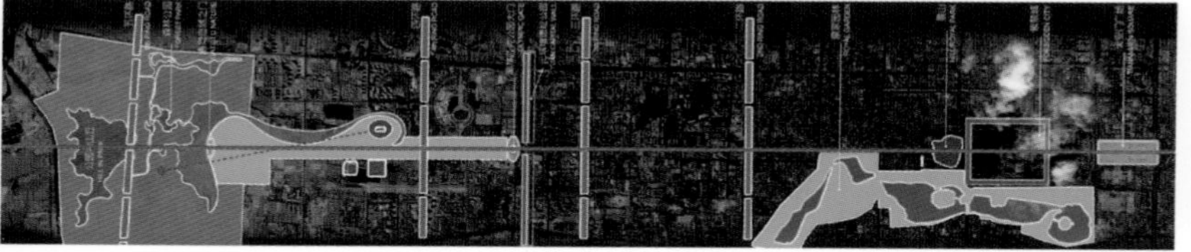

Plan diagram (north at left), indicating axial link to **Jingshan Park** (p. 076), **Forbidden City** (p. 074), and **Tian'anmen Square** (p. 072). **Beihai Park** (p. 076) is at bottom right.

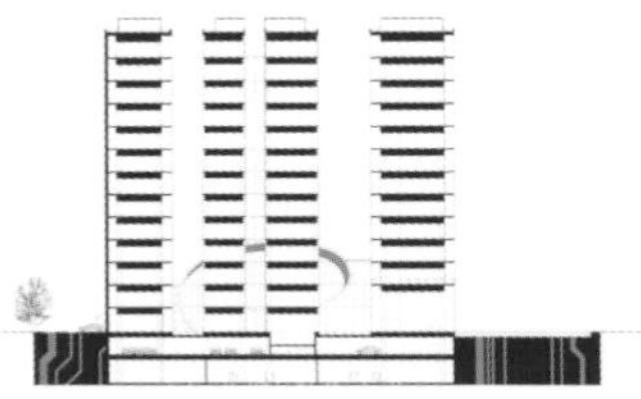
Cross section

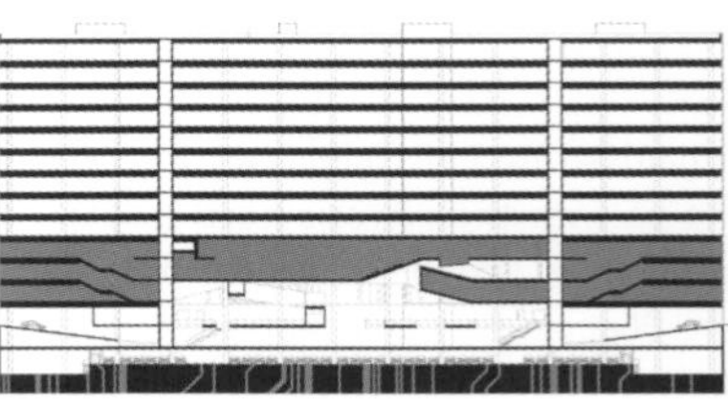
Longitudinal section

Digital Beijing
Urbanus/Studio Pei-Zhu,
2004–2008

BJ 63

数字北京/数字博物馆
北京市朝阳区北辰西路12号
12 Beichen West Road, Chaoyang
❖ 39.9940, 116.3819

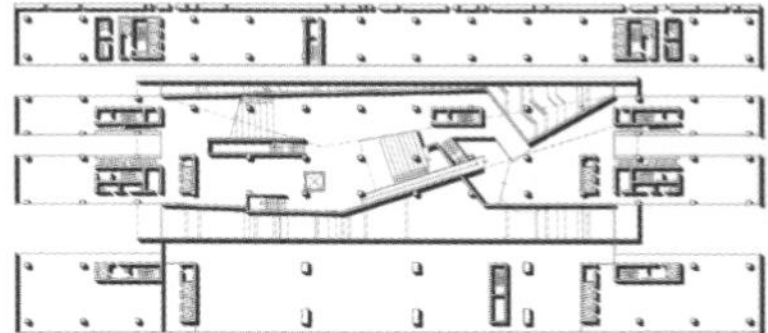
Third-floor plan

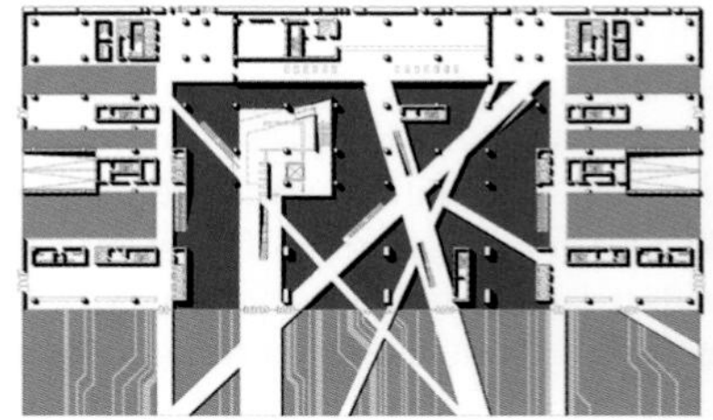
Ground-floor plan

This piece of the Olympic Green, which coincided with ZHU Pei's departure from Urbanus to found his own firm, is a billboard for the technology behind the "Digital Olympics"; it housed computers and other electronic equipment for coordinating and broadcasting the games. The mass is broken into four structurally independent slabs that reduce the visual "weight," and evoke the heat-sinks over computer CPUs, while perhaps accomplishing similar thermal-management goals. It was intended that some of the ground-floor public space would become a "virtual museum" or a showcase for electronics manufacturers; try to get a peek at the main space, where catwalks criss-cross a graceful concrete swoop. The surface pattern is meant to evoke a circuit board, a bar-code, or the 0s and 1s of binary machine language. According to Zhu, the architects were "trying to reveal an enlarged micro world suggestive of the microchips abundant but ignored in our daily life." It's an interesting attempt to give architectural presence to an order which is fundamentally invisible – and civic presence to a data centre, a programme that typically favours the protective qualities of a windowless bunker, as in old telephone exchanges. The well-made curtain wall and the abstraction of the "circuit board" motif save us from kitsch.

National Swimming Centre

BJ 64

CSCEC, PTW, CCDI and Arup, 2003–2008

北京国家游泳中心，北京奥林匹克公园
Beijing Olympic Park
❖ 39.9915, 116.3841

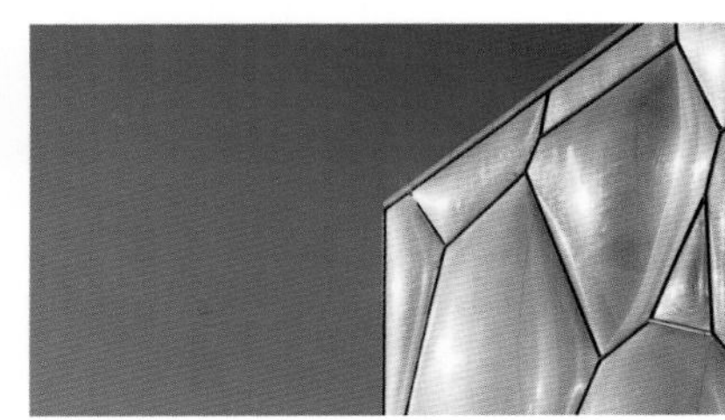

Inspired by the efficient soap-bubble mathematics of Weaire-Phelan foam, the international team saw the building not as “a pattern carved into a box,” but “a box carved from a theoretically perfect and repetitious array of bubbles.” With the square given in the master plan (and a fortuitous shape in Chinese tradition) the bubble isn’t fully exploited structurally, but the skin remains quite smart: two layers of ETFE “pillows” protect the structural steel from humidity, while reducing weight and improving the pool area’s acoustics. The double skin creates a ventilation zone, opened for convection-driven breezes in summer and closed for greenhouse-effect warmth in the winter. The bubbles also capture rainwater and solar energy. All told, the operating energy cost savings of using the skin were “equivalent to cladding the whole building with solar panels.” It’s also a visual delight: reflective and scaly in strong light, and a deep membrane revealing bubbles beyond bubbles on overcast days. The secondary pool has become a water park; the major one is still a pool, also used for performances.

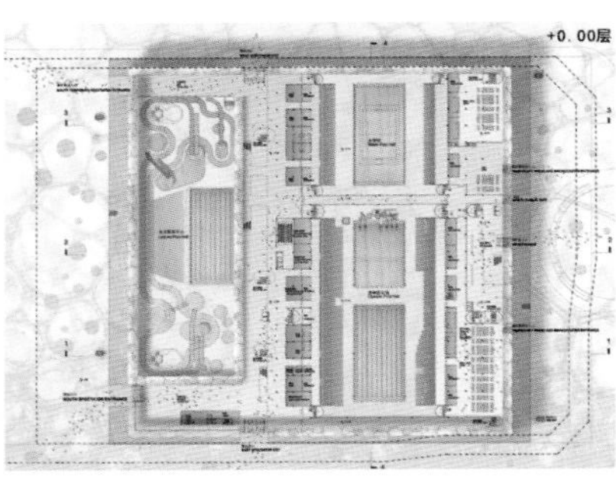

Main-level plan

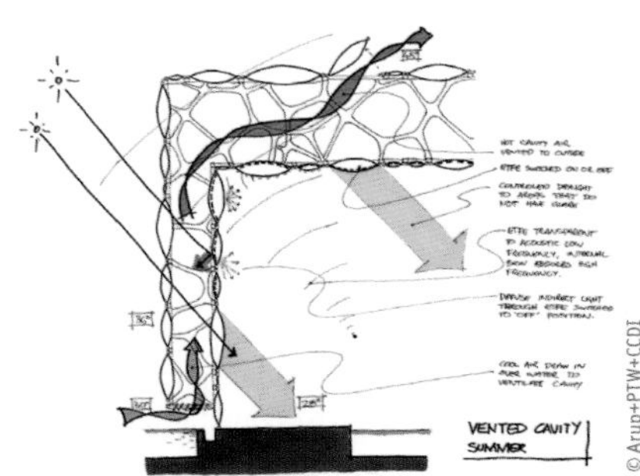

Vented cavity in summer

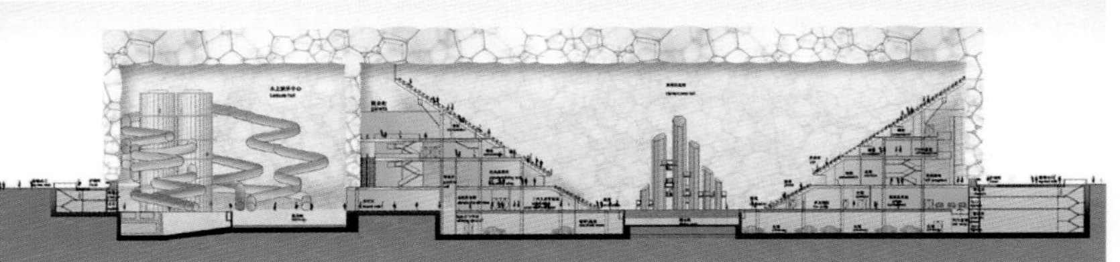

Section

Beijing National Statium (Bird's Nest)

BJ 65

Herzog & de Meuron, Arup, FAKE Design (AI Weiwei), 2002–2008

北京国家体育场（鸟巢）
北京市朝阳区国家体育场南路1号
1 S. National Stadium Road, Chaoyang
❖ 39.9916, 116.3905

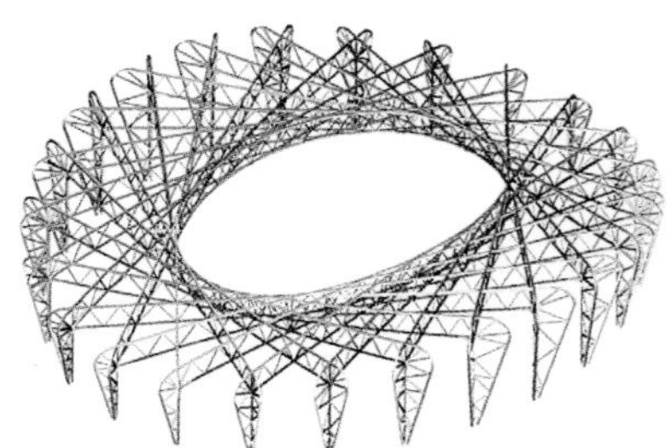

Primary structural members

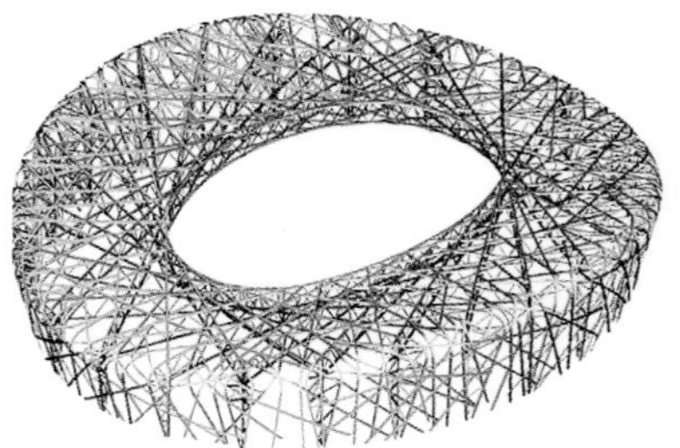

The complete "nest"

Conceived as a meditation on order and chaos, the design's wild slashes contrast with the more regular site planning of the Olympic Green. As the architects suggest, the seeming clarity of the object from a distance dissolves into a field condition up close, as what seems to be the taut outer wrapper of the "basket" reveals itself to involve multiple layers. Indeed, the scale and diffusion of the elements makes the basket itself disappear; rather, one now wanders an "artificial forest," exploring within the thickness of what had appeared to be a flat, decorative membrane. Only twenty-four of the arced steel columns carry the structure, and other elements are scaled up to match, dissolving the visual sense of support, and paradoxically making the building appear lighter. This merging of graphics and structure is a theme for the architects (see the **Jinhua Structure I-Cube**, p. 286, or Tokyo's Prada Epicenter), but finds its ultimate expression here. Similarly, the double-curved saddle form makes the building seem to change shape when seen from different directions. The stadium sits atop an artificial ground: visitors approach through a forest of columns to discover the sunken pitch within, and are treated to an overview from an elevated vantage. Along the way, they also enjoy peculiar views out, between the lattice lines, which make even more ordinary buildings unfamiliar and new. The Bird's Nest thus tests whether the provocative unfamiliarity of a park pavilion can scale up effectively, to become "something anti-monumental," to "insert an intimate space into the middle of public space." In this light, the shift from object to field may suggest a transformation from monumentality (Olympics *à la* Berlin, 1936) to an architecture so diaphanous it's barely there (Olympics *à la* Munich, 1972); Jacques HERZOG compares it instead to the space *under* the Eiffel Tower. These moves are all to avoid "the insistent sameness of technocratic architecture dominated by large spans and digital screens." Ai, in the end, withdrew from the Olympic proceedings, without disavowing this provocative design. Today, it's home to an artificial snow park and other attractions – worth the ticket for the in-between spaces. All quotes from architects' website or their remarks in *El Croquis* #129/130, 2006.

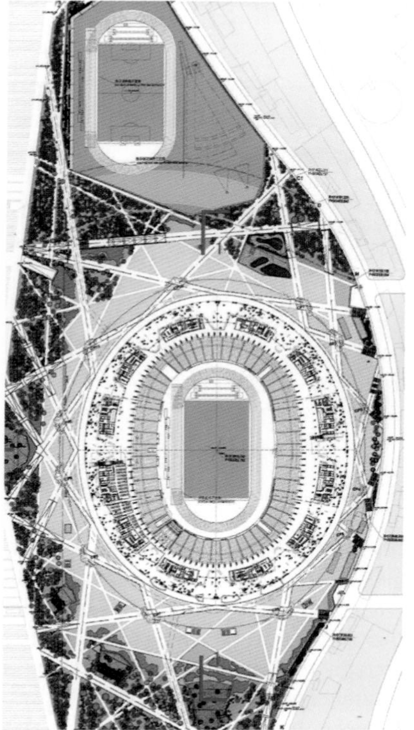

Site plan

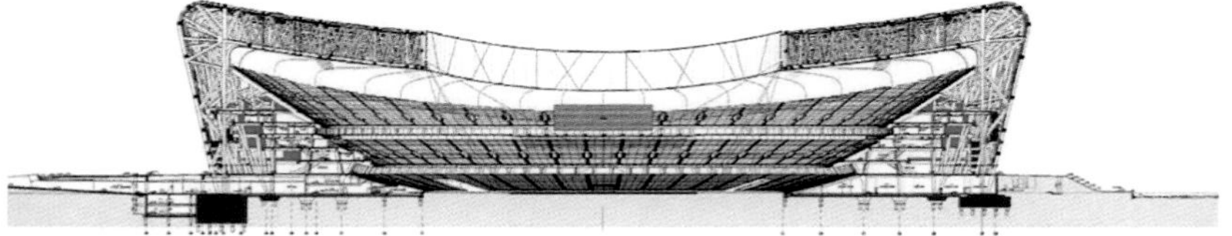

West–east section

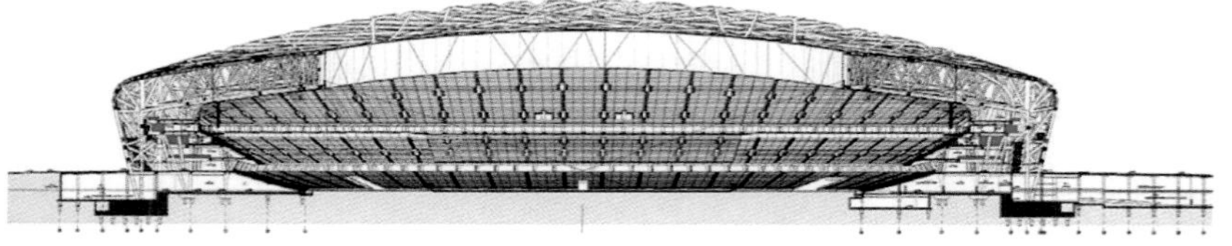

North–south section

798 Arts District

BJ 66

Original buildings, 1956. Master plan by Sasaki Associates, 2006. Galleries by various architects.

798艺术区 – 朝阳区酒仙桥路4号
4 Jiuxianqiao Rd, Chaoyang
❖ 39.9828, 116.4898

Beijing's premier gallery district has become a major tourist attraction, revitalising this once-remote corner of the city and playing a major part in the explosive growth of China's art market. Originally housing a multi-block electronics factory complex, most of the structures here were designed and built in collaboration with East German Modernist engineers. The unadorned structures of concrete and brick feature distinctive sawtooth skylights, providing ample natural light. As in many "functionalist" projects, the engineer's logic can almost, but not quite, explain the striking elegance of the structural elements, here including vaguely sickle-shaped pieces that unite the diagonal braces for the skylight lintels with the curving roof beams. The factory complex stayed in operation into the early 1990s; in 1995, Beijing's Central Academy of Fine Arts (see **CAFA Museum,** p. 103), seeking cheap, well-lit workspace, moved into one defunct building. Over the next decade, the area attracted artists and designers, and later, galleries and small shops. As its reputation spread, the district became a centre of Beijing's arts community, but the city considered demolishing the old factory buildings, now seen as insufficiently dense. A 2006 master plan by Sasaki Associates helped win support for the old structures, and proposed enhancing the existing pedestrian network with "courtyards, corridors and passageways." One suspects that 798's popularity may stem in large part from it just being a pleasant place to stroll around. High-rises, including hotels and convention centres serving the growing number of software, publishing, and design concerns, are kept to the edge of the district, and larger-scale museums are incorporated into the fabric. The district's survival, absent rent control, forces a trade-off: many artists have been priced out, with some establishing studios in nearby **Caochangdi village** (p. 102) or more remote points like **Songzhuang** (p. 105). At the same time, a certain 798–ish quality has begun to crop up in other renovated industrial spaces, and in new buildings for the arts. Compare to **22 Art Plaza** (map p. 115), **Meridian Space** (p. 078), the new **Chinese Academy of Oil Painting,** and, further out, the **Red Brick Art Museum** (both on map p. 118).

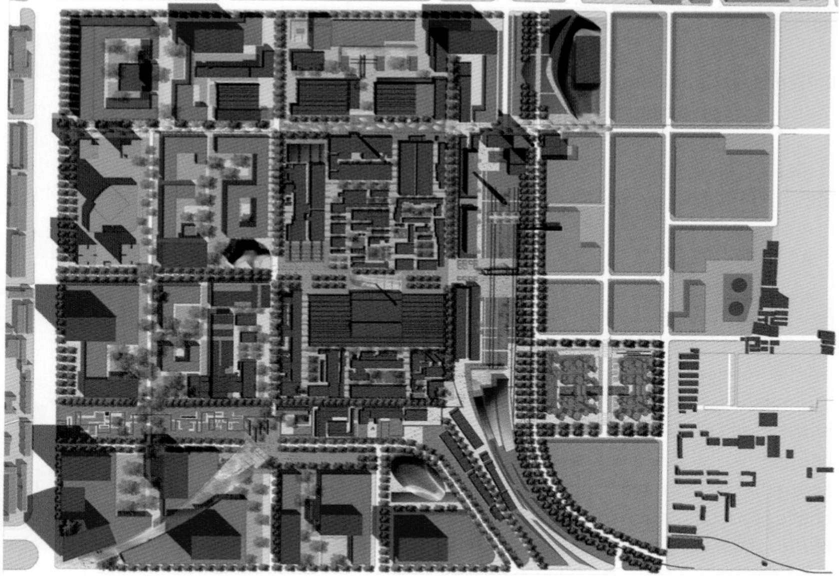

Courtesy Sasaki Associates

2006 Master Plan

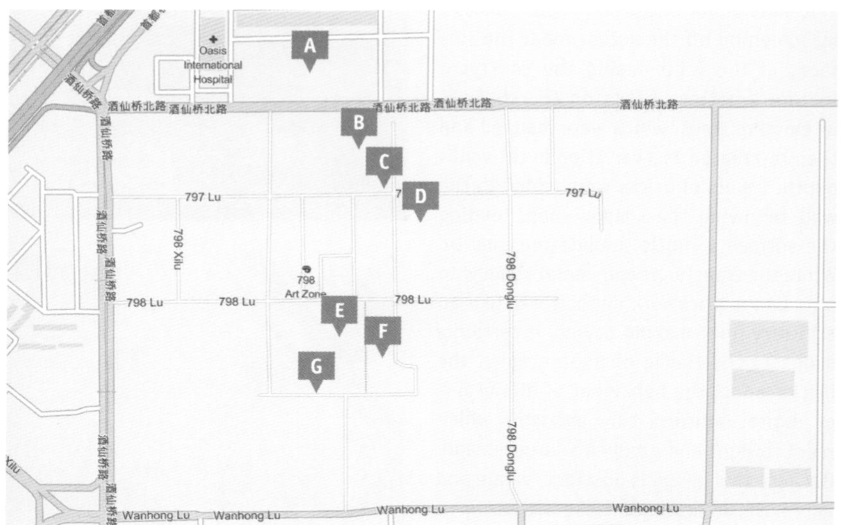

A. 798 Museum/Minsheng MOCA *Studio Pei-Zhu*. Factory renovation, under construction. **B. PACE Gallery** *Studio Pei-Zhu*. Renovation of sawtooth industrial building. **C. Yue Art Gallery/Enjoy Museum** *Tao Lei Studio*. Sleek white volumes contrast with the brick factory shell. **D. 2010 Art Space** *Thanlab/HAN Tao, 2011*. Distorted cubic volume, concealing a lively branching interior structure which perforates floors to maximise light and views. **E. Ullens Centre for Contemporary Art** *Jean-Michel Wilmotte, MADA s.p.a.m., 2007*. Two 9.6–metre-high "naves" with diffused light falling between arched concrete beams. **F. 798 Space** Relatively intact "sawtooth" industrial space. **G. Iberia Centre** *Approach Architecture Studio, 2008*. An undulating brick façade links three industrial buildings.

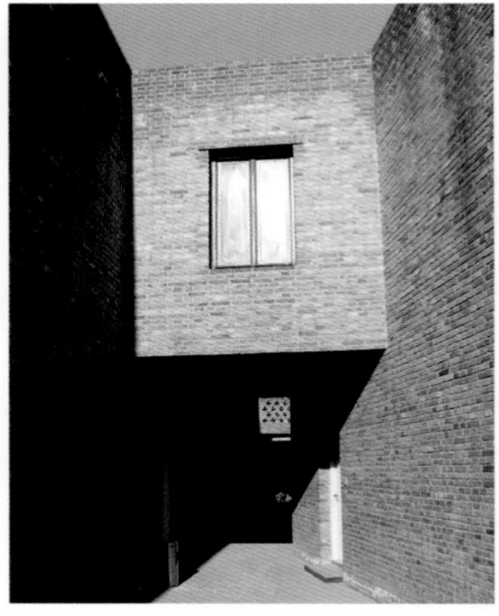

Galleries at Caochangdi

BJ 67

FAKE Design (AI Weiwei), 2000s

草场地美术馆
南皋乡草场地155号a，草场地241号
Caochangdi, various addresses
❖ 40.0002, 116.5017

As **798** (p. 100) has become more upscale and "official," many artists have relocated to the former village of Caochangdi, to the northeast. Among them is Ai Weiwei; now living in "CCD" under house arrest, he previously designed several studios and galleries. The most notable is Three Shadows, supposedly the first dedicated photo/video exhibition space in China. The "bent bar" scheme is meant to respond to existing topography, while creating "intimate public and private open spaces"; by screening off the access road. The surfaces of the walls facing the courtyard feature a pattern based on the shadows of existing trees, which were mapped and then re-created as a variation in the wall's depth. Layers of bricks were added to the wall following the shadow map, lending the surface a subtle, undulating quality. While the transfer of ephemeral shadow to permanent brickwork might seem like an arbitrary form-making device, it certainly suggests the theme of photography: the bricks model the behaviour of film grains or digital sensors, tiny particles which react to light and produce a larger image. Because this image is abstract, vague and imprecise, it demands close attention to concept and to context, and refuses clear, consumable legibility. As at **Ai Qing Park** (p. 287), Ai's strategy of architectural resistance is not the aggressive middle finger seen in his own photography. What he seems to demand is a moment to think in a country hurtling headlong into over-development. Other galleries similarly explore brick courtyard typologies: fine, understated space.

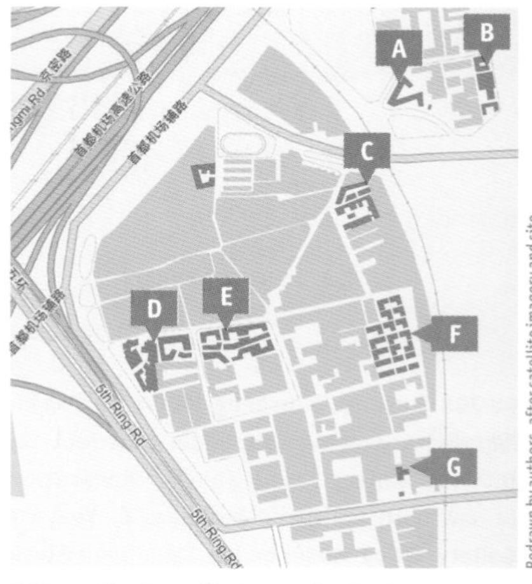

Redrawn by authors, after satellite imagery and site

A Three Shadows Photography Centre **B** CAAW **C** Courtyard 104–105 **D** Gallery Urs Meile **E** Red Brick Art Galleries **F** 17 Studios **G** Studio Ai Weiwei

Chinese Academy of Fine Arts (CAFA) Museum

BJ 69

ISOZAKI Arata, 2003–2008

中央美术学院美术馆(花家地新馆)
朝阳区花家地南街8号中央美术学院内
8 Huajiadi South Street, Chaoyang
❖ 39.9830, 116.4589

A fine addition to Isozaki's body of work, this modest museum is well worth a look. The galleries are organised along an internal ramp flanking the entry atrium, allowing visitors to view larger artworks from a variety of viewpoints. The doubly-curved form, whose two surfaces pull apart to admit light, is clad in grey slate tiles that seem to reference WU Liangyong's surrounding 1950s campus and its Modernist courtyard architecture.

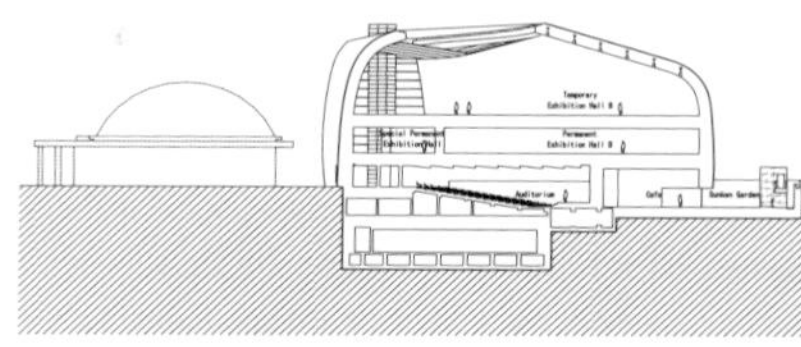

Cross section

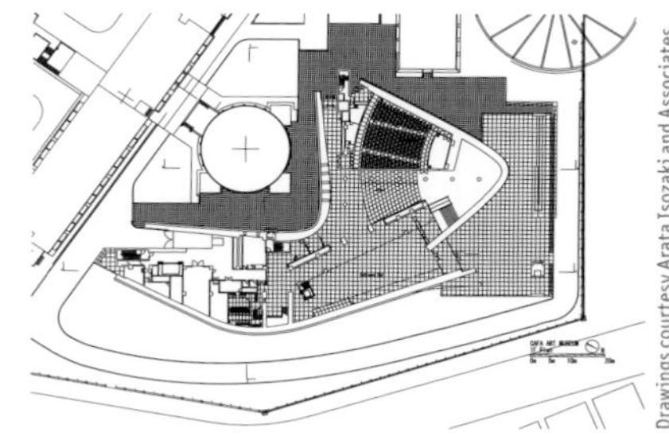

Ground-floor plan

Drawings courtesy Arata Isozaki and Associates

Wangjing SOHO

BJ 70

Zaha HADID Architects, 2009–2014

望京SOHO – 朝阳区望京街10号
10 Wangjing St, Chaoyang
❖ 39.9952, 116.4747

This scaled-up **Galaxy SOHO** (p. 081) anchors a vast, newly-developed area beyond the fourth ring road. It will be interesting to see how the different context and increase in height (from sixty to two hundred metres) affect the quality of the pedestrian space. This is also famous as the subject of legal proceedings: a copy, based perhaps on stolen plans, is rising in faraway Chongqing.

Beijing West Railway Station

BJ 71

ZHU Jialu, 1993–1996, 2000

北京西站
丰台莲花池东路118号
118 E. Lianhuachi Rd, Fengtai
❖ 39.8934, 116.3156

This mega-station, with "pagoda" roofscape, was a lightning rod for debates within China about the integration of historical and modern architecture. Such attempts at synthesis through collage were widely mocked as the clunky attachment of historical elements to a modern building, recalling the Western reception of late, kitschy Postmodernism. Worth noting, if you're passing through.

Beijing Planetarium

BJ 75

amphibianArc, 2001–2004

北京天文馆
西城区西直门外大街138号
138 Xizhimen Outer St, Xicheng
❖ 39.9363, 116.3303

This long bar, enlivened by the insertion of figural volumes housing different pieces of programme (exhibits, theatres, etc.), suggests a vague kinship with the original 1957 facility, opposite. The latter, built during the worldwide space-race-fuelled planetarium boom, is also basically linear, accented by a single dome (visible in the photograph above). The new building, whose construction in turn coincided with China's first crewed space flights, is set at a slight angle to the old, defining a figural outdoor space and perhaps linking these two historic moments of outer-space enthusiasm. The smoothly warping curtain wall, with individually curved glass elements, marks technological progress here on Earth.

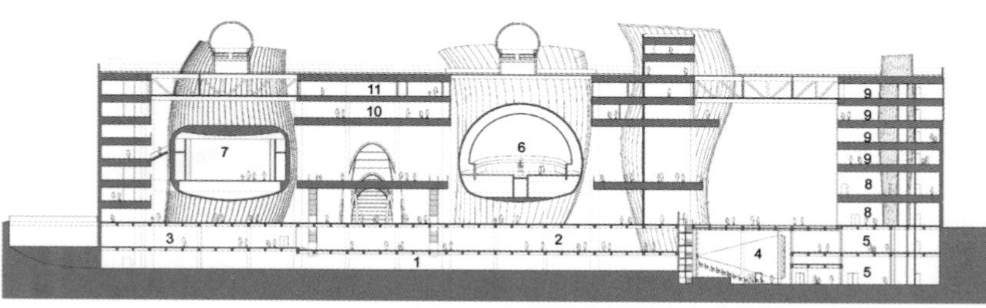

Longitudinal section

National Library

BJ 76

KSP Jürgen Engel Architekte, 2003–2008

国家图书馆新馆
北京市海淀区中关村南大街33号
33 Zhongguancun South Street, Haidian
❖ 39.9440, 116.3173

With space for twelve million books, this library's form is meant to show the innovative present (represented by a suspended, glassy volume) supported by the traditional past (an opaque pedestal, housing the archives). This seeming thematic one-liner is developed further through the spatial sequence: to experience the main space, one first travels straight to the top, then descends into the tiered volume of the reading room, as if on an archaeological dig. Past and present – stacked on the outside – turn out to interpenetrate or give rise to each other. Plan on a long wait in the baggage-checking room – it's worth it for a visit to the main space, a contemporary update of classical reading rooms (e.g. the British Library's). As with the recent Humboldt University Library in Berlin (by the German architect Max Dudler), the wide spans across the void, and the orthogonal arrangement of seating, permit a surprising sense of privacy and concentration, despite the vague sense of being under observation at all times, as in a Panoptic prison.

Artists' Residence

Songzhuang Museum

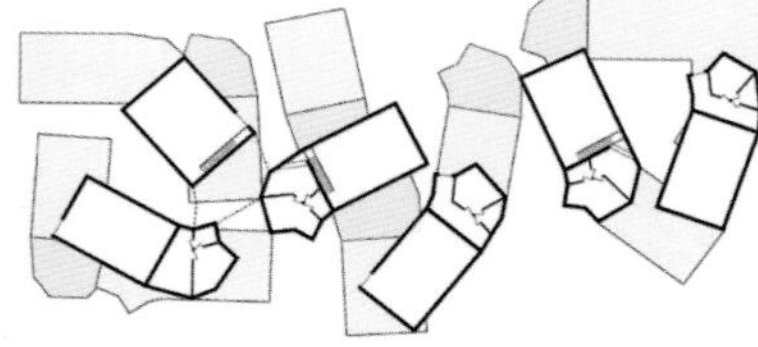

Artists' Residence, third-floor plan

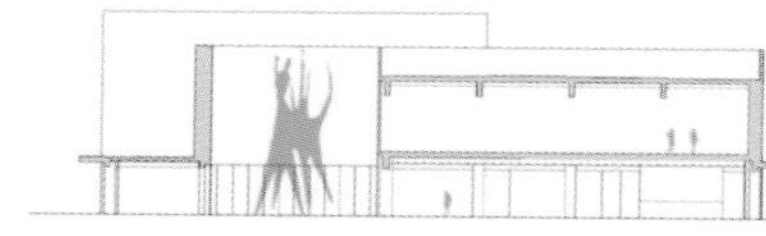

Songzhuang Museum, cross section

Xiaopu Cultural Centre, axonometric and interior photograph

Songzhuang Art Village

BJ 79

Various, 2000s+

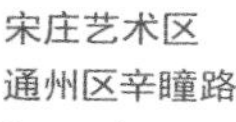

宋庄艺术区
通州区辛瞳路
Songzhuang Town, Tongzhou District
❖ 39.9456, 116.7076

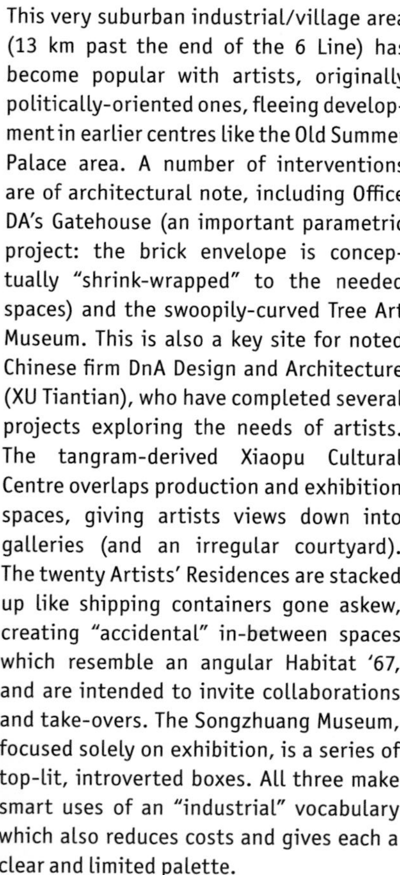

This very suburban industrial/village area (13 km past the end of the 6 Line) has become popular with artists, originally politically-oriented ones, fleeing development in earlier centres like the Old Summer Palace area. A number of interventions are of architectural note, including Office DA's Gatehouse (an important parametric project: the brick envelope is conceptually "shrink-wrapped" to the needed spaces) and the swoopily-curved Tree Art Museum. This is also a key site for noted Chinese firm DnA Design and Architecture (XU Tiantian), who have completed several projects exploring the needs of artists. The tangram-derived Xiaopu Cultural Centre overlaps production and exhibition spaces, giving artists views down into galleries (and an irregular courtyard). The twenty Artists' Residences are stacked up like shipping containers gone askew, creating "accidental" in-between spaces which resemble an angular Habitat '67, and are intended to invite collaborations and take-overs. The Songzhuang Museum, focused solely on exhibition, is a series of top-lit, introverted boxes. All three make smart uses of an "industrial" vocabulary which also reduces costs and gives each a clear and limited palette.

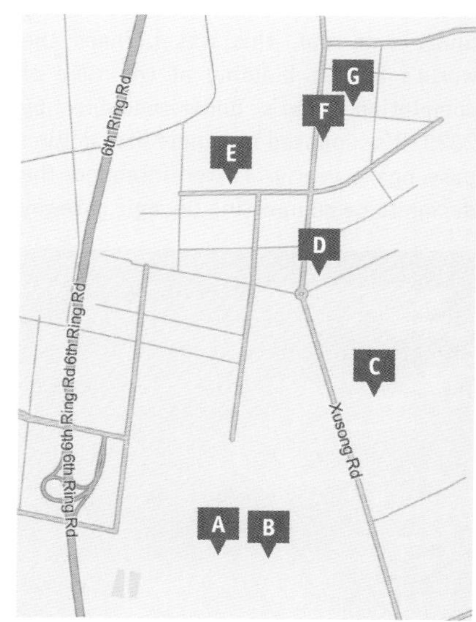

A. Artists' Residence DnA Design and Architecture, 2007–2009.

B. Xiaopu Cultural Centre DnA Design and Architecture, 2006–2007.

C. Tongxian Gatehouse Office DA, FCJZ (Yung Ho CHANG), 2001–2003.

D. Sunshine International Museum

E. Songzhuang Museum DnA Design and Architecture, 2005–2006.

F. Tree Art Museum Daipu, 2009.

G. G-Dot Art Space Atelier 100+s, 2000s.

Capital Airport, Terminal 3

BJ 80

Foster + Partners (Norman FOSTER), 2003–2008

北京首都国际机场, 3号航站楼T3
❖ 40.0642, 116.6122

With 1.3 million square metres mostly under one roof, this was perhaps the world's largest building at the time of completion. That's understandable: by 2020, it's supposed to handle fifty million passengers yearly. Foster intended the design to be an uplifting Olympic gateway with a Chinese quality, "expressed in its dragon-like form and the drama of the soaring roof that is a blaze of traditional Chinese colours – imperial reds merge into golden yellows. [The] red columns stretching ahead into the far distance [evoke] images of a Chinese temple." The triangular skylights orient southeast for maximum heat gain in the winter; between this and various other green features, the architects assert that the airport is one of the world's most sustainable buildings. One might be tempted to compare this to the **Hong Kong airport** by the same firm (p. 365), but while both strive to create vast, uninterrupted spaces, they're very different typologically. Hong Kong follows Foster's earlier Stansted model: updating the universal Modernist space of the "mat building" with a high-tech attention to mechanical services and natural light. The basic challenge of this type is getting light and a sense of orientation into a very deep floor plate. Beijing is closer to the expressive mid-century airports of Eero Saarinen, with an airy, dramatically sculpted roof that evokes the excitement and energy of air travel, now sized for a mass audience rather than a glamorous

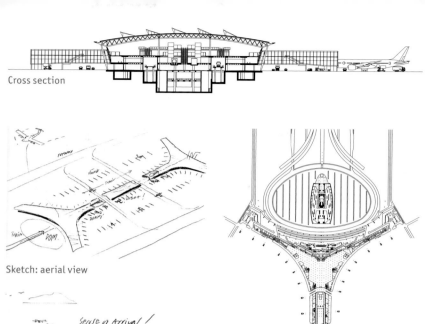

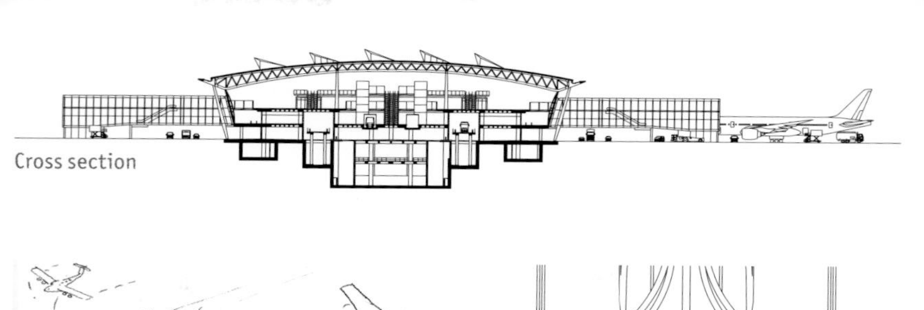
Cross section

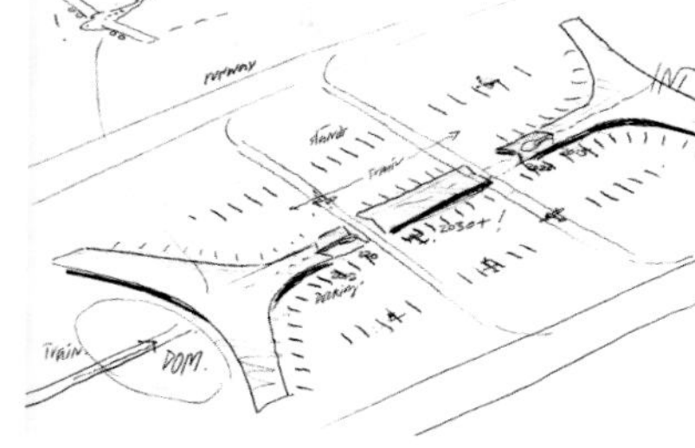
Sketch: aerial view

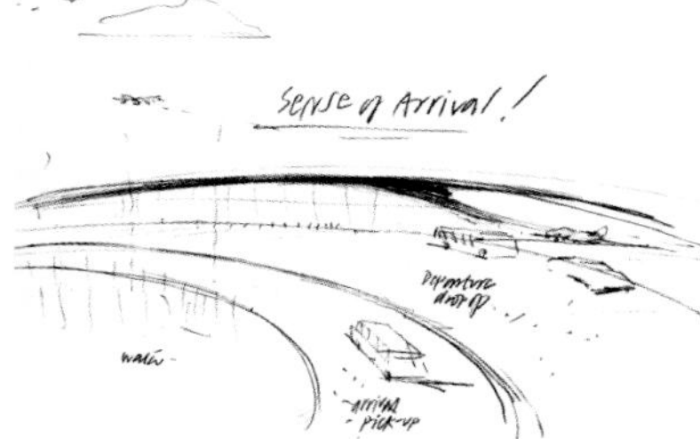

Sketch: "Sense of Arrival!"

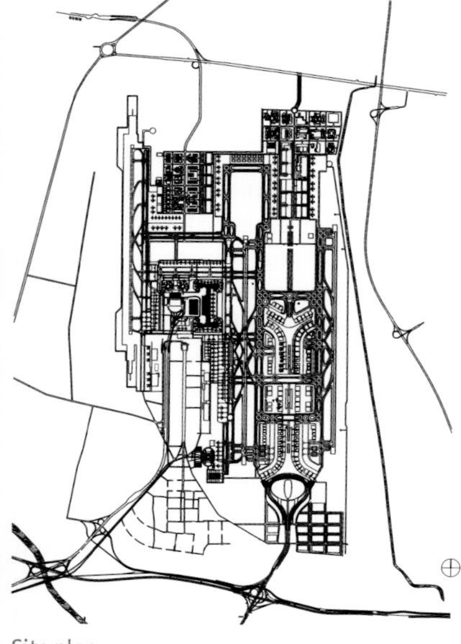
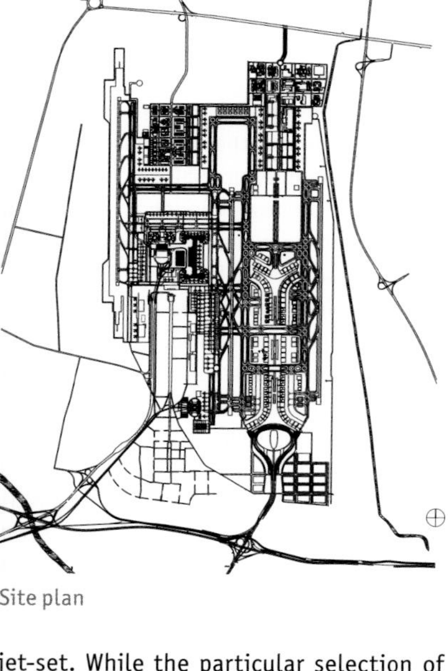
Site plan

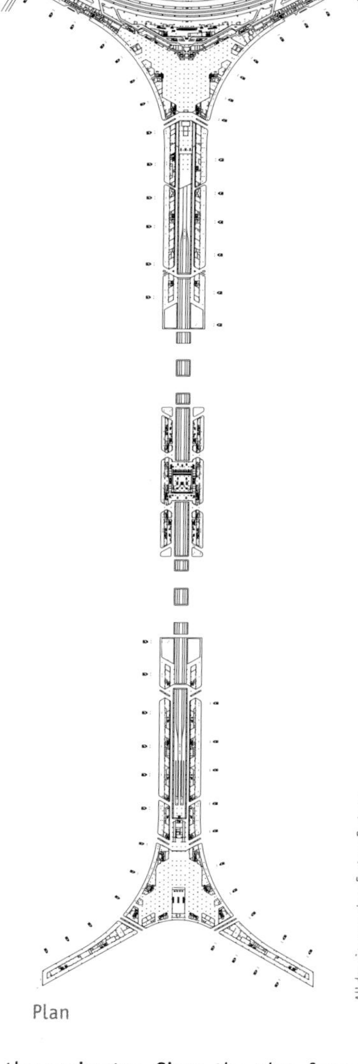
Plan

All drawings courtesy Foster + Partners

jet-set. While the particular selection of colours may be justified in client-pleasing symbolic terms, the mere presence of a colour scheme in a contemporary airport is refreshing. The gestural form makes the interior feel spacious, not least because it admits considerable natural light at the perimeter. Since the plan form is essentially linear (with a few branches), there's a *lot* of perimeter, and the payoffs are apparent. The terminal is worth a visit even if you're not flying through it; just allow for the twenty-minute journey each way on the (free) inter-terminal shuttle.

Great Wall (Mutianyu Site)
221 BCE forward

BJ 89

慕田峪长城
❖ 40.4309, 116.5642

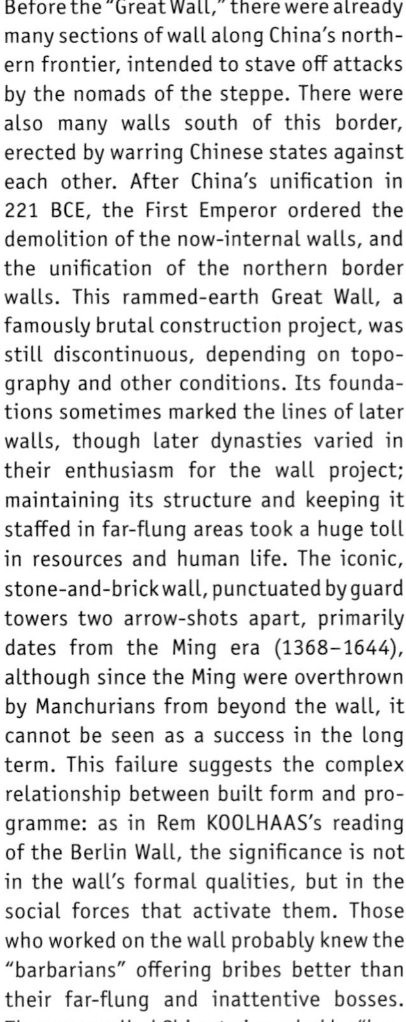

Before the "Great Wall," there were already many sections of wall along China's northern frontier, intended to stave off attacks by the nomads of the steppe. There were also many walls south of this border, erected by warring Chinese states against each other. After China's unification in 221 BCE, the First Emperor ordered the demolition of the now-internal walls, and the unification of the northern border walls. This rammed-earth Great Wall, a famously brutal construction project, was still discontinuous, depending on topography and other conditions. Its foundations sometimes marked the lines of later walls, though later dynasties varied in their enthusiasm for the wall project; maintaining its structure and keeping it staffed in far-flung areas took a huge toll in resources and human life. The iconic, stone-and-brick wall, punctuated by guard towers two arrow-shots apart, primarily dates from the Ming era (1368–1644), although since the Ming were overthrown by Manchurians from beyond the wall, it cannot be seen as a success in the long term. This failure suggests the complex relationship between built form and programme: as in Rem KOOLHAAS's reading of the Berlin Wall, the significance is not in the wall's formal qualities, but in the social forces that activate them. Those who worked on the wall probably knew the "barbarians" offering bribes better than their far-flung and inattentive bosses. Thus was walled China twice ruled by "barbarian" dynasties; the wall was breached not so much by physical force as by the loss of administrative power. Another major function of the wall was to enable signal communication along its length, from tower to tower, though its steepness works against its notional use as a road (by Chinese or barbarians). The wall's "official" significance has shifted several times. During the Civil War, the Communist Party cast it as a symbol of determination to achieve the impossible; after their victory, the wall became a reminder of the suffering of the ordinary people who died to build it. Today, as China again builds on a grand scale, it stands for cultural achievements and the organisation of vast projects. If you can handle the very steep surface, we recommend the Mutianyu site, where you can enter rebuilt Ming-style watchtowers, and peer past the trail's end at still-ruined sections. As a bonus, the management – apparently not convinced they have enough of a tourist attraction on their hands – have installed a ski lift up and a toboggan ride down.

Hongluo Clubhouse

BJ 90

MAD, IDEA Arch. Design Studio, 2004–2006

红螺会所 – 怀柔区红螺路8号
8 Hongluo Rd, Huairou
❖ 40.3606, 116.6237

This key project for MAD's MA Yansong (formerly of Zaha Hadid Architects, where he worked on the **Guangzhou Opera**, p. 300) was a landmark in the construction of continuously curved surfaces in China. The steel-built clubhouse retreats from its suburban context to sit within the lake, taking inspiration from the "undulating" landscape of water and reflected hills. Indeed, one arrives by walking "through" the water on a sunken path. While the flowing surface creates a space "without internal boundaries," varied ceiling heights suggest loose zones within.

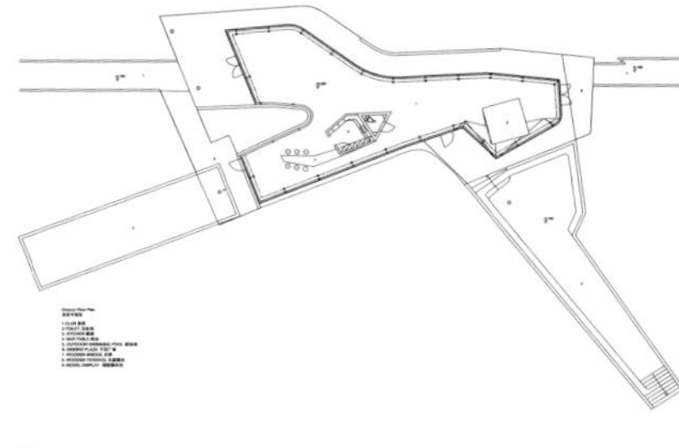

Plan

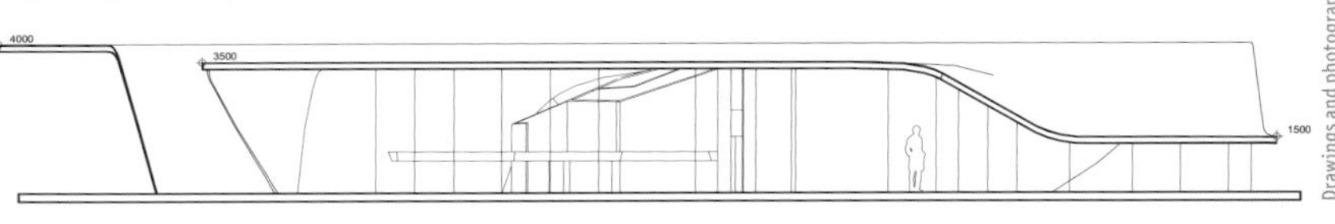

Section

Drawings and photograph courtesy MAD

Cantilever House (Antonio OCHOA)

Commune By The Great Wall

BJ 93

Various architects, 2002+

长城脚下的公社
延庆京藏高速公路53号出口（水关）
Exit #53 (Shuiguan), G6 Highway, Yanqing
❖ 40.3389, 116.0490

Bamboo Wall House (KUMA Kengo)

Photographs CC BY 2.0 Flickr user bracketing_life; cropped.

This high-end hotel consists of forty villas by twelve noted Asian architects. A number of the units deserve close attention, but given the distance from the city centre, and the likelihood that you won't be able to see every villa, we recommend this only to those making extended stays in Beijing. Tours are sometimes possible, depending on vacancy; contact SOHO (*commune.sohochina.com*) for details. Highlights: the Airport House (CHIEN Hsueh-Yi), Bamboo Wall House (KUMA Kengo and Associates), Cantilever House (Antonio OCHOA/Red House China), Clubhouse (SEUNG H-Sang/IROJE architects & planners), Distorted Courtyard House (Rocco YIM/Rocco Design Architects Limited), Forest House (NOBUAKI Furuya/Studio NASCA), Furniture House (BAN Shigeru), Shared House (Kanika R'KUL), Split House (FCJZ/Yung Ho CHANG), Suitcase House (Gary CHANG), Twin House (Kay Ngee Tan), and See & Seen House (CUI Kai).

Ming Tombs

BJ 94

Various, 1415–1644

明十三陵
定陵 (Dingling); 神道 (Spirit Way)
Changchi Road, Changping
❖ 40.2928, 116.2225 (Parking: Dingling)

Thirteen funerary complexes, across a large area well to the city's northwest: for two centuries, this was the major necropolis of the Ming emperors. The site had good *feng shui*: it was ringed by hills on the west, north and east, and two smaller hills formed a natural southern gate (augmented by the long processional "Spirit Way"). These are the same principles that would guide the siting of a city for the living, and each tomb complex displays a similar plan order, though their individual placement seems looser, permitting each tomb to have the most ideal topographical arrangement available in its vicinity. While the diagram of the emperor's burial place resembles that of the emperor's workplace and worship-space, each has a different landscape idea: here, the pavilions, though walled off, are released from the city grid and approach nature-as-nature. The Yongle Emperor, who began the complex, has the largest and most prominent tomb (the Changling), but all follow basically the same format: a series of three gateways gives way to a courtyard in front of a rectangular pagoda for ceremonies, beyond which a square bastion leads to the circular mound of the tomb proper. Compare to the first Ming Tomb (Nanjing's **Ming Xiaoling Mausoleum**, p. 132) and contrast to the much earlier tombs near Xi'an (map p. 395). The interiors were palaces for the deceased, although this is

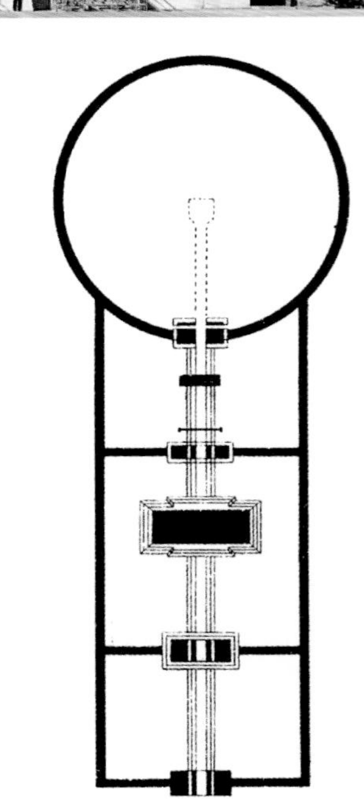

Changling: overall plan

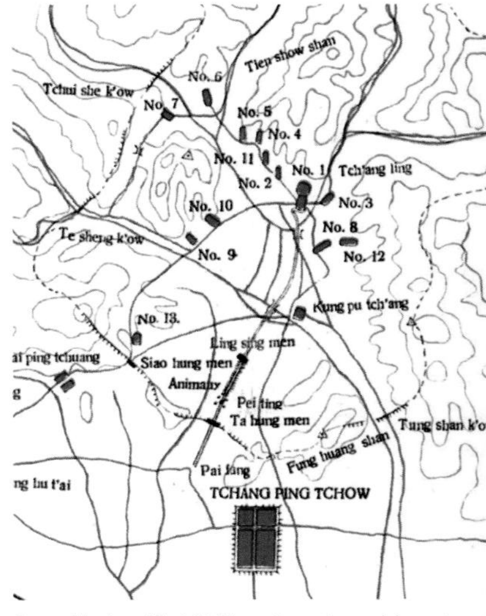

Overall plan (Spirit Way at centre; old centre of Changping town at bottom)

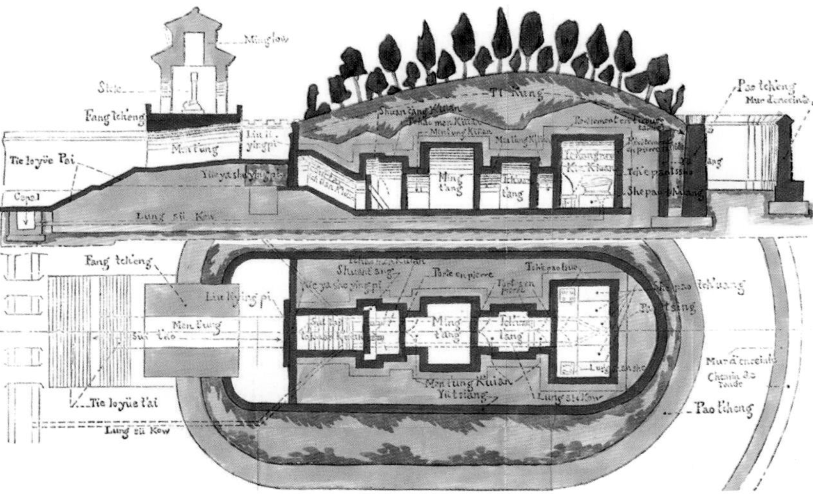

Section and plan (south at left), typical tumulus

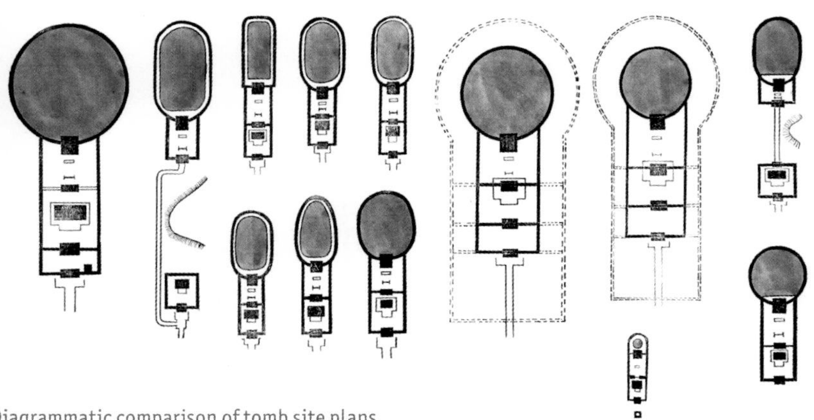

Diagrammatic comparison of tomb site plans

hard to perceive from the one tomb (the Dingling) whose *tumulus* may be visited, which is stripped of its contents and feels more like a fallout shelter. The tomb's unadorned, denatured quality is due to a rush job on the 1950s excavation, when many of the artefacts were ruined by exposure to the elements. Still more were destroyed, and the head archaeologist murdered, by Cultural Revolution zealots who saw the whole project as a monarchical throwback. Current policy forbids the excavation of any further tombs, a choice which places the long-term survival of heritage above the confidence of present-day experts.

Nanluogu Xiang *hutong* (map p. 114)

Beijing is a huge city, and can be somewhat overwhelming. Much of the urban fabric is automobile-scaled, especially the Ring Roads – multi-lane highways with few pedestrian crossing points. Major blocks are approximately one kilometre to a side; "a few blocks" on the map can easily turn into a long hike. Taxis are plentiful, but can be frustrating in peak hours due to Beijing's infamous traffic. The extensive subway network can be a bit tricky due to its ring-and-spoke model. We recommend grouping sites near stops on the same subway line, then using taxis for short-range surface travel. The following pages divide the city into rough geographical regions, working outwards from the centre. We recommend exploring Beijing in this sequence, starting with the major historical sights and contemporary work in the city centre (maps A and B), then expanding your itinerary based on time and your interests. The Summer Palace area, the Olympic grounds, and the 798 vicinity (maps C, D, and E) can be linked by taxi trips from the northern arc of the #10 subway line, for a (very full) day of sight-seeing. More remote sites (notably the Ming Tombs and the Great Wall) require surface transportation.

Second Ring Road from Galaxy SOHO (p. 081)

Hutong northeast of **Jingshan Park** (p. 076)

BJ Beijing

Beijing Region, p. 119

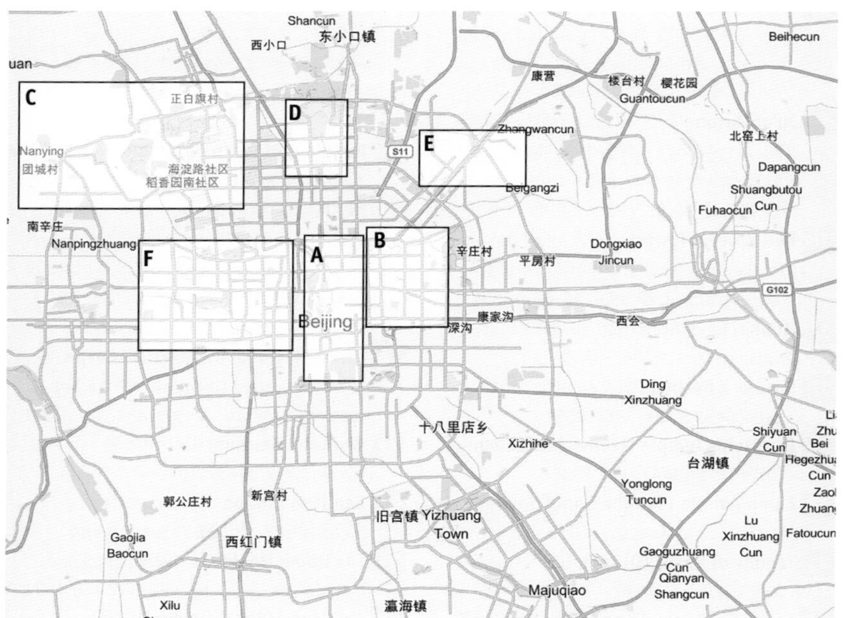

Beijing Metropolitan Area, p. 118

A. Central Beijing, p. 114
B. Beijing New CBD, p. 115
C. Summer Palace, p. 116
D. 2008 Olympic Grounds, p. 116
E. 798 & CCD Arts District, p. 117
F. West Beijing, p. 117

01 Tian'anmen Square *1651, 1958+.* ❖ 39.9031, 116.3914

02 Redwall Teahouse *CutscapeArchitecture, 2014.* Cellular insertions at a break in the old wall. ❖ 39.9089, 116.3957

03 Forbidden City *1406–1420, with additions.* ❖ 39.9157, 116.3908

04 Jingshan Park *1302+* ❖ 39.9233, 116.3903

05 Beihai Park *1179+.* ❖ 39.9243, 116.3829

06 National Grand Theatre *Paul ANDREU, 1999–2007.* ❖ 39.9031, 116.3834

07 Zhengyang Gate/Qianmen Landmark gate, commercialised imperial axis, and bits of *hutong*. ❖ 39.8980, 116.3917

08 Mausoleum of Mao Zedong *HUA Guofeng, 1977.* ❖ 39.9008, 116.3916

09 National Museum of China *LIANG Sicheng, 1959; GMP, 2011.* See #01. ❖ 39.9043, 116.3957

10 Hotel Kapok/Blur Hotel *Studio Pei-Zhu, 2004–2006.* ❖ 39.9137, 116.3993

11 National Art Museum *DAI Nianci, 1958–1962.* One of the "Ten Great Buildings." ❖ 39.9242, 116.4079

12 Meridian Space *Origin Architect, 2014.* ❖39.9263, 116.4027

13 Nanluogu Xiang Hip *hutong* area with boutique shops. ❖ 39.9338, 116.3970

14 Hutong Bubble 32 *MAD (MA Yansong, et al.), 2008–2009.* Test of planned *hutong* renewal, with bubbles. Private but visible. ❖ 39.9350, 116.4000

15 Ju'er Hutong *Tsinghua Univeristy Team (WU Liangyong), 1989–1992.* New courtyard housing, multi-storey for density. ❖ 39.9378, 116.3998

16 Bell & Drum Towers, *1272.* Imperial timekeepers anchor a vibrant district. Reconstructed. ❖ 39.9410, 116.3896

17 Houhai Lake Area Historic buildings, ice skating. ❖ 39.9406, 116.3819

18 Studio-X Beijing *OPEN Architecture, 2009.* ❖ 39.9424, 116.4055

19 Confucius Temple & Imperial Academy *1302+* ❖ 39.9447, 116.4085

20 Lama Temple (Yonghe Gong) *1694+* ❖ 39.9467, 116.4115

21 Temple of Earth (Di Tan) *1530+* ❖39.9512, 116.4097

22 Temple of Agriculture (Xiannong Tan) ❖ 39.8768, 116.3877

A. Central Beijing (Map 01–23)

23 Temple of Heaven (Tian Tan) *1406–1420+* ❖ 39.8789, 116.4073

24 Beijing Railway Station *YANG Tingbao, CHEN Deng-ao, 1959.* One of the "Ten Great Buildings." ❖ 39.9023, 116.4209

25 Galaxy SOHO *Zaha HADID Architects, 2008–2013* ❖ 39.9203, 116.4276

26 China National Offshore Oil Corp *KPF, 2006.* Rounded triangle with a wood-screened atrium. ❖ 39.9238, 116.4260

27 Workers' Stadium *BIAD, 1959* ❖ 39.9296, 116.4410

28 Sanlitun Village *Various architects, 2005–2008.* ❖ 39.9335, 116.4486

29 The Opposite House *KUMA Kengo and Associates, 2008.* ❖ 39.9360, 116.4491

30 Sanlitun SOHO *KUMA Kengo and Associates, 2010.* ❖ 39.9309, 116.4477

31 Hotel Conrad *MAD, Metamax, BIAD, 2008–2013.* ❖ 39.9264, 116.4550

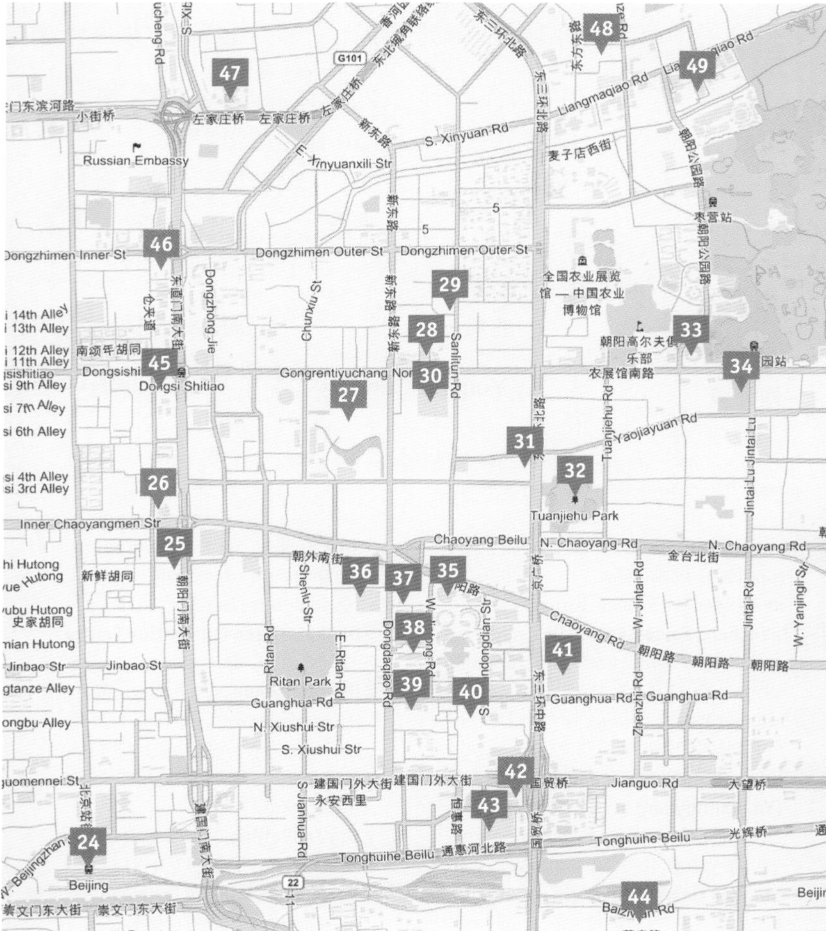

B. Beijing New CBD (Map 24–49)

32 Tuanjiehu Park *1958+* ❖ 39.9244, 116.4585

33 Phoenix Int'l. Media Centre *BIAD/UFo, 2008–2012.* ❖ 39.9332, 116.4676

34 Chaoyang Park Towers *MAD (MA Yansong, et al.), 2016.* Karst-mountain inspired towers. ❖ 39.9311, 116.4720

35 Chaowai SOHO *SEUNG H-Sang/IROJE architects&planners, 2006+.* ❖ 39.9187, 116.4485

36 Parkview Green Fangcaodi *Integrated Design Associates (Winston SHU), Arup, ca. 2010.* ❖ 39.9183, 116.4434

37 Shangdu SOHO *LAB Architecture Studio, 2004–2007.* ❖ 39.9175, 116.4453

38 The Place *Kritzinger & Rao, 2000s.* ❖ 39.9151, 116.4460

39 Guanghualu SOHO *MADA s.p.a.m. (Qingyun MA), 2008.* ❖ 39.9116, 116.4461

40 China World Trade Centre, Tower III *SOM, 2010.* ❖ 39.9109, 116.4521

41 CCTV Station & Headquarters *OMA (Rem KOOLHAAS), ECADI, 2002–2013.* ❖ 39.9140, 116.4581

42 Yintai Centre *John PORTMAN & Associates, 2007.* ❖ 39.9060, 116.4534

43 Jian Wai SOHO *YAMAMOTO Riken, 2004* ❖ 39.9040, 116.4521

44 22 Art Plaza & Today Art Museum *FCJZ (Yung Ho CHANG), WANG Hui, 2009.* Dramatic entry to a sealed old box. ❖ 39.8987, 116.4616

45 New Poly Plaza *SOM, 2007.* ❖ 39.9312, 116.4260

46 Raffles City *SPARK.* Mall, with some neat quasi-blobs. ❖ 39.9387, 116.4265

47 Linked Hybrid *Steven HOLL Architects, 2003–2009.* ❖ 39.9491, 116.4318

48 US Embassy *SOM, 2008.* Tightly-secured neo-Modernism. ❖ 39.9530, 116.4601

49 Sino-Japanese Youth Centre *KUROKAWA Kishō, 1987–1990.* ❖ 39.9498, 116.4678

C. Summer Palace Area (Map 50–58)

50 Fragrant Hill Hotel *Pei Cobb Freed (Ieoh Ming PEI), 1979–1982.* ❖ 39.9886, 116.1885

51 Tuancheng Fortress *1749.* Well-preserved walled Qing Dynasty military training ground. ❖ 39.9839, 116.2032

52 Summer Palace *Various, twelfth century forward.* ❖ 39.9969, 116.2755

53 Ruins of Old Summer Palace (Yuanmingyuan) *Various architects, 1709+.* Marker indicates the "Western Mansions." ❖ 40.0056, 116.3085

54 Tsinghua University Original Campus *Henry MURPHY, CHUANG Tsin, others, 1917+.* Jeffersonian & Beaux-Arts planning, plus a Qing-era Imperial garden. Home to a major architecture school. ❖ 40.0016, 116.3187

55 Tsinghua University Library *Mario BOTTA, 2011.* ❖ 40.0028, 116.3225

56 Tsinghua Environmental Science Building *Mario CUCINELLA Architects.* Steppy sustainability, with crisply detailed pergolas. ❖ 39.9968, 116.3288

57 Peking University *1919/1952+.* Campus buildings on former Yenching Univ. and Qing garden site. ❖ 39.9906, 116.3038

58 Christian Church *GMP (von GERKAN, MARG, and Partner), 2004–2007.* ❖ 39.9821, 116.3015

59 Olympic Green Tennis Court *BVN Architecture (BLIGH VOLLER NIELD), 2007.* ❖ 40.0194, 116.3734

60 Olympic Green "Siheyuan" Promenade *QI Xin, 2007–2008.* Sunken courtyards hugging the edge of the lake. ❖ 40.0006, 116.3878

61 Olympic Green Convention Centre *RMJM, 2008.* ❖ 39.9984, 116.3837

62 Olympic Green *Sasaki Associates, with Tsinghua University (implementation of Forest Park) and Steven HANDEL (ecological strategies), 2002–2008.* ❖ 39.9931, 116.3871

63 Digital Beijing *Urbanus/Studio Pei-Zhu, 2004–2008.* ❖ 39.9940, 116.3819

64 National Swimming Centre *CSCEC, PTW, CCDI and Arup, 2003–2008.* ❖39.9915, 116.3841

65 Beijing National Statium (Bird's Nest) *Herzog & de Meuron, Arup, FAKE Design (AI Weiwei), 2008.* ❖ 39.9916, 116.3905

D. 2008 Olympic Grounds (Map 59–65)

E. 798 & CCD Arts District (Map 66–70)

66 **798 Arts District** *Original buildings, 1950s. Master plan by Sasaki Associates, 2006. Galleries by various architects.* ❖ 39.9828, 116.4898

67 **Galleries at Caochangdi** *FAKE Design (AI Weiwei), 2000s.* ❖ 40.0002, 116.5017

68 **National Film Institute** *RTKL, BIAD, 2007* ❖ 39.9951, 116.5158

69 **Chinese Academy of Fine Arts (CAFA) Museum** *ISOZAKI Arata, 2003–2008.* ❖ 39.9830, 116.4589

70 **Wangjing SOHO** *Zaha HADID Architects, 2009–2014.* ❖ 39.8934, 116.3156

71 **Beijing West Railway Station** *1993–1996, 2000.* ❖ 39.8934, 116.3156

72 **China Millennium Monument** *2001.* Giant post-socialist sundial. Nearby: the military museum. ❖ 39.9103, 116.3154

73 **White Cloud Temple (Baiyun Guan)** ❖ 39.8993, 116.3381

74 **Bank of China Building** *Pei Partnership Architects, 1995–2001.* ❖ 39.9067, 116.3666

75 **Beijing Planetarium** *amphibianArc, 2001–2004.* ❖ 39.9363, 116.3303

76 **National Library** *KSP Jürgen Engel Architekte, 2003–2008.* ❖ 39.9440, 116.3173

77 **No. 59–1 Fuxing Road** *LI Xinggang, 2004–2006.* ❖ 39.9067, 116.2869

78 **BUCEA Student Services Building** *BIAD, 2009–2011.* Offset grids, varying skylights, nice materials. ❖ 39.9096, 116.2752

F. West Beijing (Map 71–78)

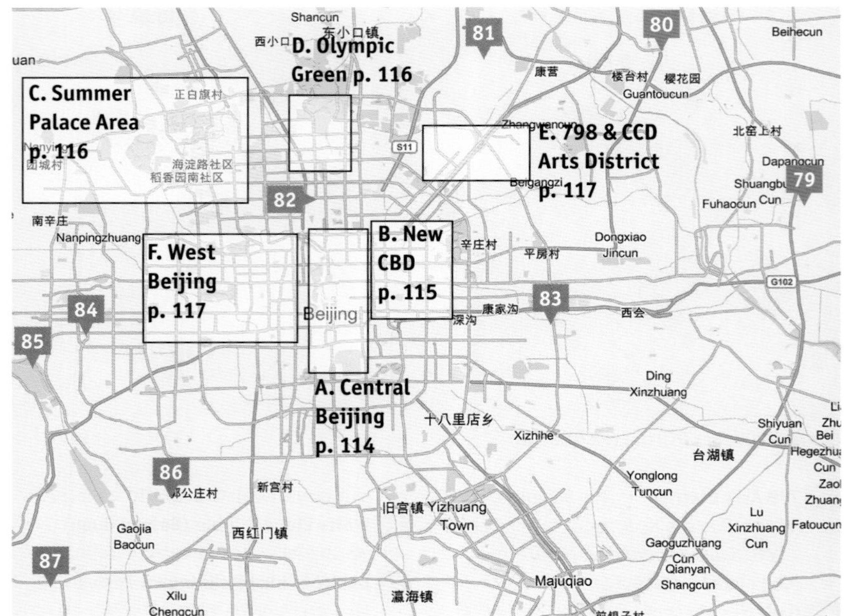

Beijing Metropolitan Area (Map 79–87)

79 Songzhuang Art Village *Various, 2000s+* ❖ 39.9456, 116.7076

80 Capital Airport, Terminal 3 *Foster + Partners (Norman FOSTER), 2003–2008.* ❖ 40.0642, 116.6122

81 Red Brick Art Museum *DONG Yugan, XIAO Ang, 2007–2012.* Fine spaces inside and out, with brick as conceptual and tectonic theme: Louis Kahn for the BIM age. ❖ 40.0414, 116.4943

82 Beijing Publishing Corporation *Studio Pei-Zhu (ZHU Pei, WU Tong), 2006–2008.* ❖ 39.9666, 116.3825

83 New Studio For Chinese Academy of Oil Painting *Thanlab (HAN Tao), 2005–2007.* Government renovation of an industrial building, with concrete studio spaces and a glass-floored corridor that doubles as gallery space. ❖ 39.8993, 116.5377

84 1/2 Stadium *Interval Architects, 2013.* Smart interventions framing an existing sports field. ❖ 39.8936, 116.2287

85 Museum of Chinese Gardens Institutionally-scaled traditional architecture. ❖ 39.8780, 116.1712

86 World Park *1993.* Theme park with miniatures of famous buildings. Nearby, a Vanke sales pavilion by OPEN Architecture, possibly temporary. ❖ 39.8099, 116.2817

87 No. 4 Middle School, Fangshan Campus *OPEN Architecture (LI Hu & HUANG Wenjing), 2010–2014.* A “tree-like” school integrated with its landscape; permission may be needed. ❖ 39.7588, 116.2037

88 Liyuan Library *LI Xiaodong Atelier, 2011.* A remote, twig-screened gem, for long-term visitors only. Check website for hours and bring books to donate. Note: due to the topography, it's further from Mutianyu than it looks. ❖ 40.4637, 116.6011

89 Great Wall at Mutianyu *221 BCE forward.* ❖ 40.4309, 116.5642

90 Hongluo Clubhouse *MAD, IDEA Arch. Design Studio, 2004–2006.* ❖ 40.3606, 116.6237

91 Longshan Chapel (Xinxin Town) *WSP Architects, 2007.* Contemporary church, nice detailing. ❖ 40.2850, 116.6255

92 Great Wall at Badaling Most popular segment of the wall, closest to Beijing and clogged with tourists in good weather. 1950s restoration. See entry for #89. ❖ 40.3544, 116.0077

93 Commune By The Great Wall *Various architects, 2002+.* ❖ 40.3389, 116.0490

94 Ming Tombs *Various, 1415–1644.* ❖ 40.2928, 116.2225

Beijing Region (Map 88–100)

95 Museum of the Fangshan Geopark *BIAD, 2009.* Folded planes, stepped approach, and an all-stone palette for a "geological" effect.
❖ 39.5839, 115.8685

96 Great Wall at Simatai One of the more rugged and authentic of the Great Wall segments near Beijing, though partially restored in 2014. Experienced hikers may consider a trek along the deteriorating wall, to another access point, and restored segment, at Jinshanling (map #97).
❖ 40.6564, 117.2715

97 Great Wall at Jinshanling Very rugged, partially restored; for the fit and seasoned hiker. See Simatai (map #96).
❖ 40.6862, 117.2420

98 Chengde Mountain Resort *1703–1792.* 230 km to Beijing's northeast, this huge garden/palace complex dates from the same era as the Summer Palace (p. 093) and Old Summer Palace (p. 094). Also near the heart of Chengde are eight colossally-scaled "outer temples," built around the same time, in different architectural styles. Taking in the geographic sweep of the empire, these include a replica of the Potala Palace in Lhasa (Tibet), 4,000 km away, and together suggest the reach and the power of the early Qing dynasty.
❖ 40.9873, 117.9385

99 Zunhua Eastern Qing Tombs *1636–1908.* 125 km east-northeast of Beijing, the six mausoleums here are the principal successors to the Ming Tombs (p. 110), and reconstitute the same typology, though at slightly grander scales. After 1737, Qing Emperor burials were split between these, and the Western Tombs (map # 100). ❖ 40.1870, 117.6395

100 Western Qing Tombs (Qing Xiling) *1737–1913.* 140 km to Beijing's southwest lies this complex of four royal mausoleums, initiated when the Yongzheng Emperor refused burial at the Eastern Tombs (map #99). Later Qing Emperors were buried either here or in the Eastern Tombs, the more major of the two sites.
❖ 39.3683, 115.3451

南京
Nanjing

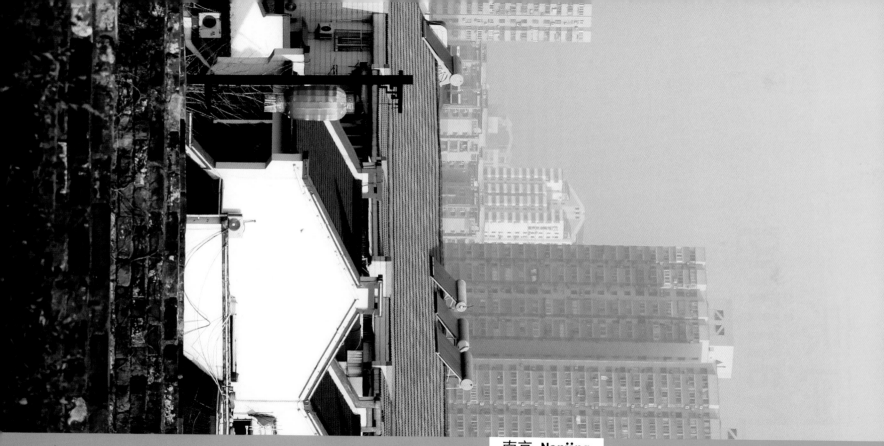

南京 Nanjing

Nanjing (formerly romanised as "Nanking") is a city of great symbolic and cultural significance in China; it has been the capital of the country on several occasions, and a major economic centre through the ages. Nanjing is located directly on the Yangtze River (just upriver from the vast, fertile delta) and ringed on the landward side by hills. In other words, it has access to river transportation as well as being a strategically defensible site, making it the perfect base for anyone looking to maintain control over the river and the immensely productive surrounding region.

Unsurprisingly, then, Nanjing (or Jiankang as it was known in earlier times) was founded as a garrison in the fifth century BCE, when China south of the Yangtze was still sparsely populated. The city centre's distance from the river (compare to Ningbo or Shanghai) and the compact, gridded arrangement of the historic city plan, still suggest the fortress-town typology. Remote Jianking seems to have had an attraction for regimes fleeing chaos in their prior bases of power. Several medieval kingdoms would set up their capitals there before the old city was totally destroyed in 589 by the first Sui emperor as part of a reunification campaign. The Sui's **Grand Canal** (see p. 226), which passed nearby, may have helped Jianking bounce back from destruction. By 1297 some 90,000 people lived within its walls, and it was already home to a major university and an important centre of Confucian study (**Fuzimiao,** map p. 138). Its key moment of development arrived in the mid-fourteenth century, when the peasant-born ZHU Yuangzhang, the first Ming Emperor, drove the Mongol Yuan dynasty out of China, and established Jianking as his new base, renaming it "Nanjing," or "Southern capital." The Ming became famous for their arts, learning, and commercial achievement. Under them, Nanjing grew to become the early fifteenth-century world's most populous city, carrying on trade across the Far East and acquiring a reputation for printing and shipbuilding as well as its established textile and agricultural economy. Even after the Ming rulers decamped to Beijing in 1421 – and modelled their **Forbidden City** (p. 074) on the one built here – Nanjing maintained its economic and cultural importance.

Zhu was an able administrator, and had strong engineers and military advisors. Swamps east of the city were drained to make way for a new capitol complex, with its dominant axis roughly parallel to that of the existing centre. The biggest project was a new city wall, completed after twenty-one years' toil by some 200,000 labourers. Zhu, not much attached to tradition, discarded the "magic square" diagram of most Chinese walled cities. His walls took long detours to exploit existing

Previous spread: traditional urbanism and recent high-rises, from **Zhonghua Gate** (p. 129)

High-rise apartments, seen hazily from Nanjing's surviving **City Wall** (p. 129)

topography, encircling major hills so that the latter could not be exploited by attackers. As in Hangzhou, this imperial capital phase came late in the city's development and made little impact on the fabric we see today; the palace complex was destroyed in 1645 (at the outset of the Qing dynasty), and most of the other old relics were destroyed by the Qing forces in the 1850s, when the Taiping Rebellion established the city as its capital for symbolic reasons. Despite all this, the walls remain largely intact, a testament to the Ming-era construction techniques which also produced the current **Great Wall** (p. 108).

The most important legacy the Ming left in Nanjing was likely symbolic. The Qing who succeeded them (and became China's last dynasty) were seen as foreigners: Manchus from the northeast, who had adopted some Chinese customs in their centuries of rule. In the Republic of China period, the nationalistic desire to assert China's pride after centuries of Western interference, coupled with an inability to hold the northeast against pretenders and warlords, suggested Nanjing, the capital of the last "Chinese" dynasty. As well, by this point, Nanjing was geographically in the middle of the country, and close to the big centres of international trade (particularly Shanghai). So it was that CHIANG Kai-Shek, the emergent leader of a notionally united Republic of China, established the capital in Nanjing in 1927, following the earlier wishes of revolutionary leader SUN Yat-Sen.

Nanjing at this time was still underpopulated after its mid-nineteenth-century destruction, and was thus seen as an ideal site for demonstrating the new Republic's governing and planning principles. An engineering group, including several American-educated experts and led by Harvard-trained LIN Yimin, pursued the creation of a twentieth-century Washington, D.C., with studies of more recent capital developments in Paris, New Delhi, and Canberra. Such sources demonstrate the complexity of expressing Chinese independence through a modernity still seen as belonging to the West. At the same time, the team sought to incorporate traditions of Chinese urbanism and monumentality, in contrast to the later approach of the Mao-era government in Beijing (see p. 067). Attempts at a grand administrative centre, complete with diagonal boulevards and a national mall, fell through under budgetary and political pressures, but the Guomindang's planners did begin to transform the city's fabric, widening major streets and tearing out several of the old city gates in favour of modern, automobile-ready crossings.[1]

The "Nanjing Decade" was a rocky one for China. 1927 saw the outbreak of civil war between Chiang's Nationalists and the Communist Party of China (not yet under the sole leadership of MAO Zedong). The Republic was in chaos, and Japan, now under a military autocracy, took advantage of the situation by first

Greater Nanjing in the Ming era. Note the irregular outer wall, and the development of the **lake** (p. 130). The denser inner city, with its southern end at **Zhonghua Gate** (p. 129), is still the city's most scenic corridor, especially along the Qinhuai River near **Fuzimiao** (map p. 138). The wooded hills to the east of the lake are the home of the one local **Ming tomb** (p. 132).

Central Nanjing in 1945. Note the concentration of development near **Zhonghua Gate** (p. 129), and the presence of the **Dr. Sun Yat-Sen Mausoleum** (p. 133) to the east of the Ming tomb site.

City Wall (p. 129) and **Xuanwu Lake** (p. 130)

taking Manchuria as a puppet state in 1931, and then surging into mainland China in 1937. The invading army drove straight for the Republican capital, and its generals promised their soldiers free rein to pillage. Animated by years of racist and nationalist ideology, the Japanese army, after taking the city in December 1937, began a six-week period of massacre, plunder, and organised rape, enabled in part by the physical barrier of the city's old walls. Estimates of the death toll range as high as 300,000 – possibly more than those who died from the atomic bombings of Hiroshima and Nagasaki combined, and dwarfing the casualties from the firebombing of Dresden. In short, the Nanjing Massacre must be ranked one of the century's most terrible war crimes. It has contributed to ongoing tension between China and Japan, aggravated by a small but vocal movement in Japan, which denies the scope of the atrocities.[2] Partly in response to a wave of such denials in the 1980s, the **Nanjing Massacre Memorial Hall** (p. 128) was built in 1985, on the site of a mass grave.

The events of 1937 may be unfamiliar to Western readers, but for many Chinese of recent generations, they are the defining event in the city's history. As discussed in the preceding historical sketch, Nanjing's heritage goes much further back, and a number of contemporary architectural works reflect its continuing status as an important and growing Chinese city, even as it has struggled to shift from its post-1950s role as a centre of state-backed heavy industry to today's consumerist economy. Though slow to reach completion, the **CIPEA site** (p. 134 forward), reflects the desire for a hip, forward-thinking design and economic culture, as do bourgeois night spots like the **1912 District** (map p. 139). A few sections of the famous city walls have been removed to accommodate automobile traffic, and dubious urban-renewal and commercial developments limit the old centre's picturesque qualities.

1. See Musgrove, "Building a Dream," cited below.

2. The Japanese pacifist left, on the other hand, has made a point of marking these terrible events as proof of the madness of militarisation.

Practical Considerations

A two-day visit is about right to do justice to the most famous architectural sites, including a bit of old and new. Several key buildings, including the **Massacre Museum** (p. 128), are within the city centre. **Xianlin Campus** (p. 131), including several interesting buildings, is further out, but with its own subway stop. The largest collection of recent work is at **CIPEA** (p. 134), about twenty kilometres (45–60 minutes) from the city centre. You will need to hire a car, but the collection of buildings is well worth it – particularly if the **Sifang Museum** (p. 137) happens to be open.

Sources and Recommended Reading

Joshua A. FOGEL, ed., *The Nanjing Massacre in History and Historiography*, Berkeley: University of California Press, 2000. Not a chronicle of the massacre, but a history of its interpretations, putting narratives (including Iris CHANG's controversial *The Rape of Nanking*) into context.

Charles D. MUSGROVE, "Building a Dream: Constructing a National Capital in Nanjing, 1927–1937," in Joseph W. Esherick, ed., *Remaking the Chinese City: Modernity and National Identity, 1900–1950*, Honolulu: University of Hawaii Press, 2002. Republican-era interventions, realised and unrealised.

ZHU Jianfei, "The Architect and a Nationalist Project, Nanjing 1925–37," in *Architecture of Modern China* (London: Routledge, 2009). A great summary of the various stylistic and political forces shaping architectural design in the "Nanjing Decade."

Nanjing Massacre Memorial and Museum

NJ 01

QI Kang, 1985, 1995, 2005

侵华日军南京大屠杀遇难同胞纪念馆
建邺区水西门街418号
418 Shuiximen St, Jianye District
❖ 32.0373, 118.7394

Completed in several phases and distinct architectural styles, this memorial hall and burial ground commemorates the lives lost in the brutal Japanese occupation of Nanjing in late 1937, when, over the course of two months, tens, or even hundreds of thousands, of Chinese civilians were killed by the invading army. Thousands were buried on this site in mass graves, several of which form the centre of the memorial grounds. The excavated burial sites, now capped with tumulus-like roofs, invite comparison to ancient mortuary architecture (see **Xi'an,** p. 395). Surrounding the tomb enclosures, a field of raked gravel suggests the city's wartime desolation, and draws uncomfortable comparisons to Japanese dry garden design. Beyond the graves to the west, an axial reflecting pool terminates with a statue of the "Goddess of Peace," flanked by a similarly literal Socialist-Realist relief. East of the graves, the 2007 expansion shifts languages, abandoning historical references for a set of fractured, angular forms. While these devices have become common in museum and memorial design since Daniel LIBESKIND's "deconstructivist" Jewish Museum (Berlin, 1989–2001), they are no less effective here: coupled with the exhibition design, the canted walls produce a sense of disorientation befitting the horror of war. Worth visiting for the exhibit alone, the memorial complex also demonstrates the evolving approach to memorial design over recent decades, as all phases depart in some way from the Mao era's thudding pseudo-Classicism (see **Tian'anmen,** p. 072).

Zhonghua Gate (Jubao Gate) and Nanjing City Wall

NJ 02

1360–1386

中华门 / 明城墙遗址，中华路
❖ 32.0148, 118.7766

Over 35 km long, Nanjing's Ming Dynasty walls (1360–1386) are arguably the longest set in the world, and among China's best-preserved. Unusually, they follow the contours of the landscape (taking the strategic high ground), rather than the rectangular footprint favoured by geometers and geomancers alike. They were commissioned by the first Ming emperor, who, being a peasant-born rebel leader, was more attached to military practicality than tradition. The gates are fortifications as well as access points: four walled courtyards, with space above for archers. A few original gates remain in varying states of disrepair and restoration. This, the largest, is missing its upper tier of buildings, but it is open to the public. Worth a visit for the spatial experience of the layered gates alone, it's also a fine access point for a hike along the city wall.

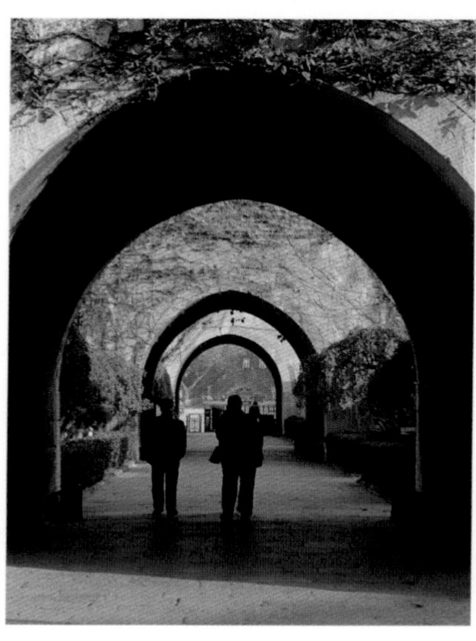

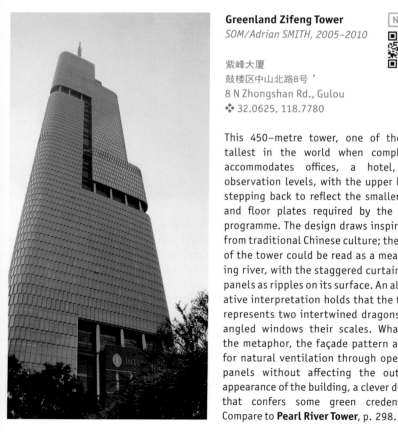

Greenland Zifeng Tower

SOM/Adrian SMITH, 2005–2010

紫峰大厦
鼓楼区中山北路8号
8 N Zhongshan Rd., Gulou
❖ 32.0625, 118.7780

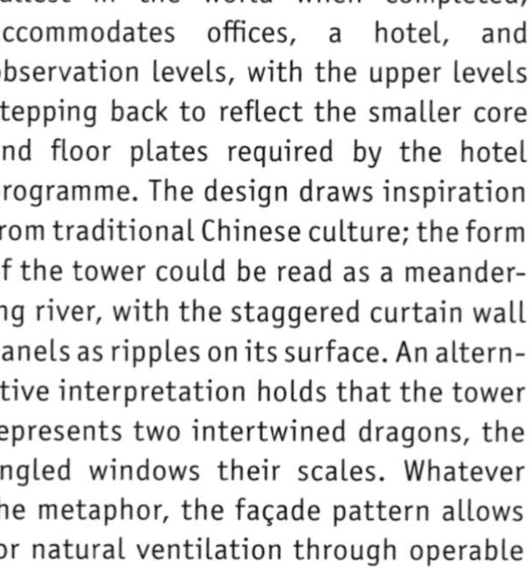

This 450-metre tower, one of the ten tallest in the world when completed, accommodates offices, a hotel, and observation levels, with the upper levels stepping back to reflect the smaller core and floor plates required by the hotel programme. The design draws inspiration from traditional Chinese culture; the form of the tower could be read as a meandering river, with the staggered curtain wall panels as ripples on its surface. An alternative interpretation holds that the tower represents two intertwined dragons, the angled windows their scales. Whatever the metaphor, the façade pattern allows for natural ventilation through operable panels without affecting the outward appearance of the building, a clever design that confers some green credentials. Compare to **Pearl River Tower**, p. 298.

Jiming Temple

NJ 13

1387+ (current design)

鸡鸣寺 – 鸡鸣寺路1号

1 Jimingsi Road, Xuanwu District

❖ 32.0632, 118.7902

One of Nanjing's oldest temples, with roots going back to the fifth century CE, this complex occupies a unique site in the urban fabric. The typical temple form of sequential halls and courtyards is distorted by the hillside topography – which only accentuates the hierarchical progression of space as one moves through the complex. The temple's rear connects to a spur of Nanjing's **city wall** (see p. 129), with views out over **Xuanwu Lake**.

Xuanwu Lake

NJ 14

玄武湖

❖ 32.0715, 118.7936

This large, natural lake lies at the centre of Nanjing, between the main train station and the old city centre. Though the lake is natural, it has been enhanced substantially through landscape design inspired by Hangzhou's justifiably-famous **West Lake** (p. 256), including a number of artificial islands connected by narrow causeways. Like West Lake, it was once at the edge of the city, but has become central as a result of twentieth-century expansions. The adjacent park features a number of small, traditionally-styled pavilions.

First Nanjing Yangtze River Bridge

NJ 16

1961–1968

南京长江大桥

❖ 32.0632, 118.7902

One of the largest infrastructure projects of its era, this bridge was a major work of civil engineering and a key marker of China's ongoing series of Five-Year modernisation plans under Mao. While this was the third major bridge to be constructed across the Yangtze (after ones in Wuhan and Chongqing), it was the first constructed by the Chinese alone, after Russian engineers departed following the 1960 Sino-Soviet split. Thus, the bridge served a propagandistic as well as a functional role, and imagery of the bridge – thronged with trucks bearing red-coloured goods and parading Red Guards – were widespread in state media. The bridge began construction in the immediate aftermath of the Great Leap Forward/Great Famine of 1958–1961, and was thus well underway before the infamous Cultural Revolution (begun in 1966) had reached

its destructive peak. This period of (relative) stability surely facilitated its construction, though later Communist Party messaging held that the bridge was completed by ordinary workers who wrested control from over-educated engineers – a great victory for "Mao Zedong Thought." Both the rail and auto decks remain in heavy use, though as crossing options have multiplied, the bridge is now reserved for vehicles with Jiangsu Province plates. The top deck is pedestrian-accessible, and features heroic Socialist-Realist statues, evocative relics of an era best left behind.

© Yao Li, courtesy AZL

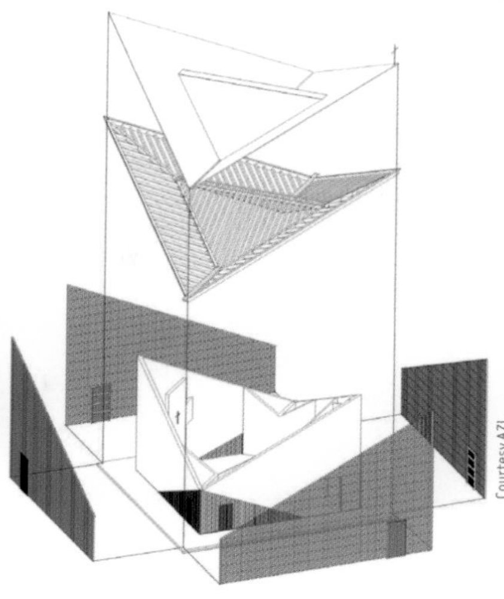

Courtesy AZL

Exploded isometric

Wanjing Garden Chapel

NJ 17

AZL (Atelier ZHANG Lei), 2014

望京 礼拜堂 / 河西万景园教堂
南京市建邺区扬子江大道228号
滨江公园万景园
Riverside Park, near 228 Yangtze River Rd.
❖ 32.0401, 118.7141

This small chapel wrestles with the concept of a centralised church, by inserting an octagonal space within a square perimeter and orienting seats, altar, and roof along the diagonal. The roof's folds, and the strip skylight, bring in light and dramatise the major axes. A narrow walkway surrounds the church, screened by vertical planks (braced by metal brackets). As with the asphalt roof shingles, details are simple, to control costs and to express a humble austerity. The layered design is meant to eschew both the closed traditional volume, and the open Modernist one.

Performing Arts Centre

NJ 21

Preston Scott COHEN, 2007–2009

表演艺术中心
栖霞区仙林大道163号
南京大学仙林校区
Nanjing University Xianlin Campus,
163 Xianlin Ave, Qixia
❖ 32.1155, 118.9521

This complex unites two building forms; a lower structure contains meeting and performance spaces, while respecting the scale of the surrounding buildings, while the tower (dramatically wrapped by the fire stair), is intended as a landmark for this vast campus of isolated object-buildings. The roof is a hyperbolic paraboloid, a complexly curved form that can be approximated by a ruled surface of straight elements. It is thus relatively easy to construct, in this case out of poured-in-place concrete. The surface is faced with a herringbone pattern of small tiles, another smart way to accommodate curvature with straightforward techniques; the shiny tiles, from even a few yards away, dissolve into a smoothly rippling surface, like the scales of a fish. To the east, note the dramatic, tripartite University Library (AZL, 2009). The Liberal Arts Buildings (Nanjing Institute of Design, 2012), straight back from the arts centre, tame the irregular courtyards, masonry and breezeways of Amateur Architecture's **Xiangshan Campus** (p. 264).

Ming Xiaoling Mausoleum

NJ 22

1381–1405

明孝陵
玄武区紫金山南独龙阜玩珠峰下
Ming Xiaoling Scenic Area, Xuanwu
32.0585, 118.8351

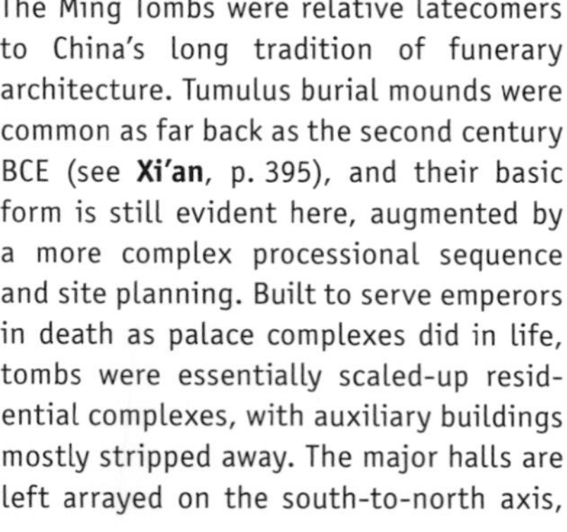

The Ming Tombs were relative latecomers to China's long tradition of funerary architecture. Tumulus burial mounds were common as far back as the second century BCE (see **Xi'an**, p. 395), and their basic form is still evident here, augmented by a more complex processional sequence and site planning. Built to serve emperors in death as palace complexes did in life, tombs were essentially scaled-up residential complexes, with auxiliary buildings mostly stripped away. The major halls are left arrayed on the south-to-north axis, culminating in the burial mound. Thus, the typical hall-courtyard-hall arrangement is blown apart to reveal isolated buildings in the landscape. This tomb was built for the founder of the Ming Dynasty, ZHU Yuanzhang (see Nanjing introduction, p. 124), and like his new city walls, it was a huge construction project, including a twenty-three-kilometre perimeter wall. It was the only tomb completed here; Zhu's successors, following an ugly power struggle, relocated to Beijing and built the later **Ming tombs** (p. 110) there.

Site plan, with old palace site at bottom left

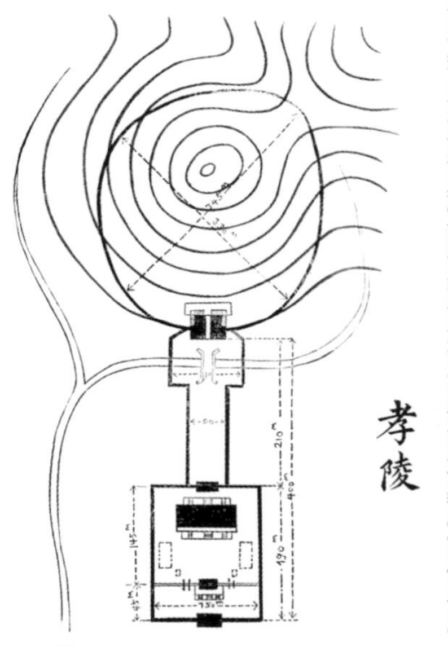

Plan

Dr. Sun Yat-sen Mausoleum

LU Yanzhi, 1925–1931

NJ 23

中山陵
玄武区中山门外石象路7号
7 Shixiang Rd, Xuanwu
❖ 32.0643,118.8482

Before his death, Nationalist revolutionary and Guomindang party leader SUN Yat-sen had expressed his desire to be interred, like Lenin, in a public monument. The site, in the hills just east of ZHU Yuanzhang's tomb (**Ming Xiaoling Mausoleum**, opposite), linked the overthrower of the Qing with the overthrower of the Yuan. Extending the comparison, the site plan included a reinvented "Spirit Way" leading to a tomb, where citizens were encouraged to pay ritualistic respect to the modern nation's founder. As historian Delin LAI argues, the mausoleum served the Guomindang's larger goals of promoting the cult surrounding the unifying figure of Sun, while symbolically invoking his goal of modernising China to keep pace with the West. The international design competition (significantly, China's first) drew many entrants from the United States and the Soviet Union, but projects that simply scaled up familiar Chinese forms were beaten out by Lu's subtler synthesis with the Beaux-Arts approach he learned at Cornell in the teens. The "Spirit Way" is stripped of decorative (Qing-style) statuary, and non-traditional granite and marble clad the concrete structure. The massing, and placement of the required statue of Sun, recall then-recent American monuments; the Western press admired the resemblance to Grant's Tomb (1897) and the Lincoln Memorial (1922).

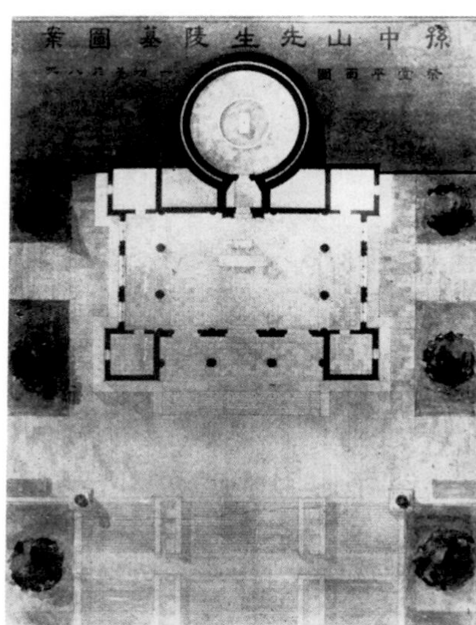

Plan of main hall

Section through main hall and mausoleum

As Lai observes, the act of crafting the ostensible "synthesis" itself helped to establish an emerging canon of principles and features constituting a single "classical Chinese architecture."

Redrawn: underlay courtesy Arata Isozaki & Associates

CIPEA

NJ 24

Various. Master plan by Paul ROSENAU/EKISTICS, with ISOZAKI Arata, 2003+

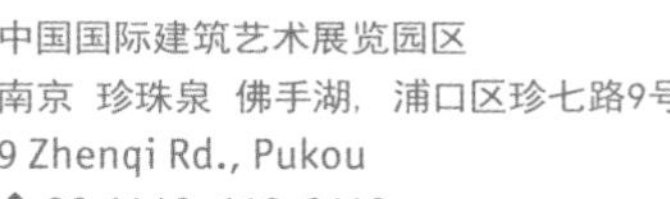

中国国际建筑艺术展览园区
南京 珍珠泉 佛手湖, 浦口区珍七路9号
9 Zhenqi Rd., Pukou
❖ 32.1140, 118.6413

The "China International Practical Exhibition of Architecture," on a hilly, 120-hectare site abutting a national park, brought together twenty-four international architects to produce an exhibition of buildings, rather than drawings and models. The first (and likely only) phase includes twenty single-family houses and four public buildings. Chinese architects were recruited by LIU Jiakun, and foreigners by ISOZAKI Arata. The goal was to open the site as a tourist attraction in 2006; budget, code, and local-foreign coordination issues have been blamed for delays in completion. As of this writing, a number of buildings are complete, enough to justify the twenty-kilometre trek from the city, though several others are incomplete or non-existent.

■ Complete as of 2012
■ Incomplete/status unknown

A Recreation Centre Ettore SOTTSASS
B Conference Centre ISOZAKI Arata (p. 136)
C Sifang Museum of Art and Architecture Steven HOLL Architects (p. 137)
D Visitors Centre Jiakun Architects (LIU Jiakun) (p. 136)
E Matti & Pirjo SANAKSENAHO (opposite)
F ZHOU Kai
G MADA s.p.a.m. (Qingyun MA) – "Pipe House"
H SANAA (opposite)
I AZL (Atelier ZHANG Lei) (opposite)
J Matthias KLOTZ
K Hrvoje NIJRIC + Arhitekti
L David ADJAYE Associates (opposite)
M Mansilla+Tuñón (opposite)
N Sean GODSELL
O Studio Odile DECQ – "Flying Horse House"
P NODE (Doreen Heng LIU) "Folded House"
Q YAO Renxi
R Gábor BACHMAN Architects, or Philip YUAN
S Tanghua Architects (TANG Hua)
T Amateur Architecture (opposite)
U FAKE Design (opposite)
V FCJZ (Yung Ho CHANG)
W KAI Cui
X Alberto KALACH

E. *Matti & Pirjo SANAKSENAHO*. This copper-clad funnel, spreading and rising towards the lake, collects images: a boat, a theatrical grand stair, or perhaps the Surrealist Villa Malaparte.

H. *SANAA (SEJIMA Kazuyo and NISHIZAWA Ryue)*. A minimalist underground retreat-to-be.

I. *AZL (Atelier ZHANG Lei)*. Stacked concrete volumes, with undulating surfaces, add up to a contemporary "pagoda." The views out through the slots are meant to create a "Chinese landscape scroll" effect while minimising openings.

M. *Mansilla+Tuñón (Luis Moreno MANSILLA and Emilio TUÑÓN)*. This undulating house of sticks, set in the trees, commingles interior and exterior.

L. *David ADJAYE Associates*. This elegant box in concrete, slate and bamboo aims for a "collage" in elevation and a "mosaic" in interior plan.

U. *FAKE Design (Ai Weiwei)*. The "six rooms" of the design, linked by a long glazed corridor, present solid, blocky concrete façades to the road. On the interior, these spaces are linked by a long glazed corridor that frames panoramic views of the valley below.

T. *Amateur Architecture (WANG Shu and LU Wenyu)*. In this modest residence, two parallel bars with curved roof profiles frame a small courtyard in a scaled-down version of the design strategies the architects developed at their **Xiangshan Campus** (p. 264) in Hangzhou.

CIPEA Conference Centre

NJ 25

ISOZAKI Arata, 2013

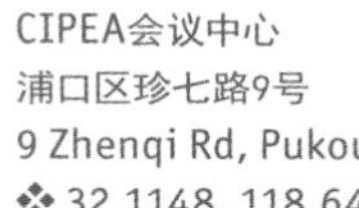

CIPEA会议中心
浦口区珍七路9号
9 Zhenqi Rd, Pukou
❖ 32.1148, 118.6401

Occupying a dip in the hillside, and following the topography to frame views out over the valley beyond, the Conference Centre is one of CIPEA's main public venues. Considering its prime real estate at the centre of the development, its unobtrusive form is something of a surprise, especially considering that Isozaki was one of the coordinators of the master plan. Perhaps by carving this building into the landscape, the architects hope to comment on the role of monumentality in architecture, or simply to preserve the landscape and the views for others. The bold geometry in plan lends a certain severity to the public gathering spaces, but abundant natural light enlivens the interiors.

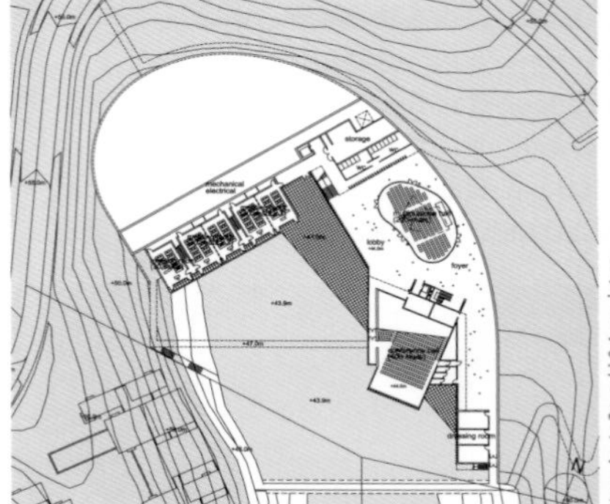

Site plan

Courtesy Jiakun Architects

CIPEA Visitors Centre

NJ 26

Jiakun Architects (LIU Jiakun), 2003+

CIPEA酒店 – 浦口区珍七路9号
9 Zhenqi Rd, Pukou
❖ 32.1138, 118.6401

This large welcome facility/hotel is broken down into smaller volumes to better address the hillside and the scale of the CIPEA houses. Meeting halls, dining rooms and reception are set into the terraces that step down the hill, while the guest rooms individuate themselves as another set of "houses," coupling distinctive gabled roof profiles with courtyards. This approach, evoking both the "international" and the "Chinese" aspects of the development, may be a wry commentary on historical domestic typologies, or an evocation of rural Chinese mountain villages. The dam downhill from CIPEA has also been cited as an inspiration. The architects are known for their sensitive use of local materials (see **Chengdu**, map p. 388); here, the walls are double-layered constructions of concrete block and clay bricks, two modular systems both easily assembled by available labour.

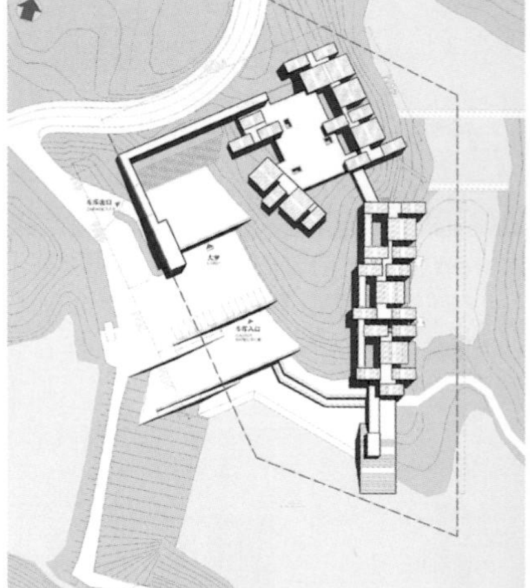

Site plan

Sifang Museum

Steven HOLL Architects,
2003–2013

NJ 28

四方当代美术馆
浦口区珍七路9号
9 Zhenqi Rd, Pukou
❖ 32.116355, 118.638551

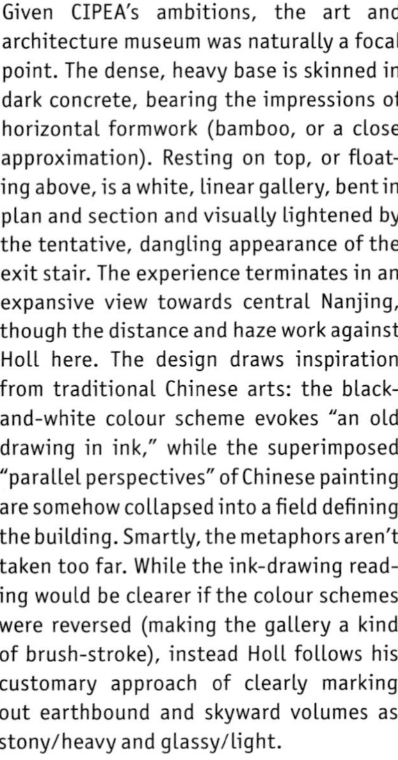

Given CIPEA's ambitions, the art and architecture museum was naturally a focal point. The dense, heavy base is skinned in dark concrete, bearing the impressions of horizontal formwork (bamboo, or a close approximation). Resting on top, or floating above, is a white, linear gallery, bent in plan and section and visually lightened by the tentative, dangling appearance of the exit stair. The experience terminates in an expansive view towards central Nanjing, though the distance and haze work against Holl here. The design draws inspiration from traditional Chinese arts: the black-and-white colour scheme evokes "an old drawing in ink," while the superimposed "parallel perspectives" of Chinese painting are somehow collapsed into a field defining the building. Smartly, the metaphors aren't taken too far. While the ink-drawing reading would be clearer if the colour schemes were reversed (making the gallery a kind of brush-stroke), instead Holl follows his customary approach of clearly marking out earthbound and skyward volumes as stony/heavy and glassy/light.

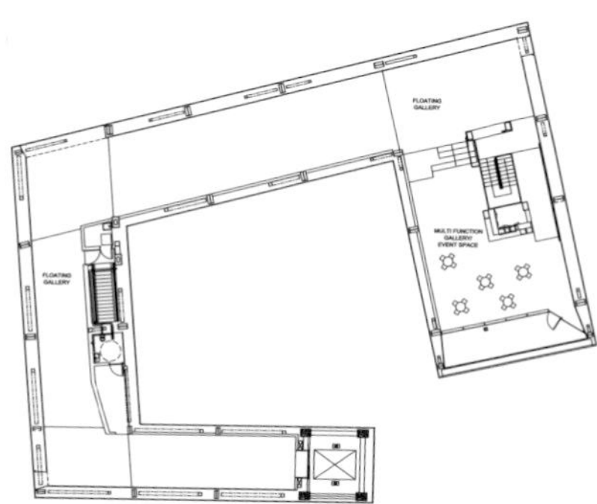

Gallery-level plan

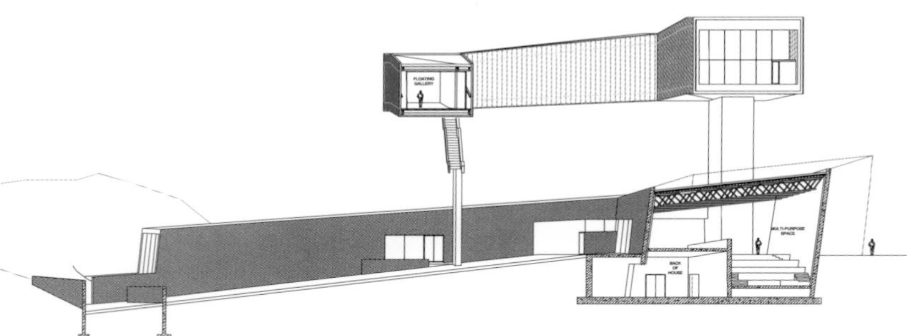

Section

NJ Nanjing

Central Nanjing (Map 01–15)

01 **Nanjing Massacre Museum** *QI Kang, 1985, 1995, 2005.* ❖ 32.0373, 118.7394

02 **Zhonghuamen (Gate of China)** ❖ 32.0145, 118.7772

03 **Jinling Art Museum/J Art Gallery** *LIU Ke-cheng & XIAO Li, 2011–2013.* A deep surface of patterned depressions, plus some new/old street fabric. ❖ 32.0148, 118.7817

04 **Outlook Garden (Zhan Yuan)** Late Qing or even more recent construction. ❖ 32.0231, 118.7802

05 **Confucius Temple/Fuzimiao** *1034.* Temple complex and vibrant canal-side historic district; its 1980s reconstruction prompted a trend of such developments. ❖ 32.0227, 118.7839

06 **Aqua City** *HMA Design, Kingdom Architecture, 2008.* A memorably over-the-top mall with indoor/outdoor water features and a sort of Bird's Nest-ish roof. ❖ 32.0258, 118.7812

07 **Jiangsu Art Museum** *KSP Jürgen Engel Architekten, 2010.* Two interlocking stone "U"s, with an atrium in between, and a major collection of historical Chinese art. ❖ 32.0437, 118.7938

08 **Six Dynasties Museum** *Pei Partnership Architects, 2014.* ❖ 32.0448, 118.7943

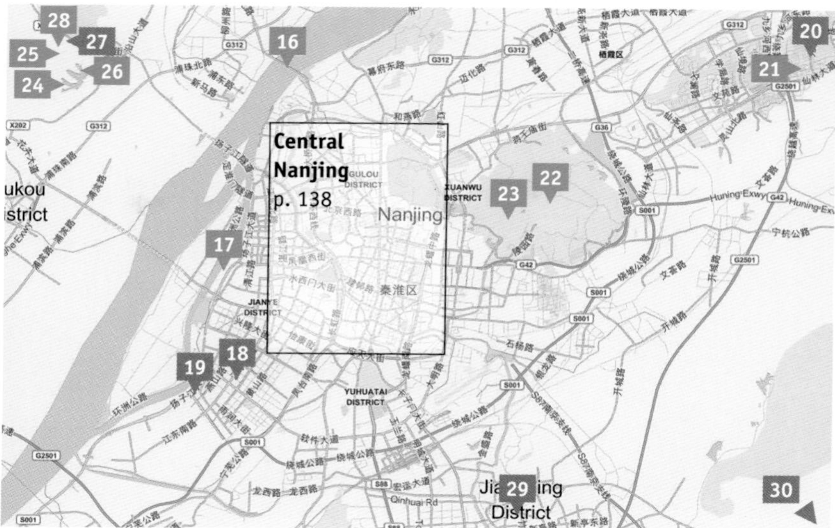

Greater Nanjing (Map 16–30)

09 **1912 District** A number of Republic-era buildings converted into restaurants, bars and clubs. ❖ 32.0474, 118.7906

10 **Wutaishan Gymnasium** *1975.* A period piece: late Mao-era public architecture. ❖ 32.0510, 118.7671

11 **Drum Tower Hospital** *Lemanarc (Vincent Zhengmao ZHANG), 2004–2012.* A double-doughnut scheme supports multi-scaled outdoor space – a "Gardenised Architecture;" the modular skin (with numerous planters) also softens things up. ❖ 32.0573, 118.7783

12 **Greenland Zifeng Tower** *SOM, 2005–2010.* ❖ 32.0625, 118.7780

13 **Jiming Temple** *1387* ❖ 32.0632, 118.7904

14 **Xuanwu Lake** ❖ 32.0715, 118.7936

15 **Nanjing Railway Station** *1968.* ❖ 32.0885, 118.7931

16 **Nanjing Yangtze River Bridge** *1968.* ❖ 32.1108, 118.7482

17 **Wanjing Garden Chapel** *Atelier ZHANG Lei, 2014.* ❖ 32.0401, 118.7141

18 **Jinao Tower** *SOM 2004–2014.* Faceted, ventilating double-skin. Part of a fast-rising new business district. ❖ 31.9999, 118.7197

19 **Nanjing International Youth Cultural Centre** *Zaha HADID Architects, 2014.* A swooping centrepiece of the new Hexi District CBD. ❖ 31.9939, 118.7033

20 **Xianlin Campus Library** *AZL (Atelier ZHANG Lei)* ❖ 32.1163, 118.9551

21 **Xianlin Campus Performing Arts Centre** *Preston Scott COHEN, 2009.* ❖ 32.1155, 118.9521

22 **Ming Xiaoling Mausoleum** *1381–1405.* ❖ 32.0585, 118.8351

23 **Dr. Sun Yat-Sen Mausoleum** *LU Yanzhi 1926–1929.* ❖ 32.0643, 118.8482

24 **CIPEA** *Various. Master plan by Paul ROSENAU/EKISTICS, with ISOZAKI Arata, 2003+.* ❖ 32.1140, 118.6413

25 **CIPEA Conference Centre** *ISOZAKI Arata, 2013.* ❖ 32.1148, 118.6401

26 **CIPEA Visitor's Centre** *Jiakun Architects, 2003+.* ❖ 32.1138, 118.6401

27 **CIPEA Clubhouse** *Ettore SOTTSASS, 2003.* A cluster of cubic volumes with punched windows, resembling a displaced Postmodern Italian hill town. ❖ 32.1140, 118.6413

28 **Sifang Museum** *Steven HOLL Architects 2011.* ❖ 32.1147, 118.6406

29 **Eastern Jin Dynasty Museum** *Southeast University Group, 2011.* A notable collection of artefacts; the building has some contemporary touches (vertical cladding pattern, offbeat window arrangement). ❖ 31.9503, 118.8388

30 **New Fourth Army Museum** *AZL (Atelier ZHANG Lei), 2006–2007.* 114 km southeast of central Nanjing (near Liyang), this museum's exterior – a severe granite rectilinear block – contrasts with a faceted red interior wrapper which carves irregular interior courtyards from the volume. ❖ 31.5096 119.3372

上海
Shanghai

上海 Shanghai

Shanghai occupies a position of critical importance at the mouth of the Yangtze, Asia's longest river and one of China's fundamental spines of development since ancient times. It may then come as a surprise that Shanghai's history can be traced back "only" about a thousand years. River deltas expand with the alluvial deposit of silt washed down from the interior, so when China was first united (mid-200s BCE), the area now occupied by Shanghai was in the Pacific Ocean, and during the early dynasties it was not much more than a tidal mud flat. While it's grown up from the mud to become the world's most populous city proper (over 17 million people) and its fifth largest financial centre, Shanghai is not an "instant city" in the Shenzhen mode. It has gone through several distinct phases of growth, and several evolutions in the politics of control. These have all left visible traces in the urban fabric, and opened unique discussions on the state of historic preservation in contemporary China. The result is an incredibly complex, heterogeneous city that defies easy characterisation. Shanghai is a testing ground, an alluvial sandbox whose history contains few periods of stasis.

Shanghai's rise starts, roughly, in 1074 CE, when the village was upgraded to "market town" status by the ruling Song dynasty (960–1279 CE). The centre was not directly on the Yangtze (where it would have been flooded regularly), but rather on a tributary, the Huangpu river, which takes a bend shortly before emptying into the Yangtze. The west side of this bend enjoys easier currents than the east, and thus was the site of the first landings. The Huangpu opens a route to Suzhou, the regional political and economic power centre at the time. Shanghai thus enjoyed a natural economic advantage: large ocean-going vessels could exchange goods with shallow-hulled riverboats, with the defensive support of the regional administrative capital. Through Suzhou's **Grand Canal** connection (see p. 226), Shanghai and the Yangtze were connected to the wider national economy – which in imperial times hinged on internal region-to-region trade, not international trade through seaports.

Late in the Song era, a sea wall was built to hold back the tides of the Huangpu, and the city entered a long, slow period of development. This culminated in 1554 CE, when a defensive, inner city wall was built, indicating the strategic value of the city at the time (or just the growing threat of marauding Japanese pirates). The walls enclosed the area which already contained most of the temples and bureaucratic

Previous spread: **Jin Mao Tower** (p. 178) and the **World Financial Centre** (p. 180) by night

Nanjing Road

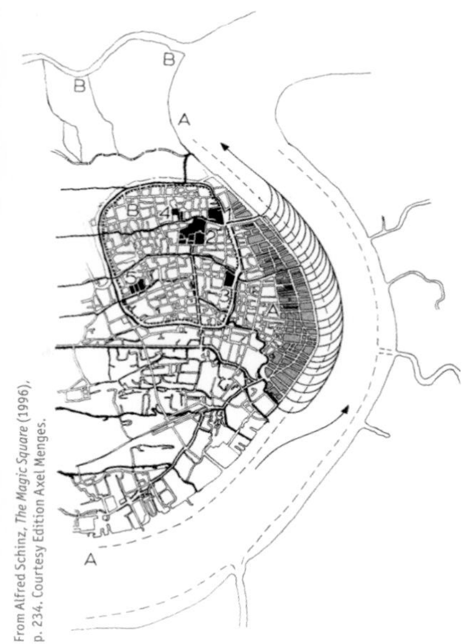

From Alfred Schinz, *The Magic Square* (1996), p. 234. Courtesy Edition Axel Menges.

Shanghai during the southern Song dynasty

offices; the dockside landings and market streets, which drove the city's economy, had become a kind of suburb, as in Guangzhou (p. 294). It was at this point that Shanghai temporarily fell victim to wider Chinese trade policy, as the Ming Emperor Jiajing cut off foreign trade in 1525 (see **Macau**, p. 374). Aside from curtailing China's "Age of Exploration," such realignment of trade priorities put seaport cities like Shanghai at a great disadvantage relative to Grand Canal cities like Suzhou, which enjoyed its golden age at this point. This embargo was lifted in 1684, and in 1732 the emperor gave Shanghai exclusive control over customs for Jiangsu province; these two events propelled Shanghai to a position of prominence (or confirmed its ongoing rise), and it soon overtook Suzhou as the economic centre of the region, despite a lower political rank.

As it developed into a major port, Shanghai grew into a dense network of narrow lanes and inward-focused courtyard houses, punctuated by temple complexes, all contained within the city walls. Lacking open public spaces and the clear, centrally planned geometry of China's political capitals (see **Beijing**, p. 064), this district would seem an impenetrable, chaotic warren to later foreign observers, who were content to write "Chinese City" on the map, with little consideration of the streets (or people, or conditions) within. "Old Town" (in today's Huangpu district) still retains this footprint, and it's easy to lose oneself in the narrow alleyways, appreciating the mix of private and public space. The life of the neighbourhood spills out into the lanes, and the sense of community is palpable. The old city walls came down in the 1920s, in a classic gesture of "modernisation," but their urban form is still evident in the ring road that surrounds the "old town" south of Fuxing Lu near the river.

With China continuing to develop and re-connect with the outside world in the sixteenth and seventeenth centuries, Shanghai became more and more appealing to foreigners seeking fame and fortune in "the Orient." By the nineteenth century, the empire was having increasing difficulty fending off European incursions (see **Guangzhou**, p. 294). The British found Shanghai attractive for its established mercantile economy and its proximity to the Yangtze, and the city was located a comfortable distance from the more fully fortified and monitored town of Jingjiang. British China policy in this period was complex, but one of their basic strategies was to keep the Qing weak, but not antagonise them so much that they would put up stiff resistance (or fall to rebels who would). This was ultimately not a sustainable strategy, and it gave way to the First Opium War (1839–1842, again see Guangzhou), during which the British

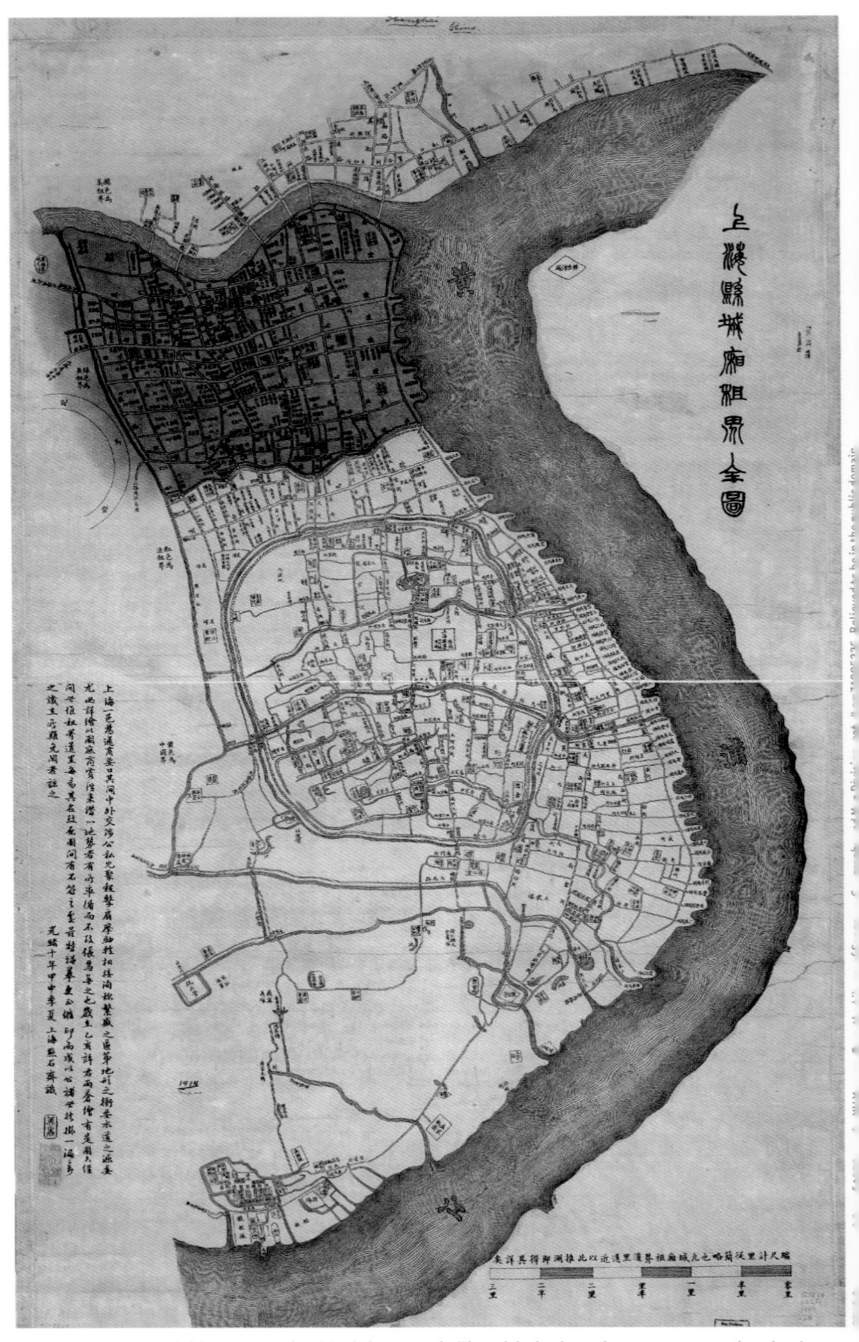

Shanghai in 1884 (Chinese map by QING Guangxu). The old city's major streets are clearly shown and labelled,along with important landmarks. The grain of the surrounding dockside city – with streets pulling back from the waterfront – can also be seen. The colour-code at the top indicates foreign concession territory.

Navy briefly occupied the city. Afterwards, the effectively colonial invaders gained long-term unrestricted trade access to Shanghai in the Treaty of Nanking (and several subsequent "unequal treaties"), which established international enclaves to the north and west of the sovereign Chinese walled city. Following the establishment of the foreign concessions, the city entered a tremendous period of sustained growth – on European terms – and rose to international prominence as a major world centre of trade and finance. The concessions were initially populated sparsely by the

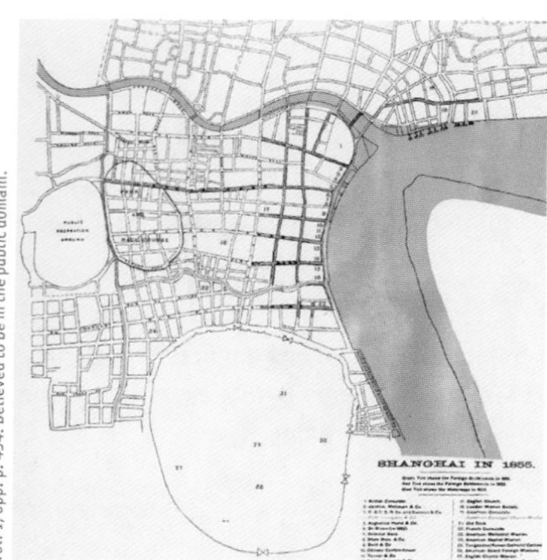

Shanghai in 1855 (map of 1910 by the American customs agent Hosea MORSE). Note that the walled city, despite numbered points of foreign interest (like the missionary chapel), is rendered as an un-mappable blank.

foreigners, but beginning with the chaos of the Taiping Rebellion (1850–1864), Chinese refugees began fleeing into the concessions, which began admitting them formally in 1854.

The "old city" acted primarily as a collection point for imports and their associated tariffs or "tribute." Proceeding north along the Huangpu, the colonial settlements of France, Britain, and the United States each claimed a linear stretch of waterfront, anticipating the huge economic value of Shanghai as a major international port, and ensuring their own access. The embankment of the British concession became known as **the Bund** (p. 156), after a Hindi word for quay or levee; even place names reveal the global extent of Britain's colonial project.

This linear waterfront grew organically out of a Western desire to maximise the profitability of Chinese concessions: with more land along the river, the colonialists could construct more docks, and carry on a greater volume of trade. The city's primary economic focus remained this littoral space along the Huangpu, even as the concessions spread inland, west and north of the river. Each concession was maintained by its respective colonial government, with differences in planning strategies still evident in today's street layout, architectural styles, and landscaping. It's revealing to compare the major thoroughfares of the French and British Concessions, which both draw on Western urban planning strategies of the era. The axial design of the French Concession's Avenue Joffrey (now Huaihai Lu) could have been taken directly from Haussmann's plan of Paris (1853–1870), while British Bubbling Well Road (now Nanjing Lu) takes a meandering path towards an ideal of picturesque Romanticism (map p. 199). The borders of the former concessions are still evident today: in the late twentieth century, they provided conveniently open right-of-ways for Shanghai's elevated highways.

Architecturally, while we can identify obvious foreign influence in the villas of the French Concession and the Neoclassical edifices of the Bund, it is in the *shikumen* ("stone gate") blocks – the housing typology that once comprised much of the urban fabric – that foreign and local influences found true synthesis. The *shikumen* combined aspects of traditional Chinese courtyard houses with a European row-house typology, as if a Beijing *siheyuan* had been compressed in plan and stacked vertically to fit a narrow British terrace house plot, with the vestigial courtyard transformed into a small, open-air vestibule. The *shikumen* form developed both from the clash of cultures after the opening of the foreign concessions, and from the accelerated residential construction necessitated by rapid population growth in an increasingly industrial city. Foreign and local developers alike embraced this dense typology, and constructed entire unified mega-blocks as profit-driven, speculative developments. At the urban scale, their form, evolving from the 1850s to the 1930s, was that of the dense *lilong* or "neighbourhood lane." In the *lilong*, a city block is defined by major streets; at ground level, it's ringed by small shops and restaurants, a visual and auditory buffer punctured by entry gates which mark the ends of the primary axes of the housing block. The street is wide enough to accommodate automobiles, but narrow enough to discourage through-traffic. Narrow lanes branch off of the primary axes, only wide enough for pedestrians, scooters, and the informal congregation of neighbours. Off these secondary lanes are the eponymous stone gates, behind which lie the small entry courtyards of individual houses.

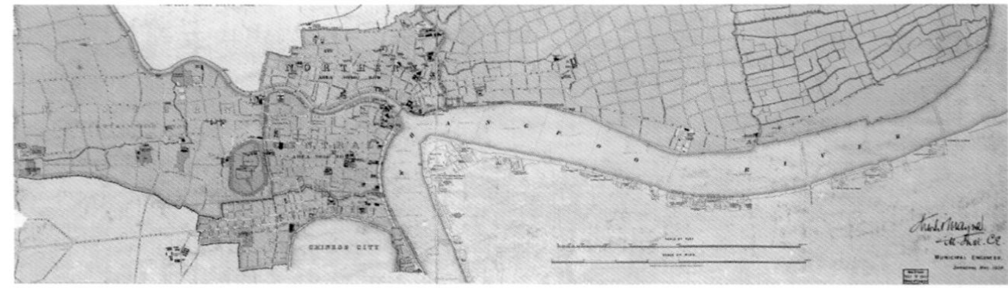

The growing city in 1904 (British map, in apparent collaboration with city engineers). Colour coding distinguishes Chinese neighbourhoods from foreign settlements. Note expansion to the east and west. Again, the "Chinese City" is posited visually as an ineffable mystery.

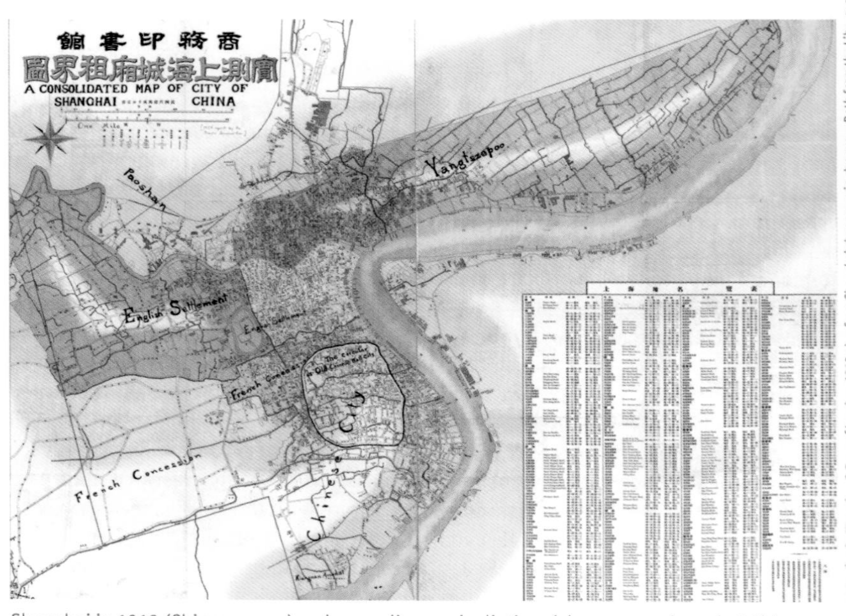

Shanghai in 1913 (Chinese maps); colour coding again distinguishes concessions, but Chinese and foreign cities are rendered with the same detail

This progression – from boulevard to lane, to alley, to courtyard – establishes a hierarchy of space with a "public" gradient considerably more layered than that of the *hutong* (see **Beijing,** p. 064). This ensures a high level of security and fosters a strong sense of social cohesion despite an enormous population of new arrivals to the city. Any strangers to a particular block become more and more visible the deeper they venture into the complex.

The formal markers of precinct, boundary, and threshold are clearly evident in Shanghai's surviving *lilong* blocks, where the sense of a thriving, vital community is strong. There are still numerous existing *shikumen* blocks, in various states of repair. **Cité Bourgogne** (p. 168) is finely restored, but perhaps more exciting for visitors is **Tianzifang** (p. 170), where the houses have been subdivided, converted into shops and restaurants, and capped with precarious additions, among other transformations. The thriving arts-district-turned-tourist-hot-spot provides a unique opportunity to size up the altered state in which most of Shanghai's *shikumen* now exist, without infringing on residents' personal space.

Shanghai's capitalist boom continued through the fall of the Qing dynasty and the rise of the Republic of China. By 1936, it was one of the world's largest cities, and perhaps China's most modern, cosmopolitan locale, home to industry, cinema, the Chinese pop music industry, and a local version of Art Deco architecture (with "oriental" motifs). In 1929, plans were drawn up for a new city centre in the Beaux Arts and/or City Beautiful tradition. Featuring grand, radiating boulevards while acknowledging the surrounding street grain,

A typical *lilong* lane

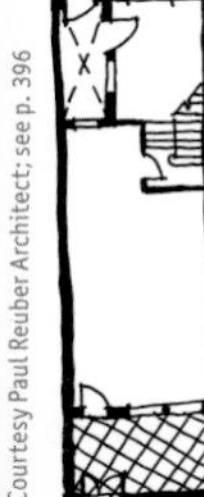

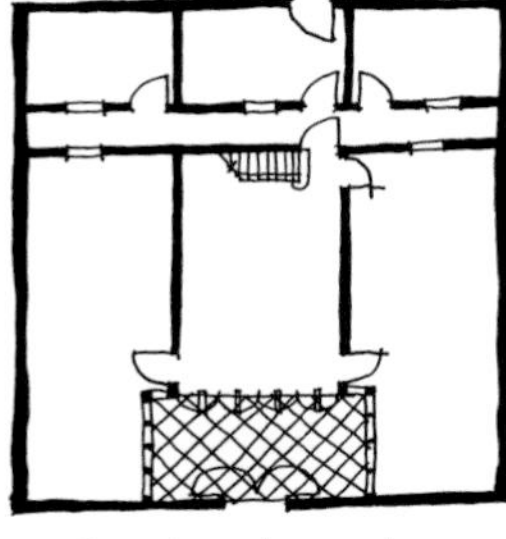

Courtesy Paul Reuber Architect; see p. 396

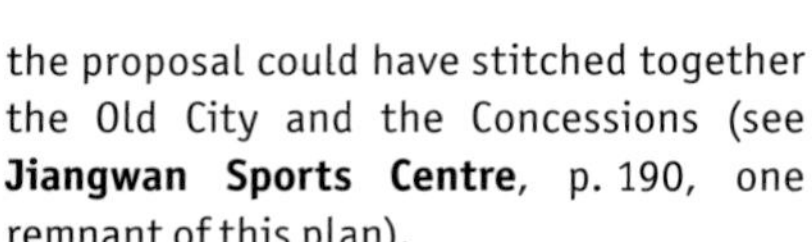

Shikumen rowhouse plans (one-bay and three-bay units)

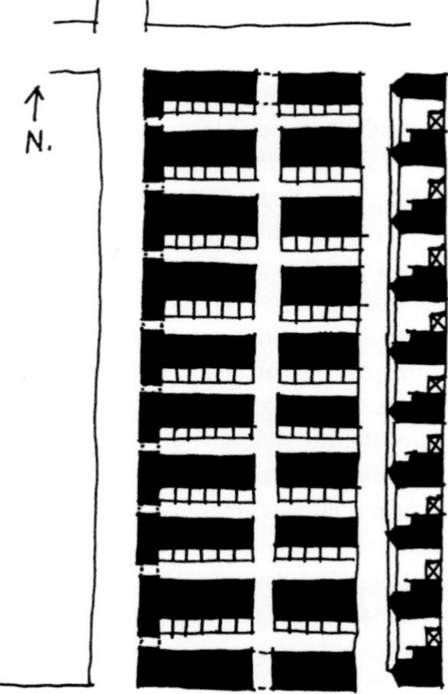

Courtesy Paul Reuber Architect

A *lilong* neighbourhood plan. Note entry courtyards and "blocked" perimeter.

the proposal could have stitched together the Old City and the Concessions (see **Jiangwan Sports Centre**, p. 190, one remnant of this plan).

However, all efforts to plan Shanghai in this period would be trumped by larger events. Removed from the warlord power struggles that undermined the authority and power of the Republic, prosperous Shanghai ("Paris of the East, New York of the West") was nonetheless beset by tremendous inequality between the landlord *comprador* class (a mix of the foreign and Chinese bourgeoisie) and the masses of industrial and shipping workers. It was thus a heady place, where foreign ideas found fertile soil: the Communist Party of China was founded in Shanghai in 1921. The Communists were violently suppressed in 1927 by an alliance between the Guomindang and the *comprador* authorities (see **Longhua Martyrs Cemetery**, p. 174), an incident that would crystallise the new Chinese political situation, with the increasingly rightist stance of CHIANG Kai-Shek's new government in Nanjing inspiring opposition (soon to spark civil war) from Communist cells nationwide. Shanghai's "glory days" came to a close with the onset of the Second Sino-Japanese War, when Japan's imperial ambitions led it beyond its puppet state in Manchuria to the heart of China.

This period was disastrous for Republican China, not least for Shanghai, which the Japanese army invaded in autumn of 1937. The Battle of Shanghai (the first major battle of the war) involved nearly a million troops fighting street-by-street for three months, as well as Japanese aerial bombardment. The city suffered greatly, and many surviving factories were dismantled and evacuated to the Chinese interior. Under Japanese control, the foreign concessions were disbanded, and the city briefly became a haven for refugees fleeing the wider world war. Later, the Japanese, under German pressure, began ghettoising foreigners, particularly Jews and those from Allied countries. Concentration camps were established in 1943.

While the war ended in 1945, the Civil War, which had effectively been put on hold out of mutual desperation, broke out again. Shanghai fell to the Communists in May 1949, after which the city's development mirrored that of China as a whole. The capitalist excesses of earlier years had no place in MAO Zedong's China. While the state built factories, China's new number-one trading partner was the Soviet Union, closer by rail than by ship. The closing of China to the West put Shanghai in the same awkward role it had occupied in the sixteenth century: a shipping powerhouse with nowhere to ship anything.

With the end of the Mao era, and following the runaway success of DENG Xiaoping's "Special Economic Zones" in the south (see **Shenzhen**, p. 316), Shanghai was poised to regain some of its former glory. In 1992, the "Pudong New Area" (across the river from the Bund) was granted SEZ status, and opened to foreign investment. Since then, the area has exploded into the vertical business hub seen today, though, as always, the Party-line hype (that the city was no more than a fishing village before Deng) should not be believed. The rapid development of Pudong is not primarily an urban or architectural experiment, but rather an exercise in branding. Since the mid-1990s, China has positioned itself as a major player in the world market and a successful exemplar of capitalism (or, rather, of "Socialism with Chinese Characteristics") and it needs an appropriate postcard skyline. As Jeffrey WASSERSTROM suggests, in his "fragmented" history, Shanghai is a city of façades, of appearances, and above all of exhibition. To some, the old, concession-era skyline represented European economic might and an outpost of civilisation, while to others it manifested offensive imperial encroachment. While China recovered from the Cultural Revolution and began its series of economic reforms in the 1980s, postcard views focused on the ships in the harbour, with the old Bund buildings obscured or even out of frame. Then, when Pudong was opened as a Special Economic Zone, and increasingly tall, proudly "Chinese" towers began construction, China's postcard photographers seemed to collectively turn 180 degrees, catching a new city seemingly emerging from marshland and paddy fields, bereft of imperialist influence.

Punctuated by structurally ambitious and eccentrically shaped towers, such as the **Oriental Pearl** (p. 182), the **Jin Mao** (p. 178), and the **World Financial Centre** (p. 180), the Pudong skyline became the public face of Shanghai, a calling-card establishing that this mainland city was every bit as modern and global as Hong Kong. Built at colossal scale and embracing functional zoning, sectional stratification of circulation, and a typology of towers in a park, Pudong's urbanism recalls such visions of the future as Le Corbusier's unnerving *Plan Voisin* of 1925 or Sant'Elia's *Citta Nuova* of 1914. Yet the paucity of life on the streets of the financial district suggests that Pudong is a failed experiment, an exemplar of Modernist planning principles long discarded in the West.

But if Pudong represents the failures of Modernism, similarly Modern and drastic interventions across the river, in Shanghai's historic centre, have proven more successful. Elevated highways, now a largely abandoned concept in the United States and Europe, seem to work fairly well here. They alleviate congestion and provide quick links across the city, while the multi-level stack interchanges, illuminated at night, become massive, infrastructural sculptures. Though these flyovers surely required a substantial amount of demolition, they largely follow previously existing boundary lines and thus are less destructive to historic fabric than one might expect. Meanwhile, in the run-up to Expo 2010, the Shanghai Metro expanded to become the longest system in the world, an indicator of the city's commitment to public transit. As well, the Bund was reworked as a pedestrian promenade, a welcome addition to the city. Perhaps the Bund may yet re-emerge as the face of Shanghai.

Until recently, "preservation" was quite literally a foreign concept. In traditional Chinese architecture, building materials were short-lived: wooden temples would naturally decay in a shorter time than the stone monuments of European antiquity, and the philosophical underpinnings of classical Chinese society stressed repetition and renewal. The physical makeup of a historic building was less important than its cultural position. Yet with China's culture itself having undergone tumultuous change, what is the role of traditional architecture? During the World Expo, and continuing today, Shanghai's self-congratulatory propaganda and advertisements have re-engaged history to a surprising extent. The stone gateways of *shikumen* adorn liquor bottles, souvenirs, and construction fencing; they even appear as topiary in public parks. **Xintiandi** (p. 171), a quasi-restoration that leaves

Shanghai in 1937. See detail p. 025.

Shanghai in 1983; detail showing Pudong before its redevelopment. Note presence of port facilities and factories producing cars, textiles, paper, tobacco, etc. Across the river, the old Bund buildings, having lost their significance in the Communist era, largely go unmarked.

few original *shikumen* standing, still almost single-handedly raised awareness of Shanghai's rich architectural heritage. By showing that the *shikumen* can be as profitable in its re-created, representational form as it was in its original speculative heyday, Xintiandi has proven (in economic terms) that the past is not always something to be discarded, and numerous restoration projects can now be found around the city, often citing the "Xintiandi effect" as a guarantee of economic success.

Beneath Yan'an Elevated Road near Jing'an Temple (formerly Avenue Edward VII, the boundary between the French Concession and International Settlement)

Lighting effects, Former French Concession

In spite of the tremendous growth and transformation of the city proper, Shanghai's most prominent recent developments have taken place in outlying areas. Wide-ranging regional plans can be traced back at least to the turn of the twentieth century, when city planners (influenced by Ebeneezer Howard) suggested a ring of satellite cities around Shanghai. Over the years, various plans have been proposed and approved, but none was implemented until 2001's "One City, Nine Towns" plan. This plan followed a multi-nodal approach to urban development that owes a great deal to Howard's strategy of concentrating growth into urban cores, linked by transit and surrounded by unspoiled farms or parks. Oddly enough, such an approach may have seemed a perfect fit for late twentieth-century China. As in turn-of-the-century Britain, expanding cities threaten to consume the agricultural land that sustains them, but unlike Britain, twenty-first-century China has an autocratic government with deep pockets and the authority to implement giant-scale urban schemes. "One City, Nine Towns" was itself part of Shanghai's "1–9–6–6" regional plan, which called for one central metropolis, nine new cities, 60 new towns, as well as 600 new villages. The "nine new cities" were all to be newly constructed, most in "European style" according to the best practices of the new towns' selected nations (see **Anting**, p. 188, **Luodian**, p. 191, **Gaoqiao**, p. 191, **Pujiang**, p. 191 and **Songjiang**, p. 193).

Of course, the eclectic strategy of assembling varied townscapes from abroad risks an "EPCOT Centre" approach to world architecture, and the vacant, faux half-timbered store-fronts of **Thames Town** (**Songjiang**, p. 193) have received their share of criticism. Even so, several of the new towns have become vibrant urban centres. **Qingpu/"Chinese Town"** (from p. 186) was planned from inception to be well integrated with the established nearby town of **Zhujiajiao** (p. 188), and the local administration's willingness to engage architects has given rise to a lively and prosperous urban core. **Pujiang/"Italian Town"** (p. 191) was designed as a hybrid of ancient Chinese and Roman town planning, with a rigid grid and street hierarchy softened by canals and augmented by International-Style villas. Though there is no sure-fire way to generate the kind of city that grows organically over centuries, copying European historic urbanism may be as valid an approach as any. The "nine towns" project was officially discontinued in 2006. Often purposefully lacking public transit links back to the city (intended to "self-select" a certain class of buyers), most of the satellite cities suffer from a high degree of vacancy. Many units were purchased solely as investments, in the absence of safer investment vehicles in China's financial markets. As these satellite cities become knitted more closely together with the historical centre (via the ever expanding Shanghai metro), observers will get a better sense of their successes and failures.

Today's enthusiasm for unbridled economic growth and ever-taller skyscrapers has numerous parallels in Shanghai's modern history, from the birth of a socialist utopia in 1949, to the 1911 revolution that toppled the Qing dynasty, to the influx of foreign entrepreneurs following the establishment in 1842 of a treaty port on the Huangpu. All of these, including the present developments, were significant events suffused with excitement for the future. By naively ignoring or consciously suppressing the past (in favour of an unrestrained future), Shanghai planners have often considered the city a *tabula rasa*, and thereby given themselves free rein to construct as they wished – whether their aim was to recreate the streets of Paris, or to build a skyline to rival Hong Kong. This attitude has defined the city we see today: a multi-layered, hybrid metropolis that serves as a living museum of urban planning – a laboratory for experimental urbanism.

Practical Considerations

While it's difficult to explore all of Shanghai's varied districts in a short time frame, ambitious travellers could put together a three or four day itinerary that covers the highlights. Shanghai's centre is relatively compact, and several districts can be productively grouped into long walking tours. Wandering through Old Town can easily take a few hours, depending on how long you wish to linger at Yuyuan. A walk from the Bund to Nanjing Road and onward into the Former French Concession can take a good half-day with occasional cafe breaks. The major sights of Pudong are clustered near the Lujiazui Metro station, though block sizes here are large, and it can be easy to underestimate distances. Shanghai's Metro is clean, efficient, extensive and cheap, though it can become quite crowded during rush hour. Taxis are ubiquitous (just raise your hand), and for trips further afield (out to the suburban New Towns, for instance) a hired driver may save a substantial amount of travel time.

Sources and Recommended Reading

Ackbar ABBAS, "Play it Again Shanghai: Urban Preservation in the Global Era" in Mario Gandelsonas, ed., *Shanghai Reflections: Architecture, Urbanism and the Search for an Alternative Modernity*, Princeton, NJ: Princeton Architectural Press, 2002. Shanghai-specific preservation issues, situated within its modern history.

Alan BALFOUR and ZHENG Shiling, *World Cities: Shanghai*, Chichester: Wiley-Academy, 2002. Coffee-table book with an architectural emphasis; good essays, including tons of historical background.

Renee CHOW, *Changing Chinese Cities: the Potentials of Field Urbanism* (2015). Forthcoming volume, developing the author's ongoing and very interesting work on urban forms including *lilong* and *shikumen*.

Harry den HARTOG, et al. *Shanghai New Towns*, Rotterdam: 010 Publishers, 2010. The essential document of "1–9–6–6" planning, with overall planning history, redrawn plans of the Nine Towns, etc.

LIU Wujun & HUANG Xiang, *Shanghai Urban Planning* (2007). Dry and textbook-like, but with lots of maps and specifics on particular urban features

QIAN Guan, *Lilong Housing, a Traditional Settlement Form* (1996). Master's thesis, available online, including excellent detail on the evolution of *shikumen* and *lilong*.

Peter G. ROWE and Seng KUAN, eds. *Shanghai: Architecture and Urbanism for Modern China* (2004). A range of essays on Shanghai, linking the city's urban form to specific aspects of its historical and contemporary culture.

Wan-Lin TSAI, *The Redevelopment and Preservation of Historic Lilong Housing in Shanghai* (2008). Another *lilong* thesis, with more emphasis on the present day.

Jeremy E. TAYLOR, "Littoral Space of the Bund," in *Social History* #27/2, 2002. An excellent social history, examining foreign concessions as constructs of power, and the Bund as a manifestation of Victorian-era mercantile capitalism.

Jeffrey WASSERSTROM, *Global Shanghai*, Chicago: Chicago University Press, 2009. An examination of the city at key points in history, focusing on the portrayal of the city in period media (and propaganda).

Yu Garden & Bazaar

SH 03

PAN Yunduan, et al., 1559+

豫园和集市 – 黄浦区安仁街218号
218 Anren St., Huangpu
❖ 31.2290, 121.4873

Yu Yuan, screened from the bustling bazaar in the Old City, is the best-preserved Ming-era garden in Shanghai, a densely-layered synthesis of landscape and architecture. In contrast with the rigid axial symmetry of traditional architecture and urban planning, classical gardens seem a study in chaos: the overlapping of contradictory elements and the intricate interlocking of building and landscape create complex, three-dimensional spatial sequences that eschew plan legibility. Porticoes flanking the small pavilions peel off to become covered walkways, slices of garden seem to get trapped in narrow courtyards behind wooden screens, and hallway ceilings are pulled back from the walls to allow sunlight to wash over planters. Compared to the Suzhou gardens (from p. 218), this can feel almost maze-like, as the high walls and rockeries divide the space into discrete zones, including the "Inner Garden" sometimes marked out separately as the *Nei Yuan*. The bazaar, though worth a visit, is a heavily-reconstructed tourist trap; the surrounding streets, including older concrete apartment blocks and downmarket malls, give a better sense of everyday urban life.

Yu bazaar

Jiushi Corp. Headquarters

Foster + Partners (Norman FOSTER) with ECADI, 1995–2001

久事公司总部
黄浦区中山南路28号
28 South Zhongshan Road, Huangpu
❖ 31.2270, 121.4952

Construction on this, the firm's first project in mainland China, began shortly after the ban on foreign architects was lifted. The form of the tower curves towards the river, and the core is offset to ensure good views of both Pudong and The Bund. At the base, a retail podium responds to the smaller scale of the surrounding neighbourhoods. The tower's design, featuring sky-gardens and an innovative triple-skin glazing system, is a close relative of Foster's celebrated Commerzbank HQ (Frankfurt, 1991–97), and a forerunner of the "Gherkin" in London (1997–2004), at least in terms of public space, sustainability, and technical detailing. Representing international best practices of the time, the tower heralded the re-emergence of Shanghai as a forward-thinking global city.

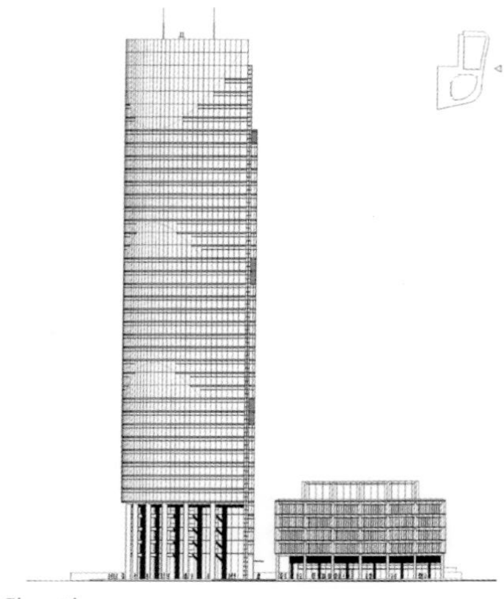

Elevation

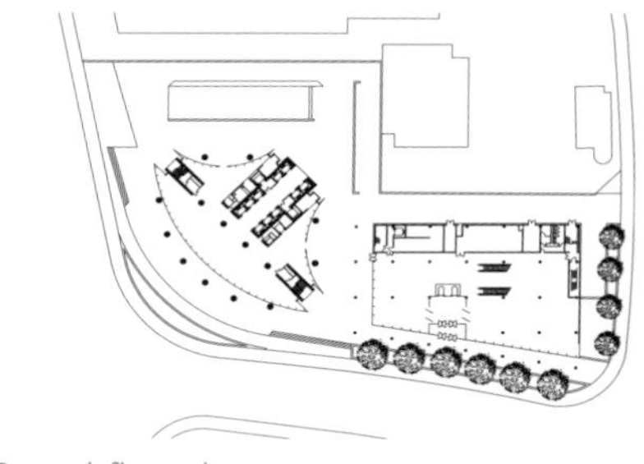

Ground-floor plan

Drawings courtesy Foster + Partners

Waterhouse Hotel

Neri&Hu Design and Research Office (Lyndon NERI & Rossana HU), 2010

水舍 – 南外滩精品酒店
黄浦区毛家园路1 – 3号
1–3 Maojiayuan Rd., Huangpu
❖ 31.2222,121.5011

Originally built in the 1930s as the Japanese occupation army headquarters, and later used as a warehouse, this space has been transformed into a boutique hotel whose oxidised steel addition references the rusting ships in nearby docks, and whose courtyard-facing rooms seem to comment on the voyeuristic potential of shared social space. The ageing surfaces of the interior are brought into dialogue with clean gallery-white surfaces throughout, sparking a discussion on the value of historic architecture during an economic boom. In the "post-**Xintiandi**" era (p. 171), such renovation projects became potentially lucrative alternatives to *tabula-rasa* development. The rooftop bar, with fine views, is publicly accessible.

© Derryck Menere, courtesy Neri & Hu

Longitudinal section

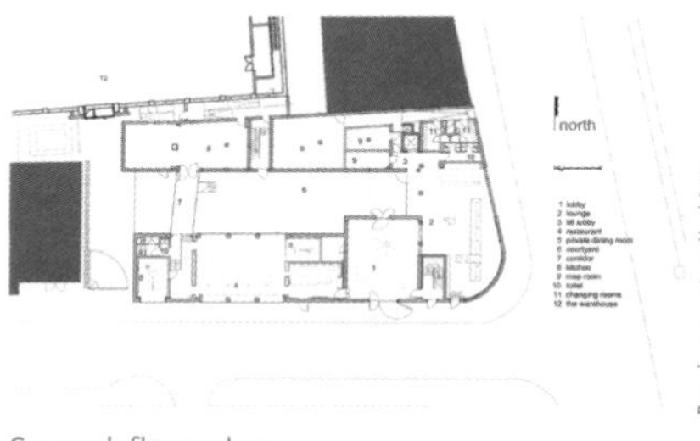

Ground-floor plan

Drawings courtesy Neri & Hu

The Bund/Wai Tan

SH 09

1842–1930s

外滩
黄浦区中山东一路
Zhongshan East 1st Rd., Huangpu
❖ 31.2385, 121.4859

Shanghai's famous Concession-era waterfront skyline was constructed first as a series of simple trading houses and docks in the years after the 1842 Treaty of Nanking "opened" China to wider foreign trade through a number of port cities. The trading houses were eventually replaced by ever-grander structures, and by Shanghai's 1930s heyday, this quay along the Huangpu River had been transformed into the banking centre of East Asia, the impressive Neo-Classical and Art Deco façades representing the flow of international capital through Shanghai. The **China Merchants' Building** (H, p. 158) is a remnant of the Bund's first incarnation, with a recessed upper portico typical of trading halls of the time, and a restrained material palette of stone and brick. The **Hong Kong & Shanghai Bank** (I, p. 159) and the Customs House (J) represent a second phase of development, with a more elaborate ornamental programme. In the late 1930s, the style of structures on the Bund started to shift towards a monolithic Art Deco style, with emphasis on clean vertical lines and minimal yet deeply symbolic ornamentation, as at the **Bank of China** (R, p. 160). When the foreign institutions were removed from their offices (and the country) following the communist revolution of 1949, many of the Bund's buildings became home to government offices, and were thus spared demolition. Meanwhile, in the century-plus since the Bund was first developed, Shanghai has been literally sinking due to aquifer depletion, and today the street level can in fact be lower than the river level, depending on the season. This is the reason for the raised waterfront promenade, completed in 2010 to coincide with the World Expo. This raised platform not only provides great views of Shanghai's other, newer skyline across the river in Pudong's Lujiazui district, but acts as a retaining wall holding back the river. The latest landscape and urban revitalisation project was led by Chan Krieger Sieniewicz (now NBBJ Boston).

The Bund: Elevations, drawings courtesy Simon Fieldhouse

The Bund

A. Meteorological Signal Tower (now Bund Museum), 1908 **B. McBain Building (No. 1)** (now Asia Building), 1916 **C. Shanghai Club (No. 2)** (now Waldorf Astoria), 1910 **D. Union Building (No. 3),** Palmer & Turner, 1922 **E. Nissin Building (No. 5),** 1925 **F. Russel & Co. (No. 6)** (now China Merchants' Bank), 1897 **G. Great Northern Telegraph Corporation (No. 7)** (now Bangkok Bank), Atkinson & Dallas, 1908 **H. China Merchants' Company Building (No. 9)** (now China Merchants' Bank), 1901 **I. Hong Kong & Shanghai Banking Corporation (No. 12)** (now Shanghai Pudong Development Bank), Palmer & Turner, 1921–1923 **J. Jianghai Custom House (No. 13)** (now Shanghai Customs House), 1927 **K. China Bank of Communications (No. 14)** (now Shanghai Council of Trade Unions), C. H. Gonda, 1948 **L. Russo-Chinese Bank (No. 15)** (now Shanghai Gold Exchange), Heinrich Bake, 1901 **M. Bank of Taiwan (No. 16)** (now China Merchants' Bank), 1924 **N. North China Daily News (No. 17)** (now AIA Insurance), 1921 **O. Chartered Bank of India, Australia, & China (No. 18)** (now Standard Chartered Bank), Tug Wilson of Palmer & Turner, 1923 **P. Palace Hotel (No. 19)** (now Peace Hotel south building), 1906 **Q. Sassoon House & Cathay Hotel (No. 20)** (now Peace Hotel), Palmer & Turner, 1929 **R. Bank of China, 1937 (No. 23) S. Yokohama Specie Bank (No. 24)** (now Industrial & Commercial Bank of China), Tug Wilson and Frank Collard of Palmer & Turner, 1924 **T. Yangtze Insurance Association (No. 26)** (now Agricultural Bank of China), Palmer & Turner, 1920 **U. Jardine Matheson & Co. (No. 27)** (now Foreign Trade Mansion/EWO), 1920–1922 **V. Glen Line Eastern Agencies (No. 28)** (now Shanghai Broadcasting Board), Tug Wilson of Palmer & Turner, 1922 **W. Banque de l'Indochine (No. 29)** (now China Everbright Bank), Atkinson & Dallas, 1914 **X. Consulate General of the UK (No. 33)** (now Peninsula Hotel), 1871–1873 **Y. Monument to the People's Heroes**, 1993 **Z. Waibaidu Bridge (Garden Bridge)**, 1906

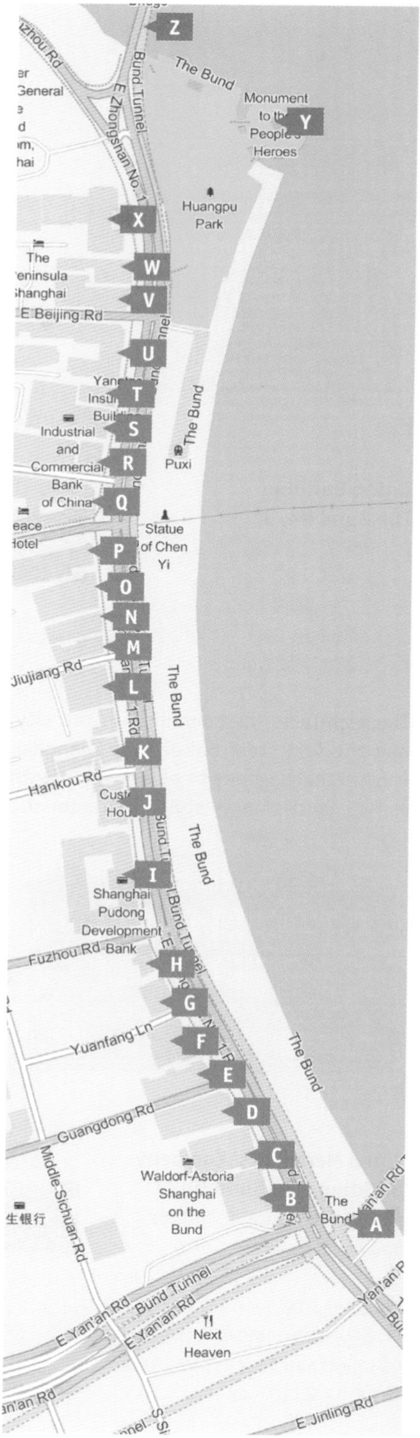

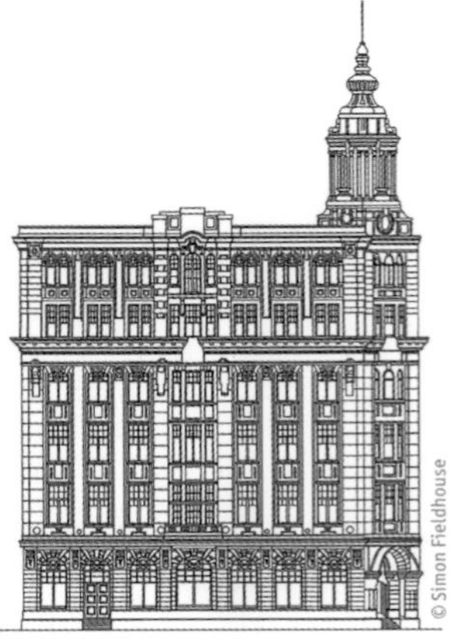

Elevation

Union Building
The Bund No. 3
PALMER & TURNER, 1916

SH 10

外滩三号，黄浦区中山东一路3号
3 Zhongshan East 1st Rd., Huangpu
❖ 31.2361, 121.4865

The architects' first building in the city, and the first steel building in Shanghai, it nevertheless hews to older models with a neo-Renaissance style characteristic of the second wave of construction on the Bund (compare to older structures like the **China Merchants' Company Building**, below). A 2004 restoration by Michael GRAVES added a narrow atrium, and a more recent intervention by Neri & Hu Design Research Office stripped down the top floor to its structure, in an appealingly elemental restaurant design.

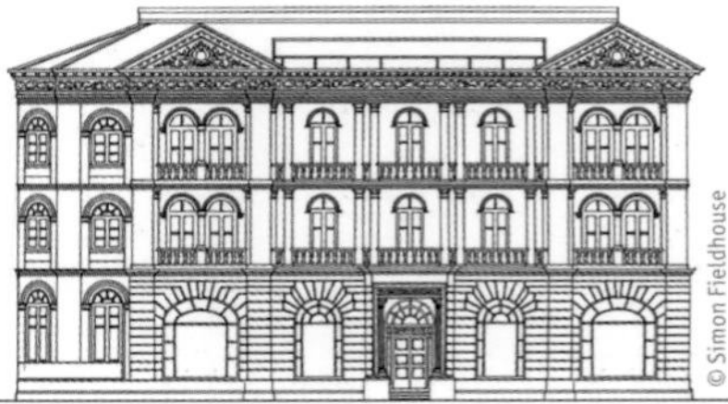

Elevation

China Merchants' Company Building, The Bund No. 9
Atkinson & Dallas Architects and Civil Engineers, 1901

SH 11

旗昌洋行大楼
黄浦区中山东一路9号
9 Zhongshan East 1st Rd., Huangpu
❖ 31.2374, 121.4859

This, one of the oldest buildings on the Bund, features an upper-level arcade typical of trading houses in hotter, more humid, parts of Southeast Asia; a structure such as this would have been typical in Hong Kong or Guangzhou at the time. The stripped-down Neo-Classical, tripartite façade marks this as a stylistic import, while the upper-level portico indicates some concession to the climate. It is one of two red-brick structures amid the Bund's grey-stone architecture (with the South Building of the Peace Hotel), and may thus be compared to Shanghai's *shikumen* blocks, of the same era and material. This is a transitional project, representing encroaching modernity; the structure is primarily stone, brick, and timber, but the external corridors are supported by eight steel columns, an innovation for Shanghai at the time. After a period of disrepair, restoration work was initiated by CHANG Qing Studio in 2001.

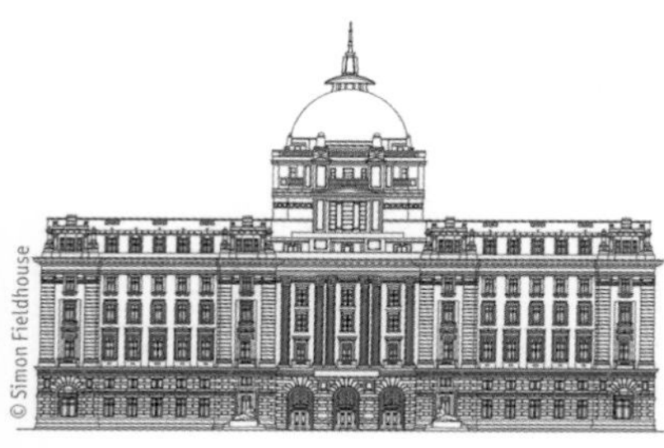

Elevation

HSBC Building (Hongkong and Shanghai Banking Corporation) The Bund No. 12

SH 12

PALMER & TURNER, 1923

汇丰银行大楼
黄浦区中山东一路12号
12 Zhongshan East 1st Rd., Huangpu
❖ 31.2380, 121.4856

The largest bank building in Asia, and second-largest in the world at the time of completion, this building represents the power, prestige and influence the bank had in Concession-era Shanghai. Neo-Classical in style, the façade is characterised by tripartite divisions both vertically and horizontally, with a recessed portico at the centre (perhaps referencing the older trading houses – see the **China Merchants' Company Building**, opposite), and capped by a distinctive central dome. Under the dome, in the opulent polished-marble lobby, mosaics depict the twelve signs of the zodiac and the eight world cities where HSBC had a presence at the time, each personified as a Greek god. Its classical pretensions and stone cladding conceal a modern steel structure, in the typical duality of the late Beaux-Arts. Two bronze lions flank the door, named after managers in Hong Kong and Shanghai. Another pair guarded HSBC in Hong Kong.

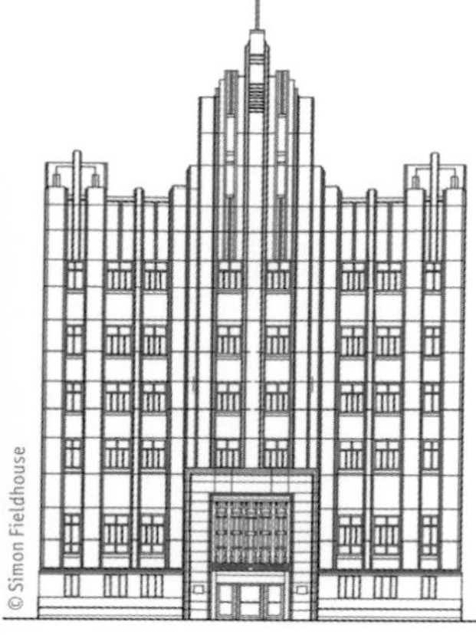

Elevation

China Bank of Communications The Bund No. 14

SH 13

C. H. GONDA , 1948

上海市总工会，黄浦区中山东一路14号
14 Zhongshan East 1st Rd., Huangpu
❖ 31.2391, 121.4855

Designed in the 1930s but delayed by a decade of war, this was the last building built on the Bund before the 1949 Communist victory. The somewhat severe Art Deco, lacking regional motifs, is less eclectic than that of the **Bank of China** (p. 160); it approaches the "Stripped Classicism" popular worldwide in these years. The façade's vertical emphasis seems to want a taller structure, though the rhythmic composition is charming.

Peace Hotel
The Bund No. 20

PALMER & TURNER, 1926–1929

SH 14

和平饭店（沙逊大厦）
黄浦区南京东路20号
20 East Nanjing Rd., Huangpu
❖ 31.2412, 121.4852

Restored to glory after years of alternating usage as a hotel or municipal offices, the former Cathay Hotel (or simply, "Sassoon House") was Sir Victor Sassoon's crowning achievement, representing the pinnacle of his family's domination of Shanghai business and real estate in the early twentieth century. Such was Sassoon's political pull that no taller building was built on the Bund during Shanghai's late-colonial boom. The building is a monumental Art Deco pastiche with slight regional flavour in ornamentation, but primarily composed of abstract forms like the pyramidal copper roof, faced with copper. Today the Peace Hotel has expanded to The Bund No. 19 (across the road to the south), a Neo-Renaissance brick structure dating to 1906.

Elevation

Bank of China
The Bund No. 23

PALMER & TURNER, with LU Qianshou, 1937

SH 15

中国银行大楼
黄浦区中山东一路23号
23 Zhongshan East 1st Rd., Huangpu
❖ 31.2415, 121.4853

One of the last structures completed on the Bund, and one of the tallest at seventeen floors, the Bank of China represents the best of Shanghai's distinctive Art Deco style. Its monolithic massing is emphasised by vertical slot windows, and "oriental" ornamentation is reduced to abstract pattern, aside from the distinctive pagoda roof. The massing, structural systems and ornamentation can be fruitfully compared to the Royal Asiatic Society (now **Rockbund Art Museum**, opposite) as representative of the architects' evolving style through the 1930s.

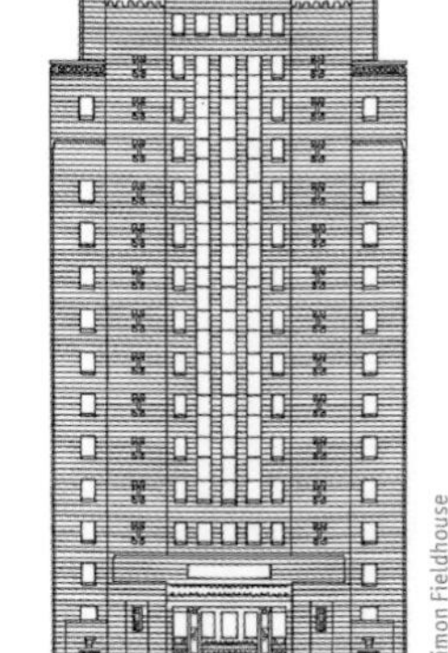

© Simon Fieldhouse

Elevation

Exterior view

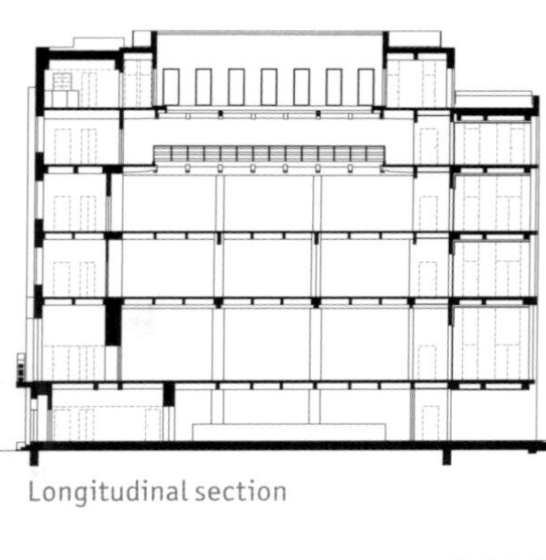
Longitudinal section

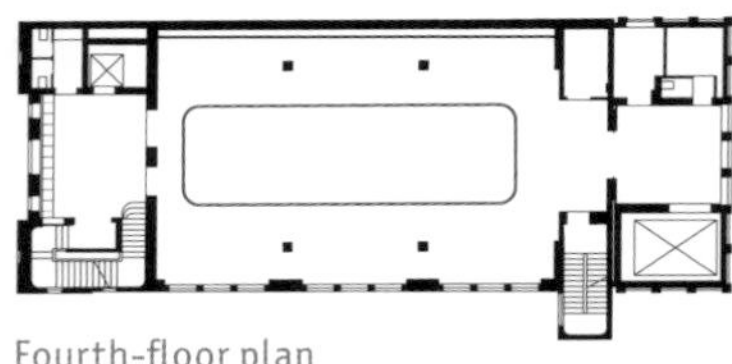
Fourth-floor plan

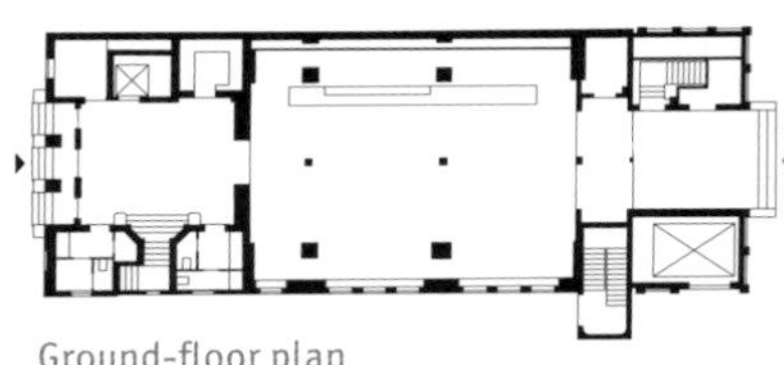
Ground-floor plan

Interior view

Site plan

All images courtesy David Chipperfield Architects

Rockbund Art Museum

SH 16

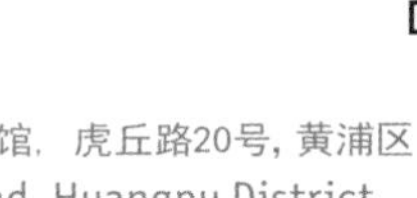

PALMER & TURNER, 1932
David CHIPPERFIELD Architects, 2006–2010

上海外滩美术馆，虎丘路20号，黄浦区
20 Huqiu Road, Huangpu District
❖ 31.2432, 121.4832

This contemporary art gallery was created through creative renovation of the Art Deco gallery-museum of the British Royal Asiatic Society. The original ornamental programme, typical of Western work in Asia at this date, makes use of such "oriental" motifs as oracle-bone script, *I Ching* hexagram grilles, and stone-bridge balustrades. The renovation leaves intact the stoic exterior massing and front façade, adding a new block at the rear to accommodate museum services and an service lift. Inside, the architects carve out a triple-height atrium overlooked by the surrounding galleries. This has given new opportunities for curation; several site-specific pieces have exploited the opportunity to encounter the same piece from multiple levels. The museum anchors the redevelopment of the whole block: eleven restoration-conversions, all under the auspices of David Chipperfield Architects.

China Baptist Publication Building and Christian Literature Society Building
László HUDEC, 1932

SH 17

真光大楼
黄浦区圆明园路209号
209 Yuanmingyuan Rd., Huangpu
❖ 31.2450, 121.4830

Connected mid-block, this pair represents Hudec at his most eclectic, applying Neo-Gothic ornamentation to otherwise modern buildings. In each, a central tower anchors a façade with progressive setbacks, a legally unnecessary but surely appreciated design that would allow daylight to reach the streets below. Hudec was likely aware of New York's 1916 zoning resolution that led to similar typologies there. While Hudec was capable of working in Art Deco or Streamline-Moderne style, here he seems to have consciously selected a style appropriate for his pious clients. This is most evident in the pointed cathedral arch that anchors the façade of the Christian Literature Society Building, though his angular treatment of Gothic arches is also suggestive of German brick Expressionism. The central tower of the China Baptist Publication Building could be read as a precursor to the architect's masterpiece, the Park Hotel, and both are worth comparing to, say, Raymond HOOD's Radiator Building of ten years earlier, in New York.

Broadway Mansions
PALMER & TURNER, with Bright FRASER, 1934

SH 18

百老汇大厦，虹口区北苏州路20号
20 Bei Suzhou Road, Hongkou District
❖ 31.2462, 121.4853

Shanghai's second-tallest building at the time of its construction, this late Concession-era apartment block remained one of the city's most prominent buildings until high-rise construction resumed in earnest in the 1980s. Palmer & Turner designed a large number of buildings in Shanghai, but until the early 1930s they tended to work in a Neo-Classical style. Broadway Mansions represents a shift in the firm's work towards a simplified Modernism, and was seen at the time as confirmation of Shanghai's cosmopolitan character. The plan arrangement was based loosely on a figure eight, a lucky number in Chinese culture. Functioning today as a luxury hotel, this Art Deco ziggurat acts as a visual terminus for the Bund promenade, offering excellent views of the Concession-era waterfront skyline.

Park Hotel

SH 26

László HUDEC, 1934

国际饭店，黄浦区南京西路170号
170 W Nanjing Rd., Huangpu
❖ 31.2354, 121.4671

Considered Hudec's masterpiece, the Park Hotel is a dark, Gothic Art Deco design modelled on New York skyscrapers of the era, if not on Raymond HOOD's Radiator Building explicitly. Here, Hudec shows a clear awareness of the evolution of skyscraper design after the 1922 Chicago Tribune competition, when Hood (along with winner Eliel SAARINEN) proved the suitability of quasi-Gothic verticality to unite a skyscraper's main block and upper setbacks while emphasising vertical thrust. The continuity of line running up the façade means that neither the exterior "piers" nor the upper "buttresses" can be purely structural: without their aesthetic contribution, the building would have appeared somewhat squat, with an awkward transition to the "crown." Hudec's eclectic stylistic range is evident when comparing this (and the similar **Baptist Publication** and **Christian Literature Society Buildings,** opposite) with the **Grand Cinema**, just down the block. But all make clear an interest in strong geometric massing, worldly inspiration, technological sophistication, as well as an enthusiastic, client-pleasing attitude.

Grand Cinema

SH 27

László HUDEC, 1932

大光明电影院，
黄浦区南京西路216号
216 W Nanjing Rd., Huangpu
❖ 31.2348, 121.4665

Demonstrating Hudec's eclecticism and knowledge of global design trends, this brightly-lit, Streamline-Moderne cinema is perhaps the most modern of the architect's designs. Its minimal, volumetric form is emphasised through material and light.

Shanghai Museum of Art (Shanghai Race Club)

SH 29

1933

上海美术馆，黄浦区南京西路325号
325 W Nanjing Rd., Huangpu
❖ 31.2328, 121.4665

This eclectic building demonstrates the transition from a strict Neo-Classical to a regionalist Art Deco style during Shanghai's Concession-era economic heyday. Formerly, it was the clubhouse for the British racecourse (now People's Park).

Tomorrow Square

SH 30

John PORTMAN & Associates, with SIADR, 1997–2003

明天广场
黄浦区南京西路399号
399 W. Nanjing Rd., Huangpu
❖ 31.2322, 121.4653

One of the tallest in Shanghai, this hotel and office tower marks its programmatic transition with a mid-tower 45-degree rotation, lending the tower its distinctive profile. The retail podium strives for the sectional interest of Portman's best work, with triple-height slices of space and bridges connecting tower to base, but the constrained site limits spatial complexity.

Shanghai Grand Theatre

SH 31

Arte CHARPENTIER Architects, 1998

上海大剧院
黄浦区人民大道300号
300 Renmin Ave., Huangpu
❖ 31.2314, 121.4676

Also known as the Shanghai Opera House (after its most popular resident performing company), the theatre sits prominently on the north side of People's Square. Together with the **Shanghai Museum** and the **Urban Planning Exhibition Centre** (below), it forms a core of a cultural district, formed during Shanghai's 1990s shift to a service and creative-class economy.

Shanghai Museum

SH 32

Shanghai Xian Dai (XING Tonghe), 1993–1995

上海博物馆，黄浦区人民大道201号
201 Renmin Ave., Huangpu
❖ 31.2304, 121.4708

One of the major cultural venues of People's Square, and one of China's first major museums, the design is based on the traditional cosmological model that describes heaven as round and the earth as square (see **Temple of Heaven,** p. 080), and also bears some resemblance to the archaeological objects displayed within, including Chinese coins and ancient cooking vessels.

Shanghai Urban Planning Exhibition Centre

SH 33

LING Benli/ECADI, 2000

上海城市规划展示馆，黄浦区人民大道100号
100 Renmin Ave., Huangpu
❖ 31.2333, 121.4707

This large museum of urbanism is of note mainly for its giant model of central Shanghai, showing the projected shape of the city in 2020 and beyond. The building's design is a cluttered collision of metaphors: the symmetrical block is apparently inspired by the gates in ancient city walls, while the sprouting parasol roof is modelled loosely on blooming magnolia flowers.

Jingan Temple

SH 35

Various, 1216–2010

静安寺，静安区南京西路1686号
1686 W. Nanjing Rd., Jing'an
❖31.2252, 121.4407

Lending its name to a district and a subway interchange, the "Temple of Peace and Tranquillity" appropriately marks the end of bustling Nanjing Road. Placards claim an "ancient" origin in 247 CE, but admit it had a different name and location. The temple was relocated here in 1216 CE, and has been here since, except for a period when it was replaced with a plastics factory (shuttered in the 1980s). The current structure is of recent vintage.

Plaza 66

SH 41

Kohn Pedersen Fox (KPF), Frank C. Y. FENG Architects, ECADI, 1994–2001

恒隆广场 – 静安区南京西路1266号
1266 W. Nanjing Rd., Jing'an
❖ 31.2291, 121.4489

Plaza 66 is one of the earliest and best examples of a now-common typology: the tower supported on a full-block, mixed-use podium. The five-level retail base, meant to respond to the scale of *lilong*, provides shopping and dining amenities for the office towers, which were intended to be linked by a bridge (see elevation). When completed, the 66-floor (288 m) Tower One was among the four tallest in Shanghai.

Shanghai Centre

SH 40

John PORTMAN & Associates 1990

上海商城，静安区南京西路1376号
1376 W. Nanjing Rd., Jing'an
❖ 31.2286, 121.4473

In this early mixed-use tower-and-podium scheme, the retail block is carved away at the lower levels, allowing hotel drop-offs and creating an interesting multi-level pedestrian circulation scheme. "Oriental" details, like over-scaled column capitals that mimic traditional wood joinery, now seem dated, but spatially the complex is quite successful, and the covered plaza provides respite from the summer sun.

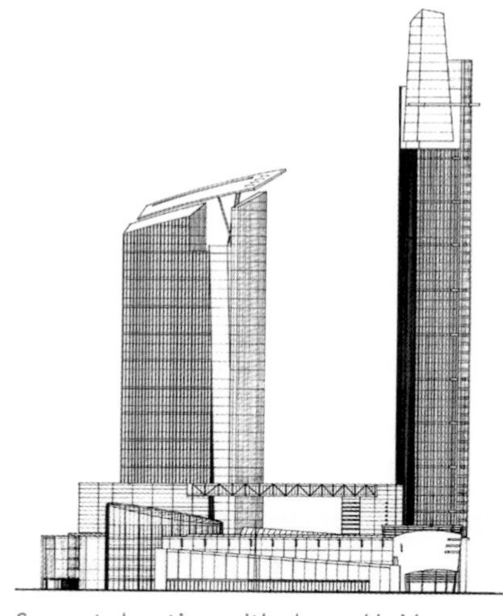

Concept elevation, with planned bridge

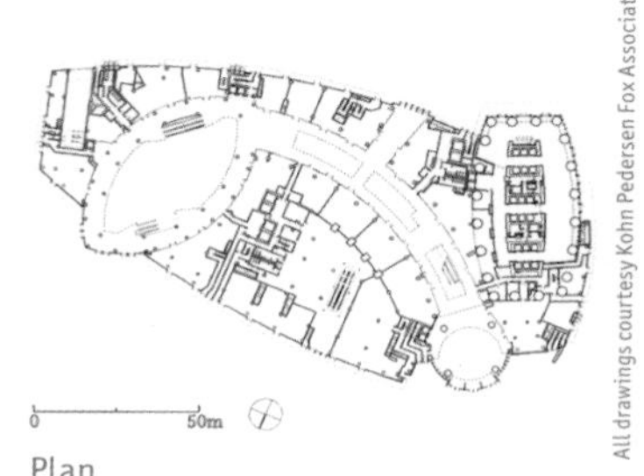

Plan

All drawings courtesy Kohn Pedersen Fox Associates

© Christian Dubrau

Shanghai Exhibition Centre

SH 43

ANDERLEV & JISLOVA/CHEN Zhi
1955

上海展览中心
静安区延安中路1000号
1000 Middle Yan'an Rd., Jing'an
❖31.2263, 121.4483

Originally known as the "Sino-Soviet Friendship Hall," this exhibition hall and conference centre was built to house an exhibit highlighting Soviet industrial and cultural achievements. The central tower, capped with a red star, is apparently modelled on St Petersburg's Admiralty Building, and was the tallest structure in Shanghai from its construction until 1988. While the ornate imperial/Neo-Classical design may seem odd for a building built to celebrate the mutual admiration of two Communist regimes, the Socialist-Realist style is in line with lingering Stalinist architectural policy in the Eastern Bloc, which sought representative "palaces for the people." The exhibition centre remains one of Shanghai's largest cultural venues, and hosts events throughout the year.

Shanghai Municipal Council Abattoir (Old Millfun/1933)

SH 46

C.H. STABLEFORD, 1933
RENEW (ZHAO Chongxin), 2010

1933 老场坊
虹口区沙泾路10号
No. 10 Shajing Lu, Hongkou
❖ 31.2565, 121.4877

A fascinating remnant of Shanghai's colonial past, this slaughterhouse, built to British designs by Chinese labour, is essentially a machine for killing. Animals were led up a system of ramps in the perimeter block, then crossed bridges to the central, cylindrical tower (automatically sorted, thanks to the bridges' varying widths). From the top of the tower, the animals were systematically eviscerated, moving downward step by step, culminating in the loading of raw meat into trucks at the ground floor. With hindsight, these logistically-derived forms take on a gestural energy, not dissimilar from the work of architects self-consciously celebrating the expressive potential of concrete for its own sake. A recent, tasteful renovation has transformed this Piranesian, proto-Brutalist space into a mixed-use development with restaurants, boutique shops, and an event space atop the central core. While its retail success seems questionable, the "Old Millfun" remains popular with architectural tourists and wedding photographers.

M50 Urban Renovation

SH 49

DAtrans Architecture Office, 2000–2005+

M50创意园，普陀区莫干山路50号
50 Moganshan Rd., Putuo
❖ 31.2495, 121.4446

One of Shanghai's "Creative Clusters" (government-sanctioned districts devoted to "creative industry" functions), this collection of former factory buildings has been converted into an arts district, populated by small galleries and a few artists' workshops. From the year 2000 onwards, artists began moving into the vacated spaces to take advantage of low costs. Over time, as the complex became more and more popular and rents began to rise,

artists' studios were replaced with galleries, cafés, and offices for creative design agencies. The district remains one of the better spots to see Chinese contemporary art in Shanghai, but it has lost the ad-hoc character of its early days. M50 is often seen as an early indicator of Shanghai's post-industrial transformation into a global city of arts and culture.

Cité Bourgogne

SH 55

China Jianye Real Estate Company, 1930

步高里
黄浦区陕西南路287号
287 S. Shaanxi Rd., Huangpu
❖ 31.2090, 121.4579

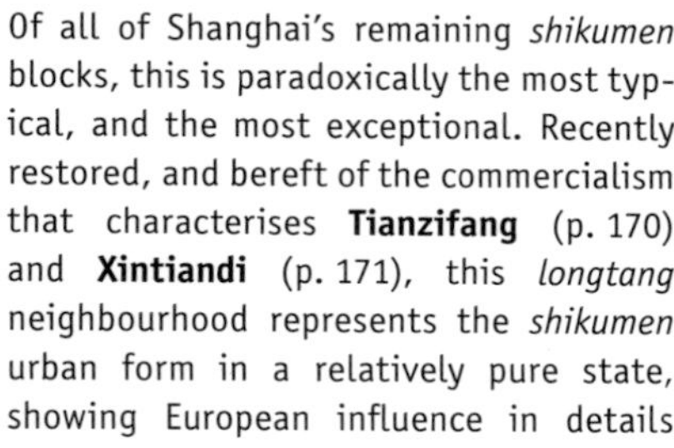

Of all of Shanghai's remaining *shikumen* blocks, this is paradoxically the most typical, and the most exceptional. Recently restored, and bereft of the commercialism that characterises **Tianzifang** (p. 170) and **Xintiandi** (p. 171), this *longtang* neighbourhood represents the *shikumen* urban form in a relatively pure state, showing European influence in details

and Chinese planning in organisation. The block is defined by arterial roads at the perimeter, cut north-south by a major internal lane, and further divided east-west by narrow alleys that lead to small entry courtyards behind stone gates. All this creates a fine social gradient from public to private – one that visitors would do well to respect.

Taikang Terrace

SH 56

A00 Architecture, 2009–2012

黄浦区建国中路169号
169 Middle Jianguo Rd., Huangpu
❖ 31.2102, 121.4629

Modelled as an extension of the wildly successful **Tianzifang** redevelopment (p. 170), this small retail, restaurant, and entertainment complex is woven into the fabric of an historic *shikumen* block. Several renovated structures with crisply-detailed brick, steel and glass store-fronts are linked by open-air corridors. Upper-level spaces are accessible only via exterior staircases, where one can gain views over the surrounding blocks of the former French Concession.

Sinan Mansions

SH 57

Arte CHARPENTIER Architects, 2010

思南公馆，黄浦区思南路51号
51 Sinan Rd., Huangpu
❖ 31.2166, 121.4641

This cluster of French Concession mansions has been completely reconstructed, transforming the private residential district into a retail and entertainment complex on the "Xintiandi" model. The redevelopment is not quite so successful here, as attention to detail has been sacrificed somewhat, and the majority of the "public" space is given over to private gardens for the (fenced off) hotel suites that form the majority of the complex.

The Bridge 8

SH 58

HMA Architects, 2005

八号桥
黄浦区建国中路10号
10 Middle Jianguo Rd., Huangpu
❖ 31.2124, 121.4663

One of Shanghai's "creative clusters," this complex of former auto shops has been converted into office and exhibition space for the creative industries. A large bridge connects the two sides, but functions primarily as an elevated exhibition hall, with views down the tree-lined street. The north side is especially worth exploring for its mix of post-industrial spaces and variety of creative-industry tenants.

The industrial origins of the structures are emphasised through the ample use of skylights, exposed trusses, and cantilevered stairs, but the skin of the complex is redesigned to tie the disparate buildings together. The name "Bridge" refers not only to the sky-bridge and catwalks linking the buildings together, but also to symbolic ambitions to link past with present and foreign with local.

Tianzifang/Taikang Road Arts District

SH 59

1930s/2000s

田子坊，黄浦区泰康路210号
210 Taikang Rd., Huangpu
❖ 31.2099, 121.4647

One of Shanghai's major attractions over the past two decades, this *shikumen* block gradually transformed from a quiet residential neighbourhood to a hub for Shanghai's nascent arts scene, then to a bustling commercial district, full of boutique shops, restaurants, and (inevitably) tourists. The appeal is hard to deny, as this is one of the few places in town where outsiders have unfettered access to a traditional lane-house residential block, albeit one that has been radically transformed over the years. Many original structures remain, and dining here can offer a taste of life in a traditional *shikumen* lane house. Formally, like all *longtang* neighbourhoods, the large block is surrounded on the perimeter by large arterial streets, cut north-south through the centre by several smaller lanes, which

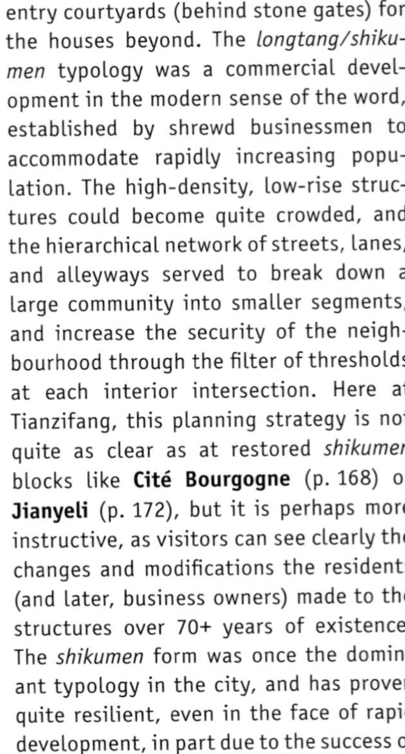

in turn feed narrow alleyways that lead to entry courtyards (behind stone gates) for the houses beyond. The *longtang/shikumen* typology was a commercial development in the modern sense of the word, established by shrewd businessmen to accommodate rapidly increasing population. The high-density, low-rise structures could become quite crowded, and the hierarchical network of streets, lanes, and alleyways served to break down a large community into smaller segments, and increase the security of the neighbourhood through the filter of thresholds at each interior intersection. Here at Tianzifang, this planning strategy is not quite as clear as at restored *shikumen* blocks like **Cité Bourgogne** (p. 168) or **Jianyeli** (p. 172), but it is perhaps more instructive, as visitors can see clearly the changes and modifications the residents (and later, business owners) made to the structures over 70+ years of existence. The *shikumen* form was once the dominant typology in the city, and has proven quite resilient, even in the face of rapid development, in part due to the success of Tianzifang and **Xintiandi** (opposite).

All photos courtesy Studio Shanghai

Xintiandi

Studio Shanghai, 2001

SH 60

上海新天地
黄浦区兴业路123弄
123 Xingye Rd., Huangpu
❖ 31.2217, 121.4703

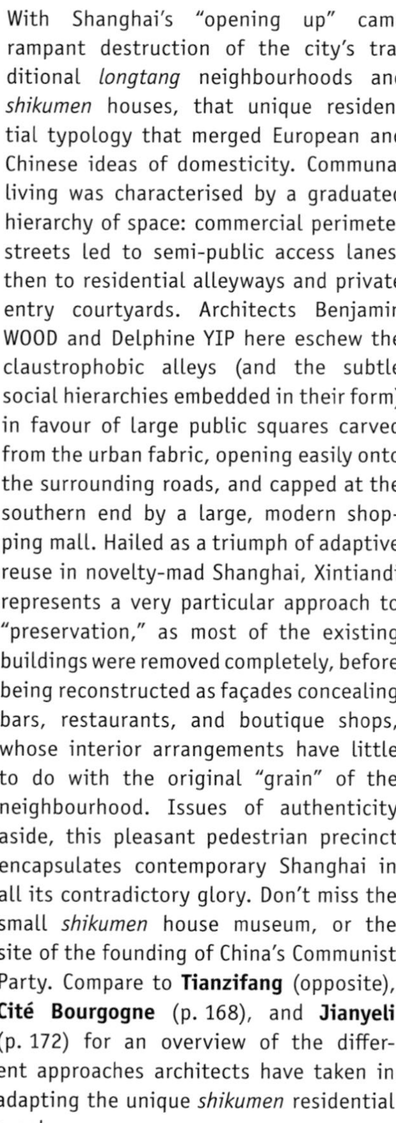

With Shanghai's "opening up" came rampant destruction of the city's traditional *longtang* neighbourhoods and *shikumen* houses, that unique residential typology that merged European and Chinese ideas of domesticity. Communal living was characterised by a graduated hierarchy of space: commercial perimeter streets led to semi-public access lanes, then to residential alleyways and private entry courtyards. Architects Benjamin WOOD and Delphine YIP here eschew the claustrophobic alleys (and the subtle social hierarchies embedded in their form) in favour of large public squares carved from the urban fabric, opening easily onto the surrounding roads, and capped at the southern end by a large, modern shopping mall. Hailed as a triumph of adaptive reuse in novelty-mad Shanghai, Xintiandi represents a very particular approach to "preservation," as most of the existing buildings were removed completely, before being reconstructed as façades concealing bars, restaurants, and boutique shops, whose interior arrangements have little to do with the original "grain" of the neighbourhood. Issues of authenticity aside, this pleasant pedestrian precinct encapsulates contemporary Shanghai in all its contradictory glory. Don't miss the small *shikumen* house museum, or the site of the founding of China's Communist Party. Compare to **Tianzifang** (opposite), **Cité Bourgogne** (p. 168), and **Jianyeli** (p. 172) for an overview of the different approaches architects have taken in adapting the unique *shikumen* residential typology.

Site plan

Courtesy Studio Shanghai

Jianyeli Shikumen Block

John PORTMAN & Associates, 2008–2013

建业里，徐汇区建国西路440号
440 W Jianguo Rd., Xuhui
❖ 31.2056, 121.4476

The *shikumen* typology (see Shanghai overview, p. 144) had always been a developer-driven way to address new populations in Shanghai (while enabling a rich spatial and social sequence in its interior lanes). Portman's project updates these features for a wealthier twenty-first century clientele, retaining the specific urban form of the site's lanes while adding modern amenities to the dwellings. The serviced apartments (essentially luxury hotel suites) to the west retain their original structure, but everything else has been reconstructed, in order to add a two-level basement (including private garages for each home, and an additional living level). The new town-houses often sprawl across three or four bays, enabling interior light-wells to serve the basements. At the street level, this does result in occasional "gates to nowhere;" a trade-off for retaining the rhythm of the old elevations. The end result: luxurious apartments in previously cramped conditions. Some local controversy has predictably resulted due to high prices displacing those who formerly lived in the block. On a strictly architectural level, Jianyeli offers hope that in some form or another, Shanghai's unique urban invention need not be swept aside by contemporary development. Compare to **Xintiandi** (p. 171).

Twelve at Hengshan

SH 65

Mario BOTTA, 2013

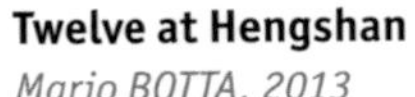

衡山路十二号酒店
徐汇区衡山路12号
12 Hengshan Rd., Xuhui
❖ 31.2069, 121.4416

This appealing luxury hotel sits along one of Shanghai's most popular nightlife streets, Hengshan Road, which was a major thoroughfare of the former French Concession. While somewhat out of scale with its context of old European-style villas, the architects' use of stark geometry has some great pay-offs, including a pleasant rooftop deck and an elliptical garden courtyard. The crisply-detailed terracotta façade is worth a close look.

Normandie Apartments

SH 67

László HUDEC, 1927

武康大楼
淮海中路1850号
1850 Middle Huaihai Rd., Xuhui
❖ 31.2062, 121.4336

A fine "flatiron" building on a triangular block, this apartment building represents Hudec at his most conservative, with an interpretation of the Italian *palazzo*. The tripartite organisation of the façade is typical for Neo-Classical buildings of the era, with a stone base giving way to brick infill above. The ground-level covered walkway provides shelter from the summer sun and winter rains, and evokes comparison with the arcades of Bologna.

Elevation

Z58 (Zhongtai Box)

KUMA Kengo, 2003–2008

SH 69

Z58创意之光，长宁区番禺路58号
58 Panyu Rd., Changning
❖ 31.2112, 121.4246

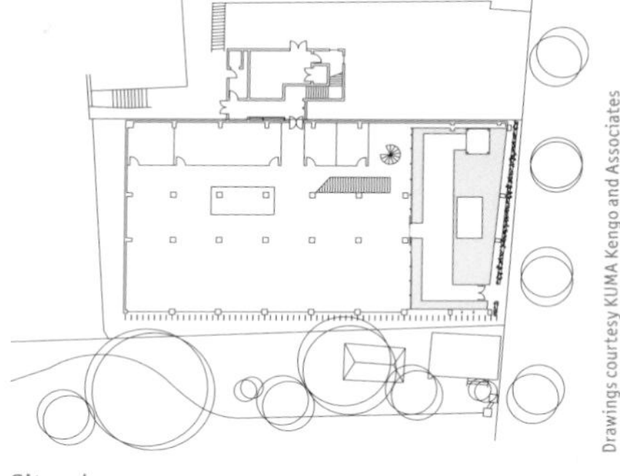

Site plan

Drawings courtesy KUMA Kengo and Associates

This small office building, notable mainly for its façade, features a fine entry lobby, seemingly inspired by the bridges and paths of traditional Chinese gardens, here abstracted as a linear causeway across a shallow reflecting pool. Beyond this, the building consists mainly of typical, if nicely-detailed, office space, flanked by a private garden. The façade, with its alternating bands of mirrored glass and dangling vegetation, is at once a denial and celebration of transparency. While no views are possible through this barrier, the panels reflect the street's pleasant canopy of plane trees, suggesting a deeper space beyond, and complicating conventional inside/outside relationships.

Red Town/Shanghai Sculpture Space

Taranta Creations, 2011

SH 70

红坊创意园区，
长宁区淮海西路570号
570 W. Huaihai Rd., Changning
❖ 31.2004, 121.4194

As in other "Creative Clusters," a number of industrial buildings have been renovated, but here a sculpture-peppered lawn provides one of Shanghai's rare open public spaces. Galleries, cafés, and restaurants vie with hip, post-industrial office suites. The long shed-like Shanghai Sculpture Space features a rotating collection of contemporary sculpture for free, public view. Taranta's own office is set inside the simple box of the former metalworks, with two floors joined by a twisted, tornado-shaped stair. The depth of an existing truss made it impossible to organise two habitable floors within the existing envelope, thus the entire upper floor was conceived as a continuous work surface, with work stations recessed within the depth of the structure.

SPSI Art Museum

SH 73

WANG Yan, 2010

上海油雕院美术馆
长宁区金珠路111号
111 Jinzhu Rd., Changning
❖ 31.2004, 121.3955

This small museum takes its structure and its name from the former occupant of the space, the Shanghai Painting and Sculpture Institute, but little else remains of the old studios. A large blank wall greets visitors across a paved plaza, and inside an off-centre sculptural staircase divides the plan into several smaller, but still connected, galleries. A narrow courtyard to the back completes the sequence.

Courtesy Atelier Deshaus

Long Museum (West Bund)

SH 78

Atelier Deshaus, 2011–2014

龙美术馆
3398龙腾大道，滨江，徐汇区
3398 Longteng Ave., Binjiang, Xuhui Dist,
❖31.1860, 121.4605

On a post-industrial site, with dimensions cued by pre-existing parking structures and coal equipment, this ensemble of half-vaults, cantilevered from their supporting walls with skylight gaps between, is one of the most interesting projects of the last few years. The acknowledged influence of Louis KAHN hints at Modernist priorities of space, light, module, and structure, and a love/hate relationship with industry.

Longhua Martyrs' Cemetery

SH 79

龙华烈士陵园
龙华西路180号
180 Longhua Lu, Xuihui
❖ 31.1786, 121.4443

This pleasant memorial park with a loaded history was once a part of the adjacent Longhua Temple's gardens. In 1927 the site was used as a prison and execution ground in a Guomindang purge of suspected communists. Ten years later, Japanese occupation forces operated Shanghai's largest civilian internment camp on the site (a development fictionalised in J.G. Ballard's *Empire of the Sun*). Today, anchored by a pyramidal mausoleum, spacious lawns are punctuated by large memorial sculptures in the late Socialist-Realist style, a rare and anachronistic sight in today's Shanghai. A portion of the site is dedicated to the preservation of several structures remaining from the war years. The Longhua Temple complex, a good example of Song Dynasty architecture, is worth a look, though most of its buildings are relatively recent reconstructions.

Power Station of Art

SH 86

Original Design Studio (ZHANG Ming & ZHANG Zi), 2006–2012; original power station, 1985

上海当代艺术博物
花园港路200号
200 Huayuangang Rd., Huangpu
❖ 31.2030, 121.4938

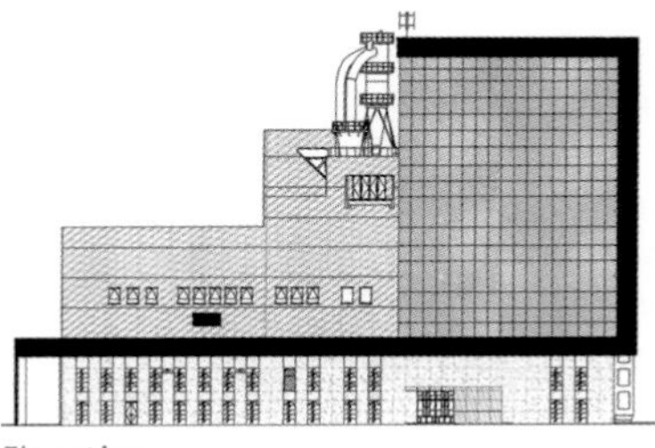

Elevation

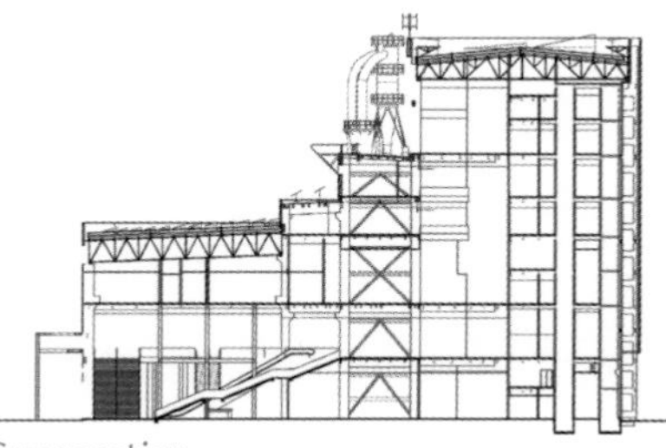

Cross section

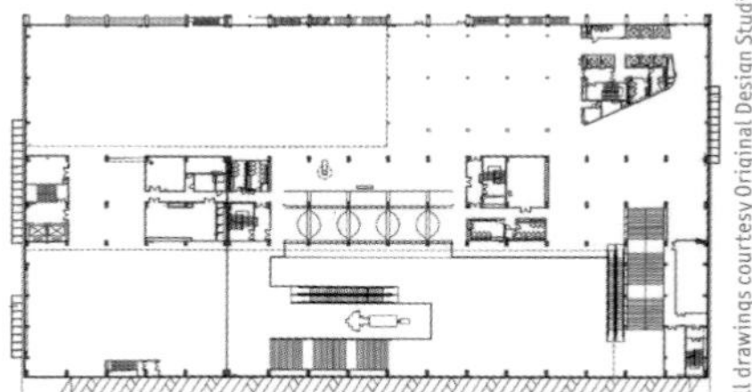

Plan

All drawings courtesy Original Design Studio

Alternatively known as Shanghai Museum of Contemporary Art (and thus, easily confused with the **Shanghai MoCA**, map p. 198), this former power plant was first converted into an exhibition hall in 2010, as the "Pavilion of Urban Future" for the World Expo. As a venue for world-class exhibitions, the building represents Shanghai's ambition to transform into a destination for arts and culture, not just commerce, and can thus be seen as an indicator of Shanghai's post-industrial evolution. Urbanistically, the Power Station acts as a beacon, its smokestack transformed into a giant LED thermometer, visible at some distance, thanks to its prominent waterfront location. The transformation of a power station into an art museum has a clear precedent in London's wildly successful Tate Modern (Herzog & de Meuron, 1994–2000), and while the large entry gallery here lacks the stark power of the Tate's Turbine Hall, a series of escalators and walkways that culminate in a large exterior terrace gives the building spatial interest and encourages curators to find unique ways to stage their exhibits. The key intervention was to open the building up, particularly by replacing the short ends and the top level (by the terrace) with glazed curtain walls. The architects later returned to add a rather stylish concrete parking garage, wrapping the smokestack. As of 2014, the surrounding area contained mostly fenced-off remnants of the 2010 Expo, but the museum aims to become an anchor for a new cultural district.

Houtan Park

Turenscape, 2010

SH 87

后滩公园，浦东新区世博大道
Shibo Ave., Pudong
❖ 31.1871, 121.4712

A legacy of the 2010 World Expo, this waterfront park was designed as a regenerative wetland: a demonstration of how a landscape design can act as a natural water purification system, a flood control mechanism, and a pleasing waterfront promenade. Water from the heavily-polluted Huangpu River enters at one end of the park, and progresses through a series of basins, where carefully selected plant life and water features act as natural filters. After processing, the water is safe enough for irrigation and other non-potable uses. The constructed wetland, replacing a concrete flood-wall, acts as a natural barrier where native plant species protect the soil from erosion and provide a habitat for local fauna. While the park lacks the spatial complexity of China's classical gardens (See Suzhou p. 210), a meandering path is nonetheless able to frame the scattered post-industrial follies that populate the park, and alternately mask and reveal views out to the river. As part of a city-wide initiative to increase green space in Shanghai, the park will eventually connect to a waterfront green-way that stretches from the former Expo site to Lujiazui and beyond.

Mercedes Benz Arena

WANG Xiao An/ECADI, 2009

SH 88

梅赛德斯-奔驰文化中心
浦东新区世博大道1200号
1200 Shibo Ave., Pudong
❖ 31.191291, 121.489391

Built for the 2010 World Expo, this performing arts centre houses a large 18,000 seat auditorium and a number of smaller theatres and cinemas, both within the upper "UFO," and below the artificial hill on which it sits. Access to the theatres occurs along the upper-level gallery, showcasing the 360-degree views. Along with the Expo Axis and China Art Palace, the arena is meant to serve as an anchor for a new cultural district on the former Expo site. As of 2014, this area remains somewhat underdeveloped, but this has become a fairly successful concert venue for internationally touring musicians, and its unique form and prominent site mark it as a major landmark on the southern Pudong waterfront.

River Mall (Expo Axis)

SBA International/ECADI
Knippers-Helbig, 2010

SH 91

中国2010年上海世博会世博轴
周家渡路，浦东
1368 Shibo Ave., Pudong
❖ 31.1858, 121.4880

This public retail and circulation spine was constructed for the 2010 World Exhibition, and remains as one of the few permanent structures from that event. The architects pierce the floor plates with doubly-curved "light cones" and cap the linear mall with a membrane roof. These ambitious, structurally-efficient forms can be fruitfully compared to the lightweight structures common to world exhibitions and Olympic venues for the past 60 years, and it's worth noting that both SBA and Knippers-Helbig hail from Stuttgart, whose Institute for Lightweight Structures has led research in this area since its founding by Frei Otto in 1964. Unfortunately, the Expo site has been slow to regain the vitality it had during the main event, but this building, at least, has recently reopened and once again provides a comfortable pedestrian path from the south Pudong waterfront to points of interest further from the river, like the **China Art Palace** (below) and **Mercedes Benz Arena** (opposite). While a true cultural district has so far failed to materialise here, this southern bank of the Huangpu remains an area to watch.

China Art Palace

South China Univ. Team
(HE Jingtang), 2010

SH 92

中华艺术宫
浦东新区上南路161号
161 Shangnan Rd., Pudong
❖ 31.1863, 121.4898

One of the few permanent structures of the 2010 World Exhibition, the former China Pavilion now houses a museum dedicated to (Party-approved) modern art. Known as the "Eastern Crown," the design is based on the corbelled *duogong* ("cap and block") brackets found in traditional architecture. The museum may soon be the anchor of a new cultural district.

Shanghai South Station

AREP/ECADI, 2006

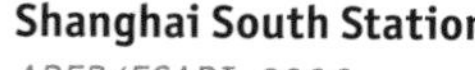

SH 93

上海南站，徐汇区动力北一路
Dongli North 1st Rd., Xuhui
❖31.1549, 121.4248

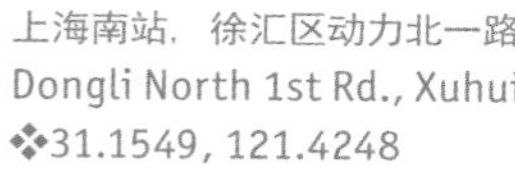

This modern, airy rail terminal consists of three main levels devoted to arrivals, platforms and departures, respectively. Such layered design aids efficiency in the loading and unloading of trains and provides complete separation between circulation paths, a boon to security. Sectionally, the building takes its cues from modern airport design, e.g. that of Foster + Partners (see **Capital Airport**, p. 106, and **Chek Lap Kok**, p. 365).

Photo courtesy SOM | Nick Merrick © Hedrich Blessing

Jin Mao Tower

SOM, SIADR, 1994–1998

SH 96

金茂大厦
浦东新区世纪大道88号
88 Century Ave., Pudong
❖ 31.2370, 121.5011

This stunning tower encapsulates the ambition and capabilities of architectural design in China in the late 1990s. Called the "Golden Prosperity Building," it was the tallest building in the PRC for a decade, and signalled the beginning of a period of unprecedented architectural production. Though now dwarfed by the **WFC** (p. 180) and **Shanghai Tower** (p. 181), this super-tall tower is perhaps the most stylish of the trio, and best expresses Shanghai's past and future at the turn of the millennium. The design is a pleasing synthesis of a variety of references; based in part on a traditional Chinese pagoda, the tower also fits comfortably into the grand tradition of the super-tall skyscraper. With its strong vertical emphasis, and stepped, illuminated crown, comparisons to the classic New York skyscrapers of the late 1920s and early 1930s are inevitable, and in the Jin Mao's Postmodern styling we find echoes of Shanghai's Art Deco heritage. The design is infused with auspicious numbers, from the octagonal core wall to the 88 occupiable floors, to the street address and 8 major super-columns. Programmatically, the tower consists of retail space at the base, offices above, and a hotel at the top, capped by an observation deck and several

Photo courtesy SOM | Nick Merrick © Hedrich Blessing

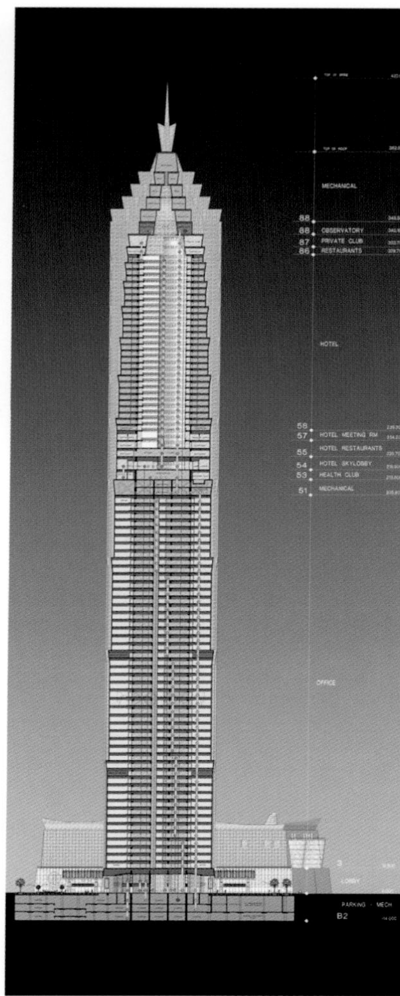

Section

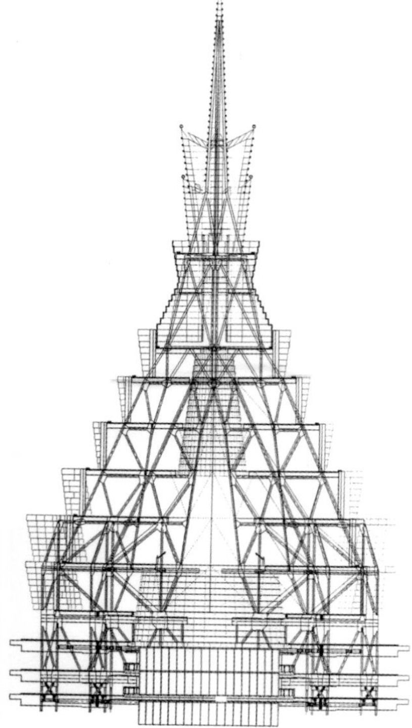
Structural section through pinnacle

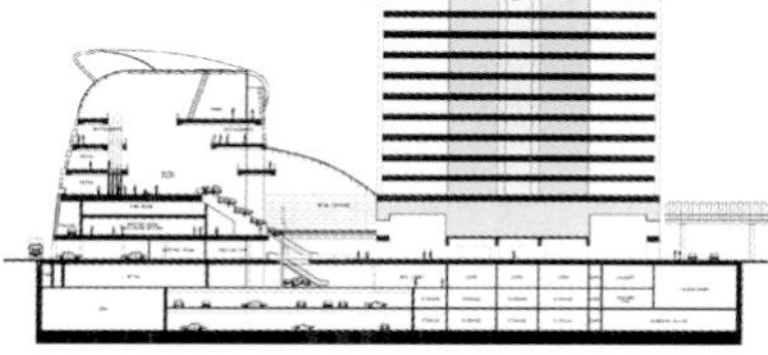
Section through podium

bars and restaurants. The hotel's thirty-storey internal atrium is one of the tallest in the world at around 150 metres clear, top to bottom. The spiral of balconies and the high-contrast lighting give visitors a sublime sense of vertigo. Featuring a number of structural innovations, the Jin Mao tower was a key project for architect Adrian SMITH, who would go on to design the **Zifeng Greenland Tower** in Nanjing (p. 129), **Pearl River Tower** in Guangzhou (p. 298), the Burj Khalifa in Dubai, and a number of ever-taller structures.

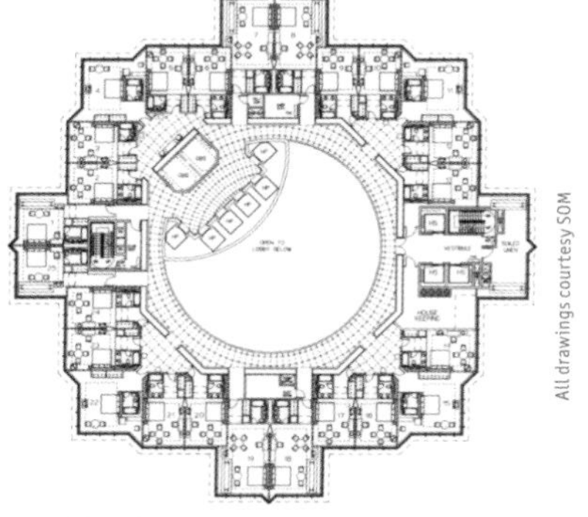
Hotel-level plan, with atrium

All drawings courtesy SOM

Photo by H. G. Esch; courtesy Kohn Pedersen Fox Associates

World Financial Centre

Kohn Pedersen Fox (KPF), 1997–2008

SH 97

上海环球金融中心
浦东新区世纪大道100号
100 Century Ave., Pudong
❖ 31.2363, 121.5030

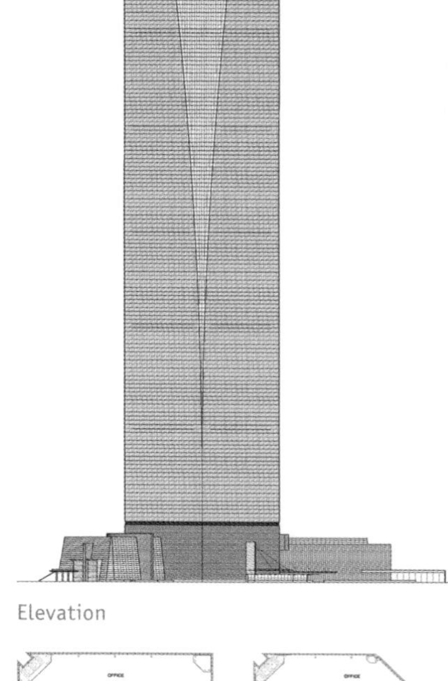

Elevation

Plans: office levels

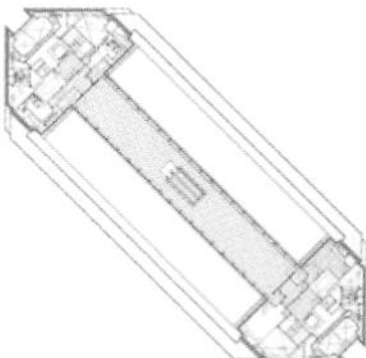

Plans: hotel, observation deck

Nicknamed "the bottle opener" for its distinctive, tapering profile and large crowning void, in fact the building's form is functionally driven. The lower levels are devoted to office space with deep floor plans, while upper levels are dedicated to hotel suites where a smaller, more efficient floor plan is more desirable. While the tapered form results in unique plans for nearly every floor, the simple sculptural profile makes a bold impact on Shanghai's Lujiazui skyline. The original design called for a circular void (based ostensibly on the "moon doors" of traditional Chinese gardens), but this was modified when comparisons were made to Japan's "rising sun" iconography, a suspicious reference given the project's Japanese developer (Mori Building Company). Formally, the tower represents a certain point in time when architectural design technology was dominated by bold, Boolean geometry, and can be fruitfully compared to the **Shanghai Tower** (opposite) with its formally plastic "parametric" design.

Shanghai Tower
Gensler, Thornton Tomasetti (engineer), TJAD, Shanghai Construction Group, 2010–2015

SH 98

上海中心大厦 花园石桥路 ， 浦东
Huayuanshiqiao Rd., Pudong
❖ 31.2355, 121.5009

China's tallest building, and the world's second-tallest, the Shanghai Tower is the third and final piece of Pudong's "supertall" cluster, an urban composition in the works since the early 1990s. The tower features the now-familiar mix of office space and hotel suites, anchored by a retail podium. In addition to height, the tower competes with its neighbours **Jin Mao** (p. 178) and **WFC** (opposite) in green technology *bona fides*: the tower is wrapped in sky-gardens, which act as an expanded double-skin, reducing interior heat gain. These serve a social function as well, housing observation decks, restaurants, and other public spaces, in a stated attempt to reconstitute Shanghai's vernacular courtyards and neighbourhood parks. Compare to the handling of sky-gardens at **Jiushi Corp.** (p. 155), **Hysan Place** (p. 361), and in different typologies, the **Vertical Courtyards** (p. 263), and **Poly U** (map p. 368). The twisted, asymmetrical form, rotating 120 degrees through its height, was chosen based on wind-tunnel studies; it's meant to reduce wind loading by nearly one quarter, permitting a massive savings in structure with the aid of parametric design tools to implement the requisite 7,000+ unique shapes of curtain wall panels. Seismic design also plays a role: the stiffened and weighted central "trunk" supports "branches" every 12 to 15 levels. These thickened refuge and mechanical areas extend to the outer surface and divide the building into nine structural and functional zones. To our eyes, this gives the super-tall building a visually comprehensible scale, and enhances the illusion that the building not only twists, but *spirals* upward.

All images © Gensler

Cutaway rendering of sky-gardens, showing extension of "branch" levels to outer surface

Oriental Pearl Tower

SH 99

JIANG Huan Chen, LIN Benlin, and ZHANG Xiulin/SIADR, 1994

浦东新区世纪大道1号
1 Century Ave., Pudong
❖ 31.2420, 121.4951

The first tower constructed in Pudong after the district was “opened” as a Special Economic Zone, the design today seems an anachronistic novelty, a cousin of Berlin’s Alexanderplatz TV Tower (1969) or the Atomium in Brussels (1958). Like those projects, the tower represents a vision of the future, with ideal platonic forms linked in a spatial composition that denies historical precedent and embraces “new” technologies, like television broadcasting. Here the re-emergence of China as a major player in the global capitalist economy is indicated by the 1950s throwback design, as if the designers recognised a need to restart stylistic development where they left off.

Lujiazui Pedestrian Loop

SH 100

SOM, 2006

浦东陆家嘴人行桥
世纪大道陆家嘴环路，浦东新区
❖ 31.2399, 121.4961

A major component of Lujiazui’s rapidly expanding grade-separated pedestrian network, this large circular walkway links the International Finance Centre (map p. 202), the **Super Brand Mall** (this page), the Lujiazui subway station, the **Oriental Pearl Tower** (above), and connects to elevated spurs that lead to the **WFC** (p. 180) and **Jin Mao** (p. 178) towers. The loop has become a major public gathering space for Shanghai’s new CBD.

Super Brand Mall

SH 101

Jon JERDE Partnership/ECADI 2002

正大广场
浦东新区陆家嘴西路168号
168 W Lujiazui Rd., Pudong
❖31.2387, 121.4947

While not among Jerde’s best work, this mall does feature a fairly interesting sequence of interior platforms that step up through the building mass and connect to an upper level “canyon.” Despite the confusing circulation path – or perhaps because of it – the mall seems successful, with a hectic energy not found amid the nearby **IFC’s** (map p. 202) luxury brands.

Apple Store

SH 102

Bohlin Cywinski Jackson, 2010

苹果商店，陆家嘴
浦东世纪大道8号
8 Century Avenue, Pudong
❖ 31.2394, 121.4968

A cylindrical version of Apple's flagship Fifth Avenue cube in New York City, the glass structure here is even more impressive for the curvature of the panels. As in its NYC predecessor, a glass spiral staircase leads to the underground shop, where minimalist fixtures display the latest Apple products. The store is also accessible directly from the **International Finance Centre** (map p. 202) shopping mall.

Agricultural Bank of China

SH 104

Arquitectonica/ECADI, 2011

浦江双辉大厦
浦东新区银城路9、55、99号
9, 55, 99 Yincheng Rd., Pudong
❖ 31.2443, 121.5047

Twin towers frame a negative space that resembles a ship's hull in profile. This reference to the dockyards that formerly stood on site also serves to create a kind of gateway, framing a public square that leads down to the Pudong waterfront promenade. In addition to the two office towers, the complex includes a hotel & spa, and luxury serviced apartments in lower bars that complement the high-rises.

Diamond Exchange

SH 108

Goettsch Partners, 2005–2009

中国钻石交易中心
浦东新区世纪大道1701号
1701 Century Avenue, Pudong
❖ 31.2263, 121.5322

This rather sharp office building consists of two thin slabs flanking a soaring atrium, enclosed at one end by an impressively-scaled, cable-supported curtain wall. The atrium is an appealing public space, featuring some small shops and restaurants, but the separation of the two slabs serves a functional purpose as well. The primary tenant wanted to ensure privacy and security for their market operations,

so their offices are separated from the other tenants by the atrium void, and accessed via dedicated elevators. The diamond business inspired many details of the design, and diamond patterns can be found throughout, from the skylights down to the atrium floor's paving pattern.

Oriental Arts Centre

SH 109

Paul ANDREU, ECADI, 2004

东方艺术中心
浦东新区丁香路425号
425 Dingxiang Rd., Pudong District
❖ 31.2249, 121.5367

Ostensibly taking the form of a butterfly orchid, the "petals" provide variably-sized auditorium halls, elevating the design beyond facile metaphor. The bold sculptural form is in line with Andreu's work of this period, like the more ambitious **National Grand Theatre** in Beijing (p. 077), completed a few years later. The presence of the theatre here suggests a hope that Pudong's CBD could evolve into a cultural, as well as financial, district.

Science & Technology Museum

SH 111

LIU Xiaoguang, RTKL, SIADR, 2001

上海科技馆,
浦东新区世纪大道2000号
2000 Century Ave., Pudong
❖ 31.2199, 121.5375

A sweeping roof, punctuated by a distinctive sphere, creates a memorable profile for this large museum that anchors Century Park and serves as a terminus for the grand Century Avenue (both map p. 202). In addition to the museum, an underground subway station here connects to a vast fabric market and "fake market" selling custom-tailored clothes, luggage, and a wide variety of electronics and other goods of dubious provenance.

Zendai Himalayas Centre

SH 115

ISOZAKI Arata, 2010

正大喜马拉雅中心
浦东新区樱花路869号
869 Yinhua Rd., Pudong
❖ 31.2117, 121.5577

This mixed-use complex combines hotel and office suites with a museum and retail, and connects below to the Shanghai subway system. Each programme area is coded with a different material treatment on the façade. The museum and retail levels are indicated by an abstract pattern inspired by Chinese characters, and the main public entry occurs through a cavernous open-air entry hall at ground level, with stalactite-esque columns framing views within.

The podium base is capped with several towers with typical curtain wall façades. As often is the case in China, metaphors sell the scheme. The canted columnar structure on the exterior has been compared to "an organic forest," and the perforated, undulating surfaces on the interior to *taihu* rocks or Himalayan Buddhist hermitages.

Courtesy Atelier Deshaus

Qingpu Youth Centre

SH 117

Atelier Deshaus, 2012

青浦区青少年活动中心
上海市青浦区
华科路和华青路交汇处
Huake Rd. & Huaqing Rd., Qingpu
❖ 31.1582, 121.1270

Courtesy Atelier Deshaus

In an interesting reading of the programme, Atelier Deshaus note that what teenagers really want is "a small town," with numerous smaller-scaled places for "destination, wandering, and meeting with the unexpected." The building is thus broken up into micro-pavilions, with irregularly (but not childishly) disposed windows, set apart by small, alley-like gaps. Simple volumes with whitewashed façades recall both China's traditional typologies and the white boxes of Modernism.

Qingpu Library/Thumb Island

SH 118

MADA s.p.a.m. (Qingyun MA), 2005

青浦图书馆，青浦新城
青龙路60号
60 Qinglong Rd., Qingpu
❖ 31.1504, 121.1311

This low-slung building is striking for its diagrammatic clarity: strips of ground are pulled up to form enclosure, and the linear plan projects into an artificial lake. These narrow strips are separated to allow natural daylight to penetrate the interior. The architects establish a formal language that works well as a diagram, and also creates perceptual shifts similar to those found in traditional Chinese architecture. The "strips" serve to capture courtyard space, and a number of walkways, catwalks, and passages criss-cross the roof-scape, making for an appealing walk around and over the building. The interiors are more ordinary, aside from several double- and triple-height spaces, and portions of the roof are unfortunately fenced-off, but this remains an impressive project.

Courtesy Jiakun Architects

Qingpu Exhibition Centre

SH 120

Jiakun Architects (LIU Jiakun), 2005

青浦区规划展示馆
青浦新城华青南路767号
767 S Huaqing Rd., Qingpu
❖ 31.1526, 121.1286

Carefully detailed in glass and black stone, this exhibition hall and office building stretches out to a length of 190 metres in an attempt to address the sprawling scale of the highway and adjacent lake (driven, perhaps, by the urban scale of Qingpu's new town centre). The beautifully-detailed minimalist bar is divided into three functional zones by courtyards, landscape terraces and pools, which create a gradation from "public to half-public to private" and recall the themes of China's classical gardens. Materials are deployed carefully, with the dark stone sun-shading fins detailed to make their irregularity and thickness clear (the veneers on the base are more vague). The only let-down here is the context: the terraced journey up to the building does buffer the over-scaled road, but it begs to grow out of a more coherent urban space. The planners' insistence on giving each of the new town centre's major civic buildings its own discrete, oversized plot has made for no coherent centre at all.

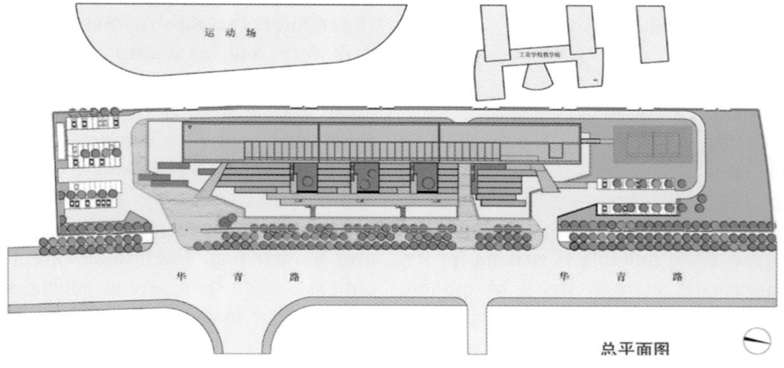

Courtesy Jiakun Architects

Site plan

Office Building for Qingpu Business Association

SH 121

Atelier Deshaus, 2003–2005

私营企业协会办公中心
青浦新城青龙路
Qinglong Rd., Qingpu
❖ 31.1509, 121.1362

A square block of offices hoisted on *piloti* wraps a courtyard, and is itself wrapped in a double-layer screen-printed glass façade, which doubles as a noise barrier. Between these two layers of glass is a thick zone of bamboo planters, refracted by the glass, lending a layered ambiguity to the surface. While the office is private, one can still sense the visual layering and the courtyard's terraces from the outside.

Qingpu Footbridge

SH 122

CA-Design, 2004–2008

青浦步行桥
青浦区浦仓路湖滨路
Pucang Rd. at Hubin Rd., Qingpu
❖ 31.1442, 121.1169

Linking two sides of the river in a single span, this bridge takes the form of a distorted truss, with density of structural members increasing in areas of greater load. The form is generated from a desire to continue the paths of two (seemingly minor) roads on either side of the river, resolving their misalignment with a kink in plan. The bold structure is capped with a wooden roof in reference to traditional building materials.

Qiaoziwan Shopping Centre & Qushui Park Edge Garden

SH 124

MADA s.p.a.m. (Qingyun MA), 2003, 2004

青浦桥梓湾购物中心和曲水园
青浦新城公园路700号
700 Gongyuan Rd., Qingpu
❖ 31.1503, 121.1097

As in the firm's work at **Y-Town** (p. 237) and **Tianyi Square** (p. 240), the shopping programme is imagined as a group of buildings related to urban space, rather than a closed mall. Here, that space is formed into a slightly irregular trapezoidal figure reminiscent of a smallish Italian *piazza* – perhaps a canal-inspired borrowing from Venice. The detailing, which may appear fussy or materially busy to some tastes, does help to further break down the scale and make the development feel less like a single homogeneous project. The adjacent "Edge Garden" wraps the perimeter of a classical garden (1745+); both are worth a visit. While most Chinese gardens are self-contained worlds, restrained by their perimeter walls, here the older garden is enlivened by its newly thickened edge. A covered walkway, out of the traditional playbook, is made contemporary and unfamiliar through sculptural form and ornamental details. At the terminal corner, a small jog in the walkway roof serves to capture a small courtyard space, and a pavilion hints at more complexity beyond.

Zhujiajiao Canal Town

SH 128

300+ CE

朱家角
❖ 31.1095, 121.0500

Perhaps the best-preserved canal town within metropolitan Shanghai (see also p. 226), Zhujiajiao provides a grounded counterpoint to the ambitious new structures in nearby **Qingpu** (p. 185). The narrow lanes here are a slice of old China, and the preserved area is large enough for long walks along the canals. The Fangsheng Bridge (1571 CE) is especially impressive. Though Zhujiajiao was founded over 1,700 years ago, most of the structures here date to the Qing dynasty, and encroaching development and commercialisation threaten to overwhelm the old town.

Zhujiajiao Administrative Centre

SH 129

MADA s.p.a.m. (Qingyun MA), 2004

青浦区朱家角镇人大,
青浦区沙家埭路18号
18 Shajiadai Rd., Qingpu
❖ 31.1054, 121.0415

Tradition and modernity are bridged through vernacular elements like wood, slatted screens, gable roofs, and water gardens, along with Modernist devices that favour light, space, and the open plan. While no one would mistake this for the adjacent "ancient town," the inspiration is clear, and we find the firm seeking a stylistic and formal design approach informed by myriad, wide-ranging influences.

Anting New Town/ German Town

SH 131

Albert SPEER & Partner, 2001

安亭新镇
嘉定区安德（环）路
Ande (Ring) Rd., Jiading
❖ 31.2717, 121.1659

A study in European-style low-rise, high-density housing, this new town is primarily composed of perimeter blocks, each enclosing a large semi-private courtyard for the residents' use. This typology, more than any of the details, is very much of Berlin. The blocks are bordered by automobile access roads, and cut across by a pedestrian parkway. A commercial and civic hub, located in the centre of the development, features larger buildings and a hard-scape public square. Marketing materials claiming "Bauhaus Style" seem a bit of a stretch, but there are certainly echoes of interwar German architecture, particularly the *Siedlungen* of Bruno Taut, Ernst May and others. The planning, landscaping, comfortable scale and lively colours make this one of the more appealing "One City, Nine Towns" projects.

Photo: Shanghai Auto Museum

Shanghai Auto Museum

SH 132

Atelier Brückner, IFB Dr. Braschel AG, Architectural Design & Research Institute of Tongji University, 2007

上海汽车博物馆
嘉定区安亭博园路7565号(近墨玉南路)
7565 Boyuan Rd. (near S Moyu Rd), Anting, Jiading District
❖ 31.2801, 121.1659

Anting, a major centre for automotive manufacturing, has turned its primary industry into a tourist theme. This museum takes the form of a flowing ribbon, perhaps inspired by the movement of the cars displayed inside, or the swooping forms of highway interchanges, or the nearby **International Circuit** track (map p. 204).

School of Communication and Art

SH 134

ZHENG Qun, WEN Xiaoqin, ZHANG Yan, 2009

同济大学嘉定校区惟新馆
嘉定区曹安公路4800号
4800 Cao'an Rd., Jiading
❖ 31.2871, 121.2053

On Tongji University's Jiading satellite campus, the building contains a number of production studios and performance halls, detailed as volumes protruding from the mat-like base, and shifted slightly to create narrow light-well courtyards at their edges. Filtered light reaches even the lower floors, and the courtyards serve double-duty as way-finding devices. The roof is accessible and pleasant.

Jiading New Town & Pavilions

SH 137

Various, 2010s

嘉定公园及小亭子
阿克苏路天祝路
Akesu Rd. at Tianzhu Rd.
❖ 31.3517, 121.2551

Jiading is one of Shanghai's satellite cities. Like **Qingpu** (p. 185) it avoids the European branding common to most of the early-2000s new town developments. Here, theme is discarded in favour of opportunity for designers to test their ideas without restraint. The centre is organised around long Ziqi Donglai Park (Sasaki Associates), a lace of free-form paths, dotted with pavilions by Atelier Archmixing (teahouse, gallery), Scenic Architecture (bookstore), LU Di (island tea-house), and others. East, past the town centre, is Yuanxiang Park (ZHU Shengxuan, YU Zhiyuan, MA Bin, YAN Ying, ZHANG Yongang), wrapped around a lake and anchored by two "Spiral Galleries" by Atelier Deshaus, TM Studio's Lotus Courtyard, and several other structures. Also nestled in the park is the Jiading Library, by MADA s.p.a.m., which features an intriguing courtyard design that captures the appeal of vernacular forms while updating the material palette to a warm, wood-and-glass minimalism. Jiading New Town is perhaps the most successful of Shanghai's "Nine Towns," boasting a growing population in the millions. Perhaps the "new" city's success can be ascribed to its history. Jiading has long been inhabited, evinced by nearby **Nanxiang Ancient Town** (map p. 204), a well preserved Yangtze Delta canal town, similar to those found near Suzhou (p. 226), if slightly smaller. The seven-storey Fahua Pagoda (originally built in 1205, though reconstructed many times since) is worth a look, as is the Jiading Confucius Temple and Confucian Academy (which dates to 1219).

Museum of Glass

SH 143

LOGON Architects, 2011

玻璃博物馆
宝山区长江西路685号
685 W Changjiang Rd., Baoshan
❖ 31.3455, 121.4673

This multi-building renovation makes good use of the various spaces, with increasingly fine finishes paralleling the glass-working process. A glass-blowing theatre sits to the rear of the site, while the main exhibition hall sits towards the road. The dark interior lets exhibition designers focus attention on the artwork, while a skylight and double-height atrium provide contrast at the entry and upper-level cafe.

Knowledge and Innovation Community

SH 146

SOM (architecture), Tom LEADER Studio (landscape), 2006

创智天地，杨浦区淞沪路234号
234 Songhu Rd., Yangpu
❖ 31.3084, 121.5089

This campus of low-rise office buildings effectively frames a central green in a plan meant to inspire creativity and a connection to nature. Landscape ideas culled from traditional gardens enhance the office environment. The scheme benefits from sectional shifts and tight integration with the existing context, particularly respecting the axial approach to the **Jiangwan Sports Centre** (below).

Jiangwan Sports Centre (Shanghai Stadium)

SH 147

DONG Dayou, 1934

江湾体育场，杨浦区国和路346号
No.346 Guohe Road, Yangpu District
❖ 31.3080, 121.5101

In 1929, Shanghai's City Planning Commission was established to draft the "Greater Shanghai Plan." CHIANG Kai-shek wished to make Shanghai a model city, and solicited competition entries which would synthesise "scientific principles developed from Europe and America" with "excellent aspects of the artistic tradition of our nation." The emphasis on Chinese style was a specific response to the burgeoning growth of foreign Neoclassical and Art Deco buildings along the Bund. The establishment of a new centre far from the foreign concessions would, perhaps, allow the Nationalist government (which had not dissolved the treaty ports) to wrest symbolic centrality from the Europeans. Development was halted by the Japanese invasion in 1937, and many completed or partially-completed structures were damaged in the subsequent war. The civic structures in the new Jiangwan district were designed by young DONG Dayou, a recent product of the American Beaux-Arts tradition. One of the few remaining parts is the Jiangwan Stadium. The style commingles the heavy massing of Romanesque revival arches with a delicate ornamental programme, then called "Ming Dynasty revival style." The inclusion of the stadium in the master plan underscored the image, which Chiang hoped to promote, of the heroic, vital new Chinese man and woman. Site of the National Games of China in 1935 (plus 1948 and 1983), the stadium prepared Chinese athletes for participation in the 1936 Berlin Olympics: another site for the politicisation of bodies and architecture, albeit to different ends.

Luodian New Town/ Swedish Town

SH 149

Sweco Architects & KTH Urban Planning and Design, 2001–2013

罗店新镇，宝山区罗芬路689号
689 Luofen Rd., Baoshan
❖ 31.4031, 121.3501

Surprisingly one of the more active of the New Towns, Luodian has the distinct advantage of a nearby Metro station and a central, well-used lake. While the "northern European style" buildings may seem stripped-down and generic compared to the self-consciously-styled structures in nearby "European" developments, perhaps this raw functionality is part of their appeal.

Gaoqiao New Town/ Holland Village

SH 150

Kuiper Compagnons and Atelier Dutch, 2001–2004

高桥新镇，浦东新区高荷路
Gaohe Rd., Pudong
❖ 31.3352, 121.5723

Though complete with windmill, canals, and narrow, Amsterdam-style shophouses, Holland Village has little to recommend aside from the novelty of a Dutch simulacrum in the Shanghai suburbs. While convincing at a distance, nothing here is particularly well detailed, and the disconnect from regional transit leaves the town centre fairly vacant, though the scale is pleasant.

Pudong International Airport

SH 153

Terminal 1: Paul ANDREU, 1999
Terminal 2: ECADI, 2008

浦东机场，浦东新区浦东机场路
Pudong Airport Rd., Pudong District
❖ 31.1530, 121.8050

Separated by a major highway and rail lines traversing shallow pools, the two terminals are each arranged as parallel bars, effecting a gradient between ground transit and air travel. In both terminals, circulation is separated in section (on the long-standing Stansted model; see p. 106) with arrivals below and departures above beneath a large, undulating roof. Also of note is the Maglev train that zips riders to the Pudong CBD at 431 km/h.

Pujiang Italian Town

SH 155

Vittorio GREGOTTI & Associates, Centro Studio Traffico, Arup, THAPE, 2001–2004+

浦江新城，闵行区浦星路江桦路
Puxing Rd. at Jianghua Rd, Minhang
❖ 31.1046, 121.4915

One of the more successful of the "Nine Towns," financially and aesthetically, Pujiang is an effective synthesis of traditional Chinese planning techniques with Italian Neo-Rationalist architecture. Rather than the Tuscan kitsch that might be expected, we find stark Modernist structures, aligned to a grid, angled slightly towards the east for climatic and *feng shui* purposes.

Giant Interactive Group HQ

SH 156

Morphosis (Thom MAYNE), 2006–2010

巨人集团总部
松江区沪松公路广富林路路口
Husong Rd. at Guangfulin Rd., Songjiang
❖31.0570, 121.2617

Located in Shanghai's southern suburbs, on the alluvial plain of the Yangtze Delta, the architects' design seems a meditation on "ground" as theoretical construct. A canal, a lake, and a below-grade car park are carved from the earth; in response, the landscape is folded up to create a green roof, enclosing conference rooms and a gallery hall. The main office spaces are gathered in a long, thin, undulating bar that rises progressively upward. This circulation spine weaves through the amenity spaces to link the various spaces and act as an index of the "flows" embedded in architectural form (bridging through the gymnasium, for example, and across the road). In a sense, the building is a representation of the client's corporate structure: open-plan office spaces are linked most closely to the ground, private offices and conference rooms are lifted slightly (tracking with the raised green roof), while the CEO's executive suite and VIP conference room leave the ground entirely to cantilever over the adjacent pool. Any resemblance to a dragon taking flight is surely coincidental.

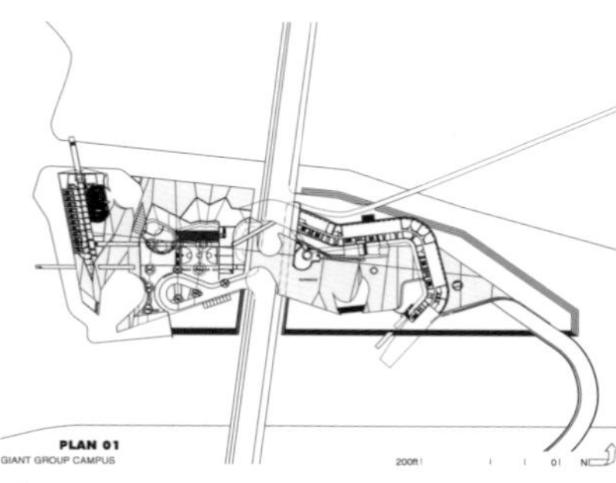

Plan

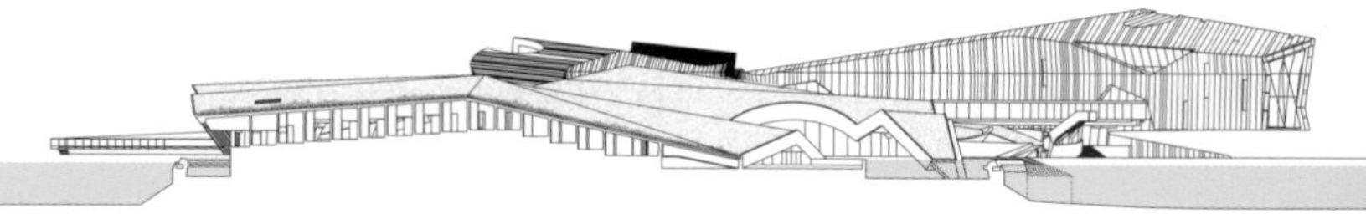

Cross section

Thames Town

Atkins Design Studio, China Shanghai Arch. Design and Research, et al., 2001–2006

SH 157

泰晤士小镇
松江区三新北路900弄
900 N. Sanxing Rd., Songjiang
❖ 31.0353, 121.1934

Among the "One City, Nine Towns" projects, Thames Town is unique. Though its convincingly cute, quasi-Tudor heart has clearly won over Shanghai's wedding photographers, most of the development slyly exploits much more recent British architectural developments, and is thus something more than a vernacular pastiche. Different shades of High-Tech (STIRLING and FOSTER) compete with Postmodernism (FARRELL and ST. JOHN WILSON). This stylistic collage, itself quite postmodern, will amuse some architects, but the scheme really works because the history lesson is collapsed into a believable and interesting master plan. Faux-Victorian lanes spill out into a spacious town square lined with modern buildings, and as in the British Picturesque and Townscape movements, there's always something interesting tempting you from just around the corner. The master plan thus develops somewhat like an "organic" city, with stylistic clashes contributing to a heterogeneous aesthetic that supports a sense of history. By "seeding" the new town with this diverse collection of styles, one hopes the architects have established a framework for varied future additions. With better transit to Shanghai, this could become the nucleus for a fully-developed, economically-diverse district, though for now it remains a somewhat underpopulated novelty.

While the maps in this book typically start in the centre of the city and move outward, for Shanghai we have provided this overview, indicating crop boxes and page numbers for the maps on the following pages. For your convenience, we refer to the districts by their most popular names in English or Chinese on a case-by-case basis. Shanghai is a huge city, but many of the city's architectural sites are "clustered" in certain districts, and easily visited on foot after short subway rides. Some of the more interesting metropolitan sites are on subway lines; others require a car. First-time visitors can find plenty to see in the centre (Maps A-C), including the old city and Pudong. Those drawn by images of the 2010 Expo (Map B) should be aware that such famed pavilions as Denmark's (Bjarke INGELS Group) and the United Kingdom's (Thomas HEATHERWICK Studio) are now gone or inaccessible, though other Expo sites have been re-used.

Shanghai Region

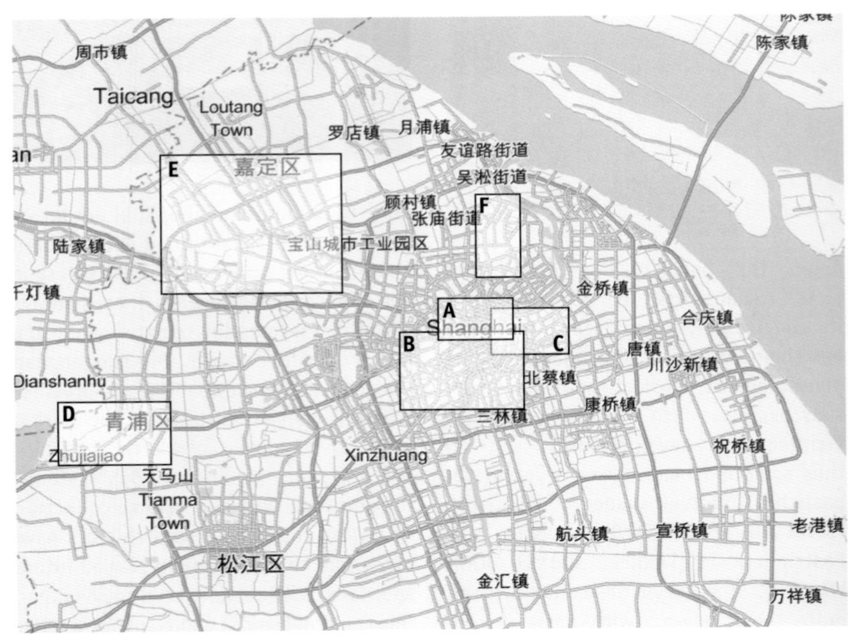

Shanghai

A. Central Shanghai, Old Town and Former International Settlement, p. 199

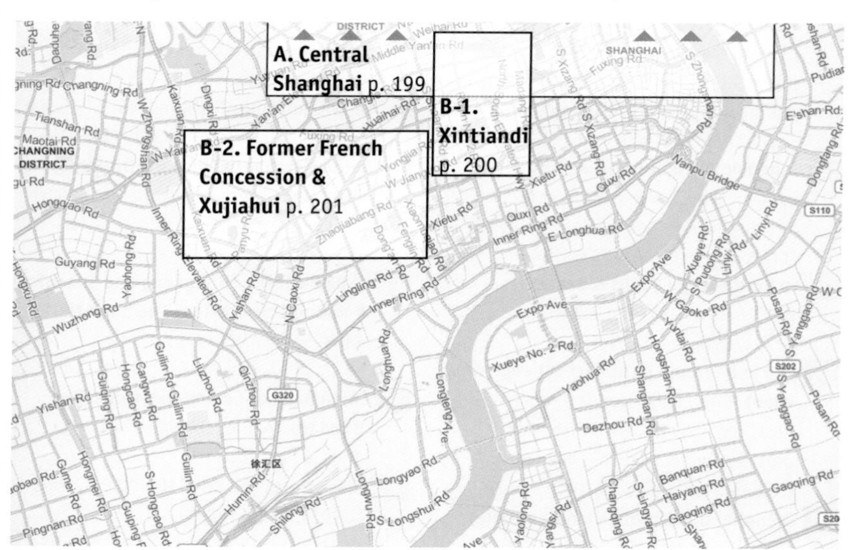

B. South Shanghai, Former French Concession, Expo Site, p. 201

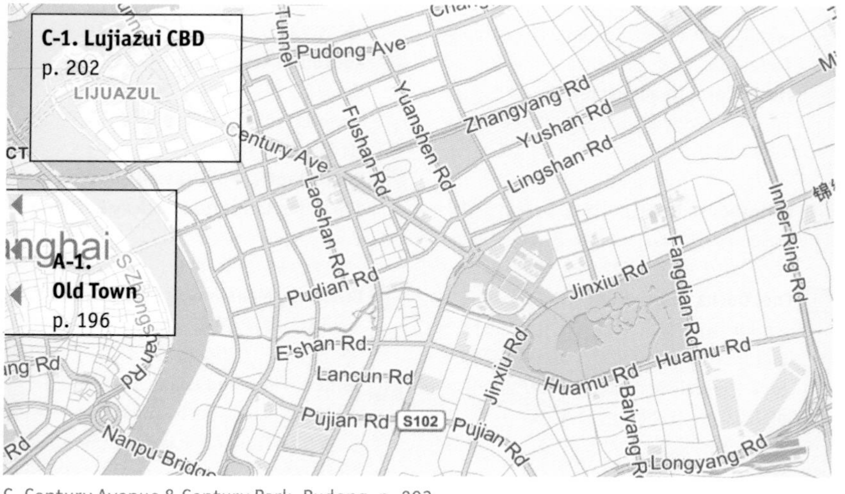

C. Century Avenue & Century Park, Pudong, p. 203

A-1. Old Town (Map 01–08)

01 Old City Wall and Dajing Ge Pavilion This fifty-metre stretch is all that remains of the old city wall. The rebuilt tower exhibits photos of old Shanghai. ❖ 31.2271, 121.4809

02 Cang Bao Antiques Market This lively four-level market is packed with antiques, regional crafts, and clever forgeries. ❖ 31.2264, 121.4844

03 Yu Gardens (Yu Yuan) & Bazaar *PAN Yunduan & Others, 1559+.* ❖ 31.2290, 121.4873

04 City God Temple & District (Chenghuang Miao) *Originally fifteenth century.* Restored in 1994, the Taoist temple presides over a lively pedestrian shopping zone. ❖ 31.2274, 121.4882

05 Shanghai Old Street (Miaoqian Dajie) *Ming & Qing dynasties, 1644–1911.* One of the main commercial streets of the Old City now caters to tourists, with shops slightly upmarket compared to nearby Yu Bazaar (#03). ❖ 31.2275, 121.4900

06 Jiushi Corp. Headquarters *Foster + Partners (Norman FOSTER) with ECADI, 1995–2001.* ❖ 31.2270, 121.4952

07 Waterhouse Hotel *Neri&Hu Design and Research Office (Lyndon NERI & Rossana HU), 2010.* ❖ 31.2222,121.5011

08 Cool Docks, South Bund *HUGE/Hongji Enterprises, 2008.* No docks; just the reuse and creation of "traditional" urban fabric for an upscale pedestrian entertainment district. ❖ 31.2214, 121.5016

Shanghai

09 The Bund (Wai Tan) *1842–1930s.* See detail map, p. 156, for full listing. ❖ 31.2385, 121.4859

10 Union Building, The Bund No. 3 *PALMER & TURNER, 1916.* ❖ 31.2361, 121.4865

11 China Merchants'Company Building, The Bund No.9 *Atkinson & Dallas Architects and Civil Engineers, 1901.* ❖ 31.2374, 121.4859

12 HSBC Building (Hongkong and Shanghai Banking Corporation) The Bund No.12 *PALMER & TURNER, 1923.* ❖ 31.2380, 121.4856

13 China Bank of Communications The Bund No.14 *C. H. GONDA , 1948.* ❖ 31.2391, 121.4855

14 Peace Hotel The Bund No. 20 *PALMER & TURNER, 1926–1929.* ❖ 31.2412, 121.4852

15 Bank of China The Bund No.23 *PALMER & TURNER with LU Qianshou, 1937.* ❖ 31.2415, 121.4853

16 Rockbund Art Museum *PALMER & TURNER, 1932 /David CHIPPERFIELD Architects, 2006–2010.* ❖ 31.2432, 121.4832

17 China Baptist Publication Building and Christian Literature Society Building *László HUDEC, 1932.* ❖ 31.2450, 121.4830

18 Broadway Mansions *PALMER & TURNER, with Bright FRASER, 1934.* ❖ 31.2462, 121.4853

19 Joint Savings and Loan *László HUDEC, 1926.* An eclectic brick and stone pile with classical detail and a corner tower, the bank is in a poor state of repair. ❖ 31.2479, 121.4808

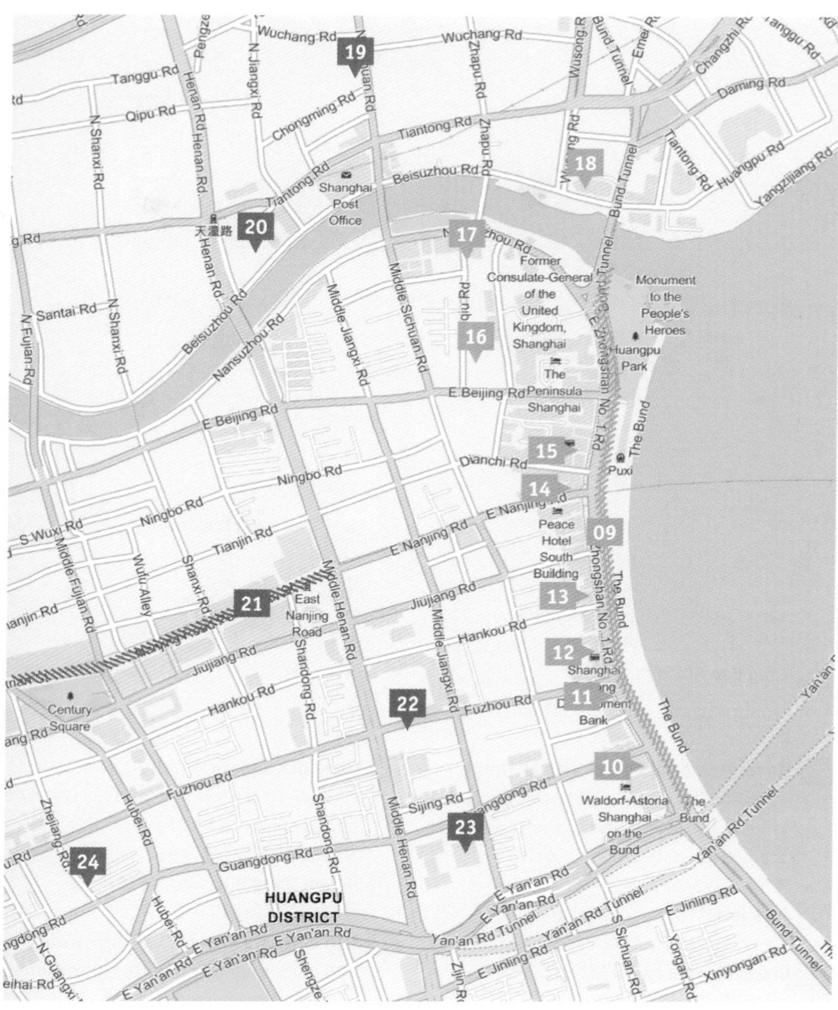

A-2. The Bund and Former British Concession (Map 09–24)

20 **Embankment Building** *PALMER & TURNER, 1933.* 400 metres long, this Streamline/Art Deco apartment block was once the world's longest. Owner Victor Sassoon offered refuge here to hundreds of Jews fleeing Germany in 1938.❖ 31.2452, 121.4791

21 **Nanjing Road Pedestrian Street** The neon-spangled shopping street extends 5.5 km west from near the Bund to Jing'an Temple, with historic department stores to the east, modern malls to the west. ❖ 31.2396, 121.4810

22 **American Club** *László HUDEC, 1922–24.* Described by the press as "American Colonial," the brick Neo-Georgian building established Hudec's reputation in Shanghai. ❖ 31.2367, 121.4819

23 **Bund Centre** *John PORTMAN and Associates, 1997–2002.* At fifty storeys, this is the tallest building in the Bund area. It features a typical Portman atrium and a giant leafy crown; the latter comes at the insistence of the client, whose corporate logo is a crown. It may also be a callback to Shanghai's Art Deco past, or simply reflect the Postmodern rediscovery of the style as the last "decorative" response to modernity. ❖ 31.2345, 121.4830

24 **Chekiang Theatre (now Zhejiang Cinema)** *László HUDEC, 1930.* Streamlined Art Deco theatre with original details intact. ❖ 31.2339 121.4755

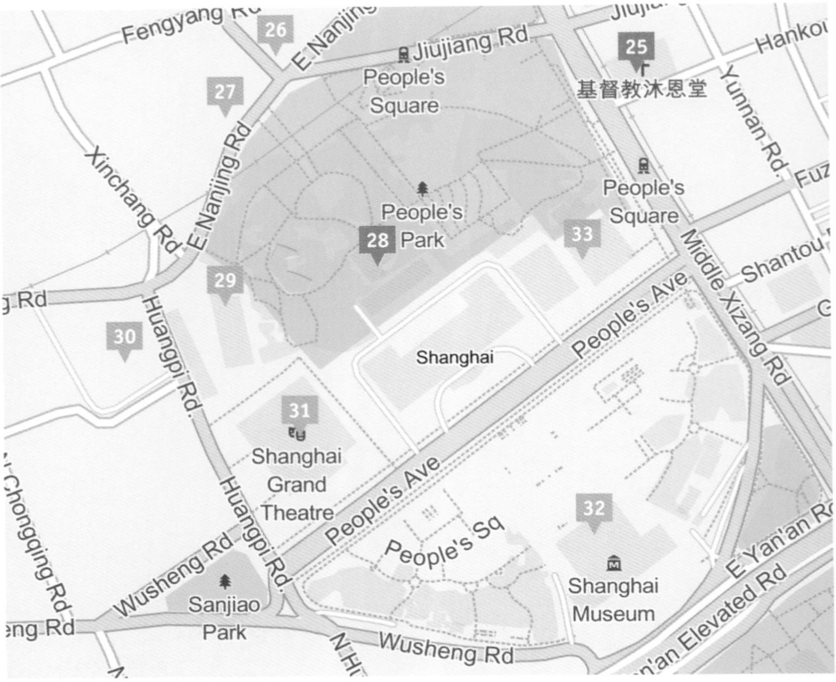

A-3. People's Square (Map 25–33)

25 Moore Memorial Church (Mu En Tang) *László HUDEC, 1929.* Vast Gothic Revival church, featuring soaring vaults and stained glass. Restored in 2010. ❖ 31.2352, 121.4711

26 Park Hotel *László HUDEC, 1934.* ❖ 31.2354, 121.4671

27 Grand Cinema *László HUDEC, 1932.* ❖ 31.2348, 121.4665

28 MoCA *Atelier LIU Yuyang Architects, 2009.* An old pavilion transformed into a contemporary art museum via black stone cladding, curved glass volumes, and ramps. ❖ 31.2332, 121.4683

29 Shanghai Museum of Art (Shanghai Race Club) *1933.* ❖ 31.2328, 121.4665

30 Tomorrow Square *John PORTMAN & Associates,with SIADR, 1997–2003.* ❖ 31.2322, 121.4653

31 Shanghai Grand Theatre *ARTE Charpentier, 1998.* ❖ 31.2314, 121.4676

32 Shanghai Museum *Shanghai Xian Dai (XING Tonghe),1993–1995.* ❖ 31.2304, 121.4708

33 Shanghai Urban Planning Exhibition Centre *Ling Benli/ECADI, 2000.* ❖ 31.2333, 121.4707

34 Wheelock Square *KPF, 2010.* The form of this 58–storey tower is "derived from the ancient Chinese art of paper folding." ❖ 31.2235, 121.4401

35 Jingan Temple *Various, 1216–2010.* ❖ 31.2252, 121.4407

36 Join-Buy City Plaza *JERDE Partnership, 2003.* A shopping mall with multi-storey atrium, glass elevators, and curved façades. ❖ 31.2257, 121.4415

37 Eddington Apartments *Eric Byron CUMINE, 1935.* A fine Art Deco survivor. ❖ 31.2263, 121.4435

38 Avenue Apartments (now Lianhua Apartments) *László HUDEC, 1931–32.* A curvilinear apartment block: Art Deco, veering towards stripped-down Functionalism. ❖ 31.2299, 121.4447

39 Pei Mansion Hotel *1934.* Deco hotel, with traditional elements, like a "spirit wall," "dragon stairs," lattice panelling, and a Suzhou-style water garden. ❖ 31.2297, 121.4461

40 Shanghai Centre *John Portman & Associates, 1990.* ❖ 31.2286, 121.4473

41 Plaza 66 *KPF, Frank C. Y. FENG Architects, ECADI, 1994–2001.* ❖ 31.2291, 121.4489

42 Burlington Rd Apts. *László HUDEC, 1928.* ❖ 31.2296, 121.4509

43 Shanghai Exhibition Centre *ANDERLEV &*

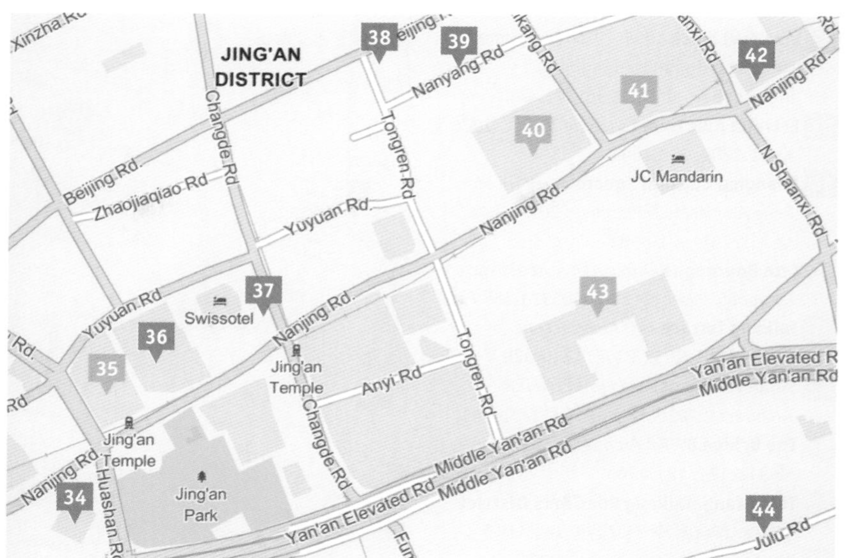

A-4 Jing'an and West Nanjing Rd. (Map 34–44)

JISLOVA/CHEN Zhi, 1955. ❖ 31.2263, 121.4483

44 Chen (Rose) Dingzhen Residence *László HUDEC, 1924.* Grand Beaux-Arts villa with a colossal Ionic portico. ❖ 31.2222, 121.4480

45 Shanghai Port International Cruise Terminal *Frank REPAS with Shanghai Arch. Des. Inst.* ❖ 31.2486, 121.4928

46 Shanghai Municipal Council Abattoir (Old Millfun/1933) *C.H. STABLEFORD, 1933, RENEW (ZHAO Chongxin), 2010.* ❖ 31.2565, 121.4877

47 Shanghai Main Railway Station Strictly functional, with a busy public plaza adjacent. ❖ 31.2514, 121.4510

48 Union Brewery *László HUDEC, 1933.* Once the largest in China, this sleek Functionalist brewery features curved ribbon windows and a crisp concrete frame. ❖ 31.2511, 121.4352

49 M50 Urban Renovation *DAtrans Architecture Office, 2000–2005+* ❖ 31.2495, 121.4446

50 Natural History Museum *Perkins & Will, Tongji Univ. Group, 2007–2014+.* ❖ 31.2368, 121.4582

51 Jingan Sculpture Park Pleasant lawns with scattered contemporary art. ❖ 31.2363, 121.4593

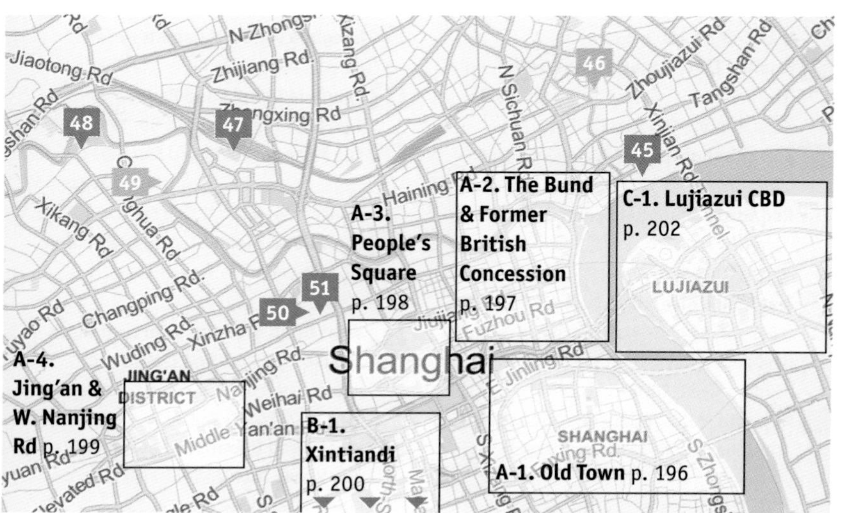

A. Central Shanghai, Old Town and Former International Settlement (Map 45–51)

52 **Six Level Stack** *1999.* "Dragon Column" supports illuminated highway interchange. ❖ 31.2236, 121.4699

53 **Estrella Apartments** *László HUDEC, 1926.* ❖ 31.2209, 121.4591

54 **Shanghai Cultural Square** *Beyer Blinder Belle Architects & Planners, 2013.* ❖ 31.2138, 121.4581

55 **Cite Bourgogne** *China Jianye Real Estate Company, 1930.* ❖ 31.2090, 121.4579

56 **Taikang Terrace** *A00 Architecture, 2009–2012.* ❖ 31.2102, 121.4629

57 **Sinan Mansions** *Arte CHARPENTIER Architects, 2010.* ❖ 31.2166, 121.4641

58 **The Bridge 8** *HMA Architects, 2005.* ❖ 31.2124, 121.4663

59 **Tianzifang/Taikang Road Arts District** *1930s/2000s.* ❖ 31.2099, 121.4647

60 **Xintiandi** *Studio Shanghai, 2001.* ❖ 31.2217, 121.4703

61 **Conrad Hotel** *KPF, 2008.* ❖ 31.2236, 121.4699

62 **L'Ecole Remi** *LEONARD, VEYSSEYRE & KRUZE, 1933.* Rare International Style in Shanghai. ❖ 31.2122, 121.4507

63 **Highstreet Loft**. *KOKAI Studios, 2006.* A fine industrial renovation. Offices and shops. ❖ 31.2072, 121.4546

64 **Jianyeli Shikumen Block** *John PORTMAN & Associates, 2008–2013.* ❖ 31.2056, 121.4476

65 **Twelve at Hengshan** *Mario BOTTA, 2013.* ❖ 31.2069, 121.4416

66 **Shanghai Library** *ZHANG Jie Zheng, 1996.* 24–storey Postmodernism, with interior garden. ❖ 31.2091, 121.4403

67 **Normandie Apartments** *László HUDEC, 1927.* ❖ 31.2062, 121.4336

68 **Huaihai Lu (Former Avenue Joffe)** *1901.* The main axis of the Former French Concession. ❖ 31.2077, 121.4361

69 **Z58 (Zhongtai Box)** *KUMA Kengo, 2003–2008.* ❖ 31.2112, 121.4246

70 **Red Town/Shanghai Sculpture Space** *Taranta Creations, 2011.* ❖ 31.2004, 121.4194

71 **JiaoTong University** *László HUDEC et al., 1896+.* Fine collegiate Gothic structures and an Art Deco Engineering Building by Hudec. ❖ 31.2008, 121.4286

72 **Xujiahui** Major retail zone and subway interchange. ❖ 31.1956, 121.4341

 Shanghai

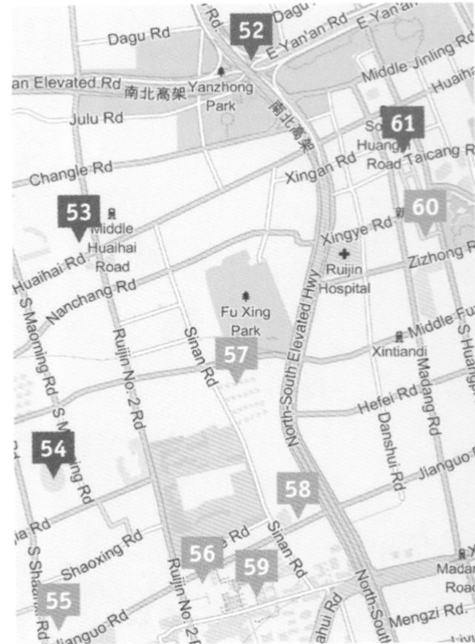

B-1. Xintiandi (Map 52–61)

73 **SPSI Art Museum** *WANG Yan, 2010.* ❖ 31.2004, 121.3955

74 **County Hospital** *László HUDEC, 1923–26.* Beaux-Arts hospital with a fine central portico and some quirky details. ❖ 31.2197, 121.4371

75 **Paramount Ballroom** *YANG Xi Liu, 1934.* Deco ballroom, partly intact/restored. ❖ 31.2065, 121.4018

76 **Gubei SOHO** *KPF, 2015+ (under construction).* ❖ 31.1994, 121.4005

77 **China Fortune Exhibition Hall/Huaxin Business Centre** *Scenic Architecture (ZHU Xiaofeng)* ❖ 31.1747, 121.4120

78 **Long Museum** *Atelier Deshaus, 2011–2014.* ❖ 31.1860, 121.4605

79 **Longhua Martyrs' Cemetery** *1995.* ❖ 31.1786, 121.4443

80 **Longhua Temple and Pagoda** *Song Dynasty/1954.* ❖ 31.1759, 121.4472

81 **Yuz Museum** *FUJIMOTO Sou, 2013.* A glass cube and old airplane hanger hold contemporary art. ❖ 31.1723, 121.4574

82 **West Bund Biennial – Cloud Pavilion** *Schmidt Hammer Larsen, 2013.* ❖ 31.1866, 121.4623

83 **West Bund Biennial – Vertical Glass House** *FCJZ (Yung Ho CHANG), 2013.* A meditation on privacy in today's city. ❖ 31.1708, 121.4596

84 **West Bund Biennial – Pavilion of Six Views** *Johnston Marklee (Sharon JOHNSTON, Mark LEE), 2013.* ❖ 31.1699, 121.4585

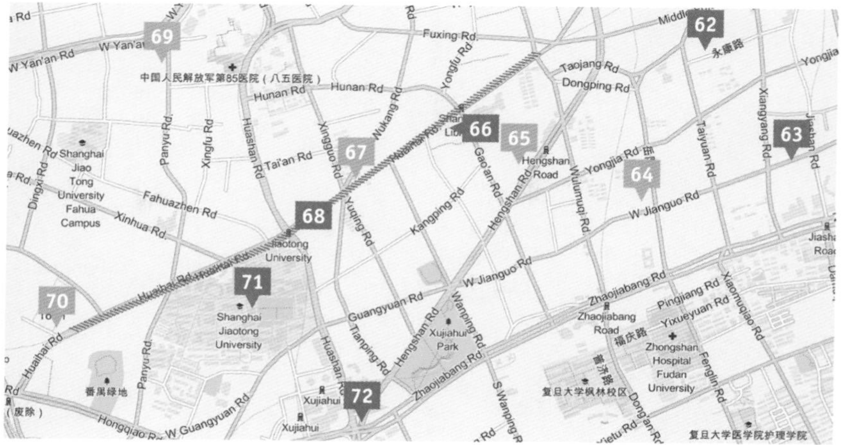

B-2. Former French Concession & Xujiahui (Map 62–72)

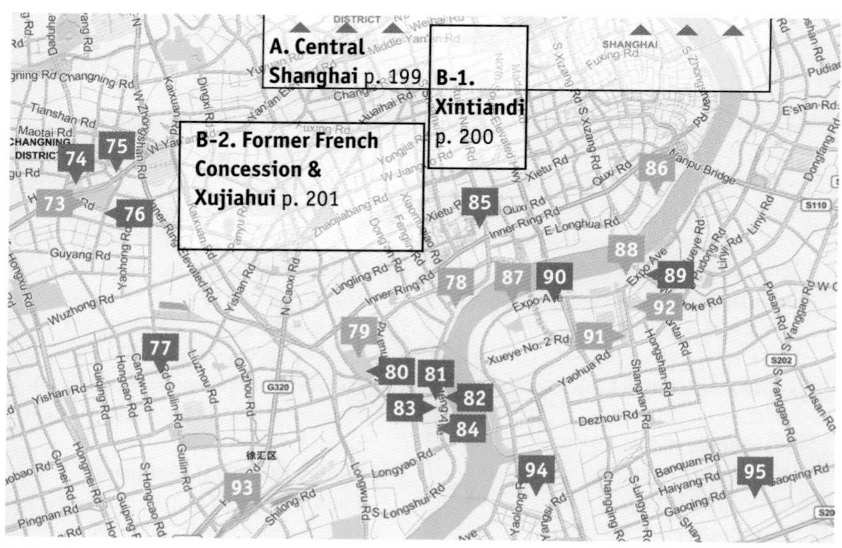

B. South Shanghai, Former French Concession, Expo Site (Map 73–95)

85 **Jade Museum** *Archi-Union (Philip F. YUAN) 2012–2013.* Digital curves dance with shuttered concrete. ❖ 31.1988, 121.4639

86 **Power Station of Art** *Original Design Studio (ZHANG Ming & ZHANG Zi), 2006–2012.* ❖ 31.2030, 121.4938

87 **Houtan Park** *Turenscape, 2010.* ❖31.1871, 121.4712

88 **Mercedes Benz Arena** *WANG Xiao An/ECADI, 2009.* ❖ 31.1912, 121.4893

89 **Saudi Arabia Pavilion. Expo 2010** *Saudi-Chinese design team, 2010.* A vast “hanging moon boat,” covered with date palms. ❖ 31.1905, 121.4914

90 **Italian Culture Centre Pavilion, Expo 2010** *IODICE Architetti, 2010.* A sliced cube represents the cultural, spatial and topographical complexity of Italian towns. ❖ 31.1856, 121.4714

91 **River Mall (Expo Axis)** *SBA International/ECADI/Knippers-Helbig, 2010.* ❖ 31.1858, 121.4880

92 **China Art Palace** *HE Jingtang, 2010.* ❖ 31.1863, 121.4898

93 **Shanghai South Station** *AREP/ECADI, 2006.* ❖ 31.1549, 121.4248

94 **Shanghai Oriental Sports Centre** *GMP (von GERKAN, MARG and Partner), 2011.* Buildings project into a lake, and a folded white triangular structure aims to evoke sails. ❖ 31.1596, 121.4730

95 **Vanke Housing** *Tsushima Design Studio, 2012.* Broken-down scale, generous landscape, and a public walkway or “threshold.” ❖ 31.1580, 121.5104

C-1. Lujiazui CBD, Pudong (Map 96–105)

96 **Jin Mao Tower** *SOM, SIADR, 1994–1998.* ❖31.2370, 121.5011

97 **World Financial Centre** *Kohn Pedersen Fox (KPF), 1997–2008.* ❖ 31.2363, 121.5030

98 **Shanghai Tower** *Marshall Strabala, Gensler, Thornton Tomasetti, TJAD, 2015.* ❖ 31.2355, 121.5009

99 **Oriental Pearl Tower** *JIANG Huan Chen, LIN Benlin, and ZHANG Xiulin/SIADR, 1994.* ❖ 31.2420, 121.4951

100 **Lujiazui Pedestrian Loop** *SOM, 2006.* ❖ 31.2399, 121.4961

101 **Super Brand Mall** *Jon JERDE Partnership/ECADI, 2002.* ❖ 31.2387, 121.4947

102 **Apple Store** *BOHLIN CYWINSKI JACKSON, 2010.* ❖ 31.2394, 121.4968

103 **Shanghai International Finance Centre (IFC)** *PELLI, CLARKE, PELLI, 2011.* Three glass and steel towers with chamfered corners perch on a four-storey shopping mall podium. ❖ 31.2385, 121.4975

104 **Agricultural Bank of China** *Arquitectonica/ECADI, 2011.* ❖ 31.2443, 121.5047

105 **Century Avenue (Shiji Dadao)** This landscaped avenue links the financial centre with Century Park. The 44.5-metre-wide north sidewalk features eight botanical gardens and a sculpture park. ❖ 31.2276, 121.5249

106 **CSCEC Tower** *Kohn Pedersen Fox (KPF), 2008.* Wrapped in blue-green glass, this triangular tower twists upward. ❖ 31.2276, 121.5249

107 **East Hope Group** *Arquitectonica, 2007.* An irregularly curved base supports a glass cube. ❖ 31.2276, 121.5293

108 **Diamond Exchange** *Goettsch Partners, 2005–2009.* ❖ 31.2263, 121.5322

109 **Oriental Arts Centre** Paul ANDREU, ECADI, 2004. ❖ 31.2249, 121.5367

110 **Parkview Hotel** Paul ANDREU, *2007.* ❖ 31.2259, 121.5386

111 **Science & Technology Museum** *LIU Xiaoguang, RTKL, SIADR, 2001.* ❖ 31.2199, 121.5375

112 **Century Park (Shìjì Gōngyuán).** This large park blends Eastern and Western features. ❖ 31.2179, 121.5468

113 **Kerry Parkside** *Kohn Pedersen Fox (KPF), 2010.* Three towers are arranged in a zig-zag fashion to maximise views to Century Park. ❖ 31.2146, 121.5599

114 **Shanghai New International Expo Centre** *MURPHY/JAHN Architects, 2001.* ❖ 31.2128, 121.5612

115 **Zendai Himalayas Centre** Arata ISOZAKI, 2010. ❖ 31.2117, 121.5577

116 **Shanghai Maglev Train Terminus** *2004.* "Downtown" station for the Magnetic levitation train to Pudong airport (in 8 minutes flat). ❖ 31.2047, 121.5536

117 **Qingpu Youth Centre** *Atelier Deshaus, 2012.* ❖ 31.1582, 121.1270

118 **Qingpu Library/Thumb Island** *MADA s.p.a.m. (Qingyun MA), 2005.* ❖ 31.1504, 121.1311

119 **Xiayu Kindergarten** *Atelier Deshaus, 2009.* A collection of colourful boxes,

SH Shanghai

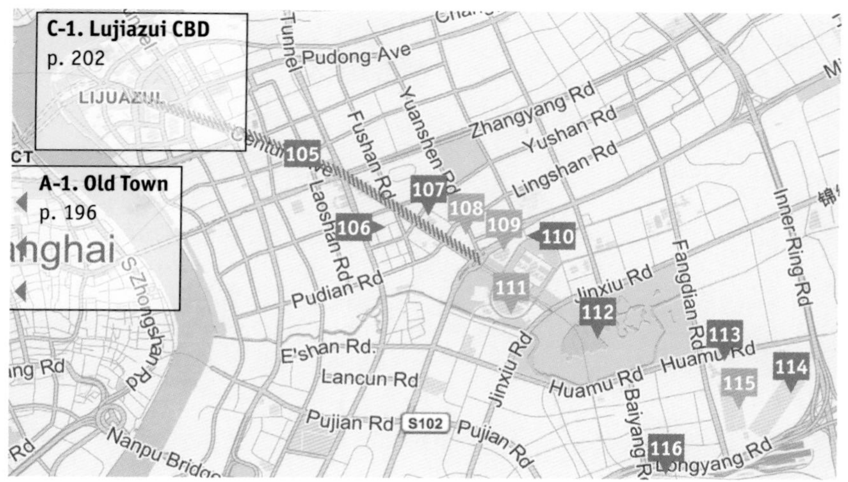

C. Century Avenue & Century Park, Pudong (Map 105–116)

wrapped by an undulating perimeter wall, suggests urbanity in a desolate new town. ❖ 31.1513, 121.1375

120 Qingpu Exhibition Centre *Jiakun Architects (LIU Jiakun), 2005* ❖ 31.1526, 121.1286

121 Office Building for Qingpu Business Association *Atelier Deshaus, 2003–2005.* ❖ 31.1509, 121.1362

122 Qingpu Footbridge CA-Design, 2004–2008. ❖ 31.1442, 121.1169

123 Qing Song Wai Garden *Scenic Architecture Office (ZHU Xiaofeng, GUO Dan), 2005.* A play of volumes in brick, wood, and Modernist-white. ❖ 31.1364, 121.1171

124 Qiaoziwan Shopping Centre & Qushui Park Edge Garden *MADA s.p.a.m. (Qingyun MA), 2004.* ❖ 31.1503, 121.1097

125 Maritime Safety Administration Building *Atelier Deshaus, 2005.* Low glass and wood structure forms a gate to the old town. ❖ 31.1149, 121.0590

126 Shangduli Leisure Plaza *Atelier FCJZ, 2004.* A dense, low-rise complex of new hotels and shopping venues. A respectful intervention in the historic water town. ❖ 31.1128, 121.0529

127 Museum of Humanities *ZHU Xiaofeng/Scenic Architecture Office, 2008.* Modern galleries inspired by canal town architecture. ❖ 31.1105, 121.0507

128 Zhujiajiao Canal Town *300+ CE.* ❖ 31.1095, 121.0500

129 Zhujiajiao Administrative Centre MADA s.p.a.m. (Qingyun MA),2004. ❖ 31.1054, 121.0415

130 Zhujiajiao Cambridge Water Town *Studio Shanghai, 2008.* Contemporary re-interpretation of a traditional water town. ❖ 31.1049, 121.0333

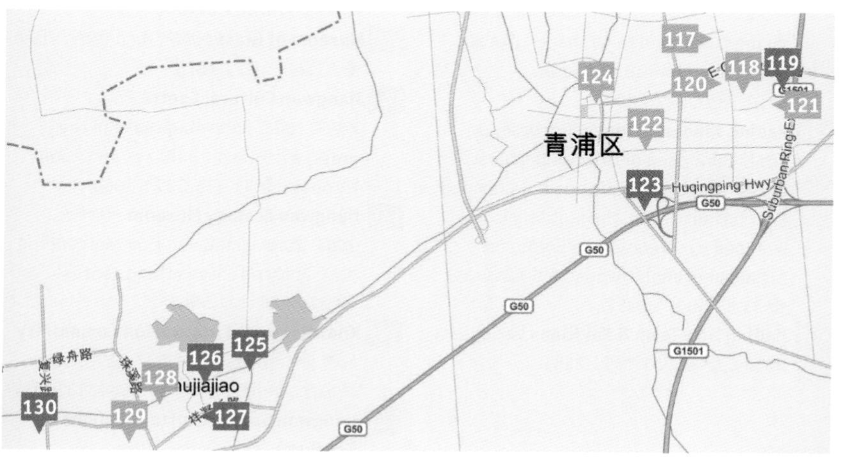

D. Qingpu & Zhujiajiao (Map 117–130)

E. Jiading and Anting (Map 131–142)

131 Anting New Town/German Town *Albert SPEER & Partner, 2001.* ❖ 31.2717, 121.1659

132 Shanghai Auto Museum *Atelier Brückner, IFB Dr. Braschel AG, Architectural Design & Research Institute of Tongji University, 2007.* ❖ 31.2801, 121.1659

133 Anting Old Street *from 220 CE.* A tourist-attraction canal street with recently-added faux-Ming and Qing buildings. ❖ 31.2989, 121.1488

134 School of Communication and Art *ZHENG Qun, WEN Xiaoqin, ZHANG Yan, 2009.* ❖ 31.2871, 121.2053

135 Shanghai International Circuit *Hermann TILKE & Peter WAHL, 2004.* Formula One racing track, said to be shaped like an auspicious Chinese character. ❖ 31.3367, 121.2208

136 Jiading Kindergarten *Atelier Deshaus, 2011.* Comprised of two zig-zag bars, one for classrooms and one for a ramped circulation atrium, the building is wrapped by screens and a colourful façade of irregularly punched windows. ❖ 31.3337, 121.2457

137 Jiading New Town & Pavilions Various, 2010s. ❖ 31.3517, 121.2551

138 Jiading Library *MADA s.p.a.m, Vermilion Zhou, 2013.* A finely detailed contemporary courtyard scheme. ❖ 31.3524, 121.2597

139 Zhouqiao Old Street A square-kilometre fragment of the old canal town. ❖ 31.3861, 121.2460

140 Garden of Autumn Vapors (Qiuxia Pu) ❖ 31.3887, 121.2486

141 Zhou Chunya Art Academy *TM Studio (TONG Ming), 2008–2009.* Brutalist/Ando-ist concrete volume, floating on water and trees. ❖ 31.3820, 121.3056

142 Nanxiang Ancient Town Charming canal town with temple, twin pagodas, gardens and pork-broth dumplings. ❖ 31.2914, 121.3110

143 Museum of Glass *LOGON Architects, 2011* ❖ 31.3455, 121.4673

144 Jiangwan Cultural Centre *RTKL, 2003–2006.* Sprawling snake in the grass, with glazed volumes punching through. ❖ 31.3363, 121.5066

145 Jiangwan Ecology Museum *PU Miao, 2004–2005.* Small museum, descending pleasantly into its wetland context. ❖ 31.3216, 121.5065

146 Knowledge and Innovation Community *SOM (architecture), Tom LEADER Studio (landscape), 2006.* ❖ 31.3084, 121.5089

147 Jiangwan Sports Centre (Shanghai Stadium) *DONG Dayou, 1934.* ❖ 31.3080, 121.5101

148 Tongji University *founded 1907.* This campus boasts one of the best architecture schools in China, housed in Building C, by Atelier Z+ (2002–04). ❖ 31.2871, 121.5013

149 Luodian New Town/Swedish Town *Sweco Architects & KTH Urban Planning and Design, 2001–2013.* ❖ 31.4031, 121.3501

150 Gaoqiao New Town/Holland Village *Kuiper Compagnons and Atelier Dutch, 2001–2004.* ❖ 31.3352, 121.5723

151 J-Office & Silk Wall *Archi-Union (Philip F. YUAN), 2009–2010.* Parametric hollow-brick wall encircles a warehouse renovation. ❖ 31.3114, 121.5429

152 Dongtan Eco-city, Chongming Island *ARUP, 2005–10.* Envisaged to become a carbon-neutral town of 500,000 by 2030, little but a wind farm has been built as of this writing (marker indicates Chongming Island only). ❖31.2914, 121.3110

153 Pudong International Airport *Terminal 1: Paul ANDREU, 1999, Terminal 2: ECADI, 2008.* ❖ 31.1530, 121.8050

154 Pudong New Library *Nihon Sekkei, Inc. 2006–2010.* ❖ 31.1942, 121.5371

155 Pujiang Italian Town *Vittorio GREGOTTI and Associates, Centro Studio Traffico, Arup, THAPE, 2001–2004+.* ❖ 31.1046, 121.4915

156 Giant Interactive Group HQ *Morphosis (Thom MAYNE), 2006–2010.* ❖ 31.0570, 121.2617

F. Jiangwan District (Map 143–148)

157 Thames Town *Atkins Design Studio, China Shanghai Arch. Design and Research, et al., 2001–2006.* ❖31.0353, 121.1934

158 Lingang New Town *GMP (von GERKAN, MARG and PARTNER), 2002.* "Water drop" rings and a greenbelt surround a circular lake. ❖ 30.9003, 121.9264

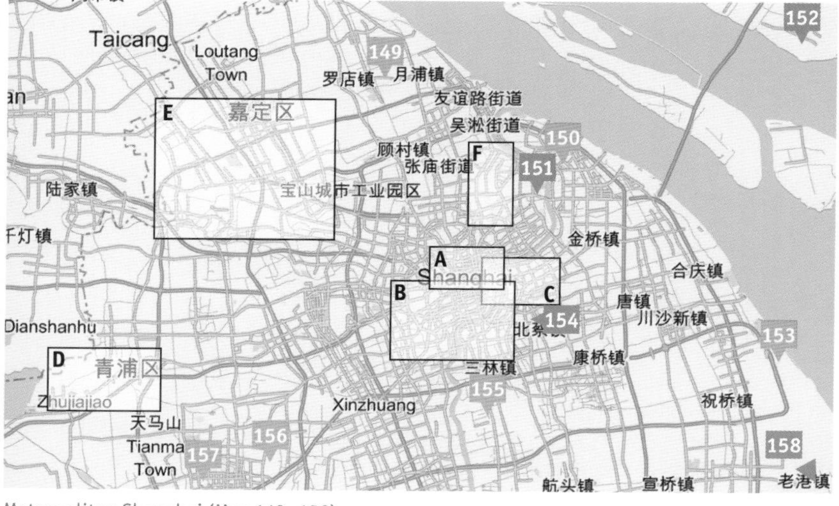

Metropolitan Shanghai (Map 149–158)

苏州
Suzhou

苏州 Suzhou

Located only 100 km west of Shanghai (now a short 25-minute ride by high-speed rail), Suzhou is, justifiably, one of China's most famous cities, most noted (and most interesting to designers) as the home of a host of world-class classical gardens of the "Southern" style. While these gardens are the main reason to make a visit, the city's historic core of gridded canals is of interest in itself, and if you somehow get tired of the gardens, a handful of worthy contemporary projects round out the experience.

Suzhou is often compared to Venice, but while both feature postcard-perfect canal scenes and were global trading hubs in their prime years, the comparisons should stop there. Venice's urbanism is defined by an irregular network of streets, fronted by structures built atop deep wooden piles on land dredged from shallower sections of the Venetian lagoon. Suzhou's plan adheres to a rigid grid that follows long-established cosmological rules of city planning, with waterways carved into the alluvial clay soil. Venice was a maritime and military power long before the city was a centre of arts and culture, and the eclectic style of Venetian architecture represents the influences of a medieval, Mediterranean trading empire. Suzhou, surrounded even today by lowland polder farming, seems more a product of the immediate environment, locked into the regional project of hydraulic engineering that transformed the Yangtze Delta into one of the most productive and populous regions on the planet. Rather than accumulating and synthesising myriad influences, the architectural style of Suzhou's buildings is a more local affair, with gardens that are arguably the pinnacle and ultimate expression of the techniques of traditional Chinese architecture.

Suzhou is said to have been founded in the fifth century BCE, situated where the fertile Yangtze Delta is politely interrupted by the hills around Taihu Lake. These hills presumably offered a strategic advantage in the very flat, hard-to-defend delta, and so Suzhou developed from an agricultural centre into the ancient capital of the Wu state. The defence problem led the first Wu king, HE Lü, to commission fortification walls in 514 BC; these would be succeeded by several later generations of walls. The completion of the **Grand Canal** (p. 226) in the sixth century CE gave Suzhou a strategic trading position, which helped usher in pre-industrial manufacturing, particularly in the fields of silk and embroidery. Another boom began in the twelfth century, as part of a larger southward

Previous spread: Layered surfaces of a canal-side building; compare to Amateur Architecture's use of masonry in the **Ningbo Urban Museum** (p. 237) and **Xiangshan Campus** (p. 264).

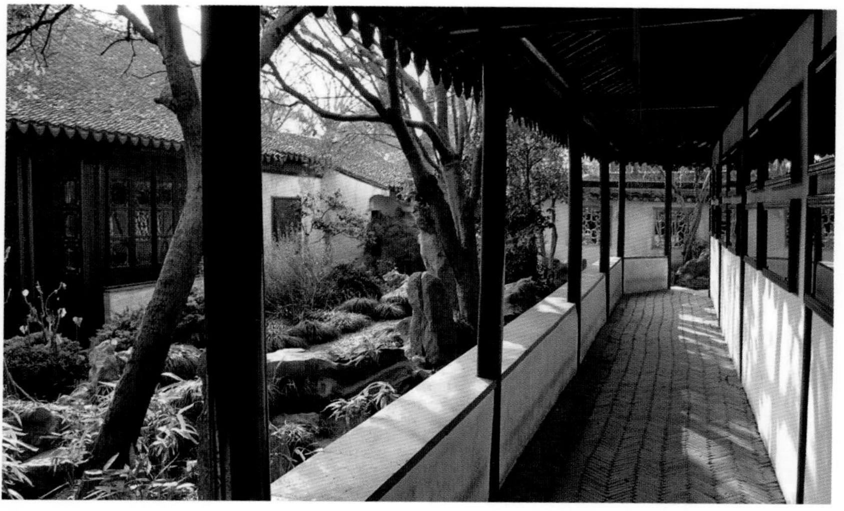

Covered walkway in Lingering Garden (p. 224)

From Alfred Schinz, *The Magic Square* (1996), pp. 253. Courtesy Edition Axel Menges.

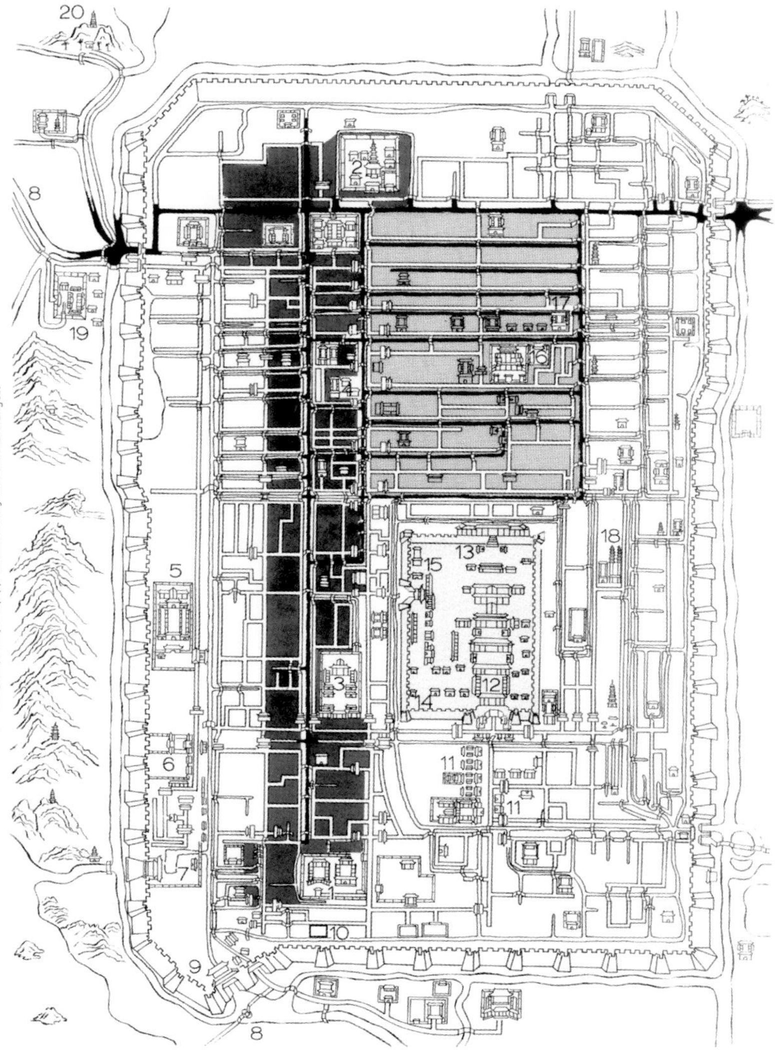

Suzhou in 1229; map based on a famous carved *stele*. The dark grey indicates the main market canal and associated streets; to its east are a palace complex and the main residential district.

Cutaway view through a typical southern Chinese covered market street and its buildings. Note the stepped sawtoothed roof which encourages ventilating breezes.

Suzhou, seen from the North Temple Pagoda

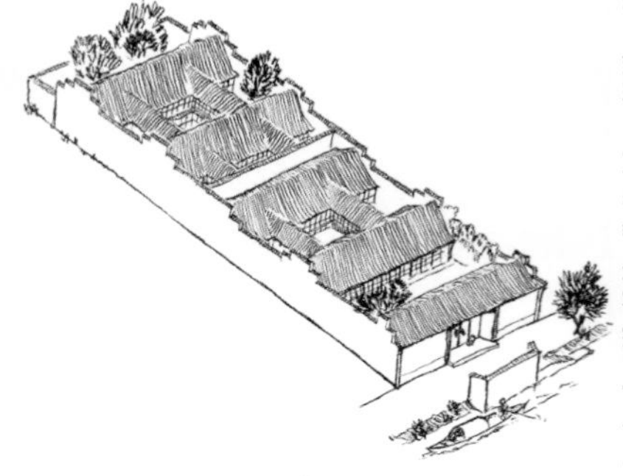

Perspective of a typical Suzhou residence

Drawings from Alfred Schinz, *The Magic Square* (1996), pp. 292, 297 Courtesy Edition Axel Menges

shift of Chinese economic activity owing to invasions in the north by Manchurians and, later, by Mongols. It was this wealth that would sponsor the creation of the city's famous gardens, in the hands of state-appointed scholars, for whom gardening was one of the high arts.

Suzhou maintained its significance throughout the Ming dynasty (1368–1644), and was mentioned by Marco Polo (ca. 1300) as "a very great and noble city" whose people lived "by their manufactures and trade" of "gold brocade and other stuffs." The city was overshadowed as Shanghai gained in prominence during the late Qing dynasty and Republic of China era, and suffered substantial ransacking and destruction in virtually every civil and foreign war in China's modern history. Its gardens have required frequent repairs, and most of their present layouts are 1950s or even 1980s reconstructions of their configurations in the late part of the Qing dynasty (1644–1912). Indeed, by the time of the People's Republic, the number of gardens was down from a peak of 271 to 188, with most in some state of decay and at least one of the "great" gardens being used as an army stables. Even as the Suzhou metropolis as a whole became one of Communist China's industrial centres, the government expropriated the gardens, and made a number of them into public parks. Many were raided again in the Cultural Revolution, leading to another round of renovations.

Though the old city centre is now peppered with twentieth-century buildings of various stripes, its general configuration and much of its fabric still date to the Song and Ming boom years. The map of the city drawn in 1229, just after a century-long rebuilding process, shows many roads and canals still recognisable today. Like many planned cities in China, the form Suzhou takes is roughly a north-south grid, with minor variations for topography, an urban form that, at this early date, had already seen thousands of years of development (see **Beijing**, p. 064).

While many cities designed on similar gridded plans aimed for the ideal of a square perimeter oriented to true north, Suzhou's grid is a little longer in the north-south direction than the east-west, and angled a few degrees off true north, perhaps a purposeful eccentricity to accommodate prevailing winds in summer, and block them in winter. Suzhou's residential blocks are generally longer in the east-west direction, bordered to the south by a road, and to the north by a canal, giving each residence land and water access.

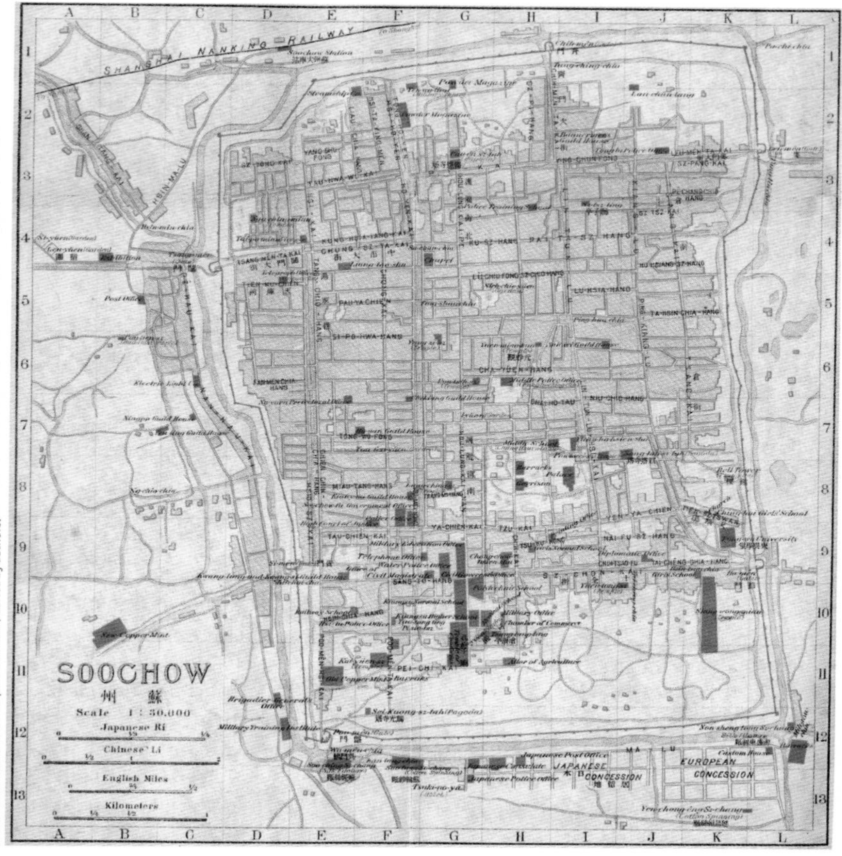

p. 217: Believed to be in the public domain; edited by authors.

"Soochow" in 1915

Today, Suzhou's streets are organised on a strict hierarchy, with automobile traffic limited to certain tree-lined boulevards, and most roads divided into bus, auto, bicycle, and pedestrian zones. The large blocks, circumscribed by the major roads, are further subdivided by smaller lanes, which give way in turn to pedestrian alleyways. Thanks to strict preservation codes, the **North Temple Pagoda** (map p. 228) remains the tallest structure in the old city; the commanding view from the top reveals a town still filled mostly with low-rise shops and houses, whose whitewashed walls and black tile roofs lend Suzhou its particular aesthetic charm.

Numerous books have been written on Suzhou's classical gardens, and for good reason. The gardens here, and across the Yangtze Delta, represent the pinnacle of classical dynastic Chinese artistry in architecture. Descriptions in English (sometimes following the canonical Chinese tomes on garden design) tend to describe in detail the essential elements of a garden, which come together in harmonious synthesis: the rockeries, the pools and water features, plantings and pavilions; all of which are ascribed various meanings and interpretations. Alternatively, reflecting on Suzhou's canals, and the surrounding rice polders carved into the alluvial plain, we can find in Suzhou's gardens a meditation on the ground plane. Pools are carved into the earth, rocks are piled up, sectional shifts expose the boundaries between earth, water, and air as porous and available for manipulation.

Similarly, in plan, the gardens reflect a dismantling of the courtyard typology. Within the perimeter walls, living areas are pushed south, with small agricultural plots abutting the canal to the north. Vestiges of this arrangement survive in many of Suzhou's gardens, perhaps most strikingly in the **Garden of the Master of Nets** (p. 221). Here the courtyard in the lower right of the plan contrasts with the marching succession of courtyards and halls towards the centre. Pergolas peel off

A canal in Suzhou

the main structure to become independent covered walkways, courtyard perimeters fragment to allow slices of views out from the corners, and windows are punched in solid walls to frame oblique views through the garden. Architecture and landscape design are so interwoven that it feels disingenuous to assign these gardens to one discipline or the other. This synthetic ambiguity is what is most striking about the gardens today, and the formal devices that allow landscape and architecture to merge are, more than material treatment or graphic symbolism, a source for inspiration in contemporary work at various scales (see **Jade Bamboo Garden,** p. 323, **Qushui Edge Garden,** p. 187, **Xiangshan Campus,** p. 264, **Jinhua Exhibition Space,** p. 281, among others).

The desire for harmony between nature and artifice is perhaps exemplified by the *taihu* stone. Carved by hand, then left to erode in nearby lake Taihu for years or decades, the smoothly perforated stones represent the combined work of man and nature. Worthy of contemplation in their own right (and often selected for this purpose), they are a microcosm of garden-making. The fact that they have been painstakingly selected and worked does not make them unsuitable as "nature."

Many analyses of the gardens focus on their role as meditative spaces for retired scholars, whom we imagine lost in solitary thought, strolling through the gardens. The cut-windows and pictorial layering make the most of limited space, illusionistically providing changes of scenery for the wandering poet. The presence of named pavilions for reading, calligraphy, listening to music, writing poetry and so on makes clear that the gardens were meant not only to be looked at, but to actively support the poet-official lifestyle. Still, we shouldn't ignore the playfulness of the stone boats, winding channels for floating wine glasses, or hidden nooks for secret dalliances. The same devices that allow for scalar ambiguity, and a dislocation between visual and physical accessibility, turn these gardens into veritable playgrounds, or at least suitable venues for entertaining guests.

Taken as a set, the gardens are fascinating in their manipulation of space, sequence, interlocking volumes, physical and visual accessibility, layering, transparency, and subtle distinctions in spatial hierarchy. As the gardens are each surrounded and defined by a solid perimeter wall, their spatial complexities are partially determined by the overall size of the parcel. In the larger gardens (such as the **Humble Administrator's Garden,** p. 218, or the **Lingering Garden**, p. 224), all architectural elements exist as independent pavilions, while at smaller gardens (**Master of Nets**, p. 221, or **Mountain Villa Embracing Beauty**, p. 223), all the same elements seem to have been folded in on each other. These extreme cases can be understood as the limits on a continuum, with each garden occupying a place along the line: from the spacious landscape dotted with free-standing pavilions, down to the compressed, ambiguous spaces, indicative of a constrained site.

The Suzhou gardens, then, are best appreciated as a typological set with scale as a variable; visitors might compare the size and density of each garden, and the range of responses to expansion and compression of the same elements. Yet one should be wary of generalising too broadly about the nature of "Chinese gardens." Everything we see here is quite recent in construction, and these reconstructions may themselves be influenced by critical perceptions of the "ideal garden." As Alison HARDIE points out, English-language scholarship has only recently begun to explore the economic and social context of the Chinese gardens, rather than simply their unique aesthetic and compositional sensibility, or their influence on Western gardens.

Today, Suzhou is undergoing a re-centring process akin to the purposeful re-location of ancient capitals by new dynasties. Recognising the economic import of Suzhou as a major tourist attraction, the government seeks to modernise through infrastructural improvements and the creation of new business and industrial districts. The model seems to be working, and while there's not yet much of interest to see in the new districts, their separate existence ensures the survival of Suzhou's remaining historic charm. Suzhou today could almost be considered part of metropolitan Shanghai: the cities are well connected by transit, linked by a near-continuous zone of urbanisation, and participate in the same schemes of economic liberalisation. Yet Suzhou retains its distinct identity, and provides an excellent model for forward-thinking urban development that foregrounds economic progress while respecting and encouraging historical preservation.

Practical Considerations

Suzhou's old city is compact, flat, and pedestrian-friendly. Its pleasant, tree-lined streets, with separated bicycle lanes, make cycling an appealing option. An expanding subway system, ubiquitous taxis, and comprehensible street grid, aid navigation. High-speed rail makes a day trip from Shanghai possible, though the city demands a longer and more relaxed itinerary. We recommend two to three days in order to take in the gardens, canal towns, and scattered contemporary works.

Sources and Recommended Reading

Rolf BORCHARD and Yali YU, *Gardens in Suzhou*, Fellbach: Axel Menges, 2003. Very helpful text, gorgeous photos, great drawings.

CHENG Liyao, *Private Gardens*, New York: Springer Verlag, 1999. Great drawings and reference material, with thorough detailing of individual pavilions, lattices, paving patterns, etc.

Ron HENDERSON, *The Gardens of Suzhou*, Philadelphia: University of Pennsylvania Press, 2012. Recent garden-by-garden breakdown by a practising landscape architect, with fresh drawings (including a comparative set).

INAJI Toshirō, *The Garden as Architecture*, Tokyo: Kodansha International, 1998. Chinese gardens in the local and international context of other building types.

R. Stewart JOHNSON, "The Ancient City of Suzhou: Town Planning in the Sung [sic] Dynasty," in *Town Planning Review* (April 1983). Deep background on urban form.

JUNHUA Zhong, *Sights and Scenes of Suzhou*, Beijing: Zhaohou Publishing House, 1983. Official government tour guide with lots of factoids and/or anecdotes about specific garden features, if you're curious.

Maggie KESWICK, with Charles JENCKS and Allison HARDIE (introduction), *The Chinese Garden: History, Art & Architecture*, Cambridge, Mass.: Harvard University Press, 2003. Great drawings and very thoughtful analysis, leavened by Hardie's even-handed introduction, relating Keswick's classic work to more recent scholarship.

XU Yinong, essays in *Studies in the History of Gardens & Designed Landscapes* (1999, 2004). More good reference material, with particular attention to the design of the Canglangting in its historical context.

Photo by Kerun Ip; courtesy Pei Partnership Architects

Photo by Kerun Ip; courtesy Pei Partnership Architects

View of great hall

Site plan

Suzhou Museum

SU 02

I.M. Pei with Pei Partnership Architects, 2002–2006

苏州博物馆
平江区东北街204号
204 Dongbei St, Pingjiang District
❖ 31.3249, 120.6237

Pei had both a loaded site (directly adjacent to the **Humble Administrator's Garden**, p. 218) and a personal connection, having spent much time in Suzhou gardens as a child. His approach tempers the elemental geometry familiar from other Pei museums (the Louvre, the Rock & Roll Hall of Fame, etc.) with references to the local white-and-grey palette, the low cornices, and the fundamental garden type: corridors and pavilions loosely enclosing an irregular pond. Modernity is suggested by the steel-framed pyramids, which also admit changing natural lighting, another garden essential. It's a fascinating project, since Pei has seemingly been trying to recreate the Suzhou gardens for years; note the elements of tradition merged with modern elements at the **Fragrant Hill Hotel** (p. 092) and the **Bank of China** (p. 354). Of course, such an attempt is not totally foreign to Pei's other work, or that of his instructors and peers way back at Harvard in the 1940s (Philip JOHNSON, Marcel BREUER, Paul RUDOLPH, et al.). The Suzhou Museum comes the closest to realising a classical design in modern materials, with the cleverest move being the series of flat rocks along the garden wall, suggesting a mountain range reflected in the pond. If it's not *as* ambiguous as a classical garden,

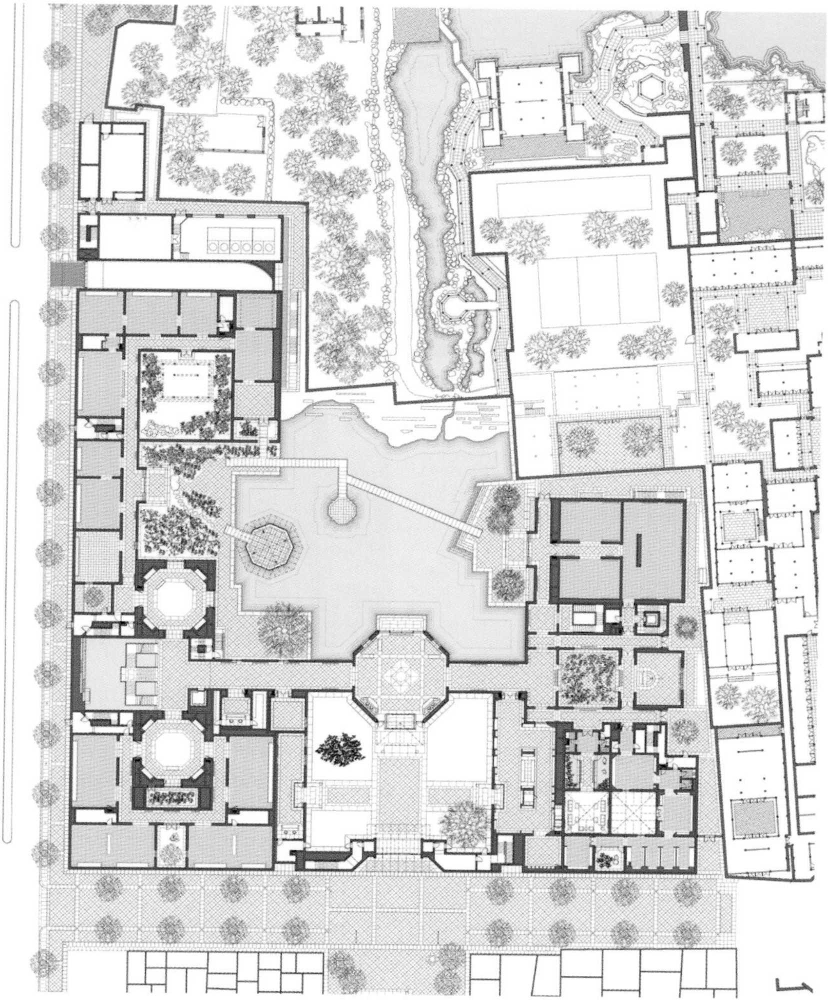

Ground-floor plan

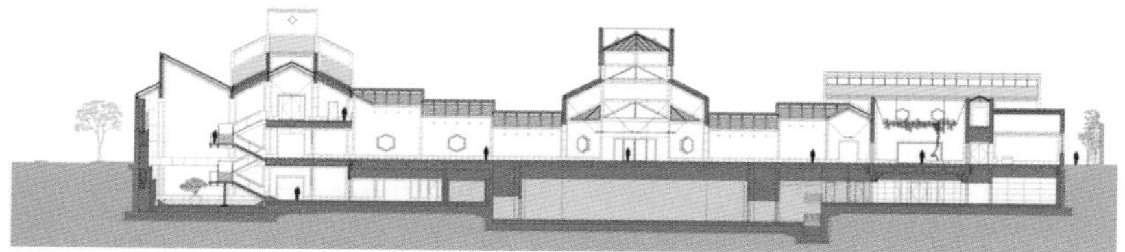

East-west section

North-south section

perhaps it's in deference to the neighbouring masterpieces, a "humble" gesture indeed. As well, most gardens begin with a regular, symmetrical house, and have attained their complexity through small edits over time; perhaps Pei is leaving bait for some future Master of Nets. Already the pragmatic incorporation of the older east wing places the building in a line of transhistorical collaboration.

Garden of the Humble Administrator
WANG Xiancheng & WEN Zhengming, 1510+

SU 03

拙政园
平江区东北街178号
178 Dongbei St, Pingjiang District
❖ 31.3256, 120.6260

Wang was a court historian run out of government by the Secret Service (!), and Wen, his assistant on the project, was one of the "Four Master" Ming painter/calligraphers, known for his studies of single landscape elements. Unusually, this garden is divided along its length into three distinct sections, whose differences were amplified when the property was broken up for sale in 1631; it was reunited in the 1950s, at which time the large East Garden was created. Thus, there are two separate pond-compositions, with the complex Middle Garden being most famous. This history, and the garden's unusual size, perhaps explain a certain diffuse quality to the spatial sequence; it's a little too easy to get your bearings and anticipate what's coming. Still, note the "borrowing" of external elements, such as the distant North Temple Pagoda. The trusty "mirroring" strategy goes as far as using an actual large mirror in one pavilion to reflect scenery from across the pond. Of particular interest is the long, rolling gallery dividing the west and middle gardens, a fine double-sided edge. The new Garden Museum is also worth a look.

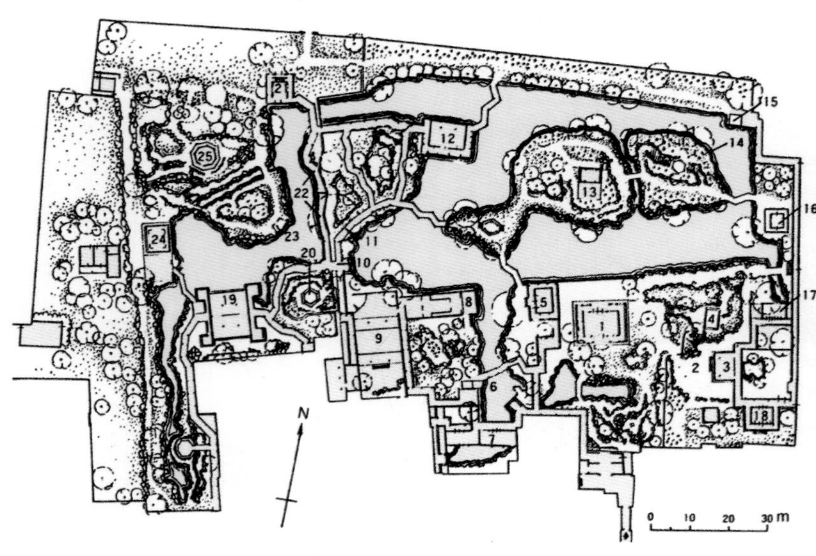

Plan (West and Middle gardens only)

Lion's Grove Garden

SU 04

WEN Tianru, et al
1342, 1589, 1771, 1917+

狮子林
平江区园林路23号
23 Yuanlin Rd., Pingjiang District
❖ 31.3228, 120.6252

Begun as a monastery garden in 1342, the "Lion's Grove" is named for the supposedly lion-esque rockery carvings (originally nine in number), or maybe the Buddhist "Lion's Roar Sutra," or maybe in honour of the builder's teacher, who had once lived at a place called Lion Cliff. In any case, the rocks probably better resembled lions before all the years of weathering; you'd need a tour guide to point out the lion forms now. The most interesting thing here is the development of the extended rockery as occupiable space; this is a small garden, and over half of it is taken up with rockeries, riddled with voids and lacking clearly-identifiable landmarks. These caves are delightful, as one can walk under spaces previously occupied, through what one would swear was the solid "ground." The view out from the grotto-like under-passage, showing the obviously artificial bridge framed by the ragged, ostens-ibly "natural" rocks, is a classic Suzhou moment. It also constitutes the direct precursor of a classic Picturesque device, in English gardens such as Stourhead (1740s-1770s), much as the over-under experience suggests post-1990s "single surface" architecture.

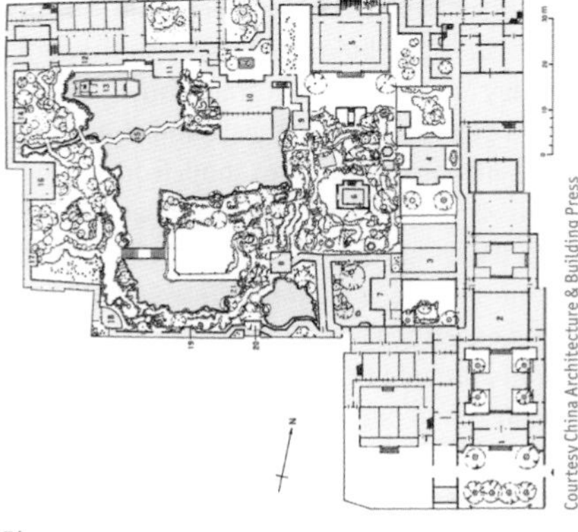

Plan

Courtesy China Architecture & Building Press

Couples' Retreat

SU 05

LU Jin, SHEN Bingcheng, 1874

耦园
平江区小新桥巷6号
6 Xiaoxinqiao Alley, Pingjiang District
❖ 31.3182, 120.6345

This mid-sized classical garden dates to the later years of the Qing dynasty, marking it one of the final constructions of the classical period. As such, the Couples' Retreat can be read as a late work, building on the innovations of past designers. Here, "couple" refers to the garden's eastern and western halves, separated by a residential core. The courtyard typology of the central complex is intact, and can be fruitfully compared to Suzhou's traditional housing stock. The east and west gardens are fairly autonomous, each featuring the spatial ambiguity and layering that make these gardens famous. Unlike many other gardens, the Couples' Retreat does have an exterior façade: at the perimeter canal, the wall is elaborated into a pavilion, and lattice windows provide views to the surrounding neighbourhood.

PingJiang Canal Street

SU 06

Song dynasty, 960–1279

平江路
❖ 31.3171, 120.6293

Historically, the cities of the Yangtze Delta were criss-crossed by canals, and inland river trade was essential to the region's economy. While many of Suzhou's canals have been filled in and paved over (see also Shanghai, p. 144), certain areas have been preserved as "cultural protection zones." Pingjiang is the central axis of a larger historic residential district, and though the cafés and boutiques that line the canal today are anything but traditional, one can still get a sense of the scale and style of the pre-modern city. The shop-fronts along this street vary in width, but are unified in style: movable wood screens provide a permeable membrane between interior and exterior space, the white-washed brick walls provide fire breaks between adjacent stores, and black tiles cap every roof. Veer off the main path, and you may still find small garden patches and other remnants of a fast-vanishing lifestyle.

Garden of the Master of Nets

SU 09

SONG Zongyuan, et al, 1785+

网师园
沧浪区带城桥路11号
11 Daichengqiao Rd, Canglang District
❖ 31.3000, 120.6299

"The Garden of the Master of Nets" (or just "Fisherman") is tiny, compared with that of the "Humble Administrator," but ranks among the city's best. The overlapping garden courtyards and pavilions have seemingly grown together so symbiotically, that it's difficult to tell where one pavilion stops and the next one begins. It's as if a larger garden has been compressed and folded in on itself to fit the small footprint, with walkways, rockeries, walls, and carved screens colliding and overlapping, creating an intricately layered space. While a garden had been on the site since 1140, it was redesigned by Song, an eighteenth-century official who aspired to the simple life and humble values of a fisherman. Later owners include a scholar (from 1795) and a master calligrapher (from 1868); each made some additions.

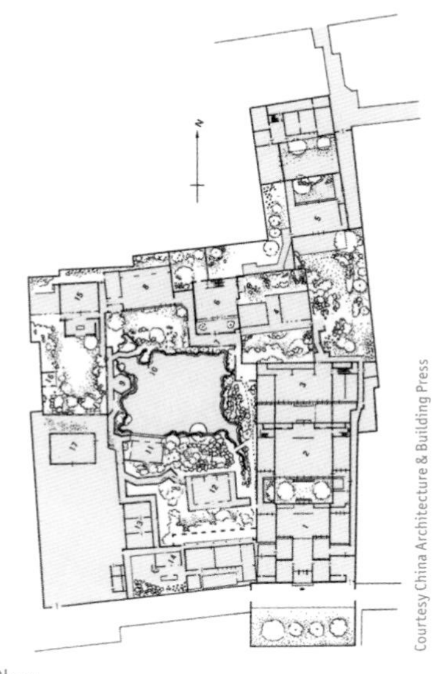

Plan

Courtesy China Architecture & Building Press

Suquan Yuan

SU 10

TM Studio (TONG Ming), 2004–2007

苏泉苑 - 十全街711号
711 Shiquan Jie, Gusu District
❖ 31.3004, 120.6252

This small development ("Spring Gardens") was inserted in the city fabric on a former parking lot, an awkward site with a "bottle-neck" entrance. Tong placed the public coffee shop towards the front, just off a major street, where it could act as a billboard for the site. The detailing establishes that the building belongs in Suzhou without falling into garden kitsch. Operable wooden screens, set frankly between concrete slabs, feature patterns simplified down to a tessellation of hexagons. The interior – two parallel rectangles in plan, with a double-height space at one end of the café – is again quite simple but effective, allowing the light passing through the screens (and the interior layer of glass) to take full effect. Tong relates the project to Le Corbusier's Dom-Ino diagram and a rationalised, Kahnian separation of "served area and servant rooms," but we're reminded most of Herzog & de Meuron's minimalist period (the Ricola warehouse, the Goetz Gallery): the building as a "skinned" effects-box, without representative façade. Compare to the same firm's extension of the **Dong Tea House** (map p. 228).

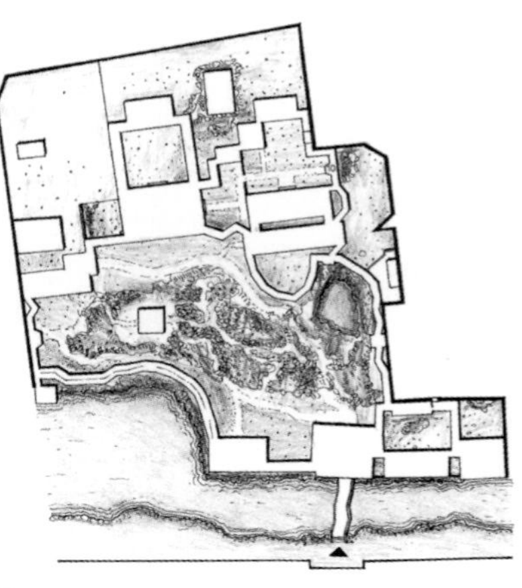

Plan

Blue Wave Pavilion

SU 11

SU Shunqin, et al. 1044+

沧浪亭
沧浪区沧浪亭街3号
3 Canglangting St, Canglang District
❖ 31.2965, 120.6221

This 1.1-hectare garden is closely identified with the Cāng Làng Tíng (Great Waves or Blue Waves Pavilion), added by the poet SU Shunqin when he purchased this former imperial flower garden (907–926 AD). The pavilion was named after a line from the sage Mencius: "If the water of the Canglang River is clear, I wash in it the ribbons of my [official] hat/If it is muddy, I use it for my feet." As with the "Humble Administrator," this is a commentary on the high-minded sage's decision to withdraw himself from the corruptions of life at court. After some years of neglect, the garden was restored in 1696 by the governor SONG Luo, who also moved said pavilion to its current location. Most of the buildings date from this renovation or later.

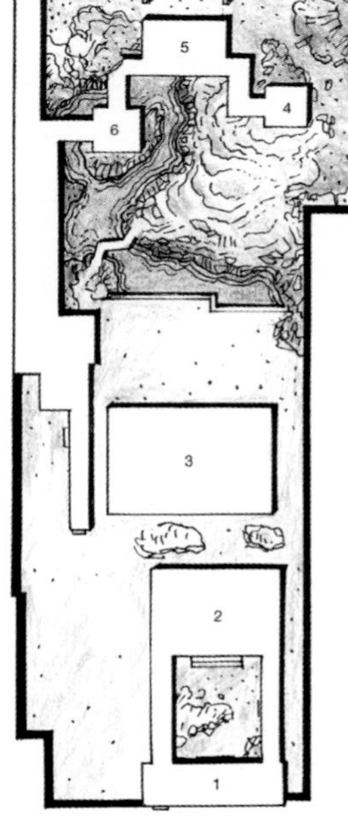

Plan

Mountain Villa with Embracing Beauty

SU 13

GE Yuliang, 1807+

环秀山庄，平江区景德路272号
272 Jingde Rd, Pingjiang District
❖ 31.3126, 120.6094

This very small and apparently simple garden is startlingly complex, with a configuration of pavilions and corridors that serve to create several distinct yet overlapping spaces. The greatest interest lies in the twisting paths of the eponymous rockery, which seems to push all other garden elements aside to occupy most of the site, with a set of pavilions perched in its heights (compare to the similarly rockery-oriented **Lion's Grove Garden**, p. 219, on a larger site). Only about six metres tall, it makes a viable "mountain" out of what could have been a mole-hill, a fine benchmark for landscape architects working on urban sites. In plan, one can see the vestiges of a typical Yangtze delta courtyard home, with a sequence of halls arrayed on a north-south axis between two canal streets, and a rough gradient from "architecture" to "landscape" as one progresses through the structure. Though the garden was rebuilt several times since its Jin Dynasty foundation, the "mountain" design dates to the Qing Dynasty.

Lingering Garden

XU Taishi, ZHOU Shicheng, et al
1593+

留园，金阊区留园路338号
338 Liuyuan Rd., Jinchang
❖ 31.3174, 120.5880

While the origins of the Lingering Garden stretch back centuries, the current design dates to 1876, when the garden was rebuilt following the Taiping Rebellion. At this relatively late point in the development of the garden type, there were plenty of precedents to draw from, and the designers here seem to have learned some lessons from other, older designs. The garden is divided into three main sections with a pool surrounded by scattered pavilions at one end and a dense zone of rockeries at the other. The centre is held by a cluster of larger buildings, where the aggregation of pavilions and courtyards form a beguiling sequence of layered, ambiguous spaces. At close to three hectares, it is one of the larger gardens, with its distinct areas bound together by a twisting walkway seven hundred metres long. As the garden plot is set forty-five metres back from the street, the arrival sequence is a major part of the promenade, with alternating closed/open and light/dark spaces along the path.

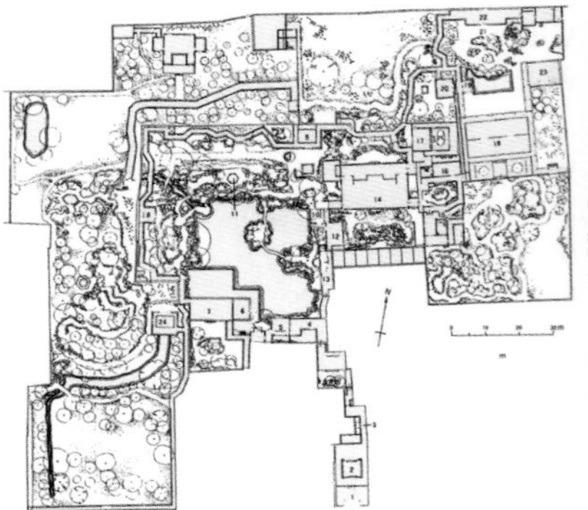

Plan

Shantang Canal Street

SU 16

山塘古街，金阊区
Jinchang District
❖ 31.3183, 120.5992

This pleasant canal street – and its surrounding neighbourhood – make for a good representation of the style of pre-modern urban development in the Yangtze Delta region. Both the restored and unrestored sections are worth exploring, though admittedly these are no substitute for a canal town visit (see p. 226).

Xi'an Jiaotong-Liverpool University Administration Information Building

Aedas (Andy WEN, project designer), 2013

SU 23

西交利物浦大学-图书馆 – 苏州市吴中区
Songtao St. & Wenjing Rd., Wuzhong
❖ 31.2748, 120.7341

Located at the intersection of two axes in the campus plan, this building was conceived as a "three-dimensional Suzhou garden" and an interpretation of the famous *taihu* stones, carved by wind and water. More interesting, perhaps, is the spatial experience of the interlocking solids and voids. Here, different programme elements are brought together around a contorted void doubling as the building's primary circulation space. Perkins & Will's campus building, opposite, does nice things with bars criss-crossed by landscape.

Courtesy Lu Wenyu/Amateur

Library of Wenzheng College

Amateur Architecture (WANG Shu & LU Wenyu), 1999

SU 22

苏州大学文正学院图书馆
吴中区吴越路
Wuyue Rd, Wuzhong
❖ 31.2212, 120.5771

In this early work, the architects favour a stripped-down modern style, without the aggressive interrogation of materials seen in their later work. The white-washed walls could be read as either a Modernist trope, or a reference to the materials of Suzhou's traditional architecture (perhaps both). The "frame" device in particular seems to anticipate later projects like the **Jinhua Ceramic House/Coffee House** (p. 283).

Photographs courtesy Aedas

Tongli and the Yangtze Delta Canal Towns

SU 24

first milenium BCE forward

(See map, p. 019.)

The waterlogged landscape of the Yangtze Delta, riddled with natural channels, has long been a centre not only for agriculture but for water-based trade. The creation of artificial canals has been undertaken since ancient times, most dramatically in the construction of the Grand Canal, an ambitious engineering project of the Sui dynasty (581–618 CE) which ran north some 1,777 km from Hangzhou to Beijing. This connected northern and southern China, and linked together all the great river systems it crossed, thus connecting the coastal provinces to the interior. Like railroads many centuries later, it helped cement "China" as an economic and cultural unity, while acting as a supply chain to troops on the frontier, far from China's bread-basket regions. The Canal, like the **Great Wall** (p. 108), was not continuous for its full length, and took advantage of many stretches of existing river; in turn, towns plugged into the existing network of rivers and canals could now benefit even further from the speed of canal shipping. All this would have appealed to the Sui dynasty, who had just reunified China after a long chaotic period; ironically, the expense and suffering of the canal project itself is sometimes cited as a reason for the dynasty's imminent downfall. The area between Taihu Lake and Shanghai is hardly the only centre of canal towns in China, but its proximity to several major cities has led to many of these towns being preserved (or "preserved") for tourist consumption. Their irregular street networks contrast sharply with Suzhou's regular canal matrix; in these towns, one might get a sense of the urban form of Shanghai or Guangzhou in pre-modern times. It's essential to visit at least one, but they are different enough that two or more can be worth your time. Boasting easy access from Suzhou, **Tongli** (同里) is likely the region's most popular town, and is notable for tasteful restoration that preserves much of the town's original aesthetic (if not the original materials). Venture off the main roads, and you'll soon find yourself passing chicken coops and small vegetable gardens mixed in with construction sites, giving the simultaneous impression of historic urbanism frozen in time, and of ever-encroaching development. Tongli is also home to the **Retreat & Reflection Garden** (1885–1887), notable for its departure from the typology: it is organised around an east-west axis (rather than north-south) and is divided into distinct eastern and western halves. Though it lacks the spatial complexity of Suzhou's best gardens, it's still a representative work of late Qing garden design. **Wuzhen** (烏鎮) directly on the Grand Canal, is among the most popular (read: sanitised) towns. While it follows the original urban plan, most of the buildings have been reconstructed for tourists, and a wrong turn may lead you to the loading docks and service entries for modern hotels hiding behind traditional store-fronts. The recent **Grand Theatre** (Kris YAO/Artech), two nested ovals, with tilted walls of brick and patterned wooden screens, fits in comfortably from certain vantage points, despite its size. By contrast, perhaps the most authentic (read: run-down) nearby town, **Xitang** (西塘) is notable for its unique covered walkways – and its fading posters for *Mission: Impossible III*, which filmed several scenes here. The majority of the structures date back to the Qing or Ming dynasties. A new entry pavilion suggests it could soon succumb to development, but as of 2014 the historic area remains knitted into the surrounding urban fabric, with few modern buildings. **Zhouzhuang** (周庄) splits the difference;

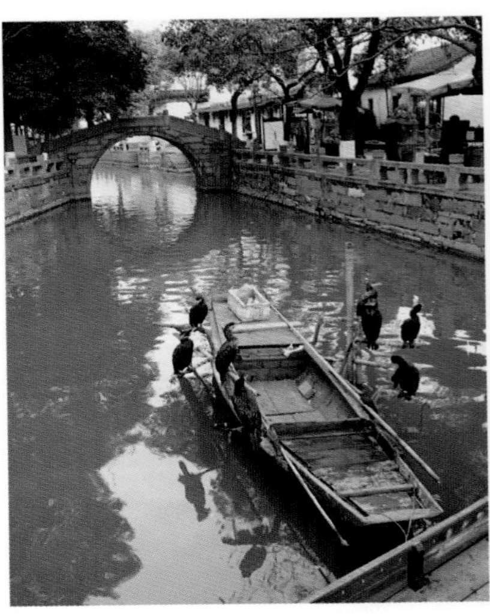

Along the canal in Tongli

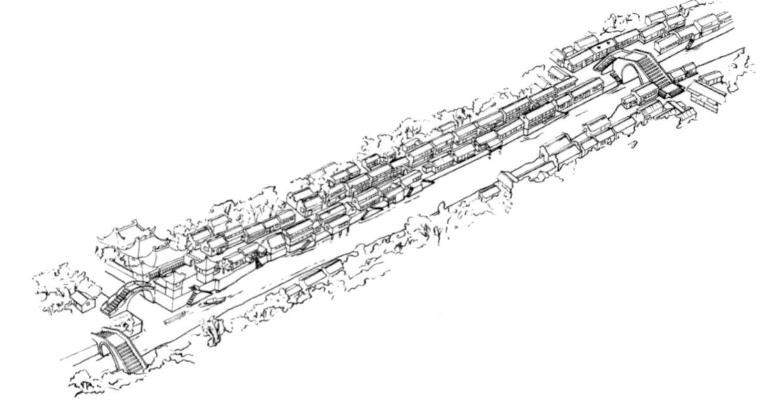
A typical Grand Canal market street

A fork in the road: Zhouzhuang

Wuzhen's canal frontage by night

The Retreat & Reflection Garden in Tongli

while commercialisation continues, its roots stretch back over 2000 years, and there are many "original" pieces here, most famously the **Chenxu Temple** (1085–1093, with extensions through 1751). This stunning example of Taoist architecture – organised on the typical axial diagram – "floats" on a shallow pool, with each hall sitting atop a platform connected to the others by bridges. Several other preserved merchants' shops and residences are included in the Zhouzhuang package ticket price, and are certainly worth a quick visit. Closer to Shanghai, consider **Zhujiajiao** (p. 188).

A covered walkway in Xitang

Central Suzhou (Map 01–17)

01 North Temple Pagoda (Beisi Pagoda, Bao'en Temple) An ancient site, a (renovated) Ming-era pagoda design, and a local landmark. (See photo, p. 043). ❖ 31.3249, 120.6237

02 Suzhou Museum *I.M. PEI with Pei Partnership Architects, 2002–2006.* ❖ 31.3249, 120.6237

03 Garden of the Humble Administrator *WANG Xiancheng & WEN Zhengming, 1510+* ❖ 31.3256, 120.6260

04 Lion's Grove Garden *WEN Tianru, et al. 1342+* ❖ 31.3228, 120.6252

05 Couple's Retreat Garden (Ouyuan) *LU Jin, SHEN Bingcheng, 1874* ❖ 31.3182, 120.6345

06 Pingjianglu Canal street ❖ 31.3171, 120.6293

07 Dong Tea House *TM Studio (TONG Ming), 2004.* A canal-side spiral of brick-screened dining on a former industrial site, attached to a courtyard house. ❖ 31.3127, 120.6304

08 Suzhou/Soochow University Original Campus *Various, 1900+.* Founded by Methodist missionaries, this leafy, European-style campus also features landscapes inspired by the classical gardens. ❖ 31.3036, 120.6374

09 Garden of the Master of Nets *SONG Zongyuan, et al., 1785.* ❖ 31.3000, 120.6299

10 Suquan Yuan *TM Studio (TONG Ming), 2004–2007.* ❖ 31.3004, 120.6252

11 Blue Wave Pavilion *SU Shunqin, et al., 1044+* ❖ 31.2965, 120.6221

12 Garden of Pleasure (Yi Yuan) A late-nineteenth century garden incorporating the "greatest hits" of earlier designs. ❖ 31.3098, 120.6171

13 Mountain Villa With Embracing Beauty *GE Yuliang, 1807.* ❖ 31.3132, 120.6089

14 Garden of Cultivation (Yipu) Small yet open, a simple and refined Ming-era garden. ❖ 31.3151, 120.6047

15 Lingering Garden *XU Taishi, ZHOU Shicheng, et al., 1593+.* ❖ 31.3174, 120.5880

16 Shantang Canal Street ❖ 31.3183, 120.5992

17 Suzhou Railway Station *KAI Cui (with CADREG), 2000s.* Vaults and materials inspired somewhat by traditional architecture. ❖ 31.3315, 120.6065

18 Xiyuan Temple (West Garden) Suzhou's largest temple complex, with structures dating to the Yuan dynasty (1271–1368)

SU Suzhou

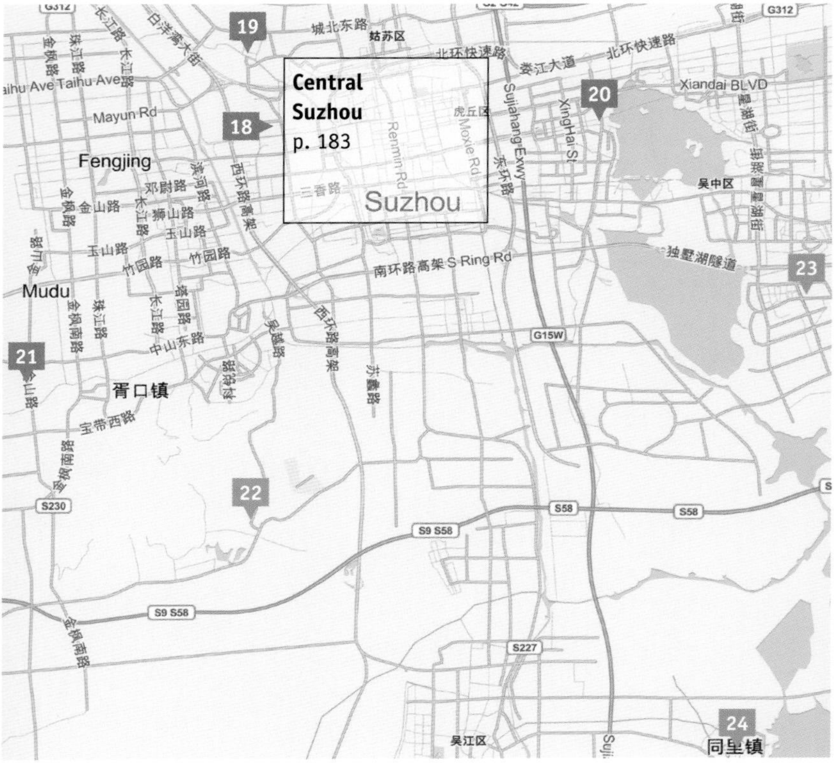

Suzhou City (Map 18–24)

and later. ❖ 31.3169, 120.5828

19 Tiger Mountain Scenic Spot Apparently shaped like a crouching tiger, this hill, capped with a famous leaning pagoda, is a popular park and tourist destination. ❖ 31.3361, 120.5756

20 Gateway to the East *RMJM, 2013.* Two mixed-use commercial towers linked at the top to form a gateway and inspire comparisons to *taihu* stones. A landmark of Suzhou's new CBD, far from the old city. ❖ 31.3185, 120.675

21 Mudu Old Town (Muduzhen) Canal town with a number of historic structures, easily accessible via subway, perhaps over-touristed. ❖ 31.2538, 120.5115

22 Wenzheng College Library *Amateur Architecture (WANG Shu & LU Wenyu), 2000.* ❖ 31.2212, 120.5771

23 Xi'an Jiaotong-Liverpool University Administration Information Building *Aedas (Andy WEN, project designer), 2013.* ❖ 31.2748, 120.7341

24 Tongli Canal Town (Tonglizhen) ❖ 31.1604, 120.7146

25 Zhouzhuang Canal Town (Zhouzhuangzhen) See entry for #24

Suzhou Region (Map 25–27)

❖ 31.1166, 120.8448

26 Xitang Canal Town (Xitangzhen) See entry for #24. ❖ 30.9422, 120.8847

27 Wuzhen Canal Town (Wuzhenzhen) See entry for #24. ❖ 30.7389, 120.4867

宁波
Ningbo

宁波 Ningbo

Ningbo (formerly Ningpo to Westerners, and Mingzhou in Asia) is China's second-busiest port after Shanghai; the greater metropolitan area has a population of 7.6 million, with 3 million in the "built-up area." Located across Hangzhou Bay from greater Shanghai, it has been inhabited for much longer, with roots going back to the Hemudu culture (5000s BCE). Its importance stems chiefly from its location at the confluence of two rivers, safely upriver from the sea and with a harbour deeper than Shanghai's (which in any case was developed much later). Thus, Ningbo has thrived whether history has favoured sea trade or river/caravan trade, and can claim to be one of the starting points of the Great Silk Road.

Ningbo's first heyday began in the Tang dynasty (618–907), with trade extending as far as the Arab world. Later, Ningbo was one of the early sites of substantial economic contact with Europeans. The Portuguese established a presence in the 1540s – a short-lived venture, as they conducted themselves atrociously, and found their settlement violently wiped out by the Chinese army. By the nineteenth century, Ningbo was an established trading port, as well as a proto-industrial centre, renowned for its furniture, jewellery, and confections. After the first Opium War, Ningbo was one of the first five ports forcibly opened to the West by the Treaty of Nanking (the first of many "Unequal Treaties"; see **Guangzhou**, p. 296). Beginning in 1842, the foreign settlement was concentrated in the "Old Bund" (*Lao Wai Tan*) across a bend in the river from the historic centre. Though much of the port infrastructure has now left this area (opening a discussion on re-use), it still retains a large collection of colonial architecture which has made it something of a tourist attraction. Ningbo's continued growth today stems from its 1984 establishment as a Special Economic Zone (see **Shenzhen,** p. 316), and from the 2007 opening of the thirty-six kilometre Hangzhou Bay Bridge, which links the city directly to the Shanghai megalopolis.

Urbanistically, old Ningbo shows little trace of planned, top-down development. Its historic grain is typical of dockside towns, with streets running perpendicular to the Fenghua river-front. Further from the river, the street network is less rigid, and seems to have been driven largely by topography. This historically residential side of town backs up against a medieval canal, functioning as a defensive moat, which effectively turned the old city centre into an island at the junction of the rivers. Following twentieth-century urban renewal, very little remains of old Ningbo's fabric, save a few pockets around **Moon Lake** (map p. 246); the **Old Bund** (p. 236) is better preserved, reflecting perhaps

Previous spread: the roofscape of the Ningbo History Museum (p. 242)

A rainy morning in **Lao Wai Tan** (p. 236)

a tendency to favour European legacies (as novel attractions for Chinese tourists) over ordinary, pre-modern fabric.

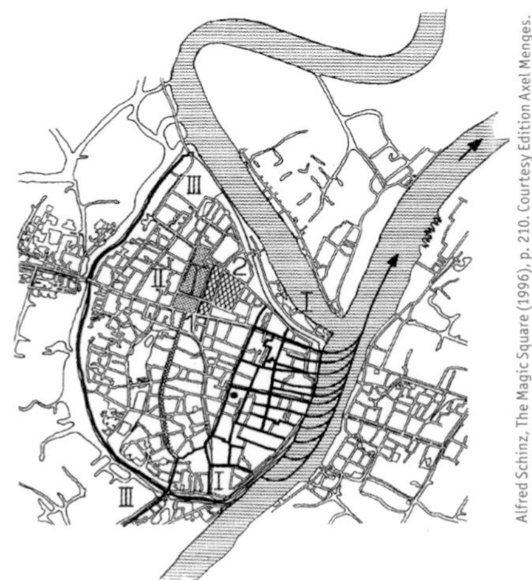

Plan, prior to development of the Old Bund in the "triangle" framed by the rivers. Arrows emphasise the grain of warehouse streets. The river branch to the northwest has since been straightened.

Alfred Schinz, The Magic Square (1996), p. 210. Courtesy Edition Axel Menges.

Practical Considerations

While Ningbo may be somewhat out of the way for most tourists, fans of contemporary architecture should consider a visit; one day should be enough, and the express trains connect to Shanghai in about two and a half hours via Hangzhou. While there are better examples of classical and colonial architecture elsewhere, the **Tianyi Pavilion** (p. 241) is well worth seeing, and the **Old Bund** (p. 236) provides an intriguing contrast with Shanghai's more famous concession-era waterfront. However, the real reason to visit is that Ningbo is home to several cultural buildings by Amateur Architecture (whose co-principal WANG Shu won the Pritzker Prize in 2012), including their most famous project, the **Ningbo History Museum** (p. 242). As a set, the projects here give a good sense of the firm's range of work and their distinctive material and spatial sensibilities.

On the "commercial" end of the spectrum, Ningbo also features several projects by MADA s.p.a.m. which explore the problem of making lively urban space from potentially bland, large-scale retail programmes. Such commissions drive much of today's Chinese building practice, so it's interesting to see a design-oriented firm giving serious attention to an indoor mall (p. 245), a large geometric plaza (p. 240), and a whole new commercial district (p. 245). A proposed ecologically oriented new town for 350,000 (HASSELL studios, 2003+) is still years away, but those interested in sustainable architecture should take a look at **CSET** (p. 241).

Sources and Recommended Reading

Eduard KÖGEL and BU Bing, eds., *Ningbo: Metamorphosis of a Chinese City* (2003). Booster-ist exhibition catalogue, with a few historic maps and other worthwhile bits of information.

Lao Wai Tan (The Old Bund)

NB 01

1850s+

老外滩
Jiangbei District, along the Yongjiang River (just north of the confluence)
❖ 29.8795,121.5562

The charming collection of colonial banks and customs houses has largely been converted into restaurants, bars, clubs, and housing. The night life is Ningbo's most lively, but conversely, it's a bit quiet during the day. In terms of historic preservation, the approach is less strict than that of **Shanghai's own Bund** (p. 156), where the façades remain pre-war postcard-perfect. There, conclusions seem binary: old building stock is either historically significant or not, thus either painstakingly restored, or demolished. Ningbo is a bit out of the spotlight, and the approach here seems more subtle and more flexible. Scattered contemporary apartment blocks rise up behind the restored treaty-port façades, and there's even a major contemporary re-do of several blocks (**Y-Town**, opposite). Just south of the district proper, past the bridge, is Pan Zhi Qin's Imperial Bank of China (1933–35, now a hotel), a blocky and restrained bit of Deco from the last pre-war days. Past that to the south, incongruously surrounded by twentieth-century parks and infrastructure, is the Cathedral of the Sacred Heart, dating to the 1870s and thus also representative of Ningbo's treaty port days; recently gutted by fire, its current status is unclear.

Y-Town

NB 02

MADA s.p.a.m. (Qingyun MA), 2000–2004

宁波老外滩
江北区江北区人民路 / 老外滩中马路
Renmin Road & Wai Mai Lu (Old Bund)
❖ 29.8792, 121.5559

A new mixed-use project on the Old Bund, with a clever, homophonous name ("Y-Town"/*Wai Tan*). The architects resisted demands for total historic preservation, but preserved certain existing features (e.g. factory chimneys) and used the older industrial vocabulary as inspiration for contemporary motifs; note the rusty colours and sawtooth roof lines. The main project involved carving out a winding sequence of pedestrian spaces with access to offices and retail. It's quite successful spatially; as at **Tianyi Square** (p. 240) it seems the architects' real interest lies in the intimately scaled and varied "street" spaces, rather than the mandatory "plaza." As at **Qiaoziwan Shopping Centre** (p. 187), the architects explore the meaning of public space.

Ningbo Urban Museum

NB 03

MADA s.p.a.m. (Qingyun MA), 2002–2003

宁波城市建设展览馆 – 外马路195
195 Waima Rd., adjacent to the Art Museum
❖ 29.8799, 121.5570

This warehouse conversion project is described by the architects in terms of urban culture in Ningbo – "an accumulation of productive human mechanisms, lifestyles and faiths, a composite of multiple layers and multiple dimensions." In practice, this means overlaying the flexible structure with a circulation trajectory, expressed on the façade. This allows a visual sculpting of the mass (suggesting an anchored ship), without subtracting much floor space. The surface is made up of glass blocks, the sides of which are painted different colours in pursuit of a variegated, shimmering effect. Compare to the blocks in the bridges off **Tianyi Square** (p. 240); here, the sheer quantity of this often-derided material bootstraps it up to elegance. Inside: maps and models of the city.

Ningbo Museum of Art

NB 04

Amateur Architecture
(WANG Shu and LU Wenyu), 2005

宁波美术馆
浙江省宁波市江北区人民路122号
122 Renmin Rd. North
❖ 29.880, 121.557

Initially, this project was planned as a rehabilitation of a 1980 "waiting-room-building," already out of date in the post-industrial port, and ultimately beyond salvage. The museum retains the original beacon tower, along with the basic layout of the old interior, organised around a set of garden courtyards. The architects recapitulate the "port" theme by organising circulation on a deck-and-gangway model, with walkways aligned to the former positions of landing bridges. The procession begins in the small courtyard on the west side; in a nod to Chinese garden tradition, this involves a couple of abrupt turnarounds, as well as a moment of window-to-a-window framing.

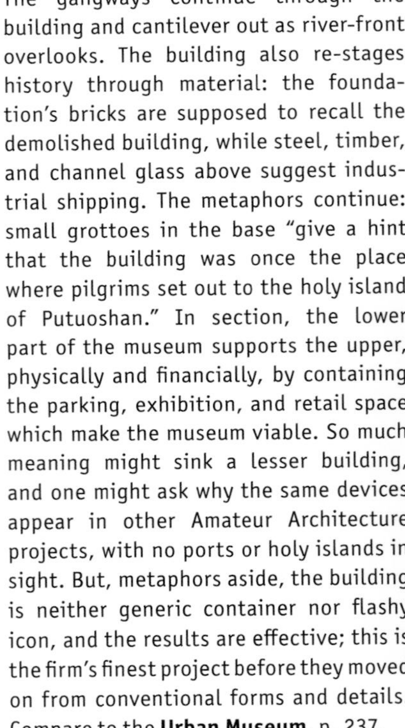

The gangways continue through the building and cantilever out as river-front overlooks. The building also re-stages history through material: the foundation's bricks are supposed to recall the demolished building, while steel, timber, and channel glass above suggest industrial shipping. The metaphors continue: small grottoes in the base "give a hint that the building was once the place where pilgrims set out to the holy island of Putuoshan." In section, the lower part of the museum supports the upper, physically and financially, by containing the parking, exhibition, and retail space which make the museum viable. So much meaning might sink a lesser building, and one might ask why the same devices appear in other Amateur Architecture projects, with no ports or holy islands in sight. But, metaphors aside, the building is neither generic container nor flashy icon, and the results are effective; this is the firm's finest project before they moved on from conventional forms and details. Compare to the **Urban Museum**, p. 237.

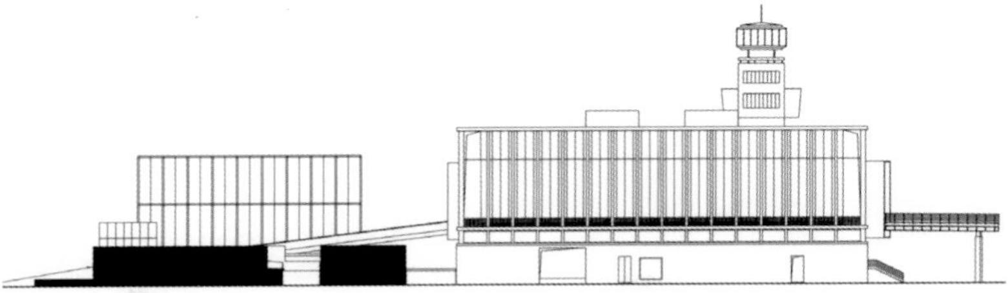

South elevation

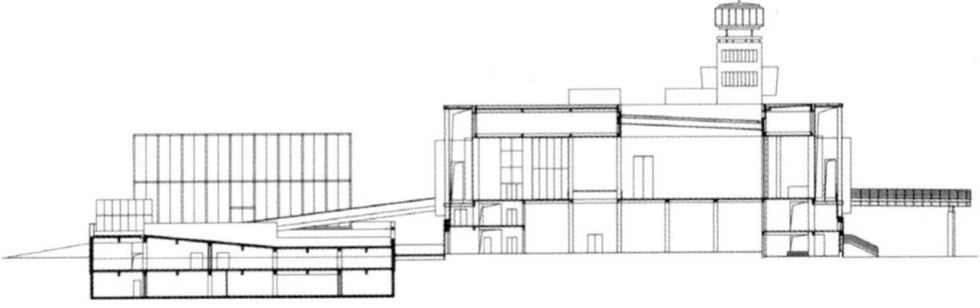

Cross section looking north

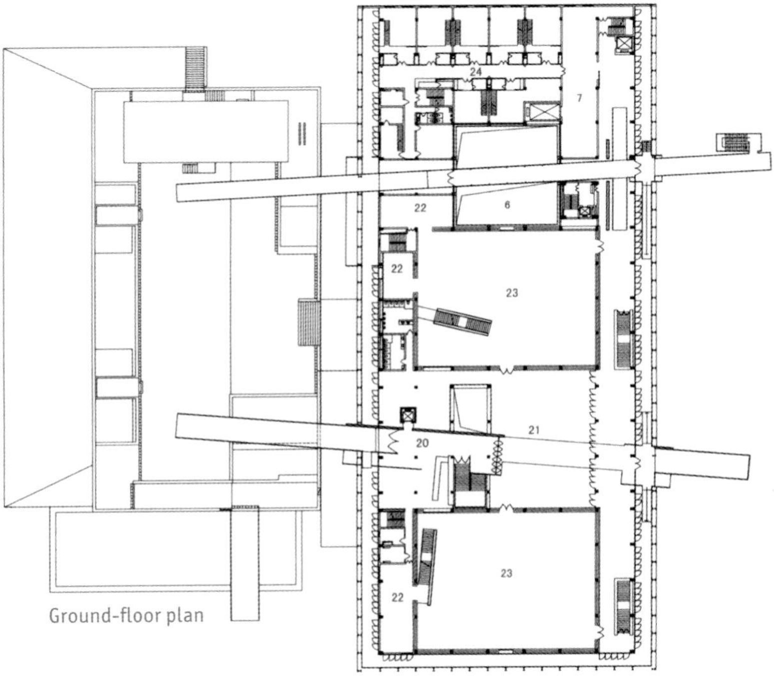

All drawings courtesy Amateur Architecture Studio

Ground-floor plan

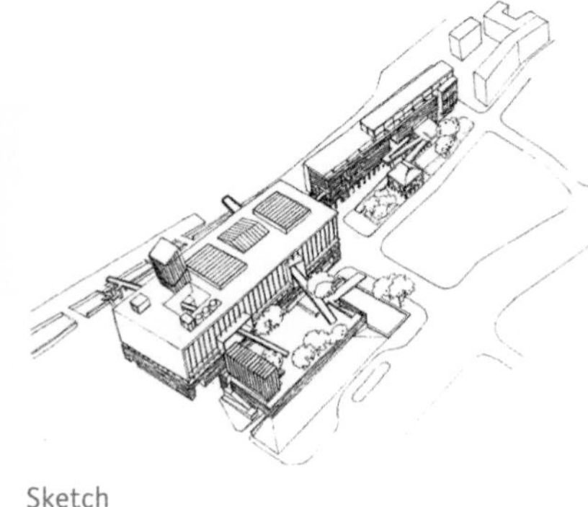

Sketch

Tianyi Square

NB 07

MADA s.p.a.m. (Qingyun MA), 2002

天一广场
海曙区开明街以东，中山东路以南，
车轿街以西、药行街以北的区域.
Zhongshan East Rd. & Medicine Store St.
❖ 29.8721, 121.5493

This circular plaza has been applauded for its use of crisply contemporary details (as opposed to stale pastiche) within the genre of enormous, geometric plazas. The central space is rather vast and empty, though enlivened by nightlife, windows, and thoughtful landscaping. But Tianyi's real attractions are the spaces ringing and radiating out from this central void: human-scaled, humming with activity, and enjoying a pleasant micro-climate, courtesy of the water features. The eastern edge features a linear reflecting pool, faced with double-height colonnades and bridged by diagonal walkways, which provide partial visual closure. It's a simple but effective combination: a flooded Uffizi in spatial terms, with late-Modern form and contemporary detailing. As with other architects of their generation, MADA s.p.a.m. seek to create a new, post-socialist public space (see also various projects by Urbanus in Shenzhen, p. 322-330).

Tianyi Pavilion (Tianyige)

NB 08

FAN Wenguang, 1665

天一阁
浙江省宁波市海曙区天一街5号
5 Tianyi Street, Hai Shu Qu
❖ 29.8741, 121.5363

Perhaps the oldest existing library in China, this complex is a garden residence in the south China tradition (see Suzhou, p. 210), with pavilions, pools, and rockeries composed to create a sequence of overlapping, ambiguous spaces. It was founded in 1561 by FAN Qin, a high-ranking Ming official with seventy thousand books to his name; the current design, attributed to his grandson, likely dates to 1665, but was largely rebuilt in 1933. While the pavilions in most traditional gardens are flexible, open, and rarely hold a fixed programme, here the necessity of book storage gives the main "chamber" a solid façade and dark interior. The book chamber became a model for libraries across dynastic China, and is a forerunner of the Wenyuan Imperial Library (1776) in Beijing's **Forbidden City** (p. 074).

Statue of Fan Qin

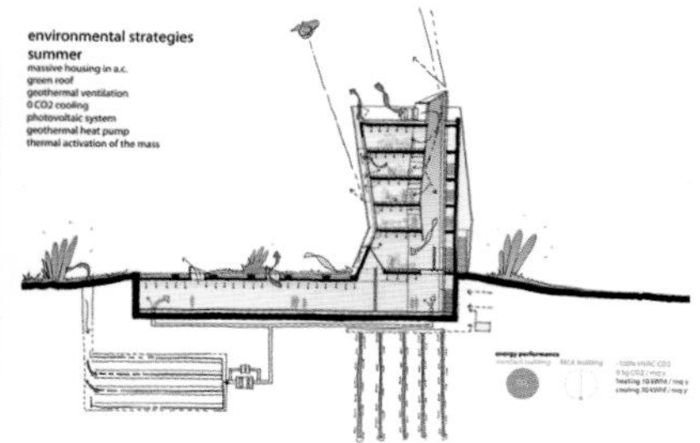

Section showing heating and ventilation

Centre for Sustainable Energy Technologies

NB 15

Mario CUCINELLA Architects, 2006–2008

宁波诺丁汉大学 - 泰康东路 199
Nottingham University, 199 Taikang E. Rd.
❖ 29.8016, 121.5588

Photo by Daniele Domenicali for MCA

For this institution devoted to green practices, the architects provide a carbon-neutral building showcasing various techniques: photovoltaic panels, geothermal heating, and stack-effect ventilation through a double skin and the light-admitting hole in the roof. The folded-plate form is meant to evoke Chinese fans and lanterns, but it also shows that sustainable architecture need not be bland. Enter the campus's north gate and head south down the main axis; CSET is to the right, on the lawn facing the water. Consider also the firm's **Tsinghua Environmental Science Building** in Beijing (map, p. 116), featuring stepped tiers of sun-screening pergolas.

Ningbo History Museum

NB 17

Amateur Architecture (WANG Shu and LU Wenyu), 2003–2008

宁波博物馆 or 宁波历史博物馆
宁波市鄞州区首南中路1000号
1000 Shounan Middle Rd., Yinzhou, Ningbo
❖ 29.8176, 121.5408

A contemporary masterpiece: a major "statement" that also works in terms of space and material. Invited to produce an isolated, monumental object, the architects picked up on the distant hills and created an "artificial mountain" with three internal "valleys" and several "caves." This topographic approach promises a variety of curatorial options. Meanwhile, the salvaged-brick façade, left partly up to the choices of mason NI Liangfu, suggests a connection to history in general, or specifically to the widespread demolition in Chinese cities. But the museum's nuanced attitude toward history involves more than devices like the recycling of materials, or the (effective) use of bamboo formwork for fine concrete. In fact, the design's big moves fall in line with contemporary, global design trends: the "randomised" and motley openings suggest digital-fabrication patterning, and the big, chunky light-and-view cuts evoke Boolean operations and blue foam models. Here, slicing away at the ideal form works to break down the scale, and recreates a kind of village-scape on the roof. The voids' angles recall vernacular pitched roofs, their size recreates the scale of pedestrian lanes, and the interlocking figure-ground evokes a pre-modern urban plan. Perhaps this is a defeated sigh: the traditional city is revealed as just another historical exhibit on a pedestal, while the new business district is framed and put at a distance. But given that the building sits in a spatial void at the heart of an underpopulated "new town centre," one might choose to interpret the building as an optimistic claim for urbanism in the contemporary city. (Compare to **Zhongshan Road,** p. 259.) Technology-driven form-making and traditional construction techniques unite in a synthesis of sculptural object and field condition that comments on its context and offers a viable alternative. Set aside time to explore: the galleries are ill-served by the usual dioramas, but the secondary spaces and courtyards reward lingering.

South elevation

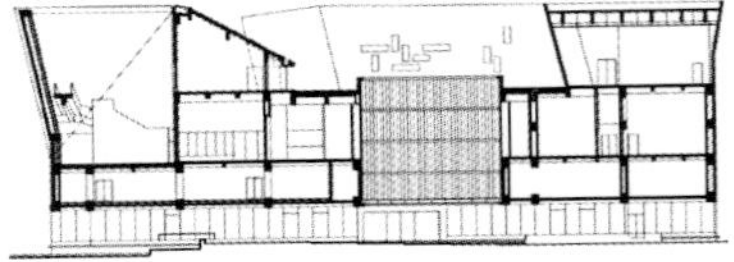

Cross section

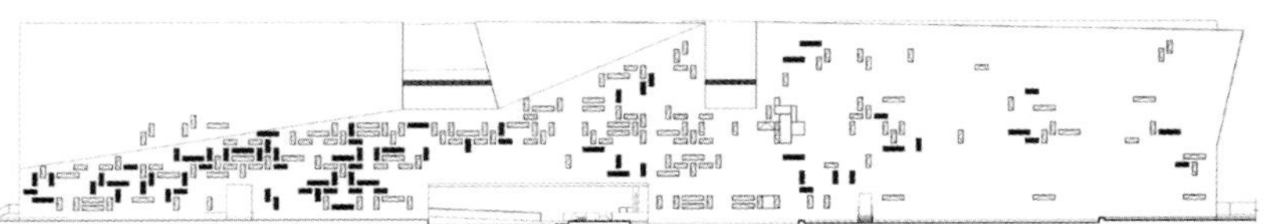

East elevation

Longitudinal section

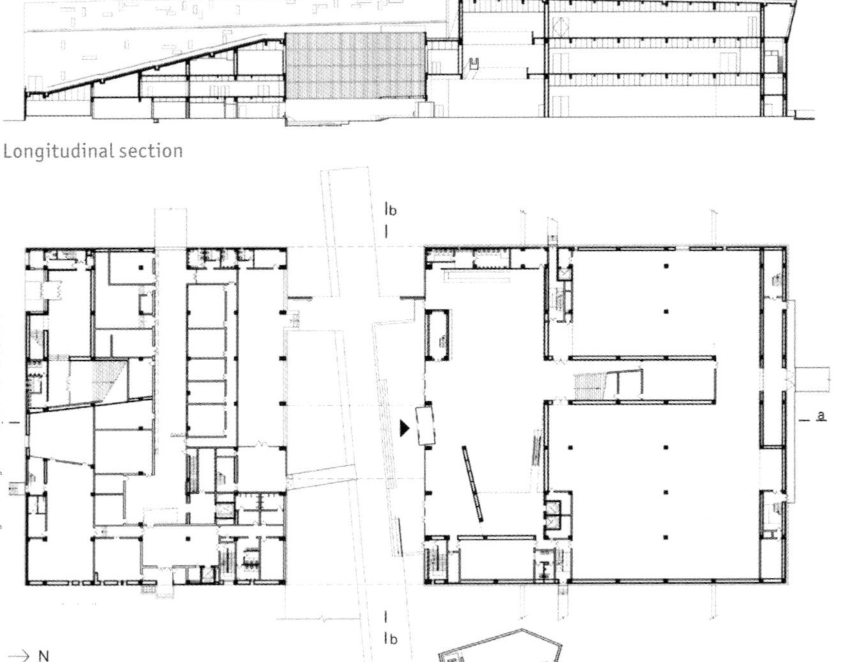

Ground-floor plan

All drawings courtesy Amateur Architecture Studio

Five Scattered Houses

NB 18

Amateur Architecture (WANG Shu and LU Wenyu), 2003–2006

鄞州公园 (Yinzhou Park)
宁波市鄞州区首南中路
Shounan Middle Road, Yinzhou
❖ 29.8133, 121.5428

A collection of pavilions or garden follies for a new park, sandwiched between the new civic centre and the **new CBD** (opposite), all far from the old city centre. In the development of Amateur's practice, these fall between **Xiangshan Phase One** (p. 264) and the **History Museum** (p. 242) – which looms in the background like an honorary "sixth house." The eclectic follies, sprinkled around an irregular pond, finds the firm at an experimental moment. The newly textured Xiangshan palette is explored across a grab-bag of new forms: folded floor plates, drooping ceilings, randomised cladding, Corbusian fin walls, dancing window openings, and elevations that suggest a flattened, graphical string of pagoda roofs. As well, we see the first wall made out of discarded roof tiles and bricks, celebrating the art of the bricklayer while critiquing the senseless demolitions that produce so much excess material. The "pagoda" façade becomes a major feature in the second phase of Xiangshan, while the "rubble" walls are now practically the firm's signature. Other moves here appear to be roads not taken – for now.

Ningbo South (Yinzhou) CBD

NB 19

MADA s.p.a.m. (Qingyun MA), 2006

宁波南部商务区
日丽中路 & 天童南路
Ri Li Zhong Lu & Tian Tong Nan Lu, Yinxian
❖ 29.8640, 121.6043

This is a denser, richer streetscape than is typical of new retail-and-office districts, and a fine alternative to the interior mall-space which could also have accommodated the programme; compare also to the vast scale of **Zhujiang** (p. 299). Though the given site is inconveniently far from the old city centre, and arguably a bit oversized, the architects introduce pockets of space at various scales, while maintaining the clarity of the axial organisation around the canal. There's a nice scaling-down of elements at the water's edge, with the canal itself visually "shrunk" by the addition of planters; compare to Amateur's tactics on **Zhongshan Road** (p. 259). Some of the details (like bridges crossing walkways at hair-clipping heights) distract, but overall, the experiment is a good one.

Courtesy Amateur Architecture Studio

Liansheng Plaza

NB 20

MADA s.p.a.m. (Qingyun MA), 2007

联盛广场
宁波鄞州区宁南北路1288号
1288 Ning Nan Bei Lu, Yinzhou
❖ 29.8264, 121.5378

This shopping mall and office tower attempts to rethink the typical podium-and-tower typology. It takes the form of a ribbon draped across the site, pulled up at one end to form a double-tower, joined at the top. It's an ambitious concept, let down somewhat by the materials and construction, which feel more ordinary. Compare to **Guanghualu SOHO** (p. 087).

Huamao Tang Art Gallery

NB 21

Amateur Architecture (WANG Shu and LU Wenyu), 2008

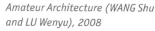

华茂堂美术馆，外国语学校
宁波市鄞县大道（中段）2号
2 Yinxian Dadao (Middle) Rd.
❖ 29.8236, 121.5433

Two concrete bars are linked by an open-air atrium, with façades punctured by patterned windows reminiscent of traditional architecture. The museum is apparently inspired by its painting collection and the books at the **Tianyi Pavilion** (p. 241). Amateur work out certain moves here which they would further develop in later projects.

Central Ningbo (Map 01–07)

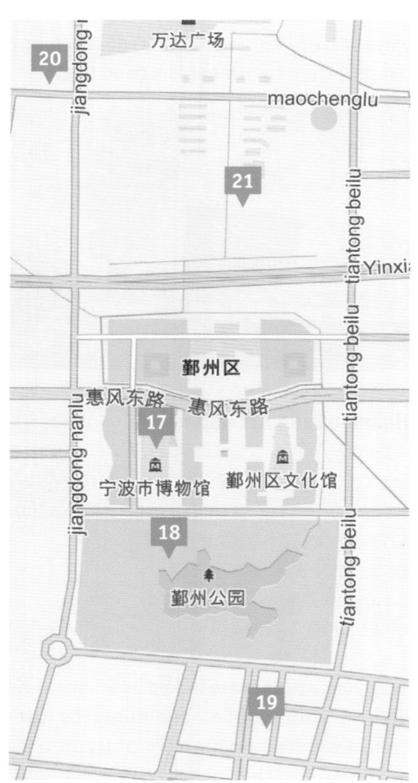

Yinzhou District (Map 17–21)

Ningbo

01 LaoWaiTan (Old Bund) ❖ 29.8795,121.5562

02 Y-Town *MADA s.p.a.m. (Qingyun MA), 2002–2004.* ❖ 29.8792, 121.5559

03 Museum of Urban Planning *MADA s.p.a.m. (Qingyun MA),* 2002–03. ❖ 29.8799, 121.5570

04 Ningbo Museum of Art *Amateur Architecture (WANG Shu & LU Wenyu), 2005.* ❖ 29.880, 121.557

05 Raffles City *SPARK, 2012.* Mall development, with green features. ❖ 29.8839, 121.5550

06 Qing'an Guild Hall (Maritime Museum) *1850.* A glimpse into the Treaty Port era. ❖ 29.8747, 121.5587

07 Tianyi Square *MADA s.p.a.m. (Qingyun MA), 2001.* ❖ 29.8721, 121.5493

08 Tianyi Pavilion (Tianyige) *1561.* ❖ 29.8741, 121.5363

09 Moon Lake Pleasant garden pond. The nearby mosque dates to 1699. ❖ 29.8718, 121.5394

10 Seven-Pagoda Temple (Qita Si) *from 858 CE.* Seven *miniature* pagodas – but fine enough. ❖ 29.8679, 121.5638

11 Yongjiang Tennis Club *WANG Cun, FANG Wei, et al., 2013.* A "landform" building with green-roof access from the adjacent park. ❖ 29.8888, 121.5669

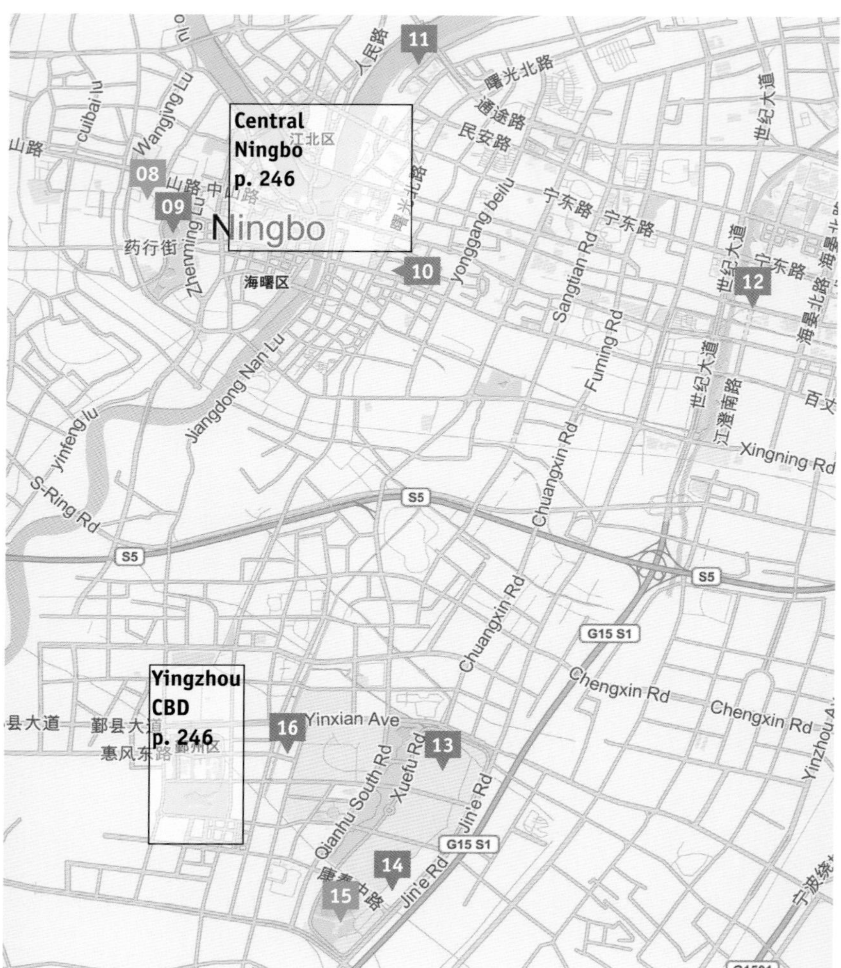

Central Ningbo p. 246
Yingzhou CBD p. 246

Greater Ningbo (Map 08–16)

12 New City Centre *Hyder, Hassell, 2003+ (planned).* This future district may someday house 350,000 residents; the "Berlin"-scaled centre will use renewable energy and stormwater-processing canals. ❖ 29.8640, 121.6043

13 Higher Education Zone Plan & Library *MADA s.p.a.m. (Qingyun MA), 1999, 2002.* A campus of parallel bands seeks an urban sense of density; library spaces are carved from a solid cube of book stacks. ❖ 29.8173, 121.5702

14 Housing for Talents, Yinzhou District *DC Alliance, 2011.* Duplex social housing units. Modernist elevations and site plan. ❖ 29.8044, 121.5647

15 Centre for Sustainable Energy Technology *Mario CUCINELLA Architects, 2006–2008.* ❖ 29.8016, 121.5588

16 Yinzhou Cultural Centre *Peter TAIGIURI, CHEN Haoru, 2013.* On the site of a demolished village, whose bricks became the History Museum façade, old foundations are exposed as a memorial. ❖ 29.8187, 121.5526

17 Ningbo History Museum *Amateur Architecture (WANG Shu & LU Wenyu), 2006.* ❖ 29.8176, 121.5408

18 Five Scattered Houses *Amateur Architecture (WANG Shu & LU Wenyu), 2003–2006.* ❖ 29.8133, 121.5428

19 Yinzhou CBD (Yinxian CBD) *MADA s.p.a.m. (Qingyun MA), 2006.* ❖ 29.8640, 121.6043

20 Liangshen Plaza *MADA s.p.a.m. (Qingyun MA), 2007.* ❖ 29.8264, 121.5378

21 Huamao Art Museum & Foreign Language School *Amateur Architecture (WANG Shu & LU Wenyu), 2008.* ❖ 29.8236, 121.5433

杭州
Hangzhou

杭州 Hangzhou

Hangzhou, which means "River-Ferrying Prefecture," is the capital city of Zhejiang province, the twelfth most populous metropolis in China. As home to the elegant West Lake, a host of temples, and the National Fine Arts Academy, it's also a cultural centre dating back centuries. One of China's key garden cities, Hangzhou has also become a very popular getaway destination, particularly for residents of Shanghai. Despite its own size and economic heft, Hangzhou is often seen as the restorative counterpart to the frenzied financial capital.

Hangzhou is located amid fertile agricultural land, just around a bend in the Qiantang River from a vast ocean bay, and protected by hills and marshlands from attackers on horseback. This area has been inhabited at least as far back as the Neolithic period, but did not become a centre for Han Chinese culture until much later. The city was founded during the Chin dynasty and given the name Hangzhou only in 589 CE. It was the southernmost sea-access port on the **Grand Canal** (p. 226), and thus a contact point for foreign merchants from as far away as the Middle East. Silk and tea made Hangzhou one of China's richest medieval cities. Capital of the Wuyue Kingdom, Hangzhou built new walls; princely sponsorship established a string of major Buddhist monasteries in the hills. As the street pattern was already well developed along organic and mercantile lines, there is little trace here of the kind of rigorous, gridded planning seen in Beijing. But royal patrons, with access to expert engineers and huge pools of labour, still left their mark in the expansion and refinement of **West Lake** (p. 256), just beyond the walls to the west, into a vast garden landscape.

A Chinese saying asserts that "In the sky there is heaven, and on Earth there are Suzhou and Hangzhou," a pairing of "garden cities" which recognises that the two are actually quite different. Suzhou's gardens, built by private individuals, are contained within walled urban lots, and many of their design innovations are attempts to create the impression of a vast, free-form natural landscape. West Lake actually is vast and free-form (though hardly natural), with an ambiguous perimeter. The **Guo Villa garden** (map p. 269), a contained space that "borrows" views of the lake, perhaps splits the difference. In imperial times, however, the lake was beyond the city walls – accessible through a few gates, but not exactly a "Central Park."

As a cultural, economic, and administrative capital, medieval Hangzhou was one of the most populous cities in the world.

Previous spread: View of **West Lake** (p. 256) and **Leifeng Pagoda** (p. 262)

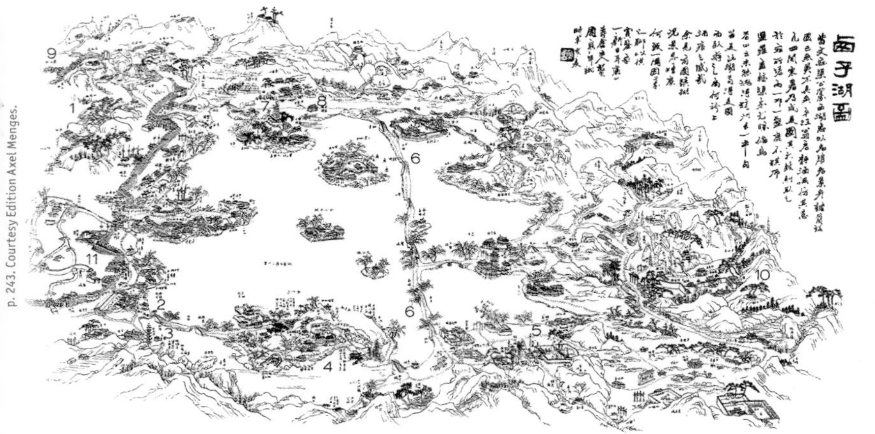

p. 243. Courtesy Edition Axel Menges.

West Lake, 1911 rendering. North is down, and the city is beyond the walls to the east/left.

Even when the Mongol Khans moved to present-day Beijing (letting the Hangzhou palace crumble without a trace), the city didn't lose its economic or artistic importance entirely. In the 1300s, Marco Polo and Ibn Battuta both found it among the finest cities they claimed to have visited. Built of wood, it caught fire several times, and the harbour began silting up in the fourteenth century. The real death blow was the Taiping Rebellion (1850–1864), when much of the surviving imperial splendour was destroyed, along with many lives. Hangzhou remained a site of religious and economic pilgrimage; the area around City-God Hill, where pilgrims arriving from the south would do business on the way to the temples, was the major economic centre. **Qinghefang Old Street** (p. 258) is a survivor of this district, and gives some sense of the pre-modern city's texture.

In the late nineteenth century, as coastal Shanghai became increasingly important, Hangzhou found itself cut out of the economic loop. Railway connection to Shanghai in 1909 cemented the shift: instead of serving as a commercial hub, Hangzhou became a convenient recreational spot for the urban office worker, especially after the Republic ushered in the seven-day calendar (and thus the weekend getaway). Equally important, the new government tore down the wall between city and lake, establishing on its footprint a new boulevard (Hubin Road) and a string of lakeside parks. The Qing dynasty's garrison town, formerly a walled-off enclave at the old city's northwest corner, was also demolished. The Republican leadership replaced it with a gridded "New Business District" full of Western-influenced buildings for commerce and government. In turn the victim of later urban renewal schemes and highway construction, the business district is now almost illegible, even in maps. Still, these infrastructural interventions effectively reoriented the city. As in Berlin after 1989, the former "edge" was now "centre," and the lake was part of the city for the first time. The incorporation of this vast park supported wider modernising impulses to provide cities with open green space, and reinforced Hangzhou's tourist-destination status. The city's image-makers began talking up the "ancient" lake, notwithstanding its many transformations over time.

In the Communist era, Hangzhou continued to expand, particularly to the north, but it suffered from something of an identity crisis; the Party celebrated its cultural significance while deriding it as a "parasitic consumer city" and promoting industrial development. More recently, with DENG Xiaoping's economic liberalisation (extended to Hangzhou in 1992), the Yangtze River Delta region as a whole embarked on a meteoric growth spurt. The Hangzhou area now includes several dedicated zones for high-tech and export-processing, and, as elsewhere, this growth has fuelled a boom in demolition and construction which can be measured in millions of square metres per year. Hangzhou considered some historic preservation regulations, for example a rule that no building could be taller than the landmark Baoshu Mountain. But even in the early

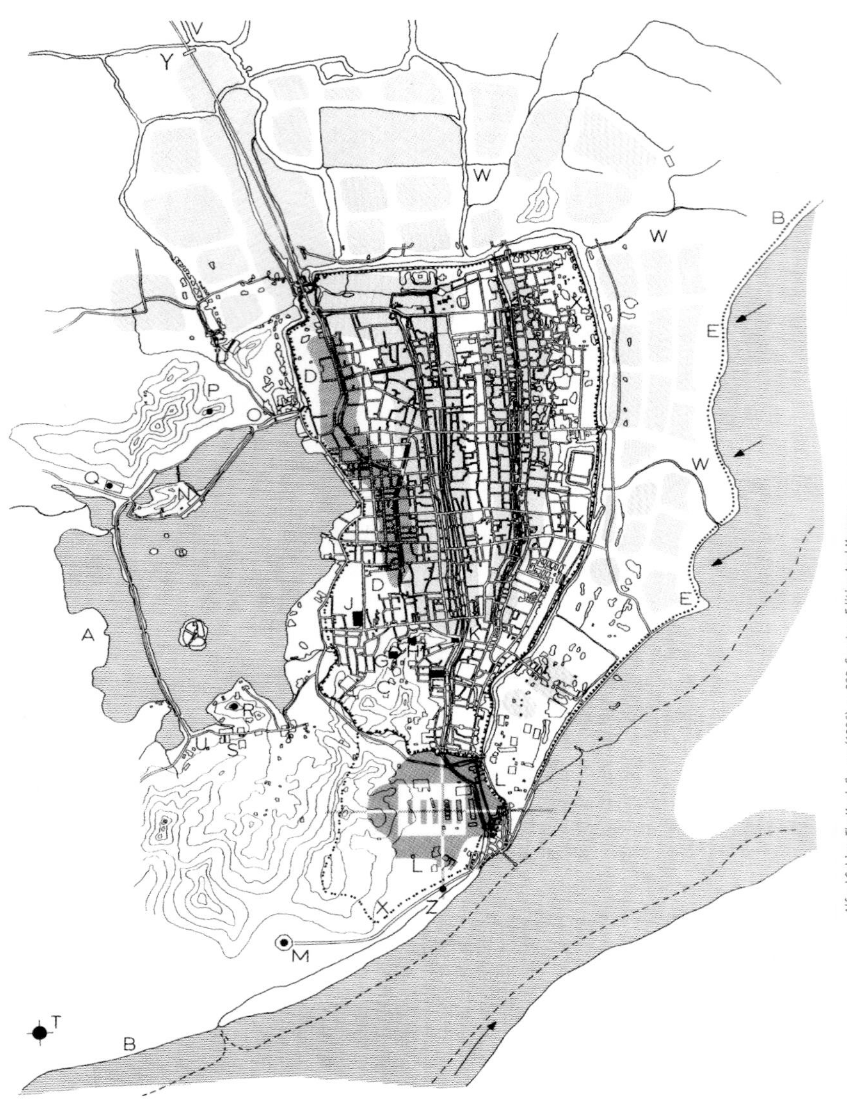

Hangzhou in the Southern Song dynasty (1127–1279). Note that the city and its walls step back from the river's floodplain, but back directly up to West Lake. The shaded zone at the southern end indicates the palace (now destroyed); City-God Hill is just northwest of that complex.

1980s, Hangzhou was building mid- and high-rise hotels for tourists exploring the newly "open" China; preservation of the skyline was a lost cause. Since the turn of the millennium, the gridded, axial **Qianjiang New Town district** (map p. 270) has tried to concentrate business and entertainment on the river-front, far from the old centres. More interesting are smaller interventions like **Zhongshan Road** (p. 259) and **Xihu Tiandi** (p. 258) – two projects different in style and ambitions, but both committed in some way to making an urbanistic "fit," unlike most master-planned developments in China.

All these developments remind us that, while Hangzhou is indeed a "garden city," it is also simply a city. The powers that created its restful attractions were first drawn to Hangzhou because it was already a commercial hub. Today, those expecting a fairy kingdom may be surprised to find a sprawling metropolis, complete with traffic, air pollution, garish signage and the other familiar woes of contemporary

"Hangchow" in 1915, with walls intact, occupying essentially the same footprint

Chinese cities. Hangzhou does, however, consistently lead its peers in Chinese quality-of-life surveys, and visitors should still be more than satisfied with the experience.

Practical Considerations

It goes against the tranquillity of a garden city to plan a jam-packed, whirlwind trip to Hangzhou. Even if time is short, we recommend spending at least one full day taking in the historic centre, including the lake and the temples. Another day can easily be spent visiting a series of suburban "showcase" sites, each with high-quality work by several architects. The spectacular **Xiangshan Campus** (p. 264) deserves at least two hours if not three. **Liangzhu Village** (pp. 266-267), a for-profit suburban scheme with ambitions of community, offers a smattering of thoughtful buildings. On the way, check out the very recent work at the southwest corner of the **Xixi National Wetlands** (p. 262, map p. 270). Still, while these projects are all undoubtedly worth seeing (and Xiangshan is a must), the conventional wisdom is right: dedicate time to the lake and the temples, and don't miss the forest for the trees.

Sources and Recommended Reading

Mathieu BORYSEVICZ, *Learning From Hangzhou,* Beijing: Timezone 8, 2009. A pop document of present-day Hangzhou, with a particular eye on its street signage.

Simon HOLLEDGE, *Hangzhou and the West Lake,* Skokie, Illinois: Rand McNally, 1981. A tourist guidebook, naturally somewhat out of date, but noteworthy for the quality of the maps and details of specific sites.

Maggie KESWICK, with Charles JENCKS and Allison HARDIE (introduction), *The Chinese Garden: History, Art & Architecture,* Cambridge, Mass.: Harvard University Press, 2003. More thorough on Suzhou, but some good Hangzhou anecdotes.

Frederick STEINER and Dean ALMY, "Conservation as Catalyst," *Topos* no. 71, 2010. A few pieces of West Lake background.

Liping WANG, "Tourism and Spatial Change in Hangzhou, 1911–1927," in Joseph W. Esherick, ed., *Remaking the Chinese City,* Honolulu: University of Hawaii Press, 2000. Filling some key modern-era gaps: changes in urban form, politics, economics, tourism.

West Lake (Xi Hu)

HZ 01

西湖

❖ 30.2450, 120.1456

Hangzhou's most magnificent attraction was not originally a lake at all, but a marshy bay or inlet of the Qiantang River. The river link began silting up early in the city's history; the locals hurried this along, perhaps to help manage flooding. Circa the second century CE, the local government began damming the water channel and dredging out the wetlands, until the former inlet became a lake. The present-day version, covering 5.6 km, is the product of some two dozen additional rounds of dredging, plus many smaller alterations and additions to the lake's perimeter. Consider a common Chinese phrase, synonymous with "gardening": "digging ponds and piling mountains." Indeed, in 927 CE, the local king established a staff of one thousand to keep the lake dredged, as erosion of the surrounding hills threatened to undermine the pristine illusion of natural peace and beauty. Intermittent major re-dredgings reflected neglect relating to political upheavals; in the Ming period, for example, private owners divided up the lake for their own enjoyment, necessitating a later re-consolidation. Early on, the lake was not reliably supplied with water, so it would flood or dry up, depending on the seasons. Gradually more advanced hydraulic systems came into play, and from 781 CE, the lake was itself a reservoir for the city's water (supplied through a system of underground clay and bamboo pipes). In the following centuries, the lake was particularly enhanced by two poets-turned-civic-leaders, BAI Juyi (772–846) and SU Shi (1037–1101) who developed both the engineering and the garden-like qualities of the lake. Each also gave it a connecting causeway (later reconstructed) for long, poetic strolls. By Su's time, this site was well established as a recreation centre, crowded with hundreds of heavily ornamented boats. It had also become a source of inspiration to landscape painters and garden designers, who would seek to imitate its qualities elsewhere in China. In 1912, amidst the collapse of the Empire, the city walls alongside the lake were torn down, finally connecting the city's centre to its most famous feature, and giving us the more or less "current" version of the lake. Altogether, this place epitomises a fundamental Chinese gardening principle: something can be "natural" even while being the product of incredible, laborious

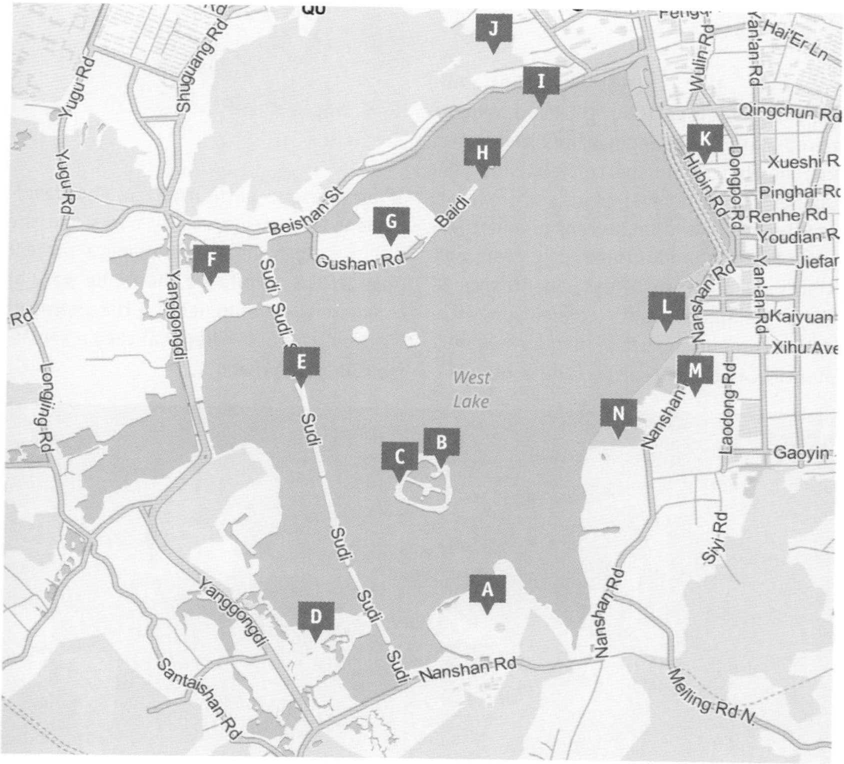

West Lake area, with major scenic viewpoints and nearby projects of note

artifice. While Western gardeners tried to make visible the geometric mastery of nature by man or God, the Chinese gardener, having mastered nature to an arguably greater degree, used these skills to produce an aestheticised, artificial *version* of nature. **Suzhou** (p. 210), and Hangzhou's own **Hu Xueyan Residence** (p. 260), show these ideas played out in an array of smaller, private gardens. Here they are writ large in one of the world's great parks. Be sure to set aside a few hours, and consider renting a bike or boat; appropriately for a Chinese garden, the lake is bigger than it looks.

A Leifeng Pagoda 雷峰塔（p. 262)
B Xiaoying Island 小瀛洲
C Three Pools Mirroring the Moon 三潭印月
D Huagang Fish-Viewing Garden 花港觀魚
E Su Shi Causeway 苏提/蘇堤
F Quyuan/Lotus Garden 曲院风荷
G Autumn Moon over Calm Lake 平湖秋月
H Bai Causeway 白堤
I Lingering Snow on the Broken Bridge
J Baochu Pagoda (map p. 269)
K Hubin Improvements (map p. 268)
L Xihu Tiandi 西湖天地（p. 258)
M China Academy of Art (old campus)
N Orioles Singing in the Willows 柳浪聞鶯

Xihu Tiandi

HZ 05

Studio Shanghai, 2004

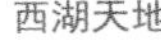

西湖天地
上城区南山路147号（近开元路）
147 Nanshan Rd., Shangcheng
❖ 30.2496, 120.1554

Following the success of **Xintiandi** (p. 171), developer Shui On Land sought to replicate the model in other cities. Here in Hangzhou, a number of lake-side villas have been redeveloped as a pleasant car-free retail and restaurant precinct. In contrast to urban Xintiandi, the design of Xihutiandi (literally "West Lake Heaven & Earth") emphasises its connection with nature through the use of long glass walls, plentiful outdoor seating, and a network of picturesque paths that tie the development to a string of city parks and the Hubin waterfront redevelopment project (map p. 268). While we should be wary of commercial development on the shores of West Lake, Studio Shanghai take a sensitive, subtle approach.

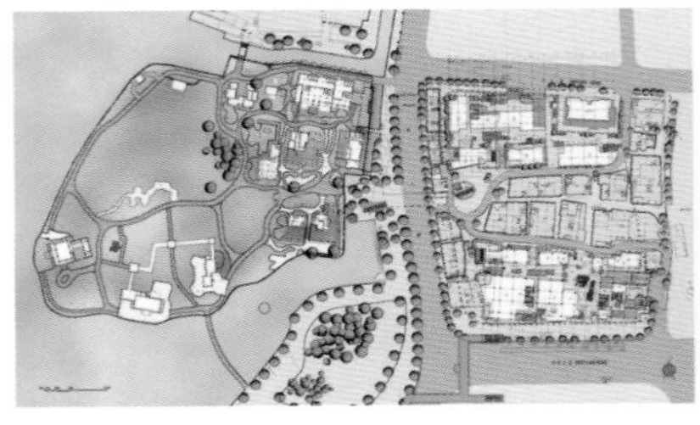

Site plan

Qinghefang Old Street

HZ 06

Ming and Qing dynasty; restoration begun 2000

清河坊路
❖ 30.2425, 120.1645

This recently-restored pedestrian street was one of Hangzhou's major commercial boulevards in the dynastic period. Now, modern infill and twentieth-century Neo-Classical façades vie for space with traditional wood-shuttered store-fronts. The surrounding neighbourhood is well worth exploring: the gridded street network and scale of space still gives an impression of pre-modern Hangzhou's urban form. Finely-carved wood details – vintage, or careful reproductions – abound.

Zhongshan Road

Amateur Architecture (WANG Shu & LU Wenyu), 2007–2009

HZ 07

中山中路
Zhongshan Lu, Hangzhou
❖ 30.2411, 120.1669/30.2478, 120.1660 (southern end/northern end)

This street, once the main approach to the Song dynasty palace, was in bad shape after the depredations of street-widening. The option of demolishing the whole stretch was on the table, but to the architects, this opened a discussion of planning values in an era of mass demolitions. If widening the street and populating it with self-contained buildings was a recipe for "US suburbanisation," this is an alternative: a return to the typical twelve-metre width of major streets in the historical city, reflecting "the true city life structure" of pedestrian and bicycle traffic. After a lot-by-lot study, Amateur accepted some demolition, but insisted that the diversity of the buildings be preserved. The approach was a kind of spatial thickening: new pavilions were added to fill the gaps and shift the building lines forward; plantings and water channels broke up the width; new gates were inserted to tie down the north-south vistas; an open area at the southern end became a legible urban room with the addition of a low building to screen the highway; existing buildings and trees were preserved where possible. The pedestrianisation of the space is effective, but more important is the refusal to accept that generic planning is the best one can do. As in other Amateur Architecture projects, we find loose, idiosyncratic touches at the heart of a thoughtful, historical project.

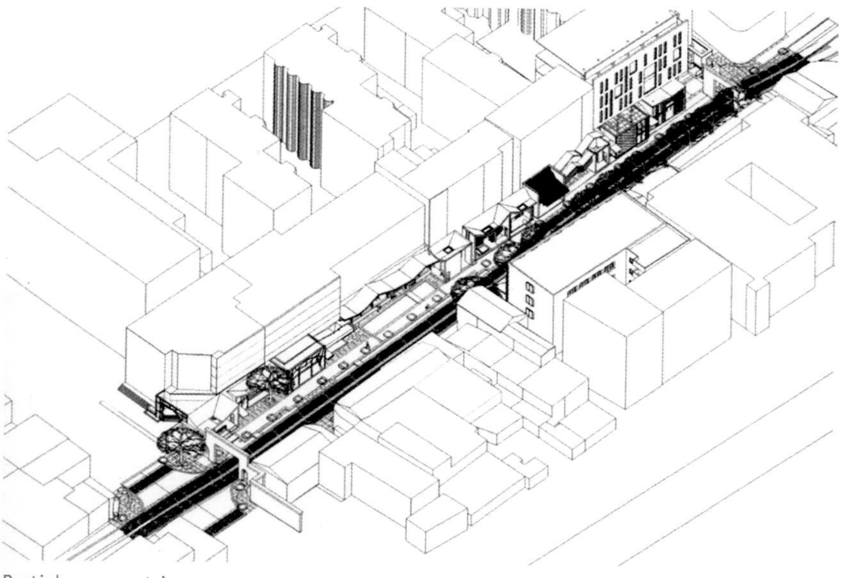

Partial axonometric

Hu Xueyan House & Gardens

HZ 10

1872–1875

胡雪岩故居
杭州市上城区元宝街18号
18 Yuanbao Street, Shangcheng
❖ 30.2397, 120.1687

The former home of an influential Qing-era merchant in silk and arms, and the founder of China's first modern naval academy. Here, he sought the traditional refuge of a merchant-scholar, as in the more famous gardens of **Suzhou** (p. 210). The gardens are tightly contained, but this only adds to the experience, as any path through the garden reveals the ambiguous, layered space that is a hallmark of late Qing dynasty garden design.

Baochu Pagoda

HZ 12

963 CE/1933 reconstruction

保俶塔
杭州市西湖区保俶路
Baochu Rd., Xihu District
❖ 30.2632, 120.1434

Located atop the ridge of Baoshishan (Precious Stone Hill) to the north of West Lake, Baochu Pagoda is a prominent landmark, easily visible from the old city. The present structure reflects one prevailing architectural style of the early 1930s, a stripped-down Art Deco with ornamental details inspired by traditional architecture. It's tempting to read the brick tower as a commentary on nearby **Leifeng Pagoda** (p. 262) which was, at the time, a burnt-out shell with only its brick core standing. The tower is inaccessible, with no internal staircase, and thus is less a work of architecture than a monumental urban sculpture. The paths up to and around the pagoda make for a short but relaxing hike, and pass by a number of Buddhist rock carvings that were severely disfigured in the Cultural Revolution.

Lingyin-Feilai Feng Scenic Area

HZ 14

328+ CE; mostly nineteenth century

灵隐寺
西湖区灵隐路法云弄1号
1 Fayun Lane, Lingyin Rd., Xihu District
❖ 30.2432, 120.0985

In the hills to the west of West Lake – best reached by car, bus, or bike – this collection of temples and carved grottoes shows a number of different approaches to sacred space in Chinese Buddhism. Before even reaching the first temples, you'll pass the Feilai Feng (飞来峰), a "flying peak" supposedly transported here from Buddhism's Indian homeland. Indian cave temples, though, tend to be sequences of small caves, open at one end, each with a separate icon. What we see here feels more like a precursor to the rockeries of a classical Chinese garden: the fine carvings are set in a landscape of winding carved passages, which in turn may invite you to undertake a refreshing hike up into the hills and back. If you can resist, the Lingyin Temple (back at the main path) is a very fine, axially-arranged complex that includes a fantastic (twentieth-century) Buddha statue, and secondary halls whose labyrinthine swastika floor plans play against the north-south clarity of the larger complex. Back out the temple gate, and further up the path, is another series of temples, more loosely arranged, since the topography becomes quite steep. If you can handle the climb, it's worth it: the integration of the axial building complexes with the trees and the waterfalls becomes almost garden-like, and the oscillations between natural and artificial are so frequent as to dissolve the difference between the two. Beyond the temple precinct proper, a number of smaller temples are scattered across the hillside, connected by trails through the dense forest; some offer distant views back to West Lake, when the fog subsides.

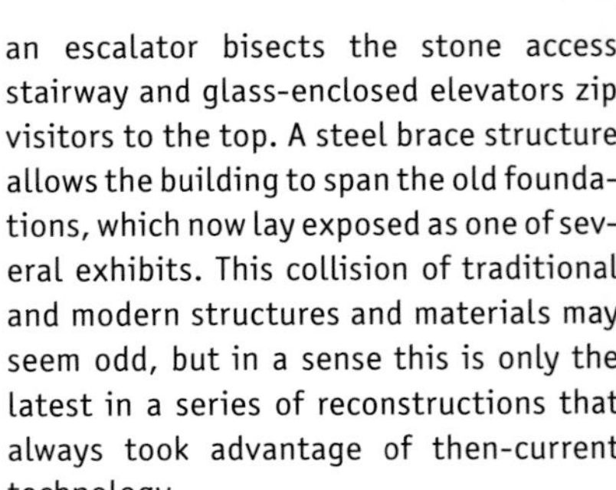

Leifeng Pagoda

HZ 15

975 CE, 1200, 1999–2002

雷峰塔
杭州市西湖区南山路15号
15 Nanshan Road, Xihu
❖30.2337, 120.1450

Dating back to 975 CE, this pagoda was built to consecrate the relic of one of Buddha's hairs. It was rebuilt in 1200 and burned by Japanese pirates around 1550, becoming a scenic ruin. The bricks, if properly ground up, were said to have healing powers; predictably, this led to the structure being undermined, and the ruins collapsed in 1924. The 2002 reconstruction is worth visiting for the lake views, and for the novelty of its structure and circulation: an escalator bisects the stone access stairway and glass-enclosed elevators zip visitors to the top. A steel brace structure allows the building to span the old foundations, which now lay exposed as one of several exhibits. This collision of traditional and modern structures and materials may seem odd, but in a sense this is only the latest in a series of reconstructions that always took advantage of then-current technology.

Courtesy AZL

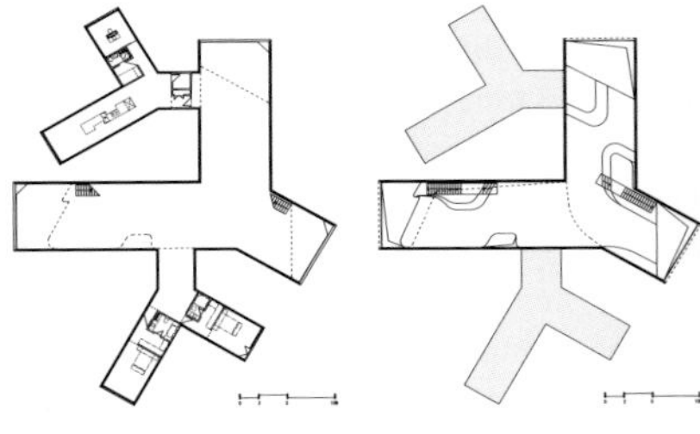

Ground- and upper-floor plans, one "cluster"

Xixi Wetlands Artists' Club

HZ 19

AZL (Atelier ZHANG Lei), 2008–2011

三期艺术集合村
杭州西溪国家湿地公园
Xixi National Wetland Park Village
❖ 30.2569, 120.0439

These wetlands, one of China's major ecological parks, are also now home to several noteworthy arts-related buildings (see map p. 270). This one is a "village" of five studio "clusters," each composed of two scales of Y-shaped pavilions. The ends of the branches are glazed to create varied, full-frame views of the surrounding landscape, or sometimes of the interesting pockets of space formed between the buildings. The large-scale Y's are concrete, while the smaller are steel-framed and clad with translucent plastic to let in diffuse light, and make the buildings into "lanterns floating on the water" by night. "Twisting fibreglass installations" on the interiors are meant to contrast with the rectilinear geometry of the building volume. It's a nice study in scale and materials, and the aggregation of individual artists into a community as "clusters" is a contemporary refresher of late-Modernist formal and social preoccupations of the 1960s-70s (Team 10, etc.). Compare to the work of AZL's peers at **Songzhuang** (p. 105).

Vertical Courtyard Apts.

Amateur Architecture (WANG Shu & LU Wenyu), 2006

HZ 22

钱江时代公寓
上城清江路346号, 近富春路
346 Qingjiang Rd., Shangcheng District
❖ 30.2372, 120.1998

Demonstrating a desire to challenge the dominant residential typology of the contemporary city, the architects insert a communal "courtyard" at every second floor and conceptually position the tower as a "tilt-up" version of a traditional urban plan. The goal is to make residents feel as if they live on the first or second storey of a traditional dwelling, rather than high in the sky. Interlocking volumes give the tower façades an appealing rhythm, and the colour palette suggests a link to the historic canal towns of the Yangtze Delta.

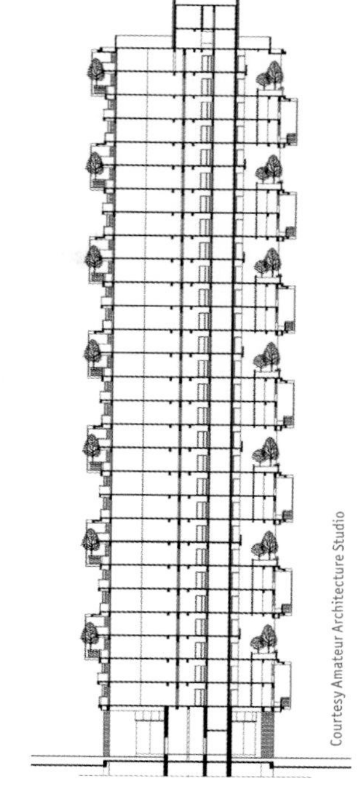

Courtesy Amateur Architecture Studio

Section

Ninetree Village

David CHIPPERFIELD Architects (architect), Zhejiang South Architectural Design Co. Ltd. (contact architect), 2004–2008

HZ 31

良渚文化博物馆 – 街道美丽洲路1号
Wuyun Mountain Road, Xihu District
❖ 30.1842, 120.1041

This private luxury development consists of twelve residential prisms set in a bamboo forest. The volumes, connected by underground parking, are set at angles to each other in response to the topography, maximising privacy and views of the landscape. Movable bamboo screens of varying density wrap peripheral "loggias," giving each dwelling its own "clearing in the forest" while reinforcing the sense of privacy. Each unit occupies a full storey, with service zones expressed as solid objects in a flowing, continuous space. Compare to **Heronshire East** at Liangzhu Village (map, p. 271), where Chipperfield applies similar site planning and massing techniques to give dignity and presence to some eight hundred walk-up units.

© Christian Richters

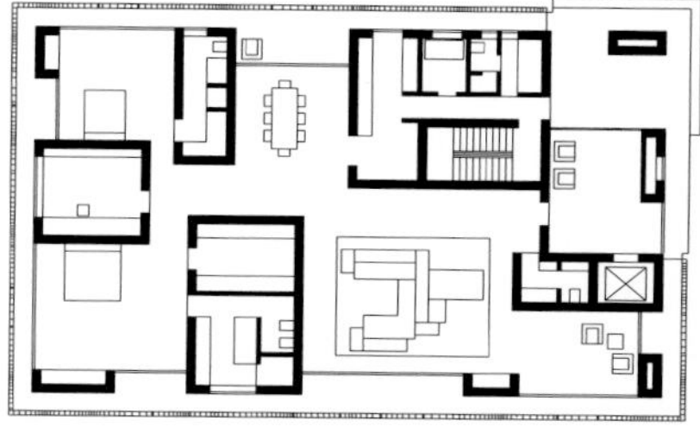

Typical floor plan

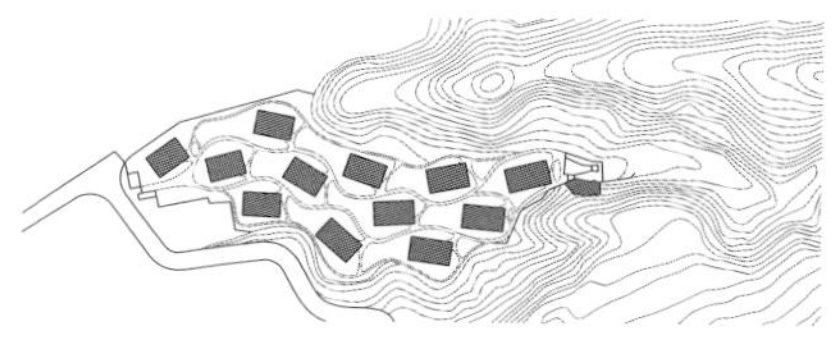

Site plan (north at right)

All images courtesy David Chipperfield Architects

China Academy of Fine Arts, Xiangshan Campus

HZ 32

Amateur Architecture (WANG Shu & LU Wenyu), 2002–2004 (Phase One), 2004–2007 (Phase Two)

中国美院象山校区
西湖区转塘镇转塘直街（近美院北路）
Zhuantang Zhi Street (near North Meiyuan Road), Zhuantang Town, Xihu District
❖ 30.1554, 120.0746

These twenty-one buildings, for the school whose architecture department Wang heads, are the architects' most ambitious work to date, a stunning realisation of design and construction techniques developed through a series of smaller projects such as the **Five Scattered Houses** (p. 244). The aesthetic marries Bauhaus-inspired functionalism with the forms and materials of traditional Chinese architecture, particularly southern China's classical gardens (see **Suzhou**, p. 210). The campus is best experienced in a clockwise progression around Xiangshan Hill, from the running track at the northwest, going first through the buildings of Phase 1. A long, low bar building marks the site's northern boundary like an ancient city wall, and a thin point tower makes a convenient landmark. But most of the buildings of Phase 1 explore the theme of a (climatically-appropriate) courtyard-building, with the occasional "missing" fourth wall allowing views out to the hills beyond. These are connected by covered walkways at multiple levels, and detailed with a mix of industrial hardware, traditional roof tiles and wooden shutters along open-air corridors. In the buildings of Phase 2, around the bend, the style shifts, becoming more formally ambitious with swooping roof profiles, concrete cantilevers, and buildings detached from the ground plane, floating above the grass as automobile and pedestrian connections cut through beneath. A miscellaneous stacking of elements appears both in the compositions of the elevations, and in the detailing of bricks and tiles. Materials were reclaimed from demolished buildings and piled up (seemingly) at random. While there are no courtyards, strictly defined, the zig-zag plans of Phase 2 still serve to define space and create a sense of enclosure. Spaces between the buildings frame the orienting central hill, which Amateur had hoped to preserve for agricultural grazing. In both phases, the buildings are constructed from a limited set of materials and construction techniques, combined in different ways to produce great variety. As in the **Ningbo Art Museum** (p. 238), there's a hint of metaphor: Phase 1 is simplified Chinese writing, and Phase 2 is traditional calligraphy. But it's in the latter where traditional forms become unrecognisable, as walkways barge into courtyards and twist up to meet sweeping roof-lines that only vaguely resemble traditional roof profiles. Recent additions to the campus, under construction as of 2014, include Álvaro SIZA's design museum at the southeast corner, and KUMA Kengo's art museum, a switch-back adventure at the joint between Phases 1 and 2. Amateur Architecture has also returned with a new guest centre ("Tiles Hill," 2013), across the canal from the southern line of Phase 2, and featuring a lively timber-trusswork roof. Uphill, a high school (SHAO Jian & ZHOU Hao) explores the courtyard-and-walkway theme, though less dramatically.

Section (Building 14)

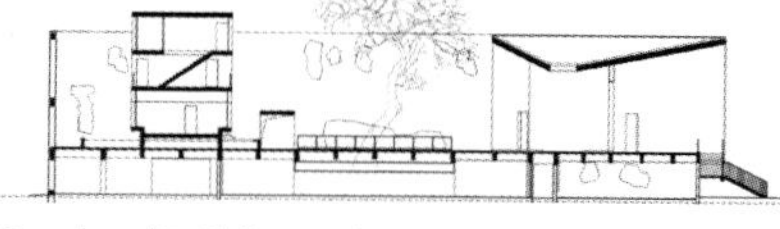

Section (Building 15)

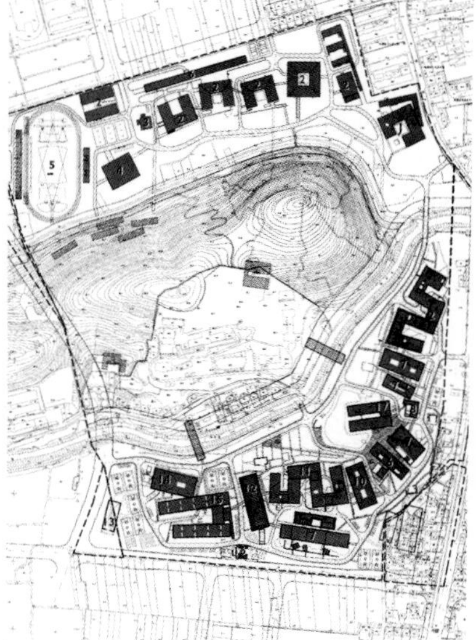

Site plan; Phase 1 above, Phase 2 below

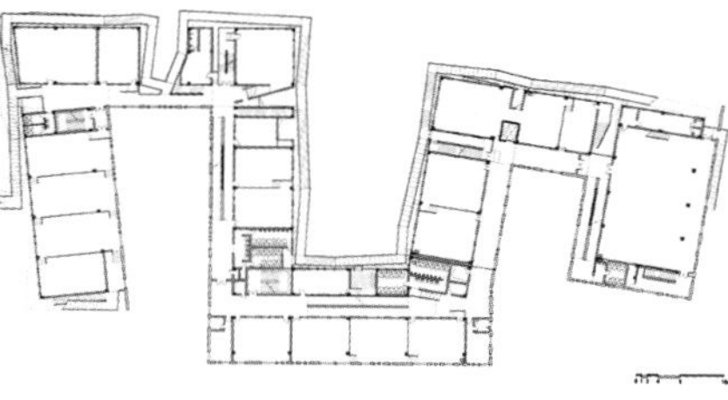

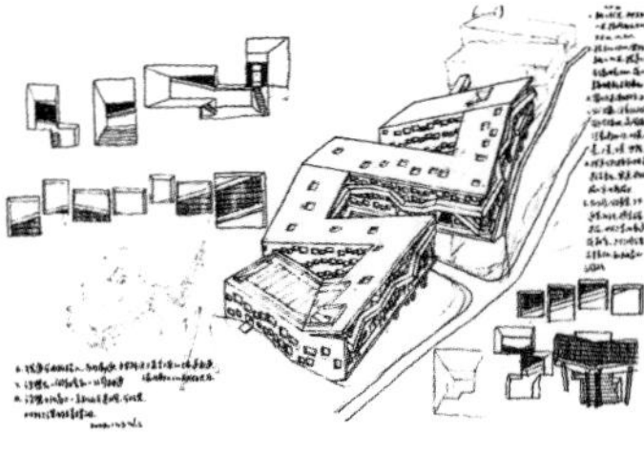

Plan and sketch (Building 11)

All drawings courtesy Amateur Architecture Studio

© Christian Richters

© Christian Richters

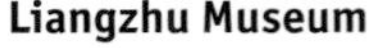

Liangzhu Museum

David CHIPPERFIELD Architects (architect), ZTUDI (contact architect), 2003–2007

良渚文化博物馆 – 街道美丽洲路1号
1 Mei Li Zhou Road, Yuhang District
❖ 30.3704, 120.0231

This piece of the Liangzhu Village development is about one kilometre north of the shopping centre, and reflects the developer's desire for the community to develop roots here. An archaeological museum, focused on the 5,000-year-old Liangzhu Culture, it is composed of four bars, each eighteen metres wide, clad in Iranian travertine. The surrounding water acts as the "organising element." Since the museum is set out on a peninsula and reached by bridges, with only limited openings to the outside, it seems to shut out its context, except for carefully-selected views of the garden landscape (by Levin Monsigny Landschaftsarchitekten). These are classic ways of creating a removed space of contemplation, but they may also be minimalist interpretations of the way Chinese garden pavilions manage views, or the inward focus of a courtyard house. The museum is staged around a set of courtyards, intended to link the exhibitions while providing a place to relax in between them. There's no fixed route through the galleries, and the spatial experience never feels particularly linear or confined; indeed, one can get a bit lost in this little world, though the distinct courtyards act as orienting landmarks (pool, trees, patio). The overall simplicity in form and material is appropriate to the Liangzhu objects on display, in particular the famous discs of jade and stone.

© Chongfu Zhao

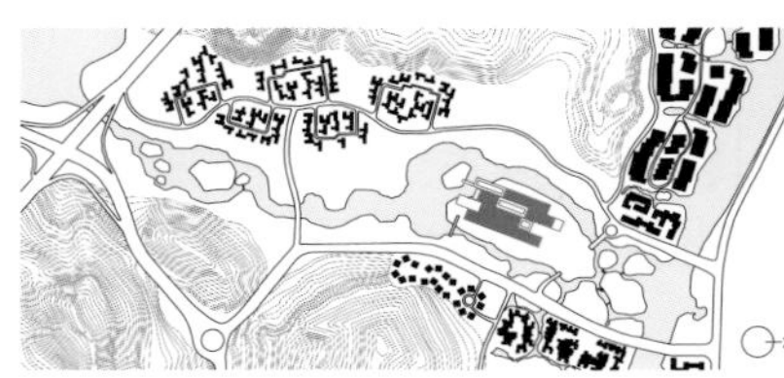

Site plan

Longitudinal section

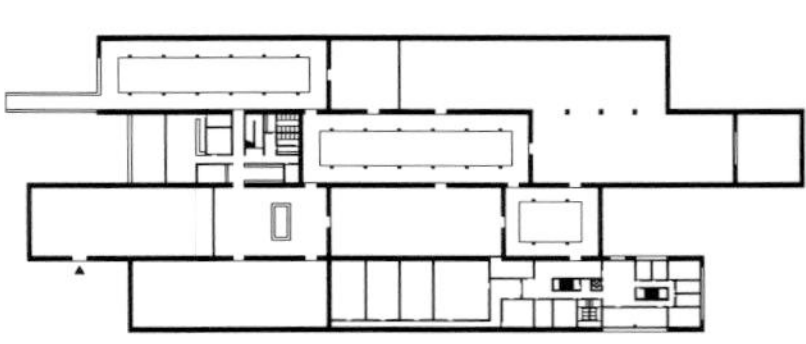

Ground-floor plan

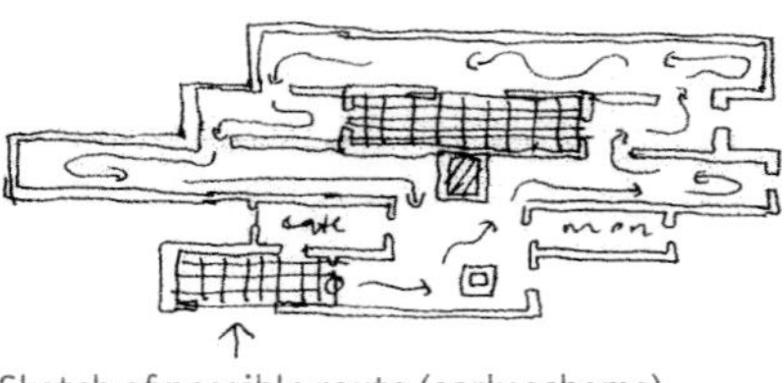

Sketch of possible route (early scheme)

All images courtesy David Chipperfield Architects

Photograph by Masao Nishikawa

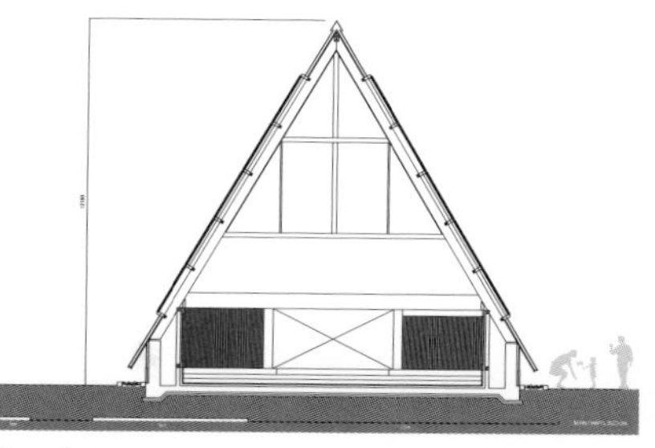

Section

Mei-Li-Zhou Church

HZ 38

Tsushima Design Studio (TSUSHIMA Toshio), ACO, PLATdesign (landscape) 2010

美利洲堂，风情大道，余杭区
Fengqing Ave., Yuhang District
❖ 30.3709, 120.0232

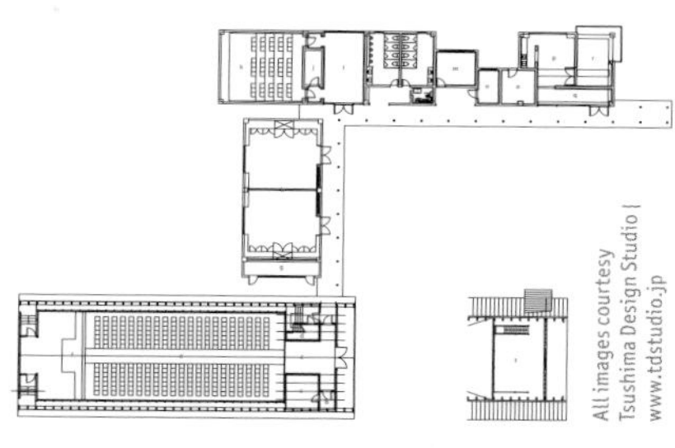

Ground-floor plan (second floor inset)

All images courtesy Tsushima Design Studio | www.tdstudio.jp

For this Protestant church, immediately northwest of **Yuniaoliusu** (below), the architects hoped to address the needs of a "sacred religious ground" as well as a non-denominational gathering-place for the Liangzhu Village community. Tsushima's design uses a limited material palette (slate, concrete, and glue-laminated cedar) to place emphasis on "sunlight, greenery, scenery and space." The goals were to seamlessly connect nature and interior, and to approach "timelessness and purity" through careful detailing and deployment of Japanese building tradition, e.g. the column-base connections outside.

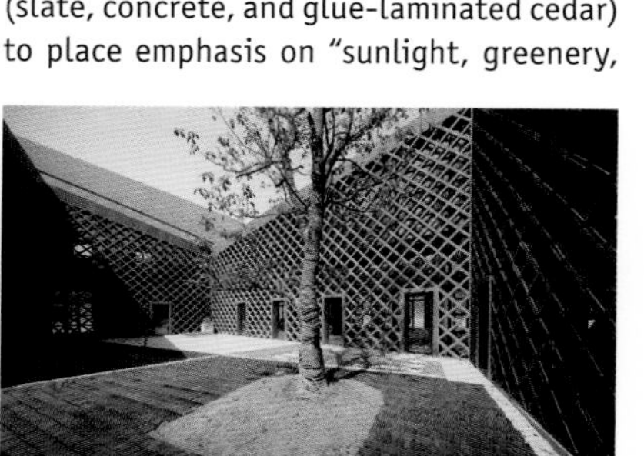

Photograph by Jia Fang, Nacasa & Partners

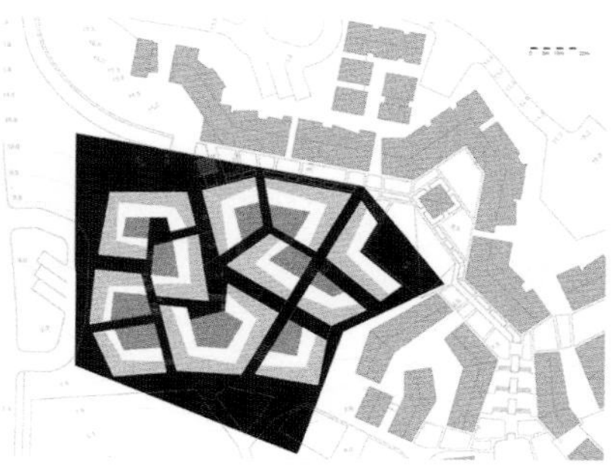

Site plan

Yuniaoliusu (YNLS)

HZ 39

AZL (Atelier ZHANG Lei), 2004–2008

玉鸟流苏
余杭区风情大道
Fengqing Ave, Yuhang District
❖ 30.3694, 120.0234

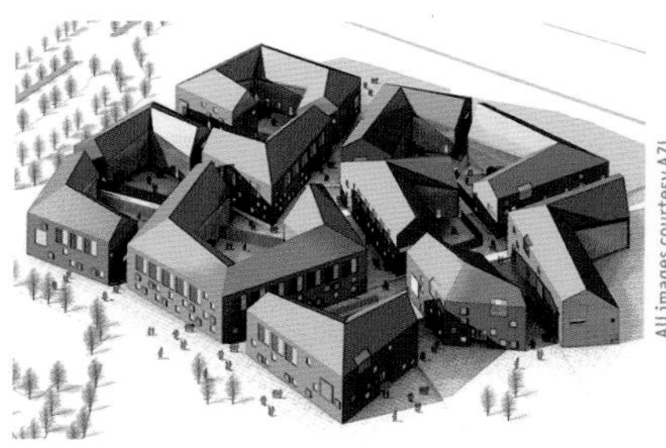

Aerial rendering

All images courtesy AZL

The retail centre (also known as "Festival Place") for the developer Vanke's Liangzhu Village project is an abstracted take on traditional courtyard units, with contemporary touches like the "folding" of the brick walls into the roofs. Offering unconventional but coherent pedestrian space on a greenfield site, AZL's buildings sit comfortably with QI Xin's more vertical contribution (the kinked bar to the north), and set up the more sober respite of the **church** (above). A planned gallery to the southeast, by ANDO Tadao, seems to be in limbo.

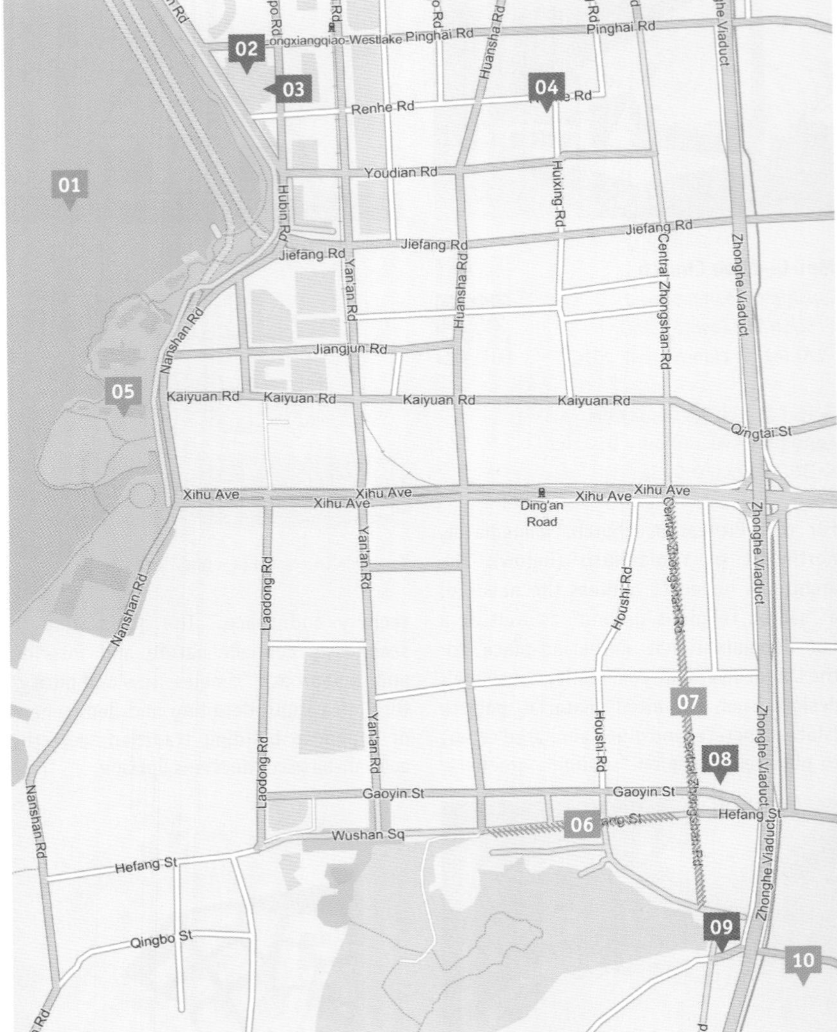

Hangzhou Old City (Map 01–10)

01 West Lake (Xihu) See area map in building entry. ❖ 30.2450, 120.1456

02 Hubin Improvements *SWA, 2002.* Re-pedestrianisation of waterfront and adjacent blocks, by deflecting auto traffic into a tunnel running parallel under the lake. Water channels, plantings, seating – familiar moves, but effective ones. ❖ 30.2563, 120.1568

03 Hubin Plot 17 *Bernhard WINKING, 2004.* New/old city fabric, contiguous with the above redevelopment. The courtyard-street seems to have been enclosed into an atrium. ❖ 30.2557, 120.1579

HZ Hangzhou

04 Wushan Night Market A typical block by day, these blocks transform into a lively market of trinket and food vendors at night. ❖ 30.2549, 120.1635

05 Xihu Tiandi *Studio Shanghai, 2004.* ❖ 30.2496, 120.1554

06 Qihefang Old Street *Renovated 2000.* ❖ 30.2425, 120.1645

07 Zhongshan Rd. *Amateur Architecture (WANG Shu & LU Wenyu), 2009.* ❖ 30.2529, 120.1657

08 White Wall House *CHEN Haoru , 2009–2013.* Pre-existing walls organise five volumes, with fascinating in-between space. ❖ 30.2431, 120.1668

09 Hangzhou Drum Tower Reconstructed in 2002, with a small (and free)

Hangzhou Old City p. 268

Central Hangzhou (Map 11–16)

exhibit hall, and decent views of the surrounding area. ❖ 30.2402, 120.1668

10 Hu Xueyan Residence & Gardens *1872–1875.* ❖ 30.2396, 120.1685

11 Alipay Headquarters *WSP Architects, 2005–2011.* Two slab towers on a podium define a courtyard. Their cladding alludes to Chinese shutters, and the garden aims at Sino-Modern fusion. ❖ 30.2751, 120.1207

12 Baochu Pagoda *963 CE/1933 reconstruction.* ❖ 30.2633, 120.1433

13 Guo Villa (Guozhuang) *1904.* Garden villa, incorporating the lake as classic "borrowed" scenery; if what one sees through one window is a garden pond, then the lake seen through another window must also be part of the garden. ❖ 30.2462, 120.1275

14 Lingyin-Feilai Feng Scenic Area 328+ CE; mostly nineteenth century. ❖ 30.2432, 120.0985

15 Leifeng Pagoda *975 CE, 1200, 1999–2002.* ❖ 30.2337, 120.1450

16 Hangzhou Railway Station *1999.* A grey behemoth, included here for reference if you're arriving by train.

❖ 30.2458, 120.1785

West Lake (p. 256)

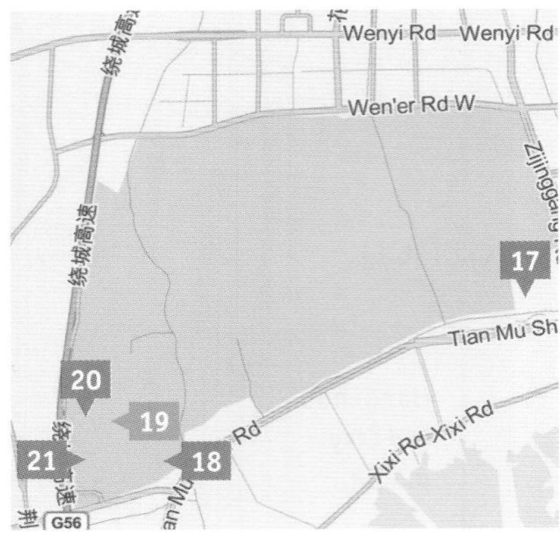

Xixi Wetlands Park(Map 17–21)

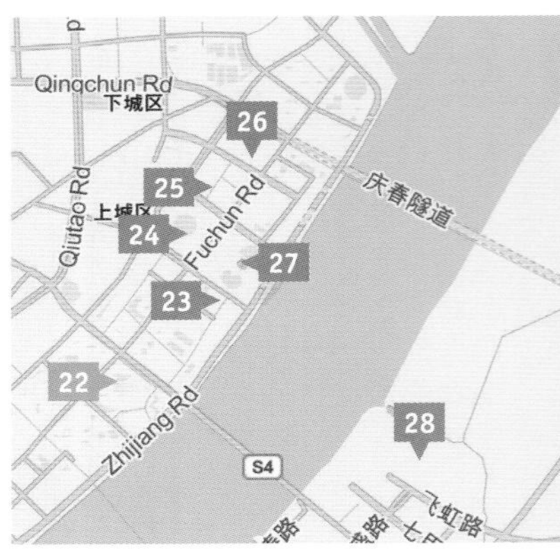

Qianjiang New Town Centre (Map 22–28)

17 Xixi China Wetlands Museum *ISOZAKI Arata, 2009.* A big, green-roofed vault, with a 40-metre "UFO"-style observation deck for an overview of China's only national-level wetland park. ❖ 30.2665, 120.0824

18 Xixi Visitors' Centre *Sunlay Design, RHINESCHEME GmbH, 2012.* Ecological exhibition, and ecological demonstration – lots of passive green features for a LEED Platinum rating. The façade treatment lends a pleasantly rustic touch, offsetting the techno-institutional quality of much current green work. ❖ 30.2575, 120.0410

19 Xixi Artists' Club *AZL (Atelier ZHANG Lei), 2008–2011.* ❖ 30.2569, 120.0439

20 Xixi Wetlands Centre *Atelier Fronti (WANG Yun), 2010.* Abandoned new-built complex of fifteen fine, minimalist volumes with call-backs to 1920s Modernism. The white colour is explained as a foil or highlight for the wetland setting. ❖ 30.2574, 120.0410

21 Xixi Wetlands Art Site *WANG Weijen, 2009–2011.* Bars of studio-residences, bent around each other with emphasis on how each will chop and re-frame views of the same landscape at different heights. ❖ 30.2537, 120.0412

22 Vertical Courtyard Apartments *Amateur Architecture (WANG Shu & LU Wenyu), 2006.* ❖ 30.2372, 120.1998

23 Citic Bank HQ *Foster + Partners (Norman FOSTER), 2015.* Bronze-coloured diagrid, unzipped at the bottom for a grand welcoming canopy that draws breezes into the ventilating atrium. ❖ 30.2432, 120.2084

24 Hangzhou Citizens Centre *XWHO, 2008.* A circle-in-square diagram organises glitzy towers surrounding a circular conference centre. ❖ 30.2489, 120.2052

25 Raffles City *UN Studio, 2008–2015 (anticipated).* A squirming high-rise, under construction, supposedly derived from the "twisting" of urban and landscape elements towards each other. "Circulation loops" in the plinth recall the firm's work at smaller scales (the Moebius House, the Mercedes Museum in Stuttgart). ❖ 30.2510, 120.2088

26 Tang Palace Restaurant *FCJZ (Yung Ho CHANG), 2010.* A fine top-floor restaurant interior. ❖ 30.2542, 120.2111

27 Qianjiang New Town Centre *2008+.* Hangzhou's grandiose new CBD, it features a yellow spherical conference centre (sun) and a silver crescent-shaped theatre (moon). ❖ 30.2462, 120.2101

28 Olympic Sports Centre *NBBJ, 2015 (construction).* Structurally-optimised "petals" (a lotus, perhaps?) surround a stadium bowl generated by minimising the distance from each seat to the pitch. ❖ 30.2314, 120.2253

29 Liuhe Pagoda *970 CE, rebuilt 1165.* Also called "Six Harmonies," the pagoda has thirteen roofs and rises 60 metres above an octagonal base. ❖ 30.1980, 120.1268

30 Cuisine Museum *KAI Cui (with CADREG) 2012.* Contemporary interpretation of the gabled house. ❖ 30.2100, 120.1383

31 Ninetree Village *David CHIPPERFIELD Architects, 2004–2008.* ❖ 30.1842, 120.1041

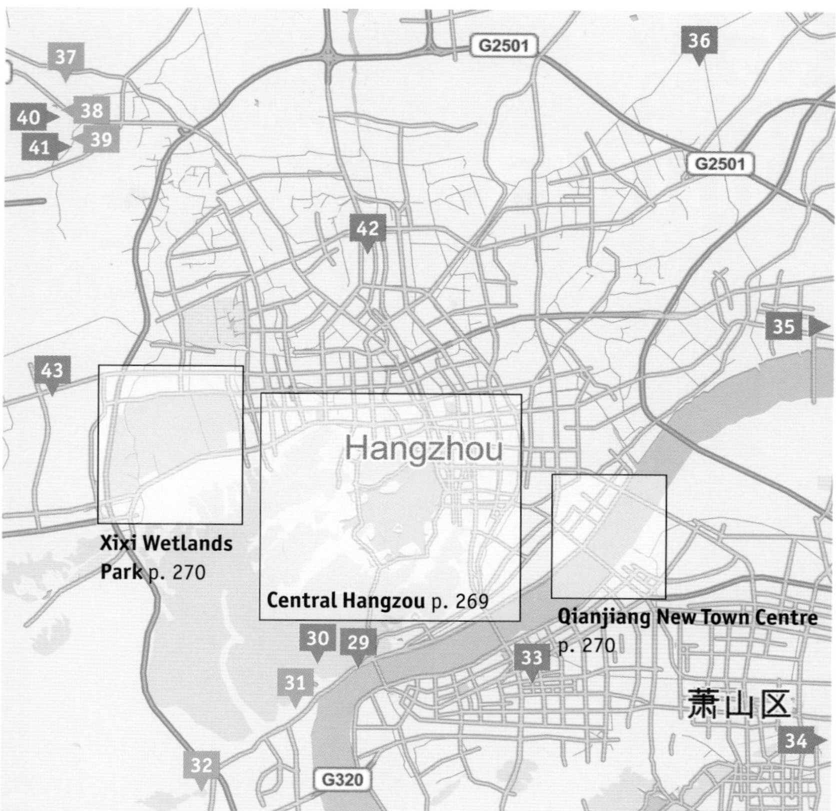

Greater Hangzhou (Map 29–43)

32 China Art Academy Xiangshan Campus *Amateur Architecture (WANG Shu & LU Wenyu), 2001–2007.* ❖ 30.1554, 120.0746

33 Alibaba Hangzhou HQ *HASSELL, 2009.* Seven bent slabs are skinned in an exaggerated garden "ice-ray" screen motif, forming courtyards, street, bridges, and terraces. Private office. ❖ 30.1925, 120.1872

34 South Railway Station Expansion *GMP (von GERKAN, MARG & Partner), under construction.* ❖ 30.1752, 120.2911

35 Duolan Mixed-Use Complex *BAU (Brearley Architects + Urbanists), 2012.* Stepped-roof park, "inside-out" mall. ❖ 30.2986, 120.3844

36 Tianducheng *2007.* A French-style development, complete with gardens and one-third-scale Eiffel Tower. ❖ 30.3864, 120.2441

37 Liangzhu Culture Museum *David CHIPPERFIELD Architects (architect), ZTUDI (contact architect), 2003–2007.* ❖ 30.3795, 120.0233

38 Liangzhu Culture Village – Mei-li-Zhou Church *Tsushima Design Studio (TSUSHIMA Toshio), ACO, PLATdesign (landscape), 2010.* ❖ 30.3709, 120.0232

39 Liangzhu Culture Village – YNLS Retail *AZL (Atelier ZHANG Lei), 2008.* ❖ 30.3694, 120.0234

40 Liangzhu Culture Village – YNLS Retail *QI Xin.* See entry for #39. ❖ 30.3701, 120.0241

41 Liangzhu Culture Village – Heronshire East *David CHIPPERFIELD Architects, 2008.* See #31. ❖ 30.3660, 120.0243

42 Gongchen Bridge *1631, 1714+.* Impressive arched stone bridge over the Grand Canal. A canal museum is on the plaza to the east, but you may find the "preserved" canal-town fabric on the west end more enjoyable. ❖ 30.3204, 120.1349

43 Alibaba Taobao City *KUMA Kengo and Associates, 2013.* Long glass volumes with various sun-shades along a wetland site. Private corporate HQ for China's answer to eBay. ❖ 30.2828, 120.0192

金华
Jinhua

金华 Jinhua

Jinhua (population 1.1 million) is a modest city by Chinese standards ; once a major grain distribution centre, it is now a burgeoning presence in miscellaneous industries, a railway hub, and, perhaps most famously for the Chinese public, the home of Jinhua cured ham. For the design tourist, the main attraction is a substantial, if badly maintained, "architecture park" featuring the work of a number of interesting architects from China and abroad. Jinhua is two hours from Hangzhou by train (four hours from Shanghai) and requires only a three-hour tour; thus, we recommend it only if you are making an extended stay in the Yangtze Delta region, or if your travel route takes you nearby. However, there are several novel buildings to examine here; together, they make up some kind of proposition on the capacity of architecture to offer meaningful alternatives to the existing cultural imaginary. These unusual goals perhaps make the park more interesting than some of contemporary China's other "variety pack" schemes, despite the shabby condition of many of the pavilions today.

The background: Jinhua was the birthplace of one JIANG Zhènghán (1910–1996), a modern poet better known by his pen name, AI Qing. A social critic and supporter of the Communist Party during the Civil War, Ai was nonetheless targeted as a reactionary in the so-called "Anti-Rightist Movement." In 1958, he and his family were exiled to a forced-labour farm in remote Xinjiang. Ai was finally released in 1979, as China stabilised in the DENG Xiaoping period. When he asked the authorities the nature of his crime, he was told, "It's a mistake." As he put it, each of those three words had cost him seven years.

Sent into exile along with Ai Qing was his son AI Weiwei, born just before the arrest. The younger Ai has become, since the 1990s, China's most famous and outspoken contemporary artist on the global stage. Over the last decade and a half, he has progressively tempted fate by finding subtle and not-so-subtle ways of critiquing the government. His artworks and writings make clear his continued dissatisfaction with the authoritarian government, and with its claims that progress could be measured simply by material accumulation. "The Chinese people," he observes, "have gone through a lot, and if it is merely about more cars and tall buildings, then it is not worth it."[1] Following a campaign to publicise the links between government corruption and the deaths of thousands of schoolchildren in the 2008 Sichuan Earthquake, Ai came under increasing pressure from the authorities. He was beaten by the police in 2009 (possibly the cause of a haemorrhage for which he was treated later that year), detained in 2010, and arrested

Previous spread: **Bridging Tea House** (p. 285), seen from **Jinhua Structure I-Cube** (p. 286)

The Architecture Park, seen from atop the **Multimedia Room** (p. 284)

on vague charges early in 2011, leading to a worldwide campaign of protest. Though released after three months, Ai remains, as of 2014, under house arrest in Beijing.

Before all that, however, Ai was a celebrated Chinese artist – and, with his company FAKE Design, an architect. Thus, it's not surprising that in the early 2000s, his father's hometown commissioned two major projects from him. The first was a **memorial park** (p. 287), dedicated to his father; the second, more ambitious project was a very large "Architecture Park," conceived as the climax or terminus of a new district called Jindong. The latter was to be designed by Ai's erstwhile collaborators Herzog & de Meuron. It was never built, but the Swiss team helped bring the Architecture Park to completion. Starting in 2002, Ai and his collaborators gathered a total of seventeen international architects to populate this new park with a string of small, vaguely programmed pavilions. Reportedly, the only Chinese architects involved were ones Ai knew personally and whose work he admired.

Such collaborative schemes are not uncommon in China. The **Great Wall Commune** (p. 109), and **CIPEA** (p. 134) both attempted something similar around the same time, arguably attaining more publicity. AI and Herzog & de Meuron even collaborated on another, the **Ordos 100 project** (p. 392). However, given the highly political nature of Ai's work, and the fact that the park across the water doubled as a tribute to the architect's father, it's appropriate to consider the Architecture Park as something more than just another showcase for star architects.

As Ai explains, "a park is a place where a person can, in a relatively short time, have a variety of different experiences, be those in terms of architectural form or architectural culture." While most Chinese parks are used primarily for fresh air and exercise, Ai imagines a park as an opportunity to experience new kinds of space. The effect this is supposed to have is not spelled out, but one can read between the lines when Ai says that the park will "allow people to use a day or a half-day of time to experience a range of possibilities, particularly young people ... If they grow up in this kind of environment, that will change their views about the world."[2] Which views exactly? Knowing Ai's politics, one can take a guess: the suggestion here is that architecture can stimulate imaginations and suggest the "possibility" of different, better worlds. This is political architecture, but not the kind that provides some socially practical function.

Indeed, hardly any of the pavilions seem conducive to the performance of any preconceived activity. Their functions, like their sites, were assigned to the architects at random, and while some certainly could support their supposed roles, it seems clear that little pressure was exerted upon their architects to make much of programme. This indifference to usefulness, in a society gone mad for capitalist productivity, may itself be a protest. If there is an activist agenda, it manifests itself neither in legible slogans or symbols, nor in what a Western audience might recognise as the space of public appearance. China hardly needs more plazas for carefully managed rallies and "protests." Rather, the optimistic promise of the Architecture Park is that the experience of unusual architecture may plant a seed that later leads one to consider unusual politics. Consider another quote from Ai:

Very small buildings are nonetheless able to wield great influence on society, and only through producing very good architectural classics can we hope to influence society. These do not need to be big buildings, nor do they require great budgets or special conditions of operation, but they do require a clear consciousness and precise grasp, as well as the diligence to complete them. If similar architectural practice occurred in other cities, it would be extremely influential for architectural taste and culture throughout China.[3]

Most of the park pavilions can be understood as passable attempts to conjure up a world of fantasy and dreams. Nearly all of them play either with unexpected scale, mis-fits between exterior and interior, or surprise induced by the "transformation" of an object seen from different angles. Of course, each building is also an architectural project in its own right, and represents the individual preoccupations of its creators. It's unclear to what extent the participants were aware of, or interested in, any political implications of the project; they may have been motivated simply by the interesting design challenges of a small garden pavilion. At times, Ai framed the park's transformative potential in terms of its possible influence on the architects themselves: "China is in desperate need of new ideas, examples of creativity both from inside and outside, and new architectural blood. Conversely, many Western architects are very familiar with architectural theory but don't get many opportunities to build."[4]

Many of the firms, both Chinese and international, made reference to what they saw as aspects of "Chinese" culture and design. These references, which might be cloying or superficial elsewhere, do seem appropriate, given the goals of the project. As well, one should note the importance of variously programmed pavilions in traditional Chinese gardens; these were similarly intended as spaces of both leisure and contemplation. One would hope the "Chinese" references in the Architecture Park turn out as serious engagements with the local artistic heritage. Since Western ideas of a garden folly were historically shaped in part through accounts of Asian landscapes, some kind of reflection on the cultural dialogue by the Western participants seems almost inevitable.

To us, then, the park poses a series of provocative and not-easily-resolved questions. To what extent can a building foster the kind of political effects Ai implies? How articulate can architecture be about the real-world political situation, or the proposal of particular alternatives? Might the same architecture give rise just as easily to dreams of *regressive* change? And, finally, to what extent does the built reality of Jinhua achieve its goals?

1. Ian LUNA and Thomas TSANG, *On the Edge: Ten Architects From China*, New York: Rizzoli, 2006, p. 145. See p. 396.
2. From the LÜ Hengzhong interview in *A & U: Architecture & Urbanism*,December 2006).
3. LÜ Hengzhong, *op. cit.*
4. From the Hans Ulrich Obrist interview in *Domus* (July-August 2006).

Practical Considerations

The Architecture Park is about six kilometres from Jinhua's train station (travelling roughly due east). A cab should get you there in fifteen minutes. The Ai Qing Culture Park is directly across the river from the Architecture Park, so if you finish at the park's east end, you can cross the nearest bridge and double back. Unless you've retained your cab, this will be a bit of a hike, but not any more so than the Architecture Park itself.

Surprisingly, given that the pavilions were finished within the last decade, many are

An overgrown path in the Architecture Park

very badly run-down. On some visits, we have found most of the interiors locked up tight, though others permit a more complete experience. The poor upkeep may simply be a budgetary issue, or alternately a consequence of Ai's thorny status in China at this time. It may be that, now that Ai is *persona non grata,* the local authorities do not want to go out of their way to advertise their city as the home of an Ai Weiwei park, or be seen as actively maintaining such a park. There may also be a more banal explanation: as the surrounding area was not developed with the intended degree of density, the park has simply lost its role as the centre of a neighbourhood. On the other hand, Amateur Architecture's pavilion received alterations or repairs in 2011–2012, perhaps a reflection of the firm's rising stature (and an anticipation of principal WANG Shu's 2012 Pritzker Prize). A few steps away, a brand-new pavilion, unseen in any previously published designs, was completed circa 2013, years after the rest of the set. Jinhua clearly has not given up on contemporary architecture. Downtown, about ten minutes from the park, is a large, brand-new cultural facility, also by Amateur Architecture, and well worth a look.

Sources and Recommended Reading

AI Weiwei and Anthony PINS, *Spatial Matters,* London: MIT Press, 2014. A valuable survey of Ai's architectural work, in the context of his art practice.

A & U: Architecture & Urbanism (December 2006). Various pavilions covered in detail, and an interview with Ai by LÜ Hengzhong.

Domus (No. 894, July-August 2006). Another spread of pavilion coverage, plus an interview with Ai (conducted by Hans Ulrich OBRIST, see below).

Toshiko MORI, "Jinhua Architecture Park, Organised by Ai Weiwei." *32: Beijing/New York* (No. 5–6, Winter 2005). Brief text with some revealing comments on the architect-selection process.

Hans Ulrich OBRIST, *Ai Weiwei Speaks,* London: Penguin, 2011. Useful, pocket-size interview volume covering Ai's background and his politics, with a few illustrations.

Welcome Centre

JH 01

tillschweizer/co, 2005

Jinhua Architecture Park
❖ 29.1131, 119.6790

This is the pavilion closest to the centre of Jinhua, and to a bend in the river, a site which afforded a long view down the river to downtown. Thus, SCHWEIZER approached the building primarily as a viewing platform which would situate new arrivals in the park, and allow tempting views of other pavilions. (It also has interior space, intended for exhibitions and/or a visitors' meeting point.) The surface of wooden lattices is meant to intensify these effects, making the volume mysterious but also invitingly porous – and creating interesting and unfamiliar views of the otherwise ordinary landscape. The shear in plan and section creates severe forced perspectives on the upper level, reminiscent of optical illusion rooms in funhouses. Given the park's overall goals, this is the right tone to set.

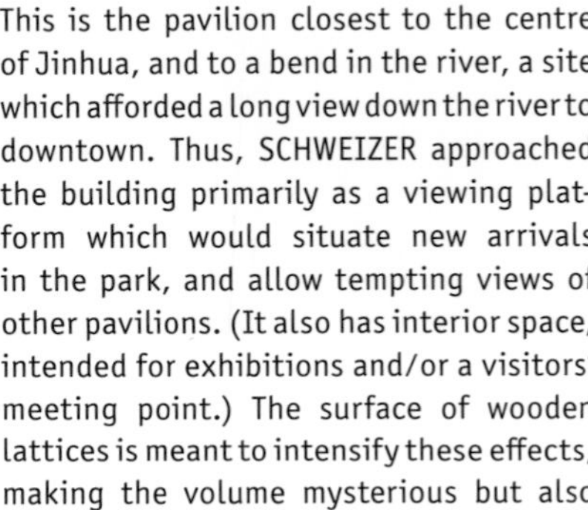

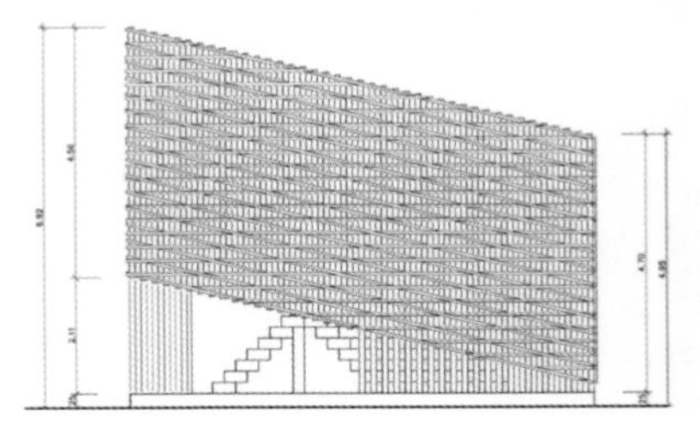

West Elevation

Courtesy tillschweizer/co

Ancient Tree

JH 02

Christ & Gantenbein, 2004–2007

Jinhua Architecture Park
❖ 29.1128, 119.68072

This concrete "tree," assembled from intersecting panels, builds on historic Chinese garden themes while going beyond the usual quotations. The abstraction and the concrete make its artificiality obvious, but its rough edges, shade, and curvature in turn suggest something more treelike than the linear garden landscape that surrounds it. It's fake nature, but more real than the real thing: see **Suzhou** (p. 210). In time, the surrounding trees will grow in, but the architects hope the "ancient" one will show its age more rapidly – a prescient thought, given the weathering seen elsewhere. The function is suitably obscure: there's nowhere to sit, and clearly any hide-and-seek games would prove suicidal.

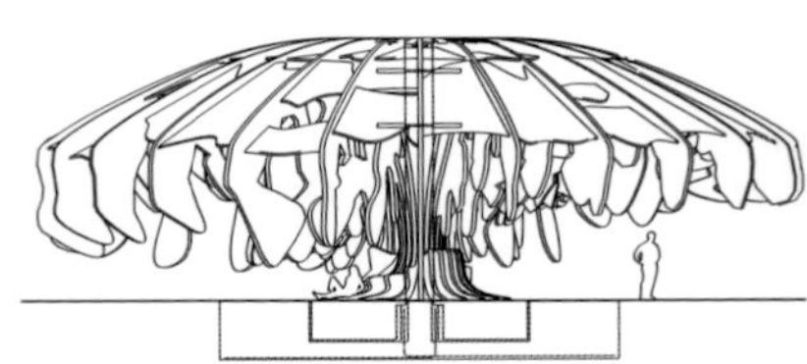

Elevation

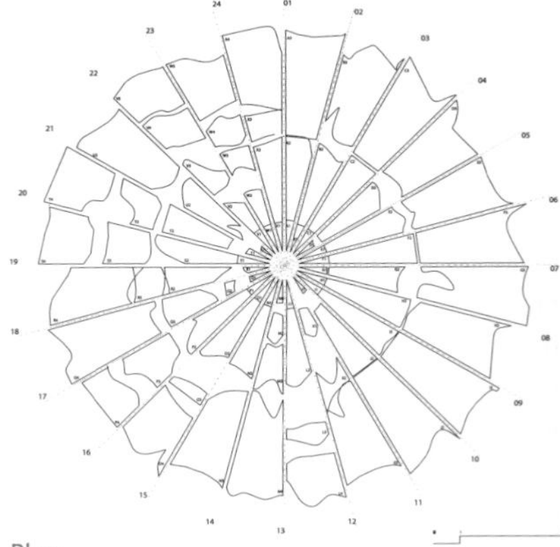

Plan

Exhibition Space

JH 03

Tatiana BILBAO/MXA, 2007

Jinhua Architecture Park
❖ 29.1122, 119.6820

Says Bilbao, "We used the architecture to frame views of the surrounding landscape, but the pavilion itself can never be surveyed entirely from a single point. One must explore it to get an idea of its form." As in Chinese gardens – compare to **Lion's Grove** (p. 219) – visual access is distinct from physical access, and multiple routes overlap in a small area. The faceted topography turns inward and plays against the linear axes of the park, while the large view-framing apertures point back out.

Baby Dragon

JH 04

HHF, 2004–2005

Jinhua Architecture Park
❖ 29.1118, 119.6827

This dyed-concrete structure was planned as a supervised play-area for children, though to be fair, few of the park's structures would fail to meet that description. It's a long wall with some roof overhang, perforated by bold geometric punches in eleven recurring shapes; children can sit in or climb through these holes. Anticipating some of the issues other foreign designers were confronted with, HHF made their design easy to construct: a concrete pour, with some holes.

Courtesy Jiakun Architects

Courtesy Jiakun Architects

Tea Rooms

JH 05

Jiakun Architects (LIU Jiakun), 2005

Jinhua Architecture Park
❖ 29.1113, 119.6839

The communal programme is split among seven small, elevated platforms. Something light and frail is put in dialogue with the heavy earthworks visible from the river, and something vertical is made to address the overall flatness of the park. The minimal structures employ a number of double-duty elements, with "electric poles used as columns," "steel platforms composed of electric pole fittings" and "channel steel used as rainwater gutters." All are typical materials for municipal/infrastructural construction, an interesting choice for the restless architects, who have done interesting work in several material languages, but are usually known for sober concrete and masonry. The Tea Rooms, unusually, feature a number of operable mechanical elements – and have thus suffered the most from the park's neglect. The wall-flaps could once be slid or folded out (flipping up, like gull wings or DeLorean car doors), but everything's either rusted, jammed, or chained in place. Though at present they make evocative, ghostly figures in the misty landscape, they would be both eerier and quirkier if seen in their intended range of transformed states. The shifting huts would also have fitted well with the park's ideas of implicit social transformation. What remains is the experience of leaving the everyday ground for a place of remove and small-group gathering: the essence of a tea room.

Courtesy DnA Design and Architecture

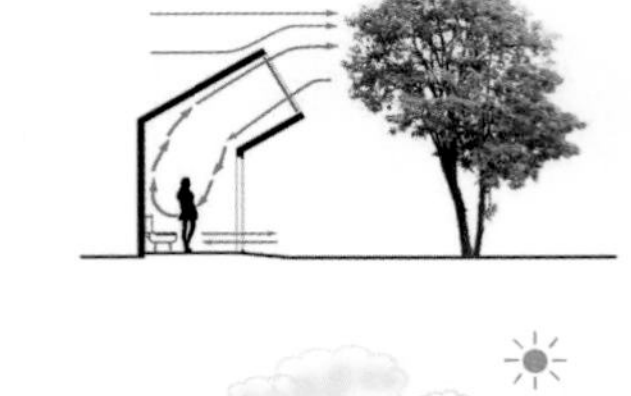

Public Toilets

JH 06

DnA Design and Architecture (XU Tiantian), 2004

Jinhua Architecture Park
❖ 29.1108 119.6847

The periscope or funnel form keeps out rain while admitting sunlight, ventilating the bathroom and maintaining privacy for the users. The minimal footprint for the buildings is meant to help them blend in with the surrounding trees, although the final landscape seems to have put more of a clearing around the buildings. Note that while the forms are rationalised functionally, the composition brings in other priorities; the buildings are arranged on the site in a scattered, semi-random fashion, giving up a little of that sunlight in order to evoke the loose, fun-loving spontaneity of the Jinhua project. As with the **Tea Rooms** (p. 281), these are currently locked up (unfortunately for visitors) and in somewhat rough shape.

Courtesy DnA Design and Architecture

Sections showing ventilation, sunlight

Manager's Room

JH 07

Buchner Bründler AG, 2007

Jinhua Architecture Park
❖ 29.1101, 119.6872

From the path, this structure presents itself as a solid wall. Behind the rectangular box is a series of angular cells: living and work spaces for the park manager. Though the walls are white concrete rather than plastered brick, the suggestion seems to be a Suzhou garden, where a secluded and irregular world is found behind an "urban" sort of wall. The forecourt behind the wall is (supposed to be) open to the public, and you can also see the ragged edge by walking around to the back side.

Multifunctional Space

JH 08

FCJZ (Yung Ho CHANG), 2006

Jinhua Architecture Park
❖ 29.1095, 119.6877

While it may have a funny name for a pavilion in a park where hardly any building seems particularly single-functional, this is an interesting solution, unique in the set. Like the **Tea Rooms** (p. 281), this space is broken up into micro-pavilions (compared by the architects to *dim sum*), which are grouped together to create an outdoor space evoking traditional urbanism. Markings on the volumes suggest patterns in garden lattice screens or paving, with a touch of contemporary graphic flatness.

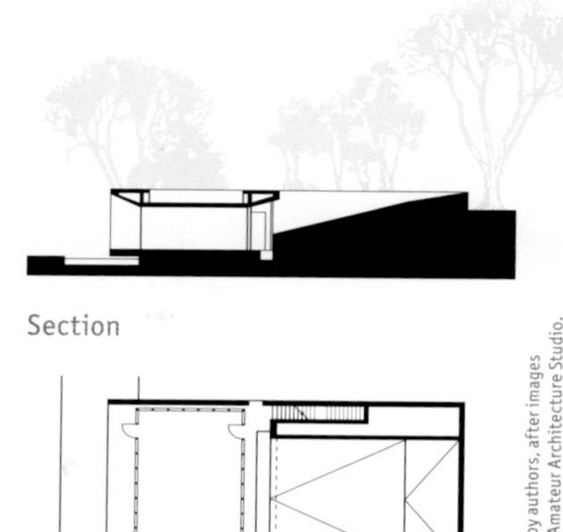

Section

Ground-floor plan

Redrawn by authors, after images courtesy Amateur Architecture Studio.

Coffee House (Ceramic House)

Amateur Architecture (WANG Shu & LU Wenyu), 2004–2006

JH 10

Jinhua Architecture Park
❖ 29.1091, 119.6891

This is yet another pavilion based around a scalar game to expand children's minds. The designers claim it's a giant-scale Song Dynasty ink basin, while the perforated surface of blocky voids suggests a shrunken version of the building's suspended, open porch. The ramp also aims to channel southeastern breezes and provide a place for contemplation under the trees. Supposedly, when one gazes up the ramp, "all evidence of perspective appears to be lost," and one sees only the tree canopy above. As the building was inspired by a traditional sculptural object, the artist ZHOU Wu was recruited to cover the building in colourful ceramic tiles, except for the numerous small openings which admit air and light. The building is thus a kind of funhouse, but a stately one for cloud-gazing daydreams shared over a grown-up's beverage, not hyperactive fantasies.

Archaeological Archive

FAKE Design (AI Weiwei), 2006

JH 11

Jinhua Architecture Park
❖29.1087, 119.6902

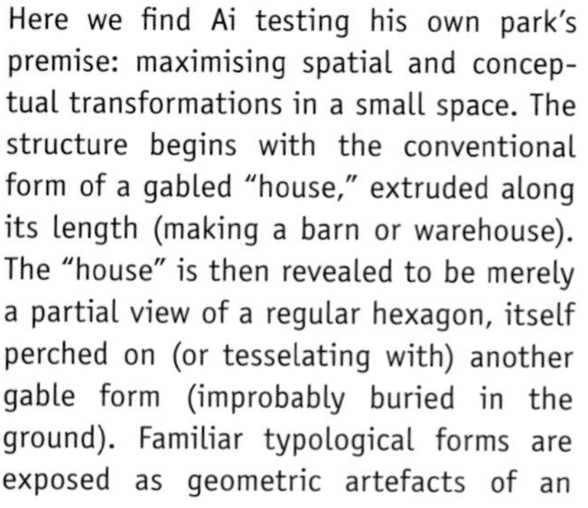

Here we find Ai testing his own park's premise: maximising spatial and conceptual transformations in a small space. The structure begins with the conventional form of a gabled "house," extruded along its length (making a barn or warehouse). The "house" is then revealed to be merely a partial view of a regular hexagon, itself perched on (or tesselating with) another gable form (improbably buried in the ground). Familiar typological forms are exposed as geometric artefacts of an abstract, cellular order, reinforced by the honeycomb-like landscape pattern. The building invites visitors to see it many different ways, and to oscillate their mental points of view between elevation and plan treatments of the same figure. It's the kind of mind-expanding provocation for which the park was intended. The stepped landscape reminds one of the earlier Ai Qing memorial (p. 287), while the explora-tion of deceptively simple extrusions suggests a mutual relationship with Herzog & de Meuron; compare to their Jinhua contribution (p. 276) and the later VitraHaus in Weil-am-Rhein. The lower level was to house some unspecified artefacts (no longer to be found), whose patterns were evoked in the bamboo-formed concrete.

Newspaper Stand

JH 12

Toshiko MORI, 2005–2006

Jinhua Architecture Park
❖ 29.1087, 119.6915

The linear "Newspaper Café" was meant to express a sharp division between its two sides: one an elevated reading overlook separates a set of newspaper racks facing the city to the north, the other a blank plaster surface facing the park to the south. The "newspaper" wall was to be animated by scalar games: at a distance, its collection of papers would dissolve into texture – an "atomised and pixelated decorative pattern." Closer up, the papers would "reveal or hide" their content as texts, depending on the viewer's angle.

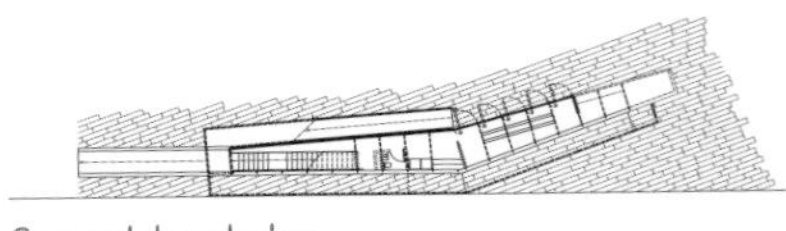

Ground-level plan

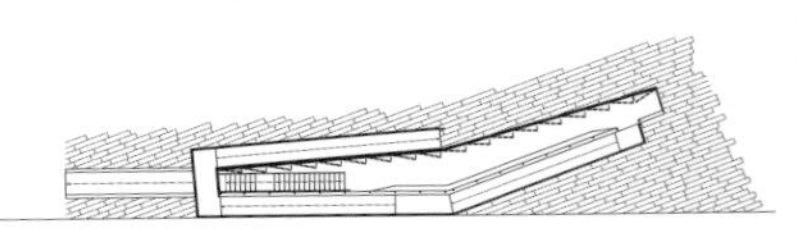

Roof-level plan

Courtesy Toshiko Mori Architects

Unfortunately, if any paper route ever covered this park, the deliveries must have stopped long ago; meanwhile, the park façade was built in exposed concrete, whose rough texture undermines the effect of neutral white scalelessness that would have contrasted with the papers. It's still a fine pavilion – just be sure to bring your own reading material.

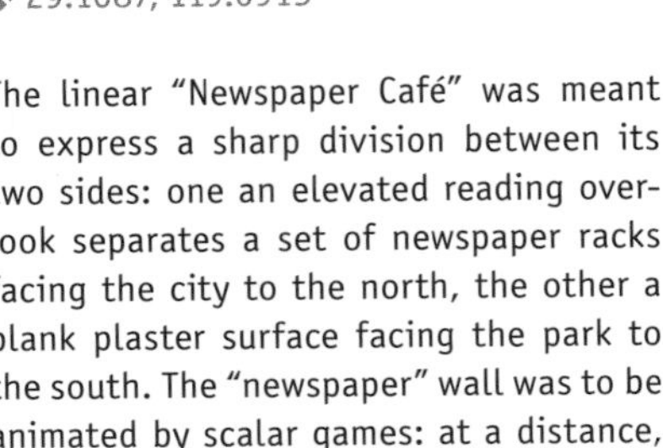

Multimedia Room

JH 13

KNOWSPACE (Erhard An-He KINZELBACH), 2005–2007

Jinhua Architecture Park
❖ 29.1084, 119.6927

An interesting little study in the distortion of form to accommodate a specific function: watching movies, inside and outside. One can picture the "original" tubular box, which has been pushed, pulled and stepped in response to the imagined light cone of a movie projector, and the needs of tiered seating (admittedly a bit steep for stepping). Tiles are used to give a slick, shiny continuity to the surface outside; weathering has been unkind.

Restaurant 13

JH 14

Fün Design Consultants (Johan DE WACHTER), 2004–2007

Jinhua Architecture Park
❖ 29.1088, 119.6933

Levels are suspended freely in space, ostensibly to accommodate different dining experiences ("street food, eating at the table, or laid back lounging"). They produce "watch-and-be-watched" relationships, and a spatial playground, reminiscent of Constant's *New Babylon* or a whimsical reinterpretation of Le Corbusier's Dom-Ino. Not all of the platforms are accessible, but at least they've helped protect the building.

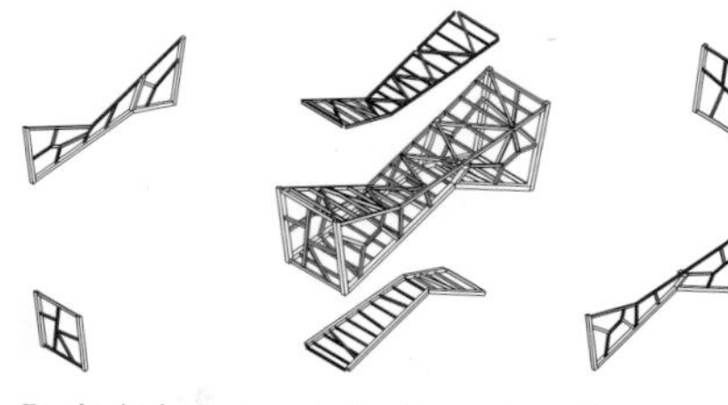

Exploded axonometric of structural frame

Bridging Tea House

LAR (now FR-EE/Fernando ROMERO), 2004–06

JH 15

Jinhua Architecture Park
❖ 29.1092, 119.6948

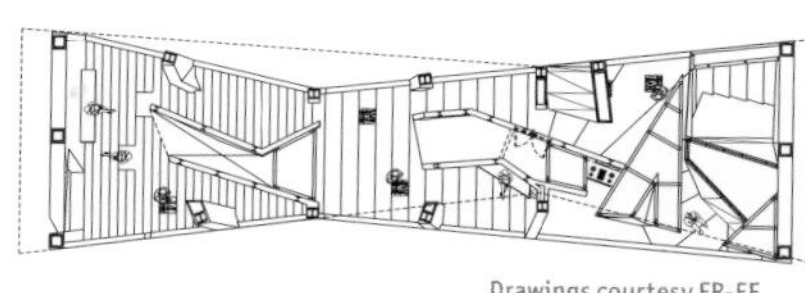

Plan

Drawings courtesy FR-EE Fernando Romero Enterprise

The architects describe this pavilion as a fusion of two fundamental Chinese garden elements: bridge and tea house. The small pocket-platforms break the space down into smaller zones, sufficiently private for contemplation of the environment, with differently-sized nooks inviting different social groupings (couples, larger families, etc.). The dividing walls double as the structural elements of the space frame which spans the erstwhile pond. Looming over the grass from a distance, it's perhaps the most surreal of all the pavilions: a big, red, weightless bow tie, drifting into one's field of vision. Inside, walls slant against the path of the stairs, adding to the funhouse experience. Revealingly, Romero asserts that, following the schematic design phase, the firm heard nothing back from the Chinese team until a year later – when photos of the finished building arrived. To the visitor, the structure as-built resembles the published designs relatively closely.

Rendering of stair geometry

Book Bar

Michael MALTZAN, 2006

JH 17

Jinhua Architecture Park
❖ 29.1102, 119.6969

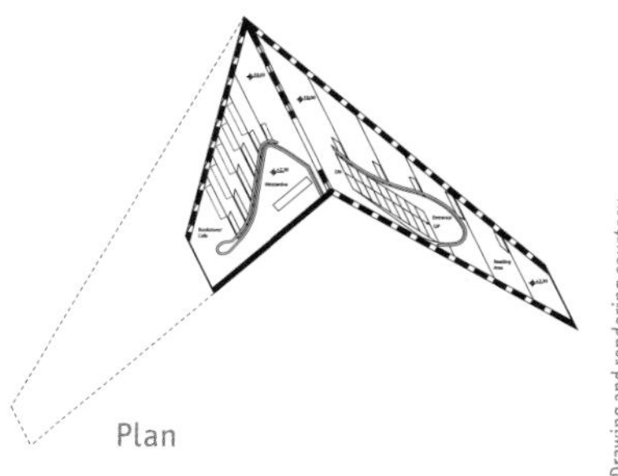

Plan

Drawing and rendering courtesy Michael Maltzan Architecture

"The pavilion's form pulls its central wall outward into two unequal, cantilevered arms, each concealing within a public space for learning" – moves notionally inspired by an incident in Chinese history, when the writings of Confucius survived burning because they had been hidden within a wall. Beyond this "confluence between the book and architecture," Maltzan was interested in the production of unusual visual effects through forced perspective and moiré-like screens. (Note the effective suppression of the adjacent roadway.) Formally, the pavilion explores the play between continuous forms, and the dividing wall through which they pass. The distorted, compressed interior indeed gives a sense of being sealed up inside a wall, while enabling quiet contemplation.

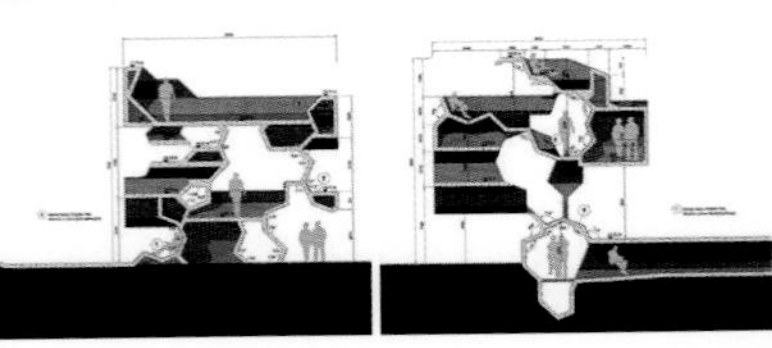

Sections

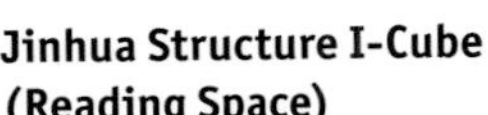

Jinhua Structure I-Cube (Reading Space)

JH 16

Herzog & de Meuron, 2004–2006

Jinhua Architecture Park
❖ 29.1098, 119.6957

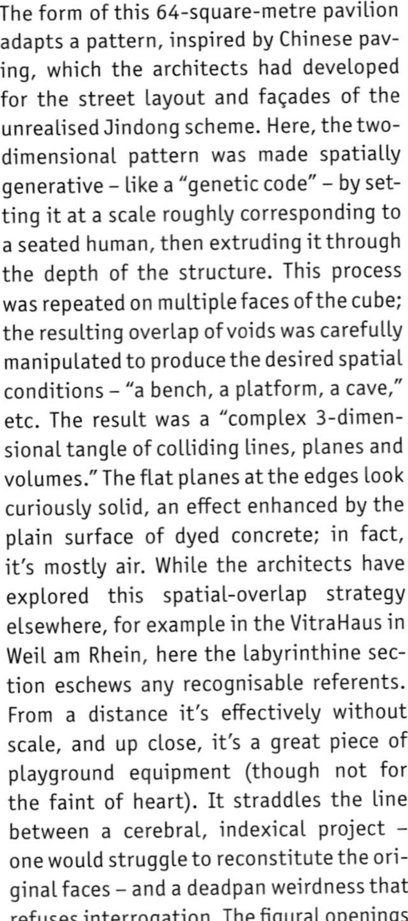

The form of this 64-square-metre pavilion adapts a pattern, inspired by Chinese paving, which the architects had developed for the street layout and façades of the unrealised Jindong scheme. Here, the two-dimensional pattern was made spatially generative – like a "genetic code" – by setting it at a scale roughly corresponding to a seated human, then extruding it through the depth of the structure. This process was repeated on multiple faces of the cube; the resulting overlap of voids was carefully manipulated to produce the desired spatial conditions – "a bench, a platform, a cave," etc. The result was a "complex 3-dimensional tangle of colliding lines, planes and volumes." The flat planes at the edges look curiously solid, an effect enhanced by the plain surface of dyed concrete; in fact, it's mostly air. While the architects have explored this spatial-overlap strategy elsewhere, for example in the VitraHaus in Weil am Rhein, here the labyrinthine section eschews any recognisable referents. From a distance it's effectively without scale, and up close, it's a great piece of playground equipment (though not for the faint of heart). It straddles the line between a cerebral, indexical project – one would struggle to reconstitute the original faces – and a deadpan weirdness that refuses interrogation. The figural openings create framed views of the neighbours, while cutting off the foreground, so other pavilions become scaleless follies floating in the landscape. Recall also Herzog's claim that "when ornament and structure become a single thing, strangely enough the result is a new feeling of freedom." All quotes from architects' website or their remarks in *El Croquis* #129/130, 2006.

Study of overlapping geometry

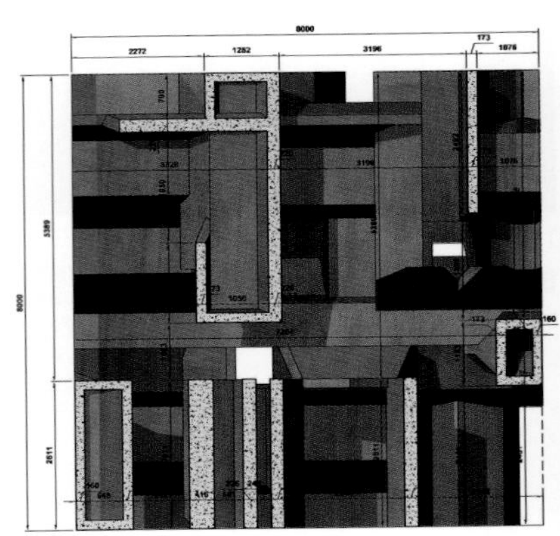

Plan

Ai Qing Culture Park

JH 18

FAKE Design (AI Weiwei), 2001–02

艾青文化公园
金华金东区艾青路（近政和街）
Aiqing Rd., Jindong, Jinhua
❖ 29.1045, 119.6920

Ai's monument to his poet father is a series of stepped granite quasi-pyramids, formed into a sawtooth confronting the riverfront, just across from the "Architecture Park." At the top of this elaborate retaining wall is a grid of pillars, shifted ever so slightly off of the axis that would have connected the park to the new Jindong district (had it been built as planned). Ai here tests his interest in whether China's new parks could offer something beyond "more leaves, cleaner air, and shade"; there are indeed, few leaves, little shade, and none of the usual self-congratulatory glitz. This severity befits a son's tribute to his father, but it also contributes to Ai's larger project of resistance. Many of FAKE's projects have a similar blankness; though their surfaces are modulated in terms of relief and texture, they refuse to offer explicit, consumable meaning, and are usually photographed without people, a striking choice at a time when clients expect to see eager, animated consumers crowding all images. Note also Ai's refusal to inscribe the pillars with his father's verses. Thus, what may seem to be a bid for timelessness is also a very timely resistance strategy: in consumerist China, a simple request for peace and quiet approaches dissent. The mute forms also help undercut any potential for "hero worship" inherent in the monumental project. If the forms are hardly as lively as those found across the river, there is still a certain uplifting presence to the outward-pointing wall of "pyramids" – perhaps an assertion of life in the face of personal or cultural oblivion.

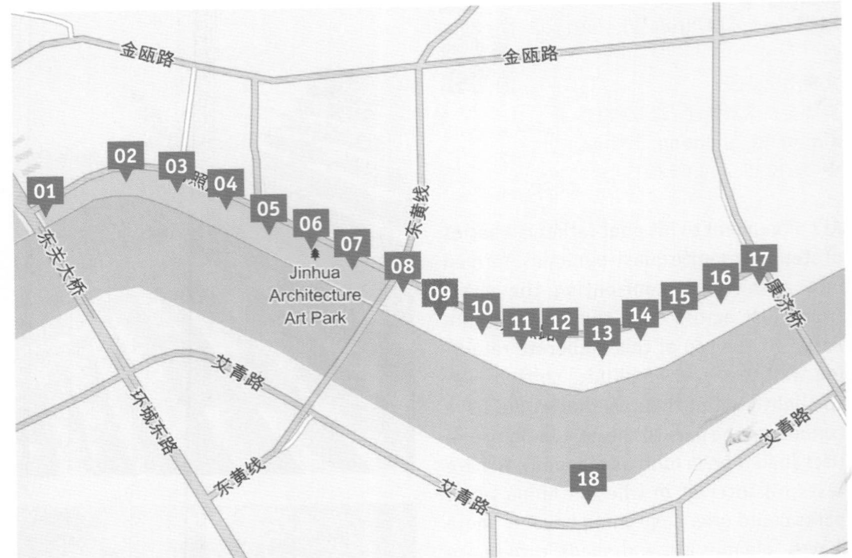

Jinhua Architecture Park – 金华建筑艺术公园 (Map 01–18)

01 Welcome Centre *tillschweizer/co (Till SCHWEIZER), 2002–2007* ❖ 29.1132, 119.6788

02 Ancient Tree *Christ & Gantenbein (Emanuel CHRIST & Christoph GANTENBEIN), 2002– 2007* ❖ 29.1128, 119.6804

03 Exhibition Space *Tatiana BILBAO/MXA, 2002–2007.* ❖ 29.1122, 119.6820

04 Baby Dragon *HHF, 2002–2007.* ❖ 29.1118, 119.6827

05 Tea Rooms *Jiakun Architects (LIU Jiakun), 2002–2007.* ❖ 29.1113, 119.6839

06 Public Toilet *DnA Design and Architecture (XU Tiantian), 2002–2007.* ❖ 29.1108, 119.6847

07 Manager's Room *Buchner Bründler AG, 2007.* ❖ 29.1101, 119.6872

08 Multifunction Space *FCJZ (Yung Ho CHANG), 2006.* ❖ 29.1095, 119.6877

09 Internet Café *DING Yi & CHEN Shu Yu.* This dense, closed-seeming 12 x 12 metre box features only one boldly-cut, unframed opening. It's a nice contrast to the expected signifiers of "electronic architecture" and/or coffee-boutique slickness; here, Internet use seems somehow monkish, deliberate, and (significantly in today's China) private. ❖ 34.2633, 108.9369

10 Coffee House (Ceramic House) *Amateur Architecture (WANG Shu & LU Wenyu), 2002–2007.* ❖ 29.1091, 119.6891

11 Archaeological Archive *FAKE Design (AI Weiwei), 2002–2007.* ❖ 29.1087, 119.6902

12 Newspaper Stand *Toshiko MORI, 2002–2007.* ❖ 29.1087, 119.6915

13 Multimedia Room *KNOWSPACE (Erhard An-he KINZELBACH), 2005–2007.* ❖ 29.1084, 119.6927

14 Restaurant *Fun Design Consultants (Johan de WACHTER), 2002–2007* ❖ 29.1088, 119.6933

15 Bridging Tea House *LAR (Fernando ROMERO, now FR-EE), 2002–2007* ❖ 29.1092, 119.6948

16 Jinhua Structure I-Cube (Reading Space) *Herzog & de Meuron, 2004–2006.* ❖ 29.1098, 119.6957

17 Book Bar *Michael MALTZAN Architecture, 2002–2007.* ❖ 29.1102, 119.6969

18 Ai Qing Culture Park *FAKE Design (AI Weiwei), 2002.* ❖ 29.1045, 119.6920

19 Jinhua West Railway Station ❖ 29.1136, 119.6313

20 Sun City *1997.* Concentric circles of retail with connecting bridges, orbiting a red dome; perhaps an interpretation of a Hakka *tulou* (see p. 386), or just a familiar circular market typology. Possibly closed, but still worth a look if you're near the station. ❖ 29.1092, 119.6302.

JH Jinhua

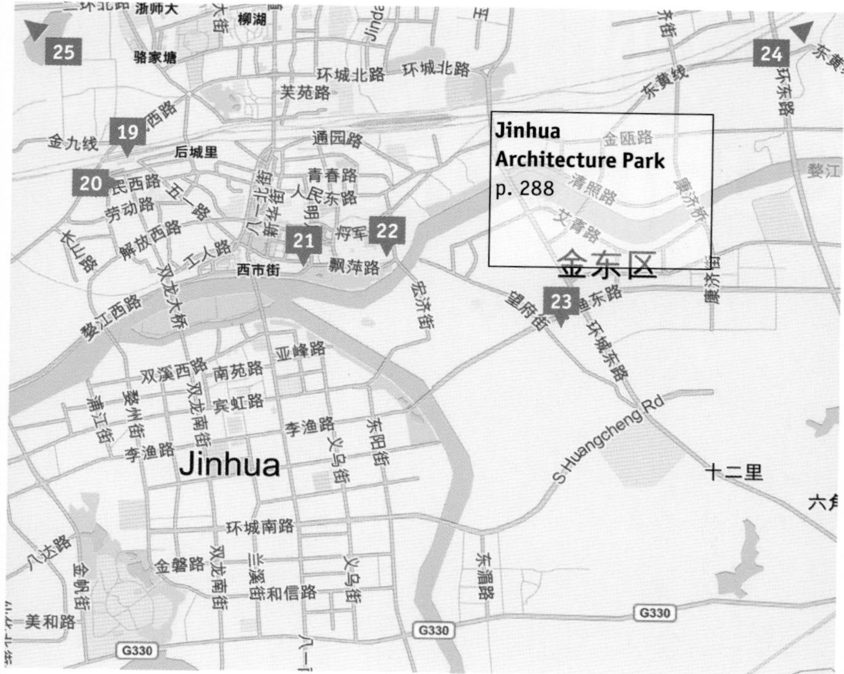

Jinhua City (Map 11–25)

21 Jinhua Culture Centre *Amateur Architecture (WANG Shu & LU Wenyu), 2010.* Stacked and sheared boxes capture ambiguous space between layered façades, while surface treatments in channel glass, stacked stones, and patterned window cuts are familiar from the firm's other projects (particularly Xiangshan Campus, p. 264). ❖ 29.1021, 119.6524

22 Wu Xichun Lane *2003.* "Historic" street (on the site of a former tea factory), lined with restaurants and several small museums. Compare to Xintiandi (p. 171) or Nanluogu Xiang (map p. 114) ❖ 29.1032, 119.6622

23 Cube Tube *SAKO Architects, 2004–2010.* An office and restaurant in the city's new Economic Development Zone. The simplified, blocky massing is enlivened by a distribution of square windows of several sizes. ❖ 29.0978,119.6869

24 Yiwu A city 65 km northeast of Jinhua, Yiwu is home to several sights. The Yiwu Museum exhibits a range of local archaeological finds, while the Yiwu Small Commodities Market is a massively scaled, multi-block wholesale shopping mall, with entire floor levels dedicated to single product types. Samples are available for sale, but the best deals are on full shipping containers for export. ❖ 29.3424, 120.1115 (Market)

25 Jiande Daci Scenic Area/Daci Rock Monastery. 57 km northwest of Jinhua, this heavily restored "hanging temple" is tucked into the base of a sheer cliff, in a foggy valley. At least a half-day's trip, but very scenic, especially if you can't make it to the one near Datong (map p. 391). This region is also home to a number of natural wonders (Shuanglong Cave, Fuxi Stone Forest, etc.) beyond the scope of this book. ❖ 29.3121, 119.2837

广州
Guangzhou

广州 Guangzhou

Guangzhou (formerly Canton, after the Portuguese Cantão) is located at a bent fork in the Pearl River (Zhujiang) just upriver from the point where it meets the South China Sea. It has thus been a key point of contact between China and the rest of the world for over 1,500 years. Today, it's the fourth largest city in China by population, and the greater Guangzhou metropolitan area effectively includes Shenzhen as well as several other cities. Guangzhou proper is the most important shipping point in a megalopolis of light industry, thus the key hand-off point for an enormous share of the "Made in China" products on which much worldwide consumerism currently depends.

Based on its convenient location, and the defensive protection of the Baiyun Hills to the north, this site became an ancient crossroads for trade between China and Southeast Asia, then India and the Middle East. When walls were finally built in the eleventh century, they incorporated the provincial palace as well as several Buddhist monasteries; this area was named "Guangzhou," but outside, the city spread east and especially west along the river, with major streets perpendicular to the waterfront. On old maps, we can read a distinction between the walled city (wider streets, with at least the major ones following a clear grid) and the bustling, irregular fabric to the west; time has not completely erased these differences.

European contact began with the arrival of the Portuguese, who briefly established a settlement in 1514. They were later forced to relocate, but maintained their trade monopoly with Guangzhou. Thus, while European contact transformed the city's economy, its urban fabric at this stage remained Chinese. With the more extensive reopening of Chinese foreign trade in 1683, Guangzhou maintained its leadership. Indeed, China's eighteenth-century trade policy was called the "Canton System": only certain cities could trade with the West, and European merchants had to deal with a middleman merchant agency (the *Cohong*), rather than with merchants directly. During the trading season, Europeans could reside in the area of the "Thirteen Hongs" (called "factories," but really warehouses and trading markets) here in Guangzhou; otherwise they were still confined officially to Macau, and were barred from bringing certain goods into China. As the Emperor put it, "Our Celestial Empire possesses all things in prolific abundance and lacks no product within its own borders."

By the 1810s, the increasingly complex economics of European colonialism were

Previous spread: **Zhujiang New Town** (p. 299)

Alfred Schinz, *The Magic Square* (1996), p. 414. Courtesy Edition Axel Menges.

Pre-Communist-era Guangzhou. Shamian Island sits at the fork between two river branches. To the east is the linear grain of factories and warehouses; to the northeast is the old walled city (including administrative and religious sub-centres).

Zhujiang New Town (p. 299): the representative space of planned public (touristic) activity, as depicted on local signage (similar graphics can be found at Edushi.com).

putting a strain on the Canton System. The British East India Company, then the *de facto* colonial government of India, had begun auctioning surplus opium to independent British merchants. The merchants, with a powerful navy on their side, sold the opium to Chinese smugglers with impunity, and at huge profits. This trade directly financed British control of India, and indirectly made possible the continuing industrialisation that underpinned further colonial adventures. In China, the rise in opium addiction precipitated massive disruptions to the economy, the army, and society itself. Protests from the Emperor were ignored by the British, until a new, hard-line commissioner was appointed to Guangdong Province in 1839. After the British ignored one last ultimatum, he sent agents into the Guangzhou harbour-front, arresting hundreds of Chinese opium merchants, confiscating thousands of pipes, and destroying thirteen hundred tons of opium. The British government sent in its navy, beginning the First Opium War (1839–1842), which is sometimes seen as the starting point of modern Chinese history. It was one-sided:

"Canton" in 1910, as seen by European businesspeople; the key emphasises bureaucratic offices and the foreign warehouses, while monasteries are reduced to pagoda icons

the modernised British Navy easily took the mouth of the Pearl and later the Yangtze, effectively seizing China's economy by the throat. What began in Guangzhou ended with the 1842 Treaty of Nanking (Nanjing), the first of what would later rightly be called "Unequal Treaties," redefining China's relationship with the West. The British required the Chinese to pay reparations for the destroyed opium, cede Hong Kong, and open five "Treaty Ports" for trade and settlement by foreign powers: Ningbo, Shanghai, Fuzhou, Xiamen, and of course Guangzhou. The Qing dynasty was humiliated, the Canton System was dead, and the opium trade was resumed. By 1881, as many as one-third of China's 370 million people may have been addicted. The Chinese leadership was increasingly split between those who believed it was necessary for China to modernise to regain its stature, and those who felt that foreign ways were the source of all the problems in the first place.

Back in Guangzhou, with the port having been forcibly opened to foreigners, the colonial presence immediately began to expand. The British and French acquired a sandbar just west of the Thirteen Hongs and shored it up into a new base of operations: **Shamian Island** (p. 305). The city remained prosperous for the same reasons as before: it occupied an excellent position at the mouth of a major river, and was only one of a few legal ports. It would continue to prosper and expand through the 1912 collapse of the Qing dynasty – an event precipitated by the very debates that had begun in Guangzhou with the Opium Wars. The new Republican government embraced Western-style, "modern" managerial bureaucracy; Guangzhou acquired new infrastructure (including wide boulevards on the lines of the old walls) and green parks, including one (**People's Park**, map p. 310) on the footprint of the old Qing administrative compound. Like Shanghai, Guangzhou prospered until World War II, but was at a loose end after the Communist victory, as its viable shipping destinations dwindled. In 1984, it became one of the second round of Special Economic Zones; since then, it has followed a pattern of unprecedented growth akin to that of Shenzhen, although in this case there was a substantial metropolis to begin with. Still, the unplanned growth has worried some, and the city has attempted to fight back with a new centre of explicitly "planned," axial urbanism (**Zhujiang,** p. 299).

If the factories of Southern China produce many of the products on sale in the world's discount retail outlets, has history in a sense reversed itself? Now it's the West whose pundits grumble that China holds too great an economic sway, with their governments unable or unwilling to defy Beijing. While the historical analogy

Suburban estates, as seen from the highway

The pedestrian city

Container shipping near Guangzhou

A drive in the hanging gardens

is reductive, it highlights Guangzhou's continuing significance in the global economy. Indeed, one could say that much of that economy takes *place* right here, and in the surrounding hinterland of light-industrial factories sprawling endlessly along the highways. The modern container ports are closer to the sea; Guangzhou proper now acts (as always) as a middleman, the old wharfs and waterfronts having largely been filled in to provide new building sites. Those interested in urban spaces and their relationships can thus find much to take in here: a countryside-city of production, a wharf city of distribution, and a monumental city of representation, all nurturing and conditioning one another.

Practical Considerations

Most of the signature new buildings are in and around the Zhujiang district; nearby are also several instances of renovated, formerly industrial "creative spaces" (see map, p. 310). The old western city is also a must-see, not as a scenic "old city" (though the surviving colonial spaces are quite interesting), but as a functional living one – don't miss **Qingping Market** (p. 306). If you have more than a day or two, consider making arrangements to see the **Tulou Collective Housing** (p. 308), the **Guangzhou Gymnasium** (p. 309), and other works further from the centre. Two brisk days should be long enough to see all the major items on our map, though it will be necessary to do a lot of driving. Conveniently, Guangzhou has some of China's most heroic traffic infrastructure, with innumerable fly-over highways gliding right through built-up areas. Even those familiar with Tokyo or Mumbai will find something distinctive here: the elevated roads' hard edges are softened by kilometres of carefully tended planters along the edges. In concert with the shade trees rising from below, this labour-intensive detail makes a hanging garden out of what would otherwise be an entirely noxious piece of infrastructure. Ignoring the traffic, there's something majestic about the experience.

If you're here for longer than a few days, consider the two-hour ride to Kaiping, where you can hire transport to see the **tower houses** (p. 309), unique to this part of China. In the other direction, halfway to Shenzhen, is the city of Dongguan, home to a cluster of contemporary university buildings as well as the world's largest, almost empty shopping mall (see Shenzhen map, p. 337).

Sources and Recommended Reading

Michael TSIN, "Canton Remapped," in Joseph W. ESHERICK, ed., *Remaking the Chinese City: Modernity and National Identity, 1900–1950*, Honolulu: University of Hawaii Press, 2000. Guangzhou's "modernisation" moment.

Tess JOHNSTON, *The Last Colonies: Western Architecture in China's Southern Treaty Ports*, Hong Kong: Old China Hand Press, 1997. Large-format treatment of colonial structures, with fine photographs.

Photo courtesy SOM | © Tim Griffith

Pearl River Tower

SOM, 2005–2008

GZ 01

珠江城大厦
天河区珠江西路金穗路
West Zhujiang Road & Jinsui Road, Tianhe
❖ 23.1271, 113.3178

Gordon GILL and Adrian SMITH of SOM produced this 71-storey tower for the China General Tobacco Company, which ironically was interested in a green, clean-air agenda (perhaps due to the new city centre's LEED requirements). Like other recent SOM projects (see p. 129, p. 307), this one tests the possibility that sustainable design might prompt tomorrow's forms, just as structural performance and industrial logistics shaped Modern architecture in the firm's first heyday. The building turns away from the north-south axis of the esplanade, favouring a southern orientation that minimises glare and catches the dominant breezes. The profile curves in towards the two mechanical levels, which contain wind turbines and generators. Thus, the entire surface of the tower acts as an aerodynamic intake funnel, increasing the turbines' output; studies anticipated outputs over eight times the output of turbines in an open field. Welcoming the wind through the building also meant that lateral, wind-resisting structural elements could be reduced. The goal was an energy-neutral building; that didn't happen, but the tower does perform 58 per cent better than required. The client liked the form's resemblance to the famed gesturing index finger of China's then-President HU Jintao, a reminder that today's green towers seek formal identity and memorable images in addition to quantifiable performance.

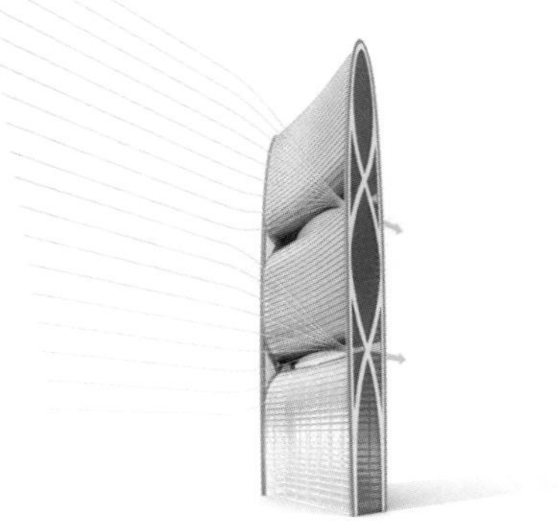

Diagram of air-flow pattern

© Adrian Smith + Gordon Gill Architecture |

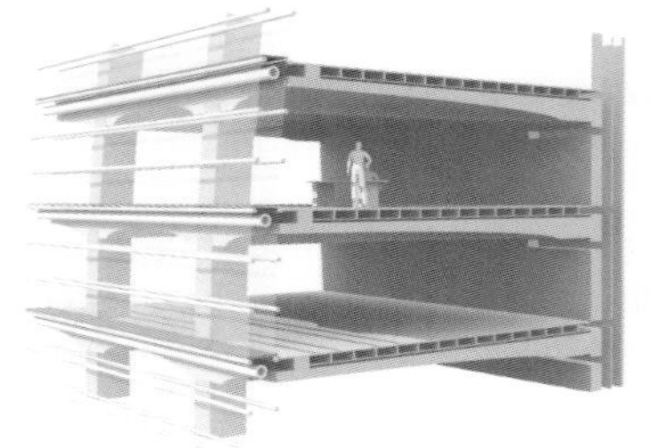

Cutaway highlighting solar panels in skin

© Adrian Smith + Gordon Gill Architecture |

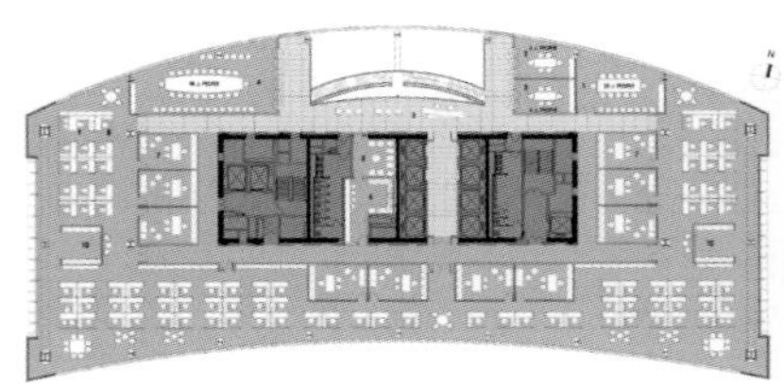

Typical floor plan

Courtesy SOM

View of turbine

Photo courtesy SOM | © Tim Griffith

Zhujiang New Town

GZ 03

珠江新城
❖23.1191, 113.3197

An archetypal 1990s–2000s new town centre: north-south axis, with a "head" of high-profile cultural buildings at the riverbank, and a skyscraper-scale central business district to the north. Compare to **Futian** (p. 320). By 2008, the government had decided that something wasn't working, especially for pedestrians arriving from the train station to the north (four kilometres from the river-front). For the link to the train station and the 2010 Asian Games site, a new "North Axis" master plan by Heller Manus Architects stresses walking, biking and transit. Plantings, water features and grade-level crossings replace vast "plazas" and China's ubiquitous pedestrian over-passes.

Guangzhou New Library

Nikken Sekkei Ltd., Guangzhou Design Institute, 2006–2011

GZ 08

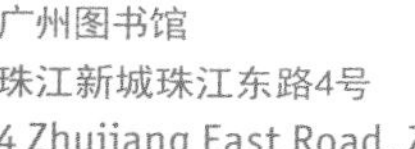

广州图书馆
珠江新城珠江东路4号
4 Zhujiang East Road, Zhujiang New Town
❖ 23.1190, 113.3206

This open-shelved library is organised by two curved bars, which frame an atrium criss-crossed by bridges. The stone façade panels are irregularly coursed to create rusticated, perforated screens, filtering daylight to the interior. This textured surface offsets the slick glass walls of the atrium, and the pattern suggests a teetering pile of stacked books. As with the **Opera House** (p. 300), we detect an effort to make the building work as an urban route as much as a monumental object.

Guangzhou Opera House

GZ 09

Zaha HADID Architects,
2003–2010

广州大剧院 / 广州歌剧院
天河区珠江西路1号
1 W. Zhujiang Rd., Tianhe
❖ 23.1178, 113.3165

At the time of the competition, Guangzhou did not have its own opera company, and was hoping to attract touring groups. The productive design forces are a tension between "fluidity and seamlessness" on the one hand, and the hard separation of the 1,800-seat opera hall and the 400-seat black box theatre into two volumes. These "boulders" (sometimes "pebbles") are explained in terms of erosion in river valleys, though the Pearl River (adjacent, sluggish and murky) might have also come into it. The folds in the "boulders" define the different spaces, separated by deep cuts which admit light and encourage north-south through-traffic. This pedestrian canyon is underused, but one of the most charming moments here; it hints at the smooth transition between figure/building and ground/landscape that drives much of Hadid's digital-era work. The two volumes, and the circulation spaces, are rendered in subdued whites and greys. This sets up the surprise of the rich-gold and red auditorium, which suggests both traditional Chinese pomp and the Baroque glitz of the European opera, and tonally matches the required medium-grey. As with many big new performance venues, the interior includes a lot of unprogrammed interstitial space, which resists falling into a clearly orchestrated promenade. Still, the exciting section and vivid play of shadows through the diamond structural grid keep things interesting. As with Hadid's MAXXI museum in Rome, and perhaps more appropriately in a theatre, these spaces detach the viewer from exterior reality and lead into the fantasy of operatic performance. The refusal to clearly choreograph this transition as a journey may be quite intentional; one of the building's strongest features is Hadid's apparent refusal to produce a fully-fledged monumental "icon" building. Approached from the **Guangdong Museum** (p. 302, a frontal, heroically cantilevered volume clearly addressing the plaza axis), the opera slouches back and tucks itself behind the trees; just when you think you've arrived, you're passing through the "canyon" and arriving at the side of the children's museum. The finished building has drawn some criticism; for reasons unknown (but probably related to a 2009 fire during construction), there are issues with construction and detailing. Surfaces are lumpy where they should be smooth, views are interrupted by sprinkler heads, and the curved, triangular tiles of the exterior surface don't tessellate correctly (and are weathering poorly besides). The technical expertise of Chinese contractors is rapidly advancing; compare the work here to that at Hadid's later **Galaxy SOHO** (p. 081) for proof. When the details do pan out, the forms are striking and attractive, taking full advantage of the strong tropical light. Step back, imagine this with the super-fluid concrete surface it clearly wants, and savour the theatrics.

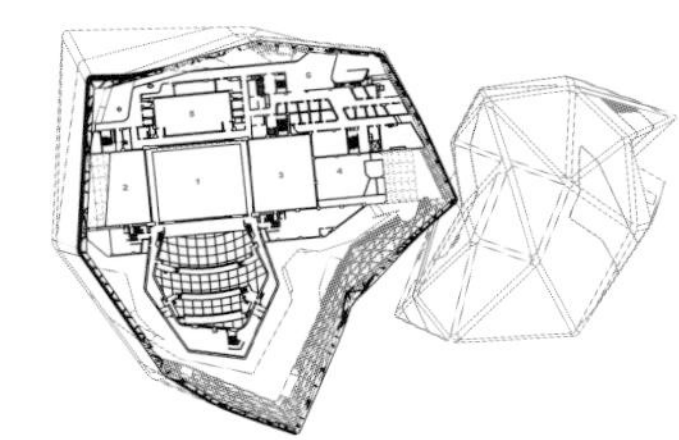

Upper-level plan

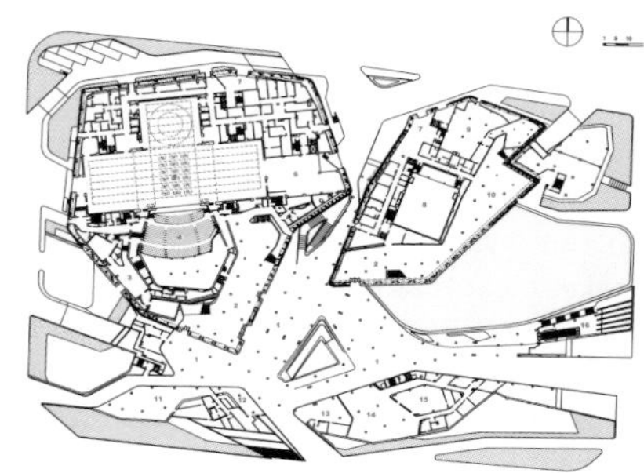

Ground-floor plan

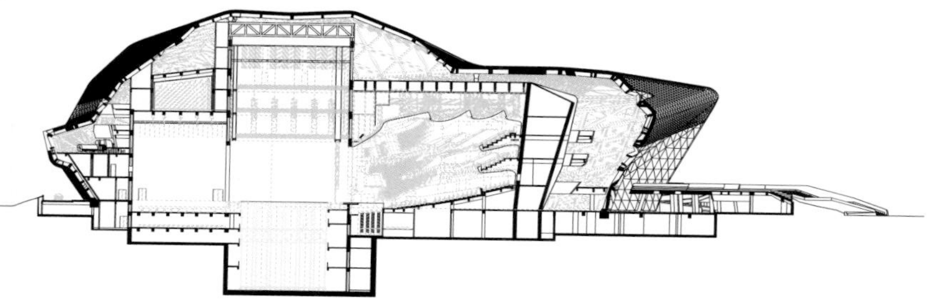

Section through main hall

Guangdong Museum

Rocco Design Architects Limited, 2004–2010

广东省博物馆
天河区珠江东路2号
2 Zhujiang East Rd., Tianhe
❖ 23.1171, 113.3213

Seeking an "identifiable cultural icon," Rocco Yim makes reference to two traditional Chinese crafts, both characterised by intricate carving: the ivory puzzle ball and the ceremonial box of jade, wood, or lacquer. Scaled up to a 646,000-ft^2 museum, these inform a series of layered walls of varying transparency, and a thick, deeply-cut façade that reveals only glimpses of the treasures inside. The surface cuts do not always correspond to sectional change on the inside; this adds to the mystery, but more importantly it makes clear that the role of the "wrapper" here is to unify the museum, which collects everything from contemporary art to dinosaur bones, into a coherent institution. The layering is strongest in the central atrium (a scaled-up residential courtyard, perhaps), where natural light scatters across hanging curtains of folded, perforated metal. At a distance, these are effectively opaque, but as you move through the space, they give gauzy impressions of the walkways and staircases beyond. Moving around and between these planes is thus a pleasant palate cleanser and optical exercise, leaving one refreshed for the next exhibit. Outside, the cantilever helps shade the ticket line.

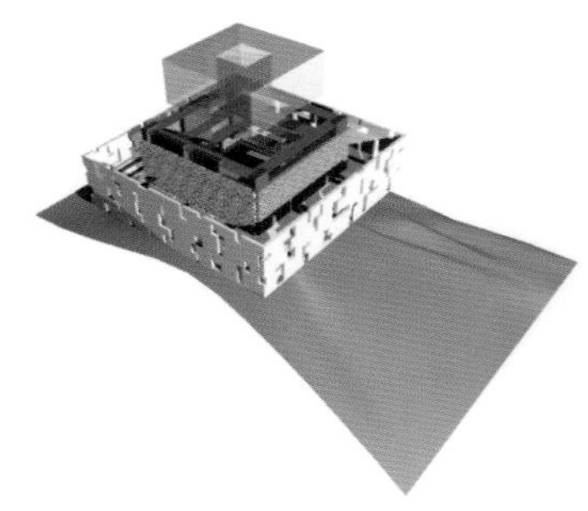

Diagram of nested spatial layers

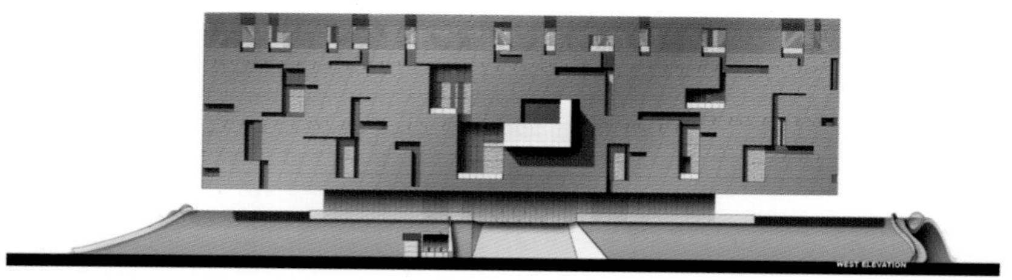

West elevation

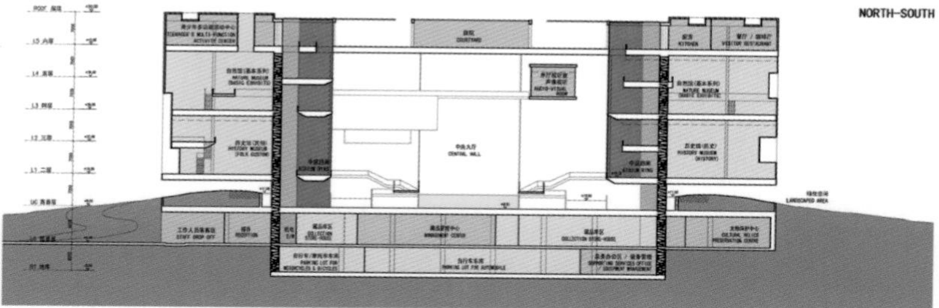

Cross section

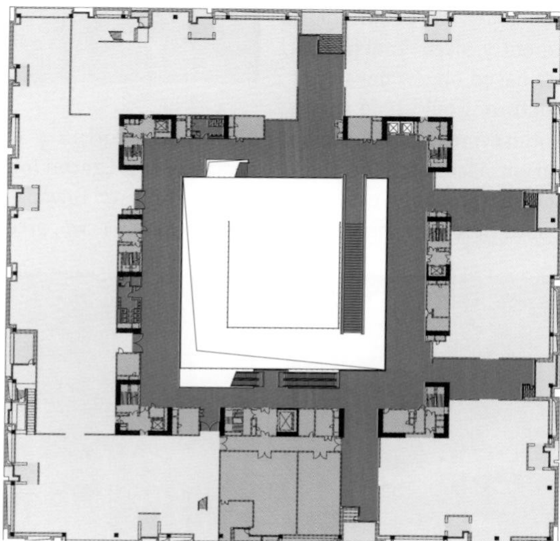

Third-floor plan

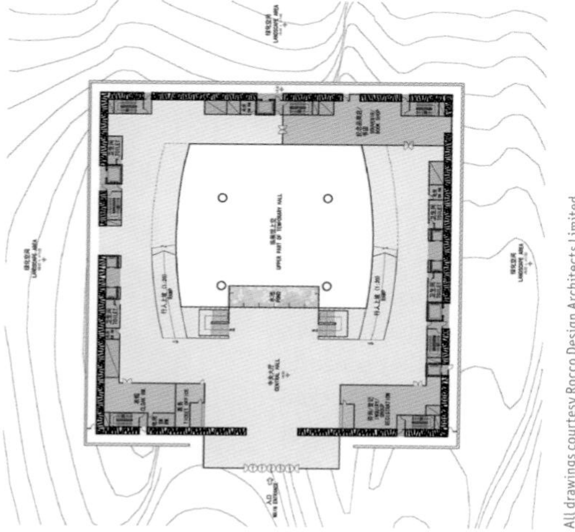

Ground-floor plan

All drawings courtesy Rocco Design Architects Limited

Canton Tower

Information Based Architecture (Mark HEMEL & Barbara KUIT)/ Arup, 2004–2011

广州塔
海珠区阅江西路222号
222 W. Yuejiang Rd., Haizhu
❖ 23.1089, 113.3191

Given a vague brief, calling for an iconic tower but almost no specific programme, IBA proposed a "system" of form-making rules concerning a hyperboloid, "twisted rope" form. Two ellipses (top and bottom) of different size and rotation are reconciled by a ruled surface of straight lines. The resulting variety in floor plate sizes could then address the needs of the programme as the client worked things out in more detail, and bumped the height up by 46 metres. Differently sized floors, with varying openness based on the density of the exterior structure, would lend themselves to different uses: restaurant, movie theatre, observation deck, etc. The thick secondary structure (probably essential for wind loads) does block the view a bit, but it's still worth the trip upstairs, even on a hazy day. Canton Tower was briefly the world's tallest "tower" (not "building"); it's now number two, after Tokyo's SkyTree.

Temple of the Six Banyans

537+ CE, 1097, 1373, 1900, etc.

六榕寺
越秀区六榕路87号
87 Liurong Rd., Yuexiu
❖ 23.1309, 113.2551

There are some banyans, but they're the poetic inspiration for the name rather than the main attraction. Indeed, what's most interesting is the way that a nearly garden-like sacred complex can be tucked into a dense urban context. The central pagoda – called Flower Pagoda as it is said to resemble a stamen – is a local landmark. Restored in 1900 to a 1300s design, the pagoda is not open to visitors.

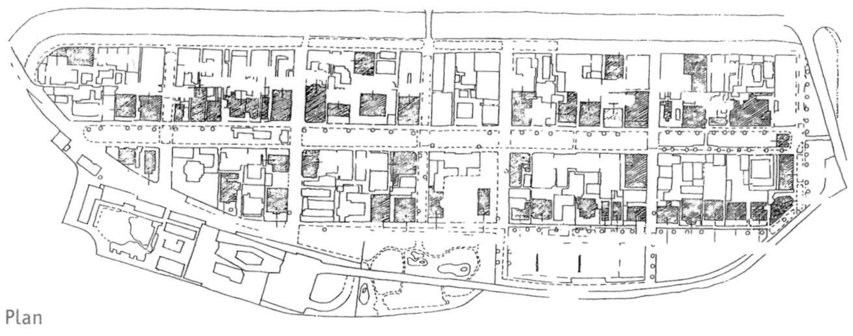

Plan

Shamian Island

GZ 18

沙面岛
Shamian Street, Liwan
❖ 23.1104, 113.2377

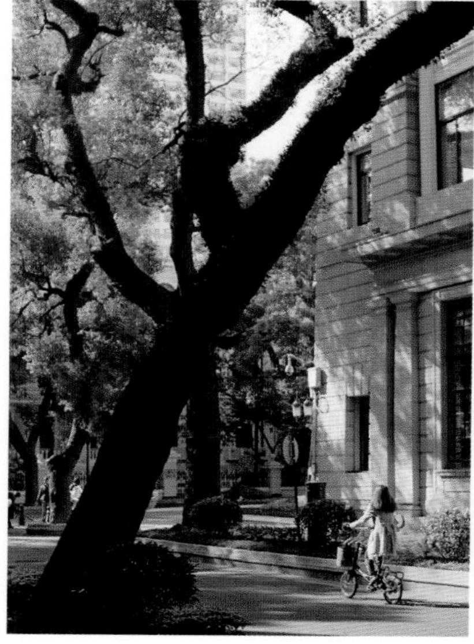

This former sandbar was formally made the foreign (British and French) Concession in 1859. It was conveniently close to the "Thirteen Factories" area, and after being enclosed and expanded by a perimeter embankment, it became a centre for banks, offices, and posh residences – an enclave of European spaces for European money and people. A stretch of green lies behind the **Bund**-like frontage (see Shanghai, p. 144) that faces the southern river embankment. The wide Central Avenue is a parallel series of small parks which bisect the island; the north-south streets are narrower, but no less leafy. After the Communist victory in 1949, Shamian's buildings were nationalised and turned into apartments. Despite later additions, the island still largely retains its colonial character, and has ironically become a desirable address for the Chinese well-to-do, reflecting a larger cultural equation of "European" with sophistication. Today, the twin barriers of murky moat and elevated road enhance the sense of separation and exclusivity. Most interesting are the collisions of colonial street-scape with Chinese open-space customs. Exercise machines, badminton enthusiasts and engagement photographers dominate.

Qingping Market Area

GZ 19

1979+ (new market buildings)

清平市场，清平路

❖ 23.1125, 113.2394

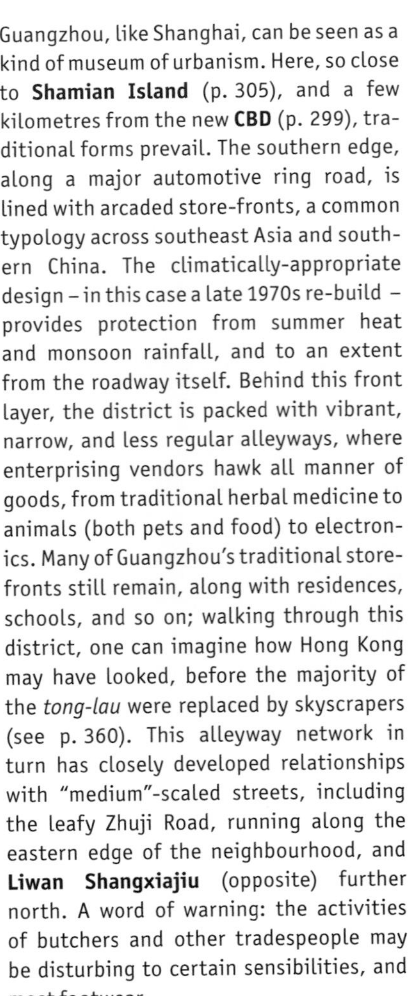

Guangzhou, like Shanghai, can be seen as a kind of museum of urbanism. Here, so close to **Shamian Island** (p. 305), and a few kilometres from the new **CBD** (p. 299), traditional forms prevail. The southern edge, along a major automotive ring road, is lined with arcaded store-fronts, a common typology across southeast Asia and southern China. The climatically-appropriate design – in this case a late 1970s re-build – provides protection from summer heat and monsoon rainfall, and to an extent from the roadway itself. Behind this front layer, the district is packed with vibrant, narrow, and less regular alleyways, where enterprising vendors hawk all manner of goods, from traditional herbal medicine to animals (both pets and food) to electronics. Many of Guangzhou's traditional storefronts still remain, along with residences, schools, and so on; walking through this district, one can imagine how Hong Kong may have looked, before the majority of the *tong-lau* were replaced by skyscrapers (see p. 360). This alleyway network in turn has closely developed relationships with "medium"-scaled streets, including the leafy Zhuji Road, running along the eastern edge of the neighbourhood, and **Liwan Shangxiajiu** (opposite) further north. A word of warning: the activities of butchers and other tradespeople may be disturbing to certain sensibilities, and most footwear.

Exterior edge

Liwan Shangxiajiu Pedestrian Street

GZ 20

荔湾上下九步行街
Shangxiajiu Pedestrian Street, Liwan
❖ 23.1163, 113.2405

This commercial strip, running along the northern edge of **Qingping** (opposite) lacks that area's complexity of scales and spaces, but the two urban spaces support each other. To the east, Shangxiajiu widens into a comfortably scaled shopping plaza – an effective cap over a through-road. To the west, where it becomes En'ning Lu, are some interesting, Asian Games-era, mid-block interventions by Atelier cnS (map p. 310), though these may now be gone.

Sacred Heart Cathedral

GZ 21

Léon VAUTRIN, 1861

广州市石室天主堂
越秀区玉子巷和元锡巷
Yuzi Lane & Yuanxi Lane, Yuexiu
❖ 23.1173, 113.2548

A remnant of Guangzhou's foreign concession days, this Neo-Gothic edifice wouldn't be out of place – or particularly notable – in Europe. Here, it is interesting mostly for the way it frames urban space and anchors a public square lined with storefronts (and former clerical housing), a reminder that European activity and architecture extended beyond the official concession boundaries on Shamian Island.

Poly International Plaza

GZ 23

SOM, SWA Group (garden), 2007

保利国际广场
海珠区阅江路688号
688 Middle Yuejiang Rd., Haizhu
❖ 23.1043, 113.3661

One of SOM's signature projects for the China Poly Group (an import/export conglomerate – see this building's Beijing counterpart, p. 089), this one is a pair of office slabs, offset for views and ventilation. In each of the high-rise slabs, the major structural elements are moved to the outside, becoming a triangular lattice. This thickening of the southern façades (the north faces are all glass) creates a deep edge zone, providing sun-shading and a loggia-like, transitional ante-lobby. The slabs are joined at the base by a plinth of exposition space and an "abstracted Chinese garden" which also refers to traditional rice paddies and thematises the slow unfolding of a "water/garden journey." In keeping with the project's green ambitions, the watercourse is also expected to manage breezes and runoff.

Photo courtesy SOM | © Tim Griffith

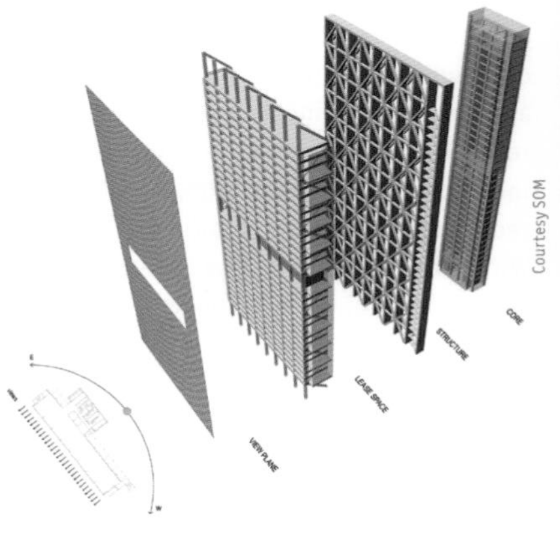

Courtesy SOM

Diagram of spatial and structural layers. From left: "View plane," "lease space," "structure," and "core."

Tulou Collective Housing

GZ 32

Urbanus, 2005–2008

万汇楼
佛山市南海区浔峰洲路（万科四季花城）
Xunfengzhou Rd., Nanhai District, Foshan
❖ 23.1502, 113.1812

Major real estate developer Vanke became interested in a vernacular housing typology: the walled *tulou* roundhouse villages of the Hakka people, built principally in the last few centuries in hillier parts of southern China. (Travellers with extra days at hand should explore these; see p. 386.) Vanke hoped the *tulou* would resonate with migrant workers arriving from rural areas, and counter the exclusivity and isolation of a gated community. To the architects, "*tulou* units are laid out along the perimeter like in modern dormitory buildings, but with greater opportunities for social interaction." This demonstration model (itself behind a gate, so write ahead for an appointment) mixes income levels by offering varied units (studios, dormitories, apartments) and incorporates a library and retail space. The brick- and wood-screen façades fit the muggy climate, hopefully reducing the need for air conditioning. With rents held slightly below market rates, the project was successful enough that Vanke is considering more.

Axonometric rendering

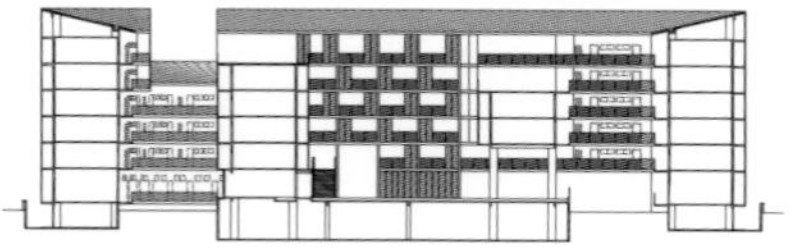

Section

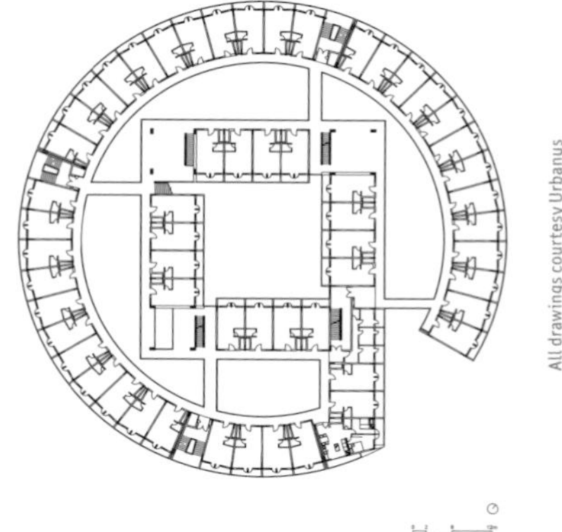

Fourth-floor plan

All drawings courtesy Urbanus

Guangzhou Gymnasium

GZ 34

Paul ANDREU, with ADPi, BIAD, 1998–2001

广州体育馆
白云区白云大道南783号
783 Baiyun South Avenue, Baiyun
❖ 23.1837, 113.2716

These three sports halls, of increasing size, elaborate on Andreu's earlier project for Charles de Gaulle Airport's Terminal 2, and step towards his **National Theatre** (p. 077). Each hall has an elongated shell roof of translucent panels, culminating in a structural spine containing the mechanical systems. Differing roof heights are meant to suggest a hierarchical ranking of the halls, and a "crescendo" evoking the nearby Baiyun hills. The roof panels were intended to admit a diffuse, calmingly "milky" light, setting a less vicious tone for competitive sports. The undulating garden-side porch is calmer still.

Kaiping Diaolou

GZ 39

Late nineteenth/ early twentieth century

广东开平碉楼旅游
❖ 22.3754, 112.5752 (Zili Village)

Zili Village

Chikan Village

Kaiping is 120 km southwest of Guangzhou (and similarly distant from Macau); it is a good base for visiting several clusters of *diaolou*. These protective "tower houses" were built principally in the chaotic early years of the twentieth century (mostly between 1900 and 1931), some by Chinese labourers returning from the U.S. It's believed that this is a source of the vaguely Western details, but the proximity to European outposts in Macau and Guangzhou shouldn't be overlooked. The concrete-framed towers projected new wealth, and the capacity to defend it against highwaymen. While they may be easier to conquer than more established typologies like the *tulou* (opposite), they also act as watchtowers, useful in a flat but tree-filled delta landscape. The height also yields welcome ventilation. In Majianglong (马降龙村, 22.2895, 112.5646) the towers punctuate a densely gridded village; in Zili (自力村) they are scattered, free-standing landmarks, and some are open to the public. They all face south, with east and west sides closed; this suggests their agglomeration in a row, as can be seen in the stoa-like form of Chikan (赤坎镇, 22.3233, 112.5815). This typology is common in the region (see **Qingping**, p. 306), so perhaps the *diaolou* are best seen as orphaned members of a series.

01 **Pearl River Tower** *SOM, 2005–2008.* ❖ 23.1271, 113.3178

02 **W Hotel** *Rocco Design Architects, Ltd. 2006–2013.* ❖ 23.1248, 113.3232

03 **Zhujiang New Town** ❖ 23.1191, 113.3197

04 **IFC Guangzhou** *Wilkinson Eyre, 2010.* Supertall tower, with appealing atrium. ❖ 23.1209, 113.3183

05 **CTF Guangzhou** *KPF, 2012+.* Supertall tower, with white terracotta verticals. ❖ 23.1204, 113.3210

06 **US Consulate** *SOM, 2013.* Dents enlarge security-limited openings, as in their Bronx call centre. ❖ 23.1193, 113.3148

07 **Guangzhou #2 Children's Palace** *Steffan BRADLEY.* ❖ 23.1192, 113.3185

08 **Guangzhou New Library** *Nikken Sekkei Ltd., Guangzhou Design Institute, 2006–2011.* ❖ 23.1190, 113.3206

09 **Guangzhou Opera House** *Zaha HADID Architects, 2003–2010.* ❖ 23.1178, 113.3165

10 **Guangdong Museum** *Rocco Design Architects Limited, 2004–2010.* ❖ 23.1171, 113.3213

11 **Canton Tower** *Information Based Architecture (Mark HEMEL & Barbara KUIT)/Arup, 2004–2011.* ❖ 23.1089, 113.3191

12 **TiT Creative Park** *Atelier cnS, 2012.* Old factory grounds, enlivened with pavilions and street furniture. ❖ 23.1024, 113.3202

13 **People's Park** *YANG Xizong, 1921.* Western-style park on the site of a former Qing dynasty administrative complex. ❖ 23.1293, 113.2589

14 **Temple of the Six Banyans** *537+, 1097, 1373, 1900, etc.* ❖ 23.1309, 113.2551

15 **Chen Clan Academy** *1888–1894.* Imperial academy, now folk art museum. ❖ 23.1297, 113.2402

16 **Liwan Lake (Lychee Wan)** Royal resort, now lake-park and scenic canal frontage. ❖ 23.1222, 113.2286

17 **En'ning Lu** *Atelier cnS, 2010.* Mid-block interventions; may be gone now. ❖ 23.1165, 113.2360

18 **Shamian Island** ❖ 23.1104, 113.2377

19 **Qingping Market Area** *1979+ (new market buildings).* ❖ 23.1125, 113.2394

GZ Guangzhou

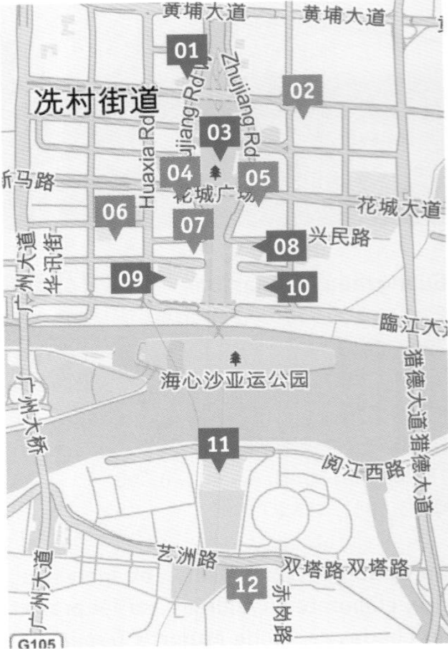

Zhujiang New Town CBD (Map 01–12)

20 **Liwan Shangxiajiu Pedestrian Street** ❖ 23.1163, 113.2405

21 **Sacred Heart Cathedral** *Léon VAUTRIN, 1861.* ❖ 23.1173, 113.2548

22 **Pearl River Promenade** ❖ 23.1087, 113.2265

23 **Poly International Plaza** *SOM, SWA Group (garden), 2007.* ❖ 23.1043, 113.3661

24 **International Conference and Exhibition Centre** *ASX Japan, South China Univ.* ❖ 23.1044, 113.3563

25 **Nanfung Mixed-Use/Hospital** *Aedas.* Strikingly shifted bars. ❖ 23.1001, 113.3534

26 **Beer Factory Landscape** *Atelier cnS 2010.* A parametrically crinkled surface forms pavilions for the 2010 Asian Games. ❖ 23.1096, 113.3360

27 **Xiaozhou Village** Scenic canal town, plus art students. ❖ 23.0620, 113.3536

28 **Shaded Mountain Cottage Garden (Yu Yinshan Fang)** *1866.* Good for a dose of garden. ❖ 23.0144, 113.3896

29 **Guangzhou South Railway Station** *TFP Farrells (Terry FARRELL), 2010.* ❖ 22.9928, 113.2654

30 **Guangzhou "Circle"** *Joseph di PASQUALE, 2013.* Round. ❖ 23.0532, 113.2537

31 **Former Sun-Yat-Sen Medical University** Colonial and Modernist campus buildings. ❖ 23.1030, 113.2939

32 **Tulou Collective Housing** *Urbanus, 2005–2008.* ❖ 23.1502, 113.1812

Guangzhou City Centre (Map 13–22)

33 **Nanyue Museum** *South China Univ. Team (HE Jingtang), 1988–1993.* Postmodern take on funerary architecture. ❖ 23.1403, 113.2557

34 **Guangzhou Gymnasium** *Paul ANDREU, with ADPi, BIAD, 1998–2001.* ❖ 23.1837, 113.2716

35 **Baiyun International Convention Centre** *BURO II, CITIC, 2007.* ❖ 23.1915, 113.2735

36 **Time's Rose Garden** *Jiakun Architects (LIU Jiakun), 2005–2006.* Public paths over private turf. ❖ 23.2256, 113.2808

37 **Guangdong Olympic Stadium** *Ellerbe Becket, 2001.* ❖ 23.1406, 113.4026

38 **Science Town Retail (Donghuicheng)** *SPARK.* Mixed-use. ❖ 23.1613, 113.4984

39 **Kaiping Diaolou Tower Houses (Zili Village)** 150 km SW of Guangzhou. ❖ 22.3754, 112.5752

Guangzhou Metropolitan Area (Map 23–39)

深圳
Shenzhen

深圳
Shenzhen

Located on a bay at the mouth of the Pearl River, and directly on the Hong Kong border, the once-obscure community of Shenzhen became famous in the last years of the twentieth century as one of the most rapidly urbanised sites in the history of the world. Almost none of its present-day fabric is older than the 1980s. All of it has been touched by the thirty-year transformation from a dispersed collection of over a thousand small villages, with an urbanised population of 30,000, into a metropolis of approximately 15 million (with 3.5 million in the urban core).

While Shenzhen is the prototypical Chinese "instant city," its rapid change belies a much longer, if quieter, history. Since ancient times, the area of Shenzhen had been a significant salt-producing zone, and in Ming times, Xin'an City (in the western part of present-day Shenzhen) rose to strategic importance as both a trade stop and naval defence point en route to Guangzhou. After an imperially mandated evacuation in 1661, Guangzhou became the only port open to foreign trade, and Shenzhen was left as something of a backwater. It remained so through the nineteenth and most of the twentieth centuries; as of the late 1970s, it was, by most accounts, a hilly collection of fishing and farming villages, with scarcely more activity in the area of the effectively closed Hong Kong border. At that moment, great changes were brewing in China. Following over a decade of violent political and economic convulsions wrought by the Cultural Revolution, and the death in 1976 of MAO Zedong, the country had a new *de facto* leader. This was DENG Xiaoping (1904–1997), an old member of the Mao circle who had suffered exile and worse for his periodic attempts to introduce measures of private ownership and capitalisation into China's communist economy. With his eyes on the success of the "Asian Tiger" economies, Deng now terminated the political chaos with a set of show trials, and called for an end to the dogmatic pursuit of party doctrine. While he resisted any move towards political freedom and democracy, and played a key role in the suppression of the 1989 Tian'anmen Square protests, his main project was the implementation of a "socialist market economy," or "socialism with Chinese characteristics." The stated theory was that China's former capitalist economy had never been advanced enough to allow it to transition successfully into Communism. Emphasising that "socialism does not mean shared poverty," he invited the local party leadership to conduct experiments, which could then be implemented on a wider scale. Meanwhile, he visited Japan and the U.S. and actively courted foreign capitalist investment in China for the first time since 1949. The centrepiece of all the reforms was the establishment of *Special Economic Zones*

Previous spread: **Citizen Square** (p. 320), from the terrace of the **Cultural Centre** (p. 321)

Billboard celebrating Deng Xiaoping

(SEZs): areas where (regulated) private business and foreign investment were permitted. The credit supply was loosened to favour light, export-friendly industry, and individual development of real estate for profit was made possible by permitting the buying and selling of long-term leases, all land still being technically owned by the state. New agricultural policies incentivised increased production by allowing farmers to keep their own crops after turning over a share to the state.

With this, our story returns to sleepy Shenzhen, cannily selected as the first SEZ in 1980. To one side was prosperous British Hong Kong; on the other was the Pearl River Delta, with millions of agricultural workers whose labour was now surplus due to the agricultural reforms, and who were thus free to pursue new kinds of work in urban industrial centres. The ingredients were in place, but the resulting growth was still almost incomprehensible. With foreign investment, factories opened, attracting the job-seeking migrants. Local small-holders capitalised on the new demand for housing, renting out rooms to the factory workers. Soon they had enough cash saved up to knock down their houses and replace them with bigger ones, renting out more rooms. The process repeated itself as development snowballed; land prices rose, and the erstwhile farmers either sold out to outside investors, or became landlords in their own right. Former villages maintained their footprints but grew vertically, growing swiftly denser in the process. Shenzhen contains over two hundred such villages, housing possibly half its population – for characteristic examples, see **Wanxia** (p. 329) and **Dafen** (p. 329). Meanwhile, Shenzhen began a process of topographic flattening, as its hills offered convenient fill material for redeveloping the wet lowlands. Growth only accelerated as neighbouring cities were added to the SEZ programme: Zhuhai in 1980, Guangzhou in 1984, and the whole of the Pearl River Delta in 1985. Shenzhen's transformation had become the engine of similarly dramatic changes across the region, an increasingly interconnected megalopolis that today includes Hong Kong and Macau.

By the 1990s, Shenzhen was an enormous and apparently permanent construction site. Buildings were going up and coming down faster than permits could be issued, and (seemingly) faster than anyone could master-plan any of it. As Shenzhen is sandwiched between the waterfront and a chain of mountains to the north, this development has largely been along an east-west linear band, with two major centres: western Shekou (the closest point to Hong Kong by sea) and eastern Luohu (closest to Hong Kong by road). While growth was carefully anticipated in terms of economic targets and methods, its physical condition at many levels has been fundamentally the unplanned product of *laissez-faire* conditions (or as close as one gets under the Communist

OCT Loft (p. 326)

Sea World (map p. 337)

Party of China). Thinkers fascinated by the idea of environments generated by economic and social forces – neo-liberal economists, or architects such as Rem KOOLHAAS – have been unable to resist the allure of this seemingly pure growth model. To Koolhaas, speaking in 1997, Shenzhen was "completely polarised," a place of "constant acceleration," "unbelievable richness and unbelievable contrasts [and] fantastic proximity." Unlikely uses of space emerged out of "sheer programmatic pressure," foreshadowing a time when "even we will not have time for 'Architecture.'" Shenzhen's growth seduces the imagination by its sheer scale and speed. Critics, however, argue that the "new China" comes at too high a price in terms of human rights abuses, environmental destruction, and lost connections to the cultural and political past.

Meanwhile, with less international attention, Shenzhen began to respond to its growth's downsides. In 1996, a comprehensive plan stressed the established centres and a new civic district called Futian. Shenzhen was to become a network between these nodes, with growth outside of them under stricter control. For example, a 2010 competition invited plans for the coherent accommodation of 1.5 million people on 4,500 acres in Qian'hai, to the city's west. The winning entry, by James CORNER Field Operations, promised a "Manhattan" for the Pearl River Delta, and seemed informed by a gridded, European-style urbanism of low-rise perimeter blocks and green boulevards, alongside more typical, freestanding skyscrapers near the waterfront. It will be years before this project is realised, but crucially, it suggests no trace of untethered, spontaneous development.

Even today, a visitor to Shenzhen may be surprised to discover how oddly "planned" and orderly the city's neighbourhoods actually seem, at least at the level of infrastructure. The roadways look like what Los Angeles was always meant to be: breezy, extensively planted, with cars cruising at high speeds alongside separate and heavily-used bicycle and pedestrian lanes. It's hardly a "natural" streetscape sprouting up magically between pockets of mutually disinterested development, nor does it seem more chaotic and under-planned than, say, Atlanta.

While the city may be "instant," it is already over thirty years old. As the new urban middle class has begun to displace light industry from the first-generation SEZs, Shenzhen can even boast at least one post-industrial arts district (**the OCT Loft,** p. 326). As well, the municipal government, apparently recognising that a city built entirely on speculative private capitalism may end up with no public space whatsoever, has experimented with smaller-scale parks and plazas. Notable in this project is the work of the firm Urbanus, covered extensively in this chapter. Its principals are all young enough to have grown up with Shenzhen as an existing place rather than a current event; their projects seem to insist on creating meaningful urban space at small scales, and on preserving existing heritage, whether that heritage is pre- or post-1980. Perhaps the process initiated by Deng may truly be coming to fruition: capitalism has given rise to a new kind of chaos, but the response to that chaos is an attempt at reason, and a public that can exist collectively without devolving into the Maoist mob. Whether that public experience is genuinely available to all, or only to the wealthier classes in an increasingly stratified China, is another question.

If Koolhaas is right, attempts at planned urbanism in the contemporary megalopolis

Dafen Urban Village (p. 329)

are always hopeless drops in a bucket, marginalised by the quantity of developer-driven construction. But however polluted, anonymous or traffic-ridden the new Chinese metropolis may appear to foreign architects and planners, it represents something else entirely to millions of Chinese: hope, progress, the escape from rural poverty, and the creation of a mass middle class. Hundreds of millions of people have been lifted out of poverty, even as inequality has grown and millions more still live under extremely difficult conditions on farms or in the minimally regulated factories and construction sites whose low prices have fuelled the boom. We are not in a position to proclaim whether China's rise has been "worth it" for those who live there. But as designers, we cannot ignore that cities like Shenzhen are now home to tens of millions of Chinese citizens; thus, their physical conditions are among the most pressing urban-design, landscape, and architectural topics of our time.

1. Rem KOOLHAAS, "Pearl River Delta" in Cynthia Davidson, ed., *Anyhow,* Cambridge, Mass.: MIT Press, 1988, p. 183.

Practical Considerations

Two full days, at a brisk pace, is enough time to at least sample the most interesting architectural sites in Shenzhen. The metro system runs very close to many of our favoured stops, though for now, you will need a car to visit the **Vanke Centre** (p. 331), **Dongguan Institute of Technology** (map p. 337) and other suburban spots.

Sources and Recommended Reading

Jonathan BACH, "Shenzhen: City of Suspended Possibility," in *International Journal of Urban and Regional Research* (March, 2011). The "economy of desire," urban myths, and the experiences of young artists (including Urbanus).

Thomas CAMPANELLA, *The Concrete Dragon,* New York: Princeton Architectural Press, 2008. A readable survey of China's recent urbanisation, packed with information.

Juan DU, "Shenzhen: Urban Myth of a New Chinese City," in *Journal of Architectural Education* (March, 2010). A cogent handling of Shenzhen's planning and urban villages.

Ma HANG and Sandra ISEMAN, "'Villages' in Shenzhen: Typical Economic Phenomena of Rural Urbanization in China," in *Chinese Sociology and Anthropology* (Spring, 2009). A treatment of the "urban village" in economic and urban-historical terms.

Rem KOOLHAAS, "Pearl River Delta" in Cynthia Davidson, ed., *Anyhow,* Cambridge, Mass.: MIT Press, 1998. A key document of Western architecture's enthusiasm for China's "instant" cities. These ideas are considerably developed, with the aid of Koolhaas's Harvard students and collaborators, in *Great Leap Forward,* Cologne, Taschen, 2002. "Copyrighted" neologisms aside, the book contains a wealth of urban-historical information and images.

Bart LOOTSMA, "Oh nooo! Shenzhen is a model city!" in *Archis* (June, 2000). An alternate take on Shenzhen, and a response to Koolhaas.

Shenzhen Stock Exchange

SZ 02

OMA/Rem KOOLHAAS, 2006–2013

深圳证券交易所营运中心
福田区福中三路和民田路
Fuzhong 3rd Rd. & Mintian Rd., Futian
❖ 22.5442, 114.0492

The Shenzhen Stock Exchange, founded in 1990, largely conducts its transactions digitally, in offices, so it does not require a trading floor. Still, OMA use the programme as an inspiration to levitate the podium base associated with the office-tower typology. As the architects put it, "the essence of the stock market is speculation: it is based on capital, not gravity" – especially in a boom town like Shenzhen. Thus, the building riffs on both Koolhaas's "delirious" New York, and on the architecturalisation of raw economic forces in the Pearl River Delta. As both places are defined by eras of egoism and laissez-faire economics, perhaps the distinction is irrelevant. The three-storey cantilever, thirty-six metres in the air, houses assembly programme, while supporting a roof garden above and shading a plaza underneath. Dramatic gaps separate it from the main volume on two sides.

Futian Centre/Citizen Square

SZ 03

Lee/Timchula (John LEE & Michael TIMCHULA), 1999+

市民广场，福中三路
Fuzhong 3rd Road, Futian
❖ 22.5444, 114.0543

The archetypal new Chinese city centre: a "cultural square" heads a monumental linear park flanked by gridded skyscrapers. Far from the ostensibly unplanned growth of the rest of Shenzhen, this suggests grand Modernist planning (Brasilia or Chandigarh) or Chinese tradition (hills to the north, open to the south). As the trees mature, the Square is becoming a bit more inhabitable and well-used, but still the scale seems out of kilter; one misses the originally proposed variety of landscapes (by Towers|Golde), and looks forward to the redesign job won by SWA in 2013. The floating behemoth is the Citizen Centre (Municipal Architects, 1998).

Cultural Centre

ISOZAKI Arata, 1997–2007

SZ 05

深圳文化中心（图书馆和音乐厅）
福田区福中一路2001号和2016号
2001 & 2016 Fuzhong 1st Rd., Futian
❖ 22.5500, 114.0522

This complex, containing a library and two concert spaces, opens up to Futian's pedestrian centre on the east side with an undulating, polyhedral glass wall, described as a "drop curtain" for the cultural facilities. The glass volumes are supported by "tree-like" structures, their "branches" and "trunks" surfaced in gold and silver. The complex arrangement of this multi-pyramidal roof structure, and the shadows cast through it, contrast with the symmetry of the overall scheme. On the north and west sides, a forty-metre-high black granite wall runs the length of the building, screening off a throughway and a major highway. The overall configuration suggests two distinct but related volumes, acting as a "gate" to the city centre, and united by the very thin connector of the entrance plaza.

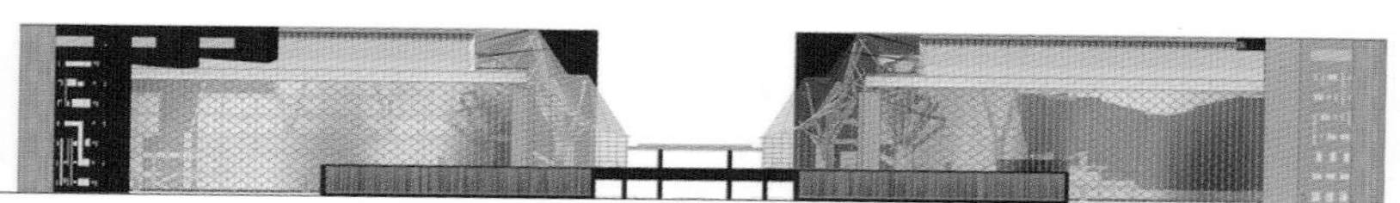

East elevation

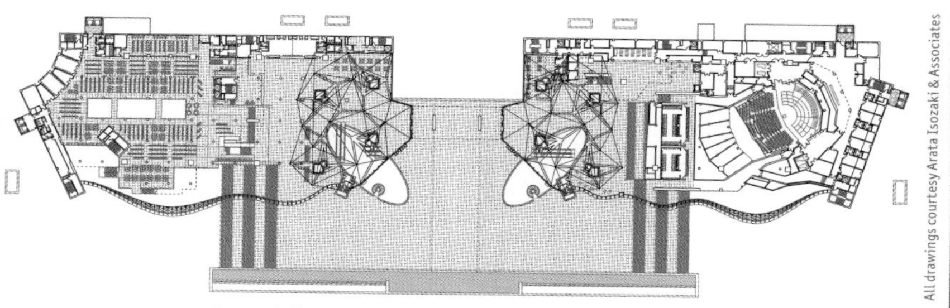

Second-floor plan

All drawings courtesy Arata Isozaki & Associates

Luohu Art Museum

Urbanus, 2000–2007

SZ 11

罗湖美术馆
罗湖区春风路和南极路
Chunfeng Rd. & Nanji Rd., Luohu
❖ 22.5458, 114.1225

The site is flat, with a less dramatic context than **Jade Bamboo** (opposite) or **Dafen Art Museum** (p. 330). But, as at the former, an underground garage is capped with public programme (art gallery, bookshop, cafe, studio), in this case broken up into one building and two minor pavilions. These join a gridded grove of trees and some water features to frame a linear plaza. The architects claim to have "remoulded, fractured, and warped" the surface to create "new urban geography"; this would be generic designer-ese elsewhere, but is potent in the context of Shenzhen, which some would say consists entirely of new urban geography. This plaza is big by the standards of local parks, but small by the standards of **Futian** (p. 320); the folded surface, the big inclined plane over the car park, the trees, the water and the little pavilions all work to make it smaller. Compare to the similar thickening of public space by Amateur Architecture at **Zhongshan Road** (p. 259). The space of Futian cannot provide the immediate local community with a sense of gathering around a unique node or landmark, something badly needed in a city whose history, for many, runs back only thirty years. Significantly, the Art Plaza is sized for a number of medium-sized collectives, not mass assemblies; Urbanus choose multiplicity over singularity. Note how the framing buildings at the perimeter lean and slump, vanishing in the foliage; they are horizontal edges, not monumental presences. Our favourite detail: the palm trees that grow up from the utilitarian parking garage, through the newly-created ground, and into the clear blue sky.

Photograph courtesy Urbanus

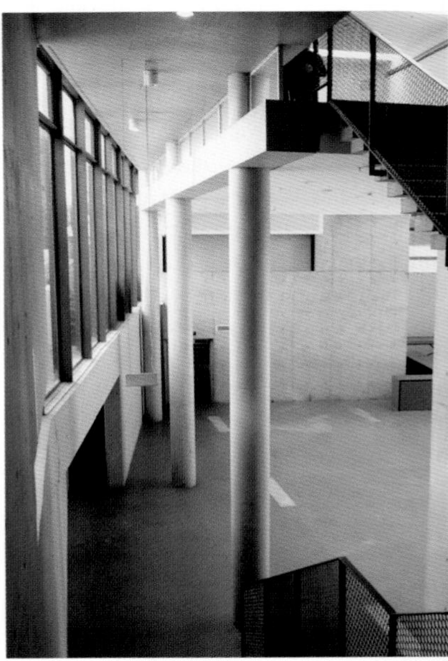

Longitudinal section

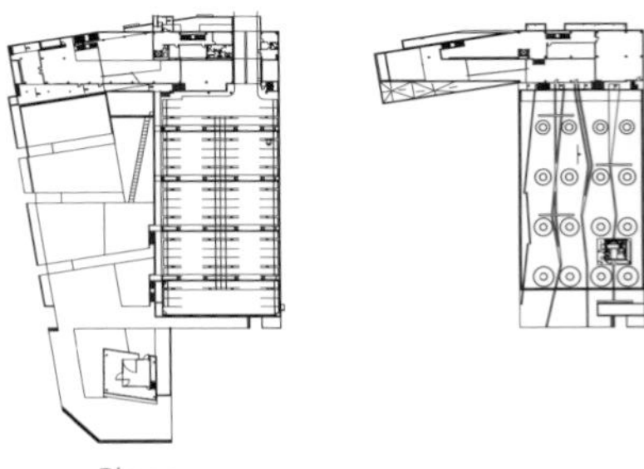

Plans

Jade Bamboo Culture Plaza

SZ 12

Urbanus, 2005–2009

翠竹公园文化广场
深圳市罗湖区太宁路
Taining Rd., Luohu District
❖ 22.5713, 114.1295

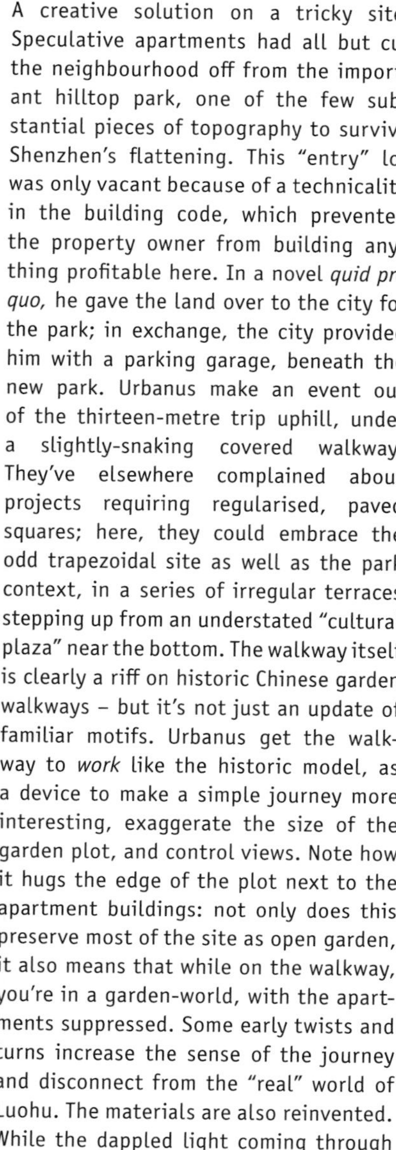

A creative solution on a tricky site. Speculative apartments had all but cut the neighbourhood off from the important hilltop park, one of the few substantial pieces of topography to survive Shenzhen's flattening. This "entry" lot was only vacant because of a technicality in the building code, which prevented the property owner from building anything profitable here. In a novel *quid pro quo,* he gave the land over to the city for the park; in exchange, the city provided him with a parking garage, beneath the new park. Urbanus make an event out of the thirteen-metre trip uphill, under a slightly-snaking covered walkway. They've elsewhere complained about projects requiring regularised, paved squares; here, they could embrace the odd trapezoidal site as well as the park context, in a series of irregular terraces stepping up from an understated "cultural plaza" near the bottom. The walkway itself is clearly a riff on historic Chinese garden walkways – but it's not just an update of familiar motifs. Urbanus get the walkway to *work* like the historic model, as a device to make a simple journey more interesting, exaggerate the size of the garden plot, and control views. Note how it hugs the edge of the plot next to the apartment buildings: not only does this preserve most of the site as open garden, it also means that while on the walkway, you're in a garden-world, with the apartments suppressed. Some early twists and turns increase the sense of the journey and disconnect from the "real" world of Luohu. The materials are also reinvented. While the dappled light coming through the wooden slats may be distantly related to the patterns of carved screen windows, few classical Chinese gardens place you on a metal grating, looking down past your feet at sun-lit plants four metres below.

Rendering, as landscape painting

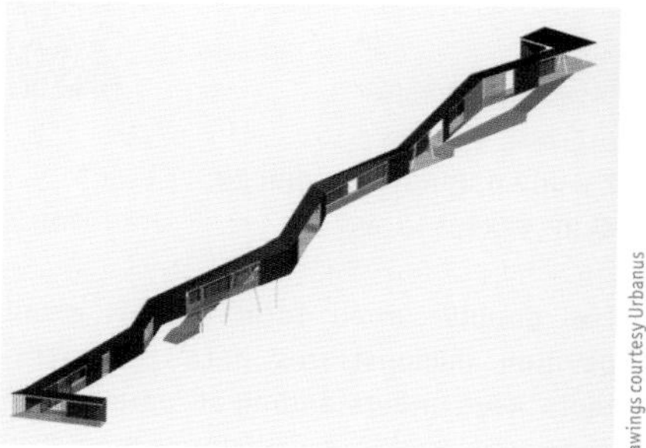

Axonometric of walkway

All drawings courtesy Urbanus

OCT Bay Clubhouse

Richard MEIER & Partners, 2008–2012

SZ 15

华侨城华会所 – 福田区白石路8号
8 Baishi Rd., Futian
❖ 22.5262, 113.9825

Located on a small island in an artificial lake, the clubhouse projects exclusivity, from the gated access road to the solidity of the entry façade. Past the entry, the building steps down towards the water, interior views enlivened and complicated by reflecting pools and polished surfaces. The white Corian (acrylic) panels yield Meier's customary monochromatic palette, though they seem to be weathering roughly here. Interestingly, while the plan geometry is a familiar assembly of prototypical forms, the vertical surfaces are slightly slanted – irregular crystals rather than Platonic volumes.

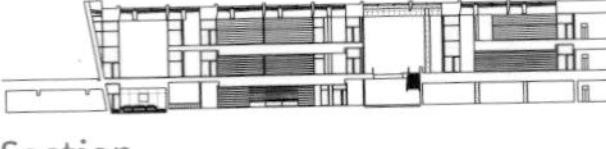

Section

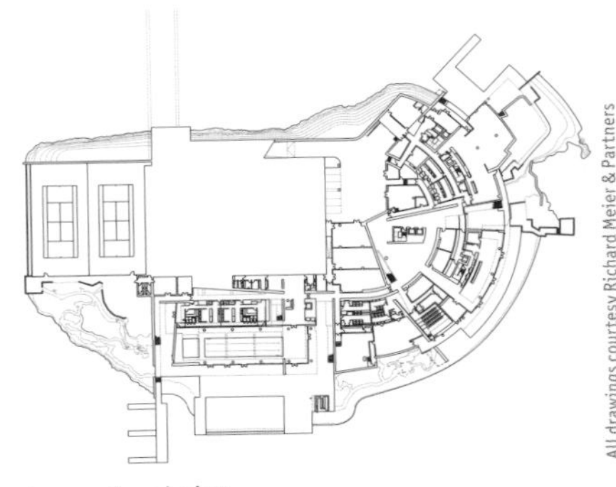

Lower-level plan

All drawings courtesy Richard Meier & Partners

Courtesy Studio Pei-Zhu

Courtesy Studio Pei-Zhu

OCT Design Museum

Studio Pei-Zhu, 2008–2010

SZ 17

华侨城设计博物馆
白石路和海园二路
Baishi Rd. & Haiyuan 2nd Rd.
❖ 22.5285, 113.9871

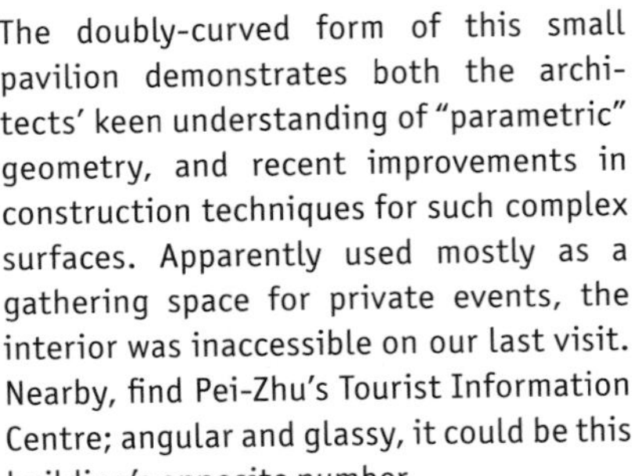

The doubly-curved form of this small pavilion demonstrates both the architects' keen understanding of "parametric" geometry, and recent improvements in construction techniques for such complex surfaces. Apparently used mostly as a gathering space for private events, the interior was inaccessible on our last visit. Nearby, find Pei-Zhu's Tourist Information Centre; angular and glassy, it could be this building's opposite number.

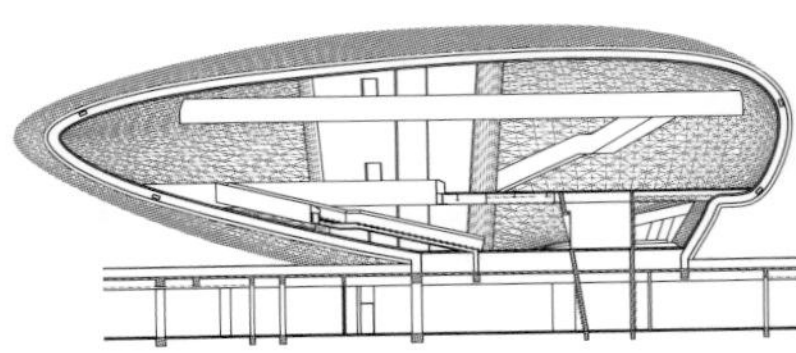

Cross section

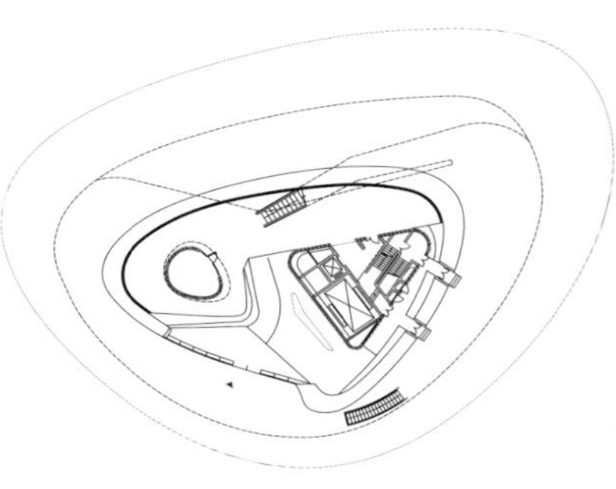

Main-level plan

OCT Art & Design Gallery (Hua Museum)

SZ 18

Urbanus, 2006–2008

华–美术馆，南山区深南大道9009号–1
9009–1 Shennan Ave., Nanshan
❖ 22.5358, 113.9780

A 1980s laundry/warehouse becomes an art gallery with the addition of a thickened wrapper of variously-scaled hexagons. Some are surface pattern, but others are extruded back into the space to form volumetric elements (e.g. seats). The challenge for the designers, then, is to make this geometry do as much as possible; stairs, for example, can't really be hexagons at this scale. At the same time, retaining some of the old building's everyday elements is both economical and another reminder that even Shenzhen has a past. It's a more sensible approach to architectural history than that offered, for example, by the adjacent theme parks.

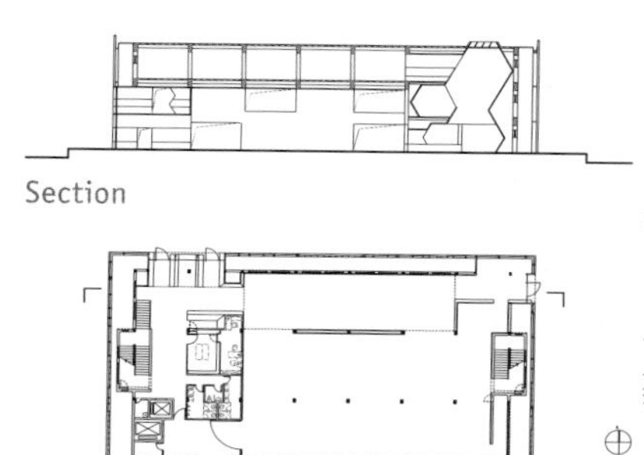

Section

Upper-floor plan

All drawings courtesy Urbanus

He Xiangning Art Museum

SZ 19

Sherman KUNG, LEE & LEE Associates, 1995–1997

何香凝美术馆
南山区深南大道9103号
9103 Shennan Ave., Nanshan
❖ 22.5359, 113.9768

Primarily devoted to HE Xiangning (1878–1972), a traditionalist painter and revolutionary activist, this mid-size museum is one of the more convincing attempts to integrate traditional Chinese planning and neo-Modern (rather than contemporary) architecture. It's not dissimilar to attempts by Kung's erstwhile associates, I. M. Pei and Richard Meier; see the **Suzhou Museum** (p. 216) or the nearby **OCT Clubhouse** (opposite). Still, the results here are particularly effective. Things which may at first appear to be formalist devices (the rotated cube, the ramp penetrating the plane) all work to orchestrate a promenade and to re-present familiar aspects of Chinese space: courtyards of house and temple, rock gardens, carefully framed views, etc. Even the "peel" of the façade is both an acknowledgement of the site's curved edge and an evocation of "the aerial perspective techniques of Chinese painting and landscaping." This could all have been a bit cheesy, but here it's done smartly, a fine precursor to the regionalist approach of followers in the 2000s.

OCT-Loft Renovation

Urbanus, 2003–2012

SZ 20

华侨城创意文化园改造
南山区恩平街
Enping Street, Nanshan
❖ 22.5403, 113.9884

A case study in post-industrial renovation, this mixed-use entertainment district was originally constructed in the 1980s as an electronics factory. Mirroring macro-economic trends in many of China's coastal cities (see introduction, p. 318), the production of televisions and refrigerators has moved elsewhere. Urbanus create a creative-class district by filling in the gaps: the old buildings, with their rusted steel, bare concrete, large wall murals, and overgrowth are preserved, supplemented by extensions and new pavilions that create a low-rise urbanism worthy of old Beijing, or Brooklyn. The result is a distinct and appealing aesthetic that seems to be working: here one finds advertising agencies, video firms, and Urbanus's own office (including a small gallery showcasing their work). In their intimacy – and shade – these projects offer an alternative to the space of **Citizen Square** (p. 320). As well, the very existence of these projects reminds us that even the "instant" city already has history – and therefore, potential for local specificity, quirks in the fabric, and layers in the urban palimpsest.

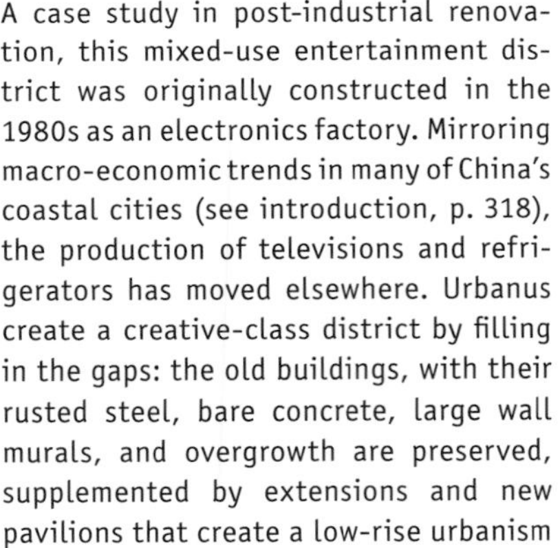

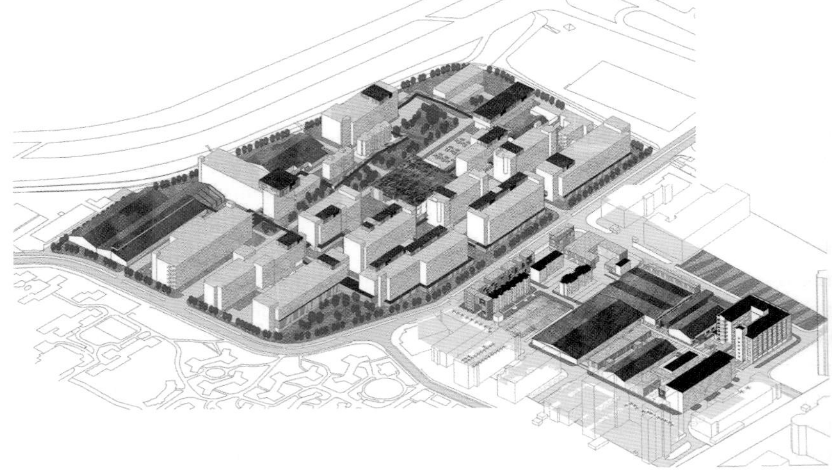

Axonometric: OCT East Factory at bottom right, OCT Loft at top left

Courtesy Urbanus

Courtesy Urbanus

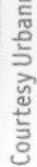

Nanshan Marriage Registration Centre

SZ 23

Urbanus, 2008–2011

南山婚姻登记中心
深圳市南山区常兴路和南头街交汇处西南角
Changxing Road & Nantou Street, Nanshan
❖ 22.5386, 113.9167

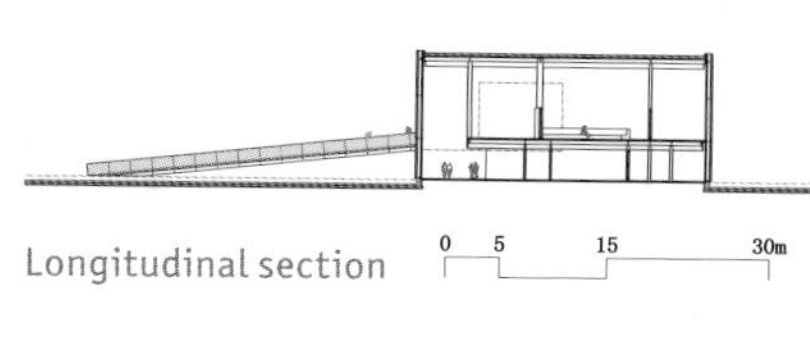

Longitudinal section

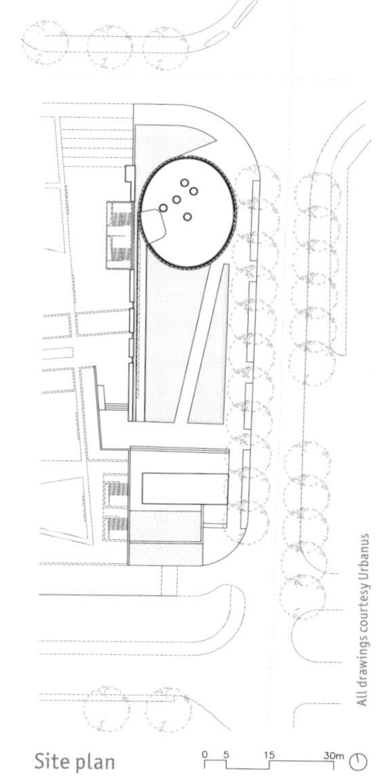

Site plan

All drawings courtesy Urbanus

While marriage celebrations can be lavish affairs, the formal act of registration with the government can be a dry, bureaucratic process. Hoping to enliven this necessary step and provide a sense of journey and ceremony, the architects designed this small office building as a circular folly, anchoring a public park; it's placed against the street edge, but closed at this point, necessitating a journey through the park and back in order to enter, perhaps representing the threshold and journey of marriage. Within, the promenade spirals around the exterior, with stops for specific events, before depositing the newly-registered couple back outside. As in the plaza at the **Luohu Art Museum** (p. 322), what could be one space is broken up into smaller ones, here for the sake of giving individuals a private, special experience. The simple design may not seem revolutionary, but when understood as a continuation of the architects' ongoing studies of public space, it does appear at least mildly subversive. In China, government buildings, and even public space, are normally characterised by tall fences, security checkpoints, and obvious surveillance systems (see **Tian'anmen Square,** p. 072). Here, the park connects directly to the street and provides seating and shade for passers-by. While the façade appears solid from some angles, the double-skin system is surprisingly porous, and dappled light comes through the "floral mesh" of aluminium to reinforce the connection between interior and exterior.

Maillen Hotel & Apartment
Urbanus, 2005–2011

SZ 32

美伦公寓+酒店
深圳南山区蛇口沿山路
Yanshan Road, Shekou, Nanshan District
❖ 22.4904, 113.9077

Courtesy Urbanus

This complex of hotel suites and serviced apartments sprawls across a hillside site. While no one would mistake this for a traditional village, the decision to limit the building height to a few storeys and distribute the programme as a long, twisted bar (single-loaded corridor throughout) pays off in the form of "captured" spaces that replicate the scale and sense of enclosure one finds in older urban configurations: "a continuous and occasionally repeating rhythm of space and form." The landscape borrows from classical garden design, with its many twisting paths, water features, framed views, and perceptual layering of spaces. As in the **Urban Tulou** (p. 308), it's clear that Urbanus are keen students of history, and determined to embrace the amenities and advantages of modernity while still respecting the past (and making use of its tools). One can imagine a greater sense of community in such a complex than in the apartment towers that make up so much of China's residential building stock.

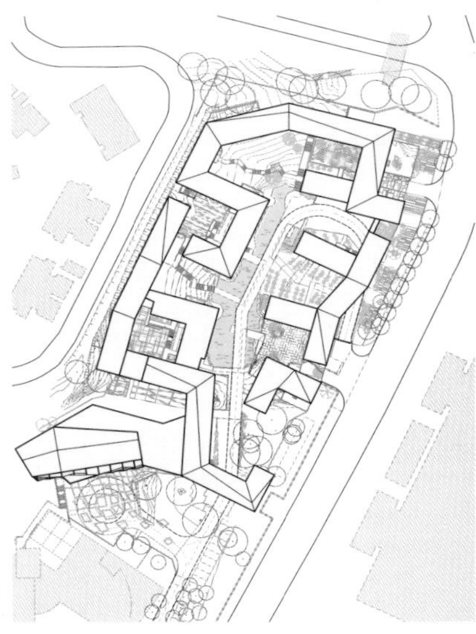

Roof plan

Section/elevation

All drawings courtesy Urbanus

Wanxia Urban Village

SZ 33

湾厦城中村，南山区湾厦路25号
25 Wanxia Rd., Nanshan
❖ 22.4946, 113.9275

One of many "fishing villages" subsumed into rapidly-expanding Shenzhen, Wanxia was originally laid out on a rough grid, typologically similar to any number of Chinese villages full of one- or two-storey courtyard homes (see **Beijing** p. 064). As the modern city grew around them, the plots remained the same size, but gradually the owners replaced their old houses: perhaps first filling in the courtyard, then replacing the whole thing with a taller building (living upstairs, renting out space below). Building higher and higher, quasi-legally, the owners re-filled

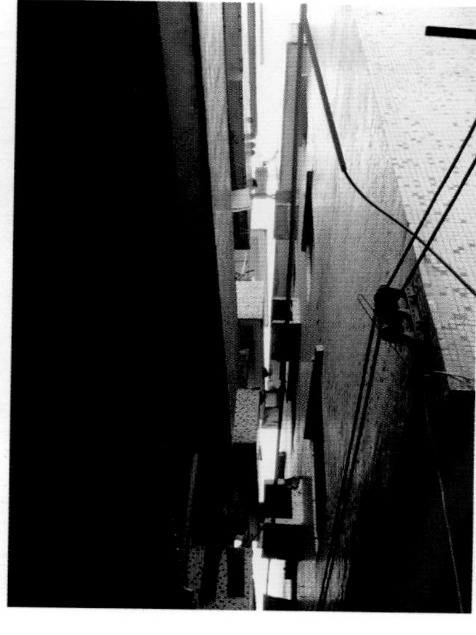

the grid with six- to ten-storey apartment buildings, sometimes with barely enough space in between to open the windows. The density makes the street life livelier than in most greenfield developments. It also belies the myth of Shenzhen springing up from nothing more than rice paddies: there were homes here, and people. Look out for the few surviving courtyard dwellings.

Dafen Oil Painting Village

SZ 34

1990s

大芬油画村内 – 深圳市龙岗区
Dafen Village, Longgang District
❖ 22.6111, 114.1312

One of Shenzhen's "urban villages" (see **Wanxia,** above), Dafen is now a tourist attraction as a result of its novel economic specialty: hand-painted replicas of famous, usually Western, paintings, for sale on the international market. While many of the buildings here date to the 1980s and earlier, Dafen's reputation as a centre for replica art began with a group of twenty or so artists who took up residence in the 1990s.

Dafen Art Museum

SZ 35

Urbanus, 2005–2007

大芬美术馆
龙岗区大芬村老围东三巷
Laowei East 3rd Alley, Dafen Village, Longgang District
❖ 22.6122, 114.1329

The city hoped to develop the sales and tourist profile of the **Dafen Art Village** (p. 329) with an art museum, despite the absence of a conventional art culture. Urbanus seek to capitalise on those urban energies which might foster a creative community. To create "a highly mixed building, a hybrid container," they connect galleries, shops, and studios with narrow pathways, which give way to larger plazas. Together, these spaces form an urban connector, passing through the building and linking the "village" to high-rise neighbourhoods uphill. On the way, the "picture frame" surface of the building makes a craggy counterpoint to the exposed bedrock, a rare glimpse of Shenzhen's often-ignored topography.

First-floor plan

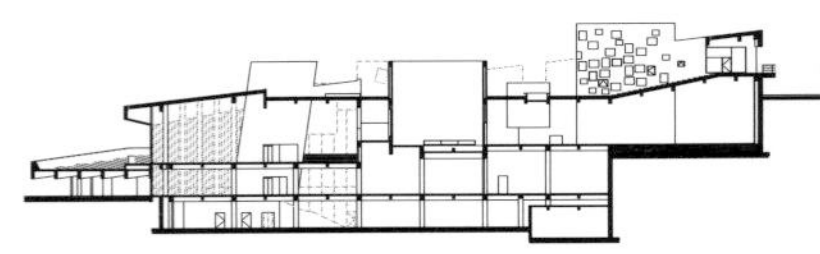

Section

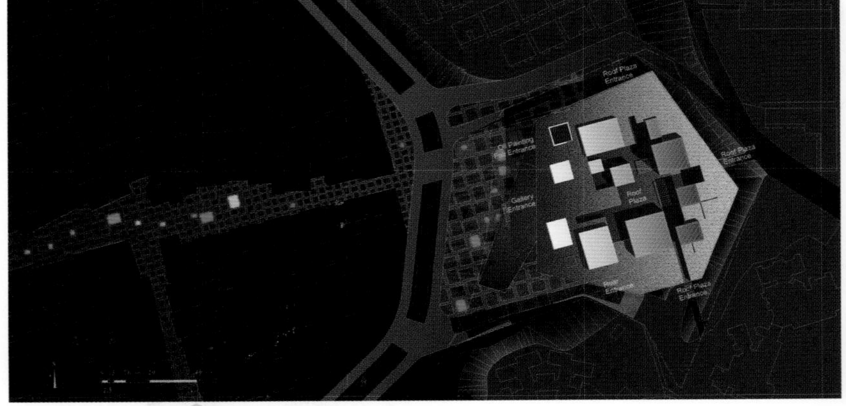

Site plan

All drawings courtesy Urbanus

Vanke Centre

Steven HOLL Architects, 2006–2009

SZ 36

万科中心（大梅沙）
盐田区环梅路68号
68 Huanmei Rd., Yantian
❖ 22.6007, 114.2999

This "horizontal skyscraper" houses the huge developer Vanke, plus a conference centre and hotel. Stepping up as much as fifty metres along its length, it becomes a floating bar that's meant to open views through to the lake and the sea beyond. A hybrid of concrete frame and cable-stayed bridge structure supports the cantilevered ends of the branching plan, while the subterranean conference centre is concealed by the free-form landscape. There are various green features (geothermal cooling, locally sourced materials, planted roof, operable shades, etc.), and a narrative: the form is like something "once floating on a higher sea; that sea has now subsided, leaving [it] propped up high on glass and white coral-like legs." As built, it's a well-detailed and pleasant complex that does a fine job breaking an enormous programme down into something manageable. It's also surprisingly spatial, framing complex and layered views of itself even before one gets inside. The landscape helps: the native-grass dunescape (a late substitution) produces visual screens, concealing the basement's huge light wells until they pop up as surprises. The skin's another winner, casting lovely shadows, diffusing the tropical sun, and visually softening the exterior surfaces. The concave section of the louvres suggests the "bamboo" concrete patterning in the **Sifang Museum** (p. 137). Vanke is thirty minutes from Shenzhen proper, but it's worth the trip and the effort to arrange a visit.

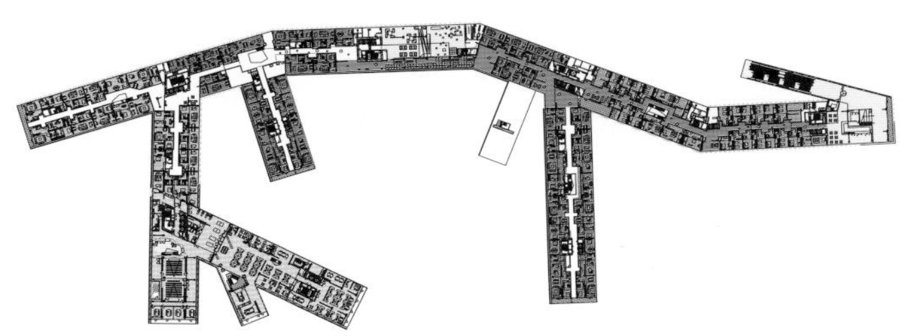

Second-floor plan

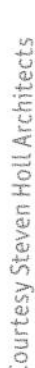

Courtesy Steven Holl Architects

© Christian Gahl | Courtesy: Architects

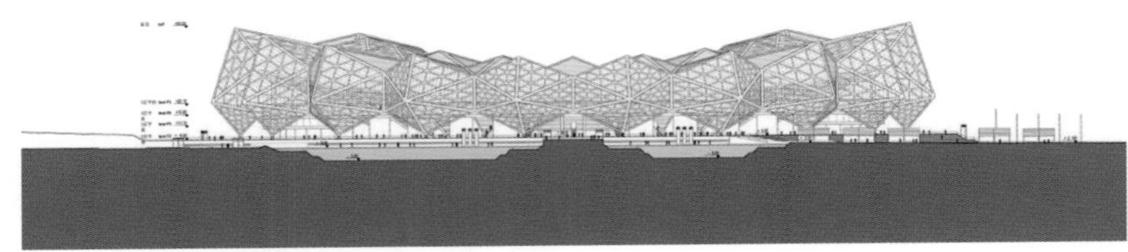
South elevation of natatorium

© Christian Gahl | Courtesy: Architects

Interior of natatorium

Plan of main arena

Universiade Arenas

SZ 39

GMP (von GERKAN, MARG and Partner), 2006–2011

深圳世界大学生运动会体育中心
龙岗区龙翔大道和黄阁路
Longxiang Ave. & Huangge Rd., Longgang
❖ 22.6968, 114.2132

Built for the 2011 Summer Universiade (a multi-national collegiate athletic event), this complex includes a football stadium, a multi-use arena, and a natatorium. United by similarly crystalline, triangulated surfaces, each has its own distinctive geometry, lending the set a subtle variety. The faceted façades are three-layered constructions: translucent membranes on the exterior and interior, with the primary steel structure and mechanical services in between, as at the **Water Cube** (p. 097). The buildings are arrayed across the site like pavilions in a traditional garden, with slight shifts in rotation avoiding an entirely axial configuration.

Site plan

This informality is reinforced by the landscape, as artificial lakes and topographic levels loosely suggest centres of post-Universiade public activity in a different way than at Beijing's **Olympic Green** (p. 095). Compare to the same firm's **Bao'an Stadium** (map p. 337).

© Leonardo Finotti

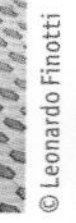

Bao'an International Airport, Terminal 3

SZ 46

Massimiliano & Doriana FUKSAS (architects), Fuksas Design (Interior Design), Knippers Helbig (structural engineering), China State Construction Engineering Corp. (general contractor), BIAD (architect of record), Speirs & Major Associates (lighting consulting), 2008–2013

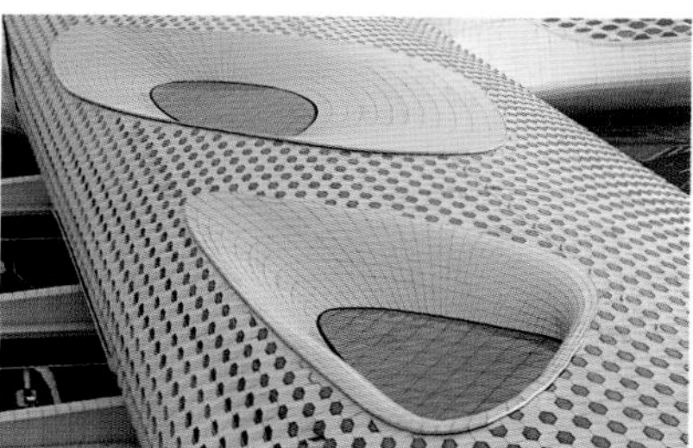

© Leonardo Finotti

深圳宝安国际机场

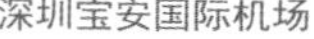

❖ 22.6328, 113.8054

© Archivio Fuksas

The branching, bird-like terminal plan is now a standard; legible in all the competition entries, it invites the architects to focus on qualities of *atmosphere,* and structural means of achieving them. Here, we find a striking, double-skinned roof, with hexagonal apertures of various sizes, parametrically designed to maximise natural light and minimise heat gain. The overall form, roughly 1.5 km in length, is described in terms of a manta ray transforming into a bird; the intended interior effect is that of a "cathedral," and so the climax is at the crossing, where a void brings filtered light through all three main levels. An "organic" sensibility unites the roofline's variations (meant to suggest the natural landscape), the amorphous white "trees" that accommodate vents and other necessities, and the "honeycomb" hexagonal pattern, which reappears in various elements. The narrow, tapered columns emphasise the roof's independent, floating quality.

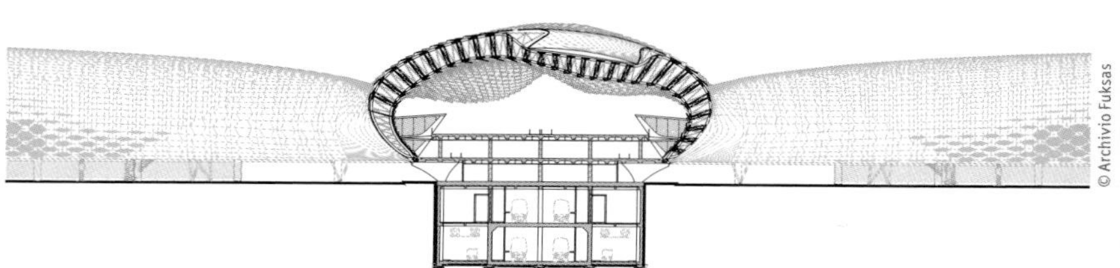

© Archivio Fuksas

Cross section

01 Ping An International Finance Centre *KPF, 2016 (anticipated).* Supertall tower, to be China's tallest (and perhaps #2 worldwide, for a time) at 600 m.
❖ 22.5367, 114.0506

02 Shenzhen Stock Exchange *OMA/Rem KOOLHAAS, 2006–2013.*
❖ 22.5442, 114.0492

03 Futian Centre/Citizen Square *Lee/Timchula (John LEE & Michael TIMCHULA), 1999+.* ❖ 22.5444, 114.0543

04 Museum of Contemporary Art & Planning Exhibition (MOCAPE) *Coop Himmelb(l)au, 2007–2015 (anticipated)* Another landmark object-building for Futian District: two distressed rectangular volumes (containing the art and planning exhibitions, respectively), conjoined by a twisty atrium.
❖ 22.5483, 114.0568

05 Cultural Centre *ISOZAKI Arata, 1997–2007.* ❖ 22.5500, 114.0522

06 Lianhuashan Park This fine hilltop park is a good spot for skyline views; note that the presence of protective hills at the north end of Futian's new civic centre is also in accordance with *feng shui*.
❖ 22.5562, 114.0523

07 KK100 (Kingkey Tower) *TFP Farrells (Terry FARRELL), 2007–2011.* The world's fourteenth-tallest tower, with a distinctive lozenge profile, and a flourish at the base.
❖ 22.5459, 114.1020

08 Sungang Central Plaza *Urbanus, 2005–2007.* A continuous brick surface unites several levels and rescues a formerly "sunken" plaza. May no longer exist.
❖ 22.5659, 114.1047

09 Dongmen Photography Plaza *Urbanus, 2009.* Making the most of on-site history, even 1980s history.
❖ 22.5492, 114.1151

10 Luo Hu Port/Lo Wu Control Point The main arrival point to Shenzhen from Hong Kong by land. Note the incredible difference in urbanisation across the river/border. ❖ 22.5300, 114.1136

11 Luohu Art Museum *Urbanus, 2000–2007.*
❖ 22.5458, 114.1225

12 Jade Bamboo Culture Plaza *Urbanus, 2005–2009.* ❖ 22.5713, 114.1295

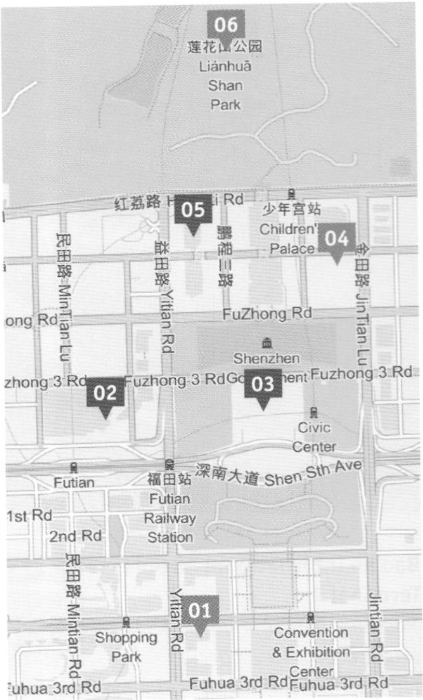

Futian & Civic Square (Map 01–06)

13 Window of the World Theme park of miniature world architecture. Irresistible photo opportunities, if you enjoy that sort of thing.
❖ 22.5389, 113.9658

14 OCT Bay *SWA Group (masterplanning & landscape)/LaGuarda Low & Associates (architecture), 2007–2011.* The fairly typical "lifestyle" retail is mirrored by a nature preserve said to be China's "only inner-city mangrove wetland."
❖ 22.5281, 113.9845

15 OCT Bay Clubhouse *Richard MEIER & Partners, 2008–2012.*
❖ 22.5262, 113.9825

16 Shenzhen Tourist Information Centre *Studio Pei-Zhu, 2012.* See entry for #17.
❖ 22.5254, 113.9864

17 OCT Design Museum *Studio Pei-Zhu, 2008–2010.* ❖ 22.5285, 113.9871

18 OCT Art & Design Gallery (Hua Museum) *Urbanus, 2006–2008.* ❖ 22.5358, 113.9780

19 He Xiangning Art Museum *Sherman KUNG, LEE & LEE Associates, 1995–1997.*
❖ 22.5359, 113.9768

20 OCT-Loft Renovation *Urbanus, 2003–2012.* ❖ 22.5403, 113.9884

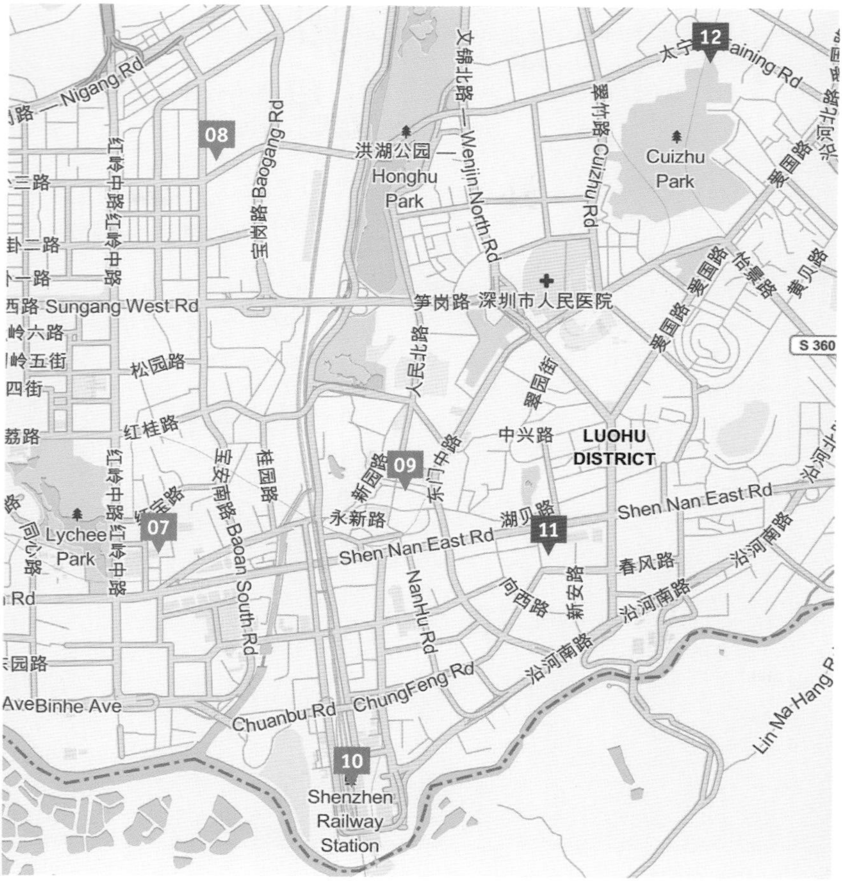

Luohu (Map 07–12)

OCT (Map 13–20)

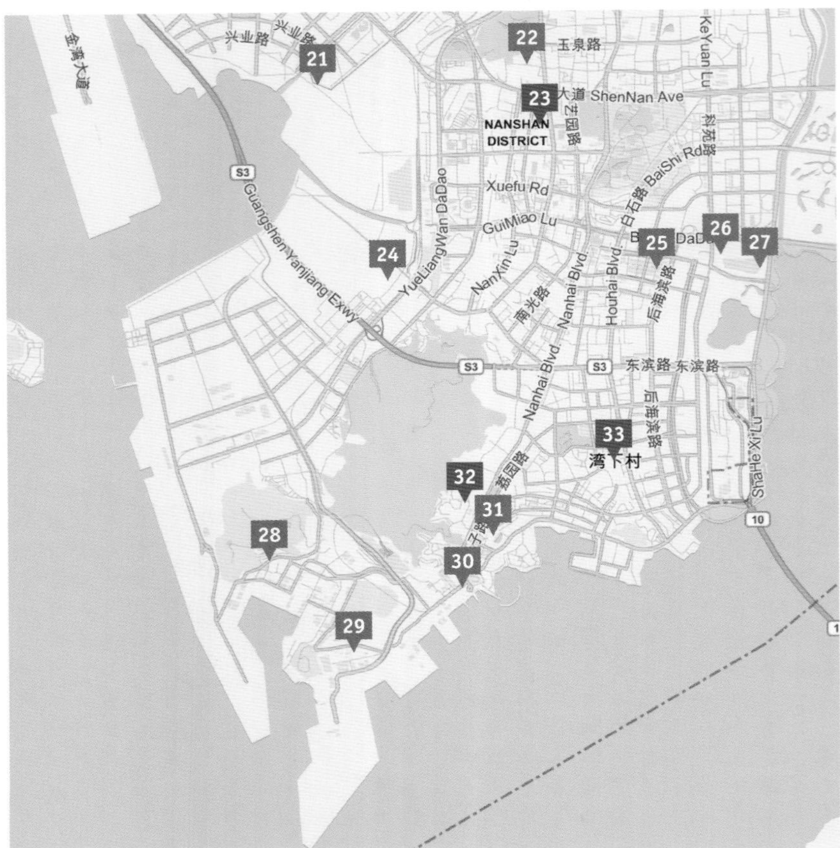

Nanshan (Map 21–33)

21 Qianhai Water City *James CORNER Field Operations, et al.* Still in planning/development, but apparently going forward. See introduction, p. 318. ❖ 22.5437, 113.8879

22 Xin'an Ancient City An urban village; see introductory text and entries for Dafen and Wanxia (both p. 329). ❖ 22.5463, 113.9157

23 Nanshan Marriage Registration Centre *Urbanus, 2008–2011.* ❖ 22.5386, 113.9167

24 Qianhai Exhibition Centre *Urbanus, 2013.* A rectilinear volume bounds a more curvaceous membrane surface. ❖ 22.5189, 113.8990

25 Poly Cultural Centre *Atelier Blur (Georges HUNG), 2009.* A performing arts centre and retail complex, featuring complex curvature in form, and a public-to-private transparency gradient in envelope. ❖ 22.5196, 113.9337

26 Hotel Kapok *Goettsch Partners, 2012* Compact, vertical prism with multi-storey atria inserted at intervals. On the grounds of the Bay Sports Centre (#27). ❖ 22.5218, 113.9422

27 Bay Sports Centre *ASX SATOW, BIAD, 2011.* A multi-use stadium complex (accommodating table tennis, swimming, football, etc.) wrapped in a doubly-curved diagrid façade. ❖ 22.5203, 113.9468

28 Tomb of the Young Song Emperor *1279/1980s.* Possible resting place of the last Emperor of the Southern Song Dynasty, "discovered" in the nineteenth century, and restored/rebuilt in the 1980s. ❖ 22.4832, 113.8816

29 Former Fufa Float-Glass Factory (2013 Biennale Pavilion) *NODE Architecture + Urbanism (Doreen Heng LIU), et al., 2013.* A "floating" pavilion above a recently-shuttered factory (1987). ❖ 22.4712, 113.8924

Shenzhen Region (Map 34–48)

30 Shekou Ferry Terminal Arrival point from Hong Kong by sea. ❖ 22.4794, 113.9091

31 Sea World Not a dolphin zoo, but a Western-style bar street (popular with expats) on an artificial pond, with façades and plaza paving borrowed from Macau. A landlocked cruise ship "anchors" the development. ❖ 22.4869, 113.9107

32 Maillen Hotel & Apartment *Urbanus, 2005–2011.* ❖ 22.4904, 113.9077

33 Wanxia Urban Village ❖ 22.4946, 113.9275

34 Dafen Oil Painting Village *1990s.* ❖ 22.6111, 114.1312

35 Dafen Art Museum *Urbanus, 2005–2007.* ❖ 22.6122, 114.1329

36 Vanke Centre *Steven HOLL Architects, 2006–2009.* ❖ 22.6007, 114.2999

37 Dawan Former Residence *1791.* More a village than a residence, this walled Hakka compound was once home to one hundred families (see p. 386). ❖ 22.6842, 114.3374

38 Crane Lake Fortified Village Showcase of the Hakka culture, including reconstructed fort-dwellings of the rectilinear type (see p. 386). ❖ 22.7305, 114.2613

39 Universiade Arenas *GMP (von GERKAN, MARG and Partner), 2006–2011.* ❖ 22.6968, 114.2132

40 Chinese University of Hong Kong (Shenzhen Campus) *Rocco Design Architects, Ltd., 2012–2015.* Stacked bars and slabs frame landscaped courtyards. ❖ 22.6919, 114.2095

41 Shenzhen Planning Building *Urbanus, 2001–2004.* A meditation on the ground plane, and a study in transparency and accessibility in government architecture. ❖ 22.5462, 114.0316

42 New Artron Art Centre *Urbanus, Wendell Burnette, 2012.* A rounded triangle in plan, containing museum galleries, a printing press, offices and retail, for a major art and architecture publisher. ❖ 22.5552, 113.9827

43 Portofino Luxurious faux-Italian residential and retail enclave. ❖ 22.5505, 113.9722

44 Library of South China University of Science and Technology *Urbanus, 2013.* Subtly-curved rectangular volume pierced by circulation pathways. ❖ 22.5981, 113.9934

45 Bao'an Sports Centre *GMP (von GERKAN, MARG & Partner), 2011.* This stadium's undulating roof rests on a forest of elongated, diagonal green steel columns, mimicking bamboo. ❖ 22.5635, 113.8794

46 Bao'an International Airport, Terminal 3 *Massimiliano & Doriana FUKSAS, et al., 2008–2013.* ❖ 22.6328, 113.8054

47 Dongguan Institute of Technology *2000s.* 37 km north of Shenzhen. Buildings by Amateur Architecture, AZL, FCJZ, Atelier Deshaus, and others. ❖ 22.9061, 113.8726

48 New South China Mall *2005.* The largest mall in the world by retail area, and 95 per cent vacant. Dongguan. ❖ 23.0375, 113.7205

香港
Hong Kong

香港 **Hong Kong**

COLORS
IN
OPTICS
昌明眼鏡
押
CHUEN TAK PAWN SHOP
錦城飯
Kat's beauty centre
祺斯美容中心
63088
1/F
ARTLAN
BEAUTY CEN
2/F
福珠寶
OOK JEWELLERY
citibank
FASHIONS
GHT TAILORS

ARTLAND
HAIR
&
BY APPOINTMENT
AR LAND
HAIR
&
BEAUTY
2/F
LAND
BEAUTY
금성식당
HAIR
PLAYGROUND
Hair
Design
Creation
良藥·香水化粧
ASTER CUSTOM TAILOR
EXCLUSIVE LADIES & GENTS
Suki Nail
ARTLAND
HAIR & BEAUTY
2/F
PERFEC

香港 Hong Kong

As countless visitors have discovered, Hong Kong, for reasons owing to its very peculiar history, remains something not-quite-the-same as the rest of China. Since its foundation, the city has been a gateway to the mainland, economically and culturally an exchange point both for Westerners coming in and Chinese heading out. Quintessentially Chinese, yet wholly unique and exceptional, Hong Kong exemplifies the contradictions of China in the twenty-first century. It is one of the world's most unique and iconic cities; this, and a collection of architecture that reflects its unusual development, make it a fascinating stop for any visitor interested in urban form and architectural design.

Hong Kong is unusual first because of its youth. When the British were ceded the island of Hong Kong in 1841 (after the First Opium War – see **Guangzhou,** p. 294), they described it as a "bare, barren rock." Though there were certainly Chinese living there, from the mainland point of view it was inconvenient: offshore, and composed mostly of steep hills. The British, however, found it suitable in several ways: its deep-water harbour could accommodate the most modern shipping vessels, it was close to the major Chinese port of Guangzhou, and it was geographically central relative to other Asian trading centres: Japan, Taiwan, the Philippines, Thailand. Once the British were established, the colony in turn became attractive to Chinese people seeking either some kind of economic opportunity, particularly in the illegal but prosperous opium trade, or simply a kind of security behind British guns in times of rebellion and war. Beginning from a population of 15,000 in 1841, the colony was swelled by refugees from the Taiping Rebellion in the 1850s and 1860s, the Revolution of 1911, and then the Chinese Civil War, World War II, and finally the Communist takeover of mainland China – bringing the population to over two million by 1950. The later events of the twentieth century have combined with apparent employment opportunities to bring today's population up to 7.2 million.

These numbers are significant because the urban history of Hong Kong has in many ways reflected the collision, shaped by British colonial policy, between raw population and the topographical facts of that "bare, barren rock." Victorian Hong Kong was characterised by a sharp divide between the elegant colonial buildings (mansions, offices, banks) and the staggeringly dense, crowded, and unsanitary city in which the working-class Chinese, who constituted the overwhelming majority, had to live. Victorian London was similarly divided, but note that most of Hong Kong's development, rich and poor, was concentrated along the limited space of Hong Kong Island's sheltered northern shore, where the first administrative buildings

Previous spread: Profusion of signage on Humphreys Ave, Tsim Sha Tsui

Hong Kong Island, with Kowloon visible beyond, from Victoria Peak, map p. 367

had been established. The accounts of would-be reformers tell of the terrible living conditions in the slums: multiple families crammed together into windowless rooms, with inadequate plumbing overflowing into the street or backing up into the walls, and hardly enough fresh water to go round. An outbreak of bubonic plague in 1894 killed 93 per cent of those who even managed to be seen in the hospital. The reformers' reports were usually ignored, or implemented so sparingly as to be irrelevant, because many of those who sat on Hong Kong's legislative assembly were themselves property owners collecting rent from the slums. Sadly, the most popular British response to these conditions was to flee from them, driving Hong Kong Island's uphill expansion. The Mid-Levels district, appropriately named for being partway up Victoria Peak, was populated with upper-class villas by the turn of the century.

The other impact of the demand for land was that Hong Kong began reclaiming land from the sea. This process started very early, less than ten years after the founding of the colony, and it was never enough to meet demand. Each successive reclamation project left its mark on the city, from the level Queensway, still humming with double-decker trams, to more recent encroachments into the harbour (see p. 358). As former shorelines tend to be preserved as major roadways, each reclamation "layer" must be tied back to the previous one by sky-bridges and underground connections, giving today's Hong Kong a certain "stratified" quality both in plan and section.

More effectively, from the British point of view, Hong Kong was enlarged by extending its borders. In 1860, after the Second Opium War, the British claimed Kowloon Peninsula, the outreach of the mainland just opposite the Hong Kong settlement. Surprisingly, Kowloon still went relatively undeveloped for some time; the British saw it chiefly as a defensive buffer for their increasingly crucial outpost. Only after it was connected by railway to Guangzhou, in 1916, did Kowloon begin its own period of sustained growth; today, it's one of the most densely populated places on Earth. In 1898, the British secured a 99-year lease on the New Territories, the hilly lands between Kowloon and present-day Shenzhen.

By 1911, the British were actually attempting real reforms, but these were continually undermined and derailed by the scale of immigration following the latest difficulties on the mainland, and possibly some strain placed on the administration by World War I. Grander and grander buildings went up on the waterfront, while conditions in the Chinese districts stayed the same or got worse, and the impoverished populace built squatter settlements alongside the overcrowded tenements. The Great Depression, World War II, and the Chinese Civil War all contributed to these conditions; refugees continued to pour

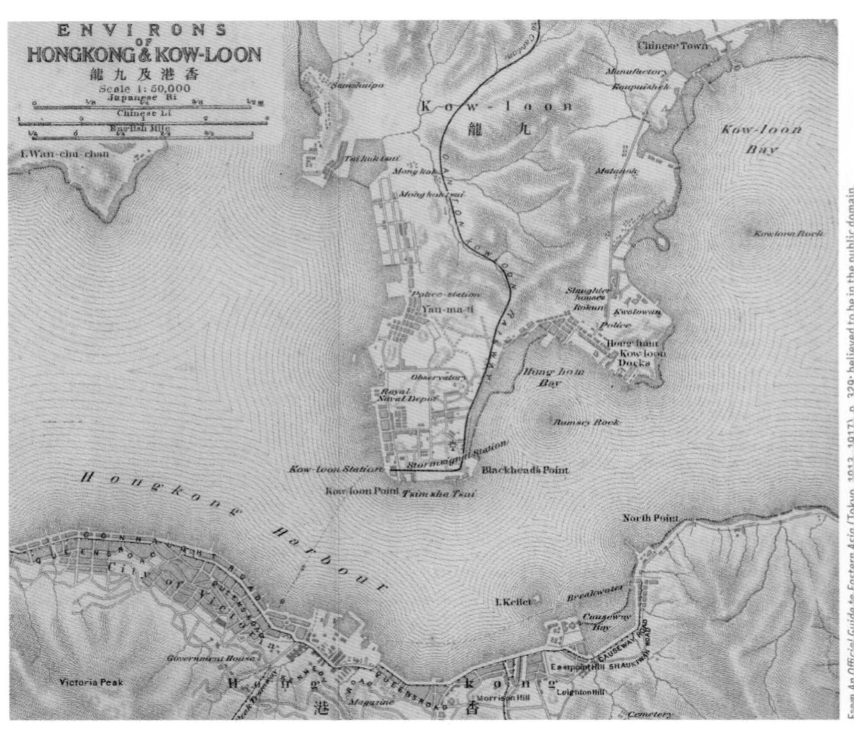

Hong Kong (below) and Kowloon (above) in 1915

in from the mainland, and the Japanese occupation government (1941–1945), in addition to committing several noted atrocities, was generally uninterested in resolving Hong Kong's domestic problems.

After 1949, though Communist China did not attempt to retake Hong Kong from the reinstated British, the new government in Beijing still had a profound effect on the colony. The arrival of another round of refugees predictably exacerbated the problems of overcrowding. Perhaps the best-known example was a Chinese border fort, later famous around the world as "Kowloon Walled City." Virtually abandoned by the Chinese government after 1949, and neglected by the British, it became one of the most infamous slums on the planet: 33,000 people living on 6.5 acres by 1987. It was supervised mainly by criminal syndicates and plagued by social problems (at least according to some critics), but sustained a community for decades. By mutual agreement between the British and Chinese governments, it was torn down starting in 1993. Its story reminds us that the bizarre effects of density, so clearly seen in Hong Kong, can be caused by administrative boundaries as much as physical limitations.

The refugees fleeing the mainland in 1949 also included a good portion of Shanghai's bourgeoisie. Seeking to reestablish themselves in a cosmopolitan, capitalist milieu, they brought with them resources and skills which helped stimulate postwar reconstruction. This was welcome, as a UN-imposed trade embargo, beginning during the Korean War, had closed the People's Republic to the west; Hong Kong's status as a port of entry was in jeopardy. The colony, with no shortage of labour, began shifting to a manufacturing economy. With the aid of British trade agreements, "Made in Hong Kong" consumer products began to appear around the world.

The physical layout of the city was altered as well; in one key redevelopment, a stretch of British military barracks in the city centre was torn down to make way for a major road, the Queensway. Today, lined with shimmering high-rises, it's one of Hong Kong's most iconic and essential thoroughfares. Perhaps more importantly, in the 1950s the government finally began to face the century-old issue of the housing shortage, partially as a result of a disastrous 1953 fire. Embracing Modernist architecture along with modern mass-production principles,

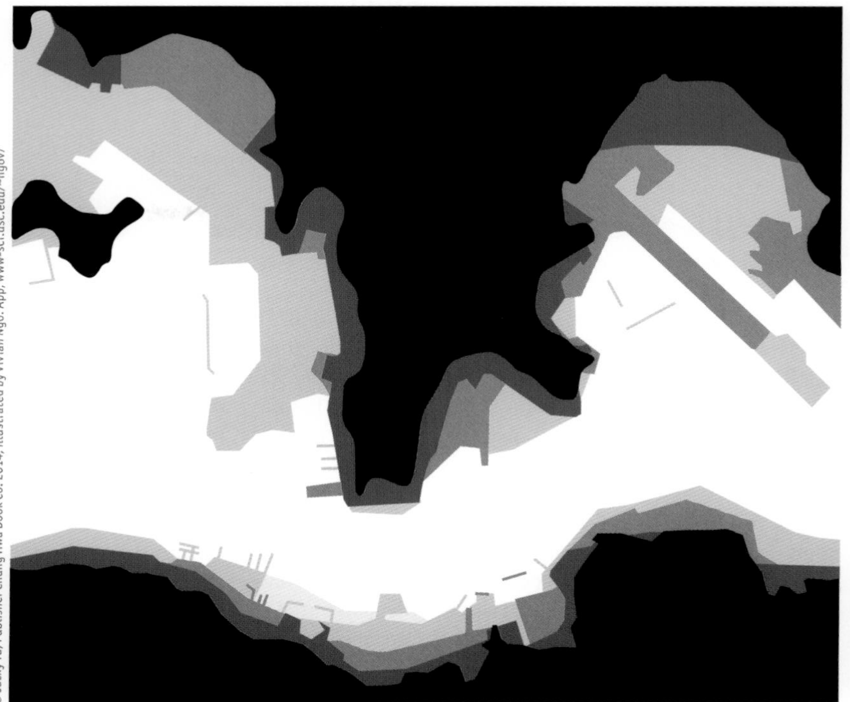

Land Reclamation: circa 1840 1850–1900 1900–1950 1950–2000 2000s

the Housing Authority began creating huge estates, housing tens of thousands of people. Initially, the programme was just to relocate squatters cleared in the process of other developments, but by 1961 applications were being taken for social housing on a general basis. Ten years later, nearly two-fifths of all households occupied a complete flat all to themselves (up from about one-tenth). For both private and public dwellings, high rises generally dominated, owing once again to the scarcity of buildable land. Today's Hong Kong, a few blocks back from the shoreline, is dominated by high-rise housing of this generation or later. Browsing window advertisements for apartments is a good way to get a feel for the intensity of the real estate market here, and the kind of living conditions that have replaced the squatter settlements and tenements.

The next major development was the beginning of a New Towns programme in the 1970s. Like New Towns in Britain, but looking more like France's high-rise *grand ensembles*, these were intended as self-contained communities complete with services and employment opportunities. Designed for an ultimate maximum of around 750,000 persons each, the New Towns that pepper the New Territories are interesting from an architectural standpoint: the building components are standardised, but owing to great variations in the topography and social conditions, each has its own character. A new transit network, built between 1979 and 1989, connected these centres with the harbourfront and Kowloon, still by far the leading areas economically. While the core remains profoundly dense, it could be argued that Hong Kong's long-term crisis of population and density was resolved by remaking the city as a polycentric network of smaller, still dense hubs with open space preserved in between. Of course, we should not pretend that today's Hong Kong has completely solved the problems of poverty and housing. Tens of thousands, for example, live in self-built, illegal "rooftop slums," left behind by the overheated housing market and the limited supply of public housing.

By the 1980s, Hong Kong's economy was poised to shift once again. As the "Asian Tiger" economies heated up, and as China's southern states became the focus of capitalistic experiments in the early 1980s (see **Shenzhen,** p. 316), Hong Kong began to transform into a sort of

Choi Hung housing estate (map p. 368)

Sha Tin New Town (map p. 368)

giant financial-services consultant. The waterfront skyline of today's Hong Kong is still dominated by the monuments of 1980s finance capital, including a string of banking headquarters, hotels and convention spaces. Hong Kong in the 1980s was thus not unlike Chicago a century earlier, or New York in the 1950s: a focal point of experimentation in high-rise typologies, as in the **HSBC Headquarters, the Bank of China building, Lippo Centre,** and others (pp. 352-355). Some of the money found its way into infrastructural improvements (such as the **Mid-Levels Escalators,** p. 350, and **Chek Lap Kok Airport,** p. 365) and public amenities (such as the conversion of the old Kowloon railway station into an arts district, see p. 361).

Even bigger changes loomed over Hong Kong in the 1980s, as the British and Chinese governments negotiated the upcoming expiry of the 99-year lease of the New Territories, which now practically meant the handover of Hong Kong and Kowloon, since the territories had become so spatially and economically interlinked in the preceding decades. With the British unwilling to give up their considerable economic interests in the colony, the result of the long and thorny negotiation was a peculiar solution: "one country, two systems." Hong Kong would return to China in 1997, but as a "Special Administrative Region" with its own currency and legal system. Free market capitalism would carry on as before – for at least fifty years. For China, it would become a source of tremendous tax revenue, a means of financing the coordinated economic reform programme of the Special Economic Zones. To some, it was also a dry run for how China and Taiwan might hypothetically be reunited, a delicate question ever since the latter became home to the Nationalist government in 1949.

In the end, the hand-over went off smoothly, though concerns have been raised periodically that the Chinese administration has not maintained the promised open society. Most recently, in September 2014, Hong Kong was the site of an enormous, sustained protest concerning plans which would effectively rig Hong Kong's future elections by limiting the candidates to those approved by Beijing. These events demonstrated that the often strange and unconventional streetscape of Hong Kong, despite being physically enmeshed with commercialised private space, could still become the site of unplanned and creative uses by an activist public. The space in front of the **HKSAR Government Headquarters** (p. 356), notionally intended for civic occupation, was thronged with protesters, but so were Gloucester Road's eight lanes of automobile space. The protests also implicitly raised the question of whether the promises of freedom for Hong Kong were intended for its public, or for its flows of capital (British, Chinese, or otherwise).

Physical changes since the handover split the difference. A few projects with quasi-public goals, like the new harbour waterfront and the under-construction **West Kowloon Cultural District** (map p. 368) demonstrate a scale of construction more akin to a twenty-first century Chinese city than a former British outpost. But as the former colony's economic success seems to have continued unabated – it has the world's sixth-highest GDP per capita, very impressive given conditions elsewhere in China – its most prominent new constructions are, as before, super-giant office towers.

Out of density, topography and individually unremarkable curtain walls and concrete slabs, Hong Kong generates an experientially rich urbanism of interpenetrating section, where every trip becomes a Piranesian expedition woven under, over, through and sometimes around the "real" ground. Here, sky-bridges and urban freeways – forms of circulation elsewhere seen as inimical to pedestrian life – are what makes that life *possible*. Pedestrian overpasses become entangled with the interiors of shopping malls, which here become integral pieces of urban tissue rather than self-isolating citadels set in parking lots. Mall owners naturally want to exploit foot traffic, and the pedestrians are happy to have access to escalators and breathing room on their way. Hence, the third floor of a building might be just as much the "entrance" level as the basement. This redundancy of infrastructural connection in section alleviates crowding in the streets themselves. Compare to the conditions in denser Kowloon, which is flatter and lacking in skyway infrastructure. There, especially around Mong Kok, the streets are often completely jam-packed with people. This may not, of course, be a negative in itself. Hong Kong's circulation is crystal-clear to locals carrying three-dimensional mental maps of every mall, subway station, and ferry terminal, but it can baffle an outsider due to the convoluted routes involved in traversing the city. While Hong Kong has several signature works of architecture, an experience of the strange topographic urbanism in Wan Chai, Admiralty, Central and, especially, the Mid-Levels may leave the more lasting impression.

Some aspects of this living laboratory for the interface between Communism and capitalism in the New China may presage changes on the mainland; others are fundamentally linked to the topography and the unique history of this place. But more than any other city in this book, Hong Kong represents the nexus of conflict between China's past and its globalised, neo-liberal capitalist future.

Practical Considerations

Hong Kong's major sights are mostly concentrated on the north side of Hong Kong Island and on the southern tip of Kowloon peninsula; ambitious visitors could tour both areas in one long day. The subway is inexpensive and convenient, though for east-to-west trips on Hong Kong island, we recommend the historic double-decker trolley. Taxis, though more expensive than in mainland China, remain a convenient mode of transport.

Sources and Recommended Reading

Juanita CHENG and Andrew YEOH, *Hong Kong: A Guide to Recent Architecture*, London: Batsford, 1998. Informative but not without personality, this little book offers considerable detail on the last two decades of British rule.

Adam FRAMPTON, Jonathan D. SOLOMON, and Clara WONG, *Cities Without Ground: A Hong Kong Guidebook*, Novato, CA: ORO Editions, 2012. The best discussion to date of Hong Kong's three-dimensional urbanism, including some drawings which will likely become iconic.

Harvard Design School, *Hong Kong: Defining the Edge*, Cambridge, Mass.: Harvard Design School, 2001. Essays and studio projects exploring the contemporary city.

Laurent GUTIERREZ, Ezio MANZINI, and Valérie PORTEFAIX, eds., *HK Lab*, Hong Kong: Map Books, 2002. Essays and journalistic photos – a sort of "Delirious Hong Kong."

Ian KELLY, *Hong Kong: A Political-Geographic Analysis*, London: Mansell, 1987. Out of date and occasionally jargonistic, but full of great historical data.

Vittorio LAMPUGNANI, ed., *Hong Kong Architecture: The Aesthetics of Density*, Rotterdam: 010 Publishers, 1993. Great, well-illustrated historic essays, particularly on housing and new towns – plus individual building coverage.

Gordon MATHEWS, *Ghetto at the Center of the World*, Chicago: University of Chicago Press, 2011. A case study of **Chungking Mansions** (p. 362), using it as a window into the complex spatial and social networks of globalisation.

Rufina WU and Stefan CANHAM, *Portraits From Above: Hong Kong's Informal Rooftop Communities*, Berlin, Peperoni Books, 2008. Photographic, architectural and face-to-face study of life in self-built rooftop dwellings.

Shun Tak Centre

HK 01

SPENCE ROBINSON, Ltd.
1983–1986

信德中心
香港中環干诺道中200号
200 Connaught Road Central
❖ 22.2879, 114.1519

This mixed-use complex combines office towers, a mall, a ferry terminal, a bus depot, taxi stands, helicopter pads, and an international border crossing (for the ferry to Macau, and beyond). The multi-modal transit hub forms the first few levels of the complex, and perfectly encapsulates the density and activity of the city. Shun Tak connects directly to Hong Kong's extensive network of pedestrian bridges; while not as stylistically ambitious as the **Lippo Centre** (p. 355), it is perhaps a fuller embodiment of late-Modern Brutalist urban planning principles, with grade- and speed-separated circulation stacked into a thickened urban field condition. The podium is topped by twin towers, distinctive for their red-highlighted exterior trusses.

Western Market

HK 02

1906/1991

上環街市
德輔道中323號
323 Des Voeux Road Central
❖ 22.2872, 114.1504

One of the oldest structures in Sheung Wan district, and the oldest existing market hall in Hong Kong, the building operated as a fresh food market until 1988. After extensive renovations by Tao HO Design Architects, it reopened in 1991, and is now home to fabric merchants, flower shops, and several cafés. As with much historic preservation in Hong Kong, it has met with criticism, but it remains a good example of early 1900s colonial architecture.

Central Star Ferry Pier

HK 03

2006

中環天星碼頭, 民光街
Man Kwong Street, Central District
❖ 22.2865, 114.1610

The Star Ferry offers a taste of Hong Kong's rapidly-vanishing past and is a fine method for a harbour crossing, with unmatched skyline views and charming, vintage ferries with both enclosed and open-air decks. The Central District terminal, however, is a recent construction, done up in faux-Edwardian imitation of an earlier terminal building. This stylistic choice has proven controversial, as the city struggles to reconcile a colonial past with an uncertain future.

International Finance Centre

HK 04

Pelli Clarke Pelli Architects (César PELLI), Rocco Design Architects, Limited, 1997-2004

香港國際金融中心, 中環金融街8號
8 Finance Street, Central
❖ 22.285, 114.159167

While now only Hong Kong's second-tallest tower (after the **ICC** across the harbour, p. 362), the IFC remains an impressive achievement. The complex consists of two towers, connected by a luxury mall. Street-level setbacks create a more varied pedestrian experience, and the mall's internal corridors connect both to the underground MTR station, and to the surrounding pedestrian network. The centrepiece is Tower Two, eighty-eight storeys high (an auspicious number – see **Jin Mao,** p. 178) and still the tallest figure on the island itself. Its elegant proportions and the gingerly "carved" massing echo traditional architecture without appeal to facile metaphors. In particular, the progressive setbacks, and the emphatic "crown" of aluminium-clad struts (a "beacon" by night), suggest an early-twentieth century high-rise. Simultaneously, the sleek curtain wall, whose crisply-profiled mullions emphasise the tower's verticality, suggests an updated international Modernism. The fusion of these two impulses reflects not only a tension between latter-day High-Tech and Postmodern sensibilities, but also, as at Jin Mao and the **Bank of China** (p. 354), a search for meaningful, locally compelling symbols in buildings whose activities tie them more to global flows of capital than to the local bedrock.

Central-Mid-Levels Escalators

HK 05

Hong Kong Transport Department, 1987–1993

中環至半山自動扶手電梯 – 些利街
Cochrane Street, Shelley Street
❖ 22.2814, 114.1527

This project combines two key pieces of Hong Kong pedestrian life, the sky-way and the escalator, addressing density and topography in one stroke. The Mid-Levels district, once home to Hong Kong's colonial mansions, is now densely packed with residential high-rises, despite the challenge of commuting up and down the steep hill. In 1987, the government decided that the choked sidewalks needed some relief. The escalators began operation in 1993, and were expected to serve about 25,000 commuters daily; twenty years later, usage is more than double that prediction. Despite the heavy traffic, some argue that the intervention was a waste of time and money, pointing out that its $30 million USD budget (more than twice the intended price) hasn't alleviated crowding, but simply moved it onto the escalators. The sidewalk, however, is freed up to accommodate retail programme, through an effective hierarchy of pedestrian travel: commuters take the escalators, while locals take the street, arguably benefiting from the shade and sense of enclosure created by the overhead walkways. Up above, the views are similar to those experienced in sky-bridges. However, with the ground below plunging steeply, the escalator often aligns with the second or third storeys of neighbouring buildings. The occupants of these buildings have taken the opportunity to turn their upper floors into showrooms, making window shoppers out of the captive audience of escalator riders. Though one would hardly compare this project's everyday, functional aesthetics to the finely-crafted jewel box of the **HSBC Headquarters** (p. 352), it's interesting to consider that both have their origins in naked problem-solving, rely on the repetition of specially-designed components, and are notionally meant to serve some infrastructural role for the surrounding neighbourhood. Though the escalators resemble a dull 1980s mall turned inside-out, they generate unique spatial and urban experiences without the traditional components of "public space," and thus encapsulate much of Hong Kong's distinctive quality. Over the years, the streets that the escalators connect have been transformed from sleepy residential zones to some of Hong Kong's most popular retail and night-life spots (with the attendant rent spikes and cries of gentrification). The government has several other public escalator projects in the works, and we expect similar transformations in those districts, for good or ill.

© Florian Meuser

Jardine House (Connaught Centre)

HK 08

PALMER & TURNER, 1970–1974

怡和大廈 / 康樂大廈
中環康樂廣場1號
1 Connaught Place, Central
❖ 22.2830, 114.1588

At 179 metres tall, this was the tallest building in Asia at the time of completion. It remains a major landmark thanks to its prominent location and its unique porthole windows, which minimally penetrate the structural outer walls. The original glass mosaic cladding kept falling off, and was replaced in the 1980s with metal panels; these overemphasise the grid, implying a non-loadbearing, clip-on façade.

Legislative Council Building (Old Supreme Court Building)

HK 11

Sir Aston WEBB and Ingress BELL, 1900–1912

立法會大樓, 昃臣道8號
8 Jackson Road at Charter Road
❖ 22.2809, 114.1603

The British architects, responsible for parts of Buckingham Palace and the Victoria and Albert Museum, here deploy an eclectic Neo-Classical style, with Ionic columns and a sculptural programme incorporating British imperial symbols. The airy design is influenced by the climate-responsive typology of the nearby trading houses (now mostly gone); compare to the **China Merchants' Company**, p. 158).

© Florian Meuser

© Florian Meuser

Central Police Station

HK 12

1864–1925/2016

中區警署 – 10荷李活道中区
10 Hollywood Rd, Central
❖ 22.2818, 114.1541

Comprised of seven blocks constructed over sixty years, the majority of the complex dates to 1910, and is now one of turn-of-the-century Hong Kong's few physical legacies, and a touchstone for conservationists. The compound is currently undergoing renovations led by Herzog & de Meuron, and will soon re-open as a contemporary art centre, with the central courtyard open to the public.

Old Dairy Farm Depot

HK 14

Danby & Leigh, 1892

舊牛奶公司倉庫, 下亚厘毕道2号
2 Lower Albert Road, Central
❖ 22.2801, 114.1557

This distinctive banded brick-and-stucco building, one of Central's oldest, was originally a cold storage facility, used to supply ice to nearby businesses and residents. The building was renovated in the 1980s following a period of disrepair, and little remains of the original interiors. It is now home to the Fringe Club (a contemporary arts venue and bar) and the Foreign Correspondents' Club.

HSBC Headquarters

HK 15

Foster + Partners (Norman FOSTER), 1979–1986

香港上海滙豐銀行總行大廈
中環皇后大道中1號
1, Queen's Road Central
❖ 22.2803, 114.1594

Arguably Foster's masterpiece, the HSBC is perhaps the clearest fulfilment of the High-Tech promise that the Modernist interrogation of structure and systems was still a viable project. At the time, the emphasis on technical priorities seemed a defiant statement against the jokey language-games and client-pleasing historicism of Postmodernism; thirty years on from its conception, it's clearer that this façade does serve a "billboard" function, representing the client's putative efficiency and forward thinking, not to mention its budgetary largesse. But the form does not derive from stylistic riffing on futurosity; rather, it embodies a series of experimental tests. By this date, the modern office tower had already become a cliché: elevator core in the centre, glassy offices at the perimeter, and a fluorescent cubicle farm in between. Foster's building returns to earlier Modernist optimism (in particular, Amancio Williams's 1946 office-tower project) to challenge these assumptions. What if all employees enjoyed natural light and a great view? What if the circulation and mechanical systems were moved to the sides, letting the middle enjoy a spectacular atrium? What if that atrium were lit by sunlight reflected through an array of mirrors above? What if the curtain wall incorporated sun-shades – and what if the shades doubled as access rigs for window-washers?

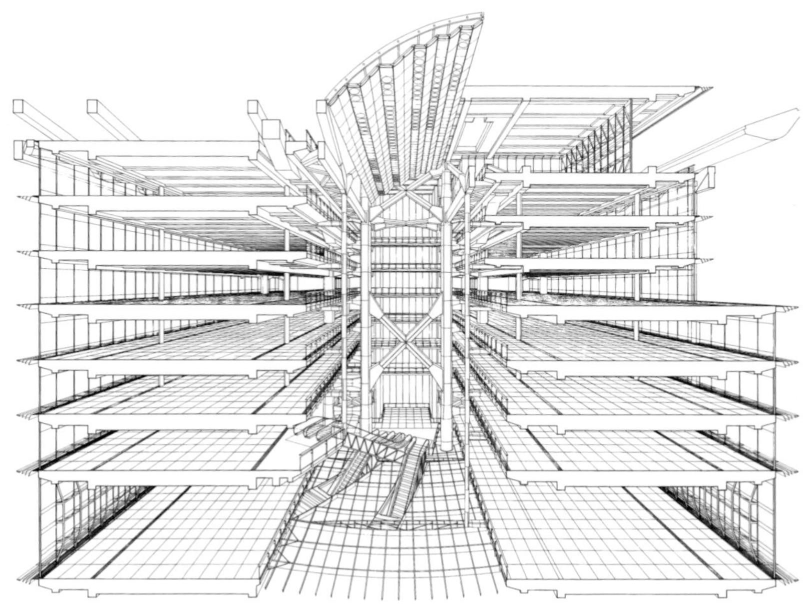

Sectional perspective through atrium

The zoning code yielded the stepped composition of the three narrow tower-masses. Politics yielded the open ground floor, connecting two public spaces and showing off the suspension of the deep floor plates from the dramatic coat-hanger trusses. The trusses also break down the curtain wall's scale, providing a "medium" level between the tower and the individual window, and helping the building address the historic bank building next door.

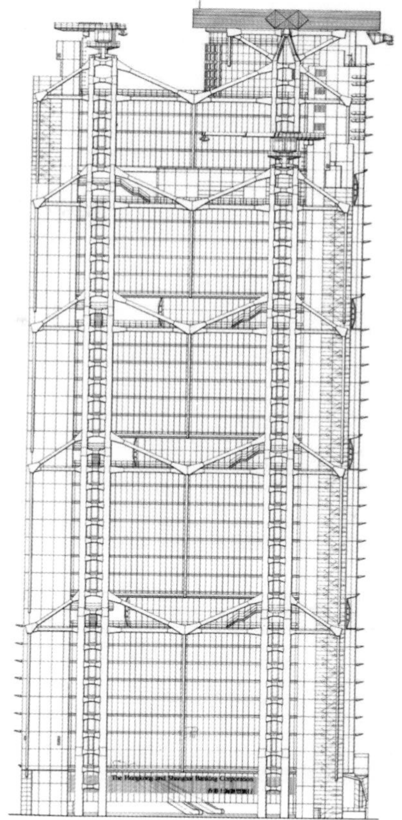

Elevation

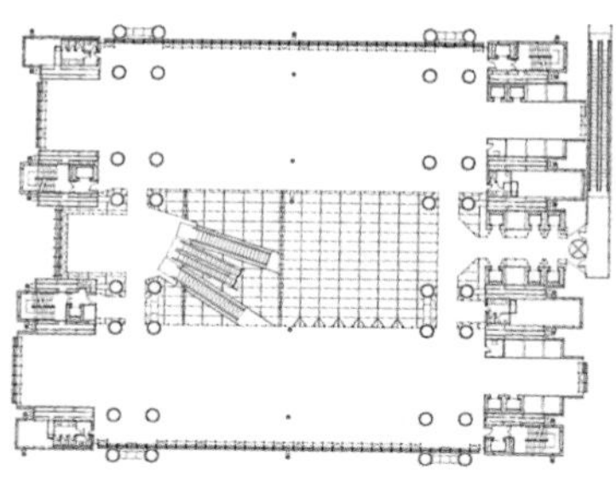

Banking Hall floor plan

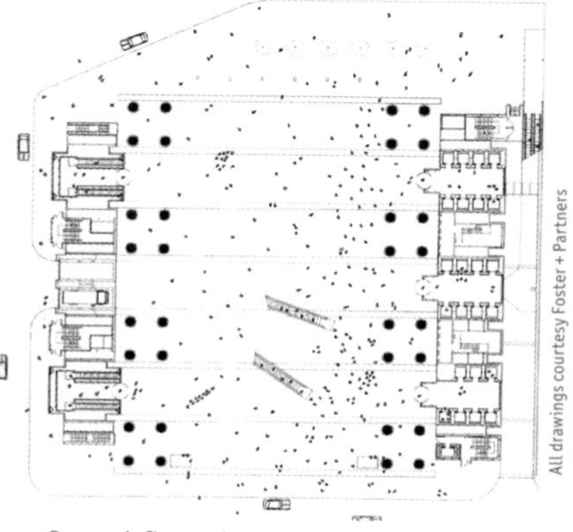

Ground-floor plan

All drawings courtesy Foster + Partners

Bank of China

Pei Cobb Freed & Partners
(Ieoh Ming PEI), 1985–1990

HK 17

中銀大廈
中西區金鐘花園道1號
1 Garden Road, Central
❖ 22.2793, 114.1616

This 70-storey office building steps into the genre of diagonally-structured towers (perhaps defined by SOM's 1969 Hancock Centre in Chicago) and re-invigorates it by imagining the diagonals as the edges of a complexly cut prism, rising from a square base and gradually shedding triangular facets as it rises. Described in terms of a bamboo plant (made rigid by its exterior structure), the tower handles typhoon-force winds with a column-free interior; all loads are directed to the four massive corner piers. These are visually slimmed, and the tower integrated with the base, through compositional devices such as a belt of overscaled curtain-wall "windows," scaling up from the punch windows further below. Abstracted Chinese motifs point ahead to the **Suzhou Museum** (p. 216).

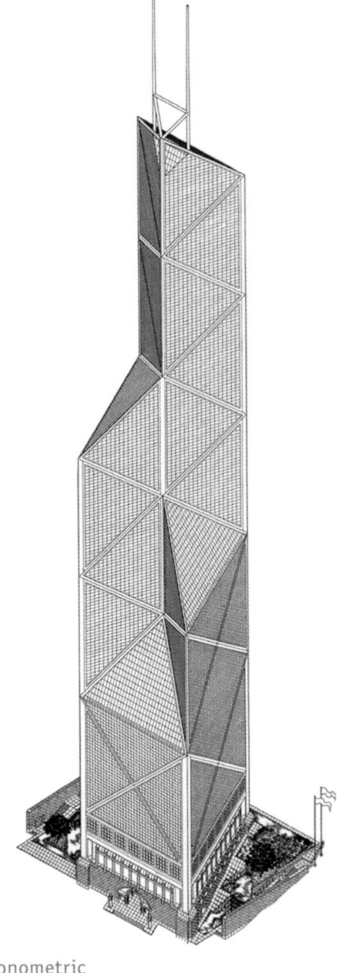

Axonometric

Typical floor plans (base and tower)

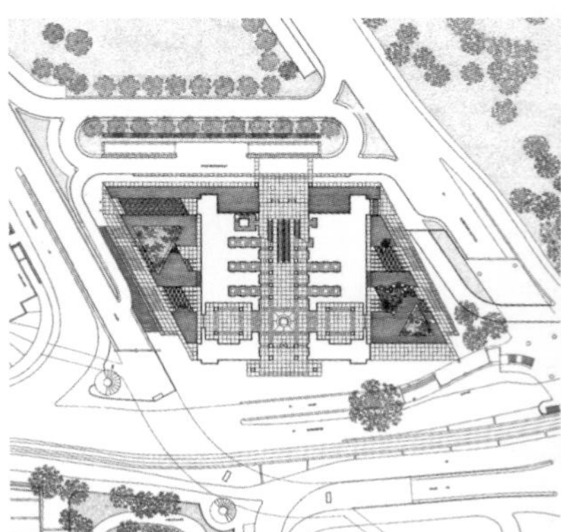

Site plan

Lippo Centre (Bond Centre)
Paul RUDOLPH, 1986–1988

HK 18

力寶中心/奔達中心
金鐘道89號
89 Queensway
❖ 22.2793, 114.1634

This pair of reflective, glassy high-rises might seem to be a departure for Rudolph, most famous for his textured, highly articulated concrete Brutalism of the 1960s. However, like that work, it demonstrates a dissatisfaction with over-simplified Modernism, in this case with the standardised curtain-wall office tower. The building, which had to perch above the new Admiralty underground station, is initially divided into two masses (thirty-six and forty storeys), and further broken down in scale by dividing each tower into nine-floor sections with the remainder at the top. The in-and-out shifting of the volumes yields twelve different basic floor plans, suggesting that even when its internal functions are fundamentally identical, a building must somehow express a messier, more complicated reality. Rudolph's other Asian towers of this period (in Singapore and Jakarta) combine similar shifts with deep-set balconies and projecting cells; in Hong Kong, the taut, solar-reflective glass wrapper still allows the sense of a sculptural volume enlivened by changing light. The scale is further humanised by the lively base, with its forest of columns rising to different heights. Grade-separated walkways and cascading staircases (suggesting impromptu theatre seating) link the building to the surrounding pedestrian network. If office space does not permit the sectional gymnastics seen in Rudolph's institutional work, the building at least seems comfortable with Hong Kong's layered ground plane.

Site section

HKSAR Government Headquarters

Rocco Design Architects Limited, 2007–2011

政府總部，金鐘添馬艦添美道2號
2 Tim Mei Ave, Admiralty
❖22.2807, 114.1654

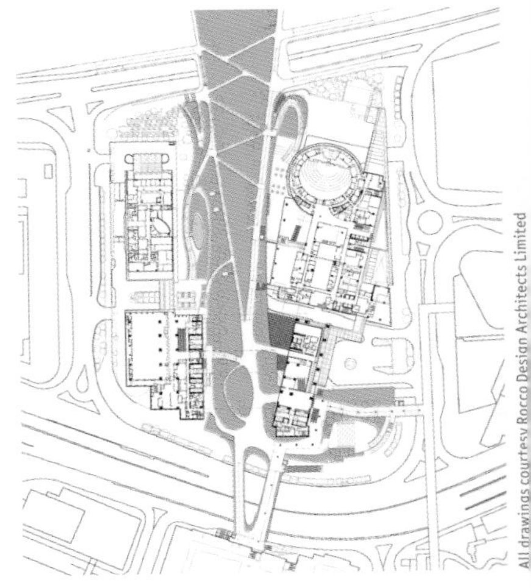

Site plan

All drawings courtesy Rocco Design Architects Limited

Characterised by the architects as an "open door" representing Hong Kong's history as a free port, its diverse cultural heritage, and its government's supposed transparency, this building's form can also be read as a provocative reflection on the commercial skyscrapers which dominate the skyline. Here, in a civic building, the tower is folded back in on itself, enabling multi-level connections and encouraging a three-dimensional urbanism, continuous with Hong Kong's already animated ground plane. Compare to the intentions and methods of **CCTV** (p. 088), and Rocco's own **W Hotel** in Guangzhou (map p. 310). While the building must be as impenetrable as most government office towers, the *complex* is made accessible; it frames a swath of pleasant greenery that slopes down to join one end of the future harbour promenade. It's a nice gesture in a dense city with few large public spaces, though it remains to be seen if the square will become a true site of dialogue between people and government.

All photographs © Michael Moran/OTTO

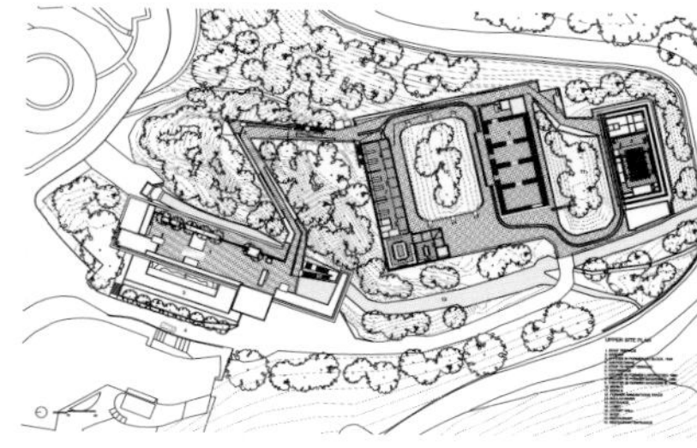

Upper-level site plan

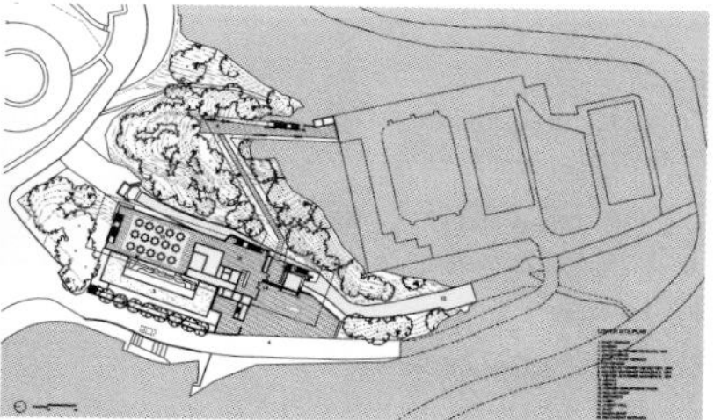

Billie Tsien Architects

Lower-level site plan

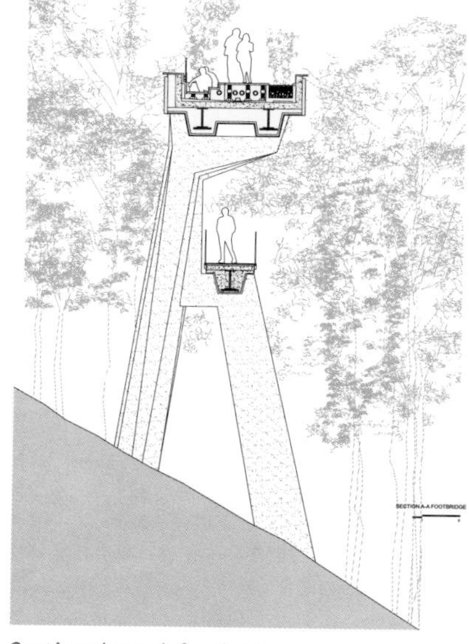

Section through footbridge

Asia Society Headquarters

HK 21

TWBTA (Tod WILLIAMS & Billie TSIEN Architects), 2012

亞洲協會香港中心
金鐘正義道九號
9 Justice Drive, Admiralty
❖ 22.2756, 114.1655

With its historically-loaded site, incorporating the former Explosives Magazine of the British Army (1860+), the Asia Society Headquarters proves the value of thoughtful restoration. The design preserves historic structures without unduly venerating their design, a careful balance in a city that still grapples with its identity in a shifting political and economic landscape. The architects demonstrate their typical flair for fine materials and details, in the new structures and old. Angling through the forest, a two-level footbridge connects the new roadside pavilion to the historic buildings nestled on the hillside; one sees the influence of Hong Kong's now-iconic pedestrian bridges. The sprawling, layered building, like the city itself, is best experienced as a cinematic progression through three-dimensional space.

Photo courtesy SOM | © James Steinkamp Photography

Hong Kong Convention and Exhibition Centre

HK 22

SOM (Larry OLTMANNS, design partner), 1998/1997/2009

香港會議展覽中心, 灣仔展覽道1號
1 Expo Drive, Wanchai
❖ 22.2834, 114.1731

This landmark conference centre sits on a reclaimed peninsula which juts forth from a cluster of hotels in Wan Chai. Like other recent waterfront projects in Hong Kong, this large cultural venue has tight security, and has been criticised for encroaching on the harbour while leaving the surrounding neighbourhood behind. However, it should be noted that the immediate context,

Photo courtesy SOM | © Hedrich Blessing

a series of freestanding high-rises occupying recently-reclaimed land, is hardly Hong Kong's liveliest spot. This centre's move into the water differentiates it from that skyline, creating a visible icon. This approach is likely inspired by Jørn UTZON's Sydney Opera House (1957–1973), which also counts on a sculptural roof to establish identity; this one has been said to resemble birds, flowers, sea turtles, etc.

CC BY-SA 2.0 Flickr user FHKE; cropped

Central Plaza

HK 23

Dennis LAU & NG Chun Man Architects & Engineers, 1992

中環廣場
灣仔港灣道18號
18 Harbour Road, Wan Chai
❖ 22.2799, 114.1736

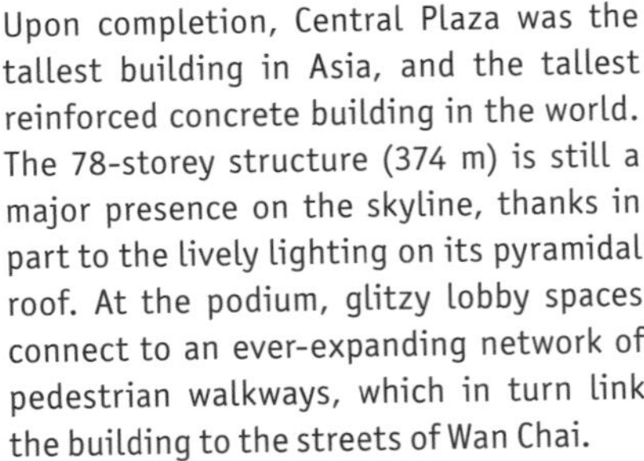

Upon completion, Central Plaza was the tallest building in Asia, and the tallest reinforced concrete building in the world. The 78-storey structure (374 m) is still a major presence on the skyline, thanks in part to the lively lighting on its pyramidal roof. At the podium, glitzy lobby spaces connect to an ever-expanding network of pedestrian walkways, which in turn link the building to the streets of Wan Chai.

Wikipedia user Chong Fat; public domain

Hong Kong Academy for the Performing Arts

HK 24

Simon KWAN and Associates, 1985

香港演藝學院 香港灣仔告士打道一號
1 Gloucester Road, Wan Chai
❖ 22.2800, 114.1702

This arts centre gathers recital halls, studios, and open-air theatres around a central atrium. The site was somewhat fractured by a transit station and its associated infrastructure below; the prismatic form of the building represents a reconciliation between these constraints and the sculptural expression of the creative arts within. In contrast, the exterior landscape emphasises curves.

Courtesy the Tao Ho Foundation; from the opening of "TaHo 70/30" in June 2006

Hong Kong Arts Centre

Tao HO Design, 1974–1977

HK 25

香港藝術中心
香港湾仔港湾道2号
2 Harbour Road, Wan Chai
❖ 22.2802, 114.1708

Hong Kong's former British colonial status makes it home to several fine late-Modern and Brutalist buildings at scales rarely seen in mainland China, where the chaos of the 1960s and 1970s generally made such things infeasible. Like the nearby **Academy for the Performing Arts** (opposite), this project features confident volumetric massing in response to site pressures, a carefully-worked-out section, and plenty of exposed concrete. Ho had a narrow site between two buildings, and lots of programme, including a tower's worth of cultural-organisation offices (which pay for the arts space). He shifted most of the support programme to the solid edges, giving the offices an atrium (renovated in 2000 by Edge Design), and leaving room for the the arts centre to accommodate its auditoria and some tall, sectionally off-set gallery space. Planned pedestrian links to the waterfront were not built, for budget reasons. The triangular plan modules respect the long-spanning, tetrahedral floor structure (reminiscent of Louis KAHN's Yale Art Gallery). These deep floors are expressed on the exterior with trusses that break down the scale of the elevation nicely; they have been compared to the levels of a pagoda, but to us they suggest then-current megastructural projects worldwide (Raj REWAL in Delhi, TANGE Kenzō in Kofu). In the Sixties, Ho had worked closely under Walter GROPIUS (his teacher at Harvard); he then helped introduce up-to-date Modernism to Hong Kong, and this building is formally and materially tougher, but spatially livelier, than most of Gropius's postwar work with The Architects' Collaborative. Worth a close look, especially if you tire of Hong Kong's later, glossier turn.

Front elevation

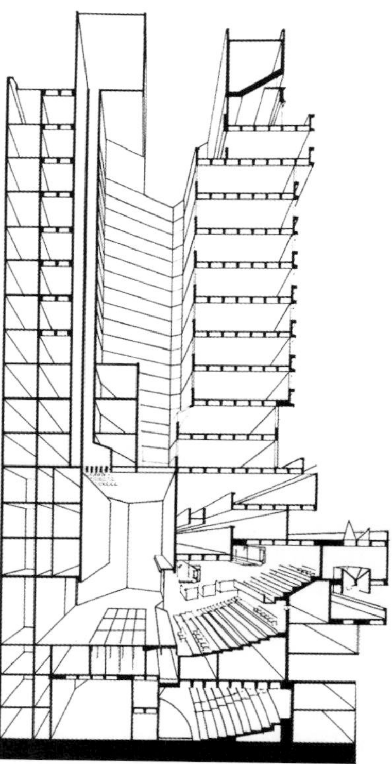

Section-perspective

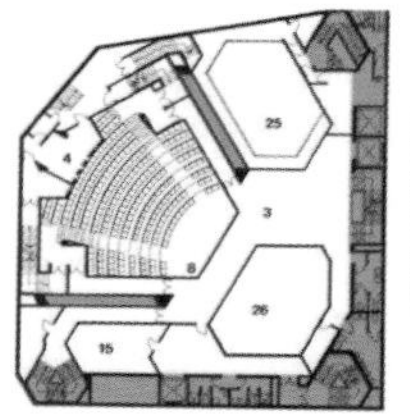

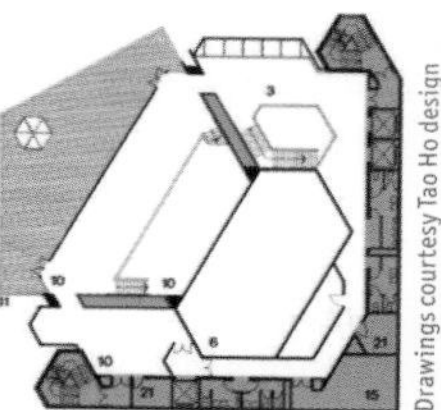

Plans: theatre level, gallery level

Drawings courtesy Tao Ho design

The Pawn

1888/2003

HK 26

灣仔莊士敦道62號
62 Johnston Road, Wan Chai
❖ 22.2763, 114.1715

This bar and restaurant, formerly the Woo Cheong Pawn Shop, is an example of the rapidly-vanishing *tong lau* typology. Such buildings proliferated throughout Hong Kong, Macau, and Southern China from the late 1800s through the 1960s, when they were supplanted by higher-density high-rise apartment blocks. Characterised by ground-floor shops fronted by a covered pedestrian walkway, with residential levels above, the "balcony-style tenement house" was a highly adaptable type (see p. 306, p. 309). The Pawn has been criticised for a heavy-handed, overly-sanitised restoration, but it nonetheless represents Hong Kong's growing preservation movement, and an easily-accessible example of this type. Across the street (plied by historic double-decker trams), note Southorn Playground, one of Wan Chai's few open public spaces.

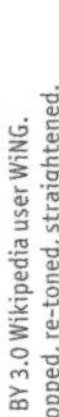

One Wan Chai (Wan Chai Market)

1937/2013

HK 28

灣仔街市，灣仔皇后大道東264號
264 Queen's Road East, Wan Chai
❖ 22.2745, 114.1737

Previously a thriving wet market, this Streamline-Morderne hall demonstrated the period's abundant enthusiasm for both speed and dynamism. Threatened with demolition, it became a touchstone for preservation advocates, and the market façade has since been incorporated into a high-rise development.

Blue House

1920s

HK 29

藍屋
灣仔石水渠街72 – 74A
72–74A Stone Nullah Lane, Wan Chai
❖ 22.2739, 114.1741

Blue House is one of the last few balcony-type *tong lau* tenements in Hong Kong (see **The Pawn**, above). While most *tong lau* feature a ground level arcade below deep upper-level balconies, here the delicate balconies project only slightly over the sidewalk. Inside is the Wan Chai Livelihood Museum, organiser of local heritage walks.

Hysan Place

HK 35

Kohn Pedersen Fox (KPF), Dennis LAU & NG Chun Man Architects and Engineers, Benoy (retail), 2012

希慎廣場，銅鑼灣軒尼詩道500號
500 Hennessy Road, Causeway Bay
❖ 22.2798, 114.1838

Plan courtesy Kohn Pedersen Fox Associates (KPF); photograph by Grischa Ruschendorf, courtesy KPF

This 36-storey mixed-use retail and office complex embraces Hong Kong's urban character as a three-dimensional matrix. The tower massing is broken into several large volumes that shift and stack to create garden terraces. These are accessible via escalators that carve through the retail podium, leaving a visible trace on the façade and emphasising the possibility of vertical circulation. At the sky-gardens, large cuts through the building volume frame views of the surrounding Causeway Bay context, and allow breezes to pass through, aiding natural ventilation. At the base, large voids open to the street and encourage entry. Sustainability was a major concern for the architects, and the building was successfully pre-certified for LEED Platinum status, Hong Kong's first.

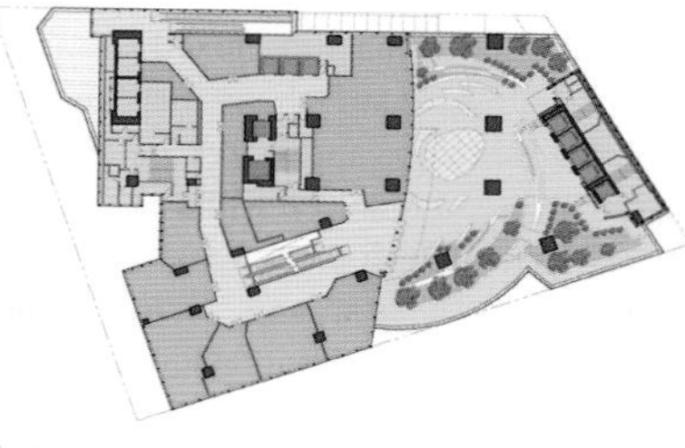

Plan

HK Cultural Centre

HK 36

Architectural Services Department of Hong Kong, 1989

香港文化中心
九龍尖沙咀梳士巴利道10號
10 Salisbury Road, Kowloon, Tsim Sha Tsui
❖ 22.2938, 114.1705

With a swooping "ski jump" roof-line concealing the fly-towers of two performance halls, this concert venue is a distinctive presence on the Kowloon waterfront. The site was formerly home to the Canton-Kowloon railway terminus, which closed in 1974 and was ultimately replaced with this complex, intended to position Hong Kong as a world-class cultural destination. The train station's preserved clock tower anchors the pleasant waterfront plaza, which is in turn framed by the curving edge of the Cultural Centre and the "Avenue of Stars" celebrating Hong Kong's film industry. The Space Museum (Joseph Ming Gun LEE/HK Public Works Department, 1977–1980) is notable for its giant hemispherical dome. Today, the **West Kowloon Cultural District** project (map p. 368), makes a similar "cultural" bid at an enlarged scale, while this park is, in turn, presently undergoing extensions by James CORNER Field Operations.

Chungking Mansions

1961

HK 39

重庆大厦，弥敦道36－44号，尖沙咀
36–44 Nathan Road, Tsim Sha Tsui
❖ 22.2964, 114.1725

Originally built for the well-to-do, today this utilitarian, seventeen-storey building is perhaps the ultimate in "mixed-use." The lower levels contain cheap restaurants, electronics shops, and wares of dubious provenance and legality, while the towers above are home to dozens of guest-houses, hostels, apartments, and various small businesses. A diverse population of African and Asian immigrants, and European backpackers seeking the thrill of Hong Kong's famous density, live in claustrophobic conditions. Gordon MATHEWS's *Ghetto at the Centre of the World* (2011) reports that up to twenty percent of Sub-Saharan Africa's mobile phones passed through Chungking Mansions at some point between manufacture and end use; this architecturally unremarkable building is thus, in a sense, a hub of global trade. Mirador Mansions, just north on Nathan Road, is similar in all aspects.

Nacasa & Partners, courtesy Kohn Pedersen Fox Associates

International Commerce Centre

Kohn Pedersen Fox (KPF), 2010

HK 41

環球貿易廣場，柯士甸道西1号，九龙西
1 Austin Road West, West Kowloon
❖ 22.3033, 114.1601

Hong Kong's tallest tower, and the seventh tallest in the world at 484 metres, it was originally intended to be nearly 100 metres taller, but was scaled back so as not to surpass the surrounding hills. The tower is split between office space and the Ritz-Carlton hotel, with a retail base where the tower connects to the Kowloon MTR station and the full-block Union Square development.

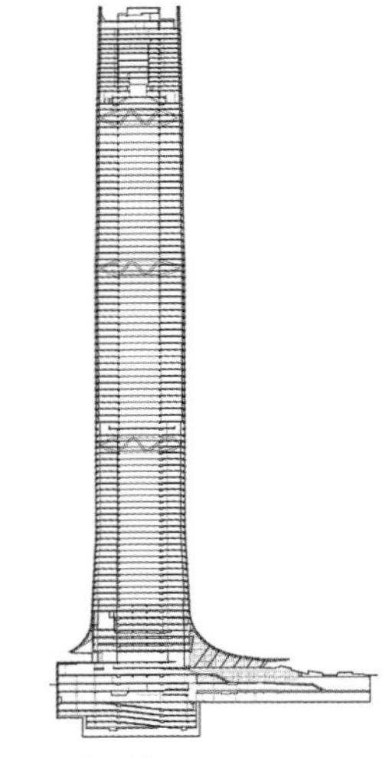

Section

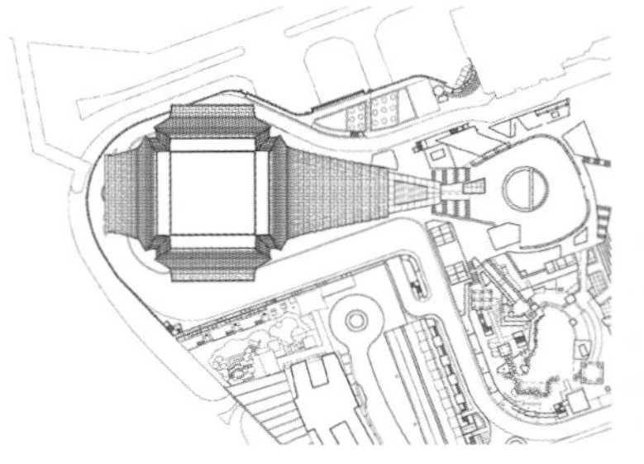

Roof plan

All drawings courtesy Kohn Pedersen Fox Associates

Courtesy the Jerde Partnership

Langham Place

HK 43

Jerde Partnership (Jon JERDE), 2005

朗豪坊，九龍旺角砵蘭街8號
8 Argyle Street, Mong Kok
❖ 22.3186, 114.1686

This two-block mixed-use structure, a monument to commerce, houses offices, hotels, restaurants, a cinema, and probably karaoke; it also has underground connections to the nearby Mong Kok MTR station. Where the fifteen-storey "vertical mall" shines is in its choreography of retail shopping as a delightful, and sales-driving, promenade. Drawn a few levels above street level, via a series of short escalators, visitors are thrust into a massive, nine-storey atrium, centred around two huge, free-standing escalators (or "expresscalators"). The temptation of this aerial journey inevitably delivers shoppers to the top of the upper "spiral" – effectively a retail street curled in on itself, descending by a few steps every bay. This creates a continuous shopping experience, which few visitors are likely to complete without passing every single store-front, though naturally, elevators and exit stairs let savvy shoppers bypass the spiral. The project was somewhat controversial, as a massive intervention in one of Hong Kong's "traditional" neighbourhoods, and a contrast with the context (small alleyway eateries and huge street markets) is apparent.

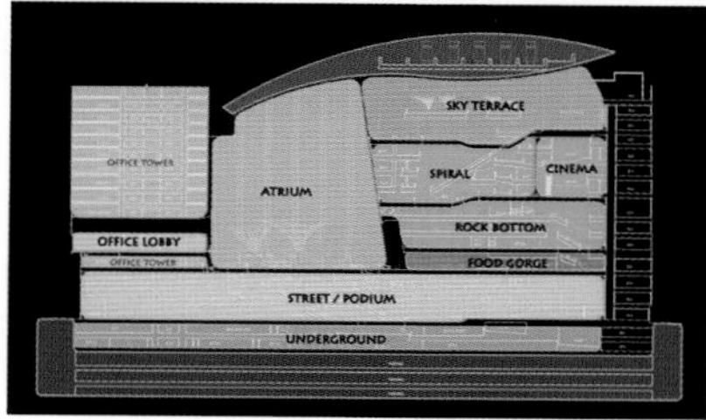

Section

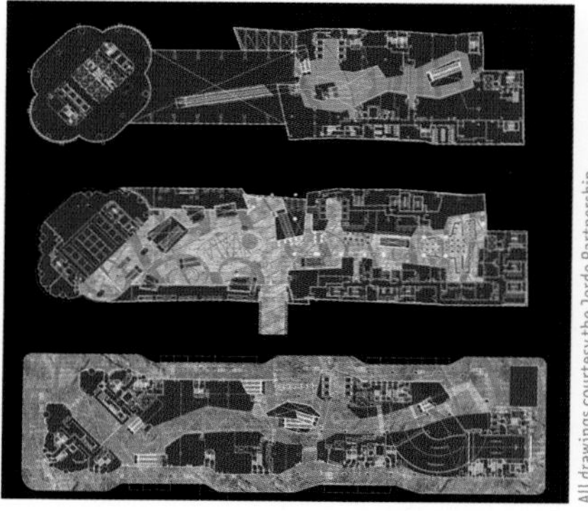

Plans, top to bottom: Level 7, Level 4, Level 1

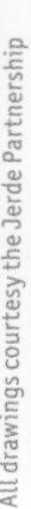

All drawings courtesy the Jerde Partnership

Jockey Club Innovation Tower

HK 45

Zaha HADID Architects, 2013

赛马会创新楼，香港理工大學
Hong Kong Polytechnic University, Kowloon
❖ 22.3052, 114.1791

Three decades after HADID's proposal for Victoria Peak helped cement her reputation, the architect completed her first built structure in Hong Kong. The form of the tower is said to derive from a merging of podium and tower into a single, fluid form, as a commentary on the dominant tower-and-podium typology. The building houses the Polytechnic University's School of Design, encompassing the environmental design, industrial and product design, visual communications, and digital design departments in one facility. (The name refers to the Hong Kong Jockey Club, the major donor.)

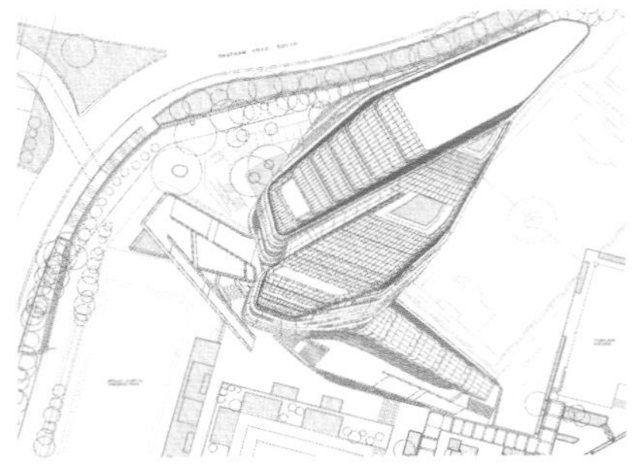

Roof plan

Section

Ho Man Tin Estate

HK 47

1972/2000

何文田邨
九龙城区何文田常富街旁
Quarry Hill, Kowloon City District
❖ 22.31537, 114.18253

Representative of more recent public housing developments, this compound consists of a number of towers of "H" or "+" configuration, connected by walkways and shopping arcades at the base. These connections are more elaborate than those found at earlier estates like **Choi Hung** (map p. 368), and seem inspired as much by speculative Brutalist schemes as by the pragmatic pedestrian walkways of Hong Kong Island. A narrow plan and modulated façade aid lighting and views.

Run Run Shaw Media Centre

HK 49

Studio Daniel LIBESKIND, 2012

邵逸夫創意媒體中心
香港城市大學，九龍塘达康路18號
18 Tat Hong Avenue, Kowloon Tong
❖ 22.3401, 114.1685

This classroom building houses the City University of Hong Kong's Computer Engineering and Media Technology departments. Various classrooms, theatres, and recording studios are housed in a faceted volume, sliced by strip windows in the architects' signature style. The interiors are detailed to match.

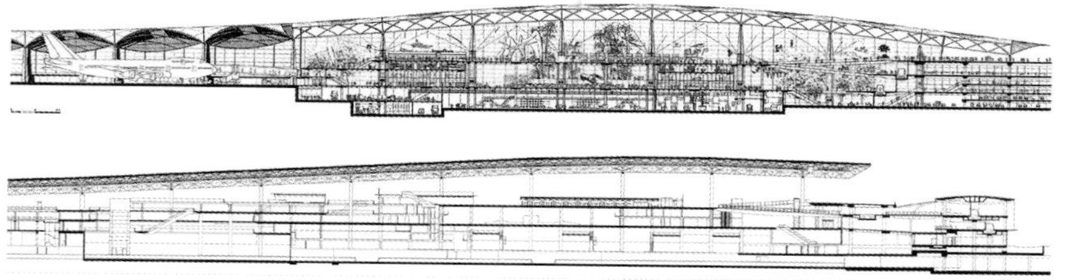

Sections

Chek Lap Kok Airport

Foster + Partners (Norman FOSTER), 1992–1998

HK 62

香港大嶼山香港國際機場 翔天路1
1 Sky Plaza Road, Lantau Island
❖ 22.3088, 113.9144

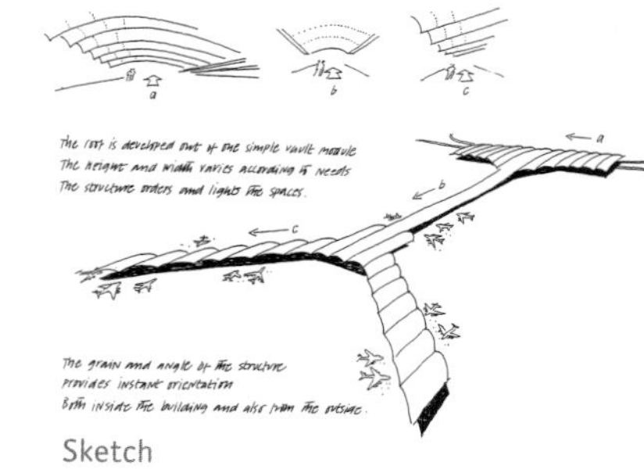

Sketch

Conceived and built during a flurry of infrastructural improvements in the 1990s, the design here solidifies Foster's experiments at Stansted (1981–1991) into a repeatable typology: circulation pathways are separated out in section, with service and arrivals below, allowing the top-level departure zone to take advantage of panoramic views and abundant natural light. Capped with a soaring canopy roof that seems to imply the lightness and freedom of aviation, the basic diagram has become a global standard, from the plan arrangement and section, to the abundance of retail outlets along the departure path, all still in evidence in new designs of nearly twenty years later (see **Shenzhen Bao'an Airport**, p. 333, and **Beijing Capital Airport,** p. 106). In addition to the forward-thinking design, the construction of Chek Lap Kok involved a major land reclamation project, as its site was once a 100-metre island peak, now flattened to seven metres above sea level, and spread over an area the size of Kowloon Peninsula. New road and rail links connected the airport to Hong Kong Island and Kowloon. The airport was home to the world's largest terminal building when first opened, and today remains one of the world's busiest, ranking first in cargo and eleventh in passenger traffic.

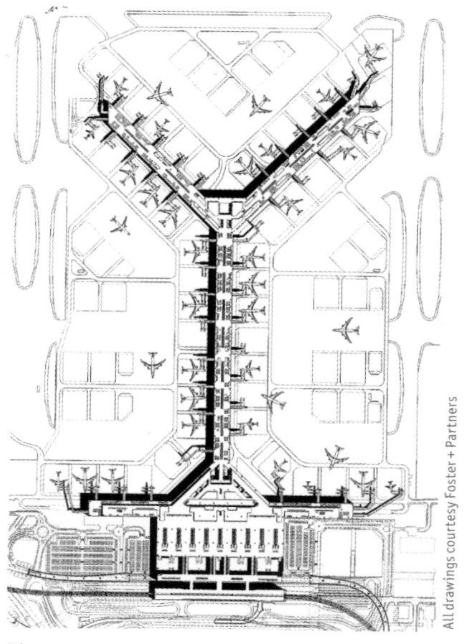

Plan

All drawings courtesy Foster + Partners

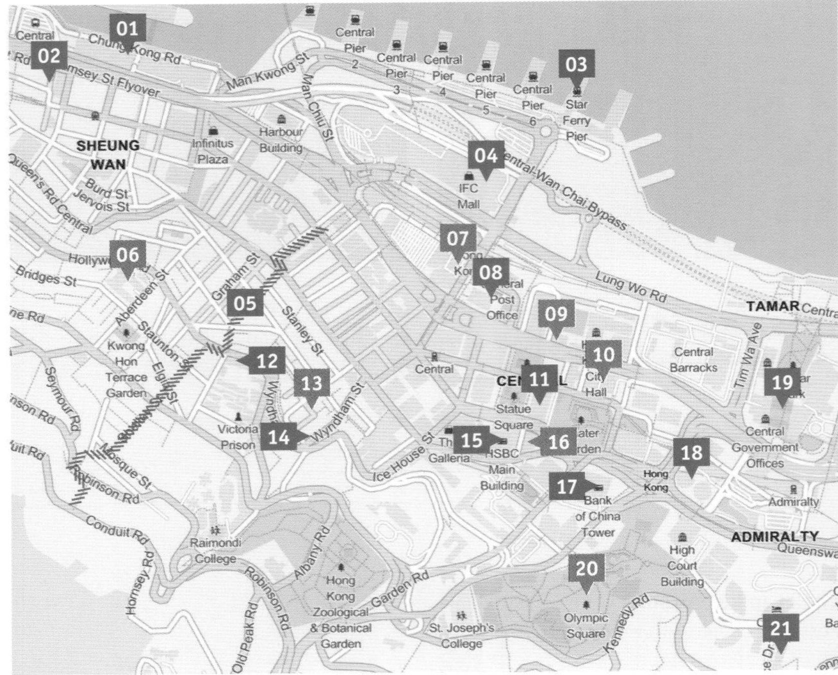

Central & Admiralty (Map 01–21)

01 **Shun Tak Centre** *SPENCE ROBINSON, Ltd., 1983–1986.* ❖ 22.2879, 114.1519

02 **Western Market** *1906/1991.* ❖ 22.2872, 114.1504

03 **Central Star Ferry Pier** *2006.* ❖ 22.2865, 114.1610

04 **International Finance Centre** *Pelli Clarke Pelli (César PELLI), 2003.* ❖ 22.2850, 114.1592

05 **Central-Mid Levels Escalators** *Hong Kong Transport Department, 1987–1993.* ❖ 22.2814, 114.1527

06 **PMQ (Police Married Quarters)** *1951/2013.* Modernist family dormitory, turned arts venue. ❖ 22.2834, 114.1518

07 **Connaught Place** Multi-level pedestrian plaza sandwiched between buildings, and linked to Central's extensive pedestrian circulation network. ❖ 22.2835, 114.1589

08 **Jardine House** *Palmer & Turner, 1970–1974.* ❖ 22.2830, 114.1593

09 **City Hall** *Ron PHILLIPS and Alan FITCH, 1956.* A fine International Style block, with a large public plaza on axis. ❖ 22.2821, 114.1608

10 **AIA Central** *Skidmore, Owings & Merrill (SOM), 2005.* ❖ 22.2813, 114.1618

HK Hong Kong

11 **Legislative Council Building** *Sir Aston WEBB and Ingress BELL, 1912.* ❖ 22.2809, 114.1603

12 **Central Police Station Compound** *1864–1925/2016* ❖ 22.2818, 114.1541

13 **Lan Kwai Fong** A lively expatriate bar district. ❖ 22.2808, 114.1557

14 **Old Dairy Farm Depot** *William DANBY and Robert LEIGH, 1892.* ❖ 22.2801, 114.1557

15 **HSBC** *Foster + Partners (Norman FOSTER, 1979–1986.* ❖ 22.2803, 114.1594

16 **Old Bank of China Building** *PALMER & TURNER , 1952.* ❖ 22.2803, 114.1601

17 **Bank of China** *Pei Cobb Freed & Partners (Ieoh Ming PEI), 1985–1990* ❖ 22.2793, 114.1616

18 **Lippo Centre** *Paul RUDOLPH, 1986–1988.* ❖ 22.2794, 114.1635

19 **HK SAR Government HQ** *Rocco Design Architects, Ltd., 2013.* ❖ 22.2807, 114.1654

20 **Hong Kong Park** *Wong TUNG and Partners, Arup, 1991.* A welcome respite, with sectional interest as it travels uphill, with treetop bridges through a cable-net aviary. ❖ 22.2768, 114.1617

21 **Asia Society Headquarters** *Tod WILLIAMS & Billie TSIEN/TWBTA, 2011.* ❖ 22.2759, 114.1654

22 **Hong Kong Convention and Exhibition Centre** *SOM (Larry OLTMANNS, design partner), 1997/2009*
❖ 22.2834, 114.1731

23 **Central Plaza** *Dennis LAU & NG Chun Man Architects & Engineers, 1992*
❖ 22.2799, 114.1736

24 **Hong Kong Academy for the Performing Arts** *Simon KWAN & Associates, 1985.*
❖ 22.2800, 114.1702

25 **Hong Kong Arts Centre** *Tao HO Design, 1974–1977.* ❖ 22.2802, 114.1708

26 **The Pawn** *1888/2003.*
❖ 22.2763, 114.1715

27 **Hopewell Centre** *Gordon Wu, WMKY Limited, 1980.* Hong Kong's tallest for most of the 1980s; a notable circular-plan tower. ❖ 22.2747, 114.1720

28 **One Wan Chai (Wan Chai Market)** *1937/2013.* ❖ 22.2746, 114.1737

29 **Blue House** *1920s.*
❖ 22.2739, 114.1741

30 **The University of Hong Kong Campus**
❖ 22.2830, 114.1371

31 **Victoria Peak Garden**
❖ 22.2742, 114.1443

32 **Peak Tower** *Terry FARRELL & Partners, 1997.* Prominent bowl-shaped observation tower, upper terminus for the Peak Tram, and tourist-clogged entertainment centre. Great views from the top, or from the surrounding hillside trails.
❖ 22.2711, 114.1500

33 **Aberdeen Country Park** *1931.*
❖ 22.2616, 114.1603

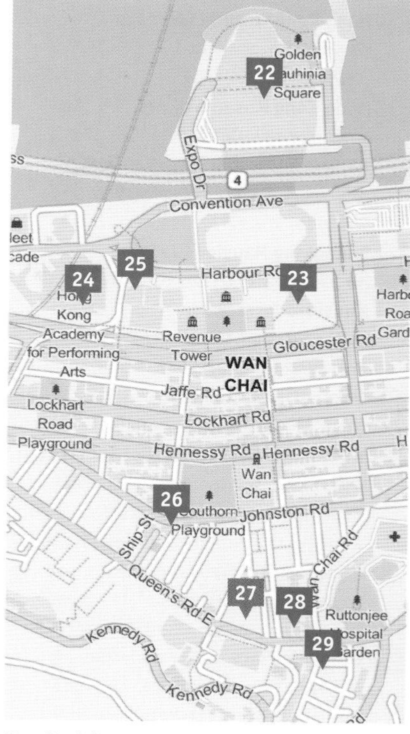

Wan Chai (Map 22–29)

34 **Opus Hong Kong** *Frank GEHRY, 2012.* High-end hillside apartments in a slightly-tilted tower.
❖ 22.2742, 114.1655

35 **Hysan Place** *Kohn Pedersen Fox (KPF), Dennis LAU & NG Chun Man Architects and Engineers, Benoy (retail), 2012*
❖ 22.2798, 114.1838

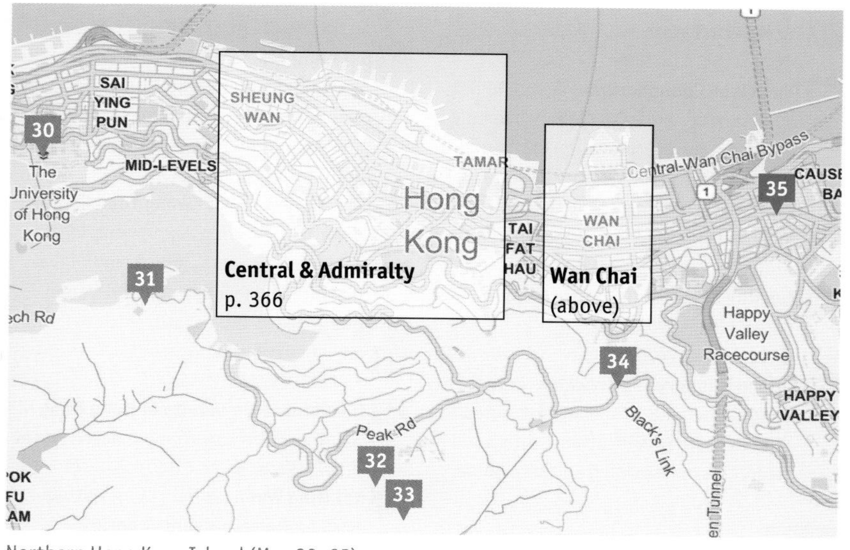

Northern Hong Kong Island (Map 30–35)

36 Hong Kong Cultural Centre *Architectural Services Department, 1989.* ❖ 22.2938, 114.1705

37 Hong Kong Museum of Art *1991.* See entry for #37. ❖ 22.2935, 114.1721

38 HK Space Museum *Joseph Ming Gun LEE/HK Public Works Dept., 1980.* See entry for #37. ❖ 22.2943, 114.1719

39 Chungking Mansions *1961.* ❖ 22.2964, 114.1725

40 Knusford Terrace A lively pedestrian-only street, lined with bars and restaurants. ❖ 22.3013, 114.1746

41 International Commerce Centre *KPF, 2010.* ❖ 22.3034, 114.1602

42 West Kowloon Cultural District (WKCD) *2015–2026 (projected).* A massive development, meant to transform Hong Kong into a world destination for arts and culture. Herzog & de Meuron are set to build the cornerstone "M+" museum, years from now. ❖ 22.3016, 114.1622

43 Langham Place *Jerde Partnership (Jon JERDE), 2005.* ❖ 22.3186, 114.1686

44 Mong Kok Street Markets A bustling district packed with street vendors and food stalls. ❖ 22.3202, 114.1705

45 Jockey Club Innovation Tower *Zaha HADID Architects, 2013.* ❖ 22.3052, 114.1791

46 Poly U Vertical Campus *WANG Weijen, 2009.* "Courtyards" as sectional voids in a high-rise; garden terraces spiral up and provide "activity centres" for each of the shifted classroom blocks. ❖ 22.3036, 114.1850

47 Ho Man Tin Estate *1972/2000* ❖ 22.3154, 114.1825

48 Tsuen Wan Columbarium *Dennis LAU & NG Chun Man, 1987.* Deep, leafy balconies line a stately interpretation of the dense, terraced hillside cemetery (a sight in itself). Unusual sobriety from architects known for their commercial work. ❖ 22.3606, 114.1156

49 Run Run Shaw Media Centre *Studio Daniel LIBESKIND, 2012.* ❖ 22.3401, 114.1685

50 Chi Lin Nunnery *1934/1990.* A large Buddhist temple complex constructed to Tang Dynasty specifications, with wood structures built using traditional joinery techniques and no iron nails. ❖ 22.3407, 114.2054

51 Choi Hung Estate *P&T Group (formerly PALMER & TURNER), 1962.* One of Hong Kong's oldest public housing estates (see introduction, p. 344). Residential slab towers are arrayed around communal courtyards, and linked by shopping arcades. ❖ 22.3355, 114.2062

52 Hong Kong Design Institute *CAAU, 2011.* Heroically suspended mega-box, with a UFO's escalator stylishly enabling entry. ❖ 22.3058, 114.2539

53 One Island East *Hargreaves, 2011.* A landscaped urban plaza that links a residential and commercial tower. ❖ 22.2861, 114.2134

54 Hong Kong Museum of Coastal Defense *1887.* Overlooking the eastern approach to Victoria Harbour, this former British colonial fortress now hosts an exhibit on Hong Kong's historical defensive strategies. ❖ 22.2818, 114.2356

55 The Repulse Bay *KNW Architects & Engineers, 1989.* Curved-plan slab apartment tower, inspired by Miami Art Deco, with a square cut-out for *feng shui.* ❖ 22.2394, 114.1942

56 Murray House *1844/2002.* This former officers' barracks is one of Hong Kong's oldest buildings. The tripartite classical composition features open-air verandas at the upper level, a concession to the local climate. Formerly located where the Bank of China tower (p. 354) now stands, it was dismantled and relocated in the 1980s. ❖ 22.2181, 114.2098

57 Sai Kung This rapidly-gentrifying small town retains some traditional charm, with fishmongers vying for space with boutique shops and galleries. A pleasant day trip. ❖ 22.3823, 114.2744

58 Sha Tin New Town: Kwong Yuen Estate *Hong Kong Housing Department, 1991.* Residential towers sit on a multi-level platform of meandering, landscaped public space and quasi-traditional community buildings. ❖ 22.3812, 114.2151

59 The Chinese University of Hong Kong *W. SZETO and Partners (campus development plan), 1960s.* ❖ 22.4199, 114.2074

60 Kat Hing Wai A walled village dating back to the seventeenth century. ❖ 22.4397, 114.0642

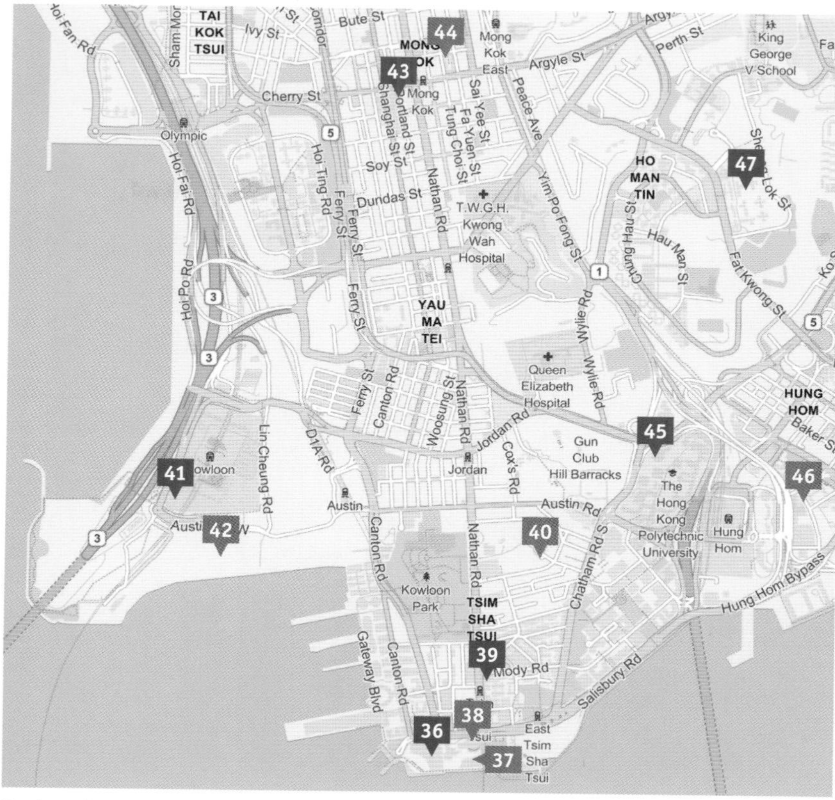

Kowloon (Map 36–47)

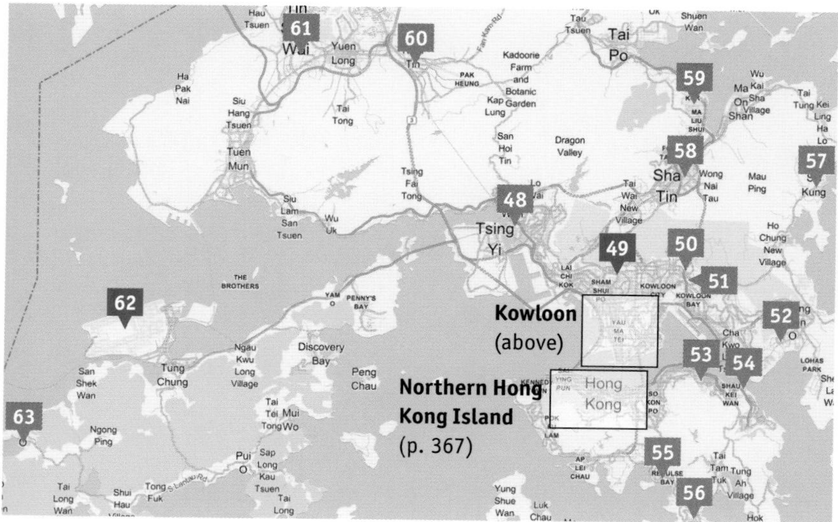

Hong Kong SAR (Map 48–63)

61 Ping Shan Heritage Trail Scenic walk including reconstructed pre-colonial buildings. Tours can be arranged with the Antiquities and Monuments office.
❖ 22.4442, 114.0082

62 Chek Lap Kok Airport *Foster + Partners (Norman FOSTER), 1998.*
❖ 22.3088, 113.9144

63 Tai O A "stilt village" with unique housing built on piles on the water, Tai O has somehow escaped redevelopment.
❖ 22.2569, 113.8577

澳门
Macau

澳门
Macau

Macau (or Macao) is sometimes described as the "Las Vegas of Asia," but it might be more apt to call Las Vegas the Macau of the United States. Macau's thirty-three casinos now take in several times the annual income of Vegas, but its glitzy skyline contrasts sharply with the tangled streets of the UNESCO-protected historic district. Neither seems particularly "Chinese" at a glance. Indeed, Macau's story begins late in China's history, and is bound up in the particular fortunes of the Ming dynasty, faraway Portugal, and East Asia's modern entertainment economy. Despite the rapid pace of change, legacies of the city's origins can be seen everywhere in its streets and its architecture; we recommend taking the ferry ride from Hong Kong and spending a day or more exploring beyond the casino floor.

Macau's transformation from a southern Chinese fishing village to a world destination has its origins in the political transformations of Renaissance Europe. Since the expulsion of Islam from Iberia, the Portuguese had been developing Europe's leading merchant marine, particularly as the fall of Constantinople in 1453 had made older channels of Asian trade inaccessible or prohibitively expensive. Portugal's naval expertise (derived in part from contact with Muslim North Africa) enabled them to begin exploratory and colonial missions around the southern tip of Africa to India. By 1510, the Portuguese were Europe's best-connected traders, with colonies growing in Brazil, Mozambique, Angola, Goa, and Sri Lanka – some of which the Portuguese state retained, through coercion and violence, until the 1970s. Intrigued by Chinese goods (such as porcelain) traded by third parties, the sixteenth-century Portuguese pressed on in search of the "Chijns," who had withdrawn from foreign trade in pursuit of economic and cultural self-sufficiency. Initial attempts to reach Beijing by Jesuit missionaries came to nothing, and several early colonial ventures went completely awry due to reprehensible behaviour on the part of the Portuguese. In this period, a sparsely populated peninsula jutting off the southern coast of Guangdong province, called Ma-Kok, became one of several bases of Portuguese operation. It was conveniently close to the mouth of the Pearl River, but as it was connected to the mainland only by a narrow isthmus, it was relatively easy to defend. The Chinese were justifiably suspicious, but the Portuguese continued in their efforts, and made a good impression by joining the fight against the scourge of Japanese piracy.

Meanwhile, the isolationist policy was turning sour for the Ming economy. China was losing access to certain goods and silver, while smugglers and pirates grew rich. The Portuguese offered themselves as

Previous spread: the **Grand Lisboa** (p. 378) and old Macau, from the **Fortaleza do Monte** (p. 380)

Senado Square (map p. 382)

middlemen for the wider foreign trade, and after much negotiation and several setbacks, the Portuguese were given settlement rights to Ma-Kok ("Macau") in 1557. In the following decades, it survived pirate and Dutch incursions, as well as violent battles with the mainland authorities, to become a boom town. The Portuguese had a monopoly on direct trade with China, in exchange for annual rent, plus tariffs. From the Emperor's perspective, it was probably a win-win situation: the Portuguese were paying taxes to perform the services of getting the silver flowing, taking care of the pirates, and giving Chinese riverboat traders access to the goods of the Indian Ocean and beyond. For the Portuguese, Macau acted as both a trading post and an entry point for missionaries seeking access to mainland China. These efforts were often unsuccessful, but those envoys who did establish themselves in Beijing became important early figures of intellectual and cultural contact between China and Europe. (Consider the Baroque ruins at Beijing's **Old Summer Palace**, p. 094.)

At least some of the trade profit went into the development of Macau itself, which soon enjoyed protective forts, schools, a cathedral, mansions, and Portuguese-style urbanism. On the southern half of the peninsula, encircled by city walls built in the 1620s, narrow streets pulled off of the waterfront (the Praia Grande), widening here and there into *largos* (small squares), with a few major plazas as well. Today, this Portuguese fabric, sometimes heavily reconstructed, is a great part of Macau's tourist appeal. But, as Paula MORAIS has shown, the establishment of these spaces, often adorned with statues symbolising Portuguese military victories over China, was also a way of projecting colonial control on a piece of land with a primarily (later, overwhelmingly) Chinese population.

Macau's fortunes declined sharply in the Qing period (beginning 1644), in part because of the European turn against the influential and wide-reaching Jesuit order. More important, perhaps, was the expansion of European competition, which also prompted the decision by the Japanese to close down their own foreign trade in the hope of protecting their society from Western influence. This inevitably dampened the port activity in Macau. The early Qing years were also a high point of Chinese power, and the first Qing rulers were considerably more able and forceful than the late, bureaucratic Ming. In 1685, China ended the Portuguese monopoly, establishing trade relations with other European countries. Guangzhou became the new sole outlet for European trade, and while Macau remained a centre for business with the rest of East Asia and Oceania, its heyday was over. Even with the general weakening of China's enforcement powers under European pressure, and Portugal's dubious claim that the territory was

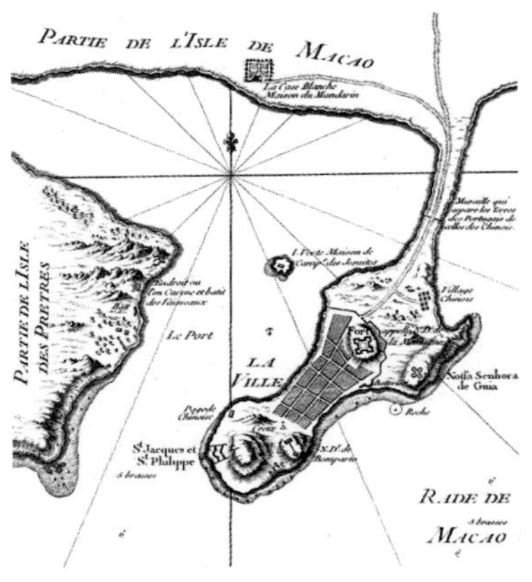

Jacques Nicolas Bellin, *Le Petit Atlas Maritime* (Paris, 1764) Library of Congress, Geography and Map Division, cat. #2002628198. Believed to be in the public domain. Edited.

Macau in 1764

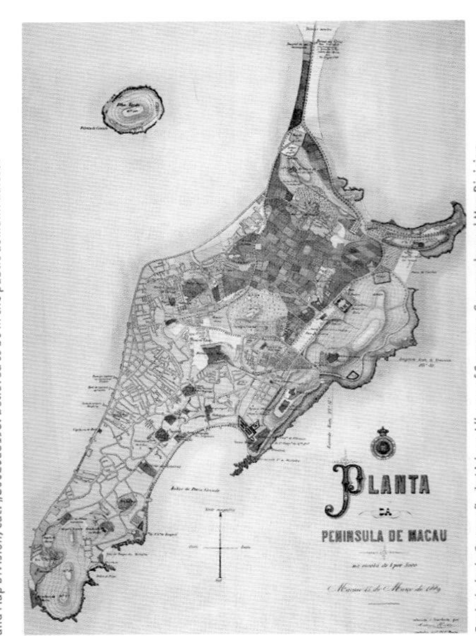

Sociedade de Geografia de Lisboa; Library of Congress, Geography and Map Division,

Macau in 1889

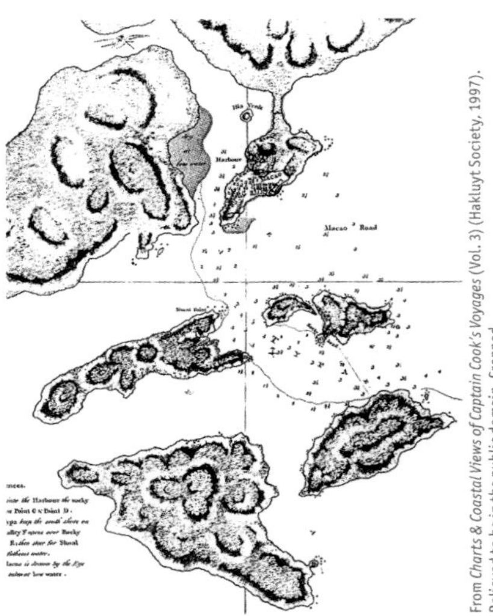

From *Charts & Coastal Views of Captain Cook's Voyages* (Vol. 3) (Hakluyt Society, 1997). Believed to be in the public domain. Cropped.

Macau area, 1785: narrow connection to mainland; separate Taipa and Coloane islands

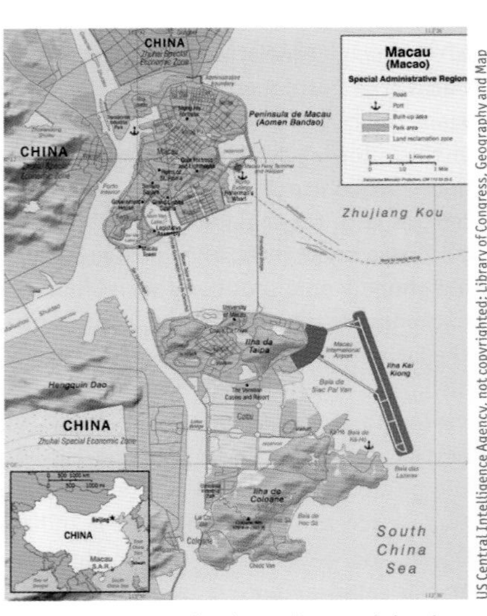

US Central Intelligence Agency, not copyrighted; Library of Congress, Geography and Map

Macau area, 2008: border strip at mainland; Cotai reclamation unites Taipa and Coloane

independent of China (rather than rental property), Macau remained in a slump.

After the nineteenth-century Opium Wars, Portugal's shaky territorial claims would ultimately be ratified by an Unequal Treaty, but Macau remained just one point of contact among many, and its harbour, rapidly silting up, was ill-suited for modern ships, especially with Hong Kong so close by. The first licensed gambling establishments appeared in the mid-nineteenth century, just slightly before the first successful industrial works; the latter necessitated the reclamation of former docklands. Though reclamation of land in Macau goes back to the early colonial days, it would become a key trend particularly after the 1920s, when the new Portuguese republic would finally invest in a major new port area, built on the silt and gravel dredged from the harbour. The clear grid and large scale of this "Porto Exterior," east of the old centre, is still legible against the old, irregular street pattern. The port facilities are gone, along with most of the 1920s boom's buildings, which synthesised local styles and an up-to-date Beaux Arts from Portugal.

As in Hong Kong, the chaos of the 1930s and 1940s brought waves of Chinese refugees to this neutral ground. The new port (finished just before the global Depression) had not brought back the glory days, and gambling, assigned to syndicate monopolies in 1934, grew in significance. In the 1960s, new casino managers brought ferry connections to Hong Kong, and Western games, particularly baccarat (popular in cultures mistrustful of the casino as a player). Macau became a regional tourist hub, with enough seedy glamour to attract even James Bond (in 1974's *The Man With The Golden Gun*), while bridges and further land reclamations expanded the colony onto the neighbouring islands of Taipa and Coloane. Growth in this period doomed much of the 1920s fabric, prompting a preservation movement which has helped Macau's core survive despite today's super-development.

Macau's fate, however, was again the product of political shifts half a world away. Even as the Bond crew headed home, Portugal's dictatorship, staggering from its long, brutal attempt to maintain colonies in Angola and Mozambique, collapsed bloodlessly in the "Carnation Revolution." The new democratic government began to slowly shed the legacy of the Portuguese Empire; Macau's handover was not complete until 1999, when it returned to Chinese administrative control. Like Hong Kong, Macau is now a "Special Administrative Region" with a multi-party elected legislature maintaining the old Portuguese code of law, under a Beijing-appointed executive. Its entertainment economy has benefited tremendously from the opening of the border to the mainland, where most forms of gambling remain illegal, if widespread. As well, the expiry of the syndicate monopolies in 2002 allowed numerous international casino chains to enter the market. The Sands Company, for example, financed the new **Cotai Strip** (p. 381), a pancake-flat reclamation zone uniting the former islands of Taipa and Coloane. Ironically, the world's gambling capital has truly come into its own under Communist leadership. This recent period produced most of Macau's signature, glitzy skyline; as in Vegas, the casino-hotel as a signature form, promising entertainment for the whole family, supplants the sealed, low-rise box.

The "one country, two systems" policy still leaves open one big question: what exactly will happen in 2049, when, according to the prior agreement, Beijing could implement state Communism in Macau? Given China's capitalistic trajectory, it is uncertain whether we would even notice a difference.

Practical Considerations

For the architectural visitor, Macau's interest lies in the close proximity of alternative worlds: traditional and contemporary urbanism, Portuguese colonial space, and the interior fantasy realms of the new casinos. One full day is enough to at least encounter all of these, though two would be better if you really want to explore. If you develop a taste for the famous egg tarts, don't worry: a mediocre facsimile is available at every KFC in China.

Sources and Recommended Reading

Arts of Asia (Jan./Feb. 1986) Spotlight issue on Macau for the fine-arts crowd. Well illustrated, if now a bit dated, with several good introductory articles.

R. D. CREMER, ed., *Macau: City of Commerce and Culture*, Hong Kong: UEA Press, 1987. Various scholarly essays on Macau's political, urban, economic and cultural history.

Tom DANIELL, "Nothing Serious," in *Log* (#27, Spring 2013). A critical focus on Cotai's development, with a look back through Macau's history.

Peter HABERZETTL & Roderich PTAK, "Macao and its Harbour: Projects Planned and Realised (1883–1927)," in *Bulletin de l'Ecole française d'Extrême-Orient* (#78, 1991). Silt, money and diplomacy.

Paula MORAIS, "The Politics of Space Prouction: the Case of Macau," in *Explorations in Urban Design* in Matthew CARMONA, ed., Farnham: Ashgate, 2014. On the projection of colonial power through spatial planning.

C. X. George WEI, ed., *Macao: The Formation of a Global City*, London: Routledge, 2014. Up-to-date scholarly essays on a range of topics from the pre-colonial period to the present day.

Portuguese School of Macau

MC 01

Raúl CHORÃO RAMALHO, 1963

澳門葡文學校，澳門殷皇子大馬路
Avenida do Infante D. Henrique
❖ 22.1912, 113.5429

Originally the Escola Comercial Pedro Nolasco, and now known as the Escola Portuguesa de Macau (EPM), this private high school is focused on a Portuguese educational curriculum. The architect deploys a regionally-inflected Modernism typical for the period (compare to Edward Durell STONE): at the street edge, visitors are greeted by a low-rise, rough concrete frame, filled in with panels clad in Portuguese *azulejo* tilework. This low bar proves to be one of several arrayed across the site, connected by a taller three-storey linkage perpendicular to the major road. In a sense, the design serves the same purpose as the façade of **St Paul's** (opposite) or the European Neoclassicism of the historic city centre: all are stylistic imports with no reference to any native local culture; these architectural imports projected and reinforced the power of the dominant colonial occupiers. Today, the building is at perpetual risk of demolition, but the recent addition of an award-winning reading room, (Rui LEÃO and Carlota BRUNI, 2012) makes a case for preservation in rapidly-changing Macau.

Grand Lisboa Hotel

MC 02

Dennis LAU & NG Chun Man Architects & Engineers, 2008

澳门新葡京酒店
新口岸南湾区交界葡京路2 - 4号
2–4 Avenida de Lisboa, Macau
❖ 22.1906, 113.5430

The tallest building-proper in Macau at 48 floors above grade and 258 metres (somewhat short of the 338-metre **Macau Tower**, p. 381), this golden monument was designed at the height of Macau's recent resurgence, and completed amidst the first rumblings of the global financial crisis. The tower is an unapologetic, ostentatious celebration of profit, whose conflation of floral and showbiz motifs – alternately a "lotus blossom" and a showgirl headdress – could well be read as an index of Macau's rise as a world casino destination. While most new casinos lie on the **Cotai Strip** (p. 381), the **Grand Lisboa**'s prominent location near Macau's old waterfront draws it into a discussion on preservation, as casinos and hotels continue to encroach on the historic centre.

Ruins of St. Paul's Cathedral

MC 09

Carlo SPINOLA, 1582–1627; Fernando António BAPTISTA PEREIRA, et al., 1990–1996

大三巴牌坊
Calçada de S.Paulo/Rua de São Paulo
❖ 22.1975, 113.5405

Perhaps the city's most famous landmark, this intricately-carved façade is all that remains of this early outpost of Catholicism in Asia. The sculptural programme augments Jesuit imagery with Chinese inscriptions, tying Biblical tales to local religious traditions with typical missionary zeal. The building was destroyed by fire during an 1835 typhoon; the façade stands almost like a ghost of the former Portuguese colonial presence. It also works urbanistically, as a Baroque stage backdrop defining one edge of the adjacent square. This space, and nearby **Senado Square** (map p. 382), provide moments of relief from the narrow alleys of Macau's historic centre. The recent renovation reinforced the ruin with a concrete and steel backing structure, incorporating a viewing platform. Behind this, a gridded pavement reveals the dimensions of the original structure, and a small viewing gallery abuts the recently-excavated crypt. The adjacent Na Tcha Temple (1888) is also worth a look.

Fortaleza do Monte/ Museu de Macau MC 10

Anonymous, 1617–1626/ Carlos MORENO & Carlos BARACHO, 1995–1998

大炮台 / 澳門博物館 – Monte Hill
❖ 22.1971, 113.5424

In the last years of Portuguese occupation, the main colonial fortress, once intended to prevent Chinese insurrection as much as European competition, was hollowed out and re-filled with a new museum. Replete with the usual dioramas of the colony's history, the museum is a pleasant little surprise: unpretentious, but with a bit of sectional interest drawing visitors up to the hilltop garden and Macau's best views.

Casino Oceanus MC 15

Paul STEELMAN, 2009

海立方娱乐场
1470 做马路罗理基博士
1470 Avenida do Dr. Rodrigo Rodrigues
❖ 22.1971,113.5559

A theme casino with an unusually contemporary angle, the Oceanus takes its inspiration from Beijing's **National Swimming Centre** (p. 097). As impersonations go, it's a good one; the bubbled façade mimics the dynamic lighting effects as well as the patterning of the original, though of course it's skin-deep here. There is no hotel, but a prominent location near the ferry terminal ensures a steady stream of gamblers.

Macao Science Centre MC 17

Pei Partnership Architects with I. M. Pei Architect, 2006–2009

澳門科學館 – 澳門孫逸仙大馬路
Avenida Dr. Sun Yat-Sen
❖ 22.1861, 113.5567

Photo by Kristopher Grunert;

This waterfront science museum, near the Hong Kong ferry terminal, is one of the first and most prominent cultural venues to open in Macau since the handover to China. Like Pei's **Rock and Roll Hall of Fame** (Cleveland, 1995), the massing is a collection of platonic forms articulating different functions. Here, the dominant one is a truncated, aluminium-clad cone, housing a large atrium and circulation pathways that connect the various galleries. An elevated observation deck affords a 360-degree view of the city and the water.

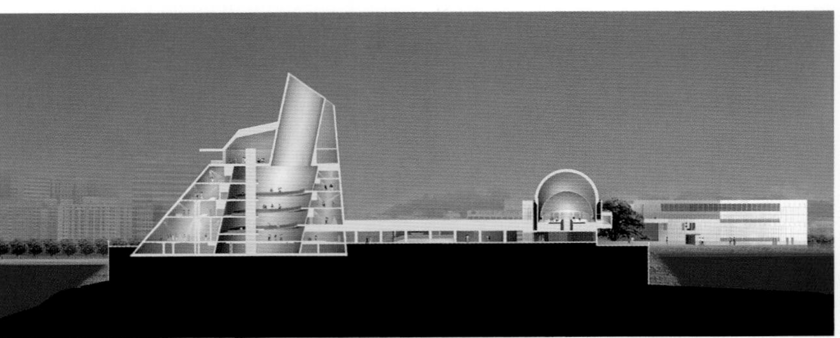

Site section

Courtesy Pei Partnership Architects

Macau Tower

MC 18

Gordon MOLLER, 1998–2001

澳門旅遊塔會展娛樂中心
观光塔澳门
Largo da Torre de Macau
❖ 22.1797, 113.5366

At 338 metres, this observation and telecommunications tower is the tallest structure in the city, and a major presence on the skyline. The upper levels house restaurants, observation decks, a "skywalk" and a bungee-jump facility. At the base, theatres and a shopping mall fill out the programme. Completed soon after the handover to China, the tower is an early indicator of Macau's role as a luxury playground for the PRC.

The Venetian Macau

MC 22

Aedas and HKS, Inc, 2007

澳門威尼斯人度假村酒店
望德聖母灣大馬路, 路氹金光大道
Estrado de Istmo, Cotai
❖ 22.1470, 113.5598

Significantly larger than its Las Vegas predecessor, this hotel, retail and casino complex was among the world's ten largest buildings at the time of completion, and remains inconceivably huge with 980,000 square metres of enclosed floor space. A study in simulacra, the building's exterior is a beguiling collage of Venice's most famous monuments, at nearly full scale. Purposefully, and perfectly, disconnected from the outside world, the interior is an endless sea of gaming tables, meeting rooms and entertainment venues, bookended by the attached hotels' lobbies. A clear highlight is the retail level: a network of crystal-clear canals, plied by costumed gondoliers, one tall storey above ground, with replicated *palazzo* façades and dynamic digital "sky." First-rate kitsch.

Cotai Strip

2002+

路氹連貫公路
❖ 22.1405, 113.5630

Macau's newest district and the new heart of the city's gaming industry, the Cotai Strip was built on reclaimed land between the former islands of Taipa and Coloane. The development expanded rapidly, from a small causeway between the islands to the zone of mega-scale casino-hotel compounds we see today. The scheme – sold as a housing and university district – was led by the Las Vegas Sands Corporation, in cooperation with the Macau government, and became home to a number of Sands properties, most designed by Aedas.

Central Macau (Map 01–11)

01 Portuguese School of Macau *Raúl Chorão RAMALHO, 1963.* ❖ 22.1912, 113.5429

02 Grand Lisboa Hotel *Dennis LAU & NG Chun MAN Architects & Engineers, 2008.* ❖ 22.1906, 113.5430

03 Macau Government Headquarters *Tomás de AQUINO, 1849.* Portuguese colonial *pombaline* style, with a large garden. ❖ 22.1899, 113.5381

04 Casa da Cheang *1869.* ❖ 22.1886, 113.5344

05 St. Joseph's Seminary & Church *1746–1758.* Portuguese Baroque, wilting into a somewhat bland Neo-Classicism. ❖ 22.1917, 113.5373

06 Dom Pedro V Theatre *1860.* Neo-Classical theatre. ❖ 22.1918, 113.5382

07 Senado Square (Senate Square) Macau's historic centre: a UNESCO World Heritage Site with European colonial architecture and "wave"-patterned tile ground. ❖ 22.1918, 113.5382

08 Ponte 16 *Jerde Partnership (Jon JERDE), 2008.* Old port site, now a Postmodern-Colonial casino, with ambitions of plugging into the "warren" of old city streets. The drawings imagined something a bit more plaza-like, but casino real estate and tourist-friendly exhibits seem to have squeezed this out. ❖ 22.1973, 113.5361

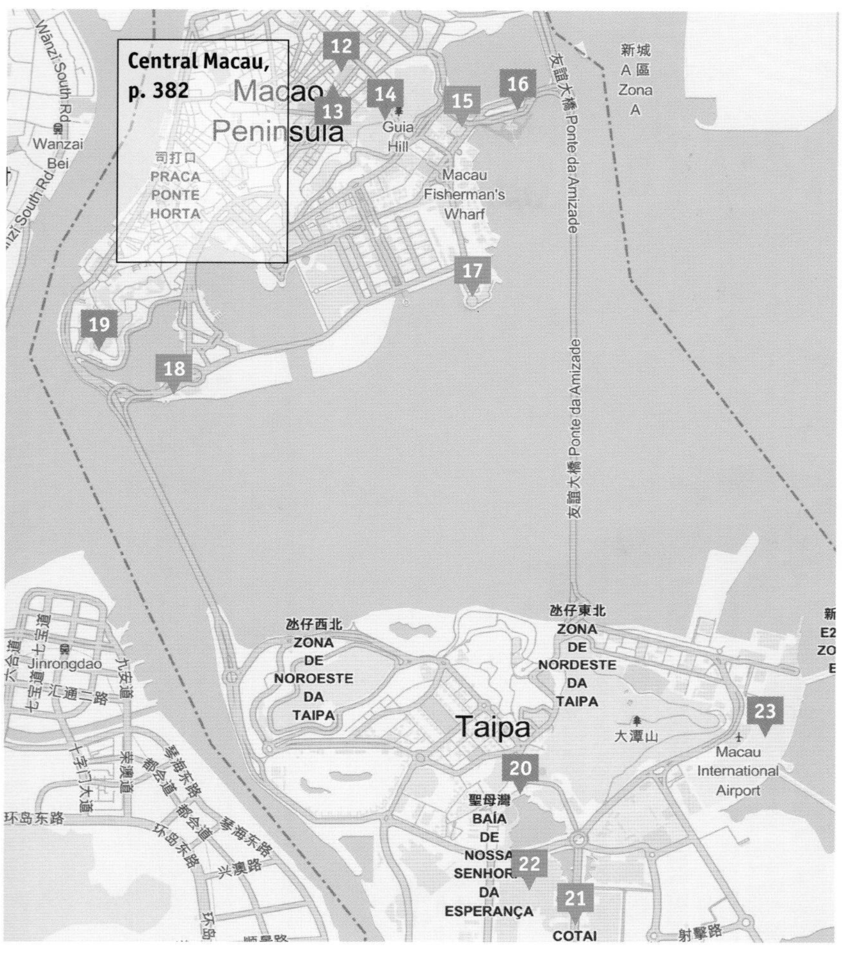

Macau SAR (Map 12–23)

09 Ruins of St. Paul's Cathedral *Carlo SPINOLA, 1582–1627; Fernando António BAPTISTA PEREIRA, et al., 1990–1996.* ❖ 22.1975, 113.5405

10 Fortaleza do Monte/Museu de Macau *Anonymous, 1617–1626/Carlos MORENO & Carlos BARACHO, 1995–1998.* ❖ 22.1971, 113.5424

11 Jardim de Luís de Camões Urban park, with hilltop view. ❖ 22.2014, 113.5400

12 Lou Lim-Leok Garden *1906.* Copy of a Suzhou garden, wrecked by use as a school in the 50s, restored in the 70s. Not bad for Macau. ❖ 22.2006, 113.5477

13 Avenida Conselheiro Ferreiro de Almeida Row of colourful twentieth-century colonial buildings, restored as government offices. ❖ 22.1990, 113.5473

14 Guia Lighthouse & Fortress *1638/1865.* UNESCO-listed; Macau's highest point. ❖ 22.1965, 113.5498

15 Casino Oceanus *Paul STEELMAN, 2009.* ❖ 22.1971,113.5559

16 Macau Ferry Terminal Your likely arrival point. ❖ 22.1981, 113.5595

17 Macao Science Centre *Pei Partnership Architects with I.M. PEI Architect, 2006–2009.* ❖ 22.1861, 113.5567

18 Macau Tower *Gordon MOLLER, 2001.* ❖ 22.1797, 113.5367

19 Pousada de São Tiago (Fortaleza de Barra) *1629, 1980s.* Historic fort, turned five-star hotel. Worth a peek for what's preserved. ❖ 22.1828, 113.5309

20 Taipa Houses Museum *ca. 1920.* Colonial houses, with period furnishings. ❖ 22.1539, 113.5600

21 Cotai Strip *2002.* ❖ 22.1405, 113.5630

22 The Venetian Macau *Aedas and HKS Inc, 2007.* ❖ 22.1470, 113.5598

23 Macau Airport ❖ 22.1578, 113.5764

参考
Reference

其他城市 Other Cities

The preceding chapters are, of course, by no means a complete record of modern and contemporary architecture in China. As a supplement, we have also assembled short descriptions and maps for cities which today may seem further afield for the first-time visitor. All will surely become more accessible – and more densely populated with contemporary architecture – over the next few years, as China's economy continues to shift from agrarian, to industrial, to post-industrial creative industries, on a roughly east-to-west trajectory.

Xiamen (formerly Amoy) was originally a Ming-dynasty garrison town, and an early stop for Portuguese traders. The city was one of the first Treaty Ports opened to Europe in the 1840s and, similarly, one of the first four Special Economic Zones in the 1980s. Though home to a growing collection of contemporary buildings, and some scenic historic urban fabric on pedestrian-only Gulanyu Island (the former British Concession), the city is perhaps more interesting as a base from which to visit the famous clusters of *tulou* communal dwellings scattered in the hilly countryside to the west. These rammed-earth structures are closely associated with the Hakka people, who speak a distinct dialect of Chinese and are thought to have migrated from central China centuries ago. The *tulou*, usually square or circular, are sometimes concatenated into larger complexes, and provided thermal insulation and shelter from bandits and earthquakes. Some are as old as the fourteenth century (possibly a time of major Hakka migrations) but they continued to be built into the twentieth. To see several clusters, take the 45-minute train ride to Longyan and hire a car; for just one visit, it may be more efficient to find transportation directly from Xiamen.

Gulanyu Island (鼓浪屿). This pleasant pedestrian-only island was once home to Xiamen's International Settlement, a legacy evident in the numerous Victorian mansions in various states of repair. ❖ 24.4475, 118.0627

Shapowei Art Zone Refrigeration Plant Renovation *WANG Zhenfei, 2013–2014.* Interior and exterior attempts at reinvigoration. ❖ 24.440232, 118.0827

Gaobei *tulou* cluster, near Xiamen (exterior)

Gaobei *tulou* cluster, near Xiamen (interior)

Previous spread: Typical high-rise apartments under construction in Datong, 2013

Saint Sophia Cathedral, Harbin

A view down a major street in Pingyao

Dalian International Conference Centre

Inside the Wang Family Compound, Pingyao

Tianluokeng Area (田螺坑土楼群) Tourist entry point; the surrounding valleys are rife with *tulou*. ❖ 24.5903, 117.0602. The Gaobei Cluster (高北土樓群), pictured, is a little further northwest, at ❖ 24.6638, 117.0026.

Bridge School *LI Xiadong Atelier, 2008–2009*. A community centre in a zig-zag bridge, connecting two of a village's several *tulou*. ❖ 24.2932, 117.0738.

Dalian was sparsely populated until the Russians constructed a modern port here in 1898, marking the endpoint of the Trans-Siberian Railway. The city fell into Japanese hands following the Russo-Japanese war (1904–1905), but construction largely followed Russian-imposed Beaux-Arts urban planning techniques, with traffic circles and public plazas connected by axial boulevards (see plan, p. 019).

International Conference Centre *Coop Himmelb(l)au 2012*. A tortured "parametric" wedge twists on the waterfront. ❖ 38.9282, 121.6682

Maritime Museum of Art *Urbanus, 2008*. An "artificial hill" and a folded-up boardwalk frame views of art and the waterfront beyond. ❖ 39.0305,121.7508

Starwood Hotel A heroically pumped-up Bavarian castle, for kitsch collectors. ❖ 38.8777, 121.5911

Xinghai Square Actually an oval, and over a million square metres: the world's largest plaza? ❖ 38.9114, 121.6122

Pingyao is an extraordinarily well-preserved traditional Han Chinese city, founded in the fourteenth century, and a centre for banking and finance through the late Qing era. Most structures within the old city walls date to the Ming or Qing Dynasty. (See discussion of urban planning in Beijing introduction, p. 064).

Pingyao City Wall (North Gate) *1370*. ❖ 37.2098, 112.1754

Pingyao City Tower The tallest structure in town (18 m), on a traditional shop street. ❖ 37.2035, 112.1792

Qiao Family Compound *1756+*. Courtyards, raised "Red Lantern." ❖ 37.4060, 112.4295

Wang Family Compound *1762–1820*. Huge hillside courtyard complex, 50 km from Pingyao. ❖ 36.8958, 111.8666

Harbin was founded by Russia in 1898, as a station on a branch of the Trans-Siberian railway line. Like Dalian, it followed then-current European planning practices; today, it's best known for the annual Ice Festival.

Saint Sophia Cathedral *1907*. Ornate Russian Orthodox church, now a museum and gallery. ❖ 45.7679, 126.6218

Wood Sculpture Museum *MAD, 2009–2013*. An icy, twisted bar of reflective steel; rippled openings light the galleries. ❖ 45.7317, 126.5561

Qunli Park *Turenscape, 2006–2011*. Footbridges criss-cross a water-managing wetland. ❖ 45.7269, 126.5475

Central Chengdu (Map 01–11)

01 MOCA Chengdu *Jiakun Architects (LIU Jiakun), 2011.* Museum capped by a sloped and planted archi-landscape, meant to compensate for the trackless software-park surroundings. Varied but not fussy; see CIPEA (p. 134). ❖ 30.5439, 104.0690

CD Chengdu

02 Contemporary Art Centre *Zaha HADID Architects, 2010+.* An asymmetrical swoop, perhaps to cancel out the behemoth opposite. Under construction. ❖ 30.5718, 104.0699

03 Century Global Centre *2013.* Shopping, entertainment, indoor beach: the world's largest building by floor area. ❖ 30.5717, 104.0619

04 Tianfu Int'l Finance Centre *Paul ANDREU, 2004.* ❖ 30.5846, 104.0643

05 Raffles City (Sliced Porosity Block) *Steven HOLL Architects, 2007–2012.* Cousin of Linked Hybrid (p. 090) – no bridges, but the terraced court flows from the street in a more effectively "public" way. ❖ 30.6337, 104.0660

06 Shuijingfang Museum *Jiakun Architects (LIU Jiakun), 2008–2013.* Distillery. Old and new stitched together with catwalks and taste. ❖ 30.6475, 104.0833

07 Wuhou Shrine *300s/1672.* Temple and memorial complex dedicated to ZHUGE Liang (181–234 CE), Three Kingdoms-period military strategist. Qing dynasty reconstructions. ❖ 30.6481, 104.0450

08 Chengdu City Museum *Sutherland Hussey Architects, 2007.* Pedestrian cuts through the faceted block reduce the scale and provide public access. The patinated bronze façade alludes to the passage of time, and the artefacts within. ❖ 30.6593, 104.0613

09 Green Ram Temple/Qingyang Palace *500s/1670s.* Taoist temple complex that served for a time as an imperial palace. ❖ 30.6602, 104.0413

10 Tomb of Wang Jian Mausoleum of the first Shu emperor (847–918 CE) with unique above-ground burial chamber. ❖ 30.6750, 104.0446

11 Wenshu Monastery *600s/1697.* Buddhist temple compound with extensive grounds. Qing reconstruction. ❖ 30.6736, 104.0743

12 MixC Garden City *Callison, 2012.* Outdoor retail, with Jerde-esque terraces. ❖ 30.6515, 104.1129

13 Jinsha Archaeological Site *c. 1200–650 BCE/2001.* Ruins and artefacts of a major political centre of the ancient Sanxingdui & Jinsha cultures. ❖ 30.6836, 104.0101

14 Sky Courts *HÖWELER + YOON, 2012.* Courtyard houses, deformed

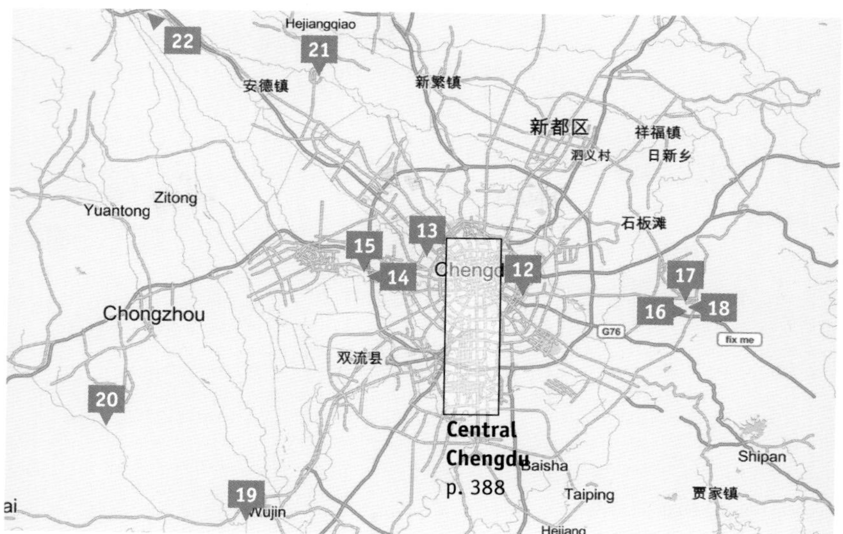

Greater Chengdu (Map 12–22)

and agglomerated into a clubhouse for the Intangible Cultural Heritage Park. ❖ 30.6676, 103.9323

15 Lanxi Curtilage & Tulou Theatre *Archi-Union (Philip F. YUAN), 2011.* Parametric regenerations of traditional architecture. ❖ 30.6691, 103.9302

16 Luodai Tulou *2010s.* Replica of the roundhouses in faraway Fujian (p. 386); Luodai is predominantly Hakka-descended. ❖ 30.6375, 104.3272

17 Luodai Ancient Town Reconstructed and touristy, but scenic nonetheless. ❖ 30.6420, 104.3216

18 Luodai Art Granary *DC Alliance (DONG Yi, CUI Zhe, et al.), 2010–2012.* Post-industrial site, with art spaces in a beehive of hexagons. ❖ 30.6412, 104.3222

19 Xinjin Zhi Museum *KUMA Kengo and Associates, 2008–2010.* Diaphanous façade of suspended, diagonal roof tiles. ❖ 30.4005, 103.8010

20 Jianchuan Museum Cluster *Various architects (FCJZ, Jiakun, et al.), 2000s–2010s.* A history-buff developer presents over a dozen museums, some by major talents. ❖ 30.5033, 103.6184

21 Luyeyuan Stone Carving Museum/Mrgadava Museum *Jiakun Architects (LIU Jiakun), 2001–2002, 2003–2005.* The firm's signature work, beautifully integrated with the landscape. Brick walls were used as concrete formwork to make the most of local expertise. Open irregularly – check website and contact in advance. ❖ 30.8845, 103.8672

22 Epicentre Memorial Hall *South China Univ. Team (HE Jingtang), 2010–2012.* An elemental block, fractured by skylights and gardens, honours the victims of the 2008 earthquake. ❖ 31.0576, 103.4835

Chengdu is the capital of Sichuan province, a major business and transportation hub, and the country's fourth-largest city by population (2010 census). While most tourists will encounter it primarily as a transfer point to regional scenic spots and panda habitats, it has naturally accumulated its share of contemporary architecture. Particular attention should be paid to the work of Jiakun Architects, who have built their reputation primarily on a series of forceful and thoughtfully-detailed projects in the area. Conveniently, several other recent major works are all along the north-south metro line, but you will need a driver to reach peripheral sites, of which the Luyeyuan Museum, Epicentre Memorial Hall (map no. 19), and Jianchuan Museum Cluster (map no. 13) may be the most interesting. The city's history goes back for millennia, as indicated by the region's many archaeological sites, but its fabric has been heavily altered by twentieth-century interventions, as well as the devastating 2008 Wenchuan Earthquake, from which many villages may never recover.

Central Datong (Map 01–09)

01 Huayan Temple Complex *907–1125 CE.* Largest and best-preserved Liao Dynasty monastery and temple complex. The halls face east in a break from typology. ❖ 40.0912, 113.2881

02 Nine Dragon Screen *1271–1368.* Glazed tile "spirit wall" marking the entrance to the long-gone Ming Dynasty palace complex. ❖ 40.0906, 113.2992

03 Shanhua Temple *1100s CE.* Liao Dynasty temple complex, with several restored original halls and several 1950s and 2000s reconstructions. ❖ 40.0824, 113.2919

04 Datong City Wall *2010s.* Recent reconstruction, built amid the city's attempted transition to a service economy and history-focused tourism. One rarely finds steel-framed city walls and a brand-new concrete moat. ❖ 40.0824, 113.2956

05 Yudong New Area Datong Art Museum *Foster + Partners (Norman FOSTER), 2012+ (under construction).* An "erupted landscape": four nested, Cor-Ten pyramids form a thick barrier against the cold winters. ❖ 40.0865, 113.3579

06 Yudong New Area Datong Museum *KAI Cui (with CADREG), 2010+ (under construction).* A snailish, "dragon"-ish form, reportedly inspired by the Yungang Grottoes. ❖ 40.0895, 113.3578

07 Yudong New Area – Datong Grand Theatre *ISOZAKI Arata, 2009+ (under construction).* "Mountains and clouds" are draped over the halls, reminding us also of a steppe nomad's tent, and the grotto-like spaces of the firm's Zendai Himalayas Centre (p. 184). ❖ 40.0895, 113.3618

08 Yudong New Area Library *Preston Scott COHEN, 2009–2013.* Quiet work space and public halls vie parametrically for space around a shared courtyard. ❖ 40.0864, 113.3618

09 Yudong New Area – Sports Centre *Populous, 2010+ (under construction)* . Arenas clad in blobbish titanium shells, again with grotto inspiration. A bit menacing at this scale. ❖ 40.0759, 113.3609

10 Yungang Grottoes Museum *Do Union Architecture, 2011.* Not the old museum at the entrance, but a rippling roofline flowing out of the landscape. Pass the grotto area and head down the wooded path. ❖ 40.1084, 113.1205

11 Yungang Grottoes *465–525 CE.* Spectacular Buddhist cave temples. A UNESCO World Heritage Site and an absolute must-see. ❖ 40.1078, 113.1379

12 Jinhuagong National Mining Park Museum *2012.* An oddly festive take on coal mining, across the valley from the grottoes. ❖ 40.1028, 113.1301

13 Xuankong Temple (Hanging Monastery) *491+ CE.* Small temple complex, perhaps a Ming- or Qing-era reconstruction, grafted onto a sheer cliff, 65 km southeast of Datong. More than worth the trek. ❖ 39.6598, 113.7087

DT Datong

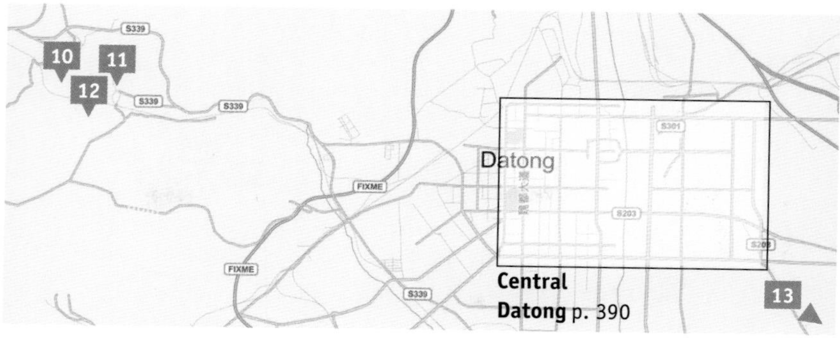

Datong Region (Map 10–13)

Yungang Grottoes

Xuankong Temple

City wall and moat under construction (2013)

A very old caravan stop and later a regional capital, Datong in the twentieth century became a classic Five-Year-Plan coal mining town. It still feels like one, even as it attempts to supplement its mining and heavy-industry sectors with business and tourism. Despite the severe air pollution and the hassles of getting around, it remains popular with tourists as a base for visiting two first-rate sites from its heyday: the Yungang Grottoes, on the city's northwestern periphery, and the "hanging" Xuankong Temple, a longer trek to the southeast. Conventional wisdom is right: these are amazing places, and you should see them before anything else. Of the various means of doing this, we recommend finding some friends and splitting the cost of a driver who will take you to both places in a day; in our experience, other methods are just too stressful or time-consuming. With those checked off, consider some of central Datong's remaining historic sites, and take in the sublime absurdity of the newly-built historic walls. The Yudong New Area (御东新区), a short cab ride east of the centre, was still under construction on our last visit, but looking close to completion; it epitomises Datong's attempted economic transition, with a new central business district anchored to a "cultural plaza" very much akin to **Shenzhen's** (p. 320) or **Guangzhou's** (p. 299). Four signature buildings sit in a Soviet-scaled wasteland, a particularly bad idea considering Datong's rough winters. Note the attempts by some of the architects to model their buildings on some kind of protective, sheltering "grotto."

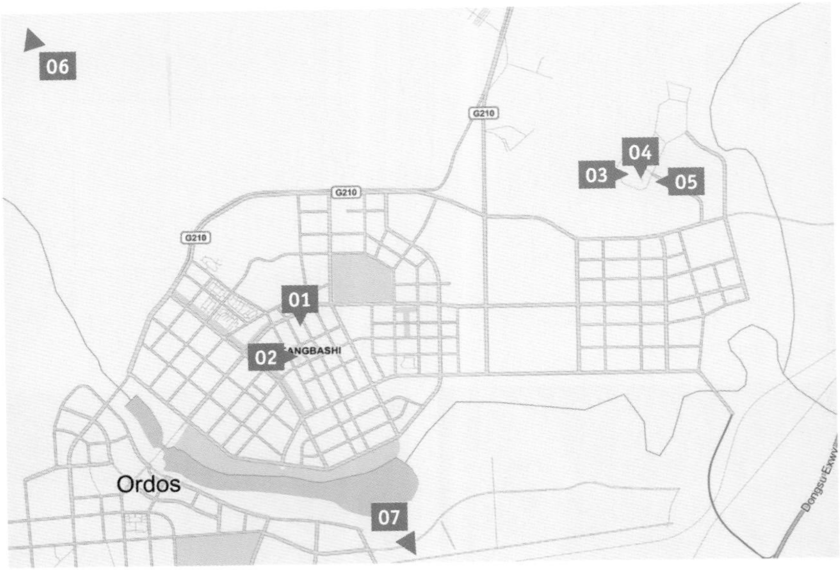

OD Ordos

Ordos (Map 01–07)

01 Genghis Khan Square Centre of the new town proper, and seemingly bigger than the Khan's empire. ❖ 39.6038, 109.7796

02 Ordos Museum *MAD (MA Yansong, et al.), 2005–2011.* An irregular "nucleus" whose shiny surface distorts its over-planned surroundings and contains an ambitious and bizarre organic space. Picking up themes of the Guangzhou Opera (p. 300) on which Ma worked, it's now one of China's highest-profile examples of the type. ❖ 39.6000, 109.7790

03 Ordos 100: Zone E *Various, 2008+.* See below. ❖ 39.6239, 109.8376

04 Art Gallery, Kokoshina Cultural District *DnA Design and Architecture (XU Tiantian), 2005–2007.* Torqued Moebius strip on a hillside, with a nice interior sequence. To the north, the restaurant (by Cannon Design's Yazdani Studio). To the south, studios (by FAKE Design/AI Weiwei), duplicating ones at Caochangdi (p. 102). ❖ 39.6232, 109.8384

05 Ordos Art Hotel *EXH, 2007+.* Distorted hexagons, ostensibly "yurt"-derived. ❖ 39.6229, 109.8407

06 Inner Mongolia Desert Museum *Inner Mongolian Grand Arch. Design 2011.* 160 km northwest of Kangbashi. ❖ 40.3906, 109.4333

07 Ordos Ejin Horo Airport 18 km southeast of Kangbashi. ❖ 39.4988, 109.8609

Ordos, specifically Kangbashi or "New Ordos" (康巴什新区), is a new town for 1,000,000, constructed on the steppe-like Ordos Desert of Inner Mongolia. It lies roughly 750 km west of Beijing, and 30 km southwest of Dongsheng (东胜, now effectively "Old Ordos") where the train station is. It's received a lot of high-handed attention in the West, partly as an exemplar of new Chinese "ghost towns," though it appears to be (very slowly) filling up (and not just with absentee real estate speculators). It was also the site of the "Ordos 100" scheme, wherein AI Weiwei, with Herzog & de Meuron, invited one hundred lucky architects to build one house each, and a handful of public buildings. In hindsight, one suspects that Ai may have been having a bit of a joke: seize the developer's drive to market a string of "unique" designer houses, then watch as the world's architects race to build bizarre fantasies that in the end, all feel somewhat the same. But there may be a more pedestrian explanation for why only the first five villas (exactly whose is hard to say) got built. Ordos is a coal-mining boom town, booms imply busts, and the Chinese credit market isn't what it used to be. Ordos is not convenient, but the very curious archi-traveller (with a lot of extra time) might consider it.

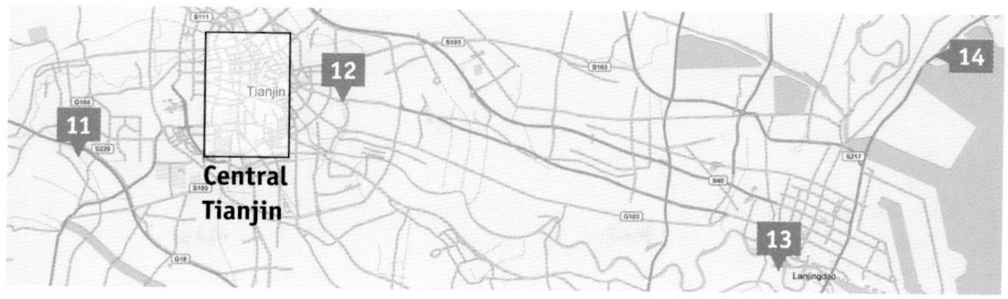

Greater Tianjin (Map 11–14)

01 West Railway Station *GMP, et al., 2007–2011.* A bright and mighty vault. ❖ 39.1572, 117.1570

02 Drum Tower Centre of the recently-destroyed old city. Fake old street, fake Drum Tower, and more obviously contemporary additions to the sides. ❖ 39.1404, 117.1755

03 Former Italian Concession *1901–1947.* Tianjin's concessions spread east and south along the river; all bear some traces of European planning in their layouts. ❖39.1337, 117.1925

04 Global Financial Centre *SOM, 2006–2011.* A pleated tube – slender but articulate. ❖ 39.1281, 117.1964

05 Riverside 66 *KPF, 2014 (anticipated).* Enormous, mixed-use, interior promenade. ❖ 39.1266, 117.1937

06 Tianjin University Sports Arena *KSP Jürgen Engel, 2006–2010.* A rhomboid with perforated-steel double skin. ❖ 39.1126, 117.1717

07 Feng Ji-Cai Arts & Literature Institute *Tianjin Huahui Inst., 2001–2004.* A huge, refreshingly blank volume floats silently over a pool. ❖ 39.1104, 117.1688

08 Culture Park: Art Museum *KSP Jürgen Engel, 2009–2012.* Levels suspended within a carved-out stone cube. ❖ 39.0841, 117.2059

09 Culture Park: Grand Theatre *GMP, 2009–2012.* An "open sea shell" unites major volumes. ❖ 39.0841, 117.2059

10 Culture Park: Library *YAMAMOTO Riken, 2012.* Complex, mezzanine-rich section; suspended bars create differently-scaled spaces. ❖39.0840, 117.2092

11 Zhangjiawo Elementary School *Vector Architects, CCDI, 2008–2010.* Bar with pavilions projected to create interior "mingling space." ❖ 39.0689, 117.0291

TJ Tianjin

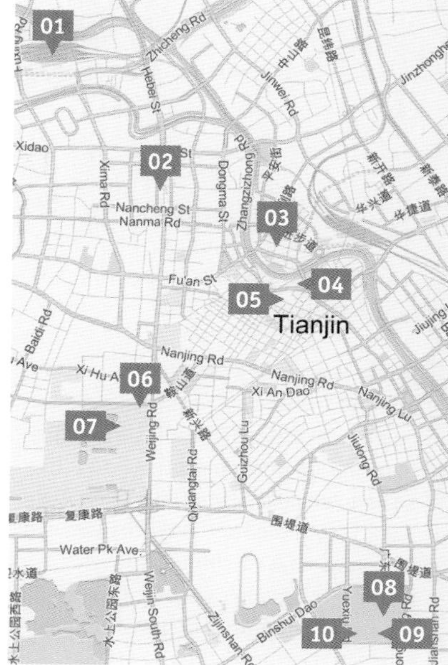

Central Tianjin (Map 01–10)

12 Qiaoyuan Bridge Culture Museum *Sunlay, 2008.* Interior topography of slanted planes, set in a former garbage dump now doing eco-work (Turenscape, 2008). ❖ 39.1175, 117.2682

13 Business District Where tall, frightening things grow apace. ❖ 38.9973, 117.6643

14 Eco-City *In progress.* Green-oriented development, now mud. Steven HOLL's museums (inversions of each other) will be great, someday. ❖ 39.1570, 117.8073

Tianjin (once Tientsin), 30 minutes from Beijing by high-speed rail, is just upriver from the sea. It was a key Treaty Port, with various European concessions, of which the Italian is most intact; others have been redeveloped with new "Italian" buildings. The Qing-era walled city was flattened after 2000 for new high-rises. An industrial and shipping hub for Beijing and the region, the city continues to grow, and the architecture is following.

Xi'an Old City(Map 01–05)

01 Great Mosque of Xi'an *742+ CE.* One of China's most famous mosques, and an indicator of Xi'an's large Muslim population, the complex is laid out like a temple, but arranged on an east-west axis to face the main prayer hall toward Mecca. Chinese architectural styles merge with Islamic ornamentation in a unique synthesis. Current structures date to the Ming or Qing dynasty. ❖ 34.2633, 108.9369

02 Drum Tower (Gu Lou) *1380/1740.* A large drum within would signal the end of the day. Qing era reconstruction in Tang dynasty style, constructed without nails. ❖ 34.2616, 108.9391

03 Bell Tower (Zhong Lou) *1384.* Dead-centre in the old city, the bell signalled the start of the day, and warned of attackers. The tower now sits sadly in a giant traffic circle. ❖ 34.2609, 108.9426

04 City Wall (South Gate) *1370.* Restored and well-maintained Ming Dynasty city walls. ❖ 34.2533, 108.9427

05 Temple of the Eight Immortals (Ba Xian An) *960–1279.* The largest Taoist temple in Xi'an, with current structures dating to the Qing dynasty. ❖ 34.2660, 108.9756

06 Museum of Tang West Market *Xi'an Arch. Univ. (LIU Ke-cheng), 2010.* Pyramidal skylight array; vast glass floor over relics and foundations. ❖ 34.2490, 108.9036

Xi'an

Central Xi'an (Map 06–10)

07 Small Wild Goose Pagoda 652/*709 CE.* Brick, Tang dynasty Buddhist pagoda with 15 tiers. ❖ 34.2407, 108.9376

08 Giant Wild Goose Pagoda *652/704 CE.* Impressive brick Tang dynasty Buddhist pagoda, with extensive repair work done in Ming Dynasty and 1960s. ❖ 34.2197, 108.9597

09 TV & Broadcast Centre (Media City) *MADA s.p.a.m. (Qingyun MA), 2003–2009.* An in-and-out wall unites diverse programme while expressing it, and hinting at Xi'an's ancient heritage. Striking, crystalline atrium *à la* Isozaki's Cultural Centre in Shenzhen (p. 321). ❖ 34.2078, 108.9721

Xi'an Region (Map 11–15)

10 Qin Er Shi (Hu Hai) Mausoleum Museum *Lacime Arch. Design, 2011.* A set of abstract, landscape-scale moves, avoiding overt imperial citations. ❖ 34.1941, 108.9798

11 HanYangLing Underground Museum (Emperor Jingdi) *Xi'an Arch. Univ. (C. Y. LEE), 1999–2006.* Atmospheric museum atop the tomb of Han Emperor Jing. Glass floors over pits reveal thousands of artefacts, and their ongoing excavation. ❖ 34.4451, 108.9444

12 Xi'an 2011 Horticultural Expo *Eva CASTRO/Plasma Studio, Groundlab, et al., 2011.* Master plan, plus various rippling groundscrapers (note the Creativity Museum). ❖ 34.3286, 109.0607

13 Chang'an Tower *ZHANG Jinqiu, 2009–2010.* Horticulture Expo landmark: a neo-pagoda in glass and steel. ❖ 34.3230, 109.0550

14 Emperor Qinshihuang's Mausoleum Museum (Terracotta Warriors) *246 BCE/1979+.* Burial site of the First Emperor, plus protective roof. A UNESCO World Heritage Site, and justifiably one of China's top tourist attractions. ❖ 34.3850, 109.2743

15 Museums at Fuping Pottery Art Village *Xi'an Arch. Univ. (LIU Ke-cheng), 2004–2006.* 60 km north. Back-to-basics brick studies: vaults, domes, light. Worth seeing if you're in town at length. ❖ 34.7724, 109.1747

One of China's oldest cities, with evidence of inhabitation dating back 6,000 years, Xi'an (formerly Chang'an) was China's imperial capital on multiple occasions under the Zhou, Qin, Han, Sui, and Tang Dynasties. It retains much of its historical character, especially within the old city walls. Xi'an marks one terminus of the Silk Road, and its architecture, food and culture show influence from afar, particularly from Central Asia and the Middle East. The Muslim quarter, north of the Drum Tower, is a matrix of lively market streets lined with tourist shops and an incredible variety of food stalls (the lamb *baozi* dumplings are a must). Xi'an's major downtown historical sights can be visited in half a day on foot. For contemporary architecture and the famous tombs, a car and driver are advised.

Xi'an's Muslim Quarter

笔记
Notes

General Sources

In addition to those volumes mentioned in the introductory texts for each city, and in the essays at the front of this book, we recommend the following to those seeking further insight into contemporary issues in Chinese design and urban culture.

Leslie CHANG, *Factory Girls: From Village to City in a Changing China*, New York: Spiegel & Grau, 2008. Documentary non-fiction, following several young women as they navigate the landscape of labour relations in factories (and sites of leisure) of the Pearl River Delta.

Nancy N. CHEN, ed., *China Urban: Ethnographies of Contemporary Culture*, Oxford: Blackwell, 2001. Cultural studies of contemporary urban Chinese life: labour conditions, rock music, the educational system, domesticity, etc.

Jae Ho CHUNG, *Cities in China: Recipes for Economic Development in the Reform Era*, London: Taylor & Francis, 1999. Case studies of cities, post-1949. Economically oriented but full of facts on development strategies, mayors' policies, etc.

Joseph Esherick, ed., *Remaking the Chinese City: Modernity and National Identity, 1900–1950,* Honolulu: University of Hawaii Press, 2000. Solid contemporary scholarship, examining various cities in the often-overlooked late Qing and Republic of China periods.

GUO Qinghua, *Chinese Architecture and Planning: Ideas, Methods, Techniques,* Stuttgart and London: Axel Menges, 2005. Thorough and well illustrated.

Michiel HULSHOF and Daan ROGGEVEEN, *How the City Moved to Mr. Sun,* Pompano Beach, FL: Sun Publishers, 2010. A journalistic examination of the strange conditions and new urban forms that result from China's rapid urbanisation – told through the stories of ordinary people swept up in this rapid change. Readable and enlightening, with a focus on the "third tier" cities that lie outside the scope of this book.

Eduard KÖGEL and Ulf MEYER, eds., *The Chinese City: Between Tradition and Modernity,* Berlin: Jovis, 2000. A dozen short essays exploring various contemporary issues in urban planning, land use, etc.; good for a sense of the issues in play in the 1990s.

Duanfang LU, *Remaking Chinese Urban Form: Modernity, Scarcity and Space, 1949–2005,* London and New York: Routledge, 2006. A journey through Communist economic planning, in spatial and political terms, with a focus on the phenomenon of the *danwei* "work unit."

Paul REUBER, series of travel articles in *Canadian Architect* (1997–2003). Observant architectural snapshots of oft-overlooked buildings, including everyday typologies; source for several images in this book.

Alfred SCHINZ, *The Magic Square: Cities in Ancient China*, Stuttgart: Edition Axel Menges, 1996. A vast study of countless Chinese cities and their symbolic and social orders, and the source for many of the redrawn historic plans reprinted in this book. Schinz's *Cities in China*, Berlin: G. Borntraeger, 1989 is less exhaustive, but may interest those studying planning after 1949.

Peter Cookson SMITH, *The Urban Design of Concession: Tradition and Transformation in the Chinese Treaty Ports*, Hong Kong: MCCM Creations, 2011). A concise, city-by-city history of the treaty ports, from the Concession Era to the present day, augmented by evocative sketches and sharp analysis of urban morphology.

Gregory VEECK, Clifton W. PANNELL, Christopher J. SMITH and Youqin HUANG, *China's Geography: Globalization and the Dynamics of Political, Economic and Social Change*, Lanham, Md.: Rowman & Littlefield Publishers, 2011. A worthy textbook, with abundant information on Chinese urban and rural space, in the shifting context of history, policy and economics.

Min-Ying WANG, *The Historicization of Chinese Architecture,* New York: Columbia University, 2010. Close reading of the period from the late Qing through the early Mao years, dealing with the "making of architectural historiography in China." For those with an interest in the meta-history of Chinese architectural discourse's internal tropes and narratives. Dissertation available online.

WU Liangyong, *A Brief History of Ancient Chinese City Planning,* Urbs and Regio, 1986. Thorough history of urban form, with a particular emphasis on capital city planning.

ZHU Jianfei, *Architecture of Modern China: A Historical Critique*, London: Routledge, 2009. An essential, exceptional history of modern architecture (and architectural discourse) in the twentieth and twenty-first centuries, concluding with a valiant attempt at a classification system for architecture in modern China's unique socio-economic climate.

Sources for Buildings and Architects

Those seeking to stay abreast of new projects should consider the major international journals. Of these, Japan's *A+U (Architecture + Urbanism)* may be particularly noted for high standards and English-language coverage. Of the Chinese magazines, *Time & Architecture (Shi Dai Jian Zhu)* can be the most illuminating, and the small but growing quantity of English language abstracts is appreciated; the Chinese *Architectural Journal (Jian zhu xue bao)* is also useful.

While we have made use of blogs and the press-release aggregator websites, readers should be warned that critical distance can sometimes be hard to perceive, and locations of projects are rarely more accurate than the correct metropolis (if that). Architects' own project descriptions have also been a useful tool when understood in context.

A number of thick, well-illustrated and thoughtful (if not portable) volumes on architecture in China were useful to us in establishing our selection of buildings, as well as providing background information on projects. All of the following are worth a look for those hoping for other windows into the Chinese scene, particularly concerning both the late 1990s and early 2000s.

Bernard CHAN, *New Architecture in China,* London and New York: Merrell Publishers, 2005; Layla DAWSON, *China's New Dawn: An Architectural Transformation,* Munich and London: Prestel, 2005; Philip JODIDIO, Architecture in China, Taschen, 2007; Ian LUNA and Thomas TSANG, *On The Edge: Ten Architects from China*, New York: Rizzoli, 2006; Peter Cachola SCHMAL & ZHI Wenjun, eds., *M8 In China; Contemporary Chinese Architects*, Berlin: Jovis, 2009; ZHI Wenjun and JIE Xu, *New Chinese Architecture* (2009). Christian DUBRAU's books, *Sinotecture: New Architecture in China* and *Contemporary Architecture in China: Buildings and Projects 2000–2020* (respectively 2008 and 2010), both from *DOM publishers,* are noteworthy for particular attention to commercially oriented work by less internationally known Chinese firms. The massive, Chinese-language *Twentieth Century Chinese Architecture* (20 世纪 中国 建筑), by YANG Yongsheng and GU Mengchao (1999) is an excellent reference for those who read the language and seek more obscure projects.

Acknowledgements

This book is a direct outgrowth of a series of study-abroad trips based out of the Ohio State University's Knowlton School of Architecture, and led by Associate Professor Jacqueline GARGUS. Special thanks must therefore be reserved for Professor Gargus, not only for her generous contributions to this volume, but also for her many years of tireless effort to offer students first-hand experiences of world architecture. These intensive trips, enriched by high-quality discussions and lectures and by a year-round project of planning, were foundational to our own architectural educations and our development as instructors. Professor Gargus's insistence on high standards for on-trip programming, research, and discussions inspired this book, which could not have come into being without her leadership, guidance and support. CHEN Zhiguo, another planner and co-leader of the Ohio State China trips, shaped them through his professionalism and insight into China's traditional and contemporary architectural cultures. Our selection of buildings, and the text of this book, were dramatically improved by his knowledge and attention. Alex Lik-Tze PUN also provided extensive input during the planning of our trips, particularly with regard to Hong Kong and the Pearl River Delta. His infectious good nature, and his insight into local planning and design issues, shaped our trips and our understanding. Douglas GRAF, Robert LIVESEY, Karla TROTT and Robert WANDEL, in addition to their many other contributions to architectural education, accompanied us in China and offered challenging readings of architectural projects and urban form. Troy MALMSTROM provided essential research and logistical support for the Ohio State China tours, while Yoyo GONG assisted with logistics, translation and interpretation, and moral support on the same. Stephanie JONES and Andrea KAMILARIS gathered information on a number of projects and planning debates, particularly with regard to Shanghai and Hong Kong. Michael ABRAHAMSON and Christophe RENAUD both provided helpful critical commentary on Evan's introductory essay. Leslie ANDERSON, Chris CAREY, Phoebe YOU, Adella MA and the staffs of the Ohio State University Office of International Affairs and the OSU China Gateway provided continuing support for the China travel programmes, while the Knowlton School of Architecture endorsed the tour's academic programme and assisted with logistics. Furthermore, this book could not have come into being without the Ohio State and Columbia University architecture libraries, and their excellent librarians. We would also like to thank all the students and staff on all our trips, who have made travelling a joy and challenged our own assumptions with pointed questions and attentive architectural criticism. A full list of the varied assistants, companions, visiting professors and others who have inspired and touched our European and Asian travels would be impossible, but particular appreciation is due to Norbert BIRNBÖCK for his professionalism, spirited conversation and quick thinking; Gregory DELANEY for his tireless energy, faith in students, and insight into urban form; and Emma GARGUS, for innumerable logistic services, personal record maintenance, and keeping our travels in good humour.

Finally, we would like to thank the following firms and individuals for their gracious provision of images for this project, and all their individual staff members who handled our enquiries with attentive grace:

Adrian Smith + Gordon Gill Architecture, Aedas, Amateur Architecture Studio, AmphibianArc, Arata Isozaki & Associates, Arup, Atelier Deshaus, AZL Architects, China Architecture and Building Press, China Architecture Design & Research Group, Christ & Gantenbein, David Chipperfield Architects, DnA Design and Architecture, Dorian Cave | Meridian Space, Edition Axel Menges, Foster + Partners, FR-EE (Fernando Romero Enterprise), Gensler, gmp Architekten (Von Gerkan, Marg, und Partner), Herzog & de Meuron, IROJE Architects & Planners, The Jerde Partnership, Jiakun Architects, Kohn Pedersen Fox Associates (KPF), KUMA Kengo and Associates, LAB Architecture Studio, LOT-EK, MAD, Mario Cucinella Architects, Massimiliano and Doriana Fuksas, Michael Maltzan Architecture, Michael Moran Photography, Morphosis Architects, Neri&Hu Design and Research Office, OPEN Architecture, Paul Reuber, Pei Cobb Freed & Partners, the Pei Partnership, Ping Xu, PTW Architects, Richard Meier & Partners Architects, Rocco Design Architects Limited, Rolf Reiner Maria Borchard, Sasaki Associates, the Shanghai Auto Museum, Simon Fieldhouse, Skidmore Owings & Merrill LLP (SOM), Steven Holl Architects, Studio Pei-Zhu, Studio Shanghai, Tao Ho Design Architects, tillschweizer/co, Tod Williams Billie Tsien Architects, Toshiko Mori Architects, Tsushima Design Studio, the University of Texas Perry-Castañeda Library Map Collection, UBC Press, Urbanus and Zaha Hadid Architects.

Image Credits

Evan CHAKROFF is a designer and critic with an interest in the urban, architectural and social implications of digital technology. While focused on computational design in practice, he remains active in academia and has published theoretical essays in *Log*, *CLOG*, *Saturated Space*, and other journals. Evan holds an M.Arch from the Knowlton School of Architecture (Ohio State University), and currently works as an architectural designer in Seattle. Previously, he has worked with Herzog & de Meuron, Massimiliano Fuksas, and NBBJ. Evan lived and worked in Shanghai from 2009 to 2013.

Addison GODEL is a Ph.D student in architecture at Columbia University, where his research concerns the myriad, two-way relationships between modern architecture and its social and political contexts, with topics including the representational paradoxes of telephone exchanges, early-modern European views of Chinese design, and the status of post-Independence Indian work in Modernist historiography. He holds an M.Arch from the Ohio State University's Knowlton School of Architecture, and publishes architectural commentary online.

Jacqueline GARGUS, RA, is an Associate Professor of Architecture at the Knowlton School of Architecture, Ohio State University. A two-time Fullbright scholar, Professor Gargus's research approaches design through an art-historical lens. Professor Gargus has led the Knowlton School's study abroad programmes to Europe and Asia for over twenty years, has taught at Harvard University and the Technische Universität Wien, published and lectured widely and has been an invited critic at MIT, UCLA and Bauhaus Universität Weimar, among other institutions.

The *Deutsche Nationalbibliothek* lists this publication in the *Deutsche Nationalbibliografie*; detailed bibliographic data are available at *http://dnb.d-nb.de*

ISBN 978-3-86922-348-3

Copy editing
Mariangela Palazzi-Williams

Proofreading
Clarice Knowles

Layout
Evan Chakroff
Addison Godel

Final artwork
Nicole Wolf

Printing
Tiger Printing (Hong Kong) Co., Ltd.
www.tigerprinting.hk

哈尔滨 Harbin
大同 Datong
鄂尔多斯 Ordos
北京 Beijing
天津 Tianjin
大连 Dalian
平遥 Pingyao
西安 Xian
南京 Nanjing
苏州 Suzhou
上海 Shanghai
杭州 Hangzhou
宁波 Ningbo
金华 Jinhua
厦门 Xiamen
广州 Guangzhou
深圳 Shenzhen
澳門 Macau
香港 Hong Kong

People's Republic of China

Beijing & Northeast China

Shanghai & the Yangtze Delta

Hong Kong & the Pearl River Delta

Introduction, Regional Maps, and Using this Book

You hold in your hands what we believe to be the best English-language resource for a visitor to China interested in modern and contemporary design, architecture, landscape and urbanism. Whether you are in China for a short visit, or staying for several months or more, we are confident that this book will allow you to explore and appreciate the range of innovative work in and around China's major cities, as well as some of the issues at stake in Chinese architectural culture today. Our visits to China, and our attention to recent Chinese architecture, have profoundly affected the ways in which we personally think about design and urban form. It's our hope that through this guide we can share that experience with you.

We believe that there is no substitute for visiting a building, urban space, or landscape. To help you make the most of your time, our emphasis is on projects which offer an *architectural experience*: that is, ones which are complete or well underway, which contribute in some way to the architectural "conversation," and which reward the visitor with something special. We've tried to balance quality with accessibility, excluding projects (however major) which are far away from other likely destinations, or which may not be open to the public. This admittedly limits the inclusion of private houses, gated communities, remote provincial museums, boutique hotels, elementary schools, and upscale luxury shops, but when time is short and traffic is tough, gazing at the exterior of a building through a crack in a fence, or pondering a retail interior that has already been gutted and replaced, seem like poor substitutes for a complete building one can walk through and touch.

Inevitably, this selection does mean that certain major Chinese firms are underrepresented in our coverage; this should not be taken as a slight on their work, but simply as an attempt to provide the short-term visitor with the richest and most varied architectural survey. Our illustrated coverage is also necessarily limited by space and the availability of images; many important buildings are confined to the map sections for each city. Nonetheless, we are pleased to present so many illustrated projects, with architectural drawings offering the visitor ways of understanding the projects not available to the naked eye. Indeed, this book was made possible by the generous support of numerous firms and individuals who permitted the use of their images, as well as those who enabled our previous trips through funding, logistical support, and friendship. A full list of acknowledgements and image credits begins on p. 398.

From experience, we know that locating projects in China can be difficult, and can consume time better spent *visiting* them. To spare you this frustration, we have provided detailed maps of the cities covered in this book. Every map entry includes coordinates synchronised to China's GPS system (look for the ❖ symbol, followed by north latitude, and east longitude). An increasing number of Chinese taxis and car services are equipped with GPS, and can use these to painlessly locate each site. In the map pages, illustrated entries are indicated by markers in the chapter's designated colour: in addition to GPS coordinates, these projects feature both English and Chinese-language names and addresses, in the body of the chapter. If you're considering a substantial detour to visit a public building, we do recommend checking the Web for opening hours or phone numbers, as many institutions keep unpredictable hours, open by request, or, in the worst case, shut their doors permanently.

While our focus is on modern and contemporary work, often we have gone beyond this mandate to highlight "must-see" masterpieces from China's very long design history. While we only include a sampling of this heritage, these gardens, palaces and urban spaces are likely to interest and inspire any curious visitor. As well, they have played a profound role in shaping China's architectural culture, and a familiarity with them will further bring into focus the design choices in many more recent projects.

China is a big country, and even its "second-tier" cities are among the world's fastest-growing. In selecting areas to cover for this volume, we have generally favoured places which have seen the most rapid, state-supported economic development over the last four decades. This has limited our focus somewhat to the major cities on and near China's east coast. Given China's growth patterns, and long-standing national policies seeking to "Open Up the West," we expect the future to offer more and more architecturally significant developments beyond this admittedly limited selection of cities. In the meantime, we have provided short introductory essays on urban form and historical development for several cities "further afield" (beginning on p. 386), to which we are unable to give full coverage. Longer-term residents in East Asia are strongly encouraged to explore beyond these cities, and to review the other guides available from *DOM publishers,* including Taiwan, Hong Kong, Japan, Tokyo, and Pyongyang.

One last note: while the compilation of an architectural travel guide necessarily involves cherry-picking individual buildings from a much wider field, it can also give rise to a dangerous tendency to think of a whole country as a set of discrete sites, between which one zips indiscriminately, without much thought for what lies in between. While it is difficult for a visitor to take stock of the entire economic, social, political and cultural context of a building, we do urge users of this guide to also consider the spaces beyond architectural monuments of interest. These spaces naturally make up the overwhelming majority of the Chinese urban environment, and you will find your trip – and your appreciation of the signature architectural works – richer if you take stock of the various spaces of work, domesticity, and leisure that make up everyday life. Not all of these are accessible to the tourist, but even keeping your eyes open and out the window as you travel can change the way you understand Chinese cities and architecture.

On Names

When crediting buildings, we have rendered family names in upper-case letters. Typically, Westerners give their family names last, and Asians give theirs first: Bill CLINTON, DENG Xiaoping. (Residents of Hong Kong and certain other places often use the Western format.) Wherever possible, we have given the preferred name of the architect or firm at the time of the building's completion. Architectural projects are inherently collaborative; many, if not most of the projects in this book would ideally have several parties listed, including the design architect(s), engineering or construction consultancies, and the local design and building institutes, critical players in Chinese practice. Where we have full credits, we have provided them, but their absence should not be taken to suggest that the given designer is solely responsible.

Using This Guide: Project Entries

Within each city, illustrated project entries have sequential numbers, corresponding to their appearance in that city's maps; in this case, the entry number is SH 143, with "SH" indicating "Shanghai." Below this is the QR code, linked to the GPS coordinates.

Project name	**Museum of Glass** SH 143
Architect(s) and date(s)	*LOGON Architects, 2011*
Project name (Chinese)	玻璃博物馆
Project address (Chinese)	宝山区长江西路685号
Project address (English)	685 W Changjiang Rd., Baoshan
GPS Coordinates	❖ 31.3455, 121.4673
Project description	This multi-building renovation makes good use of the various spaces, with

143 **Museum of Glass** *LOGON Architects, 2011* ❖ 31.3455, 121.4673

144 **Jiangwan Cultural Centre** *RTKL, 2003-2006.* Sprawling snake in the grass, with glazed volumes punching through. ❖ 31.3363, 121.5066

145 **Jiangwan Ecology Museum** *PU Miao, 2004-2005.* Small museum, descending pleasantly into its wetland context. ❖ 31.3216, 121.5065

146 **Knowledge and Innovation Community** *SOM (architecture), Tom LEADER Studio (landscape), 2006.* ❖ 31.3084, 121.5089

147 **Jiangwan Sports Centre (Shanghai Stadium)** *DONG Dayou, 1934.* ❖ 31.3080, 121.5101

148 **Tongji University** *founded 1907.* This campus boasts one of the best architecture schools in China, housed in Building C, by Atelier Z+ (2002-04). ❖ 31.2871, 121.5013

F. Jiangwan District (Map 143-148)

Using This Guide: Maps

Navigational maps are located at the end of each city chapter, in the section on additional cities (beginning on p. 386), and as sub-maps for certain project entries. Numbers on the maps correspond to the map listings, usually on the same page as the map in question. Coloured entries additionally correspond to illustrated building entries in the same chapter. In the example above, again from Shanghai (p. 205), map entries 144, 145, and 148 in grey provide basic information and GPS coordinates in the map listings. Entries 143, 146 and 147 in the Shanghai chapter colour indicate illustrated project entries; you may find them by turning back in the chapter to the corresponding numbers. While entries always appear in numerical order, not every project on the maps corresponds to an illustrated entry. Thus, the numbering of projects in the chapter may appear to have "gaps," for example between 143 and 146; these simply reflect the grey, map-only entries.

Scalelessness: Impressions of Contemporary China

Evan Chakroff

In an era of accelerating population growth, mass urbanisation, and ever-increasing pressure on natural resources and the environment, architects and urbanists have a responsibility to study the megacity in depth, to see first-hand the advantages and challenges associated with these massive urban agglomerations in order to better understand what will be the dominant urban form of the coming century. Nowhere is the megacity phenomenon more prevalent, or more accessible, than on China's eastern coast, where we find ample evidence of the "economic miracle" of the "reform and opening up" era. While all buildings are born of their distinct historical context, the general urban condition here can provide lessons for designers the world over. Each city has its own distinct history, whether as a dynastic capital, regional trading centre, global mercantile powerhouse, or foreign colony. Each has been affected profoundly by China's recent economic transition, and by studying each in turn we can begin to construct models for rapid urban growth that are applicable to other contexts.

If the next one hundred years will indeed be known as "the Chinese century" it will likely not be due to China's dominant economic position, or its military power, but because China's contemporary urbanism has become a global model that countries and cities across the economic spectrum seek to emulate. Already, new towns are being built in Africa on Chinese models, backed by Chinese investors.[1] The dominant mixed-use commercial typology – towers on a podium – has already gained traction from Kazakhstan to Kansas. There is perhaps no better architectural representation of our contemporary world: these projects are massive in scale, disorienting in urban configuration, socially and economically stratified, and often overlaid with myriad media layers in the form of integrated advertising, electronic augmentation, ubiquitous surveillance, and location-aware digital social media. The scalar shifts and formal ruptures we find in China's contemporary urban morphology can be read as a physical manifestation of our disjointed, fragmented social fabric.

In our hyper-connected world, there is no "Chinese architecture" any more than there is a single European or American style. While this essay deals with architecture in China, governed in part by local codes, the phenomena identified here – namely *scalelessness*, *fragmentation*, and *inauthenticity* – can be found world-wide. Where Western observers often label contemporary Chinese architecture as insensitive, oversized, or inhumane (even totalitarian),

Opposite: **Six-Level Stack** highway interchange, with "Dragon Column" (p. 200)

Framed and layered spaces in a dense zone of Suzhou's **Lingering Garden** (p. 224). Note rockery in the far distance.

Taihu stone on display in the **Garden of the Humble Administrator** (p. 218)

in each case there is a global precedent. Projects we find odd (or even offensive) can be rationally explained as originating in specific socioeconomic historical circumstances, and shaped by a global cultural context. Ultimately, architectural examples from contemporary China can be used to elucidate some aspects of today's worldwide socioeconomic trends.

A quality of *scalelessness* has long played a role in Chinese design practices. Scalar shifts, juxtaposition, and spatial layering (devices we may think of as modern inventions) are all in evidence in Suzhou's **classical gardens** (see p. 210), dating back centuries. In the gardens, visitors are encouraged to wander. Garden paths often take the form of covered walkways, passages that slip between buildings, or bridges that pass over tranquil ponds. The experience of the Chinese garden is one of near constant delight, as different structures frame and reframe views of the architecture and landscape in surprisingly different ways from each vantage point. Often, one will catch an oblique glimpse of a distant rockery through several layers of screens and windows, only to later arrive in that space to find that the rockery is a radically different size than anticipated. This perceptual trompe l'oeil is one of the classical gardens' greatest pleasures. It is also a key component of China's traditional arts: this ambiguity of scale, and emphasis on relativistic perception are essential to traditional landscape painting, where narrative progression and shifting perspectives animate the "reading" of a painted scroll (see discussion on p. 040). The *taihu* stones found in most gardens work in similar ways, appearing abstract or figural depending on viewing angle, and views of the full object in context are often denied by successive layers of architectural elements. In the art of *penjing* (the Chinese precursor to *bonsai*), miniature landscapes in small trays are often staged deliberately to draw comparison with framed views of "real" landscapes in the garden, beyond or its walls as "captured views." Both *taihu* stones and *penjing* trees represent a kind of synthesis, at once natural and artificial, that hints at concepts of authenticity at odds with Western traditions. Walking through the classical gardens of Suzhou, or viewing a landscape painting, one is left with the impression that scale is relative, fluid, and malleable.

This impression is only enhanced when we consider China's traditional architecture and urban planning. In pre-modern, dynastic China, many structures followed the same typological diagram, the *siheyuan* courtyard home. While many ancient

A traditional *siheyuan* in **Pingyao** (p. 387), now operating as a hostel

Varied scale of courtyards in the **Forbidden City** (p. 074)

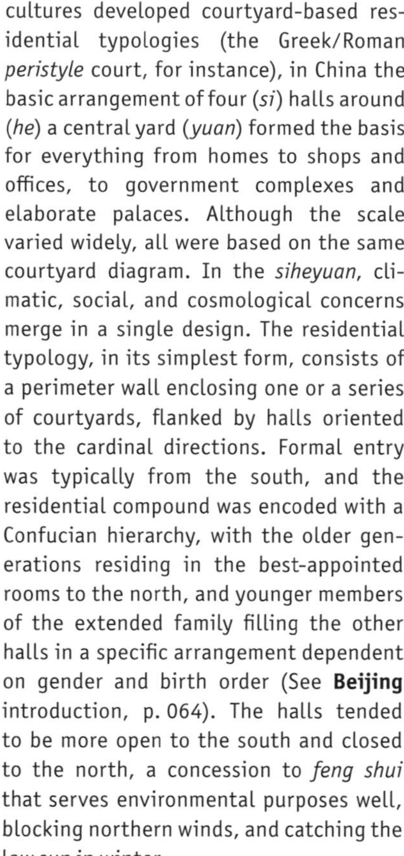

cultures developed courtyard-based residential typologies (the Greek/Roman *peristyle* court, for instance), in China the basic arrangement of four (*si*) halls around (*he*) a central yard (*yuan*) formed the basis for everything from homes to shops and offices, to government complexes and elaborate palaces. Although the scale varied widely, all were based on the same courtyard diagram. In the *siheyuan*, climatic, social, and cosmological concerns merge in a single design. The residential typology, in its simplest form, consists of a perimeter wall enclosing one or a series of courtyards, flanked by halls oriented to the cardinal directions. Formal entry was typically from the south, and the residential compound was encoded with a Confucian hierarchy, with the older generations residing in the best-appointed rooms to the north, and younger members of the extended family filling the other halls in a specific arrangement dependent on gender and birth order (See **Beijing** introduction, p. 064). The halls tended to be more open to the south and closed to the north, a concession to *feng shui* that serves environmental purposes well, blocking northern winds, and catching the low sun in winter.

When *siheyuan* complexes are arrayed on large city blocks, the residences form a *hutong* neighbourhood, with access lanes running east to west. *Hutong* blocks are divided from one another by large commercial thoroughfares, which form perimeter barriers and create the same kind of inward focus that characterises the individual family courtyard. The *hutong* block is thus delineated as a contained, legible, and repeatable unit. This urban structure is still evident in many of Beijing's older neighbourhoods (though perhaps best-preserved in smaller walled cities like **Pingyao**, p. 387). The *siheyuan* informs the *hutong*, and the *hutong* informs the city.

The nested recursions of familiar form give the city a fractal quality, with local, perceptual scale determined through intricately woven social, economic, and cosmological relationships. The design of the Imperial City manifested scale mapped to power, with the city's concentric grid focused on the palace, a conduit to the divine. Successive concentric layers of the city each represented a step down in scale and a step away from divinity, and this grid system extended out to the countryside, throughout the empire, and out to the wider world in an extensive grid (see diagram, p. 066) that simplified administrative duties, surely, but also emphasised the power and divinity of the Emperor. Thus, in dynastic China's urban planning, the scale of the city is defined as a continuum associated with the dominant social hierarchy. China's traditional forms of architecture and urban planning developed over thousands of years, deeply entwined with social constructs. These social and economic relationships have been imprinted on China's urban form.

Subtle shifts in architectural style aside, China held to its traditional understanding of the world for millennia, and these

Great Hall of the People, across wind-swept **Tian'anmen Square** (p. 072)

values were made manifest in the built environment.[2] Foreign influence was kept at bay by limiting access to China's heartland, and by confining foreign traders to specially designated zones, such as at the Thirteen Hongs of Canton, (see **Guangzhou**, p. 294). However, once China's borders were thrown open in the wake of the Opium Wars, the process of modernisation (or perhaps, Westernisation) accelerated, driven by both internal and external forces as various parties from within and without sought to bring China into the modern, already-globalised world.

In the late nineteenth and early twentieth centuries, the long-standing scalar relationships in urban form came under strain, with the Qing Dynasty losing its hold on power, and traditional culture upended by the influx of European traders and would-be conquerors. Grand, Western-inspired structures, and wider streets for carriages, trams, and (later) automobiles defied the subtle hierarchies of traditional urbanism. Commercialism reigned, and capitalist real-estate pressures directed urban development in ways that ignored the old concentric logic, a development pattern that would continue through the tumultuous 1930s and 1940s.[3] Scale lost much of its significance as new values displaced the old cosmology.

The national planning strategies of MAO Zedong's China were often disruptive and inhumane. Official aggrandisement of the agricultural proletariat ostensibly justified the forcible relocation of many urban dwellers to the rural hinterlands. Both urban and rural residents were organised into socialist work units (*danwei*) and housed in communal dormitories (*tongzilou*). The *danwei* complexes were often arranged around courtyards and featured alternating pedestrian and automobile roads, both lined with trees that now form pleasant canopies. While the social and economic structure of the *danwei* represented a radical break with the past, the spatial arrangement of communal life around shared courtyards might have held a nostalgic appeal, which may have helped to legitimise the new socialist government.[4] Such strict government control over work and housing certainly sounds stifling, but the low-rise, high-density blocks built in this era form surprisingly appealing neighbourhoods. The walk-up residential structures rarely exceeded six storeys, and these districts maintain a pleasant, human scale. Even today, the streets buzz with the sort of activity one associates with the older *hutong* neighbourhoods, and with great urban space in general. The contrast in scale between these housing blocks and the massive civic projects of the Mao era seems almost dogmatic, as if government structures were purposefully massive as a demonstration of power and assertion of dominance.[5]

From the 1950s to the 1980s, the architectural works of China's state design institutes were mainly functional and pragmatic. After Mao's death and the rise of DENG Xiaoping, the Special Economic Zone model (see **Shenzhen**, p. 316) would be adopted by numerous cities and districts, and the scalar relationships

CCTV New Headquarters (p. 088) as iconic urban landmark

between the monumental and the collective would again take on strong symbolic meaning. By the 2000s and 2010s, China was ascendant. The fanfare surrounding the 2008 Olympics was hard to ignore. Reports of inadequate worker safety measures, human rights violations, or pollution were countered by ever-more extravagant architectural or infrastructural feats, like the rapid expansion of Beijing's subway system, the construction of world-class airports, or the reconfiguration of vast swaths of urban fabric. In the years between the Olympics and the 2010 World Exposition in Shanghai, this flurry of activity only intensified. Architects worldwide embraced China with missionary zeal, both in the excitement with which new projects were discussed, and with the voracious appetite of firms whose home markets had collapsed. The country was regarded by many as a *tabula rasa*, and many architects embraced novelty, ignored budget, and treated the country as a sandbox in which to test their wildest architectural theories.

Recent major "civic" projects (like **CCTV,** p. 088, the **National Theatre**, p. 077, and the **National Olympic Stadium,** p. 098), are characterised by their massive size, true, but each exists as an independent object in a field, an urban sculpture with no detail betraying the relationship to human scale. They seem intended to be viewed from across town (smog permitting), from varied and multiple vantage points, much like the landforms in traditional landscape painting. While the designers of these projects sought to create cultural icons representative of an empowered nation,

Referencing tradition, a covered path at **Jade Bamboo Plaza** (p. 323)

other developers chased after more easily measured superlatives. The race continues, with the mega-tall **Shanghai Tower** (p. 181) now complete, and Shenzhen's **Ping An Finance Centre** (map p. 334) soon to overtake it as the world's second-tallest skyscraper.[6] Chendgu's **Century Global Centre** (map p. 388), meanwhile, claims status as the world's largest building by floor area, its 1.7 million square metres containing an enclosed mall, a waterpark with indoor beach, numerous hotels and restaurants, a recreation of a Mediterranean village, even, allegedly, an artificial sun.

To outside observers, the scale of these projects can be shocking (as can the speed and danger of construction), but rather than ascribe the frenzied construction to something inscrutable about the Chinese character, we can find historical precedent both in China and abroad, and view the current wave of megaprojects in their proper historical context. As in the past, these massive feats of architecture and engineering are most often built as representations of power, with each superlative achievement wielded like a trophy. The vast scale of China's urban landscape

Subtle intervention by Amateur Architecture, **Zhongshan Road** (p. 259), Hangzhou

can be disconcerting, but it flows from China's long history, in which large building complexes were symbolic of the dominant power of each age. The spatial and scalar gradient between these and the vernacular residential blocks has been a normal condition of China's urban morphology for centuries, if not millennia.[7]

Today the economy is cooling somewhat, but ambitious new projects are still proposed daily. However, the tone and style of projects have shifted somewhat. In projects of the 1990s–2000s there was an emphasis on culturally relevant metaphor as a driver of form (the dragon, the phoenix, the lotus flower, the *taihu* stone, etc.), but following the 2008 recession we see a tendency towards more specifically architectural referents: the traditional carved wood screen, the canal street, the apothecary, the *siheyuan* courtyard, the traditional store-front. Architects like Amateur Architecture, Urbanus, and LIU Jiakun are at the forefront of this movement as they turn away from vacuous symbolism towards models that concern the arrangement of architectural elements in space. Though the scale of projects remains almost inconceivably large, we can begin to see an appreciation for human-scale details and craft returning to the profession.[8]

While China's cities are characterised by a condition of scalar fluidity and ambiguity, this scalelessness is best appreciated in plan or diagram as an academic exercise. Alternatively, approaching the same spaces through direct, phenomenological observation, we find that the experience of the contemporary Chinese city is fragmented and episodic. While similarities between *siheyuan* and palace layouts may be appreciated in plan, in practice the disjunction between the sacred precinct and the typical blocks of the city serves to heighten and clarify social divisions. The legacy of imperial China's urban form is the expectation that cities will feature major rifts in the urban fabric. These spatial disruptions existed in pre-modern China, amplified by historical political shifts, as when Beijing was literally re-centred with each successive dynasty (see diagram, p. 067). Cities were characterised by an ever-evolving urban design, and by a morphology that eschewed visual clarity for organisational precision, resulting in experiential sequences that unfold episodically, in urbanism as in traditional landscape painting and (especially) garden design (see discussion on p. 038).

This disjunctive aspect of China's urban morphology would only be amplified in modern times. Urban planning by colonial powers (and later by the Republic of China) would come to be dominated by Beaux-Arts strategies that emphasised axial boulevards, symmetry, and other techniques born of established European traditions; these reflected new governmental goals of "modern" planning for an efficient, hygienic, and economically competitive China. This not only meant wider roads accommodating new vehicles and infrastructure: the axial cuts of the

Pingyao (p. 387) city wall and moat

Dalian (p. 387) in 1912, under Japanese control. Note central circle, radial axes.

A restored *shikumen* gate at **Xintiandi**, Shanghai (p. 171)

new roads also separated and segregated formerly cohesive neighbourhoods (and, as in Baron HAUSSMANN's Paris, could potentially act as a means of crowd control). The varied European influences during this era led to a proliferation of eclectic styles, both in material technology and ornamentation. The mix of styles and typologies served to heighten the visual diversity of the cityscape, but also clearly indicated historical rupture. "European" styles had previously been seen as exotic novelties, as in the Western Mansions of Beijing's **Old Summer Palace** (p. 094), where a small Baroque palace was designed and built as a kind of informal tribute for the Emperor.[9] By the late 1800s, the novelty had most assuredly worn off, as European styles proliferated, carrying with them reminders of China's ongoing subjugation.

The urban designers of the concessions based their plans on their home countries' best practices of the time. In Shanghai, the British concession developed around Bubbling Well Road (now Nanjing Road), whose evocative name reflected well the picturesque path the street carved from the Bund to the rural hinterlands.[10] The French Concession's Avenue Joffre (now Huaihai Road) cut a straight Hausmannian axis through the city. This large-scale Beaux-Arts approach was especially popular in northern Chinese cities with Russian (and later, Japanese) colonial histories. There, urban plans were developed around public roundabouts anchored by memorial columns or sculptures, connected by long axial boulevards, a configuration perhaps most evident in **Dalian** (p. 387). In some cities the new European-style urban plans were imposed on previously existing urban fabric (as in Beijing, where interventions in this era were more subtle than elsewhere), but typically the foreign concessions were constructed on agricultural land outside the old city walls, and grew into self-contained, relatively homogeneous zones, clearly defined by their distinctive, foreign architectural styles and planning principles. The effect of this quasi-colonial urbanism was the separation of the city into morphologically distinct zones.

If Beijing's *siheyuan*, *hutong*, and overall city plan can be taken as an example of the nested, recursive geometry of dynastic China's urban planning, Shanghai's *shikumen* ("stone gate") housing (see p. 147), arrayed in *lilong* "neighbourhood

Defensive architecture: a *diaolou* tower house in **Kaiping** (p. 309)

Controlled access: Gate D at **Beijing National Stadium** (p. 098)

Defensive architecture: a *tulou* roundhouse in Fujian province, near **Xiamen** (see p. 386)

Controlled access: gate and "traditional" perimeter wall at **Linked Hybrid** (p. 090)

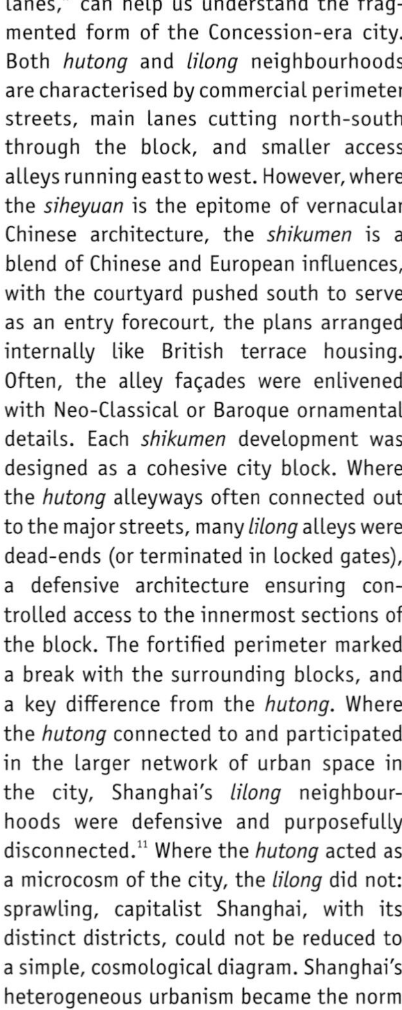

lanes," can help us understand the fragmented form of the Concession-era city. Both *hutong* and *lilong* neighbourhoods are characterised by commercial perimeter streets, main lanes cutting north-south through the block, and smaller access alleys running east to west. However, where the *siheyuan* is the epitome of vernacular Chinese architecture, the *shikumen* is a blend of Chinese and European influences, with the courtyard pushed south to serve as an entry forecourt, the plans arranged internally like British terrace housing. Often, the alley façades were enlivened with Neo-Classical or Baroque ornamental details. Each *shikumen* development was designed as a cohesive city block. Where the *hutong* alleyways often connected out to the major streets, many *lilong* alleys were dead-ends (or terminated in locked gates), a defensive architecture ensuring controlled access to the innermost sections of the block. The fortified perimeter marked a break with the surrounding blocks, and a key difference from the *hutong*. Where the *hutong* connected to and participated in the larger network of urban space in the city, Shanghai's *lilong* neighbourhoods were defensive and purposefully disconnected.[11] Where the *hutong* acted as a microcosm of the city, the *lilong* did not: sprawling, capitalist Shanghai, with its distinct districts, could not be reduced to a simple, cosmological diagram. Shanghai's heterogeneous urbanism became the norm in the early decades of the twentieth century, as European powers moved into mainland China, eventually settling dozens of foreign enclaves, each one controlled by a different governing body, with distinct (if sometimes disputed) boundaries.[12] The fragmentation of China's cities continued after the Communist revolution, as *danwei* work units were established and the socialist government's mechanisms of hierarchy and control were encoded in the urban form of the city. By the 1980s, China's cities were an amalgam of traditional urban planning and foreign enclaves, overlaid with Mao-era monuments and workers' precincts.

From the 1990s onwards, the mixed-use tower block has become China's dominant urban typology; each one is a self-contained enclave.[13] Unlike Hong Kong's commercial developments, where emphasis on connectivity and access is key, retail environments in mainland China are often accessible from only a few points, ensuring security when needed (and evincing a certain paranoia on the part of the developers). Such strict delimitation of space and vigilance in the establishment of boundaries may seem strange, but defensive, enclave architecture has a centuries-long precedent in China,[14] and such "enclave urbanism" is increasingly common the world over. New apartment complexes are similarly fortified, offering

A side street in **Thames Town** (p. 193): faux half-timber façades may be kitsch, but the narrow lanes, wide sidewalks, and low-rise fabric make for an appealing pedestrian experience

distinct themes to their residents, or simply featuring the latest in security technology. These walled complexes are often larger than similar enclaves constructed inthe past, but they limit movement through the city in similar ways, and contribute to the economic and social fragmentation of the city. Such disruptions in urban fabric are, of course, characteristic of any city with a long enough history, but in China the process of fragmentation is continual, ongoing, and has become an essential quality of the urban design. Protests occasionally erupt over new, disruptive construction projects (and associated relocation of residents, often in their thousands), but the general acceptance of such disjunction in urbanism is China's historical legacy: the fragmented city is the normative urban condition.[15]

In the 2000s, foreign architects' attempts to mitigate this fragmented condition were largely unsuccessful. The original design of OMA's **CCTV** (p. 088) featured an internal public "loop" that would pass by television studios and offices, revealing the process behind the production of the day's news, and, in theory, increasing transparency and accountability for this state-run media conglomerate.[16] In practice, the public loop was cut from the design (or perhaps survives, off limits), and today the building is surrounded by a secure perimeter fence, and accessible only to those with the proper credentials and connections. The "Bird's Nest" **National Stadium** (p. 098) seems to have a similar social ambition, as access to the stadium was to occur through a field of canted columns. With no monumental entrance or predetermined entry sequence, the vectors of public access were to be as random and free as the façade's structural pattern. Today, the stadium is fenced off, accessible via several entry gates for ticketed visitors. Beijing's **Linked Hybrid** (p. 090), intended to engage the surrounding blocks with numerous entry points, finds its "porous" perimeter sealed with a long wall capped with a traditional Chinese tile roof. Even Urbanus, who have made accessible, public space a top priority in their work, find themselves hemmed in: see the unfortunate fence at **Luohu Art Plaza** (p. 322), or the walls surrounding the **Maillen Hotel & Apartment** (p. 328); both projects seem to push for greater connectivity across boundaries, only to be denied at the perimeter. It's tough to call such appealing buildings failures, but in each case the architects' social ambitions have been stymied by the forces that compel clients and owners to wall off these complexes from their context. Though knowing China's urban history, this should come as no surprise.

"iPhono," "SciPhone," ePad," and "iRobot" devices at a Shanghai "fake market," which are renowned for selling a vast array of cheap merchandise

As the reader has seen above, modern China's urban morphology is defined by continuously variable scalar gradient and a fragmentation of urban form, resulting in heterogeneous cities composed of distinct enclaves designed in wildly diverse architectural styles, from the traditional to the modernist, to global contemporary. This diversity is testament to a turbulent history, but to contemporary observers, the various styles may be dismissed as imposed, and thus inauthentic, and not reflective of the "natural" state of Chinese architecture. In studying the architecture of twenty-first century China, we inevitably come across "copy" architecture, described with various derogatory terms: replica, clone, knock-off, pirated, "duplitecture," and almost universally derided by the (Western) media.[17] Insinuating that "the Chinese" have no ideas of their own, these critics reveal their own biases, and fail to recognise the historical context in which these odd constructions are realised.

For the uninitiated, **Thames Town** (p. 193) provides a good introduction. Designed by Atkins, and described as "a simulacrum," this mixed-use residential development features suburban villas grouped around a commercial core modelled on Victorian England. Concrete structures are dressed up in half-timber drag, and the pedestrian street network is designed to mimic the twisting alleyways of pre-modern London. One of the development's major landmarks is a "cathedral" that serves primarily as a backdrop for wedding photographers. The design in fact reflects a keen and expansive appreciation of British architectural history. Not only is there an abundance of reference to Olde England, but there is even a circular plaza which is ringed with buildings that seem to echo James STIRLING'S late work, and a small restaurant by the waterfront is housed in a geodesic dome, (after Buckminster FULLER and his UK High-Tech followers like Nicholas GRIMSHAW). In fact, the spatial composition of Thames Town is a kind of temporal gradient, with the Victorian centre giving way to more modern forms. To dismiss Thames Town as a "copy" is to deny it its unique qualities; "simulacrum" is indeed the better term, as this "copy" exists with no original referent. Similar examples of "copy architecture" are to be found across the country, from Hangzhou's Eiffel Tower (**Tianducheng**, map p. 271) to a recreation of Hallstatt, Austria, to the controversial "copy" of Zaha HADID'S **Wangjing SOHO** (p. 103) by a Chinese developer in Chongqing. While the (Western) media love to deride these projects as knock-offs or counterfeits, the reality is much more nuanced, and ties into a deep cultural tradition of iterative artistic emulation.[18]

A common point of comparison is the *shanzhai* culture that exists in the world of consumer goods. Chinese "knock-offs" of everything from luxury handbags to iPhones have spread world-wide, and over time these "fake" products have improved to the point where they now rival the originals in build quality and features. *Shanzhai* clothing and luggage are often made, after hours, in the same factories that produce the "real" brands.[19] Fake iPhones are often built with multiple SIM card slots and removable batteries, features that could be viewed as improvements upon the original. In *shanzhai*, as in the traditional arts, iteration and gradual refinement are considered higher arts than wholesale invention.[20]

Consider "Along the River during the Qingming Festival," (ZHANG Zeduan, 1085–1145) one of China's most famous and striking scroll paintings. Reading the painting from right to left, we see a wild landscape, then signs of human

Along the River during the Qingming Festival, detail at city gate and bridge; twelfth-century original by ZHANG Zeduan

Along the River during the Qingming Festival, detail at city gate and bridge; remake by Qing Dynasty court painters CHEN Mu, SUN Hu, JIN Kun, DAI Hong and CHENG Zhidao, 1736

settlement: a few thatched huts, then sturdier structures flank the river's edge. Large ships reveal these as trading houses. An arched wooden bridge crosses the river, and we see a bustling town centre; beyond this we reach a large stone gate tower, and still-bigger structures, cut off awkwardly at the end of the scroll. The painting is beautiful, as impressive for its technical mastery as for its exquisitely detailed, documentary vignettes of daily life. It was remade many times over the following centuries, and while none of these later scrolls can claim wholesale originality of subject, many represent marked improvements in technical ability, ambition, and thematic resonance. Consider an eighteenth-century remake: like the original, the scroll ostensibly depicts a city on a festival day. Reading from right to left, we see agricultural fields, a small theatre pavilion, then the boats and merchant houses, then the bridge. Notably, the bridge here is stone, not wood, and features a higher arch. The city gate, too, is more impressive, and now connects to a long city wall that disappears behind a low cloud. The city beyond the wall is much more developed than in the original, and seems to stretch over a much greater area. At the left end of the scroll, far beyond where the original cut off, we see the river tamed in narrow canals, until the bustle of the city is abruptly stopped by the wall of a palace complex, where gardens lead to a large temple. While

Along the River during the Qingming Festival, Animated media wall, Expo 2010

this scroll can be read, like the original, as a documentary, day-in-the-life urban scene, the inclusion of the water garden and temple indicates a deeper theme. In a sense, the painting is a chronicle of the development of civilisation, from the wild landscape of pre-agricultural China, to engineering masterworks like the stone bridge and canals, to the refinement of the palace grounds, whose water garden appears like a civilised mirror of the wild swamps at the right end of the scroll. The scroll ends, quite naturally, with the palace, the height of civilisation. While this is all contained within the Qing-era painting itself, it's worth noting again the "upgrades" to the original: the stone bridge, the large city wall, the updated clothing (and even mannerisms!) of the people. By acting as a commentary on the original, the copy not only transforms and updates the subject matter, but it imbues both with an enhanced thematic programme: now the collection of all possible copies together form a kind of meta-artwork with no single author and much deeper

Steel structure emerges from wood frame at **Leifeng Pagoda** (p. 262)

European-style plaza at **Xintiandi** (p. 171), with fountain and cafe seating

Internal courtyard (and parking entrance) at **Jianyeli** (p. 172), a reconstructed *shikumen*

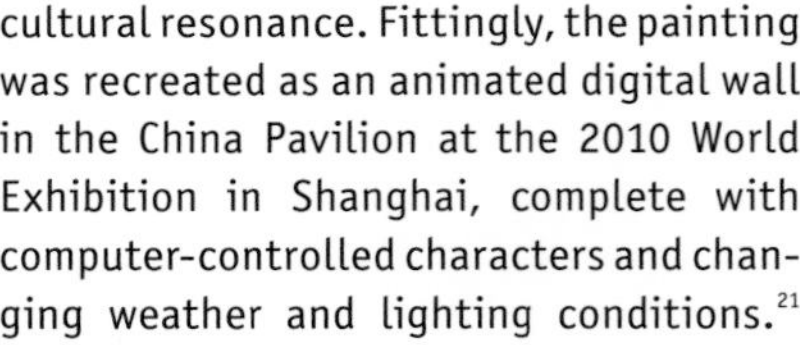

cultural resonance. Fittingly, the painting was recreated as an animated digital wall in the China Pavilion at the 2010 World Exhibition in Shanghai, complete with computer-controlled characters and changing weather and lighting conditions.[21]

This is just one example from an artistic tradition that emphasises iteration and gradual improvement, a familiar philosophy, considering Confucian tenets like filial piety and Buddhist concepts like *samsara* (the repeating cycle of life and death) and *nirvana*. Far from "copies," the traditional arts in China are focused on continual refinement of timeless models, in a potentially endless cycle. *Shanzhai* products, viewed in the West with a lighthearted disdain, can therefore be seen as a font of innovation. In architecture as in art and product design, "copying" thus does not bear the same negative connotation it does in the West, and cannot be judged by criteria that hold the original as sacred and copies as inferior by definition.

Furthermore, the European concept of originality and authenticity in architecture has little bearing on building practices in East Asia. While of course China has plenty of examples of masonry construction, the primary construction material throughout history has been wood, requiring frequent maintenance, repair, and, often, wholesale reconstruction. As in painting, reconstruction was a chance to improve upon the original model, and thus most buildings we now consider the very best of Chinese architecture are only the latest iteration of a centuries-long design process that was able to incorporate advances in technology to improve stability, aesthetics, and thematic content (through, for example, ornamental programme or typological reference). This is particularly evident in the gardens of **Suzhou** (p. 210) whose designs evolved continuously over time, until such modifications were curtailed by UNESCO World Heritage status.

One illuminating example is Hangzhou's **Leifeng Pagoda** (p. 262), recently rebuilt in steel and concrete, with glass elevators that whisk visitors to the topmost level. The pagoda is accessed via a long escalator that slices through a historic stone stairway. While this could be seen as an unfortunate collision of modernity and tradition, it is better viewed as a traditional structure updated with the latest available technology, as it would have been in the past. In Shanghai's **Jing'an Temple** (p. 165) a plaque claims a founding date over one thousand years ago, when the temple had a different name and was located across town. Visitors may find this absurd, but it demonstrates that in traditional Chinese society, architecture was not venerated for its physical form but for its social function, in which case the issue of material authenticity simply falls away.

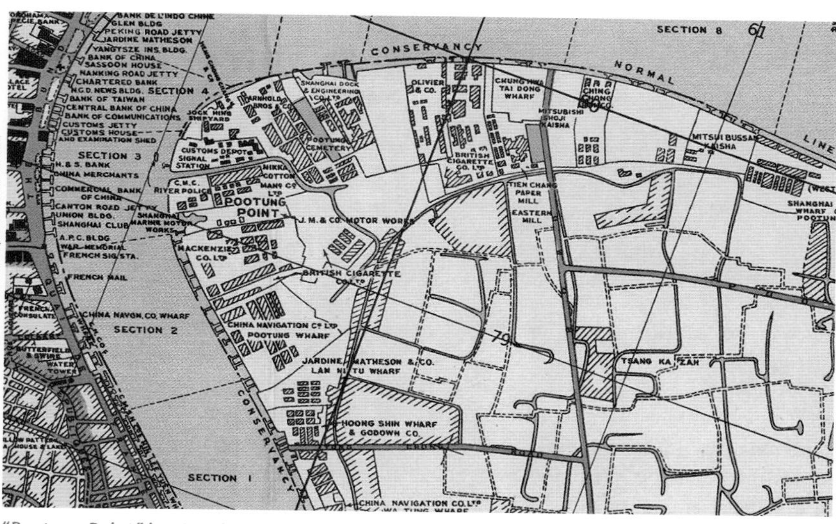

"Pootung Point" in 1937. Note such idyllic agrarian pursuits as British Cigarette Co, Tien Chang Paper Mill, J.M. & Co. Motor Works, etc. (see also full map, p. 151)

Even the specific practice of "copying" architecture and urbanism enjoys a long history. Dynastic China's tribute system encompassed architecture as well as goods and artefacts, and Emperors (and Empresses) would often reconstruct portions of distant cities as a way of asserting their power (real or imagined) over distant lands. Beijing's **Summer Palace** (p. 093) is the exemplar with its "copy" of Hangzhou's **West Lake** (p. 256), crossed by narrow causeways and punctuated by picturesque pavilions. Also within the Summer Palace complex, Suzhou Street is an eighteenth-century interpretation of that city's distinctive architecture and canalside urbanism. At **Chengde Mountain Resort's** "Outer Temples" (map p. 119), buildings as distant as Lhasa's Potala Palace were recreated. The "Western Mansions" at Beijing's Old Summer Palace, discussed above, were completed long before the Opium Wars, when the Europeans were still viewed as trading partners, not would-be conquerors. The European style must have been appealingly exotic, but it also proved that Chinese craftsmen had mastered the art of European architecture, thus folding Europe into a worldwide tribute system, with China at the centre. Such practices are not unique to China; many regimes across history have deployed architecture as a means of suggesting their imperial sweep.

As these examples demonstrate, both the physical form and ornamentation of architecture are less important than a building's social function, which may explain contemporary China's seemingly odd approach to historical preservation. Shanghai's most famous "preservation" case study is **Xintiandi** (p. 171). Ostensibly a renovation of an old *shikumen* block, it is in reality an entirely new structure, whose thin façades are reconstructions. In a loose interpretation of the original plan, tight alleyways have been replaced by European-style mid-block plazas. While the architects of Xintiandi pitched the project as a veneration of Shanghai's history, very little remains of the original residential block. Physically, the block has been transformed, but visually and perceptually, the project retains an aura of history, and has been cited as a prime example of the economic value of historical preservation. Lesser projects across China take the same approach, reconstructing faux-historic districts with various degrees of success.

If we understand the role of architecture in China as primarily a support for social structures and as a bearer of meaning, then structures like **Datong's New City Wall** (map p. 390), constructed on a steel frame with brick façade panels, begin to make sense: the original bricks may be long gone, and the city wall an outdated mode of defence, but the symbolic import remains: the wall signifies the role of the city as a bastion of traditional culture. In Thames Town, the representation of

Roofscape of Amateur Architecture's **Ningbo History Museum** (p. 242)

an English village battles with urban functionality. In Xintiandi, the image of historic fabric is promoted over any original spatial qualities of the *shikumen* block. In these and countless other cases, representation of the project becomes as important as its physical form.

This hyper-real aspect of contemporary Chinese architecture reaches its apogee in the skyline of Lujiazui, Pudong's new CBD. Though Lujiazui has its share of great individual buildings (the trio of **Jin Mao**, **WFC**, and the **Shanghai Tower**, starting p. 178), as a whole this spectacular district can be appreciated as a branding exercise at the scale of a city. Where the Concession-era Bund once represented the economic might of a dignified European-style Concession government (an outpost of civilisation to some, an oppressive colonial occupation to others), Pudong's skyline reflects China's growing role on the world stage, a new city emerging from marshland and paddy fields, bereft of imperialist influence. The "rice paddies" myth is easily dispelled with a look at a map of Shanghai in the 1930s, which shows the east bank of the Huangpu littered with factories and workers' dormitories, but the fact remains that Pudong's skyline has become the face of modern China. And so we see that "authenticity" (in the Western sense) has as little bearing on the world of branding and urban boosterism as it does on physical structures. Viewing contemporary China through a lens of "authenticity" only leads to frustration, and we must accept a greatly diminished role for "authenticity" if we hope to understand the essential condition of China's contemporary urbanism and architecture.

In the preceding text, we've identified three key aspects of contemporary Chinese urbanism. The condition of *scalelessness* that characterises China's urban form is driven by historical social hierarchy, but is evolving into a new physical representation of the dominant societal power structure. The *fragmentation* of urban form is the result of long-standing Confucian/Taoist urban models, augmented by Concession-era capitalist development and overlaid with socialist interventions. The resulting normative urban condition is one of fragmentation and disjunction. Finally, questions of *authenticity* in architecture and urban design are ultimately unproductive, as China's art-historical tradition follows a path that emphasises perfection through repetition, where authorship is less venerated than it is in European cultures. While these qualities of urban form and architecture can of course be found worldwide, they reach their apotheosis in contemporary China.

Chinese architects today tackle the incomprehensible challenge of engaging with the nation's long history, modern disruptions, and contemporary ascendance with admirable aplomb and keen aesthetic sensibility. To take one example, Pritzker Prize winner Wang Shu's firm Amateur Architecture completed the **Ningbo History Museum** (p. 242) in a second-tier city far from international scrutiny. The site planning aligns the museum's rectangular floor plate in a symmetrical arrangement with several other major civic structures in a new district. The museum faces the central plaza of this new city centre, and forms one of the four "halls," if we consider the new CBD as an inheritor of the *siheyuan* urban typology. The Ningbo museum acts as a sculptural object in the landscape, but its form is more complex than just that: at the upper level, the volume is carved away to create pathways and staircases, and impromptu auditoria, and at the upper, accessible, rooftop level, the sharply cut forms of the building start to resemble factory sheds and rural houses. The museum is at once a massive civic venue aligned with a capital-socialist CBD master plan, and a celebration of the rapidly vanishing ex-urban village typology, both in material quality (through reclaimed bricks) and in spatial organisation.

AI Wei Wei's **Archaeological Archive** (p. 283) is more explicitly narrative in its design. The artist's skill as a sculptor becomes apparent as one orbits the building, which offers up multiple, often contradictory associations from different vantage points. From one end, the elevation is the ideal of a simple farm-house (or perhaps a primitive hut), nestled in overgrown grassland. Moving around the building, the profile extrudes and elongates into an industrial shed. Further around, the sunken plaza reveals a mirror-image of the "*ur*-house" and confirms its geometry as an imposed, hexagonal, geometric order. Continuing around, the house profile is re-established, now under-cut and destabilised by the "excavation" of the sunken plaza adjacent. Reading the pavilion from this cinematic sequence of views, we can conclude that accelerating modernisation has literally stripped away the foundation of traditional society, a commentary on architecture's role in a rapidly changing culture.

Ai Wei Wei's **Archaeological Archive** (p. 283), from different vantage points

Similar social commentary seems encoded in the work of many young archi-tects across the country, and we would be foolish to deny the political aspects of Urbanus's numerous plazas designed for Shenzhen (see p. 322), Amateur Architecture's urban plans for Hangzhou's **Zhongshan Lu** (p. 259) and **Xiangshan Campus** (p. 264), MADA s.p.a.m.'s urban planning, or MAD's radical proposals for megastructures negating Beijing's urban hierarchy. These complex ideas emerge in projects that, simultaneously, demon-strate the architects' deft understand-ing of the various groups their projects serve: their financiers, the public, and the global architectural press. Where foreign firms viewed China as a *tabula rasa* and designed accordingly, Chinese designers are charting a new path that shows a deep appreciation of historical traditions, while still accepting the potentially radical nature of a design culture that eschews material authenticity. Their keen observation reminds us that the world is defined by coexisting constituencies that are spatially contiguous but separated by invisible socioeconomic boundaries. Such radical juxtaposition is physically and visually clear in China, but the cultural divisions exist throughout the world. Ours is not an era of boundless transparency and democracy, but one where society exists as an intricate web of relationships, and one's access to the varied planes of society is limited by one's connections and place within the global hierarchy.

Though this conclusion may be distressing, there is hope yet. The qualities of contem-porary urbanism identified above apply equally well to the hyper-real, digital space of "the Cloud." Online, there is no physicality, no historicity: the hypertext web is infinitely fragmented and discrete, and the question of authenticity is moot in a virtual space where all cultural pro-duction is reduced to bits of raw data. Urbanism, of course, pre-dates the virtual layers we find augmenting our physical experience of the city, but could life in the contemporary city still be seen as an analogue of this digital commons? Could the experience of navigating the disjunct city prepare rising generations for the digital-hybrid public "space" we find emerging before our eyes? When considering the role of the city in politics and society, we must also consider the digital layers now overlaid on physical space. As a coda, consider two final examples.

In late 2014, the "Umbrella Movement" protests swept Hong Kong for months; a continuation and intensification of long-standing dissent in opposition to Beijing's increasing political control over the SAR. While the protests began in the forecourt of the **HKSAR Government Headquarters** (p. 356), they soon spilled into the streets of Central and, later, Mong Kok, across the harbour. Blocking major highways, the protesters soon arranged themselves into micro-urbanisms, established food distribution networks, set up ranks of study carrels, founded "residential" zones lined with tents, etc; "occupying" Hong Kong's major arterials. Meanwhile, a parallel protest played out online through location-aware mobile apps that were able to bypass government firewalls and signal disruption. The emergence in Hong Kong of the "Great Firewall" is unfortunate, but like its physical namesake, it is a barely secured patchwork. There are always ways around the wall.

While the Hong Kong protesters politely asserted their right to democratic elections and the right to a physical space for civil discourse, Ai Wei Wei staged a protest of his own, remotely exhibiting "@Large" at Alcatraz, while under house arrest in Beijing. The ironically titled and digitally-inflected show engaged directly with themes of incarceration, freedom, and, ultimately, the state of the world as both infinitely expansive, and oppressively intimate. Increasingly, this digital-physical bifurcation is thematised in Ai's work which – while exhibited widely – will without doubt be experienced more often through digital screens than through physical proximity.

We can consider China's nascent hybrid digital urbanism as a new form of public commons – but one still divided along socioeconomic lines, with every different group barred access from certain enclaves, and admitted to others. These limits and boundaries, though present, are kept mostly hidden in the United States and the Western world, but in China, both the physical and virtual dimensions of segregation are plain to see. Barriers, checkpoints, fences, walls, and firewalls all serve to dispel the pretence of an increasingly open society. The modern Chinese city allows the existence of multiple, disparate ontologies in the same physical space. Today hyper-capitalism is married to a watered-down authoritarian socialism. For "both-and" there's no better example than China.

If architecture is to be a reflection of society and a physical manifestation of a civilisation's hopes and dreams, then there is no better representation than the architecture and urbanism of contemporary China. Architecture is a kind of calcification and fossilisation of civilisation, a permanent record with each architectural age representing the ambitions and dreams of the era. No place on earth better represents today's globalised, media-saturated culture than China's coastal megacities.

Notes

1. Michiel HULSHOF and Daan ROGGEVEEN's "Go West Project" studies this phenomenon in depth. See http://www.gowestproject.com/portfolio/urban-china-chinese-cities-in-africa/.
2. See discussion on traditional architecture and the *Yingzao Fashi*, starting p. 031.
3. See ZHU Jianfei, "The Architect and a Nationalist Project" in *Architecture of Modern China* (2008), full citation below, and Michael TSIN, "Canton Remapped," in Joseph W. ESHERICK, ed., *Remaking the Chinese City: Modernity and National Identity, 1900–1950*, Honolulu, University of Hawaii Press, 2000).
4. For more on the relationship between the *danwei* and traditional settlement patterns, see Yuwei WANG, "The Chinese Unit" (2013), a thesis project for the "Projective Cities" programme at the Architectural Association (London). Abstract and link to dissertation: http://projectivecities.aaschool.ac.uk/portfolio/yuwei-wang-the-chinese-unit/.
5. See ZHU Jianfei, "A Spatial Revolution" in *Architecture of Modern China* (2008).

6. At the time of writing, the Council for Tall Buildings and Urban Habitat lists the top three tallest completed buildings as Dubai's Burj Khalifa (828 m), Mecca's Makkah Royal Clock Tower Hotel (601 m), and New York City's One World Trade Center (541.3 m). Shanghai Tower recently topped out at 632 m and the Ping An Finance Centre is set to reach 660 m when completed in 2016, though both will soon be surpassed. For current listings, see http://skyscrapercenter.com/buildings.
7. Of course grand projects are common to all civilisations, but China is unique in that building morphology of such complexes has undergone continuous refinement over thousands of years. Note, for instance, the persistence of mortuary typologies, from the earliest **Qin Dynasty tombs** (p. 395), through to twentieth century monuments like the **Sun Yat-Sen Mausoleum** (p. 133), or the survival of the basic layout of administrative compounds.
8. See ZHU Jianfei, "Twenty Plateaus" in *Architecture of Modern China* (2008). It is likely that Zhu would file these architects under "Critical/Experimental Regionalism" in his classification system.
9. See discussion of the "Western Mansions of the Old Summer Palace in ZHU Jianfei "Perspective as Symbolic Form," in *Architecture of Modern China* (2008).
10. This picturesque approach to planning may have been influenced by earlier European scholarship on China. See discussion, p. 044
11. The development of the shikumen residential typology is studied in depth in QIAN Guan's excellent thesis "Lilong Housing, A Traditional Settlement Form" (McGill University, 1996). See http://www.mcgill.ca/mchg/student/lilong.
12. Peter Cookson SMITH, *The Urban Design of Concession: Tradition and Transformation in the Chinese Treaty Ports* (2012) provides a history of the treaty ports from their inception to present day, augmented by evocative sketches.
13. The path of historical development of the podium-tower typology is unclear, though it has been suggested that the type originated in postwar Britain, and was then exported to Hong Kong and Singapore. See, for example, http://www.cleanbiz.asia/blogs/curious-history-podium-tower.
14. China is home to a number of other defensive residential types, like the *diaolou* (p. 309) and the *tulou* (p. 386).
15. On protests over land grabs in China, see http://www.scmpcom/news/china/article/1108543/land-grabs-are-main-cause-main-land-protests-experts-say.
16. Koolhaas: "A public loop offers visitors access to all major components of the building." Quoted in Newsweek. http://www.newsweek.com/architect-rem-koolhaas-and-next-world-wonder-65503.
17. See, for example, Bianca BOSKER, *Original Copies,* cited below.
18. See, for example, WEN Fong, "The Problem of Forgeries in Chinese Painting." *Artibus Asiae*, Vol. 25, No. 2/3 (1962), 95–119 (+121–140).
19. See, for example, William HENNESSEY, "Deconstructing Shanzhai – China's Copycat Counterculture: Catch Me If You Can." *Campbell Law Review* 609 (2012). http://scholarship.law.campbell.edu/clr/vol34/iss3/3/.
20. Fifth-century art historian XIE He outlined "Six Principles of Painting" in the preface to his book *The Record of the Classification of Old Painters.* One principle, "Transmission by Copying," referred to the copying of models both from life and from the works of antiquity.
21. See Zhigeng PAN; Ruiying JIANG; Gengdai LIU; Cailiang SHEN, "Animating and Interacting with Ancient Chinese Painting – Qingming Festival by the Riverside," *Second International Conference on Culture and Computing,* 2011, vol., no., pp.3,6, 20–22

Sources and Recommended Reading

Bianca BOSKER, *Original Copies: Architectural Mimicry in Contemporary China* (2013). A journalistic look at the phenomenon of Chinese copies of Western architectural styles. Somewhat more nuanced than the glib title and clunky neologisms (i.e. "duplitecture") would suggest.

Jeffrey WASSERSTROM, *China in the 21st Century: What Everyone Needs to Know* (2010). A concise overview of the social, political, and economic issues facing China in the wake of the 2008 Olympics and 2010 Expo. The author's *Global Shanghai, 1850–2010* (2009) deals more explicitly with that city as a theatre of representation.

ZHU Jianfei, *Architecture of Modern China: A Historical Critique* (2009). An exceptional history of the development of modern architecture (and architectural discourse) in the twentieth and twenty-first centuries.

太和殿